Laws Great Britain

Acts of Parliament and provisional orders relating to Wallasey

1809-1899

Laws Great Britain

Acts of Parliament and provisional orders relating to Wallasey
1809-1899

ISBN/EAN: 9783337152918

Printed in Europe, USA, Canada, Australia, Japan

Cover: Foto ©ninafisch / pixelio.de

More available books at **www.hansebooks.com**

LOCAL ACTS.

Acts of Parliament

AND

Provisional Orders

RELATING TO

WALLASEY.

1809-1899.

LIVERPOOL:
C. TINLING & CO., PRINTERS, 53, VICTORIA STREET.

1899.

PREFACE.

This volume contains a compilation of the Acts of Parliament and Provisional Orders relating to Wallasey at present in force, together with the Liscard and Wallasey Inclosure Acts and the Awards of the Commissioner appointed by the authority of those statutes.

Local Government in the district dates from the passing of the Wallasey Improvement Act, 1845, which provided, *inter alia*, for "paving, lighting, watching, cleansing, and otherwise improving" the parish. For the purpose of administering that Act twenty-one Commissioners were appointed. These were superseded by a Local Board of Health, elected in pursuance of the Wallasey Order, 1852 (confirmed by the Public Health Supplemental Act, 1853). By this Order the Public Health Act, 1848, was applied to an enlarged area called the Wallasey District, which was comprised within the jurisdiction of the Local Board. The Public Health Act, 1875, which repealed that of 1848, consolidated and amended the laws relating to public health in England. For the purposes of that statute the area of the Local Board's jurisdiction was further extended, the "Wallasey Order (No. 2) 1877," declaring that "all that part of the Parish of Wallasey which is comprised in the Rural Sanitary District of the Birkenhead Union shall be included in and shall be deemed to form part of the Local Government District of Wallasey."

PREFACE.

The Wallasey Local Board was succeeded by the Wallasey Urban District Council, which was elected in pursuance of the Local Government Act, 1894, Urban Sanitary Authorities becoming by the operation of that statute "Urban District Councils."

In addition to the duties which are common to all Municipal bodies, the Wallasey Urban District Council, by virtue of its statutory powers, has the administration, control, and working of ferries, and of gas, water, and electric lighting undertakings. These powers are set out in the ensuing pages. Where provisions have been amended, or qualified by later enactments, explanatory notes have been appended, and those which have been expressly repealed have been omitted.

I am indebted to Mr. H. W. Cook, Clerk and Solicitor to the Council, for useful advice and suggestions.

J. W. ROSS BROWN.

STEPHENSON CHAMBERS,
    LIVERPOOL, *March 30th, 1899.*

CONTENTS.

	PAGE.
Chronological Table...	1
The Liscard Inclosure Act, 1809	12
The Wallasey and West Kirby Inclosure Act, 1814	46
The Wallasey Improvement Act, 1845	144
The Wallasey Order, 1852 (confirmed by the Public Health Supplemental Act, 1853, No. 1)	158
The Wallasey Improvement Act, 1858 ..	165
The Wallasey Improvement Act, 1861	187
The Wallasey Order, 1863 (confirmed by the Local Government Supplemental Act, 1863, No. 2) ...	193
The Wallasey Improvement Act, 1864	196
The Wallasey Improvement Act, 1867	212
The Wallasey Order, 1870 (confirmed by the Local Government Supplemental Act, 1870)	230
The Wallasey Improvement Act, 1872	233
The Wallasey Order, 1876 (confirmed by the Local Government Board's Provisional Orders Confirmation (Birmingham, &c.) Act, 1876	243
The Wallasey Order (No. 1) 1877	246
and	
The Wallasey Order (No. 2) 1877 (confirmed by the Local Government Board's Provisional Orders Confirmation (Caistor Union, &c.) Act, 1877)	250
The Wallasey Order, 1878 (confirmed by the Local Government Board's Provisional Orders Confirmation (Bristol, &c.) Act, 1878)	253
The Wallasey Order, 1881 (confirmed by the Local Government Board's Provisional Orders Confirmation (Acton, &c.) Act, 1881)	256
The Wallasey Order, 1883 (confirmed by the Local Government Board's Provisional Orders Confirmation (No. 7) Act, 1883)	260
The Wallasey Order, 1888 (confirmed by the Local Government Board's Provisional Orders Confirmation (No. 4) Act, 1888)	268
The Wallasey Local Board Act, 1890	272
The Wallasey Order, 1892 (confirmed by the Local Government Board's Provisional Orders Confirmation (No. 12) Act, 1892)	301

CONTENTS.

	PAGE.
The Wallasey Order, 1894 (confirmed by the Local Government Board's Provisional Orders Confirmation (No. 2) Act, 1894)	307
The Wallasey Order, 1895 (confirmed by the Local Government Board's Provisional Orders Confirmation (No. 1) Act, 1895)	309
The Wallasey Order, 1896 (confirmed by the Local Government Board's Provisional Orders Confirmation (No. 4) Act, 1896)	312
The Wallasey Urban District Council (Promenade) Act, 1896...	315
The Wallasey Electric Lighting Order, 1897 (confirmed by the Electric Lighting Orders Confirmation (No. 6) Act, 1897) ..	335
The Wallasey Order, 1897 (confirmed by the Local Government Board's Provisional Orders Confirmation (No. 2) Act, 1897)	368
The Wallasey Order, 1898 (confirmed by the Local Government Board's Provisional Orders Confirmation (No. 2) Act, 1898)	374
The Wallasey Tramways and Improvements Act, 1899... ...	377

CHRONOLOGICAL TABLE.

Statute, Chapter, Year.	Titles of Acts.	How repealed or otherwise affected.
49 Geo. III. ch. 103. (1809).	An Act for Inclosing Waste Lands in the Township of Liscard, in the Parish of Wallasey.	By the Wallasey Improvement Act, 1845, sec. 84, lands allotted under this Act for stone and marl, when exhausted, may be sold; and by the Wallasey Improvement Act, 1858, sec. 68, and the Wallasey Improvement Act, 1864, sec. 20, may be either sold, let, exchanged, or otherwise appropriated.
54 Geo. III. ch. 87. (1814).	An Act for Inclosing Waste Lands in the Parishes of Wallasey and West Kirby.	Sec. 17.—Lands allotted for stone and marl, when exhausted, may be sold, let, exchanged or otherwise appropriated (Wallasey Improvement Act, 1845, sec. 84; Act of 1858, sec. 68, and Act of 1864, sec. 20). Sec. 23.—Sandhills left as protection against sea, placed under control of Commissioners. (Wallasey Improvement Act, 1845, sec. 85).
8 Vict. ch. 6. (1845).	The Wallasey Improvement Act, 1845.	Secs. 1 to 5.—Repealed by the Wallasey Order, 1852. Secs. 7 to 16.—Repealed by the Wallasey Order, 1852. Secs. 18 to 62.—Repealed by the Wallasey Order, 1852. Sec. 63.—Repealed by the Wallasey Order, 1870, art. 4. Secs. 64 to 68.—Repealed by the Wallasey Order, 1852. Sec. 69.—Repealed by the Wallasey Order, 1870, art. 4. Secs. 70 to 83.—Repealed by the Wallasey Order, 1852. Sec. 84.—Extended by the Wallasey Improvement Act, 1858, sec. 68, the Wallasey Improvement Act, 1864, sec. 20; and the Wallasey Order (No. 1), 1877, art. 1. Sec. 87.—Power to hire and charter, the Wallasey Improvement Act, 1858, sec. 37. Sec. 89.—The limits were extended by the Wallasey Order, 1852, the Wallasey Order (No. 2), 1877, and the Wallasey Local Board Act, 1890, sec. 5.

Statute, Chapter, Year.	Titles of Acts.	How repealed or otherwise affected.
8 Vict. ch. 6. (1845.)	The Wallasey Improvement Act, 1845. *Continued.*	Secs. 90 to 117.—Repealed by the Wallasey Order, 1852. Sec. 118.—*Vide* Wallasey Local Board Act, 1890, sec. 24. Secs. 119 to 141.—Repealed by the Wallasey Order, 1852. Secs. 143 to 152.—Repealed by the Wallasey Order, 1852. Secs. 157 to 165.—Repealed by the Wallasey Order, 1852. Secs. 166 to 171.—Repealed by the Wallasey Order, 1870, art. 4. Secs. 172 to 181.—Repealed by the Wallasey Order, 1852. Secs. 183 to 186.—Repealed by the Wallasey Order, 1852. Secs. 189 to 191.—Repealed by the Wallasey Order, 1852. Secs. 192 to 197.—Repealed by the Wallasey Order, 1870, art. 4. Secs. 199 to 235.—Repealed by the Wallasey Order, 1852. Secs. 236 and 237.—(So much as relates to drivers of hackney carriages), repealed by the Wallasey Order, 1852. Secs. 238 and 239.—Repealed by the Wallasey Order, 1852. Sec. 240.—(So much as relates to drivers of hackney carriages), repealed by the Wallasey Order, 1852. Sec. 241.—Repealed by the Wallasey Order, 1852. Secs. 242 and 243.—(So much as relates to drivers of hackney carriages), repealed by the Wallasey Order, 1852. Sec. 244.—Repealed by the Wallasey Order, 1852. Sec. 245.—In part repealed by the Wallasey Order, 1852. Secs. 247 to 250.—Repealed by the Wallasey Order, 1852. Secs. 252 to 255.—Repealed by the Wallasey Order, 1852. Secs. 258 to 277.—Repealed by the Wallasey Order, 1852. Secs. 278 to 280.—Repealed by the Wallasey Order, 1870, art. 4. Secs. 281 to 292.—Repealed by the Wallasey Order, 1852.

Statute, Chapter, Year.	Titles of Acts.	How repealed or otherwise affected.
8 Vict. ch. 6. (1845.)	The Wallasey Improvement Act, 1845. *Continued.*	Sec. 293.—Repealed, with proviso, by the Wallasey Order, 1870, art. 1, which proviso was repealed by the Wallasey Improvement Act, 1872, sec. 20. Secs. 295 to 299.—Repealed by the Wallasey Order, 1852. Secs. 301 to 323.—Repealed by the Wallasey Order, 1852. Secs. 325 and 326.—Repealed by the Wallasey Order, 1852. Sec. 327.—Inclusion of "omnibus" in definitions of "hackney carriage" and "carriage" repealed by the Wallasey Order, 1888, art. 4. Sec. 328.—Repealed by the Wallasey Order, 1852. The Wallasey Order, 1852, also repealed "so much of any unrepealed part" of this Act "as fixes the amount of any penalty for any offence under the said Act, wherever the penalty for such offence is fixed by the Public Health Act, or any Act hereby incorporated therewith, or by any Byelaw of the Local Board of Health, at an amount other than that fixed by the said local Act." (*Vide* Schedule to the Wallasey Order, 1852.) The powers granted by the unrepealed parts of this Act were by art. 9 of The Wallasey Order, 1852, transferred to a Local Board of Health, created in pursuance of the Public Health Act, 1848. By art. 11 of the same Order the unrepealed parts of the Act were incorporated with the said Public Health Act. The Public Health Act, 1848, was repealed by the Public Health Act, 1875 (sec. 343 and sched.), which consolidated and amended the Acts relating to Public Health in England.

Statute, Chapter, Year.	Titles of Acts.	How repealed or otherwise affected.
16 Vict. ch. 24. 1853.	The Public Health Supplemental Act, 1853 (No. 1), confirming the Wallasey Order, 1852.	*Order.—Art. 1.*—The District was further extended by the Wallasey Order (No. 2), 1877; and the sea and river boundary is defined by sec. 5 of the Wallasey Local Board Act, 1890. *Arts. 2 to 5.*—The constitution and elections of Local Boards were subsequently governed by the Public Health Act, 1875, which repealed the Public Health Act, 1848. Local Boards were superseded by District Councils constituted under the Local Government Act, 1894.

21 & 22 Vict. ch. 63. (1858).	The Wallasey Improvement Act, 1858.	Sec. 11.—Part repealed by sec. 18 of the Wallasey Improvement Act, 1864.
		Sec. 22.—Altered by sec. 13 of the Wallasey Improvement Act, 1867.
		Sec. 23.—Altered by sec. 14 of the Wallasey Improvement Act, 1867.
		Secs. 39 and 40—Power to alter Ferry tolls conferred by the Wallasey Improvement Act, 1864, sec. 16, tolls altered, Wallasey Improvement Act, 1867, sec. 20.
		Secs. 42 to 44 and secs. 46 to 50.—Incorporated with the Wallasey Improvement Act, 1867, by sec. 23 of that Act.
		Sec. 46.—Extended by sec. 26 of the Wallasey Improvement Act, 1867, and sec. 15 of the Wallasey Improvement Act, 1872.
		Secs. 52 to 59.—Applied to bye-laws under the Wallasey Improvement Act, 1867, by sec. 29 of that Act.
		Sec. 60.—Borrowing Powers extended:—
		  Water, Act of 1861, sec. 3; Order 1863; Order 1870, art. 6; Act of 1872, sec. 17.
		  Gas, Act of 1861, sec. 3, Act of 1867, sec. 30; Order (No. 1), 1877, art. 2; Order 1883, art. 1; Order 1892, art. 2; Order 1896, art. 1; and Order 1898, art. 1.

Statute, Chapter, Year.	Titles of Acts.	How repealed or otherwise affected.
21 & 22 Vict. ch. 63. (1858).	The Wallasey Improvement Act, 1858. *Continued.*	Sec. 60—*Continued.* Ferries, Act of 1861, sec. 3; Act of 1864, sec. 21; Act of 1872, sec. 17; Order (No. 1), 1877, art. 3; Order 1881, art. 1; Order 1883, art. 2; Order 1895, art. 1, and Order 1897, art. 1. Sec. 62.—Altered and amended by the Wallasey Order, 1883, art. 9. Sec. 68.—Extended by the Wallasey Improvement Act, 1864, sec. 20, and the Wallasey Order (No. 1), 1877, art. 1. Secs. 69 to 79.—Repealed by the Wallasey Order, 1870, art. 3. As to repayment of moneys borrowed and sinking fund, *vide* the Wallasey Order, 1883, arts. 4 and 7.
24 Vict. ch. 4. (1861).	The Wallasey Improvement Act, 1861.	Sec. 2.—The Public Health Act, 1848, and the Local Government Act, 1858, were repealed by the Public Health Act, 1875, which consolidated and amended the Acts relating to public health. Sec. 3.—Borrowing powers extended:— 1. Water: The Wallasey Order, 1863. The Wallasey Order, 1870, art. 6. The Wallasey Improvement Act, 1872, sec. 17. 2. Gas: The Wallasey Improvement Act, 1867, sec. 30. The Wallasey Order (No. 1), 1877, art. 2. The Wallasey Order, 1883, art. 1. The Wallasey Order, 1892, art. 2. The Wallasey Order, 1896, art. 1. The Wallasey Order, 1898, art. 1. 3. Ferries: The Wallasey Improvement Act, 1864, sec. 21. The Wallasey Improvement Act, 1872, sec. 17. The Wallasey Order (No. 1), 1877, art. 3.

Statute, Chapter, Year.	Titles of Acts.	How repealed or otherwise affected.
24 Vict. ch. 4. (1861).	The Wallasey Improvement Act, 1861. *Continued.*	Sec. 3—*Continued.* The Wallasey Order, 1881, art. 1. The Wallasey Order, 1883, art 2. The Wallasey Order, 1895, art. 1. The Wallasey Order, 1897, art. 1. Sec. 5.—Altered and amended by The Wallasey Order, 1883, art. 9, *Vide* also arts. 4 and 7 of the same order for provisions as to repayment of loans and sinking fund.
26 & 27 Vict. ch. 64, (1863).	The Local Government Supplemental Act, 1863 (No. 2), confirming the Wallasey Order of 1863.	Order, art. 1.—Power to mortgage works and water rents as well as rates. The Wallasey Improvement Act, 1864, sec. 28. Borrowing powers extended by the Wallasey Order, 1870, art. 6 (repealed by the Wallasey Order, 1894, art. 1.)
27 & 28 Vict. ch. 117. (1864.)	The Wallasey Improvement Act, 1864.	Sec. 2.—The Public Health Act, 1848, and the Local Government Act, 1858, repealed by the Public Health Act, 1875, and its provisions substituted (sec. 313). Sec. 16.--Incorporated with the Wallasey Improvement Act, 1867 (sec. 23 of that Act). Sec. 20.—Extended powers by the Wallasey Order(No.1),1877,art.1. Sec. 21.—As to application of moneys borrowed, repealed by the Wallasey Improvement Act, 1867, sec. 37. Further Borrowing Powers : Ferries— The Wallasey Improvement Act, 1872, sec. 17. The Wallasey Order (No. 1), 1877, art. 3. The Wallasey Order, 1881, art. 1. The Wallasey Order, 1883, art. 2. The Wallasey Order, 1895, art. 1. The Wallasey Order, 1897, art. 1.

Statute, Chapter, Year.	Titles of Acts.	How repealed or otherwise affected.
27 & 28 Vict. ch. 117. (1864).	The Wallasey Improvement Act, 1864. *Continued.*	Sec. 22.—The Public Health Act, 1848, and the Local Government Act, 1858, repealed by the Public Health Act, 1875; provisions substituted, sec. 313. Sec. 23.—Altered and amended by the Wallasey Order, 1883, art. 9. Sec. 25.—As to priority, *vide* the Wallasey Order, 1883, art. 9. Secs. 25 to 27.—Applied to mortgages under the Wallasey Improvement Act, 1867; *vide* sec. 33 of that Act. Sec. 27.—Repealed by the Wallasey Order (No. 1), 1877, art. 4. Amended provisions for repayment, the Wallasey Order, 1883, arts. 4 to 8. Sec. 30.—*Vide* the Wallasey Local Board Act, 1890, sec. 26. Sec. 31.—*Vide* the Wallasey Local Board Act, 1890, sec. 35. Sec. 36.—Repealed by the Wallasey Order, 1870, art. 5.
30 & 31 Vict. ch. 132. (1867).	The Wallasey Improvement Act, 1867.	Sec. 9.—Altered and amended by The Wallasey Order (No. 1), 1877, art. 5, and The Wallasey Order, 1892, art. 1. Sec. 15.—*Vide* The Wallasey Local Board Act, 1890, sec. 70. Sec. 18.—*Vide* The Wallasey Local Board Act, 1890, sec. 72. Sec. 26.—*Vide* The Wallasey Improvement Act, 1858, sec. 46, and The Wallasey Improvement Act, 1872, sec. 15. Sec. 27.—Extended by The Wallasey Local Board Act, 1890, sec. 74. Sec. 28.—Extended to Seacombe Ferry, The Wallasey Improvement Act, 1872, sec. 14. Sec. 30.—Further Borrowing Powers—Gas:— The Wallasey Order (No. 1), 1877, art. 2. The Wallasey Order, 1883, art. 1. The Wallasey Order, 1892, art. 2. The Wallasey Order, 1896, art. 1. The Wallasey Order, 1898, art. 1.

Statute, Chapter, Year.	Titles of Acts.	How repealed or otherwise affected.
30 & 31 Vict. ch. 132. (1867).	The Wallasey Improvement Act, 1867. *Continued*.	Sec. 31.—Altered and amended by The Wallasey Order, 1883, art. 9. Sec. 32.—The Public Health Act, 1848, and the Local Government Act, 1858, repealed by the Public Health Act, 1875. Sec. 33.—As to priority, The Wallasey Order, 1883, art. 9, and as to repayment and sinking fund, the same order, arts. 4 and 7. Sec. 38.—The Bankruptcy Act, 1861, repealed by the Bankruptcy Repeal and Insolvent Court Act, 1869, sec. 20. As to priority of rates in bankruptcy, *vide* The Preferential Payments in Bankruptcy Act, 1888, sec. 1. Sec. 39.—The Nuisances Removal Act, 1855, repealed by the Public Health Act, 1875.
33 & 34 Vict. ch. 114. (1870.)	The Local Government Supplemental Act, 1870, confirming The Wallasey Order, 1870.	Art. 2 of the Order repealed by the Wallasey Improvement Act, 1872, sec. 20. Art. 6.—Repealed (except so far as may have been acted upon or so far as relates to the repayment of money borrowed in pursuance thereof) by The Wallasey Order, 1894, art. 1.
35 & 36 Vict. ch. 125. (1872).	The Wallasey Improvement Act, 1872.	Sec. 15.—*Vide* the Wallasey Improvement Act, 1858, sec. 46; the Wallasey Improvement Act, 1867, Secs. 26 & 27, and the Wallasey Local Board Act, 1890, sec. 74. Sec. 17.—Further Borrowing Powers—Ferries:— The Wallasey Order (No. 1) 1877, art. 3. The Wallasey Order, 1881, art. 1. The Wallasey Order, 1883, art. 2. The Wallasey Order, 1895, art. 1. The Wallasey Order, 1897, art. 1. Sec. 18.—*Vide* the Wallasey Orders of 1881 and 1883. Sec. 19.—Altered and amended by the Wallasey Order, 1883, art. 9.

CHRONOLOGICAL TABLE. 3

Statute, Chapter, Year.	Titles of Acts.	How repealed or otherwise affected.
35 & 36 Vict. ch. 125. (1872.)	The Wallasey Improvement Act, 1872. *Continued.*	Sec. 21.—The Bankruptcy Act, 1869, repealed by the Bankruptcy Act, 1883, sec. 169. As to priority of "parochial or other rates" in bankruptcy, *vide* the Preferential Payments in Bankruptcy Act, 1888, sec. 1, and the amended Act of 1897 (60 and 61 Vict., c. 19, sec. 1). Sec. 22.—Altered and amended by the Wallasey Order, 1883, art. 3.
39 & 40 Vict. ch. 202. (1876).	The Local Government Board's Provisional Orders Confirmation (Birmingham, &c.), Act, 1876, confirming the Wallasey Order of 1876.	
40 & 41 Vict. ch. 227. (1877).	The Local Government Board's Provisional Orders Confirmation (Caistor Union, &c.) Act, 1877, confirming The Wallasey Order (No. 1), 1877, and The Wallasey Order (No. 2), 1877.	Order No. 1, art. 2.—Further Borrowing Powers.—Gas: The Wallasey Order, 1883, art. 1. The Wallasey Order, 1892, art. 2. The Wallasey Order, 1896, art. 1. The Wallasey Order, 1898, art. 1. Order No. 1, art. 3.—Further Borrowing Powers.—Ferries: The Wallasey Order, 1881, art. 1. The Wallasey Order, 1883, art. 2. The Wallasey Order, 1895, art. 1. The Wallasey Order, 1897, art. 1. Order No. 1, art. 4.—*Vide* The Wallasey Order, 1883, arts. 4 to 8. Order No. 1, art. 5.—Altered by The Wallasey Order, 1892, art. 1. Order No. 2, art. 3.—The Wallasey Improvement Act, 1858, also applied by The Wallasey Order, 1878, to the extended district. Sea and River boundary of district defined, The Wallasey Local Board Act, 1890, sec. 5.
41 Vict. ch. 8. (1878).	The Local Government Board's Provisional Orders Confirmation (Bristol, &c.) Act, 1878, confirming The Wallasey Order, 1878.	

Statute, Chapter, Year.	Titles of Acts.	How repealed or otherwise affected.
44 & 45 Vict. ch. 162. (1881).	The Local Government Board's Provisional Orders Confirmation (Acton, &c.), Act, 1881, confirming The Wallasey Order, 1881.	Order.—Art. 1.—Further Borrowing Powers—Ferries— The Wallasey Order, 1883, art. 2. The Wallasey Order, 1895, art. 1. The Wallasey Order, 1897, art. 1. *Vide* The Wallasey Order, 1883, arts. 4 to 8; provisions for repayment and sinking fund.
46 & 47 Vict. ch. 137. (1883).	The Local Government Board's Provisional Orders Confirmation (No. 7) Act, 1883, confirming The Wallasey Order, 1883.	Order.—Art. 1.—Further Borrowing Powers—Gas— The Wallasey Order, 1892, art. 2. The Wallasey Order, 1896, art. 1. The Wallasey Order, 1898, art 1. Further Borrowing Powers—Ferries— The Wallasey Order, 1895, art. 1. The Wallasey Order, 1897, art. 1.
51 & 52 Vict. ch. 62. (1888).	The Local Government Board's Provisional Orders Confirmation (No. 4), Act, 1888, confirming The Wallasey Order, 1888.	
53 & 54 Vict. ch. 121. (1890).	The Wallasey Local Board Act, 1890.	Secs. 38 to 55.—These sections are in general similar to the provisions contained in the adoptive "Private Street Works Act, 1892," secs. 5 to 21 (55 & 56 Vict. ch. 57). Sec. 75. – The Merchant Shipping Act Amendment Act, 1862, was repealed by the Merchant Shipping Act, 1894; *vide* now sec. 503 of the later statute (57 and 58 Vict. ch. 60).
55 & 56 Vict. ch. 223. (1892).	The Local Government Board's Provisional Orders Confirmation (No. 12) Act, 1892, confirming the Wallasey Order, 1892.	Order, art. 11 (sub. sec. 1).— Borrowing Powers—Gas: Extended by The Wallasey Order, 1896, art. 1; The Wallasey Order, 1898, art. 1.
57 Vict. ch. 20. (1894).	The Local Government Board's Provisional Orders Confirmation (No. 2) Act, 1894, confirming The Wallasey Order, 1894.	

Statute, Chapter, Year.	Titles of Acts.	How repealed or otherwise affected.
58 & 59 Vict. ch. 40. (1895).	The Local Government Board's Provisional Orders Confirmation (No. 1) Act, 1895, confirming The Wallasey Order, 1895.	Order, art. 1.—Power to borrow a further sum of £10,600 for the purpose of a Dredger is given by The Wallasey Order, 1897, art. 1.
59 Vict. ch. 29. (1896).	The Local Government Board's Provisional Orders Confirmation (No. 4) Act, 1896, confirming The Wallasey Order, 1896.	Order, art. 1.—Further altered to "one hundred and twelve thousand pounds" by The Wallasey Order, 1898, art. 1.
59 & 60 Vict. ch. 209. (1896).	The Wallasey Urban District Council (Promenade) Act, 1896.	
60 & 61 Vict. ch. 66. (1897).	The Electric Lighting Orders Confirmation (No. 6) Act, 1897, confirming the Wallasey Electric Lighting Order, 1897.	
60 & 61 Vict. ch. 68. (1897).	The Local Government Board's Provisional Orders Confirmation (No. 2) Act, 1897, confirming the Wallasey Order, 1897.	
61 Vict. ch. 32. (1898).	The Local Government Board's Provisional Orders Confirmation (No. 2) Act, 1898, confirming the Wallasey Order, 1898.	

THE LISCARD INCLOSURE ACT, 1809.
(49 Geo. III. c. 103.)

ARRANGEMENT OF SECTIONS.

	SECTION
Preamble.	
Commissioner	1
For appointing new Commissioner	2
Notice of meetings to be given	3
Other notices	4
Commissioner to settle Disputes	5
Power to assess Costs	6
Allowing parties to try their Rights at Law	7
Action not to abate	8
In cases of deaths of parties before actions brought, the same to be carried on and defended in their names	9
Persons in possession not to be molested without due course of Law	10
Encroachments	11
Allotment for sale to defray expenses	12
Allotments of Residue	13
For making exchanges	14
Expenses of exchanges or partitions by whom to be paid	15
Proprietors to pay their own expenses at Meetings	16
Wills and Settlements not to be revoked or altered by this Act	17
Allotments to be of the same Tenure as Lands allotted were	18
Allotments to be fenced	19
Power to sell Rights before the Execution of the Award	20
Rights of common to be extinguished	21
Commissioner's Allowance	22
Commissioner to Account	23
Persons advancing money to be repaid with interest	24
Directing where the Award shall be deposited	25
Roads may be made of less width than forty feet, but not less than thirty	26
Altering the time for giving Notices in certain cases	27
Allowing an Appeal	28
General saving of Rights	29
Act may be given in evidence when printed	30

49 Geo. III.   *The Liscard Inclosure Act*, 1809.   ch. ciii.   13

AN

ACT

for inclosing Waste Lands in the Township of Liscard, in the Parish of Wallasey, in the County Palatine of Chester.

20TH MAY, 1809.

WHEREAS there are within the township of Liscard, in the parish of Wallasey, in the County Palatine of Chester, divers commons and waste lands, containing about four hundred and sixteen acres of land (statute measure) lying open and uncultivated: and whereas John Penkett, Esquire, is or claims to be Lord of the Manor of Liscard, in the said County: and whereas the Reverend George Briggs is Rector of the Rectory and Parish Church of Wallasey, in the said County Palatine of Chester: and whereas the Reverend Sir Henry Poole, Baronet, James Mainwaring, Esquire, the said John Penkett, John Tobin, Esquire, John Dean, Thomas Molyneux, Gerard Stanley and several other Persons, are owners or proprietors of divers messuages, tenements, lands, and hereditaments within the said Township, and as such are entitled to right of common on the said commons and waste lands: and whereas an Act was passed in the forty-first year of the Reign of His present Majesty intituled an Act for consolidating in one Act certain provisions usually inserted in Acts of inclosure, and for facilitating the mode of proving the several facts usually required on the passing of such Acts: and whereas the said commons and waste lands in their present state are of little value; but if the same were divided and allotted into specific shares unto and amongst the proprietors thereof and persons interested therein, and such allotments inclosed, they would be considerably improved; but such division, allotment, and inclosure, cannot be made and rendered effectual without the aid and authority of Parliament; may it therefore please your Majesty that it may be enacted; and be it enacted by the King's most Excellent Majesty, by and with the advice and consent of the Lords Spiritual and Temporal, and Commons, in this present Parliament assembled, and by the authority of the same, that the said commons and waste lands shall be set out, allotted and divided as soon as conveniently may be after the passing of this Act; and that James Boydell, of Rossett, in the County of Denbigh, Gentleman, and his successor, to be appointed in the manner hereinafter mentioned, shall be and he is hereby appointed the Commissioner for setting out, allotting and dividing the said several commons and waste lands, and for carrying this and the said recited Act into execution, subject

Commissioner.

Sec. 2—6 to the regulations of the said recited Act, except in such cases where the same are hereby varied or altered.

For appointing new Commissioner.

2. And be it further enacted, that if the said James Boydell shall die or refuse to act, or be rendered incapable of acting by sickness or any other cause, it shall be lawful for a majority in value, such value to be ascertained by the Land Tax Assessment for the said township of the land owners within the said township, by writing under their hands, to appoint another Commissioner (not interested in the said commons and waste lands) in the room or place of the said James Boydell, within three weeks next after such death, refusal, or incapacity shall be made known; and every such new Commissioner so to be appointed, having taken and subscribed the oath appointed to be taken by the said recited Act, shall have such and the like powers and authorities by virtue of this Act as if he had been named and appointed a Commissioner in and by this Act.

Notice of Meetings to be given.

3. And be it further enacted, that the said Commissioner shall and he is hereby required to cause notice to be inserted in one of the Liverpool weekly newspapers of the time and place of his first sitting to put this Act in execution, at least ten days before the day of such sitting, which said sitting shall be held at some convenient place within the said township, or within eight miles of the boundary of the said parish, and the said Commissioner shall and may afterwards proceed in the execution of this Act, and from time to time adjourn to such time and place as he shall think proper.

Other notices.

4. Provided always, and be it further enacted, that all other notices requisite or necessary to be made and given by the said Commissioner, for the purpose of carrying this and the said recited Act in execution, shall be made and given by advertisement in one of the said Liverpool newspapers, and that fourteen days shall be deemed sufficient notice of such sittings respectively.

Commissioner to settle disputes.

5. And be it further enacted, that if any dispute or difference shall arise between any of the parties interested or claiming to be interested in the lands and grounds to be allotted and divided in pursuance of this Act or any part thereof, touching or concerning the several rights and interests which they or any of them shall have or claim to have in, over, upon or out of the said lands and grounds or any part thereof, or touching or concerning any matter or thing relating to the said allotment, division and inclosure, it shall be lawful for the said Commissioner and he is hereby authorised to examine into, hear, and determine the same: Provided always, that nothing in this Act contained shall authorise the said Commissioner to determine the title to any messuages, lands, tenements or hereditaments whatsoever.

Power to assess costs.

6. And be it further enacted, That in case the said Commissioner shall upon the hearing and determination of any claim or claims, objection or objections, to be delivered to him in pursuance of this Act, see cause to award any costs, it shall be lawful for him, and he is hereby empowered, upon application made to him for that purpose, to settle, assess and award such costs and charges as he shall think reasonable, to be paid to the party or parties in whose favour any determination of the said Commissioner shall have been made by the person or persons whose claim or claims, objection or objections, shall be thereby disallowed or overruled; and in case **Sec. 7** the person or persons who shall be liable to pay such costs and charges shall neglect or refuse to pay the same on demand, then it shall and may be lawful for the said Commissioner, and he is hereby required and authorised, by warrant under his hand and seal directed to any person or persons whomsoever, to cause such costs and charges to be levied by distress and sale of the goods and chattels of the person or persons so neglecting or refusing to pay the same, rendering the overplus (if any) upon demand to the person or persons whose goods and chattels shall have been so distrained and sold, after deducting the costs and charges attending such distress and sale.

7. Provided always, and be it further enacted, That in case any person or persons interested or claiming to be interested in the said intended allotments, shall be dissatisfied with any determination of the said Commissioner, touching or concerning any claim or claims or other rights or interests in, over, or upon the lands and grounds hereby directed to be divided, allotted, and inclosed, or any part thereof, it shall be lawful for the person or persons so dissatisfied to proceed to a trial at law of the matter so determined by the said Commissioner, at the then next or at the following Great Sessions or Assizes to be holden for the said County Palatine of Chester, and for that purpose the person or persons who shall be dissatisfied with the determination of the said Commissioner shall, upon giving notice to the said Commissioner of his, her, or their intention to bring such action, within three calendar months after such determination shall be made, cause an action to be brought upon a feigned issue against the person or persons in whose favour such determination shall have been made, within six calendar months next after the determination of the said Commissioner shall be so made; and the defendant or defendants in such respective action or actions shall, and he, she, and they is and are hereby required to name an attorney or attornies, who shall appear thereto or file common bail, and accept one or more issue or issues, whereby such claim or claims and the right or rights thereby insisted on may be tried and determined, such issue or issues to be settled by the proper officer of the court in which the said respective action or actions shall be commenced, in case the parties shall differ about the same; and the verdict or verdicts which shall be given in such action or actions shall be final, binding, and conclusive, upon all and every person and persons whomsoever, unless the court wherein such action or actions shall be brought shall set aside such verdict or verdicts and order a new trial to be had therein, which it shall be lawful for the court to do as is usual in other cases; and after such verdict or verdicts shall be obtained and not set aside by the court, the said Commissioner shall and he is hereby required to act in conformity thereto, and to allow or disallow the claim or claims thereby determined, according to the event of such trial or trials: Provided always, that the determination of the said Commissioner, touching such claim or claims of right to the soil of the said commons and waste lands, or other rights or interests in, over, or upon the lands and grounds hereby directed to be divided, allotted, and inclosed, or any part thereof, which shall not be objected to, or being objected to, the party or parties objecting not causing such

Allowing parties to try their rights at law.

Sec. 8—11 action at law to be brought and proceeded in as aforesaid, shall be final and conclusive upon all parties.

8. And be it further enacted, That if any of the parties in any action to be brought in pursuance of this Act shall die pending the same, such action shall not abate by reason thereof, but shall be proceeded in as if no such event had happened.

In cases of deaths of parties before actions brought, the same to be carried on and defended in their names.

9. Provided always, and be it further enacted, That if any person or persons in whose favour any such determination as aforesaid shall have been made, and against whom any such action or actions might have been brought if living, shall die before any such action or actions shall have been brought, and before the expiration of the time hereinbefore limited for bringing such action or actions, it shall be lawful for the person or persons who might have brought such action or actions against the person or persons so dying, to bring the same within the time so limited as aforesaid, against such person or persons as if actually living, and to serve the Clerk to the said Commissioner with process for commencing such action or actions, in the same manner as the party or parties might have been served therewith if living; and it shall thereupon be incumbent on the heir or heirs, or other person or persons who shall claim the benefit of such determination as aforesaid, to appear and defend such action or actions in the name or names of the person or persons so dead, or in his, her, or their own name or names, and proceedings shall be had therein in the same manner as if such person or persons had been actually living; and the rights of all parties shall be equally bound and concluded by the event of such action or actions.

Persons in possession not to be molested without due course of law.

10. Provided also, and be it further enacted, That nothing in this Act contained shall extend to enable the said Commissioner to determine any right between any parties contrary to the possession of any of such parties (except in cases of encroachments as hereinafter mentioned); but in case the said Commissioner shall be of opinion against the right of the person or persons so in possession, he shall forbear to make any determination thereupon, until the possession shall be given up by or recovered from such person or persons by ejectment or other due course of law.

Encroachments.

11. And be it further enacted, That it shall be lawful for the said Commissioner to enquire into and determine what inclosure or inclosures, encroachment or encroachments hath or have been made upon or from the said commons or waste lands by any person or persons whomsoever, and that all such inclosures and encroachments as shall have been made upon or taken from the said commons and waste lands, within twenty years previous to the passing of this Act, shall be deemed part of the said commons and waste lands, which said encroachments the said Commissioner is hereby directed to allot to the persons respectively who now hold the same, as part of their respective shares of the said commons and waste lands; but in the valuation of such encroachments respectively, the said Commissioner shall not take into his consideration any improvements which may have been made thereon, nor estimate the same at any higher rate or value than the same respectively would have been estimated at had they remained part of the said commons and had not been inclosed; and all inclosures or encroachments from the said commons or waste lands, which have been held for twenty years or upwards, shall remain and be the property and as part of the ancient estate of the person or persons to whom the same respectively now belong, in respect of any such land so inclosed for twenty years or upwards.

Sec. 12—14

12. And be it further enacted, That the said Commissioner (after setting out the roads and ways in, over, and upon the said commons and waste lands, in the manner prescribed by the said recited Act) shall and he is hereby authorized, directed, and required to set out and allot such part or parts of the said commons and waste lands, as will in his judgment by sale thereof, in the manner and subject to the regulations and directions contained in the said recited Act, raise a sum of money sufficient to pay the charges and expenses incident to and attending the obtaining and passing of this Act, and of carrying the same and the said recited Act in all respects into execution; and in case any surplus shall remain, after all such costs and charges shall have been fully paid and satisfied, such surplus shall be divided and apportioned between the several proprietors of the lands and grounds hereby directed to be allotted, divided, and inclosed, according to their several and respective interests therein, in case they shall be tenants thereof in fee simple, or otherwise the same shall be applied and disposed of in manner directed by the said recited Act, whenever money is to be paid for the purchase or exchange of any lands, tenements, or hereditaments, or of any timber or wood growing thereon, and which money ought to be laid out in the purchase or exchange of other lands, tenements, or hereditaments to be settled to the same uses.

Allotment for sale to defray expenses.

13. And be it further enacted, That the said Commissioner shall and he is hereby directed and required to allot, set out, and divide the residue and remainder of the said several commons and waste grounds, unto and amongst the several persons who, at the time of making such allotments and division, shall be entitled to right of common on the said several commons and waste grounds, in proportion and according to their respective rights, property, and interest therein.

Allotments of residue.

14. And be it further enacted, That it shall be lawful for the said Commissioner to set out, allot, and award any lands, tenements, or hereditaments whatsoever, within the said township of Liscard and parish of Wallasey or either of them, in lieu of and in exchange for any other lands, tenements, and hereditaments whatsoever within the said township and parish or either of them, or within any adjoining parish, hamlet, manor, township, or place, provided all such exchanges be ascertained, specified and declared in the Award of the said Commissioner, and be made with the consent of the owner or owners of the lands, tenements, or hereditaments which shall be so exchanged, whether such owner or owners shall be a body or bodies politic, corporate, or collegiate, or a tenant or tenants in fee simple, or in fee tail general or special, or for life, or by the courtesy of England, or for years determinable on any life or lives, or with the consent of the guardians, trustees, feoffees for charitable or other uses, husbands, committees or attornies of or acting for any such owners as aforesaid, who at the time of making such exchange or exchanges shall be respectively infants, femes covert, lunatics, or under any other legal disability, or who shall be beyond the seas, or otherwise disabled to act for themselves, himself, or herself, such consent to be testified in

For making exchanges.

Sec. 15—19
writing under the common seal of the body politic, corporate, or collegiate, and under the hands of the other consenting parties respectively; and all and every exchange and exchanges so to be made shall be good, valid and effectual in the law to all intents and purposes whatsoever: provided nevertheless, that no exchange shall be made of any lands, tenements, or hereditaments held in right of any church, chapel or other ecclesiastical benefice, without the consent testified as aforesaid of the patron thereof, and of the Lord Bishop of the diocese in which such lands, tenements, or hereditaments so to be exchanged shall lie and be situate.

Expenses of exchanges or partitions by whom to be paid.
15. And be it further enacted, That the costs, charges, and expenses attending the making and completing of any exchanges or partitions to be made under and by virtue of the said recited Act, or this Act, shall be borne, paid, and defrayed by the several persons proposing or consenting to the making of such exchanges or partitions, in such manner and in such shares and proportions as the said Commissioners shall by their Award order and direct.

Proprietors to pay their own expenses at meetings.
16. And be it further enacted, That the said proprietors, their attornies and agents shall pay their own expenses when they or any of them shall attend the said Commissioner at any of his sittings to be holden in pursuance of this Act.

Wills and settlements not to be revoked or altered by this Act.
17. Provided always, and be it further enacted, That nothing herein contained shall extend or be construed, adjudged, deemed or taken to revoke, make void, alter or impeach any settlement, deed, or will whatsoever, or to prejudice any person or persons having any right, title, interest, claim, charge, or incumbrance whatsoever, in, out of, upon, or affecting any parts of the land or ground to be allotted, divided and inclosed as aforesaid, or any part or parcel thereof, but that the respective shares of the said commons or waste lands so to be allotted or exchanged, shall immediately after such allotments or exchanges be remain and enure, and be held and enjoyed, and the several persons to whom the same shall be allotted or given in exchange shall from thenceforth stand and be seized and possessed thereof respectively, for such estates, upon such and the same uses, for such trusts, and with such and the same powers, and subject to such and the same wills, limitations, conditions, settlements, trusts, provisions, remainders, reversions, debts, charges, and incumbrances, as the several messuages, lands, tenements, or hereditaments in respect whereof such allotments or exchanges shall be made, were held and stood severally limited, or subject or liable unto at the time of making such allotments or exchanges.

Allotments to be of the same tenure as lands allotted were.
18. And be it further enacted, That the lands and grounds which shall be allotted to any of the said proprietors by virtue of this Act shall be held by the same tenures by which the lands and grounds in respect whereof such allotments shall be made, are now held.

Allotments to be fenced.
19. And be it further enacted, That it shall be lawful for all and every person or persons to whom any allotment or allotments shall be made by virtue of this Act, from time to time during the term of seven years from the signing the said Award, to set down posts and rails or other fences on the outside of the ditches, bounding any highway or uninclosed lands adjoining to his or their allotment or allotments, for the preservation of the quicksets, not exceeding five

feet from the line of inclosure, and at any time before the end of the said term to remove and carry away such posts, rails, and fences.

Sec. 20—23

20. And be it further enacted, That it shall be lawful for any person or persons interested in the commons and waste lands to be inclosed by virtue of this Act, at any time before the execution of the Award hereinafter directed to be made by the said Commissioner, to sell and dispose of all such estate, right, and interest, as he, she or they now hath or have, or shall or may hereafter have in or to any right of common in and upon the said commons and waste lands, or in or to any allotment or allotments to be made in respect thereof by virtue of this Act, separate from such estate in right whereof he, she, or they, is, are, or shall be so entitled; and that in case of any such sale it shall be lawful for the said Commissioner, and he is hereby authorized and required to allot the same to the purchaser or purchasers thereof respectively, who shall and may immediately after the execution of such Award as aforesaid, have, hold, use and enjoy such allotments so to be allotted and laid out, in lieu of the right of common or other interest, so by him, her, or them purchased as aforesaid, and shall and may have, use, and exercise any Act of Ownership in, upon, over and to the same, and be seized and possessed thereof, in as full, large, ample, and beneficial a manner to all intents and purposes whatsoever, as the former proprietor or vendor thereof could or might have done in case such sale or sales had not been made, but subject nevertheless to the several rules, orders, conditions, and restrictions mentioned and contained in this and the said recited Act.

Power to sell rights before the execution of the Award.

21. And be it further enacted, That the several allotments, partitions, divisions, exchanges, and determinations to be made, declared or approved by the said Commissioner, in and by his Award or instrument to be made in pursuance of the said recited Act, shall be and are hereby declared to be final, binding and conclusive unto and upon the several parties interested in the said commons or waste lands, and all other persons, bodies politic and corporate whomsoever; and from and immediately after the execution of the said Award or instrument, and the publication thereof as aforesaid, all right of common, in, over, or upon the said several commons and waste lands shall cease and be for ever extinguished.

Rights of common to be extinguished.

22. And be it further enacted, That out of the money which shall be raised for defraying the expenses of obtaining and executing this Act, there shall be paid to the said Commissioner, as a recompense for his pains and trouble, the sum of two pounds twelve shillings and sixpence for each day he shall respectively act or travel for the purpose of acting; and that at all meetings to be held in pursuance of this Act, the said Commissioner shall defray his own expenses.

Commissioner's allowance.

23. And be it further enacted, That once at least in every year during the execution of this Act (such day to be computed from the day of passing thereof), the said Commissioner shall and he is hereby required to make a true and just statement or account of all sums of money by him received and expended, or due to him for his own trouble and expenses in the execution of this Act; such statement or account when so made, together with the vouchers relating thereto, shall be by him laid before any two justices of the peace for the

Commissioner to account.

Sec. 24—28

County of Chester, to be by them examined and balanced, and such balance shall be by such justices stated in the books of accounts to be kept in the office of the Clerk to the said Commissioner; and no charges or items in such accounts shall be binding on the parties concerned, or valid in law, unless the same shall have been duly allowed by such justices.

Persons advancing money to be repaid with interest.

24. And be it further enacted, That if any person shall advance any sum or sums of money for the purpose of defraying the expenses of obtaining and passing this Act, or of carrying the same into execution, every such person shall be repaid the same, with interest, at the rate of five pounds per centum per annum, out of the first monies that shall be raised for defraying such expenses by virtue of this Act.

Directing where the Award shall be deposited.

25. And be it further enacted, That the Award to be made by the said Commissioner, after being enrolled in the manner directed by the said recited Act, shall be deposited in the said Parish Church of Wallasey.

Roads may be made of less width than forty feet, but not less than thirty.

26. And whereas the said commons adjoin chiefly on the coast or shore of the River Mersey, and there is not nor ever can be much passing over the public roads to be made in, over, upon or across the said commons; be it further enacted, That the said Commissioner shall have and hereby hath full power given to him, to set out all and every or any the public highways and roads, in, over or across the said commons, of less width than forty feet, so as none of such public roads shall be set out less than thirty feet wide.

Altering the time for giving notices in certain cases.

27. And whereas the giving six weeks notice for some of the purposes by the said recited Act to be given, hath been found by experience to occasion not only great delay but considerable expense; be it further enacted, That for the purposes of this Act three weeks notice of any thing to be done in pursuance of this Act, or the said recited Act, shall be deemed sufficient notice; anything in the said recited Act contained to the contrary notwithstanding.

Allowing an appeal.

28. And be it further enacted, That if any person or persons, bodies politic or corporate, shall think himself, herself, or themselves aggrieved by any thing done in pursuance of this or the said recited Act (except as to such claims, matters, and things as are hereinbefore directed or authorised to be tried, settled, or determined by the verdict of a jury, or where any of the clauses or provisions of the said recited Act or of this Act shall express that the same shall be final and conclusive), then and in every such case, he, she or they may appeal to the General Quarter Sessions of the Peace to be held at Chester, in and for the said County Palatine of Chester, within four calendar months next after the cause of complaint shall have arisen; and the justices at the said Quarter Sessions are hereby required to hear and determine the matter of every such appeal, and to make such order and award such costs as to them in their discretion shall seem reasonable, and by their order and warrant to levy the costs and damages which shall be awarded by the said justices, by distress and sale of the goods and chattels of the party or parties liable to pay the same, rendering the overplus (if any) to the owner or owners of such goods and chattels, deducting the reasonable charges of every such distress and sale; which determination of the said justices shall be final and conclusive to all parties concerned, and shall not be removed by certiorari or any other writ or process whatsoever into any of His Majesty's Courts of Record at Westminster, or elsewhere; but in case such appeal shall appear to the said justices to be frivolous, vexatious or without foundation, then the said justices shall award such costs to be paid by the appellant or appellants, as to them in their discretion shall seem reasonable.

Sec. 29—30

29. Saving always to the King's most Excellent Majesty, his heirs and successors, and all and every person and persons, bodies politic and corporate, his, her and their successors, executors, and administrators (other than and except the several persons, bodies politic and corporate, to and amongst whom the said commons or waste lands shall be allotted and divided in pursuance of this Act), all such right title and interest (other than and except such as are hereby intended to be barred and destroyed), as they, every, or any of them had and enjoyed, of, in, to or out of the said several commons or waste lands at the time of passing this Act, or would or might have had or enjoyed in case this Act had not been made.

General saving of rights.

30. And be it further enacted, That this Act shall be printed by the printer to the King's most Excellent Majesty, and a copy thereof so printed shall be admitted as evidence thereof by all judges, justices, and others.

Act may be given in evidence when printed.

[By the Wallasey Improvement Act, 1845, sec. 84, lands allotted under this Act for the purpose of getting stone and marl therefrom, and of a watering pit for the use of the landowners within the township may, when exhausted and dried up, be sold; and by the Wallasey Improvement Act, 1858, sec. 68, and the Wallasey Improvement Act, 1864, sec. 20, may be either sold, let, exchanged, or otherwise appropriated.]

COMMISSIONER'S AWARD.

(*Under* 49 *Geo. III. cap.* 103.)

LISCARD INCLOSURE.

TO ALL PERSONS TO WHOM these presents shall come, I, James Boydell, of Rossett, in the County of Denbigh, gentleman, the Commissioner named and appointed in, and by an Act of Parliament made and passed in the forty-ninth year of the reign of His present Majesty King George the Third, intituled an Act for "Inclosing waste lands in the Township of Liscard, in the Parish of Wallasey, in the County Palatine of Chester," having taken and subscribed the oath directed to be taken by the Act of the forty-first year of the reign of His present Majesty intituled "An Act for consolidating in one Act certain provisions usually inserted in Acts of Inclosure and for facilitating the mode of proving the several facts usually required on the passing of such Acts, which oath is written on parchment and annexed to this my Award, and having made the survey and valuation of all the messuages, tenements and inclosed lands or inlands in the said township of Liscard and also made a plan and admeasurement of the said commons and waste lands setting forth the true contents or as near thereto as may be of the said commons and waste lands in statute measure, by which measure the said commons and waste lands contain four hundred and seven acres and thirty-nine perches or thereabouts, and in which measure I declare the contents of all and every the parts and parcels of the said commons and waste lands by me hereinafter assigned and allotted are so assigned and allotted and in further execution of the said several Acts I caused the several notices by the said several Acts directed to be given to be given accordingly as well for receiving the claims of the several persons claiming right of common on the said several commons and waste lands as for making objections thereto, and some claims having been made and objected to I proceeded to the hearing and determining the same as by the said several Acts is directed. And the boundaries of the said township of Liscard being doubted or disputed I proceeded to enquire into the boundaries of the said township of Liscard as by the said recited Act of the forty-first year of His present Majesty is directed, and having given the several notices by the same Acts directed to be given in the manner described by the said Act, and having examined several witnesses on oath respecting such boundaries I proceeded to ascertain, set out, determine and fix the same, and having acted in all other respects pursuant to the directions of the said recited Acts and completed the division and allotment of the said commons and waste grounds I, the said Commissioner, have therefore drawn up this my Award in writing with such map or plan as aforesaid thereunto annexed, which I direct to be taken as part of this my Award.

Now know ye that I the said Commissioner in pursuance of all powers and authorities in anywise enabling me in this behalf do by this my Award fairly engrossed or written on parchment, and read and executed by me in the presence of the proprietors now attending at a special meeting duly called by notice for that purpose award, order and determine in manner following that is to say.

[Commissioners are authorized to determine the boundaries of parishes, &c , by virtue of sec. 3, of 41 Geo. III., c. 109 (1801), which consolidates certain provisions usually inserted in Acts of Inclosure.]

I do ascertain, determine and fix the boundaries of the said Township of Liscard as follows, that is to say, the boundaries of the said Township of Liscard begin at the low water mark of the river Mersey opposite to the southeastwardly corner of a close or parcel of land in Liscard aforesaid belonging to Thomas Wilson called the Rice Hey, and extend from thence westwardly along the south fence of the said close to another close in Liscard aforesaid belonging to Thomas Molyneux called the Pike Hey, and extend along the same close southwardly to the southeastwardly corner of the said close called the Pike Hey, and from thence in a westwardly direction along the south side of a certain close called the Weedy Meadow also belonging to the said Thomas Molyneux, to the southwesternmost corner of a certain other close called the Weedy Hey, also belonging to the said Thomas Molyneux, and from thence in a northwestwardly direction along the southwestwardly fence of the said close, called the Weedy Hey, to another close in Liscard aforesaid, called the Moor Hey, also belonging to the said Thomas Molyneux, and from thence in a westwardly direction along the south fence of the said close, called the Moor Hey, to the southwestwardly corner of the said close, called the Moor Hey, and from thence in a southwardly direction along the ancient fence of a close, called the Lower Moor Hey, in Poulton-cum-Seacombe, belonging to the said Thomas Molyneux, until they come within four yards, or nearly as may be, of the gate in the said field adjoining the common, and from thence along a slack or hollow place across the highway or road leading from Seacombe into Liscard, to the extent of fifteen feet westwardly beyond the centre of the said highway, and from thence in a southwardly direction to the northeastwardly corner of the ancient enclosed lands in the township of Poulton-cum-Seacombe aforesaid, belonging to James Mainwaring, Esq., in the holding of Mr. Wm. Webster, adjoining to Liscard Moor and thence along other ancient enclosed lands in Poulton-cum-Seacombe aforesaid, adjoining to Liscard Moor aforesaid, to the south-east corner of William Pritchard's buildings, and thence in the same direction to the southeastwardly corner of the said William Pritchard's garden and thence along the ancient fence to the north-east corner of a croft in Poulton-cum-Seacombe aforesaid, belonging to the said James Mainwaring, in the holding of George Bird, and from the said corner of the said croft and in a westwardly direction along the fence of the said croft and alongside the house and buildings there in the possession of the said George Bird, and from thence in same direction along the fence of the garden in the possession of the said George Bird, adjoining Mill Lane, to the north-west corner of the said garden, and from thence in a direct line across Mill Lane into and across ancient inclosed lands in Wallasey aforesaid, called the Moor Hey and the Meadow, late the inheritance of Francis Richard Price, Esquire, and now of John Tobin, Esquire, to an ancient boundary stone dividing the said Township of Liscard from the Township of Wallasey aforesaid, near to the southeastwardly corner of a cottage there in the Township of Wallasey aforesaid, in the possession of Margery Smallwood, and from thence across the highway or road leading from Liscard Moor to and into Wallasey to the westwardly corner of a close in Liscard aforesaid, called the Kennions Yard, belonging to Thomas Twist, in the possession of Jane Hasler, and from thence along the westward, northward, and part of the eastward fence of the said croft, to another close in Liscard aforesaid, called the Lower Yard, belonging to Daniel Deane, and from thence along the westward fence and north corner of the said close to another close called Runcorns Yard, belonging to John Deane, senior, hereinbefore described as in his own possession, and thence along the westward fence of another close in Liscard aforesaid, called the Higher Yard, belonging to the said Thomas Molyneux, in his own possession, and from thence along the westward fence of the said close called the Higher Yard until it comes to a stile in the said fence or an ancient foot-path there leading from Liscard and from that stile along the said foot-path which runs in a northwestwardly direction into and across a close called the Marled Butt Hey, belonging to Mr. John Leigh, in the possession of John Hilliard, and from that close still along the said footpath into and across another close called the Higher Hey, belonging to John Egerton, Esquire, in the possession of Thomas Deane, and from the said last mentioned close into and across the westwardly corner of another close called the Higher Heys, belonging to the said John Egerton, in possession of the said Thomas Deane, to the southwardly corner of a close called the Cerpeseech Hey belonging to Ann Thompson, in the possession of William Ledder, and from thence along the westward fence of the said field to the northward corner of such field and from thence to a boundary stone between the said Townships of Wallasey and Liscard, near to the house of the said William Ledder, and from thence in a north-westwardly direction to a boundary near to a pit in Liscard aforesaid, called Captain's Pit, and from thence in the same direction to another stone near Gill's house, and from thence to a hole lately made in the form of a cross on the summit of a hill called Stone Bank hill, and from thence in the same direction to the westernmost rock there near the strand of the sea called Watts Hole, and from thence in the same direction to the low water mark.

And having so ascertained, set out determined and fixed the said boundaries, I caused the several notices by the said Act of the forty-first year of His present Majesty of my having so done to be given, and against which determination no appeal was made, and before I proceeded to make any allotment of the said commons and waste lands in the said Township of Liscard, I ascertained set out and appointed the public carriage roads and highways through and over the lands and grounds intended to be divided, allotted, and inclosed, and the public carriage roads and highways so by me set out and appointed being thirty feet wide at the least are set out in such directions as upon the whole appear to me most commodious to the public. And I also ascertained the same by marks and bounds and prepared a map in which such roads are accurately laid down and described, and signed the same and deposited such plan as by the said last mentioned Act is directed, and gave and affixed the several notices by the same Act directed to be given and affixed of my having set out such roads and deposited such map and also of the general lines of such intended carriage roads, and in and by the said notice appointed a meeting to be held as by the same Act is directed, and some objections being made to the mode of setting out some of the said roads, I, the said Commissioner, together with the Reverend Roger Jackson, Clerk, one of his Majesty's Justices of the Peace, acting in and for the division of the said County of Chester, in which the said commons lie, and not being interested in the same who attended such meeting, proceeded to hear and determine such objections and all other objections thereto, and I, the said Commissioner, and the said Roger Jackson, according to the best of our judgment upon the whole, ordered and finally directed how the said carriage roads should be set out, and having made some trifling alterations in the said map of the said roads, we then confirmed the same, and the said public carriage roads so set out as aforesaid are particularly described in the said map annexed to and forming a part of this my Award, and the general lines of such roads are hereinafter set forth (that is to say)

One public carriage road and highway within and part of the said commons in Liscard aforesaid, marked upon the said map with the letter A, beginning near and opposite a gate leading into a close of ancient inclosed lands belonging to Thomas Molyneux, called the Lower Moor Hey, at the south-east corner of Liscard Moor, and extending from thence across the said Moor in a northwardly direction until it meets the road D, hereinafter described at a place near a barn belonging to the said Thomas Molyneux, containing in length one thousand one hundred and ten yards or thereabouts, and in breadth ten yards.

One other public carriage road and highway within and part of the said commons in Liscard aforesaid, marked upon the said map with the letter B, beginning at the end of the ancient road at the north-east angle of Liscard Moor, near to a house belonging to John Carter, in possession of Daniel Bather, and running alongside or near to the inclosed lands in the township of Liscard into the road marked A, at or near the south-west corner of a close there belonging to Sir Henry Poole, Baronet, in the holding of Mr. John Penkett, containing in length three hundred and twenty yards or thereabouts, and in breadth ten yards.

One other public carriage road and highway within and part of the said commons in Liscard aforesaid, marked upon the said map with the letter C, beginning in a certain lane called Mill Lane, opposite the north-west corner of a garden in the possession of George Bird, and leading in an eastwardly direction past the house in the possession of the said George Bird to the road marked A, nearly opposite to a cottage belonging to Bethia Andley, in the possession of James Wade, containing in length three hundred and fifty-two yards or thereabouts, and in breadth ten yards.

49 Geo. III. *Commissioner's Award,* **ch. ciii.**
Liscard Inclosure.

One other public carriage road and highway within and part of the said commons in Liscard aforesaid, marked upon the said map with the letter D, beginning at that part of the ancient road in Liscard aforesaid, near to Jonathan Deane's house, and extending in a southwestwardly direction alongside of or near to the ancient inclosed lands in Liscard aforesaid, to the high road leading to Wallasey, containing in length three hundred and thirty-six yards or thereabouts, and in breadth ten yards.

One other public carriage road and highway within and part of the said commons in Liscard aforesaid, marked upon the said map with the letter E, beginning at the bank of the River Mersey on Liscard Common, nearly opposite to the Powder Magazines, and extending from thence in a westwardly direction alongside of and near to the inclosed lands in Liscard to the boundary line dividing the Townships of Wallasey and Liscard, where the same ends, containing in length one thousand five hundred and thirty-six yards or thereabouts, and in breadth ten yards.

One other public carriage road and highway within and part of the said commons in Liscard aforesaid, marked upon the said map with the letter F, beginning near and opposite to a cottage in the possession of Henry Bird on the ancient road leading past William Groom's house to Liscard Common, and leading northwestwardly into the last mentioned road E, containing in length eighty-six yards or thereabouts, and in breadth ten yards.

And having set out the public carriage roads as aforesaid, I proceeded as by the said last mentioned Act I am required and empowered to set out and appoint the private roads following:—

I do hereby set out and appoint the same accordingly, that is to say I set out and appoint one private way or road marked upon the said map with the letter a, beginning near to the east end of the new road, on the said map marked A, and extending in a northeastwardly direction to a field of John Carter, in length about sixty-five yards, and in breadth four yards.

One other private way or road marked upon the said map with the letter b, beginning at the north-east end of the road marked B, opposite the house of the said John Carter, and extending from thence in a southeastwardly direction alongside of or near to ancient inclosed lands in Liscard aforesaid, to premises belonging to John Tobin, Esquire, in length about one hundred and thirty-six yards, and in breadth five yards.

One other private way or road marked upon the said map with the letter c, beginning at the north-east end of the road marked D, opposite a house in the occupation of Jonathan Deane, and extending thence in a southwardly direction along ancient inclosed lands in Liscard aforesaid to the south side of a cottage belonging to the said Jonathan Deane, occupied by William Preston, in length about forty-nine yards and in breadth five yards.

One other private way or road marked upon the said map with the letter d, beginning at that part of the new road marked C, opposite George Bird's house, and extending thence northwardly to a cottage in the occupation of Thomas Leather, in length forty-nine yards and in breadth four yards.

One other private way or road marked upon the said map with the letter e, beginning at that part of the road marked C, at the north-east corner of George Bird's garden and extending thence south-eastwardly along ancient inclosed lands in the Township of Poulton-cum-Seacombe to the south-east side of a cottage in the occupation of William Pritchard, in length about two hundred and thirty-three yards and in breadth five yards.

One other private way or road marked upon the said map with the letter f, beginning at that part of the road A, near to the south-west end of the road marked B, and extending thence southwestwardly to a cottage in Poulton-cum-Seacombe aforesaid in the possession of Jane Wilcox, Widow, in length about one hundred and ninety-one yards and in breadth five yards.

One other private way or road marked upon the said map with the letter g, beginning at that part of the road marked E, at the north-east corner of a garden in the occupation of William Peers, and extending in a southwardly direction along the said garden, in length about eighty yards and in breadth ten yards.

One other private way or road marked upon the said map with the letter h, beginning at that part of the road E, at the north-east corner of the said William Peers' garden and extending thence in a northwestwardly direction to the Magazine, in length about sixty-eight yards and in breadth five yards.

One other private way or road marked upon the said map with the letter i, beginning at that part of the road marked E, opposite to a field belonging to James Mainwaring, Esquire, on the west side of a house belonging to Alexander Bibby and extending thence north-wardly to an allotment of the said commons made to John Penkett, Esquire, in length about two hundred and nineteen yards and in breadth ten yards.

One other private way or road marked upon the said map with the letter k, beginning at that part of the road nearly opposite to a windmill belonging to Mr. Penkett, and extending thence northwest-wardly to several allotments made to Mr. Penkett and Mr. Tobin, in length about seven hundred and ninety yards and in breadth ten yards.

One other private way or road marked upon the said map with the letter l, beginning at that part of the road marked E, opposite a house belonging to Peter Ledder, and extending thence in a south-wardly and westwardly direction to the said Peter Ledder's house, in length about one hundred and thirty-seven yards and in breadth five yards.

One other private road or foot-path marked upon the said map with the letter m, beginning at that part of the road marked A, opposite the south-west end of the road marked B, and extending from thence across an allotment marked C, sold to John Tobin, Esquire, to the south corner of a house in the occupation of William Pritchard.

And in further execution of the said recited Acts I allot and set out a piece of land part of the said commons for the purpose of getting stone for the use of the lord and land owners in the said Township of

Liscard, that is to say a piece or parcel of land containing two acres marked upon the said map No. 2a, bounded on the north and west sides by an allotment No. 52, to Gerard Stanley on the east by the private road marked i, and on the south by the public road marked E.

And in further execution of the said Acts I allot and set out another piece of land, part of the said commons on Liscard Common, for the purpose of getting marl for the use of the lord and land owners within the Township of Liscard aforesaid, that is to say, a piece or parcel of land containing one acre marked upon the said map No. 3a, bounded on the north and west by an allotment No. 43, to John Penkett, Esquire, on the south by an allotment by me sold to the said John Penkett, and by him since sold to Thomas Twemlow and Samuel McDowall, marked upon the said map D, and on the east by the strand or shore of the River Mersey.

I also allot and set out another piece of land, part of the same commons for the like purpose, that is to say a piece or parcel of land containing one acre marked upon the said map No. 4a, bounded on the north by an allotment No. 35 to the said John Leigh, on the east by an allotment No. 30 to William Meadowcroft, on the south partly by the said allotment No. 30, and partly by an allotment No. 28 to Ann Thompson, and on the west by a road leading to Wallasey, in the Township of Wallasey.

And in further execution of the said Acts, I have also set out and allotted from and out of the said commons in Liscard aforesaid, the several parcels of land hereinafter mentioned for sale towards defraying the charges and expenses incident to and attending the obtaining and passing the said Act, and of carrying the same into execution, and which parcels of land are described as follows:—

One part of the said commons of Liscard Moor containing three acres and four perches, marked upon the said map with the letter A, and by me sold to John Tobin Esquire, bounded north-eastwardly by old inclosed land of John Carter, eastwardly by the private road a, southwardly by the public road marked A, and westwardly by an allotment No. 2. and No. 2* to John Tobin Esquire, and I direct the fences on the eastwardly, southwardly, and westwardly sides to be made and for ever afterwards kept in repair by the owner thereof.

One other part of the said commons on Liscard Moor aforesaid, containing twenty-three acres, marked upon the said map with the letter B, and by me sold to the said John Tobin in three lots, as advertised for sale, bounded on the northwardly side thereof by the public road marked A, on the eastwardly, southwardly, and southwestwardly sides thereof by old inclosed lands in the Township of Poulton-cum-Seacombe, and on the westwardly side by the private road marked f. And I direct the fences on the northwardly and westwardly sides thereof to be made and for ever afterwards kept in repair by the owner thereof.

One other part of the said commons on Liscard Moor aforesaid, containing eighteen acres and three perches marked upon the said map with the letter C, and by me sold to John Tobin, bounded on the northwardly side by the public road marked A, on the eastwardly and part of the southwardly sides by the private road marked f, on other part of the southwardly side by ancient inclosed lands in the Township of Poulton-cum-Seacombe and by the private road marked e, and on the westwardly side by the public road marked C. And I direct the fences on all sides of the said allotment (except where it adjoins the ancient inclosed lands in the Township of Poulton-cum-Seacombe) to be made and for ever afterwards kept in repair by the owner thereof.

One other part of the said commons on Liscard Common, containing twenty-five acres, marked upon the said map with the letter D, and by me sold to John Penkett, Esquire, and by him since sold to Thomas Twemlow and Samuel McDowall, bounded on the north in part by an allotment No. 43, to the said John Penkett, and in other part by the allotment for marl marked upon the said map No. 3a, on the east in part by the shore of the river Mersey, and in other part by part of the said commons by me sold to the said Samuel McDowall, on the southwardly side by the road marked E, on the said map, and on the west in part by the said road E, and in other part by an allotment No. 56, to the Corporation of Liverpool, but by them since sold to the said Samuel McDowall. And I direct the fences on all sides of the said allotment to be made and for ever afterwards kept in repair by the owner thereof.

One other part of the said commons on Liscard Common containing two roods and two perches marked upon the said map with the letter E, and by me sold to the said Samuel McDowall; bounded on the north-west and south sides by an allotment marked upon the said map with the letter D, by me sold to John Penkett Esq., and by him since sold to the said Thomas Twemlow and Samuel McDowall; and on the east side by the shore of the River Mersey. And I direct the fences on all sides of the said allotment to be made and for ever afterwards kept in repair by the owner thereof.

One other part of the said commons on Liscard Common containing six acres two roods and eight perches marked upon the said map with the letter F, and by me sold to the said John Tobin, bounded on the north by the strand or shore of the sea, on the east in part by an allotment, No. 43, to John Penkett Esquire, in other part by the road marked K, on the south by an allotment No. 42 to the said John Tobin, and on the west in part by the said allotment No. 42, and in other part by an allotment No. 41 to the said John Tobin. And I direct the fences on all sides of the said allotment to be made and for ever afterwards kept in repair by the owner thereof.

And I do hereby set out and allot the remainder of the said commons and waste lands in Liscard aforesaid by the said first mentioned Act directed to be inclosed as follows :—

I set out and allot unto Thomas Molyneux, his heirs and assigns, in right of his ancient inclosed lands, within the Township of Liscard aforesaid, a piece or parcel of land part of the said commons on Liscard Moor, marked upon the said map No. 1, containing three roods or thereabouts bounded on the northeastwardly side by ancient inclosed lands of the said Thomas Molyneux, in the Township of Liscard aforesaid, on the southeastwardly end by waste land in the

Township of Poulton-cum-Seacombe, on the southwardly side by the public road marked A, and on the northwestwardly side by the private road marked a. And I direct the fences on the eastwardly, southwardly, and westwardly sides of the said allotment to be made and for ever afterwards kept in repair by the owner thereof.

I also set out and allot unto the said Thomas Molyneux, his heirs and assigns, a piece or parcel of land other part of the said commons on Liscard Moor aforesaid, marked upon the said map No. 25, containing three acres, three roods and thirty-five perches, bounded on the northeastwardly side by the public road, marked A, on the southeastwardly side in part by an allotment No. 16, to the devisees in trust of Matthew Taylor, deceased, in south part by an allotment No. 17, to John Moston, on the south-west in part by an allotment No. 18, to the representatives of John Deane, Senior, deceased, and in other part by an allotment No. 24, to Sarah Strong, and northwestwardly by the public road marked D, and I direct the fences on the northeastwardly, northwestwardly, and half the southeastwardly sides of the said allotment to be made and for ever afterwards kept in repair by the owner thereof.

I also set out and allot unto John Tobin Esquire, his heirs and assigns, in right of his ancient inclosed lands in Liscard aforesaid, a piece of land other part of the said commons on Liscard Moor aforesaid, marked upon the said map No. 2, containing four acres, two roods, and 32 perches, bounded northeastwardly by ancient inclosed lands of the said John Tobin, eastwardly in part by an allotment marked A, by me sold to the said John Tobin, and in other part by an allotment No. 2*, to the said John Tobin, southwardly by the public road A, and northwestwardly in part by an allotment No. 6, to John Deane, junior, in other part by an allotment No. 5 to the said John Tobin, in right of land purchased from Thomas Martin, in other part by an allotment No. 3, to Joseph Jackson, and in other part by the private road V. And I direct the fences on the southwardly and northwestwardly sides of the said allotment to be made and for ever afterwards kept in repair by the owner thereof.

I also set out and allot unto the said John Tobin his heirs and assigns, to whom Thomas Wilson hath sold and conveyed the same a piece of land, part of the said commons on Liscard Moor aforesaid, marked upon the said map No. 2*, containing thirty-six perches or thereabouts, bounded northwardly and westwardly by the said allotment No. 2, to the said John Tobin, eastwardly by an allotment marked A, by me sold to the said John Tobin, and southwardly by the public road marked A. And I direct the fences on the southwardly and westwardly sides of the said allotment to be made and for ever afterwards kept in repair by the owner thereof.

I also set out and allot unto the said John Tobin his heirs and assigns, another piece of land, part of the said commons on Liscard Moor aforesaid marked upon the said map No. 20, containing one rood and three perches or thereabouts, bounded on the northeast by the private road d, on the southeast by the public road C, on the southwest by the boundary line dividing the Townships of Liscard and Wallasey, and on the northwest by ancient inclosed lands belonging to the said John Tobin, in the Township of Liscard aforesaid. And I direct the fences on the northeast southeast and southwest sides of the said allotment to be made and for ever afterwards kept in repair by the owner thereof.

I also set out and allot unto the said John Tobin his heirs and assigns to whom the said Thomas Wilson hath sold and conveyed the same, a piece of land other part of the said commons on Liscard common aforesaid, marked upon the said map No. 41, containing eleven acres and four perches or thereabouts, bounded northwardly by the strand or shore of the sea, eastwardly in part by an allotment marked with the letter F, by me sold to the said John Tobin, and in other part by an allotment No. 42 to the said John Tobin, southwardly in part by the said allotment No. 42, and in other part by an allotment No. 40 to John Deane, junior, and westwardly by the boundary line dividing the Townships of Liscard and Wallasey. And I direct the fences on the northwardly, southwardly, and westwardly sides of the said allotment to be made and for ever afterwards kept in repair by the owner thereof.

I also set out and allot unto the said John Tobin his heirs and assigns, to whom Thomas Martin hath sold and conveyed the same, a piece of land,part of the said commons on Liscard Moor aforesaid, marked upon the said map No. 5, containing one acre and four perches or thereabouts, bounded northwestwardly by the public road marked B, northeastwardly in part by an allotment No. 4, to John Carter, and in other part by an allotment No. 3 to Joseph Jackson, southeastwardly by an allotment No. 2 to the said John Tobin, and southwestwardly by an allotment No. 6 to John Deane, junior, and I direct the fences on the northwestwardly and southwestwardly sides of the said allotment to be made and for ever afterwards kept in repair by the owner thereof.

I also set out and allot unto the said John Tobin his heirs and assigns to whom the said Thomas Martin hath also sold and conveyed the same another piece of land other part of the said commons on Liscard Moor aforesaid marked upon the said map No. 8 containing two perches or thereabouts bounded northwestwardly by a house and outbuildings late belonging to the said Thomas Martin but now to the said John Tobin northeastwardly by an allotment No. 7 to James Mainwaring, Esquire, southeastwardly by the public road B, and southwestwardly by a garden belonging to the said John Tobin also late Martins and I direct the fences on the southeastwardly side of the said allotment to be made and for ever afterwards kept in repair by the owner thereof.

I also set out and allot unto the said John Tobin his heirs and assigns to whom the said Thomas Martin hath also sold and conveyed the same another piece of land part of the said commons on Liscard Moor aforesaid marked upon the said map No. 9 containing one perch or thereabouts, bounded northwestwardly by buildings belonging to the said John Tobin lately purchased from the said Thomas Martin northeastwardly by a garden belonging to the said John Tobin also purchased from the said Thomas Martin southeastwardly by the public road B, and southwestwardly by an allotment No. 10 to John Deane, junior, and

I direct the fences on the southeastwardly and southwestwardly sides of the said allotment to be made and for ever afterwards kept in repair by the owner thereof.

I also set out and allot unto the said John Tobin for the life of Bethia Andley and after her death to the person or persons entitled thereto under John Hough deceased according to his and their estate in the same another piece of land other part of the said commons on Liscard Moor aforesaid marked upon the said map No. 15 containing thirty-seven perches or thereabouts bounded northwardly by ancient inclosed land of Jonathan Deane, northeastwardly by ancient inclosed lands belonging to John Owens, southeastwardly by an allotment No. 14 to the Devisees in Trust of Matthew Taylor, deceased, and southwestwardly by the public road A over which allotment No. 15 the said John Owens and the owner of his estate are to have the right of passing with horses, carts and carriages, on a road of five yards wide, beginning at the westwardly corner of the said allotment adjoining the public road A along the fence of Jonathan Deane's land to the said John Owens' house, and I direct the fences on the southeastwardly and southwestwardly sides of the said allotment to be made and for ever afterwards kept in repair by the owner thereof.

I also set out and allot unto the said John Tobin his heirs and assigns, to whom the said John Owens hath also sold and conveyed the same, another piece of land part of the said commons on Liscard Common aforesaid marked upon the said map No. 42 containing six acres one rood and thirty-eight perches or thereabouts, bounded northwardly in part by an allotment No. 41 to the said John Tobin, and in other part by an allotment marked F by me sold to the said John Tobin, eastwardly in part by the said allotment marked F and in other part by the private road marked K, southwardly by an allotment No. 40 to John Deane, junior, and westwardly by the said allotment No. 41, and I direct the fences on the eastwardly side as far as the said allotment extends along the road K and on the southwardly and westwardly sides of the said allotment to be made and for ever afterwards kept in repair by the owner thereof.

I also set out and allot unto Joseph Jackson his heirs and assigns a piece of land part of the said commons on Liscard Moor aforesaid marked upon the said map No. 3 containing one acre and nineteen perches, bounded northeastwardly by the private road marked b, southeastwardly by an allotment No. 2 to John Tobin, Esquire, southwestwardly by an allotment No. 5 to the said John Tobin and northwestwardly by an allotment No. 4 to John Carter, and I direct the fences on the northeast, southwest and northwestwardly sides of the said allotment to be made and for ever afterwards kept in repair by the owner thereof.

I also set out and allot unto John Carter his heirs and assigns, a piece of land part of the said commons on Liscard Moor aforesaid marked upon the said map No. 4 containing two acres two roods and seven perches, bounded northeastwardly by the private road marked b, southeastwardly by the said allotment No. 3 to the said Joseph Jackson, southwestwardly by the said allotment No. 5 to the said John Tobin and northwestwardly by the public road marked B, and I direct the fences on the northeast southwest and northwestwardly sides to be made and for ever afterwards kept in repair by the owner thereof.

I also set out and allot unto John Deane, junior, his heirs and assigns, a piece of land part of the said commons on Liscard Moor aforesaid marked upon the said map No. 6 containing one acre and thirty-seven perches or thereabouts, bounded on the northwardly side by an allotment No. 5, to John Tobin, Esquire, southeastwardly by an allotment No. 2, to the said John Tobin, on the southwardly side by the public road marked A, and on the west and northwestwardly sides by the public road marked B, but in making such allotment to the said John Deane, it is meant and intended that Joseph Streets, who holds the lands in right of which this allotment is made for a term of twelve years, under a lease from the said John Deane, is to hold and enjoy this allotment along with his other lands during the remainder of his term in such lease, and I direct the fences on the southwardly, west, and northwestwardly sides of the said allotment to be made by the said Joseph Streets, and to be by him kept in repair during his interest in such lease, and afterwards the same are to be kept in repair by the said John Deane, junior, his heirs and assigns.

I also set out and allot unto the said John Deane, junior, his heirs and assigns, a piece of land part of the said commons on Liscard Moor aforesaid, marked upon the said map No. 10, containing ten perches or thereabouts, bounded northwestwardly by a house and outbuildings belonging to the said John Deane, in the occupation of the said Joseph Streets, northeastwardly in part by a house belonging to John Tobin Esquire, and in other part by an allotment No. 9, to the said John Tobin, southeastwardly by the public road marked B, and southwestwardly by an allotment No. 11, to Sir Henry Poole, Baronet. And I direct the fences on the southeastwardly and southwestwardly sides of the said allotment to be made and for ever afterwards kept in repair by the owner thereof.

I also set out and allot unto the said John Deane, junior, his heirs and assigns, a piece of land part of the said commons on Liscard Common, marked upon the said map No. 40, containing six acres, two roods and three perches, or thereabouts, bounded northwardly by allotments No. 41 and 42 to John Tobin Esquire, eastwardly by the private road marked K, southwardly by an allotment No. 39, to William Groom, and westwardly by the line of boundary dividing the Townships of Liscard and Wallasey, and I direct the fences on the eastwardly, southwardly, and westwardly sides of the said allotment to be made and for ever afterwards kept in repair by the owner thereof.

I also set out and allot unto James Mainwaring, Esquire, his heirs and assigns, a piece of land part of the said commons on Liscard Moor aforesaid, marked upon the said map No. 7, containing four perches, or thereabouts, bounded northwardly by ancient inclosed lands of the said James Mainwaring, Esquire, southeastwardly by the public road B, and southwestwardly by an allotment No. 8, to John Tobin Esquire, and I direct the fences on the southeastwardly and southwestwardly sides of the said allotment to be made and for ever afterwards kept in repair by the owner thereof.

I also set out and allot unto the said James Mainwaring, his heirs and assigns, another piece of land other part of the said commons on

Liscard Moor aforesaid, marked upon the said map No. 19, containing two acres, three roods and twenty-five perches, or thereabouts, bounded northeastwardly by an allotment No. 18, to the representatives of the late John Deane, senior, deceased, south and southeastwardly by the public road marked C, southwestwardly in part by the private road d, in other part by a cottage and garden in the occupation of Thomas Leather, and in other part by ancient inclosed land of John Tobin, Esquire, northwestwardly in part by an allotment No. 21, to Thomas Twist, and in other part by an allotment No. 22, to the representatives of Daniel Deane, deceased, or those next entitled after him, and I direct the fences on the northeastwardly, south, and southeastwardly, as much of the southwestwardly sides as adjoins the private road d, and northwestwardly sides of the said allotment to be made and for ever afterwards kept in repair by the owner thereof.

I also set out and allot unto the said James Mainwaring, his heirs and assigns, another piece of land other part of the said commons on Liscard Common aforesaid, marked upon the said map No. 46, containing thirteen acres two roods and three perches or thereabouts, bounded northwardly in part by an allotment No. 45 to Sarah Strong, and in other part by an allotment No. 43 to John Penkett, Esquire, eastwardly by an allotment No. 52 to Gerard Stanley, southwardly in part by an allotment No. 51 to the representatives of John Deane, senior, deceased, and in other part by an allotment No. 47 to the representatives of Daniel Deane, deceased, or those next entitled after him, and southwestwardly by the private road marked K. And I direct the fences on the southwardly and southwestwardly sides of the said allotment to be made and for ever afterwards kept in repair by the owner thereof.

I also set out and allot unto the said James Mainwaring, his heirs and assigns, another piece of land part of the said commons on Liscard Common aforesaid, marked upon the said map No. 54, containing one rood and ten perches or thereabouts, bounded northwardly by the public road marked E, southwardly and eastwardly in part by ancient inclosed lands belonging to the said James Mainwaring, in other part southwardly by a cottage and garden belonging to Henry Bird and westwardly by the public road marked F, and I direct the fences on the northwardly and westwardly sides of the said allotment to be made and for ever afterwards kept in repair by the owner thereof.

I also set out and allot unto the Reverend Sir Henry Poole, Baronet, his heirs and assigns, a piece of land part of the said commons on Liscard Moor aforesaid, marked upon the said map No. 11, containing four perches or thereabouts, bounded northwestwardly by a cottage and ancient inclosed land of the said Sir Henry Poole, northeastwardly by an allotment No. 10 to John Deane, junior, and southeastwardly by the public road B, and I direct the fences on the southeastwardly side of the said allotment to be made and for ever afterwards kept in repair by the owner thereof.

I also set out and allot unto the said Sir Henry Poole, his heirs and assigns, another piece of land part of the said commons on Liscard Moor aforesaid, marked upon the said map No. 12, containing thirty-eight perches or thereabouts, bounded northeastwardly by ancient inclosed lands belonging to the said Sir Henry Poole, southwestwardly by the public road A, and northwestwardly by an allotment No. 13 to John Moston. And I direct the fences on the southwestwardly and northwestwardly sides of the said allotment to be made and for ever afterwards kept in repair by the owners thereof.

I also set out and allot unto the said Sir Henry Poole, his heirs and assigns, another piece of land part of the said commons on Liscard Common aforesaid, marked upon the said map No. 34, containing twelve acres, three roods and seventeen perches or thereabouts, bounded northwardly by an allotment No. 38 to Edward Wilcox, northeastwardly by the private road marked K, southwardly in part by the public road E, in other part by an allotment No. 33 to Alexander Bibby, in other part by an allotment No. 32 to William Peers, and in other part by an allotment No 37 to John Egerton, Esquire, and westwardly in part by the said allotment No. 33 to Alexander Bibby, in other part by an allotment No. 31 to Elizabeth Johnson, in other part by the said allotment No. 37 to the said John Egerton, and in other part by the boundary line dividing the Townships of Liscard and Wallasey, and I direct the fences on the northeastwardly and southwardly sides and that part of the westwardly side of the said allotment which adjoins, and allotment No. 37 to the said John Egerton and also that part which divides the Townships of Liscard and Wallasey to be made and for ever afterwards kept in repair by the owner thereof.

I also set out and allot unto John Moston, his heirs and assigns, a piece of land part of the said commons on Liscard Moor aforesaid, marked upon the said map No. 13, containing one rood and six perches or thereabouts, bounded northeastwardly by ancient inclosed land of the said John Moston, southeastwardly by an allotment No. 12 to Sir Henry Poole, Baronet, southwestwardly by the public road marked A, and northwestwardly by an allotment No. 14 to the devisees in trust of Matthew Taylor, deceased. And I direct the fences on the southwestwardly and northwestwardly sides of the said allotment to be made and for ever afterwards kept in repair by the owner thereof.

I also set out and allot unto the said John Moston, his heirs and assigns, another piece of land part of the said commons on Liscard Moor aforesaid, marked upon the said map No. 17, containing one rood and sixteen perches or thereabouts, bounded northeastwardly by an allotment No. 16 to the devisees in trust of Matthew Taylor, deceased, southeastwardly by the public road C, southwestwardly by an allotment No. 18 to the representatives of the late John Deane, senior, deceased, and northwestwardly by an allotment No. 25 to Thomas Molyneux. And I direct the fences on the northeastwardly and southeastwardly sides thereof to be made and for ever afterward kept in repair by the owner thereof.

I also set out and allot unto the heir at law or the devisees of Matthew Taylor, deceased, as they may respectively be entitled thereto, a piece of land part of the said commons on Liscard Moor aforesaid, marked upon the said map No. 14, containing one rood one perch or thereabouts, bounded northeastwardly by ancient inclosed lands belonging to the said trustees, southeastwardly by an allotment No. 13 to John Moston, southwestwardly by the public road A, and northwestwardly by an allotment No. 15 to John Tobin, Esquire, which allotment to the said trustees is so made subject to such rights and interest as Berthia Andley hath therein, she holding the lands in right of which this allotment is made by a lease from John Hough, for the life of herself and her son. And I direct the fences on the south-west side of the said allotment to be made by the said Berthia Andley, and to be by her kept in repair during her interest in such lease, and afterwards the same are to be kept in repair by the owner thereof.

I also set out and allot unto the said heir at law, or the devisees of Matthew Taylor, deceased, as they may respectively be entitled thereto, another piece of land other part of the said commons on Liscard Moor aforesaid, marked upon the said map No. 16, containing one acre two roods and thirty-seven perches or thereabouts, bounded northeastwardly by the public road marked A, southeastwardly by the public road C, southwestwardly by an allotment No. 17 to John Moston, and northwestwardly by an allotment No. 25 to Thomas Molyneux, but in making this allotment to the said trustees it is meant and intended that Bethia Andley, who holds the lands in right of which this allotment is made for the life of herself and her son, under a lease from John Hough, is to hold and enjoy this allotment along with the other lands comprised in such lease during her estate and interest therein. And I direct the fences on the northeastwardly and southeastwardly sides and about two-thirds of the fence on the northwestwardly side of the said allotment to be made by the said Bethia Andley, and to be by her kept in repair during her interest in such lease and afterwards the same are to be kept in repair by the owners thereof.

I also set out and allot unto the heir at law or the devisees of John Deane, senior, deceased, as they may respectively be intitled thereto, a piece of land part of the said commons on Liscard Moor aforesaid, marked upon the said map No. 18, containing two acres two roods and twenty-nine perches, bounded northeastwardly in part by an allotment No. 25 to Thomas Molyneux, and in other part by an allotment No. 17. to John Moston, southeastwardly by the public road marked C, southwestwardly by an allotment No. 19 to James Mainwaring Esquire, and northwestwardly in part by an allotment No. 22 to the representatives of the late Daniel Deane, deceased, and in other part by an allotment No. 24 to Sarah Strong. And I direct the fences on the northeastwardly southeastwardly and northwestwardly sides of the said allotment to be made and for ever afterwards kept in repair by the owner thereof.

I also set out and allot unto the said heir at law or devisees of the said John Deane, senior, deceased, as they may respectively be intitled thereto, another piece of land other part of the said commons on Liscard Common aforesaid, marked upon the said map No. 51 containing four acres three roods and fourteen perches or thereabouts, bounded northwardly by an allotment No. 46 to James Mainwaring Esquire, eastwardly by an allotment No. 52 to Gerard Stanley, southwardly by the public road E, and westwardly by allotments No. 47 and 48 to the representatives of Daniel Deane, deceased. And I direct the fences on the south and west sides of the said allotment to be made and for ever afterwards kept in repair by the owner thereof.

I also set out and allot unto the heir at law or the devisees of Thomas Twist, deceased, as they may respectively be entitled thereto, a piece of land other part of the said commons on Liscard Moor aforesaid, marked upon the said map No. 21, containing two roods and two perches or thereabouts, bounded northeastwardly by an allotment No. 22 to the representatives of Daniel Deane, deceased, southeastwardly by an allotment No. 19 to James Mainwaring Esquire, southwestwardly by ancient inclosed land in Liscard aforesaid, belonging to John Tobin Esquire, on the west by a garden belonging to Samuel Dean, and northwestwardly by the road marked D. And I direct the fences on the northeastwardly and northwestwardly sides of the said allotment to be made and for ever afterwards kept in repair by the owner thereof.

I also set out and allot unto Sarah Strong for her life, and after her death to the person or persons entitled thereto, under Thomas Strong, deceased, according to his and their estate in the same, a piece of land other part of the said commons on Liscard Moor aforesaid, marked upon the said map No. 24, containing one rood and twenty-nine perches or thereabouts, bounded northeastwardly by an allotment No. 25 to Thomas Molyneux, southeastwardly by an allotment No. 18 to the devisees or heir at law of John Deane, senior, deceased, southwestwardly by an allotment No. 22 to the persons claiming under Daniel Deane, deceased, and northwestwardly by the public road marked D. And I direct the fences on the northeastwardly and northwestwardly sides of the said allotment to be made and for ever afterwards kept in repair by the owner thereof.

I also set out and allot unto the said Sarah Strong for her life, and after her death to the persons or person entitled thereto under the said Thomas Strong according to his her and their estate in the same, another piece of land other part of the said commons on Liscard Common aforesaid, marked upon the said map No. 45, containing twelve acres and thirty-nine perches or thereabouts, bounded northwardly by an allotment No. 44 to John Penkett Esquire, eastwardly by an allotment No. 43 to the said John Penkett, southwardly by an allotment No. 46 to James Mainwaring Esquire, and westwardly by the private road marked K. And I direct the fences on the southwardly and westwardly sides of the said allotment to be made, and for ever afterwards kept in repair by the owner thereof. And I declare that such allotment is so made part in right of the ancient inclosed lands in Liscard unsold, of which the said Thomas Strong, died, seized and in part right of lands by him sold to Jonathan Deane, Joseph Deane, and Thomas Wilson respectively, the common right in respect of which by the several conveyances thereof was reserved to the said Thomas Strong, his heirs and assigns.

I also set out and allot unto the person or persons intitled thereto in respect of the estate held by Daniel Deane, lately deceased, according to his, her or their estate, therein a piece of land other part of the said commons on Liscard Moor aforesaid, marked upon the said map No. 22, containing one acre and twenty-two perches or thereabouts, bounded northeastwardly by an allotment No 24, to Sarah Strong, southeastwardly in part by an allotment No. 18, to the representatives of John Deane, senior, deceased, and in other part by an allotment No. 19, to James Mainwaring, Esquire, southwestwardly by an allotment No. 21, to persons intitled in respect of an estate late belonging to Thomas Twist deceased, and northwestwardly by the public road marked D. And I direct the fences on the northwestwardly and northeastwardly sides thereof to be made and for ever afterwards kept in repair by the owners thereof.

I also set out and allot unto the person or persons entitled thereto in respect of the estate in Liscard aforesaid in which Daniel Deane, lately deceased, had a life estate or life interest therein according to his, her or their estate therein, another piece of land other part of the said commons on Liscard Moor aforesaid, marked upon the said map No. 23, containing one rood and thirty perches or thereabouts, bounded northeastwardly by a house and garden late in lease to James Wade, southeastwardly by the public road marked D, westwardly by ancient inclosed lands belonging to the representatives of Thomas Twist deceased, and northwestwardly by ancient inclosed lands late in lease to the said James Wade, and I direct the fence on the southeastwardly side of such allotment to be made and kept in repair by the owners thereof.

I also set out and allot unto the person or persons entitled thereto in respect of the estate in Liscard aforesaid, in which Daniel Deane lately deceased had a life estate or life interest according to his, her or their estate therein, a piece of land other part of the said commons on Liscard Common marked upon the said map No. 47, containing one acre three roods and thirty-two perches or thereabouts, bounded northwardly by an allotment No. 46, to James Mainwaring Esquire, eastwardly by an allotment No. 51, to the representatives of John Deane, senior, deceased, southwardly by an allotment No. 48, to the representatives of the said Daniel Deane, deceased, and westwardly by the private road K. And I direct the fences on the south and westwardly sides thereof to be made and for ever afterwards kept in repair by the owners thereof.

I also set out and allot unto Samuel McDowall (to whom Thomas Deane the heir at law of Daniel Deane, deceased, hath sold and conveyed the same) his heirs and assigns a piece of land part of the said commons on Liscard Common marked upon the said map No. 55, containing four acres two roods and nine perches or thereabouts, bounded on the north by an allotment No. 1a, to John Penkett Esquire, on the east by an allotment No. 56, to the said Samuel McDowall purchased from the Corporation of Liverpool, on the south by the public road marked E, and on the west by the private road i. And I direct the fences on the south and west sides of the said allotment to be made and for ever afterwards kept in repair by the owners thereof.

I also set out and allot unto the person or persons intitled thereto in respect of the estate in Liscard aforesaid in which Daniel Deane, deceased, had a life estate or life interest therein according to his, her or their estate therein a piece of land, other part of the said commons on Liscard Common aforesaid, marked upon the said map No. 48, containing two roods and thirty-three perches or thereabouts, bounded northwardly by an allotment No. 47, to the representatives of the said Daniel Deane, and eastwardly by an allotment No. 51 to the representatives of John Deane, senior, deceased, southwardly by the public road E and westwardly by the private road K. And I direct the fences on the south and west sides of the said allotment to be made and for ever afterwards kept in repair by the owner thereof.

I also set out and allot unto William Stronge, his heirs, and assigns, to whom John Penkett, Esquire, has sold and conveyed the same, and who purchased from Jonathan Deane a piece of land, other part of the said commons on Liscard Moor aforesaid, marked upon the said map No. 26, containing one acre or thereabouts, bounded eastwardly in part by the private road marked c and in other part by ancient inclosed lands belonging to Jonathan Deane, on the south-west by the public road marked A and on the northwest by the public road marked D. And I direct the fences on the eastwardly side as far as the road c extends and on the south-west and north-west sides to be made and for ever afterwards kept in repair by the owners thereof.

I also set out and allot unto the said John Penkett, his heirs and assigns, to whom the said Jonathan Deane hath sold and conveyed the same, a piece of land, other part of the said commons on Liscard Common aforesaid, marked upon the said map No. 43A, containing five acres one rood and thirty-eight perches or thereabouts, bounded on the north and east sides by an allotment No. 43 to the said John Penkett, on the south by an allotment No. 44 to the said John Penkett, and on the west by the private road K. And I direct the fences on the south and west sides of the said allotment to be made and for ever afterwards kept in repair by the owner thereof.

I also set out and allot unto the said John Penkett, to whom the said Jonathan Deane hath also sold and conveyed the same, another piece of land, other part of the said commons on Liscard Common aforesaid, marked on the said map No. 49, containing two roods and twenty-one perches or thereabouts, bounded on the north by the public road marked E, on the east in part by an allotment No. 50 to the said John Penkett, and in other part by ancient inclosed land belonging to the said John Penkett, on the south by ancient inclosed land belonging to the said Jonathan Deane, and on the south-west by ancient inclosed lands belonging to Sir Henry Poole, Baronet, and James Mainwaring, Esquire. And I direct the fences on the north and so far of the east fence as adjoins the allotment No. 50 to the said John Penkett to be made and for ever afterwards kept in repair by the owner thereof.

I also set out and allot unto the said John Penkett, unto whom the said Jonathan Deane hath also sold and conveyed the same, another piece of land, other part of the said commons on Liscard Common aforesaid, marked upon the said map No. 53, containing one rood and twenty-six perches or thereabouts, bounded on the north by the public road marked E, on the east by the public road marked F, and on the southwardly side by ancient inclosed land belonging to the said Jonathan Deane, and I direct the fences on the north and east sides of the said allotment to be made, and for ever afterwards kept in repair by the owner thereof.

I also set out and allot unto the said John Penkett, his heirs and assigns to whom Bethia Andley hath sold and conveyed the same, another piece of land other part of the said commons on Liscard Common aforesaid marked upon the said map No. 44, containing four acres, two roods and twenty-four perches or thereabouts, bounded on the north by allotment No. 43a, on the east by an allotment No. 43, to the said John Penkett, on the south by an allotment No. 45 to Sarah Strong, and on the west by the private road marked K. And I direct the fences on the south and west sides of the said allotment to be made and for ever afterwards kept in repair by the owners thereof.

I also set out and allot unto the said John Penkett, his heirs and assigns in right of his ancient inclosed lands in Liscard aforesaid, another piece of land other part of the said commons on Liscard Common aforesaid marked upon the said map No. 43, containing one hundred and forty-three acres, one rood and twenty-five perches, bounded on the north by the strand or shore of the sea, on the east by the strand or shore of the River Mersey, on the south in part by an allotment No. 3a set out as a marl pit for the use of the public, in other part by an allotment marked with the letter D, by me sold to the said John Penkett, and by him since sold and conveyed to Thomas Twemlow and Samuel McDowall, in other part by an allotment No. 56 to the Corporation of Liverpool, since sold by them to the said Samuel McDowall, in other part by an allotment No. 1a to the said John Penkett, in other part by an allotment No. 52, to Gerard Stanley, in other part by an allotment No. 46, to James Mainwaring, Esquire, in other part by an allotment No 43a to the said John Penkett and in other part by the private road K, and on the west in part by the said allotment No. 1a, in other part by an allotment No. 45 to Sarah Strong, in other part by allotments No. 44 and No. 43a to the said John Penkett and in other part by an allotment marked with the letter F, sold to John Tobin, Esquire. And I direct the fences on the south and west sides of the said allotment (except where it adjoins the allotment marked No. 3a, the allotment D sold to the said John Penkett and the allotment marked F sold to the said John Tobin), to be made and for ever afterwards kept in repair by the owners thereof.

I also set out and allot unto the said John Penkett his heirs, and assigns to whom Jonathan Deane hath sold and conveyed the same another piece of land other part of the said commons on Liscard Common aforesaid marked upon the said map No. 50, containing two roods and eleven perches or thereabouts, bounded on the north by the public road marked E, on the south by ancient inclosed land belonging to the said John Penkett, and on the west by an allotment No. 49 to the said John Penkett. And I direct the fence on the north side of the said allotment to be made and for ever afterwards kept in repair by the owner thereof.

I also set out and allot unto the said John Penkett his heirs and assigns a piece or parcel of land parcel of the said commons in Liscard aforesaid marked upon the said map No. 1A, containing six acres two roods and six perches, bounded on the north by an allotment No. 43 on the said map to the said John Penkett, on the east by the same allotment, on the south in part by an allotment

No. 56 to Samuel McDowall purchased from the Corporation of Liverpool in other part by an allotment No. 55 to the said Samuel McDowall purchased from Thomas Deane, the heir at law of Daniel Deane deceased, and in other part by the road marked I on the said map, and on the west by an allotment No. 52, to Gerard Stanley. And I direct the fences on all sides of the said allotment to be made and for ever afterwards kept in repair by the owners thereof, which said several allotments so made to the said John Penkett, are in full satisfaction, not only for his right of common upon the said several commons or waste lands, in respect of his estates and of his purchases so made as aforesaid, but also in full satisfaction for his claim on the said commons in respect to the royalty of the said Manor of Liscard.

I also set out and allot unto Ann Thompson, in respect of her estate in the said Township of Liscard, and to her heirs and assigns according to her estate therein, a piece or parcel of land, part of the said commons on Liscard Common aforesaid marked upon the said map No. 27, containing one acre one rood and twenty perches, or thereabouts, bounded northwardly by the public road E, eastwardly and southwardly by the private road i, and ancient inclosed lands belonging to Peter Ledder and the said Ann Thompson, and westwardly by the boundary line dividing the Townships of Liscard and Wallasey. And I direct the fences on the north, and so far of the east and south sides of the said allotment as adjoins the road I, and on the westwardly side to be made, and for ever afterwards kept in repair by the owners thereof.

I also set out and allot unto the said Ann Thompson, in respect of the same estate and to her heirs and assigns according to her estate therein, a piece or parcel of land, other part of the said commons on Liscard Common aforesaid marked upon the said map No. 28, containing three roods and five perches or thereabouts, bounded northwardly by an allotment No. 4A, left for a marl pit, eastwardly by an allotment No. 30, to William Meadowcroft, southwardly by the public road marked E, and westwardly by the boundary line dividing the Townships of Liscard and Wallasey. And I direct the fences on the eastwardly, southwardly and westwardly sides of the said allotment to be made and for ever afterwards kept in repair by the owner thereof.

I also set out and allot unto William Meadowcroft, his heirs and assigns, a piece of land other part of the said commons on Liscard Common marked upon the said map No. 29, containing two roods and thirty-eight perches, or thereabouts, bounded northwardly by the public road E, eastwardly by ancient inclosed lands of the said William Meadowcroft, southwardly by ancient inclosed lands belonging to Peter Ledder, and westwardly by the private road I. And I direct the fences on the north and westwardly sides of the said allotment to be made and for ever afterwards kept in repair by the owners thereof.

I also set out and allot unto the said William Meadowcroft, his heirs and assigns, another piece of land other part of the said commons on Liscard Common, marked upon the said map No. 30, containing one acre one rood and twenty-two perches or thereabouts, bounded northwardly in part by an allotment No. 4A set out for marl, and in other part by an allotment No. 35 to John Leigh, Esquire, eastwardly by an allotment No. 31 to Elizabeth Johnson, southwardly by the public road marked E, westwardly in part by an allotment No. 28 to Ann Thompson, and in other part by the said allotment No. 4A set out for marl. And I direct the fences on the east and south sides of the said allotment to be made and for ever afterwards kept in repair by the owners thereof.

I also set out and allot unto Elizabeth Johnson, in respect of her estate in the said Township of Liscard and to her heirs and assigns or according to her estate therein, a piece of land part of the said commons on Liscard Common, marked upon the said map No. 31, containing three acres, one rood and twenty-three perches, or thereabouts, bounded northwardly by an allotment No. 37, to John Egerton, Esquire, eastwardly in part by an allotment No. 34, to the Reverend Sir Henry Poole, Baronet, and in other part by an allotment No. 32, to William Peers, southwardly by the public road marked E, and westwardly in part by an allotment No. 30, to William Meadowcroft, and in other part by an allotment No. 35, to John Leigh, Esquire. And I direct the fences on the east and south sides of the said allotment to be made and for ever afterwards kept in repair by the owners thereof.

I also set out and allot unto William Peers, his heirs and assigns, a piece of land other part of the said commons on Liscard Common, marked upon the said map No. 32, containing two roods and thirty-four perches, bounded northwardly by an allotment No. 34, to the Reverend Sir Henry Poole, Baronet, eastwardly by an allotment No. 33, to Alexander Bibby, southwardly by the public road E, and westwardly by an allotment No. 31, to Elizabeth Johnson. And I direct the fences on the east and south sides thereof to be made and for ever afterwards kept in repair by the owners thereof.

I also set out and allot unto the said Alexander Bibby, his heirs and assigns, a piece of land other part of the said commons on Liscard Common aforesaid, marked upon the said map No. 33, containing two roods and twenty-six perches, or thereabouts, bounded northwardly and eastwardly by an allotment No. 34, to the Reverend Sir Henry Poole, Baronet, on the south by the public road E, and on the west by an allotment No. 32, to William Peers. And I direct the fences on the south and east sides thereof to be made and for ever afterwards kept in repair by the owners thereof.

I also set out and allot unto the said John Leigh, his heirs and assigns, a piece of land part of the said commons on Liscard Common, marked upon the said map No. 35, containing one acre and thirty-three perches, or thereabouts, bounded northwardly in part by an allotment No. 36, to the Reverend George Briggs, and in other part by an allotment No. 37, to John Egerton, Esquire, eastwardly by an allotment, No. 31, to Elizabeth Johnson, southwardly in part by an allotment No. 30, to William Meadowcroft, and in other part by an allotment No 4A, set out for marl, and westwardly by the boundary line dividing the Townships of Liscard and Wallasey. And I direct the fences on the east, on that part of the south adjoining the allotment No. 30, to William Meadowcroft, and on the west to be made and for ever afterwards kept in repair by the owners thereof.

I also set out and allot unto the Reverend George Briggs, his heirs and assigns, a piece of land other part of the said commons on Liscard Common, marked upon the said map No 36, containing one rood and twenty-two perches, or thereabouts, bounded northwardly and eastwardly by an allotment No. 37, to John Egerton, Esquire, southwardly by an allotment No. 35, to John Leigh, Esquire, and westwardly by the boundary line dividing the Townships of Liscard and Wallasey. And I direct the fences on the east, south, and west sides thereof to be made and for ever afterwards kept in repair by the owners thereof.

I also set out and allot unto John Egerton Esquire, his heirs and assigns, a piece of land other part of the said commons on Liscard Common, marked upon the said map No. 37, containing six acres and twenty-six perches, or thereabouts, bounded northwardly and eastwardly by an allotment No. 34, to the Reverend Sir Henry Poole, Baronet, southwardly in part by an allotment No. 31 to Elizabeth Johnson, in other part by an allotment No. 35, to John Leigh, Esquire, and in other part by an allotment No. 36, to the Reverend George Briggs, and westwardly in part by the said allotment No. 36, and in other part by the line of boundary dividing the Townships of Liscard and Wallasey. And I direct the fences on the south, and so far of the west fence as adjoins the boundary line aforesaid, to be made and for ever afterwards kept in repair by the owner thereof.

I also set out and allot unto Edward Wilcock, his heirs and assigns a piece of land other part of the said commons on Liscard Common marked on the said map No. 38, containing seven acres and twenty perches or thereabouts, bounded northwardly by an allotment No. 39, to William Groom, eastwardly by the private road K, southwardly by an allotment No. 34, to the Reverend Sir Henry Poole, Baronet, and westwardly by the boundary line dividing the townships of Liscard and Wallasey. And I direct the fences on the eastwardly, south, and west sides thereof to be made and for ever afterwards kept in repair by the owners thereof.

I also set out and allot unto William Groom, his heirs and assigns a piece of land other part of the said commons on Liscard Common marked upon the said map No. 39, containing five acres one rood and thirteen perches or thereabouts, bounded northwardly by an allotment No. 40, to John Deane, junior, eastwardly by a private road K, southwardly by an allotment No. 38, to Edward Wilcock, and westwardly by the boundary line dividing the townships of Liscard and Wallasey. And I direct the fences on the east, south, and west sides to be made and for ever afterwards kept in repair by the owners thereof.

I also set out and allot unto Gerard Stanley, his heirs and assigns, a piece of land other part of the said commons on Liscard Common marked upon the said map No. 52, containing fourteen acres and fifteen perches or thereabouts, bounded northwardly by an allotment No. 43, to John Penkett, Esquire, eastwardly in part by an allotment No. 1a, to the said John Penkett, in other part by the said private road I, and in other part by an allotment No. 2a, set out for a stone quarry, southwardly in part by the said allotment No. 2a, and in other part by the public road marked E, and westwardly in part by an allotment No. 51, to the representatives of John Deane, senior, deceased, and in other part by an allotment No. 46 to James Mainwaring, Esquire, and I direct that so far of the east fence as adjoins the road I, and so far of the south side as adjoins the public road E, and the fence on the whole of the west side to be made and for ever afterwards kept in repair by the owner thereof.

I also set out and allot unto Samuel McDowal, his heirs and assigns, to whom the Mayor, Bailiffs, and Burgesses of the Corporation of Liverpool have sold and conveyed the same, a piece or parcel of land other part of the said commons on Liscard Common marked upon the said map No. 56, containing five acres three roods and thirty perches or thereabouts, bounded northwardly by allotments No. 1a and No. 43 to John Penkett, Esq., eastwardly by an allotment D sold to the said John Penkett and by him since sold to Thomas Twemlow and Samuel McDowal, southwardly by the public road E, and westwardly by an allotment No. 55. to the said Samuel McDowal purchased from Thomas Deane the heir at law of Daniel Deane deceased, and I direct that the fences on the south and west sides thereof shall be made and for ever afterwards kept in repair by the owner thereof.

I also set out and allot unto the said Mayor, Bailiffs, and Burgesses of the town of Liverpool aforesaid, in right of their estate there, a piece of land other part of the said commons on Liscard Common marked upon the said map No. 57, containing one rood and sixteen perches or thereabouts, bounded northeastwardly by the public road E, southwestwardly by the private road h, and westwardly in part by the Powder Magazines and in other part by ancient inclosed lands now or late belonging to William Meadowcroft, and I direct the fences on the northeastwardly and southwestwardly sides thereof, to be made and for ever afterwards kept in repair by the owner thereof.

I also set out and allot unto the said Mayor, Bailiffs, and Burgesses of the town of Liverpool aforesaid in right of their estate there another piece of land other part of the said commons on Liscard Common, marked upon the said map No. 58, containing one rood and five perches or thereabouts, bounded northeastwardly by the private road h, southwardly by a garden belonging to William Peers. and westwardly in part by ancient inclosed lands belonging to the Reverend Sir Henry Poole, Baronet, and in other part by the Powder Magazines. And I direct the fence on the north-eastwardly side thereof to be made and for ever afterwards kept in repair by the owner thereof.

I also set out and allot unto the same Mayor, Bailiffs and Burgesses, another piece of land other part of the said commons on Liscard Common, marked upon the said map No. 59, containing two roods and thirty-two perches or thereabouts, bounded northwardly by the public road E, eastwardly by the strand or shore of the River Mersey, and westwardly by the road G. And I direct that the fences on all sides of the said allotment are to be made and for ever afterwards kept in repair by the owners thereof.

And I Award and direct that the said several allotments, so by me set out as aforesaid within the said Township of Liscard, shall be by the persons and body corporate to whom the same are so respectively allotted accepted, closed, and fenced in within three months from the date of this my Award. And that the same are in full of their respective rights of common in and upon the said several commons and waste lands so directed to be inclosed as aforesaid.

And I declare that the quantities of all the said lands to which this Award has reference are in statute measure, and that the quantities and descriptions are accurately set down in the words of this my Award, but as figures and lines on maps are more certain in the description and boundaries of small allotments than words, I do hereby declare that if any doubts should arise the map must decide the doubt.

And I order and direct, that the several private ways and roads hereinbefore set out and appointed shall be made and at all times for ever thereafter, be supported and kept in repair by and at the expense of the owners and proprietors for the time being of the lands and grounds so inclosed as aforesaid, according to an equal rate or assessment to be from time to time made as the same may become necessary.

In witness whereof I have hereunto set may hand and seal, that is to say, my hand to the first fourteen skins and my hand and seal to this fifteenth and last skin, my hand and seal this second day of November, one thousand eight hundred and thirteen.

This Award was signed, sealed and published by the said James Boydell (being first duly stamped) in the presence of
      JAMES BOYDELL. (L.S.)
    EDW. EYES.
    SYL. HEELIS.

I hereby certify that the foregoing is a true copy of a copy of an Award bearing date the second day of November, one thousand eight hundred and thirteen, under the hand and seal of James Boydell, of Rosset, in the County of Denbigh, Gentleman, the Commissioner named and appointed in and by an act of Parliament, made and passed in the forty-ninth year of the reign of his then present Majesty King George the Third, intituled "An Act for enclosing Waste Lands in the Township of Liscard, in the Parish of Wallasey in the County Palatine of Chester" deposited in the office of the Clerk of the Peace for the County of Chester, on the fourth day of November, one thousand eight hundred and fourteen. Dated this ninth day of August, one thousand eight hundred and sixty-six.

               THOMAS ROBERTS, Deputy Clerk of the
                    Peace for the County of Chester.

THE
WALLASEY & WEST KIRBY INCLOSURE ACT, 1814.

(54 Geo. III. c. 87.)

ARRANGEMENT OF SECTIONS.

	SECTION.
Preamble.	
Commissioner	1
For appointing new Commissioner	2
Notice of meeting for the appointment of a new Commissioner	3
Notice of sittings to put Act in execution	4
Other notices	5
Commissioner to determine disputes	6
Persons in possession not to be molested without due course of Law	7
Power to award Costs	8
For determining disputed Claims	9
Action not to abate by death of parties	10
In cases of deaths of parties before Actions brought, the same to be carried on and defended in their Names	11
Suits respecting Titles not to impede the execution of the Act	12
Deaths of parties not to suspend the execution of the Act	13
Commissioner to determine Encroachments	14
Drains, &c.	15
Apportioning allotments to the respective parties	16
Allotments for Stone and Marl	17
Allotment for sale to pay expenses	18
To be sold by Auction	19
Division of expenses	20
Making good Deficiency	21
Allotment of the Residue	22
Sand Hills to remain open	23
Allotment to the Rectors in respect of their Glebe Lands, to be fenced at the expense of the other Claimants	24

54 *Geo. III.* *The Wallasey and West Kirby* *ch. lxxxvii.*
Inclosure Act, 1814.

	SECTION.
Exchanges... ...	25
Not to revoke wills	26
To set posts and rails to preserve Quicksets	27
Rights in Inclosures may be sold separate from the Estate which gives the Right	28
Right of common to cease	29
Commissioner's Allowance ...	30
Accounts to be settled by Justices	31
Money advanced to be repaid with interest	32
Award to be deposited	33
Appeal	34
Saving Manorial Rights ...	35
General Saving	36
Act to be given in evidence as Public Act	37

54 *Geo. III.* The *Wallasey and West Kirby* ch. *lxxxvii.*
Inclosure Act, 1814.

AN

A C T

for inclosing Lands in the Parishes of Wallasey and West Kirby, in the County of Chester.

27th May, 1814.

WHEREAS there are within the Township of Wallasey, in the parish of Wallasey, in the county of Chester, divers commons and waste lands containing about three hundred and twelve acres of statute measure, exclusive of certain land covered with sand hills on the north-west side of part of the said commons; and there is within the said Township of Wallasey, a certain tract or parcel of open and undivided land, called Wallasey Pasture, containing about two hundred and twenty acres of statute measure; and there are within the Township of Poolton-cum-Seacombe, in the said parish of Wallasey, divers other commons and waste lands, containing eighty-two acres of statute measure, or thereabouts; and there is within the parish of West Kirby, in the said county, a certain other tract or parcel of common land, called The Carr, containing about two hundred and four acres of statute measure, adjoining the Townships of Grange, Little Meols, and Newton-cum-Larton, in the said parish of West Kirby, and on which the owners of lands in those several Townships have right of common: and whereas Robert Vyner, Esquire, and John Egerton, Esquire, are joint lords of the manor of Wallasey aforesaid; and Richard Smith, Esquire, is or claims to be lord of the manor of Poolton-cum-Seacombe aforesaid; and James Mainwaring, Esquire, also claims some right or title to, or interest in, the said last-mentioned manor; and John Leigh, Esquire, is lord of the manor of Grange, in the said Parish of West Kirby, in which manor the said piece of land called The Carr is situate: And whereas the Right Reverend the Bishop of Chester is patron of the Rectory and Parish Church of Wallasey aforesaid, and the Reverend Augustus Campbell, Clerk, is the Rector of the said Parish and Parish Church; and the Dean and Chapter of the Cathedral Church of Chester are Patrons of the Rectory and Parish Church of West Kirby aforesaid; and the Reverend Thomas Trevor Trevor, Clerk, is the Rector of the said Parish and Parish Church: And whereas the said Robert Vyner, John Egerton, Richard Smith, James Mainwaring, and John Leigh, and also Sir Henry Poole, Baronet, John Tobin, Joseph Green, Joseph Molyneux, Peter Ledsom, Joseph Jackson, George Cooper, William Bird, Robert Stanley, John Meadows, William Dean, Robinson Dean, Richard Hilliard, and several other persons, are owners and proprietors of divers messuages, tenements, lands, and hereditaments within the said Townships of Wallasey and Poolton-cum-Seacombe, and are respectively entitled to right of common on the said commons and waste lands in Wallasey and Poolton-cum-Seacombe, in which Townships their messuages,

54 Geo. III.   The Wallasey and West Kirby   ch. lxxvii.   49
Inclosure Act, 1814.

lands, and tenements respectively lie; and the said John Leigh, Sir **Sec. 2**
Thomas Stanley Massey Stanley, Baronet, the Reverend Edward
Stanley, the Reverend Roger Jackson, and several other persons are
owners of estates within the said Townships of Grange, Little Meols
and Newton-cum-Larton respectively, and are entitled to right of
common on the said piece of land called The Carr; and some of the
said persons before named, and others, are possessed of or entitled
to the said piece of land called Wallasey Pasture, in certain shares
and proportions called cowgaits; but the same cowgaits lie open to
each other, and are undivided, although the number of such cowgaits
belonging to each person is well known and ascertained, and the
owners of such cowgaits are also entitled to right of common on the
said commons and waste lands in the Township of Wallasey: And
whereas an Act was passed in the forty-first year of the reign of His 41 G. 3.
present Majesty, intituled an act for consolidating in one act certain
provisions usually inserted in acts of inclosure, and for facilitating
the mode of proving the several facts usually required on the passing
of such acts: And whereas the said several commons and waste lands,
and the said cowgaits and Carr before specified, in their present state
are of little value, and if divided into specific allotments and inclosed
would be considerably improved; but such division and inclosure
cannot be made and rendered effectual without the aid and authority
of Parliament: May it therefore please Your Majesty that it may be
enacted; and be it enacted by the King's most Excellent Majesty by
and with the advice and consent of the lords spiritual and temporal,
and commons, in this present parliament assembled, and by the
authority of the same, that the said commons and waste lands
within the said several Townships of Wallasey and Poolton-cum-
Seacombe, and the said cowgaits and Carr respectively, shall be set
out, allotted, and divided, as soon as conveniently may be; and that Commis-
James Boydell of Rossett, in the county of Denbigh, Gentleman, shall sioner.
be and he is hereby appointed the Commissioner for setting out,
allotting, and dividing the same, and for carrying this and the said
recited act into execution, subject to the regulations of the said recited
act, except in such cases where the same are hereby varied or altered.

2. And be it further enacted, that if the said James Boydell, or any For appoint-
succeeding commissioner to be appointed as hereinafter mentioned, shall ing new Com-
die, or refuse to act, or be rendered incapable of acting by sickness, missioner.
or any other cause, it shall be lawful for a majority in value (such
value to be ascertained by the Assessment of the Land Tax) of the
owners and proprietors of messuages, lands, tenements, or hereditaments in the said several townships of Wallasey, Poolton-cum-Seacombe, Grange, Little Meols, and Newton-cum-Larton, having Right
of Common there, and also of the owners of the said cowgaits, being
present at a meeting to be called as hereinafter mentioned, by writing
under their hands, to appoint another Commissioner (not interested
in the premises) in the room or place of the said James Boydell,
within six weeks next after such death, refusal, or incapacity shall
be made known, and so from time to time as such Commissioner so
to be appointed as aforesaid may happen to die, or refuse, or become
incapable to act, to appoint another Commissioner in the like
manner; and every such new Commissioner so to be appointed,
having taken and subscribed the oath required to be taken by the
said recited Act, shall have such and the like powers and authorities

E

Sec. 3—8	by virtue of this Act, as if he had been originally named and appointed a Commissioner in and by this Act.
Notice of meeting for the appointment of a new Commissioner.	3. And be it further enacted, that such meeting for the appointment of a new Commissioner shall be called of the several persons interested in the said commons and waste lands, and in the said cowgaits and Carr before specified, and shall be held at some convenient place in the Townships of Wallasey, Little Meols, or Grange, and that notice of such meeting shall and may be given by order of any five or more persons interested in the lands and grounds to be allotted, divided, and inclosed by virtue of this Act, by fixing such notice on the Parish Churches of Wallasey and West Kirby aforesaid, on three Sundays next immediately preceding such meeting, and also by publishing the same in one of the Chester newspapers fourteen days previous to such meeting.
Notice of sittings to put Act in execution.	4. And be it further enacted, that the said Commissioner shall and he is hereby required to cause notice to be inserted in one of the Chester weekly newspapers of the time and place of his first sitting, to put this Act into execution, at least twenty-one days before the day of such sitting, and which shall be at some convenient place within some one of the said Townships; and the said Commissioner shall and may afterwards proceed in the execution of this Act, and from time to time adjourn to such time and place within the said Townships respectively, or within eight miles thereof, as he shall think proper.
Other notices.	5. Provided always, and be it enacted, that all other notices requisite or necessary to be made and given by the said Commissioner, shall be so made and given by advertisement in one of the said Chester newspapers.
Commissioner to determine Disputes.	6. And be it further enacted, that if any dispute or difference shall arise between any of the parties interested, or claiming to be interested, in the lands and grounds to be divided, allotted, and inclosed in pursuance of this Act, or any part thereof, touching or concerning the several rights and interests which they or any of them have, or shall have, or claim to have, in, over, upon, or out of the said lands and grounds, or any part thereof, or touching or concerning any matter or thing relating to the said division, allotment, and inclosure, it shall be lawful for the said Commissioner, and he is hereby authorized to examine into, hear, and determine the same: provided always, that nothing in this Act contained shall authorize the said Commissioner to determine the title to any messuages, lands, tenements, and hereditaments whatsoever.
Persons in Possession not to be molested without due course of law.	7. Provided also, and be it further enacted, that nothing in this Act contained shall extend to enable the said Commissioner to determine any right between any parties, contrary to the possession of any such parties (except as hereinafter particularly mentioned); but in case the said Commissioner shall be of opinion against the right of the person or persons so in possession, he shall forbear to make any determination thereupon till the possession shall have been given up by such person or persons or recovered from such person or persons by ejectment or other due course of law.
Power to award costs.	8. And be it further enacted, that in case the said Commissioner shall, upon the hearing and determination of any claim or claims, objection or objections, to be delivered to him in pursuance of this

Act, see cause to award any costs, it shall and may be lawful for him, and he is hereby empowered, upon application made for that purpose, to settle, assess, and award such costs and charges as he shall think reasonable, to be paid to the party or parties in whose favour any determination of the said Commissioner shall be made, by the person or persons whose claim or claims, objection or objections, shall be thereby disallowed or overruled; and in case the person or persons who shall be liable to pay such costs and charges, shall neglect or refuse to pay the same on demand, then and in such case it shall and may be lawful for the said Commissioner, and he is hereby required and authorized, by a warrant under his hand and seal, directed to any person or persons whomsoever, to cause such costs and charges to be levied by distress and sale of the goods and chattels of the person or persons so neglecting or refusing to pay the same, rendering the overplus (if any), upon demand, to the person or persons whose goods and chattels shall have been so distrained and sold, after deducting the costs and charges attending such distress and sale.

Sec. 9

9. And be it further enacted, that in case any person or persons interested or claiming to be interested in the said intended division and allotments, shall refuse to leave his, her, or their claim or right to the decision of the Commissioner, or shall be dissatisfied with any determination of the said Commissioner, touching or concerning such claim or right in, over, or upon the lands and grounds hereby directed to be divided, allotted, and inclosed, or any part thereof, it shall be lawful for the person or persons so refusing to refer such claim or right, or being dissatisfied with any determination of the said Commissioner made respecting the same as aforesaid, to proceed to a trial at law of the matter in dispute at the then next or at the following Assizes to be holden for the said County of Chester; and for that purpose the person or persons who shall so refuse to refer as aforesaid, or shall be dissatisfied with the determination of the said Commissioner, shall, upon giving notice in writing to the said Commissioner of his, her, or their intention to bring an action, cause an action to be brought in one of His Majesty's Courts of Record, at Westminster, upon a feigned issue against the person or persons with whom such question of claim or right may have arisen, or in whose favour such determination shall have been made, within three calendar months next after such refusal or determination as aforesaid, as the case may be; and the defendant or defendants in such respective action or actions shall, and he, she, and they is and are hereby required to name an attorney or attornies who shall appear thereto, or file common bail, and accept one or more issue or issues, whereby such claim or claims, and the right or rights thereby insisted on, may be tried and determined, such issue or issues to be settled by the proper officer of the Court in which the said respective action or actions shall be commenced, (in case the parties shall differ about the same,) and the verdict or verdicts which shall be given upon the trial of such action or actions shall be final, binding, and conclusive upon all and every person and persons whomsoever, unless the Court wherein such action or actions shall be brought shall set aside such verdict or verdicts, and order a new trial to be had therein, which it shall be lawful for the Court to do, as is usual in other cases; and after such verdict or verdicts

For determining disputed claims.

54 Geo. III. *The Wallasey and West Kirby* ch. lxxxvii.
Inclosure Act, 1814.

Sec. 10—13 shall be obtained, and not set aside by the Court, the said Commissioner shall and he is hereby required to act in conformity thereto, and to allow or disallow the claim or claims thereby determined, according to the event of such trial or trials: Provided always, that in case such refusal to refer shall not be signified as aforesaid, or in case the determination of the said Commissioner, touching such claim or right in, over, or upon the lands and grounds hereby directed to be divided, allotted, and inclosed, or any part thereof, shall not be objected to, or being objected to, the party or parties objecting shall not cause such action at law to be brought and proceeded in as aforesaid, then the determination of the said Commissioner shall be final and conclusive upon all parties.

Action not to abate by death of parties.

10. And be it further enacted, That if any of the parties in any action to be brought in pursuance of this Act shall die pending the same, such action shall not abate by reason thereof, but shall be proceeded in as if no such event had happened.

In cases of deaths of parties before actions brought, the same to be carried on and defended in their names.

11. Provided always, and be it further enacted, That if any person or persons with whom any such question of right may have arisen, or in whose favour any such determination as aforesaid shall have been made, and against whom any such action or actions might have been brought, if living, shall die before any such action shall have been brought, and before the expiration of the time by this Act limited for bringing such action or actions, it shall be lawful for the person or persons, bodies politic, corporate or collegiate, who might have brought such action or actions against the person or persons so dying, to bring the same within the time so limited against such person or persons as if actually living, and to serve the Clerks or Clerk of the said Commissioner with process for commencing such action or actions, in the same manner as the party or parties might have been served therewith if living; and it shall thereupon be incumbent on the heir or heirs, or other person or persons, who shall question such claim or right, or demand the benefit of such determination as aforesaid, to appear to and defend such action or actions in the name or names of the person or persons so dead, and proceedings shall be had therein in the same manner as if such person or persons had been actually living, and the rights of all parties shall be equally bound and concluded by the event of such action or actions.

Suits respecting titles not to impede the execution of the Act.

12. And be it further enacted, That if any suit or suits shall be commenced or prosecuted, touching or concerning the title of any person or persons in or to any lands, tenements, or hereditaments, for or in respect of which any right or interest in, over, or upon the lands and grounds hereby directed to be divided, allotted, and inclosed, or any part thereof, shall be claimed, such suit or suits shall not impede, delay or hinder the said Commissioner from proceeding in the execution of the powers vested in him by this Act; but the said division, allotment, and inclosure shall be proceeded in notwithstanding such suit or suits, and the allotment may be had and taken by the person or persons who, upon the determination of such suit or suits, shall become entitled to the same.

Deaths of parties not to suspend the execution of the Act.

13. And be it further enacted, That if any of the parties interested in the said intended division or inclosure shall die before the same shall be completed, the powers and authorities hereby given to the said Commissioner, shall not be thereby determined or suspended, but the said Commissioner shall proceed in the execution of the powers to him given by this Act or the said recited Act, in such manner as he might have done in case such parties had not died; and the share or shares of the person or persons so dying, shall be allotted to such person or persons who by law shall become entitled to the same, and shall be accepted and fenced by him, her, or them, according to the directions of this or the said recited Act; and he, she, or they, shall be liable to the charges and expenses, and other conditions of this and the said recited Act.

Sec.14—15

14. And be it further enacted, That it shall be lawful for the said Commissioner to enquire into and determine what incroachment or incroachments hath or have been made upon or from the said several commons or waste lands, or the said Carr respectively, by any person or persons whomsoever, and that all such incroachments as shall have been made upon or taken from the said several commons and waste lands and Carr, within twenty years previous to the passing of this Act, shall be deemed part or parcel of the said several commons or waste lands, or Carr, by this Act intended to be inclosed, which said incroachments the said Commissioner is hereby directed to allot to such person or persons entitled to right of common upon the said several commons and waste lands and Carr, as is or are or shall be in the possession thereof, for or in part of the allotment or allotments to be made to him, her, or them respectively by virtue of this Act, so that such incroachment or incroachments shall not exceed the allotment or allotments to be made to such person or persons in respect of his, her, or their right of common as aforesaid, and in the valuation of which incroachments respectively the said Commissioner shall not take into his consideration any improvements which may have been made thereon, nor estimate the same at any higher rate or value than the same respectively would have been estimated at had the same remained part of the said commons and waste lands and Carr, and had not been inclosed; and all incroachments from the said commons or waste lands, or Carr, which have been held for twenty years or upwards, shall remain and be the property and as part of the ancient estate of the person or persons to whom the same respectively now belong, but no allotment shall be made to any person or persons in respect of any such lands so inclosed for twenty years or upwards.

Commissioner to determine incroachments.

15. And be it further enacted, That the said Commissioner shall, and he is hereby authorised and empowered to set out and make such roads, ditches, drains, watercourses, bridges, walls, banks, tunnels, gates, stiles, and other works, and divert, alter, or change the course of any of the present roads, ditches, drains, or watercourses in, through, over, or upon the lands or grounds hereby directed to be divided, allotted, and inclosed, and every or any of them, and also to set out and make such roads from the said lands and grounds in, through, and over the said sand hills, to communicate with the strand or shore of the sea, as he the said Commissioner shall think proper and convenient, useful, or necessary; and that all such roads, ditches, drains, and watercourses, bridges, walls, banks, tunnels, gates, stiles, and other works as shall be set out and made as aforesaid, shall be made, and from time to time amended, cleansed and repaired, by and

Drains, &c.

Sec. 16—18 at the expense of the inhabitants of such of the said townships respectively in which the same may be, or of such persons interested in any of the lands or grounds hereby directed to be divided, allotted, and inclosed, and in such manner as the said Commissioner shall in that behalf by his Award, or by any other writing or writings under his hand, order, direct, or appoint: Provided always, that no watercourse or stream shall be diverted or turned without the consent in writing of the owner or owners of the lands from which such stream or watercourse shall be intended to be diverted or turned, and of the owner or owners of the lands into which the same shall be turned.

Apportioning allotments to the respective parties.

16. And be it further enacted, That the part or share of the said commons and waste lands in the said Township of Wallasey, (exclusively of the said tract or parcel of land called Wallasey Pasture), to be allotted to the Lords of the said Manor, and also the part or share of the said commons and waste lands in the said Township of Poolton-cum-Seacombe to be allotted to the Lord of that Manor, shall be equal to one sixteenth part in value of such commons and waste lands to be inclosed respectively as the said value shall be ascertained by the said Commissioner, and that the said Commissioner shall set out and allot to the said John Leigh, as Lord of the said Manor of Grange, eleven acres (of statute measure) of the said tract or parcel of land called The Carr, by way of compensation.

Allotments for stone and marl.

17. And be it further enacted, That it shall be lawful for the said Commissioner, and he is hereby authorized and required, to allot and set out such parcel of land, in such part or parts of the said Carr, for the purpose of getting marl for the use of the land owners in the said Townships of Grange, Little Meols, and Newton-cum-Larton, and also such parcel of land in such part or parts of the commons in the said several Townships of Wallasey and Poolton-cum-Seacombe, as he shall think proper, and by his Award direct, for the purpose of getting stone and marl for the use of the land owners within those townships respectively, but such stone and marl are not to be used elsewhere than in the said townships, for the use of which the same shall be respectively set out.

[Lands allotted for stone and marl, when exhausted, may be sold, let, exchanged, or otherwise appropriated, Wallasey Improvement Act, 1845, sec. 84; Wallasey Improvement Act, 1858, sec. 68; Wallasey Improvement Act, 1864, sec. 20.]

Allotment for sale to pay expenses.

18. And be it further enacted, That the proportion of the charges and expenses incident to and attending the obtaining and passing this Act, and of carrying the same into execution, and of making any drains, watercourses, or fences, so far as regards the said piece of land called The Carr, shall be paid and borne by the several parties interested therein, according to an equal rate or assessment to be made by the said Commissioner on such several parties so interested (other than in respect of the said eleven acres so to be set out for the said John Leigh, as Lord of the said Manor of Grange); and that the said Commissioner, after the setting out such roads and ways on the said several commons and lands in the said Townships of Wallasey and Poolton-cum-Seacombe, as he may think requisite by virtue of the power herein-before given, shall set out and allot such part or parts of the said commons and lands in Wallasey and Poolton-cum-

Seacombe respectively, as will in his judgement, by sale thereof, **Sec. 19—21**
raise a sum of money sufficient to pay the proportionate charges and
expenses of obtaining and passing this act, and carrying the same
into execution, as far as regards the said commons and lands in the
said Townships of Wallasey and Poolton-cum-Seacombe respectively.

19. Provided also, and be it further enacted, that it shall and To be sold
may be lawful to and for the said Commissioner, after having set out by auction.
and allotted such part or parts of the said commons and lands in the
said Townships of Wallasey and Poolton-cum-Seacombe, as will in
his judgement be sufficient by sale thereof to pay such proportionate
expenses as aforesaid, to order and direct such part and parts of the
said commons and land to be advertised for sale, and sold by public
auction at some convenient place in the said Townships, or one of
them, at such time and times, and in such manner as he shall
think proper.

20. Provided always, that no part of the expenses which, in the Division of
judgement of the said Commissioner, may be incurred respecting the expenses.
commons and waste lands in one of the said Townships, shall be
charged to or form any part of the expenses which may relate to the
other of the said Townships; nor shall the expenses which in the
judgement of the said Commissioner, may be incurred respecting the
said parcel of land called Wallasey Pasture, be charged to the
expenses which may relate to the commons and waste lands in that
township, nor the expenses which may relate to the said piece of
land called The Carr, be charged to any other of the said townships
than those of Grange, Newton cum-Larton, and Little Meols:
Provided also, that in case any surplus shall remain after all such
charges and expenses as aforesaid shall have been fully paid and
satisfied, such surplus shall be divided and apportioned between the
several proprietors of the commons and lands hereby directed to be
divided, allotted and inclosed, according to their several and
respective interests therein, in case they shall be tenants in fee
simple thereof, or otherwise, shall be applied and disposed of in
manner directed by the said recited Act, whenever monies are to be
paid for the purchase or exchange of any lands, tenements, or
hereditaments, or of any timber or wood growing thereon; and
which money ought to be laid out in the purchase or exchange of
other lands, tenements, or hereditaments, to be settled to the same
uses.

21. Provided always, and be it further enacted, that if the Making good
monies to be produced by such sale or sales as aforesaid, shall not be deficiency.
sufficient to pay such proportionate charges and expenses aforesaid,
then the deficiency shall be borne by the proprietors of lands in the
said townships of Wallasey and Poolton-cum-Seacombe, hereby
directed to be allotted and inclosed, in proportion to the real value of
their respective divisions and allotments; such proportion to be
settled and ascertained by the said Commissioner and shall be raised
by a rate or rates, and be paid to such person or persons, and
at such time or times as the said Commissioner shall, by notice in
writing to be affixed on the outer door of the Parish Church of
Wallasey, at least twenty-one days previous to the day of payment,
order and direct; and in case any person or persons shall refuse or
neglect to pay his, her, or their share or proportion of the said

Sec. 22—25

deficiency as aforesaid, then the same shall be levied and recovered in the manner directed by the said recited Act, in case the expenses of obtaining and executing this Act, so far as regards the said commons and lands in the said townships of Wallasey and Poolton-cum-Seacombe, had been directed to be paid, in proportion, by the proprietors of lands or grounds to whom allotments shall be made, instead of being raised by sale of land as aforesaid.

Allotment of the residue.

22. And be it further enacted, that the said Commissioner shall, and he is hereby directed and required to divide, set out, and allot the residue and remainder of the said several commons and waste lands in the said several townships of Wallasey and Poolton-cum-Seacombe, and the said piece of land called The Carr, unto and amongst the several persons who, at the time of making such division and allotment, shall be entitled to right of common on such commons and waste lands, and on the said Carr respectively, in proportion and according to their respective rights, property, and interest therein ; and that the said Commissioner shall, and he is hereby directed and required to divide, set out, and allot the residue and remainder of the said tract or parcel of land, called Wallasey Pasture, unto and amongst the several persons who, at the time of making such division and allotment, shall be entitled to cowgaits on the said land, in proportion and according to their respective rights, property, and interest in the same.

Sand Hills to remain open.

23. And be it further enacted, that nothing herein contained shall be construed to authorize the said Commissioner to divide, set out, or allot any of the land covered with sand hills, on the north-west side of the said commons or waste lands, in the township of Wallasey aforesaid, beyond such line or extent of land as the said Commissioner may think fit for cultivation, but that the said sand hills shall remain uninclosed and open, for the better security and preservation of the land to the eastward and southward of the same, from the encroachments of the sea, and for which purpose such land covered with sand hills is hereby appropriated.

[These sand hills placed under control of Wallasey Commissioners.—Wallasey Improvement Act, 1845, s. 85.]

Allotment to the Rectors in respect of their Glebe Lands, to be fenced at the expense of the other claimants.

24. And be it further enacted, that the several plots of lands and grounds, which shall be set out and allotted in right of the said rectories of Wallasey and West Kirby, in respect of the glebe lands, by virtue of this Act, shall be inclosed and fenced round with ditches, posts, and rails, or other proper mounds and fences ; and that the same shall be so made and done by or under the directions of the said Commissioner, and the expenses thereof shall be borne and paid as the expenses of this Act are hereby directed to be paid ; and the said ditches and fences, when properly made, shall for ever thereafter be kept up, maintained and supported by and at the expense of the person or persons whom the said Commissioner shall direct to do the same.

Exchanges.

25. And be it further enacted, that it shall and may be lawful to and for the said Commissioner to set out, allot, and award any allotment or allotments of the said several commons or waste lands, or any other lands, tenements, or hereditaments within the said parishes of Wallasey and West Kirby, or either of them, in lieu of and in exchange for any other allotment or allotments, or any other lands, tenements, and hereditaments within the said parishes, or within any adjoining parish, hamlet, or township, provided that all such exchanges be ascertained, specified, and declared in the said Award of the said Commissioner, and be made with the consent of the owner or owners, proprietor or proprietors of the lands, tenements, or hereditaments which shall be so exchanged, whether such owner or owners, proprietor or proprietors shall be a body or bodies politic, corporate, or collegiate, or a tenant or tenants in fee simple, or for life, or in fee tail general or special, or by the courtesy of England, or for years determinable on any life or lives, or with the consent of the guardians, trustees, feoffees for charitable uses, husbands, committees, or attornies of or acting for any such proprietors or owners as aforesaid, who at the time of making such exchange or exchanges shall be respectively infants, femes covert, lunatics, or under any legal disability, or who shall be beyond the seas, or otherwise disabled to act for themselves, himself, or herself, such consent to be testified in writing under the common seal of the body politic, corporate or collegiate, and under the hands of the other consenting parties respectively; and all and every such exchange and exchanges so to be made, shall be good, valid, and effectual in the law to all intents and purposes whatsoever: provided, nevertheless, that no exchange shall be made of any lands, tenements, or hereditaments held in right of any church, chapel, or other ecclesiastical benefice, without the consent in writing of the patron thereof, and of the Bishop of the Diocese in which such lands, tenements, or hereditaments so to be exchanged shall lie and be situate: provided always, that all costs, charges, and expenses attending the making any exchanges shall be paid and borne by the several persons making such exchanges, in such manner and in such proportion as the said Commissioner shall by his Award order and direct.

26. Provided always, and be it further enacted, that nothing herein contained shall extend or be construed, adjudged, deemed, or taken to revoke, make void, alter, or impeach any settlement, deed, or will whatsoever, or to prejudice any person or persons having any right, title, interest, claim, charge, or incumbrance whatsoever, in, out of, upon, or affecting any of the lands, or grounds to be divided and inclosed as aforesaid or any part or parcel thereof, but that the respective Shares of the said commons or waste lands so to be allotted or exchanged, shall, immediately after such allotments or exchanges, be, remain, and enure, and be held and enjoyed, and the several persons to whom the same shall be allotted and given in exchange, shall from thenceforth stand and be seised and possessed thereof respectively, by such tenure, for such estates, upon such and the same uses, for such trusts, and with such and the same powers, and subject to such and the same wills, limitations, conditions, settlements, trusts, provisions, remainders, reversions, debts, charges, and incumbrances, as the several messuages, lands, tenements, or hereditaments, in respect whereof such allotments or exchanges shall be made, were held, and stood severally limited or subject or liable unto at the time of making such allotments or exchanges.

Not to revoke wills.

27. And be it further enacted, That it shall be lawful for all and every person or persons to whom any allotment or allotments shall

To set posts and rails to preserve quicksets.

Sec. 28—30 be made by virtue of this Act from time to time, during the term of seven years from the signing of the said Award, to set down posts and rails, or other fences on the outside of the ditches bounding any highway or uninclosed lands, adjoining to his, her, or their allotment or allotments, for the preservation of the quicksets, not exceeding five feet from the line of inclosure, and at any time before the end of the said term to remove and carry away such posts, rails, and fences; and it shall and may be lawful to and for the said Commissioner, by his Award, to order and direct by what person and persons the fences of the different allotments to be set out by virtue of this Act, shall be made and kept in repair.

Rights in inclosures may be sold separate from the estate which gives the right.

28. And be it further enacted, That it shall be lawful for any person or persons interested in the said commons and waste lands to be inclosed by virtue of this Act, at any time before the execution of the award herein directed to be made by the said Commissioner, to sell and dispose of all such estate, right, and interest as he, she or they now hath or have, or shall or may hereafter have, in respect of any allotment or allotments to be made by virtue of this Act, separate from such estate in right whereof he, she, or they is, are, or shall be so entitled; and that in case of any such sale it shall be lawful for the said Commissioner, and he is hereby authorized and required to allot the same to the purchaser or purchasers thereof respectively, who shall and may immediately after the execution of such award as aforesaid, have, hold, use, and enjoy such allotments, so by him, her, or them purchased as aforesaid, and shall and may have, use, and exercise any act of ownership in, upon, over, and to the same, and be seised and possessed thereof, in as full, large, ample, and beneficial a manner, to all intents and purposes whatsoever, as the former proprietor or vendor thereof could or might have done, in case such sale or sales had not been made, but subject nevertheless to the several rules, orders, conditions, and restrictions mentioned and contained in this and the said recited Act.

Right of common to cease.

29. And be it further enacted, That the several allotments, partitions, divisions and exchanges to be made, declared or approved by the said Commissioner, in and by his Award, shall be and are hereby declared to be final, binding, and conclusive upon the several parties interested in the said commons or waste lands, and all other persons, bodies politic and corporate whomsoever, and from and immediately after the execution of the said Award, and the publication thereof, all right of common in, over, or upon the said several commons or waste lands and in, over, or upon the said Sand Hills, shall cease and be for ever extinguished.

Commissioner's allowance.

30. And be it further enacted, That out of the money which shall be raised for defraying the expenses of obtaining and executing this Act, there shall be paid to the said Commissioner, as a recompense for his trouble, the sum of three pounds and three shillings for each day he shall respectively act, or travel for the purpose of acting, or be returning home from acting, in the execution of this Act, and no more; and that at all meetings to be held in pursuance of this Act, the said Commissioner shall defray his own expenses: Provided also, that all persons interested in the said intended division and inclosure, their attornies and agents, shall pay their own expenses when they, or any of them, shall attend the said Commissioner upon any occasion relative to the execution of this Act.

54 Geo. III. *The Wallasey and West Kirby* ch. lxxxvii. 59
Inclosure Act, 1814.

31. And be it further enacted, That once at least in each and **Sec. 31—34** every year, during the execution of this Act, (such year to be computed from the day of passing thereof) the said Commissioner Accounts to shall, and he is hereby required to make a true and just statement be settled by or account of all sums of money by him received and expended, or justices. due to him for his own trouble and expenses in the execution of this Act; and such statement or account when so made, together with the vouchers relating thereto, shall be by him laid before any one Justice of the Peace for the County of Chester, to be by him examined and balanced, and such Balance shall be by such Justice stated in the book of Accounts to be kept in the office of the clerk to the said Commissioner; and no charges or items in such accounts shall be binding on the parties concerned, or valid in law, unless the same shall have been duly allowed by such Justice.

32. And be it further enacted, That if any person shall advance Money any sum or sums of money for the purpose of defraying the expenses advanced to of obtaining and passing this Act, or of carrying the same into be repaid with execution, every such person shall be repaid the same, with interest, interest. at the rate of five pounds per centum per annum, out of the first monies that shall be raised for defraying such expenses by virtue of this Act.

33. And be it further enacted, That the Award to be made by Award to be the said Commissioner, when enrolled in the manner directed by the deposited. said recited Act, shall, together with a map or plan thereunto annexed, be deposited in the Parish Church of Wallasey.

34. And be it further enacted, that if any person or persons, Appeal. bodies politic or corporate, shall think himself, herself, or themselves aggrieved by any thing done in pursuance of the said recited Act or this Act, (except as to such claims, matters, and things as are hereinbefore directed or authorized to be tried, settled, or determined by the verdict of a jury, or where any of the clauses or provisions of the said recited Act, or of this Act, shall express that the same shall be final and conclusive) then, and in every such case, he, she, or they may appeal to the General Quarter Sessions of the Peace, to be held at Chester or Knutsford, in and for the said County of Chester, within four calendar months next after the cause of complaint shall have arisen, every such appellant giving ten days' previous notice in writing to the parties to be appealed against, of the intention of bringing such appeal; and the Justices at their said Quarter Sessions are hereby required to hear and determine the matter of every such appeal, and to make such order, and award such costs, as to them in their discretion shall seem reasonable; and by their order and warrant to levy the costs and damages which shall be awarded by the said Justices by distress and sale of the goods and chattels of the party or parties liable to pay the same, rendering the overplus (if any) to the owner or owners of such goods and chattels, after deducting the reasonable charges of every such distress and sale, which determination of the said Justices shall be final and conclusive to all parties concerned, and shall not be removed by certiorari, or any other writ or process whatsoever, into any of His Majesty's Courts of Record at Westminster or elsewhere; but in case such appeal shall appear to the said Justices to be frivolous, vexatious, or without foundation, then the said Justices

Sec. 35--37 shall award such costs to be paid by the appellant or appellants as to them in their discretion shall seem reasonable.

Saving Manorial rights.

35. And be it further enacted, That nothing herein contained shall extend, or be construed to extend, to defeat, lessen, or prejudice, the right, title, or interest, of the Lord or Lords of the said several manors of Wallasey, Poolton-cum-Seacombe, and Grange, or any of them respectively, for the time being, of, in, and to any quit rents, chief rents, fee farm rents, incroachment rents, or other rents now payable, or to the seigniories and royalties incident and belonging to the said manors respectively; but that the said Lord and Lords of the said manors respectively, and all and every person and persons claiming or to claim, by, from, under, or in trust for them respectively, shall and may from time to time, and at all times for ever hereafter, hold and enjoy all rents, services, courts, perquisites, and profits of courts, goods and chattels of felons and fugitives, felons of themselves and those put in exigent, deodands, waifs, estrays, forfeitures, and all other royalties, jurisdictions, privileges, pre-eminences, manorial jurisdictions, and appurtenances whatsoever, to the said manors respectively incident, appendant, belonging or appertaining (other than and except their respective rights of and in the soil of such parts of the said commons and waste grounds as shall be allotted by virtue of this Act to any person or persons), in as full, ample, and beneficial a manner, to all intents and purposes, as the said Lord and Lords could or might have held and enjoyed the same respectively, in case this Act or the said intended inclosure and division had not been made; provided also, that nothing in this Act contained shall be construed to affect, prejudice, or lessen any of the rights of the said Richard Smith in respect of his ancient ferry of Seacombe.

General saving.

36. Saving always to the King's most Excellent Majesty, his heirs and successors, and to all and every person and persons, bodies politic and corporate, his, her, and their successors, executors, and administrators, all such estate, right, title, and interest, other than and except such as are hereby intended to be barred and destroyed, as they, every, or any of them had and enjoyed of, in, to, or out of the said several commons or waste lands at the time of passing this Act, or would or might have had or enjoyed in case this Act had not been made.

Act to be given in evidence as public act.

37. And be it further enacted, That this Act shall be printed by the several printers to the King's most Excellent Majesty, duly authorized to print the statutes of the United Kingdom, and a copy thereof so printed by any of them, shall be admitted as evidence thereof by all Judges, Justices, and others.

COMMISSIONER'S AWARD.

(Under 54 Geo. III. cap. 87.)

WALLASEY INCLOSURE.

TO ALL TO WHOM THESE PRESENTS SHALL COME, I, James Boydell, of Rossett, in the County of Denbigh, gentleman, the Commissioner named and appointed in and by an   of the reign of his late Majesty King George the third, intituled " an Act for inclosing lands in the Parishes of Wallasey and West Kirby, in the County of Chester," send greeting.

 Whereas I, the said Commissioner, having   recited Act taken and subscribed the oath directed to be taken by the Act of the forty-first year of the reign of his said late Majesty intituled " an Act for consolidating in one Act certain provisions usually inserted   in the mode of proving the several facts usually required in the passing of such Acts." Which oath is written on parchment and annexed to this my Award, and having made such survey, plan admeasurement and valuation as in the said   to be made, and having given all such notices as by the said Acts or either of them are directed, and having before I proceeded to make any provision or allotment under the said Acts, set out and appointed such public carriage roads and highways through and over the lands intended to be divided, allotted, and inclosed as I judged necessary, and in such directions as upon the whole appeared to me most commodious to the public, and having ascertained the same by marks and bounds, and prepared a map in which such roads are accurately laid down and described, and deposited such map as by the said Act is directed, and having given such notices respecting such roads, and having called such meeting as by the said Act is directed. And I having also set out and appointed such private roads, footways, drains and watercourses, as I thought requisite, giving such notices in respect of the private roads or paths so set out as by the said Acts are required, and having in all other respects acted in pursuance of the directions of the said Acts, and having completed the division and allotment of the said commons and waste lands, and open and undivided and common land, by the said first-mentioned Act directed to be allotted and divided.

 Now I, the said Commissioner, do draw up, make, and publish this my Award, in writing, as directed by the said Act of the forty-first year of the reign of his said late Majesty. And I do direct that the three several maps or plans drawn on parchment and annexed to this my Award to be taken and deemed as part thereof. And I, the said Commissioner, do ascertain and find the contents of the several commons and waste lands, open and undivided land and common land, by the first-mentioned Act, directed to be divided and allotted, to be as follows, as I compute the same, that is to say, I find the contents of the commons and waste lands in the Township of Wallasey, in the Parish of Wallasey, exclusive of the open and undivided land in the said Township called Wallasey Pasture, and also of the Sandhills, left open and uninclosed, according to the directions of the first recited act to the extent hereinafter mentioned to be six hundred and forty acres and five perches in statute measure in which measure I declare the contents of all and every part and parcel of the said commons and waste lands by me hereinafter assigned and allotted, are so assigned and allotted, and I find the extent of the tract or parcel of open and undivided land in the said township of Wallasey, called Wallasey Pasture, to be two hundred and twenty acres two roods and twenty-seven perches, and I find the contents of the commons and waste lands in the Township of Poolton-cum-Seacombe in the said parish of Wallasey to be ninety-one acres two roods and twenty-five perches, and I find the contents of the tract or parcel of common land in the parish of West Kirby called the Carr to be two hundred and seven acres two roods and thirty-three perches and with respect to the said commons or waste lands in the said township of Wallasey, other than and besides and exclusive of the said open and undivided land called Wallasey Pasture, I the said Commissioner do make my Award as follows, that is to say,

Public Road E. In the first place I do hereby particularise and describe the public carriage roads highways and private roads so set out by me, through and over the same last mentioned commons and waste lands as aforesaid, in manner following, that is to say, one public carriage road and highway in the said map marked with the letter E, on part of the commons and waste lands in Wallasey commencing at the end of the lane there leading through the Village of Wallasey, to the Leasowe and continuing from thence northwardly to the allotment by me sold to the Reverend Augustus Campbell and to the northern end of the said watering place.

Public Road F. One other public carriage road and highway in the same map marked with the letter F, on part of the said commons and waste lands in Wallasey aforesaid, commencing at the said last mentioned road and running from thence eastwardly to the corner of a certain field in the occupation of George Fazakerley and from thence to a certain house there called Gills House or Hose Side.

Public Road K. One other public carriage road and highway in the same map marked with the letter K, on part of the said commons and waste lands on Wallasey Leasowe of the width of ten yards which begins at the end of a public carriage road leading through ancient inclosed lands in the Township of Moreton belonging to Robert Vyner, Esq., and forming a continuation of the public road over the pasture marked 1 in the said map, and runs from thence in a westwardly direction to the boundary between the Townships of Great Meols and Wallasey.

Public Road L. One other public carriage road and highway in the same map marked with the letter L, on part of the said commons and waste lands on Wallasey Brake of the width of ten yards beginning at the end of a public road set out by me, the said Commissioner, in the said Township of Poulton marked C in the said map hereunto annexed leading from Seacombe to Wallasey, and running in a northwardly direction along the lower side of the brake there to the southwest corner of a garden in Wallasey aforesaid belonging to George Cooper.

54 *Geo. III.*   *Commissioner's Award,*   *ch. lxxxvii.*   63
                 Wallasey Inclosure.

One other public carriage road and highway in the said map | Public Road
marked with the letters L L, on part of the said commons and waste | L L.
lands on Wallasey Brake of the width of ten yards beginning at or
near to the "Ship" public house belonging to George Cooper, and
running in a northwardly direction along the lower side of the Brake
to the southwest of ancient lands belonging to Sir John Tobin.

One other public carriage road or highway in the same map marked | Public Road
with the letter M, on other part of the said commons and waste | M.
lands on Wallasey Brake, of the width of ten yards commencing from
the west end of the lane leading from Liscard to Wallasey, and
running from thence in a northwardly direction on the eastward of
the Parish Church of Wallasey aforesaid, towards Wallasey Village
as far as the ancient highroad called Folly Lane, leading from Liscard
to Wallasey.

One other public carriage road or highway in the same map | Public Road
marked with the letter N, on other part of the said commons and | N.
waste lands on Wallasey Brake, of the width of ten yards, running
from the west side of the said last-mentioned road along the south
side of the yard of the said Parish Church towards the Rectory and
village of Wallasey.

One other public carriage road or highway in the same map marked | Public Road
with the letter O, of the width of ten yards, over part of the said | O.
commons and waste lands called Wallasey Leasowe which had been
sold to Mrs. Boode who has since given up so much of the said lot
sold to her, commencing at the strand or shore at the northwest
corner of the said allotment sold to Mrs. Boode, and running from
thence in a southwardly direction along the east side of the fence
lately made by her adjoining to the Township of Great Meols as far
as the ancient tract or road over Great Meols common which formerly
led from Wallasey towards Hoylake, but which has been lately
stopped up by me, the said Commissioner, as far as the limits of
Wallasey Common.

One other public carriage road on part of the said commons and | Public Road
waste lands on Wallasey Leasowe, of the width of ten yards, in the | P.
same map marked P, commencing from the east side of the public
road before set out by me marked F, and running from thence in a
southwardly direction as far as the entrance of the road leading to
the Magazines.

One other public carriage or highway of the width of eight yards | Public Road
on other part of the said commons and waste lands, called Wallasey | Q.
Leasowe, in the same map marked with the letter Q, commencing at
the north end of the public road over the Wallasey Pasture, in the
map marked with the letter R, and running from thence in a northwardly direction through allotments of Sir John Tobin and to the
allotment sold to the Reverend Augustus Campbell.

One private or occupation road on part of the said commons and | Private Road
waste lands on Wallasey Brake, of the width of ten yards, in the | O.
same map marked with the letter O, beginning on the east side of the
before mentioned road marked LL, running from thence in a southwardly direction along the east side of an allotment of the said
commons intended to be made to George Cooper, then turning off
and running in an eastwardly direction to a field or ancient enclosed
land in Wallasey belonging to Robert Vyner, Esquire, and then

turning off and running in an eastwardly direction along allotments No. 73 made to the said Robert Vyner, and No. 72 made to Sir John Grey Egerton, to the end of a lane leading from Wallasey to the Township of Liscard.

Private Road P. — One other private occupation road of the width of eight yards on other part of the said commons and waste lands on Wallasey Brake, in the same map marked with the letter P, commencing at the south side of the said last described private road marked O, and extending from thence in a southwardly direction along the west end of a field belonging to Sir John Grey Egerton to the public quarry in Wallasey aforesaid.

Private Road Q. — One other private or occupation road on other part of the said commons and waste lands on Wallasey Leasowe, in the same map marked with the letter Q, of the width of six yards commencing at the south end of the said public road marked P, in Wallasey aforesaid, and running from thence in a southwardly direction along an inclosure in Liscard, belonging to Mrs. Thompson, to the boundary between the Townships of Liscard and Wallasey.

Private Road R. — One other private or occupation road in the same map, marked with the letter R, on other part of the said commons and waste lands on Wallasey Leasowe of the width of six yards, commencing on the north side and at the east end of the said public road marked F, and running from thence along the west side of enclosures in the Township of Liscard, and along the east side of other part of the said commons in Wallasey, intended to be allotted to Mr. Davies and Mr. Groom to another piece of land part of the said commons intended to be allotted to Sir John Tobin, both which said roads marked Q and R, as aforesaid shall not be laid open, or the proprietors of the adjoining lands be compelled to fence the same, but that the persons for whose use they are intended and who shall be entitled thereto shall only have a right of way or passage of six yards wide through and over that part of the said allotments to Mr. Davies and Mr. Groom.

Private Road S. — Another private or occupation road on other part of the said commons and waste lands on Wallasey Leasowe, in the same map marked with the letter S, of the width of eight yards commencing from the north side of the public carriage road or highway marked F, running from thence in a northwardly direction along the west side of an allotment of the said commons sold by me the said Commissioner in pursuance of the directions of the said Act to Mr. John Davies, as far as the allotment by me sold to the Reverend Augustus Campbell in Wallasey aforesaid.

Private Road T. — Another private or occupation road on other part of the said commons and waste lands on Wallasey Leasowe, in the same map marked with the letter T, of the width of four yards commencing on the south side of the said public high road marked F, leading along the east side of an allotment sold by me to the Reverend James Smedley, to the north-east corner of a garden belonging to Mrs. Wotherspoon.

Private Road U. — Another private or occupation road on other part of the said commons and waste lands on Wallasey Leasowe, in the same map marked with the letter U, of the width of eight yards commencing from the east side of the public road marked E, and running from thence in an eastwardly direction along the north side of a cottage messuage and land in the occupation of Margaret Deane to the lane leading from thence to the sandfields.

One other private or occupation road on other part of the said commons and waste lands on Wallasey Leasowe, in the same map marked with the letter V, on other part of the said commons of the width of eight yards commencing in Wallasey aforesaid on the west side of a certain public carriage road and highway marked E, nearly opposite to the cottage belonging to Thomas Dean in Wallasey aforesaid, and running thence in a westwardly direction over that part of the said commons called the Wallasey Leasowe to an allotment of the said commons next adjoining the Leasowe Castle sold by me, the said Commissioner, in pursuance of the directions of the said Act to Mrs. Boode. *Private Road V.*

One other private or occupation road on other part of the said commons and waste lands on Wallasey Leasowe marked on the said map with the letter X, of the width of eight yards, commencing at the public road leading from Wallasey to Hoylake opposite to and running from thence northwardly to the allotment marked A, sold to Mrs. Boode. *Private Road X.*

And I, the said Commissioner, do direct that the said two private or occupation roads marked in the said map O and S, shall be for ever afterwards maintained and kept in repair by the proprietors and occupiers of lands in the Township of Wallasey, and that the four private or occupation roads marked in the said map P, Q, T and U, shall be for ever afterwards maintained and kept in repair by the owners or occupiers of the ancient lands to which the same lead, and shall be solely used and enjoyed by them, and that all other private or occupation roads by me set out as aforesaid, shall be for ever afterwards maintained and kept in repair by the several owners or occupiers of the lands adjoining to or abutting on the same, and shall be solely used and enjoyed by them.

And I, the said Commissioner, have in this my Award set out and allotted two watering places for the use and enjoyment of the inhabitants of the Township of Wallasey, one of which is mentioned and described in the allotment No. 71, hereinafter made to Sir John Tobin, and the other of which as follows, that is to say a piece or parcel of land with the watering pit thereon part of the said commons and waste lands on Wallasey Leasowe, containing two roods marked on the said map watering place, bounded northwardly and eastwardly by the allotment marked Q, and by me sold to the Reverend Augustus Campbell, southwardly by the allotment marked R, sold by me to George Peers, and westwardly by the public road E, and I direct that the walls or fences by me erected on the northward and eastward sides of the said watering place shall be for ever kept in repair by the inhabitants of the said Township of Wallasey, but that the same shall be discontinued to be a watering place on another watering pit being made and provided to the satisfaction of all the inhabitants of Wallasey aforesaid. *Watering Pit.*

And in further execution of the said recited Acts, I direct and set out a piece or parcel of land part of the said commons and waste lands on Wallasey Leasowe for the purpose of getting marl for the use of the lords and landowners within the Township of Wallasey, *Marl, 1a. 3r. 30p.*

54 Geo. III.   *Commissioner's Award,*   ch. lxxxvii.
Wallasey Inclosure.

that is to say a piece or parcel of land containing one acre three roods and thirty perches marked upon the said map with the word Marl, bounded northwardly by the public road F, eastwardly and southwardly by ancient inclosed lands belonging to Robert Vyner, Esquire, and westwardly by   No. 58 to Thomas Lowry.

Quarry, 2a. 0r. 0p.

And in further execution of the said recited acts, I direct and set out a piece or parcel of land other part of the said commons and waste lands on Wallasey Brake in the said Township of Wallasey for the purpose of getting stone for the use of the lords and landowners within the said Township of Wallasey, that is to say, of land on Wallasey Brake containing two acres marked in the said map "Quarry" bounded northwardly in part by ancient inclosed land belonging to George Cooper and in other part by the allotment No. 74 to the said George Cooper   and marked P, eastwardly by ancient inclosed lands belonging to Sir John Grey Egerton, Baronet, Robert Vyner, Esquire and Sir John Tobin, Knight, in the said Township of Wallasey, southwestwardly by the several allotments on the said   respectively to Sir John Tobin No. 76, No. 75 to Samuel Dean and by the allotment marked on the said map with the letter P, by me sold to Samuel Dean, and westwardly by the said public road L, and I direct that the site of the said   part of the said allotment shall be reserved therefrom, and also as much of the said allotment as may be necessary for a road to the said school and for the purpose of repairing and upholding the same shall be let for ever afterwards for the said purpose.

Sale allotment, Reverend James Smedley, A. 5a. 0r. 1p.

I have in the next place set out and allotted from and out of the said commons and waste lands in Wallasey aforesaid, the several parcels of land hereinafter mentioned for sale towards defraying the charges and expenses incident to and attending the obtaining, and passing the said Act, and of carrying the same into execution in the manner and as directed in the said Act, and which parcels of land are described as follows, that is to say, one part of the said commons and waste lands of Wallasey Leasowe in the said Township of Wallasey containing five acres and one perch marked upon the said map with the letter A, and by me sold to the Reverend James Smedley, Clerk, bounded northwardly by the allotment marked in the said Map Q, to the Reverend Augustus Campbell eastwardly by the public road marked on the said map with the letter E, southwardly by an allotment marked with the letter B sold to the said James Smedley, and westwardly by an allotment No. 38 to the Reverend Augustus Campbell.

Sale allotment, James Smedley, B. 4 acres.

One part of the said commons and waste lands on Wallasey Leasowe aforesaid, marked on the said map B by me sold to the said James Smedley containing four acres, bounded northwardly by the before described allotment A, eastwardly by the said public road E, southwardly in part by allotment C, in other part by allotment D, and in other part by allotment F, by me in like manner sold to the said James Smedley, and westwardly by an allotment No. 38, to the said Reverend Augustus Campbell.

Sale allotment, James Smedley, C. 1a. 0r. 0p.

One other part of the said commons and waste lands on Wallasey Leasowe aforesaid, marked on the said map C, by me sold to the said James Smedley, containing one acre, bounded northwardly by the before described allotment B, eastwardly by the said public road E, southwardly by the private road marked on the said map with the letter V, and westwardly by an allotment D, by me in like manner sold to the said James Smedley.

One other part of the said commons and waste lands on Wallasey Leasowe aforesaid, marked on the said map D, by me sold to the said James Smedley containing two acres and thirty-two perches, bounded northwardly by the before described allotment D, eastwardly by the before described allotment C, southwardly by the said private road V, and westwardly by an allotment F, in like manner sold to the said James Smedley. *Sale allotment, James Smedley, D, 2a. 0r. 32p.*

One other part of the said commons and waste lands of Wallasey Leasowe aforesaid marked on the said map E, by me sold to the said James Smedley containing two acres and thirty-two perches, bounded northwardly by the before described allotment B, eastwardly by the allotment marked D, by me in like manner sold to the Reverend James Smedley, southwardly by the private road marked V, and westwardly by the allotment No. 38 on the said Leasowe to the Reverend Augustus Campbell, and I direct that the whole of the fences to the several before described five allotments shall be made and for ever afterwards kept in repair by the owners thereof. *Sale allotment, James Smedley, E 2a. 0r. 32p.*

One other part of the said commons and waste lands on Wallasey Leasowe aforesaid, marked on the said map F, containing two acres and thirteen perches, by me in like manner sold to the Reverend James Smedley, bounded northwardly by the public road marked F, eastwardly by the private road marked T, southwardly in part by ancient inclosed lands in the said Township of Wallasey belonging to Mrs. Wotherspoon, in other part by an allotment No. 65 on the said Leasowe to the said Mrs. Wotherspoon, westwardly by the public road marked E in the said map. And I direct that all the fences to the said allotments save and except as much of the fence on the southward side as adjoins the ancient inclosed lands of Mrs. Wotherspoon shall be made and for ever afterwards kept in repair by the owner thereof. *Sale allotment, Rev. James Smedley, F, 2a. 0r. 13p.*

One other part of the said commons and waste lands on Wallasey Leasowe aforesaid by me in like manner sold to the said John Davies, marked in the said map G, containing forty-six acres one rood and fifteen perches, bounded northwardly by the allotment marked in the said map Q to the Reverend Augustus Campbell, eastwardly in part by allotment No. 48 on the said Leasowe to Sir John Tobin, Knight, in other part by another allotment No. 49 to William Groom, and in other part by another allotment No. 50 to the said John Davies, southwardly by the said public road F, and westwardly in part by the private road marked S, and in other part by the said allotment marked in the said map Q to the Reverend Augustus Campbell. And I direct that all the fences to the said allotment shall be made and for ever afterwards kept in repair by the owner thereof. *Sale allotment, John Davies, G, 46a. 1r. 15p.*

One other part of the said commons and waste lands on Wallasey Leasowe aforesaid by me in like manner sold to the said John Davies, marked in the said map H, containing one rood and twenty-three perches, bounded northeastwardly by ancient inclosed land *Sale allotment, John Davies, H, 0a. 1r. 23p.*

in the said township belonging to the said John Davies, eastwardly by the public road marked P, southwardly by an allotment No. 52 to the said John Davies, and westwardly in part by ancient inclosed land belonging to the said John Davies, and in other part by ancient glebe lands belonging to the Rector of Wallasey, reserving to the said Rector of Wallasey and his tenants the ancient road from the said glebe lands through this allotment to the public road marked P. And I direct the fences on the eastward side of the said allotment to be made and for ever afterwards kept in repair by the owner thereof.

Sale allotment, William Peers, I, 1a. 0r. 0p.

One other part of the said commons and waste lands on Wallasey Leasowe by me sold to William Peers, who never paid the purchase money for the same and is since deceased, and the Reverend Augustus Campbell having paid to me such purchase money I do hereby at his request award the following allotment to the said Augustus Campbell, his heirs and assigns, the equitable purchaser thereof, and which is marked in the said map I, containing one acre, bounded northwardly in part by an allotment marked L, sold by me in like manner to Leigh Blundell, in other part by an allotment on the said Leasowe by me made to James Horrocks marked No. 3, eastwardly in part by the public road marked E, and in other part by the allotment marked K by me sold to Elizabeth Ashbrook, southwardly in part by the said allotment sold to Elizabeth Ashbrook marked K in the said map, and in other part by an allotment on the said Leasowe by me made to Thomas Sparks marked No. 2, and westwardly by the said allotment marked L by me sold to Leigh Blundell. And I direct the whole of the fences to this allotment to be made and for ever afterwards kept in repair by the owner thereof, which allotment is subject nevertheless to such redemption as any person claiming under the said William Peers may have therein or thereto.

Sale allotment, Elizabeth Ashbrook, K, 0a. 0r. 20p.

One other part of the said commons and waste lands on Wallasey Leasowe by me sold to Elizabeth Ashbrook, marked on the said map K, containing twenty perches, bounded northwardly and westwardly by an allotment marked I by me sold to William Peers, eastwardly by the public road marked E, southwardly by an allotment on the said Leasowe by me made to Thomas Sparks, marked No. 2. And I direct the fences on the eastward and southward sides of the said allotment to be made and for ever afterwards kept in repair by the owners thereof.

Sale allotment, Leigh Blundell, L, 5a. 3r. 19p.

One other part of the said common and waste lands on Wallasey Leasowe by me sold to Leigh Blundell, Esquire, marked in the said map with the letter L, containing five acres three roods and nineteen perches, bounded northwardly by the private road V, over the said Leasowe eastwardly by the several allotments on the said Leasowe marked respectively on the said map No. 7 made to Elizabeth Smith, No. 6 made to Mary Coventry, No. 5 made to John Woodfine, No. 4 made to Margaret Jones, No. 3 made to James Horrocks, I sold to William Peers, No. 2 made to Thomas Sparks, and No. 1 to George Evans, southwardly in part by ancient inclosed lands belonging to George Evans, and in other part by an allotment on the Wallasey pasture marked No. 1, and made to the representatives of the late Reverend George Briggs, and westwardly by an allotment on the Wallasey Leasowe marked No. 8A made to the representatives of the late George Briggs. And I direct the fences on the northward side and the fences on the eastward side, except so much as adjoins the allotment marked I by me sold to William Peers and the fence on the westward side, to be made and for ever afterwards kept in repair by the owner thereof.

One other part of the said commons and waste lands on Wallasey Leasowe by me sold to Mrs. Margaret Boode marked in the said map with the letter M containing four acres and twenty-one perches bounded northeastwardly by part of the next described allotment marked with the letter N, by me in like manner sold to the said Margaret Boode eastwardly by an allotment on the said Leasowe marked No. 22 made to Robert Harrison and southwardly by ancient inclosed lands in the said Township of Wallasey belonging to the said Robert Harrison and westwardly by ancient inclosed lands belonging to Mrs. Boode. *Sale allotment, Mrs. Boode, M, 4a. 0r. 21p*

One other part of the said commons and waste lands on Wallasey Leasowe by me sold to Mrs. Margaret Boode marked in the said map with the letter N, containing nine acres three roods and ten perches being an irregular allotment bounded by the strand or shore of the sea there and by the land covered with sand hills, by an allotment marked No. 25 the said Leasowe made to Mr. Robert Harrison, by the private road marked V, by the before described allotment sold to Mrs. Boode marked M, by the garden wall and buildings belonging to Mrs. Boode by an allotment on the said Leasowe marked No. 23, made to Mr. Robert Harrison, by the end of the private road X, by ancient inclosed land in the said township belonging to the said Robert Harrison, and by an allotment marked O, by me in like manner sold to Mrs. Boode, and by the public road marked O. *Sale allotment, Mrs. Boode, N, 9a. 3r. 10p.*

One other part of the said commons and waste lands on Wallasey Leasowe by me also sold to Mrs. Margaret Boode marked in the said map with the letter O, containing nine acres, bounded northwardly in part by the end of the public road marked O, and in other part by the last described allotment sold to Mrs. Boode marked N, southeastwardly by the said allotment to Mrs. Boode marked N, southwardly in part by ancient inclosed lands belonging to Mr. Robert Harrison, and in other part by another allotment No. 24 on the said Leasowe made to the said Robert Harrison, and westwardly in part by common land in the township of Great Meols, and in other part by the public road marked O in the said map, and I direct the whole of the fences to the three last described allotments marked M, N and O to be made and for ever afterwards kept in repair by the owners thereof. *Sale allotment, Mrs. Boode, O, 9a. 0r. 0p.*

One other part of the said commons and waste lands on the Wallasey Brake aforesaid, by me sold to Henry Johnson marked on the said map with the letter P, containing one rood and thirty-two perches, bounded northeastwardly by the public stone quarry on the said brake, southwardly by an allotment No. 75 to the said Henry Johnson, and westwardly by the public road marked L. And I direct the whole of the fences to the said allotment be made and for ever afterwards kept in repair by the owner thereof. *Sale allotment, Henry Johnson, P, 0a. 1r. 32p.*

One other part of the said commons and waste lands being part of the commons in the township of Wallasey called Wallasey Leasowe, by me sold to the Reverend Augustus Campbell, marked in the said *Sale allotment, Reverend Augustus Campbell, Q, 259a. 2r. 37p.*

map or plan with the letter Q, containing two hundred and fifty-nine acres, two roods and thirty-seven perches, bounded southwardly by the several allotments on the said Leasowe, by me made to Robert Harrison No. 25, Robert Vyner, Esquire, No. 26, 27, 27F and 27G, Sir John Grey Egerton, No. 28 and 29, the public road marked on the said map with the letter Q, the allotment to Sir John Tobin No. 30, John Leigh, Esquire, No. 31, Joseph Greene, Esquire, No. 32, 32a and 33, Robinson Dean No. 34, the trustees of the late Matthew Taylor No. 35, Richard Smith, Esquire, No. 36, John Meadows No. 37, the said Reverend Augustus Campbell No. 38, the said allotment marked on the said map A, the said public road marked on the said map E, and the allotment marked on the said map R, by me sold to George Peers, the allotments made to George Cooper No. 43, to Joseph Hodgson No. 44, to Peter Ledsham No. 45, to William Dean No. 46, the heirs of Elizabeth Bird No. 47, by the private road marked on the said map S, by an allotment by me sold to John Davies marked G, and by an allotment to Sir John Tobin No. 48, eastwardly in part by the said allotment marked on the said map G, by me sold to John Davies, in other part by lands in Liscard belonging to Sir John Tobin, northwardly by lands covered by sand hills by me left open and uninclosed as directed by the said Act to the extent of one hundred yards from the high water mark of the sea, there the boundary of which said one hundred yards I have ascertained and marked by posts by me set down, there saving and reserving, nevertheless out of this allotment to all persons the road as now occupied, leading from Wallasey village to the sea-shore the road as now occupied leading under the allotment, by me sold to John Davies to the sea-shore, and also the road leading through and from the lands of Sir John Tobin to the sea-shore in the track now used; and I direct the fences on the west side of the public road E to be for ever afterwards kept in repair by the owner of this allotment.

Sale allotment, George Peers, R. 1a. 2r. 0p.

One other piece or parcel of land, other part of the said commons and waste lands called Wallasey Leasowe, marked in the said map with the letter R, containing one acre and two roods, by me sold to George Peers, bounded southwardly by allotments made to George Cooper, No. 43, and Robert Stanley, No. 42, westwardly and northwardly by the watering pit and the road leading thereto, and eastwardly by the allotment marked Q by me sold to the Reverend Augustus Campbell. And I direct the fences on the westward, northward, and eastward sides thereof to be made and for ever afterwards kept in repair by the owner thereof.

Robert Vyner, Esq. (Royalty), 21 and 26, 6a. 3r. 21p.

And I set out and allot unto Robert Vyner, Esquire, his heirs and assigns, in respect of his royalty as one of the Lords of the Manor of Wallasey aforesaid, and in satisfaction of his claims upon the said commons or waste lands as Lord of the said Manor, two pieces or parcels of land hereinafter described, and marked in the said map No. 21 and No. 26, which I estimate as equal to one-half of one-sixteenth part in value of the said commons and waste lands in the said Township of Wallasey other than the said tract of land called Wallasey Pasture, that is to say, a piece or parcel marked on the said map No. 21, containing six acres three roods and twenty-one perches, bounded northwardly by the private road marked on the said map V, eastwardly by an allotment No. 23B to the said Robert Vyner, southwardly by ancient inclosed lands belonging to

Robert Harrison, and westwardly by an allotment No. 22 to the said Robert Harrison. And I direct the fences on the northward and eastward sides thereof to be made and for ever afterwards kept in repair by the owner thereof, and also a piece or parcel of land marked on the said map No. 26, containing four acres and eleven perches, bounded northwardly by the allotment marked U, by me sold to the Reverend Augustus Campbell, eastwardly by an allotment No. 27 to the said Robert Vyner, Esquire, southwardly by the said private road V, and westwardly by an allotment No. 25 to Robert Harrison. And I direct the fences on the northward, eastward, and southward sides thereof to be made and for ever afterwards kept in repair by the owner thereof.

I set out and allot unto Sir John Grey Egerton, Baronet, his heirs and assigns, in respect of his royalty as one of the Lords of the Manor of Wallasey aforesaid and in satisfaction of his claim upon the said commons or waste lands as one of the Lords of the said Manor, two pieces or parcels of land hereinafter described and marked upon the said map No. 19 and No. 28, which I estimate as equal to one-half of one-sixteenth part in value of the said commons and waste lands in the said Township of Wallasey other than the said tract of land called Wallasey Pasture, that is to say a piece or parcel of land marked on the said map No. 19, containing two acres two roods and three perches, bounded northwardly by the said private road marked L on the said map, eastwardly by an allotment No. 18 to the said Sir John Grey Egerton, and southwardly in part by an allotment No. 8 to the said Sir John Grey Egerton on Wallasey pasture, and in other part by allotment No. 9 on the said pasture to Robert Vyner, Esquire, and westwardly by an allotment on the said Leasowe No. 20a to Robert Vyner, Esquire, and I direct the fences on the northward and westward sides thereof to be made and for ever afterwards kept in repair by the owners thereof.

Sir J. G. Egerton, Bart. (Royalty), 2, 2, 3.

A piece or parcel of land marked in the said map No. 28, containing five acres and thirty-seven perches bounded northwardly by an allotment marked Q, by me sold to the Reverend Augustus Campbell, eastwardly by the allotment No. 29 to Sir John Grey Egerton, southwardly by the said private road marked V on the said map, and westwardly by the allotment No. 27G on the said Leasowe to Robert Vyner, Esq, and I direct the fences on the northward, eastward, and southward sides thereof to be made and for ever afterwards kept in repair by the owner thereof.

Sir J. G. Egerton, Bart. (Royalty), No. 28, 5, 0, 37.

And in further execution of the said recited acts I set out and allot the residue of the said commons and waste lands in the Township of Wallasey, other than the said common land called Wallasey Pasture, in manner following, that is to say, I do set out and allot unto Sir John Grey Egerton, Baronet, his heirs and assigns, in right of his ancient inclosed lands in the said Township of Wallasey, to the uses and under the limitations in the will of Philip Egerton, late of Oulton Park, Esquire, deceased, respecting the same, a piece or parcel of land, part of the said commons and waste lands in Wallasey Leasowe, marked in the said map No. 18, containing eight acres two roods and twelve perches, bounded northwardly by the private road over the said Leasowe marked with letter V, eastwardly by the public road marked Q, between this allotment and an allotment to Sir John Tobin marked No. 17, southwardly in part by an

Sir J. G. Egerton, Bart., No. 18, 8, 2, 12.

allotment on Wallasey Pasture, made to the said Sir John Tobin, marked No. 7B, and in other part by another allotment on the said pasture made to the said Sir John Grey Egerton marked No. 8, and westwardly by an allotment on the said Leasowe, made to the said Sir John Grey Egerton in his right as lord of the said manor of Wallasey aforesaid, and marked No. 19, and I direct that the fences on the northward and eastward sides thereof shall be made and for ever hereafter kept in repair by the owner thereof.

Sir J. G. Egerton, No. 29, 17a. 3r. 11p.

I also set out and allot unto the said Sir John Grey Egerton his heirs and assigns in right of his same ancient lands and in manner as aforesaid, a piece or parcel of land other part of the said commons and waste lands in Wallasey Leasowe, marked in the said map No. 29, containing seventeen acres three roods and eleven perches, bounded northwardly by the allotment marked Q, by me sold to the Reverend Augustus Campbell, eastwardly by the public road marked Q, between this allotment and an allotment to Sir John Tobin marked No. 30, southwardly by the said private road marked V, and westwardly by an allotment heretofore made to the said Sir John Grey Egerton in his right as Lord of the said Manor and marked No. 28, and I direct the fences on the northward, eastward, and southward sides of the same allotment shall be made and for ever afterwards kept in repair by the owner thereof.

Sir J. G. Egerton, No. 54, 0, 0, 17.

I also set out and allot unto the said Sir John Grey Egerton, his heirs and assigns, in right of his same ancient lands and in manner aforesaid, a piece or parcel of land, other part of the said commons and waste lands in Wallasey Leasowe, marked in the said map No. 54, containing seventeen perches, bounded northeastwardly by the public road marked F, in the said map eastwardly by an allotment to Mr. John Davies No. 53, and southwardly by ancient inclosed lands in Wallasey aforesaid, belonging to the said Sir John Grey Egerton, and westwardly by an allotment No. 55, to Mrs. Wade, and I direct the fences on the northeastward and westward sides thereof to be made and for ever afterwards kept in repair by the owner thereof.

Sir J. G. Egerton, No. 66, 0, 0, 19.

I also set out and allot unto the said Sir John Grey Egerton, Baronet, his heirs and assigns, in right of the same ancient lands and in manner aforesaid a piece or parcel of land other part of the said commons and waste lands in Wallasey Leasowe aforesaid marked in the said map No. 66, containing nineteen perches, bounded northwardly by an allotment No. 65 to Mrs. Wotherspoon, southeastwardly by ancient inclosed land belonging to the said Sir John Grey Egerton, southwardly by an allotment to Joseph Jackson No. 67, and westwardly by the public road marked E in the said map. And I direct the fences on the southward and westward sides to be made and for ever afterwards kept in repair by the owners thereof.

Sir J. G. Egerton, No. 72, 0, 1, 1.

I also set out and allot unto the said Sir John Grey Egerton, Baronet, his heirs and assigns, in right of his ancient lands, and in manner aforesaid, a piece or parcel of land, other part of the said commons and waste lands on Wallasey Brake, marked in the said map No. 72, and containing one rood and one perch bounded northwardly by the private road marked O in the said map, southeastwardly by ancient inclosed lands belonging to the said Sir John Grey Egerton, and southwestwardly in part by ancient inclosed lands belonging to Robert Vyner, Esquire, and in other part by an allotment to the said Robert Vyner, Esquire, marked No. 73. And I direct the fences on the northward side thereof shall be made and for ever afterwards kept in repair by the owners thereof.

I also set out and allot unto the said Sir John Grey Egerton' Baronet, his heirs and assigns in right of his same ancient lands in manner aforesaid, a piece or parcel of land, other part of the said commons and waste lands on Wallasey Brake, marked in the said map No. 78, containing one acre one rood and thirty-eight perches, bounded northwardly by an allotment to Joseph Jackson No. 77, eastwardly by ancient inclosed lands belonging to the said Sir John Grey Egerton, and southwardly by an allotment to Richard Smith, Esquire, No. 79, and westwardly by the public road marked L in the said map, and I direct the fences on the southward and westward sides thereof to be made and for ever afterwards kept in repair by the owner thereof.

Sir J. G. Egerton, No. 78, 1, 1, 38.

I set out and allot unto Robert Vyner, Esquire, his heirs and assigns in respect of his ancient inclosed lands in the said Township of Wallasey a piece or parcel of land, part of the said commons or waste lands on Wallasey Leasowe marked in the said map No. 20, containing two acres two roods and twenty-eight perches, bounded northwardly by the private road marked V in the said map, eastwardly by another allotment made to the said Robert Vyner marked No. 20B, and southwardly by an allotment to the said Robert Vyner upon the Wallasey pasture No. 11, and westwardly by another allotment to the said Robert Vyner No. 20c. And I direct the fences on the northward and eastward sides thereof shall be made and for ever afterwards kept in repair by the owner thereof.

Robert Vyner, Esq., No. 20, 2, 2, 28.

I also set out and allot unto the said Robert Vyner, Esquire, his heirs and assigns in respect of his same ancient lands, a piece or parcel of land other part of the said commons and waste lands on the Wallasey Leasowe marked in the said map No. 20A, containing three acres one rood and twenty perches, bounded northwardly by the said private road V, eastwardly by an allotment to the said Robert Vyner Esquire, No. 20D, and southwardly by ancient inclosed land belonging to the said Robert Vyner, and westwardly in part by an allotment No. 20E to the said Robert Vyner and in other part by an allotment No. 20F to the said Robert Vyner, and I direct the fences on the northward and eastward sides thereof to be made and for ever afterwards kept in repair by the owner thereof.

Robert Vyner, Esq., No. 20A, 3, 1, 20.

I also set out and allot unto the said Robert Vyner, Esquire, his heirs and assigns, in respect of his same ancient lands, another piece or parcel of land other part of the said commons and waste lands on Wallasey Leasowe, marked in the said map No. 20B, containing four acres and thirty-one perches, bounded northwardly by the said private road V, eastwardly in part by an allotment No. 20E, to the said Robert Vyner, and in other part by ancient inclosed land belonging to the said Robert Vyner, southwardly in part by ancient inclosed lands belonging to the said Robert Vyner, and in other part by ancient inclosed lands belonging to Mr. Robert Harrison, and westwardly by an allotment to the said Robert Vyner, as one of the Lords of the said Manor of Wallasey No. 21, and I direct the

Robert Vyner, Esq., No. 20B. 4, 0, 31.

fences on the northward and eastward sides to be made and for ever afterwards kept in repair by the owner thereof.

Robert Vyner, Esq., No. 27. 3, 0, 29.

I also set out and allot unto the said Robert Vyner, his heirs and assigns, in respect of his same ancient lands, another piece or parcel of land other part of the said commons and waste lands in Wallasey Leasowe, marked in the said map No. 27, containing three acres and twenty-nine perches, bounded northwardly by the allotment marked Q, by me sold to the Reverend Augustus Campbell, eastwardly by another allotment to the said Robert Vyner, No. 27F, southwardly by the said private road V, and westwardly by an allotment to the said Robert Vyner as one of the Lords of the said Manor of Wallasey No. 26, and I direct the fences on the northward, eastward, and southward sides shall be made and for ever afterwards kept in repair by the owner thereof.

Robert Vyner, Esq., No. 20A, 2, 3, 21.

I also set out and allot unto the said Robert Vyner his heirs and assigns in respect of his same ancient inclosed lands, another piece or parcel of land, other part of the said commons and waste lands on the Wallasey Leasowe marked in the said map No. 20A, containing two acres three roods and twenty-one perches, bounded northwardly by the said private road V, eastwardly by an allotment to Sir John Grey Egerton as one of the lords of the said manor of Wallasey No. 19, southwardly in part by an allotment to the said Robert Vyner, Esquire, on the Wallasey pasture No. 9 and in other part by another allotment to the said Robert Vyner on Wallasey pasture No. 10, and westwardly by an allotment to the said Robert Vyner No. 20B, but in making the allotment to the said Robert Vyner, Esquire, it is meant and intended that Ann Rainford who holds the lands in right of which this allotment is made under a certain lease for three lives from Robert Vyner, Esquire, is to hold and enjoy this allotment along with the other lands comprised in such lease during her estate and interest therein, and I direct the fences on the northward and eastward sides to be made by the said Ann Rainford and kept in repair by her during her interest in such lease and afterwards the same are to be kept in repair by the owner or owners thereof.

Ann Rainford's Leasehold.

Robert Vyner, No. 20B, 1, 3, 23.

I also set out and allot unto the said Robert Vyner, Esquire, his heirs and assigns in respect of his same ancient lands, another piece or parcel of land other part of the said commons and waste lands in Wallasey Leasowe marked in the said map No. 20B, containing one acre three roods and twenty three perches, bounded northwardly by the said private road V, eastwardly by the allotment No. 20A to the said Robert Vyner, southwardly by an allotment on the said pasture to the said Robert Vyner marked No 10, and westwardly by the allotment before made to the said Robert Vyner No. 20, but in making this allotment to the said Robert Vyner it is meant and intended that John Webster who holds the land in right of which this allotment is made under a lease for the lives of himself and Susannah Egerton and Margaret Frankland from the said Robert Vyner, is to hold and enjoy this allotment along with the other lands comprised in such lease during his estate and interest therein, and I direct the fences on the northward and eastward sides thereof shall be made and kept in repair by the said John Webster during the continuance of his interest therein and afterwards that the same shall be kept in repair by the owner and owners thereof.

John Webster's Leasehold.

I also set out and allot unto the said Robert Vyner, his heirs and assigns, in respect of his same ancient lands a piece or parcel of land other part of the said commons and waste lands on Wallasey Leasowe marked in the said map No. 27G, containing twenty-two acres and two perches, bounded northwardly by the said allotment Q, by me sold to the Reverend Augustus Campbell, eastwardly by an allotment No. 28, to Sir John Grey Egerton as one of the lords of the said manor of Wallasey, southwardly by the said private road V, and westwardly by an allotment to the said Robert Vyner, No. 27F, but in making this allotment to the said Robert Vyner, Esquire, it is meant and intended that the said John Webster who holds the lands in right of which this allotment is made under the said lease for the lives of himself and Susannah Egerton and Margaret Frankland from the said Robert Vyner is to hold and enjoy this allotment along with the other lands comprised in the said lease during his estate and interest therein, and I direct the fences on the northward, eastward, and southward sides of the said allotment shall be made and kept in repair by the said John Webster during the continuance of his said lease, and afterwards shall be kept in repair by the owner or owners thereof. *Robert Vyner, Esq., No. 27G, 22, 0, 2.* *John Webster's Leasehold.*

I also set out and allot unto the said Robert Vyner, his heirs and assigns, in respect of his same ancient lands, another piece or parcel of land other part of the said commons and waste lands on Wallasey Leasowe marked on the said map No. 57, containing two acres and thirty-six perches, bounded northeastwardly by the public road F, eastwardly by an allotment No. 56 to John Leigh, Esquire, and southwardly and southwestwardly by ancient inclosed lands belonging to the said Robert Vyner, and in making this allotment it is meant and intended that the said John Webster who holds the lands in right of which this allotment is made under the said lease from Robert Vyner, Esquire, should also hold this allotment during the continuance of his said lease, and I direct the fences on the northeastward side thereof shall be made and kept in repair by the said John Webster during the continuance of his said lease and afterwards shall be kept in repair by the owner or owners thereof. *Robert Vyner, Esq., No. 57, 2, 0, 36.* *John Webster's Leasehold.*

I also set out and allot unto the said Robert Vyner, Esquire, his heirs and assigns in respect of his same ancient lands, a piece or parcel of land other part of the said commons and waste lands on the Wallasey Leasowe marked in the said map No. 20c, containing three roods and two perches, bounded northwardly by the said private road marked V, eastwardly by an allotment No. 20 before made to the said Robert Vyner, southwardly by ancient inclosed lands belonging to the said Robert Vyner, and westwardly by an allotment made to the said Robert Vyner on the Wallasey Leasowe No. 20D, but in making this allotment to the said Robert Vyner, it is meant and intended that Gerard Stanley who holds the lands in right of which this allotment is made under a lease for the lives of himself and Thomas Stanley and Elizabeth Hammond from Robert Vyner, Esquire, is to hold and enjoy this allotment along with the other lands comprised in such lease during his estate and interest therein, and I direct the fences on the northward and eastward sides thereof shall be made and kept in repair by the said Gerard Stanley during the continuance of his said lease and afterwards to be kept in repair by the owner or owners thereof. *Robert Vyner, Esq., No. 20c, 0, 3, 2.* *Gerard Stanley's Leasehold.*

54 Geo. III. Commissioner's Award, ch. lxxvii.
Wallasey Inclosure.

Robert Vyner, Esq., No. 20D, 0, 3, 32.

I also set out and allot unto the said Robert Vyner, his heirs and assigns in respect of his same ancient lands, a piece of land other part of the said commons and waste lands on Wallasey Leasowe marked on the said map No. 20D, containing three roods and thirty-two perches, bounded northwardly by the said private road V, eastwardly by an allotment No. 20C, to the said Robert Vyner, southwardly by ancient inclosed lands of the said Robert Vyner and westwardly by an allotment No. 20A, to the said Robert Vyner, but in making this allotment it is meant and understood that Peter Wilson who holds the lands in right of which this allotment is made under a lease for the lives of Rebecca Wilson, John Wilson, and Peter Wilson from the said Robert Vyner shall hold and enjoy this allotment along with the other lands comprised in such lease during his estate and interest therein and I direct the fences on the northward and eastward sides thereof to be made and kept in repair by the said Peter Wilson during the continuance of his said lease and shall afterwards be kept in repair by the owner or owners thereof.

Peter Wilson's Leasehold.

Robert Vyner, Esq., No. 20E, 3, 2, 7.

I also set out and allot unto Robert Vyner, Esquire, his heirs and assigns in respect of his same ancient lands, a piece or parcel of land other part of the said commons and waste lands on Wallasey Leasowe marked in the said map No. 20E, containing three acres two roods and seven perches, bounded northwardly in part by the said private road marked V in the said map and in other part by an allotment No. 20F to the said Robert Vyner, eastwardly in part by the said allotment No. 20F to the said Robert Vyner, in other part by the said allotment No. 20A to the said Robert Vyner, and in other part by ancient inclosed lands belonging to the said Robert Vyner southwardly by ancient inclosed lands in the said township belonging to the said Robert Vyner, and westwardly by an allotment No. 20B to the said Robert Vyner, but it is meant and intended in making this allotment that Thomas Hilliard who holds the lands in right of which this allotment is made under a lease for three lives from Robert Vyner, Esquire, shall hold and enjoy the same during his estate and interest therein, and I direct the fences on the northward side and as much of the fence on the eastward side as adjoins the allotments No. 20, No. 20F and No. 20A, shall be made and kept in repair by the said Thomas Hilliard during the continuance of his said lease and afterwards shall be kept in repair by the owner or owners thereof.

Thomas Hilliard's Leasehold.

Robert Vyner, Esq., No. 20F, 0, 0, 19.

I also set out and allot unto the said Robert Vyner his heirs and assigns in respect of his same ancient lands, a piece or parcel of land other part of the said commons or waste lands on Wallasey Leasowe marked on the said map No. 20F, containing nineteen perches, bounded northwardly by the said private road V, eastwardly by the said allotment No. 20A made to the said Robert Vyner, southwardly and westwardly by the said last-mentioned allotment No. 20E, and in making this allotment it is meant and intended that George Cooper who holds the land in right of which this allotment is made under a conveyance thereof to him from Thomas Hilliard for the lives named in the said lease to the said Thomas Hilliard from the said Robert Vyner in which the same was included shall hold and enjoy the same during his estate and interest therein and I direct the fences on the northward and eastward sides thereof to be made and kept in repair by the said George Cooper during the continuance

George Cooper, Purchase of Thomas Hilliard's Leasehold.

of his interest therein as aforesaid and afterwards to be kept in repair by the owner or owners thereof.

I also set out and allot unto the Robert Vyner, Esquire, his heirs and assigns in respect of his same ancient inclosed lands a piece or parcel of land, other part of the said commons and waste lands on Wallasey Leasowe marked in the said map No. 27F, containing three acres, two roods and twenty perches, bounded northwardly by the said allotment Q, by me sold to the Reverend Augustus Campbell, eastwardly by the allotment No. 27G to the said Robert Vyner, southwardly by the said private road V, and westwardly by an allotment No. 27 to the said Robert Vyner, and in making this allotment it is meant and intended that the said Thomas Hilliard who holds the lands in right of which this allotment is made under the said before-mentioned lease shall hold and enjoy the same during his estate and interest therein, and I direct the fences on the northward, eastward and southward sides thereof shall be made and kept in repair by the said Thomas Hilliard during the continuance of the said lease and afterwards shall be kept in repair by the owner thereof. *Robert Vyner, Esq., No. 27F, 3, 2, 20.* *Thomas Hilliard's Leasehold.*

I also set out and allot unto the said Robert Vyner his heirs and assigns in respect of his same ancient lands, a piece or parcel of land part of the said commons and waste lands on Wallasey Brake marked in the said map No. 73, containing thirteen perches, bounded northeastwardly by an allotment No. 72 made to Sir John Grey Egerton southeastwardly by ancient inclosed land belonging to Robert Vyner, Esquire, and northwestwardly by the said private road O, but it is meant and intended that the said George Cooper who holds the land in respect of which this allotment is made by virtue of a conveyance from the said Thomas Hilliard under the said lease shall hold and enjoy this allotment during his estate and interest therein, and I direct the fence on the northeastward and northwestward sides thereof shall be made and kept in repair by the said George Cooper during the continuance of his interest under the said lease and afterwards shall be kept in repair by the owner and owners thereof. *Robert Vyner, Esq., No. 73.* *George Cooper's Purchase of Thomas Hilliard's Leasehold.*

I also set out and allot unto Robert Vyner, Esquire, or to the person or persons entitled to the piece or parcel of ancient enclosed lands called the Stable Croft and for and in respect of the same lands and according to his her or their estate and interest therein a piece or parcel of land other part of the said commons and waste lands on the Wallasey Leasowe marked in the said map No. 63 containing two roods and two perches, bounded northwardly by the said public road F, eastwardly by an allotment No. 62 to Thomas Webster, southwardly by the ancient lands called the Stable Croft, and westwardly by an allotment No. 64 to Mrs. Wotherspoon, and I direct the fences on the northward and eastward sides thereof to be made and for ever afterwards kept in repair by the owner thereof. *Robert Vyner, Esq., for Stable Croft, No. 63, 0, 2, 2.*

I also set out and allot unto Sir John Tobin, Knight, his heirs and assigns in right of his ancient inclosed lands in the Township of Wallasey aforesaid a piece or parcel of land other part of the said commons and waste lands on Wallasey Leasowe marked in the said map No. 17, containing nine acres three roods, bounded northwardly by the private road V, eastwardly by an allotment No. 16 to John *Sir John Tobin, No. 17, 9, 3, 0.*

Leigh, Esquire, southwardly in part by an allotment No. 6 to the said John Leigh on Wallasey pasture, and in other part by an allotment No. 7A to the said Sir John Tobin on the said pasture and westwardly by the public road Q between this allotment and the allotment No. 18 to the said Sir John Grey Egerton, and I direct the fences on the northward, westward and eastward sides thereof to be made and for ever afterwards kept in repair by the owner thereof.

Sir John Tobin, Knt., No. 30, 16, 3, 15.

I also set out and allot unto Sir John Tobin his heirs and assigns in respect of his said ancient inclosed lands a piece or parcel of land other part of the said commons and waste lands on Wallasey Leasowe marked on the said map No. 30 containing sixteen acres three roods and fifteen perches, bounded northwardly by the said allotment Q, by me sold to the Reverend Augustus Campbell, eastwardly by an allotment No. 31 to the said John Leigh southwardly by the said private road V, and westwardly by the public road Q, between this allotment and an allotment No. 29, to the said Sir John Grey Egerton, and I direct the fences on the northward, westward, eastward and southward sides to be made and for ever kept in repair by the owner thereof.

Sir John Tobin, Knt., No. 48, 14, 1, 4

I also set out and allot unto the said Sir John Tobin his heirs and assigns, in respect of his said ancient lands a piece or parcel of land other part of the said commons and waste lands on Wallasey Leasowe, marked on the said map No. 48, containing fourteen acres one rood and four perches, bounded northwardly by the said allotment Q, by me sold to the Reverend Augustus Campbell, eastwardly in part by lands in Liscard belonging to the said Sir John Tobin, in other part by lands in Liscard belonging to John Dean the younger, and in other part by lands in Liscard aforesaid, belonging to the representatives of William Groom, southwardly by an allotment No. 49, to the representatives of William Groom, and westwardly by an allotment G. sold to John Davies in pursuance of the said act, and I direct the fences on the northward and southward sides thereof to be made and for ever afterwards kept in repair by the owner thereof.

Sir John Tobin, Knt., No. 15, 3, 0, 1.

I also set out and allot unto the said Sir John Tobin his heirs and assigns, a piece or parcel of land, part of the said commons and waste lands on Wallasey Leasowe marked in the said map No. 15, containing three acres and one perch and bounded northwardly by the said private road V, eastwardly by an allotment No. 14 to Joseph Green, southwardly by an allotment No. 5 to the said Sir John Tobin on Wallasey Pasture, and westwardly by an allotment No. 16 to the said John Leigh, and I direct the fences on the northward and eastward sides thereof to be made and for ever afterwards kept in repair by the owner thereof.

Sir John Tobin, Knt., No. 67, 0, 0, 12.

I also set out and allot unto the said Sir John Tobin his heirs and assigns, a piece or parcel of land, other part of the said commons and waste lands on Wallasey Leasowe marked in the said map No. 67, containing twelve perches, bounded northwardly by an allotment No. 66 to Sir John Grey Egerton, eastwardly by ancient inclosed lands and buildings belonging to the said Joseph Jackson, southwardly by a cottage belonging to the representatives of the late Thomas Dean, and westwardly by the said public road E, and I direct the fence on the westward side to be made and for ever afterwards kept in repair by the owner thereof.

51 Geo. III.   *Commissioner's Award,*   ch. lxxxvii.
             Wallasey Inclosure.

I also set out and allot unto the said Sir John Tobin his heirs and Sir John
assigns, a piece or parcel of land, other part of the said commons Tobin, Knt.,
and waste lands on Wallasey Brake marked on the said map No. 77, No. 77, 0, 3,
containing three roods and thirty four perches, bounded northwardly 34.
by an allotment No. 76 to the said Sir John Tobin, eastwardly by
ancient inclosed lands belonging to the said Sir John Tobin,
southwardly by allotment No. 78 to Sir John Grey Egerton, and
westwardly by the said public road marked L, the right to which
said three last mentioned allotments No. 15, 67, and 77, belongs to
Joseph Jackson in respect of his ancient inclosed lands in the said
Township of Wallasey and has been sold and disposed of by him to
the said Sir John Tobin to whom I have made these allotments in
pursuance of the said act. And I direct the fences on the southward
and westward sides thereof to be made and for ever afterwards kept
in repair by the owner thereof.

I also set out and allot unto the said Sir John Tobin, his heirs and Sir John
assigns, a piece or parcel of land other part of the said commons and Tobin, Knt.,
waste lands on Wallasey Brake marked in the said map No. 71, No. 71, 3, 3,
which together with the piece of land covered with water, and the 19.
road thereto, used as a public pit for the inhabitants of the township of
Wallasey, containing twenty-eight perches, which I also set out and
allot unto the said Sir John Tobin, his heirs and assigns, subject to
the conditions hereinafter mentioned and exclusive of half an acre
of uninclosed ancient land belonging to Sir John Tobin within this
allotment, contains three acres three roods and nineteen perches
bounded northwardly in part by ancient inclosed lands belonging to
the said Sir John Tobin, and in other part by the public road
marked on the said map with the letter N, eastwardly by another
public road marked on the said map with the letter M, southwardly
by a private road marked on the said map by the letter O, and westwardly in part by the said private road O, in other part by a public
road marked on the said map LL, and in other part by ancient
inclosed lands belonging to the said Sir John Tobin, and I direct all
the fences shall be made and for ever afterwards be kept in repair by
the owner thereof, and I have set out and allotted unto the said Sir
John Tobin the said piece of land covered with water, and the road Watering Pit
thereto upon this condition that the said Sir John Tobin, his heirs
and assigns, shall and do at all times hereafter permit and suffer
the inhabitants of the township of Wallasey aforesaid, to use and
enjoy and take water from a certain pit or watering place situate in
a certain field in Wallasey aforesaid called Little Wallacres belonging
to the said Sir John Tobin in as full free and unrestrained manner as
they heretofore might or could have used or enjoyed the said pit or
watering place as aforesaid, allotted to the said Sir John Tobin and
also that the said Sir John Tobin do and shall from time to time
cleanse the same watering pit whenever necessary.

I also set out and allot unto the said Sir John Tobin, his heirs and Sir John
assigns in respect of the said ancient inclosed lands a piece or parcel Tobin, Knt
of land other part of said commons and waste lands on the Wallasey No. 76, 1, 0
Brake marked on the said map No. 76, containing one acre and 33
thirty-three perches, bounded northwardly by an allotment No. 75, to
Henry Johnson, eastwardly by ancient inclosed lands belonging to
the said Sir John Tobin, southwardly by an allotment No. 77,
to the said Sir John Tobin, and westwardly by the public

road marked on the said map with the letter L. And I direct the fences on the southward and westward sides thereof to be made and for ever afterwards kept in repair by the owner thereof.

John Leigh, Esq., No. 16, 7, 3, 15.

I also set out and allot unto John Leigh, Esquire, his heirs and assigns, in respect of his ancient inclosed lands in the township of Wallasey aforesaid, a piece or parcel of land other part of the said commons and waste lands on the Wallasey Leasowe marked on the said map No. 16, containing seven acres three roods and fifteen perches, bounded northwardly by the said private road V, eastwardly by an allotment No. 15, to Joseph Jackson, southwardly by an allotment No. 6, to the said John Leigh, on the said Wallasey Pasture, and westwardly by an allotment No. 17, to the said Sir John Tobin, and I direct the fences on the northward and eastward sides thereof to be made and for ever afterwards kept in repair by the owner thereof.

John Leigh, Esq., No. 31, 15, 1, 29.

I also set out and allot unto the said John Leigh, his heirs and assigns, in respect of his same ancient lands a piece or parcel of land other part of the said commons and waste lands on Wallasey Leasowe marked on the said map No. 31, containing fifteen acres one rood and twenty-nine perches, bounded northwardly by the said allotment Q, by me sold to the Reverend Augustus Campbell, eastwardly by an allotment No. 32 to Joseph Green, Esquire, southwardly by the said private road V, and westwardly by an allotment No. 30 to the said Sir John Tobin. And I direct the fences on the northward and eastward and southward sides thereof to be made and for ever afterwards kept in repair by the owner thereof.

John Leigh, Esq., No. 56, 0, 0, 38.

I also set out and allot unto the said John Leigh, his heirs and assigns in respect of his same ancient land a piece or parcel of land other part of the said commons and waste lands on Wallasey Leasowe, marked on the said map No. 56, containing thirty-eight perches, bounded northeastwardly by the said public road F, eastwardly by an allotment No. 55 to Margaret Wade's Trustees, southwardly by ancient inclosed lands belonging to the said John Leigh and westwardly by an allotment No. 57 to Robert Vyner, Esquire. And I direct the fences on the northeastward and westward sides thereof to be made and for ever afterwards kept in repair by the owner thereof.

Joseph Green, Esq., No. 14, 4, 3, 34.

I also set out and allot unto Joseph Green, Esquire, his heirs and assigns in respect of his ancient inclosed lands in the Township of Wallasey aforesaid, a piece or parcel of land, other part of the said commons and waste lands on Wallasey Leasowe, marked on the said map No. 14, containing four acres three roods and thirty-four perches, bounded northwardly by the said private road V, eastwardly by an allotment No. 13 to the Reverend Augustus Campbell, southwardly in part by an allotment No. 4 to the said Joseph Green on the said Wallasey Pasture and in other part by an allotment No. 5 to Sir John Tobin on the said Wallasey Pasture and westwardly by an allotment No. 15 to the said Sir John Tobin on the said Leasowe. And I direct the fences on the northward and eastward sides thereof to be made and for ever afterwards kept in repair by the owner thereof.

Joseph Green, Esq., No. 32, 5, 2, 37.

I also set out and allot unto the said Joseph Green, Esquire, his heirs and assigns in respect of his same ancient inclosed lands a piece or parcel of land, part of the said commons and waste lands on Wallasey Leasowe, marked on the said map No. 32, containing five acres two roods thirty-seven perches, bounded northwardly by the said allotment Q by me sold to the Reverend Augustus Campbell, eastwardly by an allotment No. 32A to the said Joseph Green, southwardly by the said private road V, and westwardly by an allotment No. 31 to the said John Leigh. And I direct the fences on the northward, eastward and southward sides thereof to be made and for ever afterwards kept in repair by the owner thereof.

I also set out and allot unto the said Joseph Green, his heirs and assigns a piece or parcel of land, other part of the said commons and waste lands on the Wallasey Leasowe, marked in the said map No. 32A, containing three roods and two perches, bounded northwardly by the said allotment Q, by me sold to the Reverend Augustus Campbell, eastwardly by an allotment No. 33 to the said Joseph Greene, southwardly by the said private road V, and westwardly by the said allotment No. 32 to the said Joseph Green, the right of which said allotment marked No. 32A, belonged to the Trustees of Margaret Wade in respect of her ancient inclosed lands in the said Township of Wallasey and was sold and disposed of by the said Trustees to the said Joseph Green to whom I have made this allotment in pursuance of the said Act. And I direct the fences on the northward, eastward and southward sides thereof to be made and for ever afterwards kept in repair by the owner thereof. Joseph Green, Esq., No. 32A, 0, 3, 2. Purchase from Mrs. Wade's Trustees.

I also set out and allot unto the said Joseph Green, his heirs and assigns, a piece or parcel of land, other part of the said commons and waste lands on Wallasey Leasowe, marked on the said map No. 33, containing two acres one rood and twenty-six perches, bounded northwardly by the said allotment Q, by me sold to the Reverend Augustus Campbell, eastwardly by an allotment No. 34 to Robinson Dean, southwardly by the said private road V, and westwardly by an allotment No. 32A to the said Joseph Green, the right of which said allotment No. 33 belonged to Robinson Dean in respect of his ancient inclosed lands in the said Township of Wallasey, and was sold and disposed of by the said Robinson Dean to the said Joseph Green, to whom I have made the allotment in pursuance of the said Act. And I direct the fences on the northward, eastward, and southward sides thereof to be made and for ever afterwards kept in repair by the owner thereof. Joseph Green, Esq., No. 33, 2, 1, 26. Purchase from R. Dean.

I also set out and allot unto the said Joseph Green, Esquire, his heirs and assigns, a piece or parcel of land, other part of the said commons and waste lands on Wallasey Leasowe, marked in the said map No. 68, containing one rood and seven perches, bounded northwardly by ancient inclosed lands belonging to the representatives of the late Thomas Dean, eastwardly by ancient inclosed lands belonging to the said Joseph Green, southwardly in part by the allotment No. 69A to Isaac Brien, and in other part by an allotment No. 69 to the representatives of the late Thomas Dean, and westwardly by a public road marked on the said map with the letter E. And I direct the fences on the southward and westward sides thereof to be made and for ever afterwards kept in repair by the owner thereof. Joseph Green, Esq., No. 68, 0, 1, 7.

I also set out and allot unto the Rector of the Parish and Parish Church of Wallasey aforesaid, in respect of his glebe lands and rectorial rights in the said Township of Wallasey, a piece or parcel Rector of Wallasey, No. 13, Glebe Lands, 1, 3, 35 of land, other part of the said commons and waste lands on Wallasey Leasowe, marked on the said map No. 13, containing one acre three roods and thirty-five perches, bounded northwardly by the said private road V, eastwardly in part by an allotment No. 12 to William Bird, and in other part by an allotment No. 11 to Mrs. Wade's trustees, southwardly in part by an allotment No. 3 to Sir Thomas Stanley Massey Stanley on the said Wallasey Pasture, and in other part by an allotment No. 4 to the said Joseph Green on the said Wallasey Pasture, and westwardly by an allotment No. 14 to the said Joseph Green. And I direct the fences on the northward and eastward sides thereof to be for ever hereafter kept in repair by the owner thereof.

Rector of Wallasey, No. 38, Glebe Lands, 5, 0, 24.

I also set out and allot unto the Rector of the Parish and Parish Church of Wallasey aforesaid, in respect of his said glebe lands and rectorial rights, a piece or parcel of land, other part of the said commons and waste lands on Wallasey Leasowe, marked on the said map No. 38, containing five acres and twenty-four perches, bounded northwardly by the said allotment Q, by me sold to the Reverend Augustus Campbell, eastwardly by several allotments by me sold to the Reverend James Smedley, marked A, B, and E, southwardly by the said private road V, and westwardly by an allotment No. 37 to John Meadows. And I direct the fences on the northward and southward sides thereof to be hereafter kept in repair by the owner thereof.

Rector of Wallasey, No. 70, Glebe Lands, 0, 0, 34.

I also set out and allot unto the said Rector of the Parish and Parish Church of Wallasey aforesaid, in respect of his said Glebe lands and rectorial rights, a piece or parcel of land part of the said commons and waste lands on Wallasey Brake, marked in the said map No. 70, and containing thirty-four perches, bounded eastwardly by the said public road M, southwardly by the said public road N, and northwestwardly in part by the churchyard belonging to Wallasey Church, and in other part by ancient inclosed glebe lands. And I direct that the part of the fences which is opposite to the said glebe lands shall be kept in repair by the Rector of the said Parish and Parish Church of Wallasey for the time being, and the fence surrounding the part of the above allotment, which is now added to the said churchyard, shall for ever afterwards be kept in repair by or at the expense of the parishioners of the said Parish of Wallasey aforesaid.

John Davies, No. 50, 9, 0, 14.

I also set out and allot unto John Davies, his heirs and assigns, a piece or parcel of land, part of the said commons and waste lands in Wallasey Leasowe, marked in the said map No. 50, containing nine acres and fourteen perches, bounded northwardly by an allotment No. 49, to the representatives of William Groom, eastwardly in part by the said private road, marked on the said map with the letter R, and in other part by an allotment No. 51 to the said John Davies, southwestwardly by the said public road F, and eastwardly by an allotment G, by me sold to the said John Davies, the right of which said allotment No. 50 belonged to the Reverend James Smedley, in respect of his ancient inclosed lands in the said Township of Wallasey, and has been sold and disposed of by the said Reverend James Smedley to the said John Davies, to whom I have made this allotment in pursuance of the said Act. And I direct the fences on the southwestward side to be made and for ever afterwards kept in repair by the owner thereof.

54 Geo. III.   Commissioner's Award,   ch. lxxrvii.   83
Wallasey Inclosure.

I also set out and allot unto the said John Davies, his heirs and assigns, in respect of his ancient inclosed lands in the said Township of Wallasey, a piece or parcel of land other part of the said commons and waste lands on Wallasey Leasowe, marked in the said map No. 53, containing four perches, bounded northeastwardly by the said public road F, southwardly by ancient inclosed lands belonging to the said John Davies, and westwardly in part by ancient inclosed lands belonging to Sir John Grey Egerton, and in other part by an allotment No. 54 to the said Sir John Grey Egerton, and I direct the fences on the northeastward side thereof and so much of the fence on the westward side as is adjoining the allotment No. 54, to Sir John Grey Egerton to be made and for ever afterwards kept in repair by the owner thereof.

John Davies, No. 53, 0, 0, 4.

I also set out and allot unto the said John Davies, his heirs and assigns, a piece or parcel of land other part of the said commons and waste lands on Wallasey Leasowe, marked on the said map No. 51, containing nineteen perches, bounded northwardly and westwardly by allotment No. 50 to the said John Davies, eastwardly by the said private road R, and southwestwardly by the public road F. And I direct the fence on the south side thereof to be made and for ever afterwards kept in repair by the owner thereof.

John Davies, No. 51, 0, 0, 19

I also set out and allot unto the said John Davies, his heirs and assigns, a piece or parcel of land other part of the said commons and waste lands on Wallasey Leasowe, marked in the said map No. 52, containing one acre, bounded northwardly in part by an allotment A, by me sold to the said John Davies, in other part by the said public road P, eastwardly by the said private road marked in the said plan q, southeastwardly by land in Liscard belonging to Mrs. Thompson, and westwardly by ancient inclosed lands belonging to the said John Davies, the right to which two last-mentioned allotments No. 51 and No. 52 belong to John Leigh, Esquire, in respect of his ancient inclosed lands in the Township of Wallasey, and have been sold and disposed of by the said John Leigh to the said John Davies, to whom I have made these allotments in pursuance of the said Act. And I direct the fences on the northward side thereof to be made and for ever afterwards kept in repair by the owner thereof.

John Davies, No. 52, 1, 0, 0.

Purchase from J. Leigh, Esq.

I also set out and allot unto Robert Harrison, his heirs and assigns, in respect of his ancient inclosed lands in the said Township of Wallasey, a piece or parcel of land, other part of the said commons and waste lands on Wallasey Leasowe, marked on the said map No. 22, containing four acres one rood and thirteen perches, bounded northwardly by the said private road V, eastwardly by the allotment No. 21 to Robert Vyner, Esquire, as one of the Lords of the said Manor of Wallasey, southwestwardly by ancient inclosed lands belonging to the said Robert Harrison, and westwardly by an allotment M, by me sold to Mrs. Boode. And I direct the fences on the northward and eastward sides thereof to be made and for ever afterwards kept in repair by the owner thereof.

Robert Harrison, No. 22, 4, 1, 13

I also set out and allot unto the said Robert Harrison, his heirs and assigns, in respect of his same ancient lands, a piece or parcel of land, other part of the said commons and waste lands on Wallasey Leasowe, marked on the said map No. 25, containing three acres three roods and thirty-seven perches, bounded north-

Robert Harrison, No. 25, 3, 3, 37

eastwardly by the said allotment Q, by me sold to the Reverend Augustus Campbell, eastwardly by an allotment No. 26 to Robert Vyner, Esquire, southwardly by the said private road V, and westwardly by an allotment N, by me sold to Mrs. Boode. And I direct the fences on the northeastward, eastward, and southward sides thereof to be made and for ever afterwards kept in repair by the owner thereof.

Robert Harrison, No. 23, 0, 1, 5.

I also set out and allot unto the said Robert Harrison, his heirs and assigns, in respect of his same ancient lands, a piece or parcel of land, other part of the said commons and waste lands on Wallasey Leasowe marked in the said map No. 23, containing one rood and five perches, bounded northwardly by an allotment N, by me sold to Mrs. Boode, eastwardly by ancient inclosed land belonging to the said Robert Harrison, southwardly by the commencement of Reed's Lane leading to Bidston, and westwardly by a private road marked on the said map with the letter X. And I direct the fences on the southward and westward sides thereof to be made and for ever afterwards kept in repair by the owner thereof.

Robert Harrison, No. 24, 3, 2, 37.

I also set out and allot unto the said Robert Harrison, his heirs and assigns, in respect of his same ancient lands, a piece or parcel of land, other part of the said commons and waste lands on Wallasey Leasowe, marked on the said map No. 24, containing three acres two roods and thirty-seven perches, bounded northwardly by an allotment by me sold to Mrs. Boode in pursuance of the said Act, marked O, eastwardly by ancient inclosed lands belonging to the said Robert Harrison, southwardly by the public road marked in the said map K, and westwardly by common lands in the Township of Great Meols. And I direct the fences on the southward and westward sides thereof to be made and for ever afterwards kept in repair by the owner thereof.

Robinson Dean, No. 34, 3, 0, 5.

I also set out and allot unto Robinson Dean his heirs and assigns, in respect of his ancient inclosed lands in the said township of Wallasey a piece or parcel of land part of the said commons and waste lands on Wallasey Leasowe marked on the said map No. 34 containing three acres and five perches, bounded northwardly by the said allotment Q by me sold to the Reverend Augustus Campbell, eastwardly by an allotment No. 35 to the trustees of Matthew Taylor, southwardly by the said private road V, and westwardly by an allotment No. 33 to Joseph Green, Esquire, and I direct the fences on the northward, eastward, and southward sides thereof to be made and for ever afterwards kept in repair by the owner thereof.

Trustees of M. Taylor, deceased, No. 35, 3, 1, 17

I also set out and allot unto the trustees named and appointed in and by the last will and testament of Matthew Taylor, Gentleman, deceased, and to their heirs and assigns in respect of their ancient inclosed lands in the said township of Wallasey a piece or parcel of land, other part of the said commons and waste lands on Wallasey Leasowe marked on the said map No. 35, containing three acres one rood and seventeen perches, bounded northwardly by the said allotment Q, by me sold to the Reverend Augustus Campbell, eastwardly by an allotment No. 36 to Richard Smith, Esquire, southwardly by the said private road V, and westwardly by an allotment No. 34 to Robinson Dean, and I direct the fences on the northward, eastward and southward sides thereof to be made and for ever afterwards kept in repair by the owners thereof.

Wallasey Inclosure.

I also set out and allot unto Richard Smith, Esquire, his heirs and assigns in respect of his ancient inclosed lands in the said Township of Wallasey a piece or parcel of land other part of the said commons and waste lands on Wallasey Leasowe marked on the said map No. 36, containing three acres one rood and twenty-eight perches, bounded northwardly by the said allotment Q, by me sold to the Reverend Augustus Campbell, eastwardly by an allotment No. 37 to John Meadows, southwardly by the said private road V, and westwardly by an allotment No. 35 to the trustees of Matthew Taylor, and I direct the fences on the northward, eastward and southward sides thereof to be made and for ever afterwards kept in repair by the owner thereof.

Richard Smith, Esq., No. 36, 3, 1, 28

I also set out and allot unto the said Richard Smith, Esquire, his heirs and assigns in respect of his same ancient lands a piece or parcel of land part of the said commons and waste lands on Wallasey Brake aforesaid marked on the said map No. 79 containing one acre and thirty-two perches, bounded northwardly by an allotment No. 78 to Sir John Grey Egerton, eastwardly by ancient inclosed lands belonging to the said Richard Smith in the Township of Poolton-cum-Seacombe, and southwestwardly by the said public road L, and I direct the fences on the southwestwardly side thereof to be made and for ever afterwards kept in repair by the owner thereof.

Richard Smith, No. 79, 1, 0, 32.

I also set out and allot unto John Meadows his heirs and assigns in respect of his ancient inclosed lands in the said township of Wallasey, a piece or parcel of land other part of the said commons and waste lands on Wallasey Leasowe marked on the said map No. 37, containing three acres two roods and twenty-six perches, bounded northwardly by the said allotment Q by me sold to the Reverend Augustus Campbell, eastwardly by an allotment No. 38 to the said Rector of Wallasey, southwardly by the said private road V, and westwardly by an allotment No. 36 to Richard Smith, Esquire, and I direct the fences on the northward, eastward and southward sides thereof to be made and for ever afterwards kept in repair by the owner thereof.

John Meadows, No. 37, 3, 2, 26

I also set out and allot unto Thomas Molyneux, his heirs and assigns in respect of his ancient inclosed lands in the Township of Wallasey a piece or parcel of land other part of the said commons and waste lands on Wallasey Leasowe, marked in the said map No. 39, containing twenty-five perches, bounded northwardly by an allotment No. 42 to Robert Stanley, eastwardly by an allotment No. 40 to John Coventry and southwardly by the said public road F, and westwardly by the said public road E. And I direct the fences on the northward, southward and westward sides thereof to be made and for ever afterwards kept in repair by the owner thereof.

Thos. Molyneux, No. 39, 0, 0, 25

I also set out and allot unto John Coventry, his heirs and assigns in respect of his ancient inclosed lands in the said Township of Wallasey a piece or parcel of land, other part of the said commons and waste lands on Wallasey Leasowe, marked on the said map No. 40, containing twenty-four perches bounded northwardly by an allotment No. 42 to Robert Stanley, eastwardly by an allotment No. 41 to John Street, southwardly by the said public road F, and westwardly by an allotment No. 39 to Thomas Molyneux. And I direct the fences on the northward, southward and westward sides thereof to be made and for ever afterwards kept in repair by the owner thereof.

John Coventry, No. 40, 0, 0, 24.

54 *Geo. III.* *Commissioner's Award,* ch. lxxxvii.
Wallasey Inclosure.

Joseph Street, No. 41, 0, 0, 32.

Purchase from Ralph Hassall.

I also set out and allot unto Joseph Street, his heirs and assigns a piece or parcel of land other part of the said commons and waste lands on Wallasey Leasowe marked in the said map number 41, containing thirty-two perches, bounded northwardly by an allotment No. 42 to Robert Stanley, eastwardly by an allotment No. 43 to George Cooper, southwardly by the said public road F, and westwardly by an allotment No. 40 to John Coventry, the right of which said allotment No. 41 belonged to Ralph Hassall in respect of his ancient inclosed lands in the Township of Wallasey, and has been sold and disposed of by him to the said Joseph Street to whom I have made this allotment in pursuance of the said Act, and I direct the fences on the northward, southward, and westward sides thereof to be made and for ever afterwards kept in repair by the owner thereof.

Robert Stanley, No. 42, 0, 3, 39

I also set out and allot unto Robert Stanley, his heirs and assigns in respect of his ancient inclosed lands in the Township of Wallasey a piece or parcel of land other part of the said commons and waste lands on Wallasey Leasowe marked in the said map No. 42, and containing three roods and thirty-nine perches, bounded northwardly by the allotment marked R, by me sold to George Peers, eastwardly by an allotment No. 43 to George Cooper, and southwardly in part by an allotment No. 41 to Joseph Street, in other part by an allotment No. 40 to John Coventry, and in other part by an allotment No. 39 to Thomas Molyneux, and westwardly by the said public road E. And I direct the fences on the northward and westward sides thereof to be made and for ever afterwards kept in repair by the owner thereof.

George Cooper, No. 43, 0, 3, 32

I also set out and allot unto George Cooper, his heirs and assigns in respect of his ancient inclosed lands in the Township of Wallasey a piece or parcel of land other part of the said commons and waste lands on Wallasey Leasowe marked on the said map No. 43, containing three roods and thirty-two perches, bounded northwardly in part by the said allotment R, by me sold to George Peers, and in other part by the said allotment Q, by me sold to the Reverend Augustus Campbell, eastwardly by an allotment number 44 to Peter Ledsham, southwardly by the public road F, and westwardly in part by another allotment No. 41 to Joseph Street, and in other part by an allotment No. 42 to Robert Stanley. And I direct the fences on the northward southward and westward sides thereof to be made and for ever afterwards kept in repair by the owner thereof.

George Cooper, No. 74, 0, 1, 32

I also set out and allot unto George Cooper, his heirs and assigns in respect of his same ancient lands a piece or parcel of land other part of the said commons and waste lands on Wallasey Brake marked on the said map No. 74, containing one rood and thirty-two perches, bounded northwardly and northeastwardly by the private road marked on the said map o, eastwardly by another private road marked p, southwardly by the allotment by me hereinbefore set out and described as the allotment for stone on the said brake, and westwardly and southwestwardly in part by ancient inclosed lands belonging to the said George Cooper, and in other part by the said public road LL. And I direct the fences on the northward, northeastward, eastward, southward sides thereof, and so much of the fences on the westward side thereof as adjoins the public road LL, to be made and for ever afterwards kept in repair by the owner thereof.

54 Geo. III.   *Commissioner's Award.*   ch. lxxxvii.   87
Wallasey Inclosure.

I also set out and allot unto Peter Ledsham, his heirs and assigns, in respect of his ancient inclosed lands in the said Township of Wallasey, a piece or parcel of land other part of the said commons and waste lands on Wallasey Leasowe marked on the said map No. 44, containing one acre one rood and six perches, bounded northwardly by the said allotment Q, by me sold to the Reverend Augustus Campbell, eastwardly by an allotment No. 45 to Peter Ledsham, southwardly by the said public road F, and westwardly by an allotment No. 43, to the said George Cooper, the right to which said allotment No. 44 belonged to Joseph Molyneux in respect of his ancient inclosed lands in the said Township of Wallasey, and has been sold and disposed of by him to the said Peter Ledsham to whom I have made this allotment in pursuance of the said Act, and I direct the fences on the northward, southward, and westward sides thereof to be made and for ever afterwards kept in repair by the owner thereof.
Peter Ledsham, Purchased from Joseph Molyneux, No. 44, 1, 1, 6.

I also set out and allot unto Peter Ledsham, his heirs and assigns, in respect of his ancient inclosed lands in the said Township of Wallasey, a piece or parcel of land other part of the said commons and waste lands on Wallasey Leasowe marked on the said map No. 45, containing two acres one rood and three perches, bounded northwardly by the said allotment Q, by me sold to the Reverend Augustus Campbell, eastwardly by an allotment No. 46 to William Dean, southwardly by the said public road F, and westwardly by the said allotment No. 44 to the said Peter Ledsham, and I direct the fences on the northward, southward, and westward sides thereof to be made and for ever afterwards kept in repair by the owner thereof.
Peter Ledsham, No. 45, 2, 1, 3.

I also set out and allot unto William Dean, his heirs and assigns, in respect of his ancient inclosed lands in the Township of Wallasey, a piece or parcel of land other part of the said commons and waste lands on Wallasey Leasowe, marked on the said map No. 46, containing two acres one rood and twenty-five perches, bounded northwardly by the said allotment Q, by me sold to the Reverend Augustus Campbell, eastwardly by an allotment No. 47 to the heirs of Elizabeth Bird, southwardly by the said public road F, and westwardly by an allotment No. 45 to Peter Ledsham, and I direct the fences on the northward, southward, and westward sides thereof, to be made and for ever afterwards kept in repair by the owner therof.
William Dean, No. 46, 2, 1, 25.

I also set out and allot unto the heirs or other representatives of the late Elizabeth Bird, his, her, and their heirs and assigns, in respect of her ancient inclosed lands in the Township of Wallasey, a piece or parcel of land other part of the said commons and waste lands on Wallasey Leasowe marked on the said map No. 47, containing two acres three roods and thirty-four perches bounded northwardly by the said allotment Q, by me sold to the Reverend Augustus Campbell, eastwardly by the private road marked in the said map S, southwardly by the public road F, and westwardly by an allotment No. 46 to William Dean, and I direct all the fences thereof to be made and for ever afterwards kept in repair by the owner thereof.
Heirs of Elizh. Bird, No. 47, 2, 3, 34.

I also set out and allot unto the heirs, devisees or other representatives of William Groom, deceased, his heirs and assigns in respect of his ancient inclosed lands in the Township of Wallasey a piece or parcel of land other part of the said commons and waste
Heirs of W. Groom, No. 49, 2, 3, 14.

lands and waste lands on Wallasey Leasowe marked on the said map No. 49, containing two acres three roods and fourteen perches, bounded northwardly by an allotment No. 48, to Sir John Tobin, eastwardly by the private road marked on the said map r, southwardly by an allotment No. 50, to John Davies, and westwardly by an allotment G, by me sold to the said John Davies, and I direct the fences on the southward side thereof to be made and for ever afterwards kept in repair by the owner thereof.

Sir T. S. M. Stanley, Purchased from Trustees of Margt. Wade, No. 10, 2, 2, 38.

I also set out and allot unto Sir Thomas Stanley Massey Stanley, Baronet, his heirs and assigns, a piece or parcel of land other part of the said commons and waste lands on Wallasey Leasowe, marked on the said map No. 10, containing two acres two roods and thirty-eight perches, bounded northwardly by the private road V, eastwardly by an allotment No. 9, to Miss Jane Rainsford, southwardly in part by an allotment No. 1 A, on the said Wallasey pasture to the devisee in trust of George Briggs, and in other part by an allotment No. 2, on the said pasture to John Davies, and westwardly by an allotment No. 11, to the said Margaret Wade's trustees the right to which said allotment No. 10, belonged to the trustees of the marriage settlement of Margaret Wade in respect of their ancient lands in the said Township of Wallasey, and has been sold and disposed of by them to the said Sir Thomas Stanley Massey Stanley to whom I have made this allotment in pursuance of the said Act, and I direct the fences on the northward and eastward sides thereof to be made and kept in repair by the owner thereof.

Trustees of Margt. Wade, No. 11, 3, 0, 2.

I also set out and allot unto the said trustees of Mrs. Margaret Wade's Settlement in respect of their same ancient lands a piece or parcel of land other part of the said commons and waste lands on Wallasey Leasowe marked on the said map No. 11, containing three acres and two perches bounded northwardly in part by an allotment No. 12, to William Bird and in other part by the said private road V, eastwardly by an allotment No. 10, to the said Sir Thomas Stanley Massey Stanley and in other part by an allotment No. 2, to John Davies on the said pasture, and in other part by an allotment No. 3, to the said Sir Thomas Stanley Massey Stanley on the said pasture, and westwardly part by an allotment No. 13, to the Rector of Wallasey, and in other part by an allotment No. 12, to William Bird, and I direct the fences on the northward and eastward sides thereof to be made and for ever afterwards kept in repair by the owner thereof.

Trustees of Margt. Wade, No. 55, 0, 0, 33.

I also set out and allot unto the said trustees of Margaret Wade's Settlement in respect of their same ancient lands a piece or parcel of land other part of the said commons and waste lands on Wallasey Leasowe marked in the said map No. 55, containing thirty-three perches, bounded southeastwardly by the said public road F, eastwardly by an allotment No. 54, to Sir John Grey Egerton, southwardly by ancient inclosed lands belonging to the said trustees, and westwardly by an allotment No. 56, to John Leigh, Esquire, and I direct the fences on the northeastwardly and westwardly sides thereof to be made and for ever afterwards kept in repair by the owner thereof.

Trustees of Margt. Wade, No. 80, 0, 0, 21.

I also set out and allot unto the said trustees of Margaret Wade's Settlement, in respect of their same ancient lands, a piece or parcel of land part of the said commons and waste lands on Wallasey Brake, marked on the said map No. 80, containing twenty-one perches, bounded northwardly and northeastwardly by the public road L, and southeastwardly by an allotment No. 40 in the Township of Poolton-cum-Seacombe, and westwardly by ancient inclosed lands belonging to the said trustees. And I direct the fences on the northward and northeastward sides thereof to be made and for ever afterwards kept in repair by the owner thereof.

I also set out and allot unto Thomas Lowry, his heirs and assigns, a piece or parcel of land other part of the said commons and waste lands on Wallasey Leasowe, marked on the said map No. 58, containing one acre and twenty perches, bounded northwardly by the said public road F, eastwardly by an allotment, by me hereinbefore set out for the purpose of the inhabitants of the said Township of Wallasey getting marl in the same pursuant to the said Act, southwardly by ancient inclosed lands belonging to Robert Vyner, Esquire, and westwardly by an allotment No. 59, to William Joynson, the right to which said allotment No. 58 belonged to John Urmson, in respect of his ancient inclosed lands in the said Township of Wallasey and has been sold and disposed of by him to the said Thomas Lowry, to whom I have made this allotment in pursuance of the said Act. And I direct the fences on the northward and eastward sides thereof to be made and for ever afterwards kept in repair by the owner thereof.   *Thomas Lowry, purchased from John Urmson, No. 58, 1, 0, 20.*

I also set out and allot unto William Joynson, his heirs and assigns, in respect of his ancient inclosed lands in the said Township of Wallasey, a piece or parcel of land other part of the said commons and waste lands on Wallasey Leasowe, marked on the said map No. 59, containing two roods and twenty-eight perches, bounded northwardly by the said public road F, eastwardly by an allotment No. 58 to Thomas Lowry, southwardly by ancient inclosed lands belonging to Robert Vyner, Esquire, and westwardly by an allotment No. 60 to James Harrocks. And I direct the fences on the northward and eastward sides thereof to be made and for ever afterwards kept in repair by the owner thereof.   *William Joynson, No. 59, 0, 2, 28.*

I also set out and allot unto James Harrocks, his heirs and assigns, in respect of his ancient inclosed lands in the said Township of Wallasey a piece or parcel of land other part of the said commons and waste lands on Wallasey Leasowe, marked on the said map No. 60, containing two roods and twenty-six perches, bounded northwardly by the said public road F, eastwardly by the said allotment No. 59, to the said William Joynson, southwardly by ancient inclosed lands belonging to Robert Vyner, Esquire, and westwardly by an allotment No. 61 to Jane Hassler's representatives, the right to which allotment No. 60 belonged to Richard Hilliard who has sold and disposed of the same to the said James Harrocks to whom I have made this allotment in pursuance of the said Act. And I direct the fences on the northward and eastward sides thereof to be made and for ever afterwards kept in repair by the owner thereof.   *James Harrocks, purchased from Richard Hilliard, No. 60, 0, 2. 26.*

I also set out and allot unto the heirs, devisees, or other representatives of Jane Hassler, otherwise Harlehurst, his, her, or their heirs and assigns, in respect of her ancient inclosed lands in the said Township of Wallasey, a piece or parcel of land other part of the said commons and waste lands on Wallasey Leasowe, marked   *Heirs of Jane Hassler, otherwise Jane Harlehurst, No. 61, 0, 3, 2.*

Commissioner's Award, Wallasey Inclosure.

on the said map No. 61, containing three roods and two perches, bounded northwardly by the said public road F, eastwardly by an allotment No. 60 to the said James Harrocks, southwardly by ancient inclosed lands belonging to Robert Vyner, Esquire, and westwardly by an allotment No. 62 to Thomas Webster. And I direct the fences on the northward and eastward sides thereof to be made and for ever afterwards kept in repair by the owner thereof.

Thomas Webster, No. 62, 0, 1, 24.

I also set out and allot unto Thomas Webster, his heirs and assigns, in respect of his ancient inclosed lands in the said Township of Wallasey, a piece or parcel of land other part of the said commons and waste lands on Wallasey Leasowe, marked on the said map No. 62, containing one rood and twenty-four perches, bounded northwardly by the said public road F, eastwardly by an allotment No. 61 to the representatives of Jane Hassler, southwardly by ancient inclosed lands belonging to Robert Vyner, Esquire, or the owner of the Stable Croft, and westwardly by an allotment No. 63 to the said Robert Vyner or the owner of the Stable Croft. And I direct the fences on the northward and eastward sides thereof to be made and for ever afterwards kept in repair by the owner thereof.

Margaret Wotherspoon No. 64, 0, 0, 25.

I also set out and allot unto Margaret Wotherspoon, her heirs and assigns, in respect of her ancient inclosed lands in the said Township of Wallasey, a piece or parcel of land, other part of the said commons and waste lands on Wallasey Leasowe, marked on the said map No. 64, containing twenty-five perches, bounded northwardly by the said public road F, westwardly by the said allotment No. 63 to the said Robert Vyner or the owner of the Stable Croft, southwardly by the said ancient inclosed land called the Stable Croft, and westwardly by the private road marked in the said map with the letter t. And I direct the fences on the northward and eastward sides thereof to be made and for ever afterwards kept in repair by the owner thereof.

Margaret Wotherspoon No. 65, 0, 2, 0.

I also set out and allot unto the said Margaret Wotherspoon, her heirs and assigns in respect of her same ancient lands, a piece or parcel of land other part of the said commons or waste lands on Wallasey Leasowe, marked on the said map No. 65, containing two roods, bounded northwardly by an allotment F, by me sold to the Reverend James Smedley, southeastwardly by ancient inclosed lands belonging to the said Margaret Wotherspoon, southwardly by an allotment No. 66 to Sir John Grey Egerton, and westwardly by the said public road E. And I direct the fences on the southward and westward sides thereof shall be made and for ever afterwards kept in repair by the owner thereof.

Heirs of late Thos. Dean, No. 69, 0, 0, 14¾.

I also set out and allot unto the heirs, devisees, or other representatives of the late Thomas Dean, his heirs and assigns, in respect of his ancient inclosed lands in the Township of Wallasey, a piece or parcel of land, part of the said commons and waste lands on Wallasey Leasowe, marked on the said map No. 69, containing fourteen perches and three-quarters of a perch, bounded northwardly by an allotment No. 68 to Joseph Green, Esquire, eastwardly by an allotment No. 69A to Isaac Brian, southwardly by the private roads marked on the said map with the letters u, and westwardly by the said public road E, and I direct the fences on the southward and westward sides thereof shall be made and for ever afterwards kept in repair by the owners thereof.

I also set out and allot unto Isaac Brian, his heirs and assigns, a piece or parcel of land other part of the said commons and waste lands on Wallasey Leasowe, marked on the said map No. 69A, containing four perches and a quarter, bounded northwardly by an allotment No. 68 to Joseph Green, Esquire, eastwardly by ancient inclosed lands belonging to Sir John Grey Egerton, and southwardly by the said private road, marked on the said map with the letter u, and westwardly by the allotment No. 69 to Thomas Dean's representatives, the right of which said allotment No. 69A belonged to Thomas Dean in respect of his ancient inclosed lands in the said Township of Wallasey, and has been sold and disposed of by the said Thomas Dean to the said Isaac Brian, to whom I have made this allotment in pursuance of the said Act. And I direct the fences on the southward and westward sides thereof to be made and for ever afterwards kept in repair by the owner thereof. *Isaac Brian, No. 69a, 0, 0, 4¼, purchased from T. Dean.*

I also set out and allot unto Elizabeth Smith, her heirs and assigns, in respect of her ancient inclosed lands in the said Township of Wallasey, a piece or parcel of land, other part of the said commons and waste lands on Wallasey Leasowe, marked on the said map No. 7, containing thirty-five perches, bounded northwardly by the said private road V, eastwardly by the said public road E, and southwardly by an allotment No. 6 to Mary Coventry, and eastwardly by an allotment L, by me sold to Leigh Blundell. And I direct the fences on the northward and eastward sides thereof to be made and for ever afterwards kept in repair by the owner thereof. *Elizabeth Smith, No. 7 0, 0, 35.*

I also set out and allot unto Mary Coventry, her heirs and assigns, in respect of her ancient inclosed lands in the said Township of Wallasey, a piece or parcel of land, part of the said commons and waste lands on Wallasey Leasowe, marked on the said map No. 6, containing thirty-nine perches, bounded northwardly by the said allotment No. 7 to Elizabeth Smith, eastwardly by the said public road E, southwardly by an allotment No. 5 to John Woodfine, and westwardly by an allotment L, by me sold to Leigh Blundell. And I direct the fences on the northward and eastward sides thereof to be made and for ever afterwards kept in repair by the owner thereof. *Mary Coventry, No. 6, 0, 0, 39*

I also set out and allot unto John Woodfine, his heirs and assigns, in respect of his ancient inclosed lands in the said Township of Wallasey, a piece or parcel of land, other part of the said commons and waste lands on Wallasey Leasowe, marked on the said map No. 5, containing one rood and four perches, bounded northwardly by the said allotment No. 6 to Mary Coventry, eastwardly by the said public road E, southwardly by an allotment No. 4 to Margaret Jones, and westwardly by the said allotment by me sold to Leigh Blundell, marked L. And I direct the fences on the northward and eastward sides thereof to be made and for ever afterwards kept in repair by the owner thereof. *John Woodfine, No. 5, 0, 1, 4.*

I also set out and allot unto Margaret Jones, her heirs and assigns, in respect of her ancient inclosed lands in the said Township of Wallasey, a piece or parcel of land, other part of the said commons and waste lands on Wallasey Leasowe, marked on the said map No. 4, *Margaret Jones, No. 4, 0, 1, 11.*

containing one rood and eleven perches, bounded northwardly by the said allotment No. 5 to James Woodfine, eastwardly by the said public road E, southwardly by an allotment No. 3 to James Harrocks, and westwardly by the said allotment to Leigh Blundell, marked L. And I direct the fences on the northward and eastward sides thereof to be made and for ever afterwards kept in repair by the owner thereof.

James Harrocks, No. 3, 0, 1, 19
I also set out and allot unto James Harrocks, his heirs and assigns, in respect of his ancient inclosed lands in the said Township of Wallasey, another piece or parcel of land, other part of the said commons and waste lands on Wallasey Leasowe, marked on the said map No. 3, containing one rood and nineteen perches, bounded northwardly by an allotment No. 4 to Margaret Jones, eastwardly by the public road marked E in the said map, southwardly by an allotment by me sold to William Peers, marked I, and westwardly by an allotment sold to Mr. Leigh Blundell marked L. And I direct the fences on the northward and eastward sides thereof to be made and for ever afterwards kept in repair by the owner thereof.

Thomas Sparks, No. 2, 1, 2, 13.
I also set out and allot unto Thomas Sparks, his heirs and assigns, in respect of his ancient inclosed lands in the said Township of Wallasey, a piece or parcel of land other part of the said commons and waste lands on Wallasey Leasowe, marked on the said map No. 2, containing one acre two roods and thirteen perches, bounded northwardly in part by an allotment sold to William Peers marked I, and in other part by an allotment sold to Elizabeth Ashbrook marked K, eastwardly by the said public road E, southwardly by an allotment No. 1 to George Evans, westwardly by an allotment sold to Leigh Blundell marked L. And I direct the fences on the eastward and southward sides thereof to be made and for ever afterwards kept in repair by the owner thereof.

George Evans, No. 1, 0, 1, 36.
I also set out and allot unto George Evans, his heirs and assigns, in respect of his ancient inclosed lands in the Township of Wallasey, a piece or parcel of land other part of the said commons and waste lands on Wallasey Leasowe marked in the said map No. 1, containing one rood and thirty-six perches, bounded northwardly by the last mentioned allotment No. 2 to Thomas Sparks, eastwardly by the said public road E, southwardly by ancient inclosed lands belonging to the said George Evans, and westwardly by an allotment sold to Leigh Blundell marked L. And I direct the fence on the eastward side to be made and for ever afterwards kept in repair by the owner thereof.

Henry Johnson, No. 75, 0, 1, 10, Purchase from S. Dean.
I also set out and allot unto Henry Johnson, his heirs and assigns a piece or parcel of land other part of the said commons and waste lands on Wallasey Brake, marked in the said map No. 75, and containing one rood and ten perches, bounded northwardly by an allotment sold to Henry Johnson marked P, northeastwardly by an allotment by me hereinbefore set out for stone on the said brake, southwardly by an allotment No. 76 to Sir John Tobin, and westwardly by the public road L, the right to which said allotment No. 75 belonged to Samuel Dean in respect of his ancient inclosed lands in the said township of Wallasey, and has been sold and disposed of by him to the said Henry Johnson to whom I have made the allotment in pursuance of the said Act, and I direct the fences on the northeastward, and southward, and westward sides to be made and for ever afterwards kept in repair by the owner thereof.

I also set out and allot unto Jane Rainsford, her heirs and assigns, in respect of her ancient inclosed lands in the Township of Wallasey, a piece or parcel of land other part of the said commons and waste land on Wallasey Leasowe, marked on the said map No. 9, containing two acres and thirty-nine perches, bounded northwardly by the private road marked V in the said map, eastwardly by an allotment No. 8 to the devisee of the Reverend George Briggs, southwardly by two several allotments on Wallasey Pasture made to the devisee of the said George Briggs marked No. 1 and No. 1a, and westwardly by an allotment No. 10 to Sir T. S. Massey Stanley, and I direct the fences on the northward and eastward sides to be made and for ever afterwards kept in repair by the owner thereof. *Jane Rainsford, No. 9, 2, 0, 39.*

I also set out and allot unto the devisees in trust under the will of the Reverend George Briggs, in respect of his ancient inclosed lands in the township of Wallasey, a piece or parcel of land other part of the said commons and waste lands on Wallasey Leasowe marked on the said map No. 8, containing one acre three roods and twenty-one perches, bounded northwardly by the said private roads marked V, eastwardly by an allotment to the said devisee in trust, No. 8a, southwardly by an allotment on Wallasey Pasture to the said devisees No. 1, and westwardly by the said allotment No. 9 to Jane Rainsford, and in making this allotment it is understood and intended that John Rogers, who holds the land in right of which this allotment is made under a lease for the lives of himself and Alice Rogers his mother and William Rogers from the late Reverend George Briggs, and their assigns shall hold and enjoy this allotment, together with the other lands included in the said lease during his estate and interest therein, and I direct the fences on the northward and eastward sides thereof shall be made and kept in repair by the said John Rogers, and his assigns, during the continuance of the said lease and afterwards that the same shall be kept in repair by the owner and owners thereof. *Devisees in trust of Rev. Geo. Briggs, No. 8, 1, 3, 21. John Rogers, Leasehold.*

I also set out and allot unto the said devisees in trust under the will of the late Reverend George Briggs in respect of his same ancient inclosed lands a piece or parcel of land other part of the said commons and waste lands on Wallasey Leasowe, marked in the said map No. 8a, containing one acre two roods and ten perches, bounded northwardly by the said private road V, eastwardly by an allotment sold to Leigh Blundell marked L, southwardly by an allotment on the Wallasey pasture made to the said devisees No. 1, and westwardly by an allotment No. 8, to the said devisees, and I direct the fences on the northward side thereof to be made and for ever afterwards kept in repair by the owner thereof. *Devisees in Trust of Rev. George Briggs, No. 8a, 1, 2, 10.*

I also set out and allot unto William Bird, his heirs and assigns in respect of his ancient inclosed land in the said Township of Wallasey a piece or parcel of land other part of the said commons and waste lands on Wallasey Leasowe, marked in the said map No. 12, containing three roods and five perches, bounded northwardly by the private road V, eastwardly and southwardly by an allotment No. 11, to Mrs. Wade's trustees, and westwardly by an allotment No. 13, to the Rector of Wallasey, and I direct the fences on the northward and eastward sides thereof to be made and for ever afterwards kept in repair by the owner thereof. *William Bird, No. 12, 0, 3, 5.*

And with respect to the tract or parcel of open and undivided land in the said Township of Wallasey called Wallasey Pasture I the said Commissioner do make my Award as follows (that is to say) :—

54 Geo. III. Commissioner's Award, ch. lxxxvii.
Wallasey Inclosure.

In the first place I do hereby particularise and describe the public carriage roads, highways and private roads so set out by me through and over the same last-mentioned tract or parcel of land aforesaid in manner following (that is to say)

Public Road I. — One public carriage road and highway in the said map hereto annexed marked with the letter I on part of the said tract or parcel of land called Wallasey Pasture of the width of ten yards beginning at the end of a public carriage road and highway lately open and set out through certain ancient inclosed lands in the said Township of Wallasey aforesaid leading from the town of Wallasey to the said tract or parcel of land which said carriage road marked I runs from the said road so lately set out in a westwardly direction over the said tract or parcel of land to a field called the Chiefs belonging to Robert Vyner, Esquire, and which said carriage road and highway has been made and set out by me the said commissioner in lieu of the public carriage road formerly intended to have been set out by me leading from Thomas Dean's house in the Village of Wallasey over the Leasowe there past Mrs Boode's house, which last mentioned road is now intended and is hereinbefore mentioned to be set out and made as a private occupation road marked V.

Public Road R. — One other public carriage road or highway in the said map hereunto annexed marked with the letter R on other part of the said tract or parcel of land called Wallasey Pasture of the width of eight yards commencing on the north side of the said public road I, and running from thence northwardly to the south end of the before described public road marked Q.

Private Road Y. — One private or occupation road of the width of six yards marked with the letter Y, commencing on the south side of the said public road marked I, and running from thence in a southwardly direction to buildings in Wallasey belonging to Miss Rainsford.

Private Road Z. — Another private or occupation road of the width of eight yards marked with the letter Z being other part of the said tract or parcel of land called Wallasey Pasture commencing on the south side of the said public road marked I, running from thence in a southwardly direction to lands belonging to Miss Rainsford.

Private Road ZZ. — Another private or occupation road of the width of eight yards marked with the letters ZZ commencing on the south side of the said public road marked I, and running in a southwardly direction to two several allotments of the said tract or parcel of land made to Sir John Grey Egerton No. 31 and Robert Vyner, Esquire, No. 20.

And I the said Commissioner do direct that the said before described private or occupation road marked on the said map ZZ shall be for ever afterwards maintained and kept in repair by the owners or occupiers of the lands adjoining to or abutting on the same and shall be solely used and enjoyed by them, and that the two before described private or occupation roads marked on the said map Y and Z shall be for ever afterwards maintained and kept in repair by the owner or occupier of the ancient inclosed lands to which the same roads lead and shall be solely used and enjoyed by such owner or occupier.

Public Drain, No. 1. — And in further execution of the said Act, I have set out and made a certain public drain marked in the said map "Public Drain No. 1," commencing at the northeast corner of a field called the Chiefs, belonging to Robert Vyner Esquire, and running in eastwardly direction along the north side of the ancient fence dividing the said tract or parcel of land called the Wallasey Pasture from the Wallasey Leasowe to the north end of the public drain hereinafter mentioned, marked No. 4.

I have also set out and made another certain public drain marked in the said map "Public Drain 2," over the said tract or parcel of land called the Wallasey Pasture, commencing from the south side of the last mentioned drain marked Public Drain 1, and running southwardly between the allotments No. 7 belonging to Sir John Tobin, No. 8 to Sir John Grey Egerton, across the public road I and between the allotments No. 14, to Sir John Tobin, and No. 13, to Sir John Grey Egerton, to ancient inclosed lands in the said Township of Wallasey belonging to Miss Rainsford. *Public Drain, No. 2.*

I have also set out and made another public drain, marked in the said map "Public Drain 3," commencing on the southward side of the said Public Drain 1, and running southwardly between the allotments on the said tract or parcel of land called the Wallasey Pasture in the said map No. 5 and No. 6 to Sir John Tobin and John Leigh, Esquire, across the public road I, to the east side of the private road ZZ. and thence running in a southwardly direction along the east of the said road to the south end thereof, and thence running in a westwardly direction along the end of the said road to the centre thereof, and then turning off and running in a southwardly direction to the ancient fender or watercourse running from Newton Carr towards Wallasey. *Public Drain, No. 3.*

I have also set out and made another public drain on the said tract or parcel of land called Wallasey Pasture, marked in the said map "Public Drain No. 4," commencing at the east end of the said Public Drain 1, and thence running in a southwardly direction through an allotment to the devisees of the late Reverend George Briggs, marked No. 1, across the public road I, and between allotment 38, to Sir John Grey Egerton, 37, to Margaret Jones, and 36 to Thomas Sparks to ancient inclosed lands in the said Township of Wallasey, belonging to Thomas Sparks. *Public Drain No. 4.*

And I direct the whole of the said drains to be from time to time for ever hereafter amended, cleansed, and repaired by and at the expense of the owners of lands on the said tract or parcel of land called Wallasey Pasture, in the proportions and according to a rate by me made for the same and which is written in the margin of the map of the said tract or parcel of land on the said pasture annexed to this my award under the direction of a person or persons to be from time to time appointed by the major part in value of the owners of the several allotments on the said tract or parcel of land, according to the said rate, who shall attend at a meeting to be called for that purpose by any three of the said owners, of which meeting notice shall be given at least two Sundays in the Parish Church of Wallasey before the same shall be held. And that the fence on the southward side of the said drain, marked Public Drain 1, shall be for ever afterwards kept in repair by the owners of allotments adjoining the said drain.

And in further execution of the said Acts I have set out and allotted from and out of the said tract or parcel of land called Wallasey Pasture, in Wallasey aforesaid, the piece or parcel of land hereinafter mentioned for sale, towards defraying the charges and expenses *Sale allotment, Thomas Sparks, 3, 0, 0.*

54 *Geo. III.* *Commissioner's Award,* ch. lxxxvii.
Wallasey Inclosure.

incident to and attending the obtaining of the said Acts, and of carrying the same into execution in the manner and as directed in the said Act, and which parcel of land is described as follows : —

One part of the said tract or parcel of land called Wallasey Pasture, containing three acres, marked on the said map with the letters Q Q, by me sold to Thomas Sparks, bounded northwardly by the public road marked in the said map with the letter I, eastwardly by the allotment No. 37 to Margaret Jones and No. 36 to Thomas Sparks, southwardly by the said allotment No. 36 to Thomas Sparks, and westwardly by an allotment No. 35 to the Reverend Augustus Campbell. And I direct all the fences to this allotment to be made and for ever afterwards kept in repair by the owner thereof.

Devisee in Trust of the Rev. George Briggs, No. 1 3, 0, 17.

I also set out and allot unto the devisee in trust under the last will and testament of the Reverend George Briggs, deceased, in right of his two cowgaits on the said tract or parcel of land now in lease to John Rogers, a piece or parcel of land, part of the said tract or parcel of land called Wallasey Pasture, marked in the said map No. 1, containing three acres and seventeen perches, bounded northeastwardly in part by an allotment on the Wallasey Leasowe to Miss Jane Rainsford, No. 9, in other part by two other allotments on the said Leasowe marked respectively No. 8 and No. 8A, to the said devisee, and in other part by an allotment on the said Leasowe, sold to Mr. Leigh Blundell marked L, eastwardly in part by ancient inclosed lands in the Township of Wallasey belonging to George Evans, in other part by ancient inclosed lands in the said township belonging to the said devisee, and in other part by ancient lands in the said township belonging to Sir John Grey Egerton, and southwardly by the public road over the tract or parcel of land marked on the said map I, and westwardly by an allotment to the said devisee on the said tract or parcel of land No. 1A. And in making this allotment it is meant and intended that John Rogers, who holds the cowgaits in right of which this allotment is made under the before-mentioned lease for the lives of himself and Alice Rogers and William Rogers from the Reverend George Briggs and his assigns, shall hold and enjoy this allotment along with the other ands in the said lease during his and their estate and interest therein. And I direct the fences on the southward and westward sides thereof shall be made and kept in repair by the said John Rogers during the continuance of his said lease and afterwards be kept in repair by the owner thereof.

Same No. 1A 2, 1, 31.

I also set out and allot unto the said devisee, his heirs and assigns, in right of his one and a-half other cowgaits on the said tract or parcel of land, a piece or parcel of land, other part of the said tract or parcel of land, marked in the said map No. 1A, containing two acres one rood and thirty-one perches, bounded northwardly in part by an allotment to Sir Thomas Stanley Massey Stanley on the Wallasey Leasowe No. 10, in other part by an allotment to Miss Rainsford on the said Leasowe No. 9, eastwardly by the last-mentioned allotment No. 1 on the said tract or parcel of land, southwardly by the said public road I, and westwardly by an allotment No. 2 on the said tract or parcel of land to John Davies. And I direct the fences on the southward and westward sides to be made and for ever afterwards kept in repair by the owner thereof.

I also set out and allot unto John Davies, his heirs and assigns, a piece or parcel of land, other part of the said tract or parcel of land, marked in the said map No. 2, and containing four acres two roods and seventeen perches, bounded northwardly by allotments on the said Leasowe No. 11 to Mrs. Wade's trustees and No. 10 to Sir Thomas Stanley Massey Stanley, eastwardly by an allotment on the said tract or parcel of land No. 1A to the devisees of the Reverend George Briggs, southwardly by the said public road I, and westwardly by an allotment No. 3 to Sir Thomas Stanley Massey Stanley, the right to which said allotment belonged to the Reverend James Smedley in respect of his three cowgaits on the said aforesaid tract or parcel of land, and was sold and disposed of to the said John Davies to whom I have made this allotment in pursuance of the said Act. And I direct the southward and westward fences of the said allotment to be made and for ever afterwards kept in repair by the owner or owners thereof.

John Davies, No. 2, 4, 2, 17

I also set out and allot unto Sir Thomas Stanley Massey Stanley, Baronet, his heirs and assigns, a piece or parcel of land other part of the said tract or parcel of land, marked in the said map No. 3, containing four acres three roods and thirty-two perches, bounded northwardly in part by an allotment to the Reverend Augustus Campbell on the said Leasowe No. 13, and in other part by the allotment No. 11 on the said Leasowe made to Mrs. Wade's trustees, and eastwardly by the last-mentioned allotment to John Davies No. 2, southwardly by the said public road I, and westwardly by the allotment on the said tract or parcel of land No. 4 to Joseph Green, the right to which said allotment No. 3 belongs to the said Mrs. Wade's trustees, in respect of their three cowgaits on the said tract or parcel of land, and was sold and disposed of by them to the said Sir Thomas Stanley Massey Stanley, to whom I have made this allotment in pursuance of the said Act. And I direct the fences on the southward and westward sides thereof shall be made and kept in repair by the owner thereof.

Sir T. S. M. Stanley, purchased from Trustees of Mrs. Wade, No. 3, 4, 3, 32.

I also set out and allot unto Joseph Green, his heirs and assigns, a piece or parcel of land other part of the said tract or parcel of land marked in the said map No. 4, containing five acres, three roods and eleven perches, bounded northwardly in part by an allotment on the said Leasowe to the said Joseph Green No. 14, and in other part by another allotment on the said Leasowe No. 13 to the Reverend Augustus Campbell, eastwardly by the said allotment on the pasture No. 3 to Sir Thomas Stanley Massey Stanley by the said public road I, and westwardly by an allotment to Sir John Tobin on the said pasture No. 5, the right to which said allotment belonged to Robinson Deane in respect of his four cowgaits on the said tract or parcel of land, and has been sold and disposed of by the said Robinson Deane to the said Joseph Green to whom I have allotted the same in pursuance of the said Act. And I direct the fences on the southward and westward sides thereof to be made and for ever afterwards kept in repair by the owners thereof.

Joseph Green, No. 4, 5, 3, 11.

I also set out and allot unto the said Joseph Green, his heirs and assigns, a piece or parcel of land other part of the said tract or parcel of land marked in the said map No. 29, containing three roods and twenty-eight perches, bounded northwardly and eastwardly by the allotment No. 34 on the said tract or parcel of land to the said Joseph

Joseph Green, No. 29, 0, 3, 28.

Green, southwardly by the allotment No. 30 on the said tract or parcel of land to John Leigh, Esquire, and westwardly by the public drain marked "Public Drain 3" between this present allotment and the private road Z Z, the right to which said allotment belonged to the said Robinson Deane in respect of his four cowgaits on the said tract or parcel of land, and has been sold and disposed of by the said Robinson Deane to the said Joseph Green to whom I have allotted the same in pursuance of the said Act. And I direct the fences on the northward and westward sides thereof to be made and for ever afterwards kept in repair by the owner thereof.

Joseph Green, No. 34, 5, 1, 32.

I also set out and allot unto the said Joseph Green, his heirs and assigns, in right of his five cowgaits on the said tract or parcel of land a piece or parcel of land other part of the said tract or parcel of land marked No. 34 in the said map, containing five acres, one rood and thirty-two perches, bounded northwardly in part by an allotment on the said tract or parcel of land made to Peter Ledsham marked No. 28, in other part by an allotment on the same marked No. 35 to the Reverend Augustus Campbell, and in other part by an allotment on the same to Thomas Sparks, marked No. 36, eastwardly by ancient inclosed lands in the township of Wallasey belonging to Thomas Sparks and Robert Vyner, Esquire, southwardly in part by an allotment No. 33 on the said tract or parcel of land to Sir John Grey Egerton, in other part by an allotment to John Leigh No. 30, and in other part by an allotment on the same No. 29 made to the said Joseph Green, and westwardly in part by the allotment No. 29 to the said Joseph Green, in other part by the public drain No. 3, dividing this allotment from the private road Z Z. And I direct the fences on the northward and westward sides thereof, to be made and for ever afterwards kept in repair by the owner thereof.

Sir John Tobin, No. 5, 5, 3, 39, Purchased from Jos. Jackson.

I also set out and allot unto Sir John Tobin, his heirs and assigns, a piece or parcel of land other part of the said tract or parcel of land marked in the said map No. 5, containing five acres three roods and thirty-nine perches, bounded northwardly in part by an allotment to the said Sir John Tobin on Wallasey Leasowe No. 15, and in other part by an allotment to Joseph Green on the said Leasowe No. 14, eastwardly by an allotment on the said tract or parcel made to the said Joseph Green No. 4, southwardly by the said public road marked I, and westwardly by a public drain marked "Public Drain 3," between this present allotment and an allotment on the same to John Leigh, Esquire, marked No. 6, the right to which said allotment No. 5 belonged to Joseph Jackson in respect of his three and a-half cowgaits on the said tract or parcel of land, and has been sold and disposed of by him to the said Sir John Tobin to whom I have made this allotment in pursuance of the said Act. And I direct the fences on the southward and westward sides thereof, to be made and for ever afterwards kept in repair by the owner thereof.

John Leigh, Esquire, No. 6, 22, 0, 18

I also set out and allot unto John Leigh Esquire, his heirs and assigns, in right of his nineteen cowgaits on the said tract or parcel of land, a piece or parcel of land other part of the said tract or parcel of land marked in the said map No. 6, containing twenty-two acres and eighteen perches, bounded northwardly in part by an allotment on the said Leasowe, to Sir John Tobin, No. 17, in other part by an allotment on the said Leasowe to the said John Leigh, Esquire, marked

No. 16, eastwardly by the public drain 3, between this present allotment and an allotment on the said tract or parcel of land to Sir John Tobin, marked No. 5, southwardly by the said public road I, and westwardly by the allotment on the same to Sir John Tobin, marked No. 7a. And I direct the fences on the southward and westward sides thereof, be made and for ever afterwards kept in repair by the owner thereof.

I also set out and allot unto the said John Leigh, Esquire, his heirs and assigns, in right of his said nineteen cowgaits, a piece or parcel of land other part of the said tract or parcel of land marked in the said map No. 30, containing eight acres one rood and twenty-one perches, bounded northwardly by two several allotments on the same made to Joseph Green, Nos. 29 and 34, eastwardly by an allotment on the same to Sir John Grey Egerton, No. 33, southwardly by another allotment to the said Sir John Grey Egerton, No. 31, and westwardly by the public drain 3, between this present allotment and the said private road ZZ. And I direct the fences on the northward and westward sides to be made and for ever afterwards kept in repair by the owner thereof.

John Leigh, Esquire, No. 30, 8, 1, 21

I also set out and allot to Sir John Tobin, Knight, his heirs and assigns, in right of his twenty-two and a-half cowgaits on the said tract or parcel of land, a piece or parcel of land other part of the said tract or parcel of land marked in the said map No. 7a, containing nine acres two roods and thirty-eight perches, bounded northwardly by an allotment on Wallasey Leasowe to the said Sir John Tobin No. 17 eastwardly by an allotment to the said John Leigh on the said tract or parcel of land No. 6, southwardly by the public road I, and westwardly by the public road R, between this present allotment and an allotment No. 7B, on the same to the said Sir John Tobin, and I direct the fences on the southward and westward sides thereof shall be made and for ever afterwards be kept in repair by the owners thereof.

Sir John Tobin, Kngt., No. 7A, 9, 2, 38.

I do also set out and allot unto the said Sir John Tobin, his heirs and assigns, in right of his said twenty-two and a-half cowgaits a piece or parcel of land other part of the said tract or parcel of land marked on the said map No. 7B, containing eleven acres and twenty-four perches, bounded northwardly by an allotment on the Wallasey Leasowe, to Sir John Grey Egerton, No. 18, eastwardly by the public road R, southwardly by the public road I, and westwardly by the public drain marked No. 2, between this present allotment and an allotment No. 8, on the said tract or parcel of land to Sir John Grey Egerton, and I direct the fences on the eastward and southward and westward sides thereof shall be made and for ever afterwards kept in repair by the owners thereof.

Sir John Tobin, Kngt., No. 7B, 11, 0, 24.

I do also set out and allot unto the said Sir John Tobin, his heirs and assigns, in right of his said cowgaits another piece or parcel of land other part of the said tract or parcel of land marked in the said map No. 14, containing nine acres one rood and thirty-six perches, bounded northwardly by the said public road I, eastwardly by a private road marked Z, southwardly by ancient inclosed land belonging to Jane Rainsford, and westwardly by the public drain marked "Public Drain No. 2," between this present allotment and an allotment No. 13, to Sir John Grey Egerton on the said tract or

Sir John Tobin, Kngt., No. 14, 9, 1, 36.

parcel of land and I direct the fences on the northward and eastward sides thereof to be made and for ever afterwards kept in repair by the owners thereof.

Sir John Tobin, Kngt., No. 32, 7, 0, 19.

I also set out and allot unto the said Sir John Tobin, his heirs and assigns, in right of his said cowgaits a piece or parcel of land other part of the said tract or parcel of land marked on the said map No. 32, containing seven acres and nineteen perches, bounded northwardly by an allotment No. 33, to Sir John Grey Egerton on the same eastwardly by ancient inclosed lands belonging to Sir John Grey Egerton and Sir John Tobin, southwardly by ancient inclosed lands belonging to Sir John Grey Egerton, and westwardly by an allotment No. 31, to Sir John Grey Egerton on the same, and I direct the fences on the northward and westward sides thereof to be made and for ever afterwards kept in repair by the owner thereof.

Sir John Grey Egerton, Bart., No. 8, 9, 2, 36.

I also set out and allot unto Sir John Grey Egerton, Baronet, his heirs and assigns, to the uses and under the limitation in the will of Philip Egerton, late of Oulton Park, Esquire, deceased, respecting the same in right of his eighteen and a-half cowgaits on the said tract or parcel of land a piece or parcel of land other part of the said tract or parcel of land marked No. 8, containing nine acres two roods and thirty-six perches, bounded northwardly by allotments No. 19 and 18 to the said Sir John Grey Egerton, on the said Wallasey Leasowe, eastwardly by the public drain marked No. 2, between this present allotment and an allotment No. 7B, to the said Sir John Tobin on the said tract or parcel of land, northwardly by the said public road I, and westwardly by an allotment No. 9, to Robert Vyner, Esquire, on the same, and I direct the fences on the southward and westward sides thereof to be made and for ever afterwards kept in repair by the owner thereof.

Sir J. G. Egerton, Bart., No. 13, 3, 3, 24.

I also set out and allot unto the said Sir John Grey Egerton, Baronet, his heirs and assigns, in the manner aforesaid, in right of his said cowgaits on the said tract or parcel of land aforesaid, a piece or parcel of land other part of the said tract or parcel of land marked in the said map No. 13, containing three acres, three roods, and twenty-four perches, bounded northwardly by the said public road I, eastwardly by the public drain marked "Public Drain No. 2," between this present allotment and an allotment on the same to Sir John Tobin No. 14, southwardly by ancient inclosed lands belonging to Miss Rainsford and westwardly by the private road marked Y. And I direct the fences on the northward, eastward and westward sides thereof to be made and for ever afterwards kept in repair by the owner thereof.

Sir J. G. Egerton, Bart., No. 31, 5, 3, 20.

I also set out and allot unto the said Sir John Grey Egerton, his heirs and assigns, in right of his said cowgaits on the said tract or parcel of land a piece or parcel of land other part of the said tract or parcel of land, marked in the said map No. 31, containing five acres, three roods, and twenty perches, bounded northwardly in part by an allotment on the same to John Leigh, Esquire, No. 30, and in other part by another allotment on the same to the said Sir John Grey Egerton, No. 33, eastwardly by an allotment to Sir John Tobin, on the same, No. 32, southwardly in part by ancient inclosed lands in Wallasey aforesaid, belonging to the said Sir John Grey Egerton, and in other part by the fender or watercourse running from Newton

Carr to Wallasey, and westwardly by the public drain No. 3, between this present allotment and an allotment on the said tract or parcel of land No. 20 to Robert Vyner, Esquire. And I direct the fences on the northward side thereof to be made and for ever afterwards kept in repair by the owner or owners thereof.

I do also set out and allot unto the said Sir John Grey Egerton, his heirs and assigns, in manner aforesaid, in right of his said cowgaits on the said tract or parcel of land, another piece or parcel of land other part of the said tract or parcel of land, marked on the said map No. 33, containing six acres three roods, and thirty-five perches, bounded northwardly by an allotment No. 34 to Joseph Green, Esquire, on the same eastwardly in part by ancient inclosed lands belonging to Robert Vyner, Esquire, and in other part by ancient inclosed lands belonging to the said Sir John Grey Egerton, southwardly in part by an allotment No. 32 to Sir John Tobin on the same, and in other part by an allotment No. 31, to Sir John Grey Egerton on the same, and westwardly by an allotment No. 30 to John Leigh, Esquire, on the same. And I direct the fences on the northward and westward sides thereof to be made and for ever afterwards kept in repair by the owner thereof.

Sir J. G. Egerton, No. 33, 6, 3, 35

I also set out and allot unto the said Sir John Grey Egerton, his heirs and assigns, in manner aforesaid, in right of his said cowgaits, a piece or parcel of land other part of the said tract or parcel of land marked on the said map No. 38, containing thirty-five perches, bounded northwardly by the said public road 1, southeastwardly in part by ancient inclosed lands belonging to Robinson Deane, and in other part by ancient inclosed lands belonging to Sir John Grey Egerton, southwestwardly by ancient inclosed lands belonging to Thomas Sparks and northwestwardly by the public drain marked No. 4 between the said allotment No. 36 to Thomas Sparks and the allotment No. 37 to Margaret Jones. And I direct the fences on the northward side thereof to be made and for ever afterwards kept in repair by the owner thereof.

Sir J. G. Egerton, No. 38, 0, 0, 35

I also set out and allot unto Robert Vyner, Esquire, in right of his twenty-one and a-half cowgaits on the said tract or parcel of land, other part of the said tract or parcel of land marked in the said map No. 9, containing five acres two roods and twenty-one perches, bounded northwardly in part by an allotment No. 28 to the said Robert Vyner on the Wallasey Leasowe, and in other part by an allotment No. 19 to Sir John Grey Egerton in the said Leasowe, eastwardly by an allotment No. 8 to Sir John Grey Egerton on the said tract or parcel of land, southwardly by the said public road 1, and westwardly by another allotment No. 10 to the said Robert Vyner on the same, but in making this allotment it is meant and intended that Ann Rainsford, who holds three of the cowgaits in respect of which this allotment is made by virtue of a lease thereof from the said Robert Vyner for three lives, shall occupy and enjoy the same allotment with the other lands comprised in such lease during her estate and interest therein. And I direct the fences on the southward and westward sides thereof to be made and kept in repair by the said Jane Rainsford or her assigns during the continuance of such lease and afterwards by the owner or owners thereof.

Robert Vyner Esquire, No. 9, 5, 2, 21

Ann Rainsford's Leasehold.

54 Geo. III. Commissioner's Award, ch. lxxxvii.
Wallasey Inclosure.

Robert Vyner, Esquire, No. 10, 3, 2, 23

I also set out and allot unto the said Robert Vyner, Esquire, his heirs and assigns, in further right of his said cowgaits, a piece or parcel of land, other part of the said tract or parcel of land marked in the said map No. 10, containing three acres two roods and twenty-three perches, bounded northwardly in part by an allotment No. 20B to the said Robert Vyner on the said Wallasey Leasowe, in other part by an allotment No. 20A to the said Robert Vyner on the said Leasowe, eastwardly by an allotment No. 9 to the said Robert Vyner on the said tract or parcel of land, southwardly by the said public road I, and westwardly by an allotment No. 11 to the said Robert Vyner on the same, but in making the allotment to

John Webster's Leasehold.

the said Robert Vyner it is meant and intended that John Webster, who holds the four and a-half cowgaits in right of which this allotment is made by virtue of a lease from the said Robert Vyner for three lives, shall occupy and enjoy the said allotment along with the other lands comprised in the said lease during the continuance of his estate and interest therein. And I direct the fences on the southward and westward sides thereof to be made and be kept in repair by the said John Webster or his assigns during the continuance of such lease and afterwards by the owner thereof.

Robert Vyner, Esquire, No. 19, 3, 2, 6.

I also set out and allot unto the said Robert Vyner, his heirs and assigns, in further right of his said cowgaits, a piece or parcel of land, other part of the said tract or parcel of land, marked on the said map No. 19, containing three acres two roods and six perches, bounded northwardly in part by allotments No. 17 and 18 to the said Robert Vyner on the same, and in other part by an allotment No. 21 to the heirs of Elizabeth Bird on the same, eastwardly by an allotment No. 20 to the said Robert Vyner, southwardly by the fender or watercourse running from Newton Carr to Wallasey Pool, and westwardly by an allotment No. 16 to the said Robert Vyner on the same, but in making this allotment to the said Robert Vyner it is meant and understood that the said

John Webster's Leasehold.

John Webster, who holds the said four and a-half cowgaits in right of which this allotment is made by virtue of the lease before-mentioned, shall occupy and enjoy the said allotments along with the other lands comprised in such lease during the continuance of his estate and interest therein saving and reserving, nevertheless, out of this allotment a right of road of four yards wide along the north side thereof, for the use of the occupiers of the several allotments marked respectively No. 16, 17 and 18. And I direct the fences on the northward and westward sides thereof to be made and kept in repair by the said John Webster or his assigns during the continuance of such lease and afterwards by the owner thereof.

Robert Vyner, Esquire, No. 11, 3, 2, 23

I also set out and allot unto the said Robert Vyner, Esquire, his heirs and assigns in further right of his said cowgaits a piece or parcel of land, other part of the said tract or parcel of land marked on the said map No. 11, containing three acres two roods and twenty-three perches, bounded northwardly by an allotment No. 20 on the Wallasey Leasowe to the said Robert Vyner, Esquire, eastwardly by an allotment No. 10 to the said Robert Vyner, Esquire, on the said tract or parcel of land, southwardly by the said public road I, and westwardly by ancient inclosed lands belonging to the said Robert Vyner. And I direct the fence on the southward side thereof to be made and for ever afterwards kept in repair by the owner thereof.

54 *Geo. III.*   *Commissioner's Award,*   ch. *lxxxii.*   103
Wallasey Inclosure.

I also set out and allot unto the said Robert Vyner, Esquire, his RobertVyner,
heirs and assigns in right of his said cowgaits a piece or parcel of No. 12, 5, 2, 1.
land, other part of the said tract or parcel of land marked on the said
map No. 12, containing five acres two roods and one perch, bounded
northwardly by the said Public Road 1, eastwardly by a private road
marked on the said map Y, southwardly and westwardly by ancient
inclosed lands belonging to the said Robert Vyner, Esquire. And I
direct the fences on the northward and eastward sides thereof to be
made and for ever afterwards kept in repair by the owner thereof.

I also set out and allot unto the said Robert Vyner, his heirs and RobertVyner,
assigns in right of his said cowgaits a piece or parcel of land, other part No. 16, 4, 2, 21
of the said tract or parcel of land marked on the said map No. 16,
containing four acres two roods and twenty-one perches, bounded
northwardly by an allotment No. 15 on the same to the trustee of the
late Matthew Taylor, eastwardly by allotments No. 17 and 19 on the
same to the said Robert Vyner, southwestwardly in part by the
fender or watercourse leading from Newton Carr to Wallasey
aforesaid and in other part by ancient inclosed lands belonging to
the said Robert Vyner and northwestwardly by ancient inclosed
land belonging to Jane Rainsford, but in making this allotment to
the said Robert Vyner it is meant and intended that Thomas Hilliard Thomas
who holds three and a-half of the cowgaits in right of which this Hilliard's
allotment is made by virtue of a lease from Robert Vyner, Esquire, Leasehold
for three lives shall occupy and enjoy the said allotment together
with the right and liberty of using and enjoying the said road so
reserved from and out of the said allotments No. 19 and 20 to Robert
Vyner, Esquire along with the other lands comprised in such lease
during the continuance thereof. And I direct the fences on the
northward side thereof and so much thereof on the eastward side as
adjoins the allotment marked No. 17 to the said Robert Vyner,
Esquire, to be made and kept in repair by the said Thomas Hilliard
or his assigns during the continuance of the said lease and afterwards
by the owner thereof.

I also set out and allot unto the said Robert Vyner, his heirs and RobertVyner,
assigns in further right of his said cowgaits, a piece or parcel of land No. 17, 1, 3, 24
other part of the said tract or parcel of land, marked on the said map
No. 17, containing one acre three roods and twenty-four perches,
bounded northwardly by an allotment No. 15 to the trustee of the
said Matthew Taylor, on the same eastwardly by an allotment
No. 18 to the said Robert Vyner, southwardly by allotments No. 19
and No. 16 to the said Robert Vyner on the same and westwardly
by the said allotment No. 16 to the said Robert Vyner, and in
making the said allotment to the said Robert Vyner it is meant and
intended that Gerard Stanley who holds one and a-half of the cow- Gerard
gaits, in right of which the allotment is made for three lives, under a Stanley's
lease thereof from Robert Vyner thereof, should hold and occupy Leasehold.
this allotment, together with the privilege of using the said road,
reserved out of the allotments Nos. 19 and 20 during the continuance
of his said lease, and I direct the fences on the northward and
eastward sides thereof to be made and kept in repair by the said
Gerard Stanley during the continuance of his said lease, and afterwards kept in repair by the owner thereof.

I also set out and allot unto the said Robert Vyner, his heirs and RobertVyner
assigns, in further right of his said cowgaits, a piece or parcel of land No. 18, 1, 3, 38

other part of the said tract or parcel of land, marked on the said map No. 18, containing one acre three roods and thirty-eight perches, bounded northwardly by an allotment No. 15 to the said trustee of the late Matthew Taylor, on the same eastwardly in part by an allotment No. 23 on the same to the representatives of the late William Groom, in other part by allotment No. 22 to John Meadows on the same and in other part by an allotment on the same No. 21 to Elizabeth Bird's representatives, southwardly by an allotment No. 19 to the said Robert Vyner, and westwardly by an allotment No. 17 to the said Robert Vyner, but in making this allotment to the said Robert Vyner, it is meant and intended that Peter Wilson who holds one and a-half of the cowgaits in right of which this allotment is made, under a lease thereof from the said Robert Vyner, Esquire, for three lives, shall occupy and enjoy the same and also have the right and privilege of using and enjoying the said road, reserved from and out of the said two allotments No. 19 and No. 20, along with the other lands demised by the said lease during the continuance thereof, and I direct the fences on the northward and eastward sides thereof to be made and be kept in repair by the said Peter Wilson during the continuance of his said lease and afterwards to be kept in repair by the owner thereof.

Peter Wilson's Leasehold.

I also set out and allot unto the said Robert Vyner, Esquire, his heirs and assigns, in right of his said cowgaits, a piece or parcel of land other part of the said tract or parcel of land, marked in the said map No. 20, and containing three acres two roods and twenty-six perches, bounded northwardly by an allotment on the same No. 21 to Elizabeth Bird's representatives, eastwardly in part by the public drain No. 3, between this allotment and allotment No. 31 to Sir John Grey Egerton, on the same and in other part by the fender or watercourse leading from Newton Carr to Wallasey, southwardly and westwardly in part by the said fender or watercourse, and in other part by an allotment No. 19 on the same to the said Robert Vyner, saving and reserving nevertheless from and out of this allotment a right of road of four yards wide on the north side thereof, for the owners and occupiers of the several allotments Nos. 16 and 17 and Nos. 18 and 19, made to Robert Vyner, Esquire, and I direct the fences on the northward, eastward and westward sides thereof to be made and for ever afterwards kept in repair by the owners thereof.

Robert Vyner, Esquire, No. 20, 3, 2, 26

I also set out and allot unto the trustees made and appointed in and by the last Will and Testament of Matthew Taylor, Gentleman, deceased, in right of the eight cowgaits belonging to the said Matthew Taylor a piece or parcel of land other part of the said tract or parcel of land marked on the said map No. 15 containing twelve acres two roods and nine perches bounded northwardly by the said public road I, eastwardly in part by the allotment No. 25 on the same to John Urmson, in other part by the allotment No. 24 to Richard Smith, Esq., and in other part by an allotment No. 23 to the representatives of William Groom, southwardly by three allotments No. 18, No. 17, and No. 16 to Robert Vyner, and westwardly in part by ancient inclosed land belonging to Jane Rainsford and in other part by the said private road Z, and I direct the fences on the northward and eastward sides thereof and so much of the fence of the westward side as adjoins the said private road Z shall be made and for ever afterwards kept in repair by the owner thereof.

Trustees of Mr. Taylor, No. 15, 12, 2, 9

I also set out and allot unto the heirs, devisees, or other represen- Heirs of
tatives of Elizabeth Bird, her, his, or their heirs and assigns in right Elizabeth
of her three cowgaits on the said tract or parcel of land, a piece or Bird, No. 21,
parcel of land other part of the said tract or parcel of land marked on 3, 3, 13.
the said map No. 21 containing three acres three roods and thirteen
perches bounded northwardly by an allotment No. 22 to John Meadows
on the same, eastwardly by the said private road ZZ, southwardly by
allotments No. 19 and 20 to Robert Vyner, Esquire, on the same and
westwardly by an allotment No. 18 on the same to the said Robert
Vyner, and I direct the fences on the southward and eastward sides
to be made and for ever afterwards kept in repair by the owner thereof.

I also set out and allot unto John Meadows, his heirs and assigns, John
in right of his three cowgaits on the said tract or parcel of land a Meadows.
piece or parcel of land other part of the said tract or parcel of land No. 22, 3, 3, 14
marked on the said map No. 22 containing three acres three roods
and fourteen perches, bounded northwardly by an allotment No. 23
on the same to the representatives of William Groom, eastwardly by
the said private road ZZ, southwardly by an allotment on the same
No. 21 to the representatives of Elizabeth Bird, and westwardly by
an allotment No. 18 on the same to Robert Vyner, and I direct the
fences on the northward and eastward sides thereof to be made and
for ever afterwards kept in repair by the owner thereof.

I also set out and allot unto the heir, devisee, or representative of Representa-
William Groom his heirs and assigns in right of his three cowgaits tive of W. M.
on the said tract or parcel of land a piece or parcel of land marked on Groom,
the said map No. 23 containing three acres three roods and nine No. 23, 3, 3, 9.
perches, bounded northwardly by an allotment No. 24 to Richard
Smith, Esq., on the same eastwardly by the said private road ZZ,
southwardly by an allotment No. 22 to John Meadows on the same
and westwardly in part by an allotment No. 18 on the same to Robert
Vyner, Esquire, and in other part by an allotment No. 15 to the
trustees of Matthew Taylor, and I direct the fences on the northward
and eastward sides thereof to be made and for ever afterwards kept
in repair by the owner thereof.

I also set out and allot unto Richard Smith, Esquire, his heirs and Richard
assigns, in right of his three cowgaits on the said tract or parcel of Smith, Esq..
land a piece or parcel of land marked on the said map No. 24 contain- No. 24, 4, 0, 4.
ing four acres and four perches, bounded northwardly in part by an
allotment No. 25 on the same to John Urmson and in other part by
an allotment on the same No. 26 to James Harrocks and in other
part by an allotment No. 27 to Robert Stanley on the same, eastwardly by the said private road ZZ, southwardly by an allotment to
the representatives of William Groom No. 23 on the same, and westwardly by an allotment No. 15 on the same to the trustees of the
said Matthew Taylor. And I direct the fences on the northward and
eastward sides thereof to be made and for ever afterwards kept in
repair by the owner thereof.

I also set out and allot unto John Urmson, his heirs and assigns, John Urmson,
in right of his two cowgaits on the said tract or parcel of land a piece No. 25, 3, 0, 3.
or parcel of land other part of the said tract or parcel of land marked
on the said map No. 25, containing three acres and three perches,
bounded northwardly by the said public road I, eastwardly by the
allotment No. 26 on the same to James Harrocks, southwardly by an

allotment on the same No. 24 to Richard Smith, Esquire, and westwardly by an allotment No. 15 to the said trustee of Matthew Taylor on the same. And I direct the fences on the northward and eastward sides thereof to be made and for ever afterwards kept in repair by the owner thereof.

James Harrocks, Purchase from Richard Hilliard, No. 26, 2, 0, 35 I also set out and allot unto James Harrocks, his heirs and assigns, in right of his one and a-half cowgait on the said tract or parcel of land a piece or parcel of land other part of the said tract or parcel of land marked on the said map No. 26, containing two acres and thirty-five perches, bounded northwardly by the said public road I, eastwardly by an allotment No. 27 on the same to Robert Stanley, southwardly by an allotment No. 24 to Richard Smith, Esquire, on the same, and westwardly by an allotment No. 25 to John Urmson the right to which said allotment No. 26 belonged to Richard Hilliard who has sold and disposed of the same to the said James Harrocks to whom I have made this allotment in pursuance of the said Act. And I direct the fences on the northward and eastward sides thereof to be made and for ever afterwards kept in repair by the owner thereof.

Robert Stanley, No. 27, 2, 3, 14 I also set out and allot unto Robert Stanley, his heirs and assigns, in right of his two cowgaits on the said piece or parcel of land a piece or parcel of land other part of the said tract or parcel of land marked on the said map No. 27, containing two acres, three roods and fourteen perches, bounded northwardly by the said public road I, eastwardly by the said private road Z Z, southwardly by an allotment on the same No. 24 to Richard Smith, Esquire, and westwardly by an allotment on the same No. 26 to James Harrocks. And I direct the fences on the northward and eastward sides thereof to be made and for ever afterwards kept in repair by the owner thereof.

Peter Ledsham, No. 28, 2, 2, 29 I also set out and allot unto Peter Ledsham, his heirs and assigns, in right of his two cowgaits on the said tract or parcel of land a piece or parcel of land other part of the said tract or parcel of land marked on the said map No. 28, containing two acres, two roods and twenty-nine perches, bounded northwardly by the said public road I, eastwardly by an allotment No. 35 to the Rector of Wallasey on the same, southwardly by an allotment on the same No. 34 to Joseph Green, Esquire, and westwardly by the public drain No. 3, between this allotment and the said private road Z Z. And I direct the fences on the northward and westward sides thereof to be made, and for ever afterwards kept in repair by the owner thereof.

Rector of Wallasey, No. 35, 7, 2, 38 I also set out and allot unto the said Augustus Campbell, the Rector of the Parish, and Parish Church of Wallasey aforesaid, in right of his six and a-half cowgaits on the said tract or parcel of land a piece or parcel of land other part of the said tract or parcel of land marked on the said map No. 35, containing seven acres, two roods and thirty-eight perches, bounded northwardly by the said public road I, eastwardly in part by an allotment marked Q Q sold by me to Thomas Sparks, and in other part by an allotment No. 36 to the said Thomas Sparks on the same, and southwardly by an allotment on the same, No. 34, to Joseph Green, and westwardly by an allotment on the same, No. 28, to Peter Ledsham. And I direct the fences on the northward and westward sides thereof, to be made and for ever afterwards kept in repair by the owner thereof. And I the said

Commissioner do also direct that the drain or watercourse from the before described allotment unto the ancient watercourse running to the fender through the allotments made to Joseph Green, Esquire, Sir John Grey Egerton, and Sir John Tobin, shall be left open and cleansed whenever necessary by the owners of the said allotments.

I also set out and allot unto Thomas Sparks, his heirs and assigns, in right of his two cowgaits on the said tract or parcel of land, a piece or parcel of land other part of the said tract or parcels of land marked on the said map No. 36, containing two acres and eighteen perches, bounded northwardly in part by an allotment marked QQ, by me sold to the said Thomas Sparks, and in other part by an allotment No. 37 to Margaret Jones on the same, southeastwardly in part by the public drain No. 4, between this allotment and an allotment No. 38 to Sir John Grey Egerton, and in other part by ancient inclosed lands belonging to the said Thomas Sparks, southwardly by an allotment on the said tract or parcel of land No. 34 to Joseph Green, and westwardly in part by an allotment on the same, No. 35, to the said Rector of Wallasey aforesaid, and in other part by an allotment QQ, by me sold to the said Thomas Sparks. And I direct so much of the fences on the northward side as adjoins the said allotment No. 37 to Margaret Jones, and so much of the fences on the westward side as adjoins the said allotment No. 35, and so much of the fence on the eastward side as adjoins the said drain, to be made and for ever afterwards kept in repair by the owner thereof. *Thomas Sparks, No. 36, 2, 0, 18*

I also set out and allot unto Margaret Jones, her heirs and assigns, in right of her one cowgait on the said tract or parcel of land, a piece or parcel of land other part of the said tract or parcel of land marked on the said map No. 37, containing one acre and sixteen perches, bounded northwardly by the said public road 1, eastwardly by the public drain No. 4, between this allotment and the allotment No. 38, to Sir John Grey Egerton, southwardly by the said allotment No. 36, to Thomas Sparks on the same, and westwardly by the said allotment QQ, by me sold to the said Thomas Sparks. And I direct the fences on the northward and eastward sides to be made and for ever afterwards kept in repair by the owner thereof. *Margaret Jones, No. 37, 1, 0, 16.*

And with respect to the said commons and waste lands in the township of Poolton-cum-Seacombe, I the said Commissioner do make my award as follows, that is to say:—

In the first place I do hereby particularise and describe the public carriage roads, highways, and private roads and footways so set out by me through and over the same last mentioned commons and waste lands as aforesaid in manner following, that is to say:—

One public carriage road or highway marked in the said map with the letter A, on part of the said commons and waste lands on Seacombe Common beginning at the Seacombe Ferry house and running northwardly in an irregular line near to the cottage or dwelling house in the occupation of Ann Bennett, and then continuing northwestwardly to the end of the lane leading to Liscard and then turning westwardly towards Poolton along the present road there. *Public Road A.*

One other public carriage road or highway marked with the letter B, on part of the said commons and waste lands on Seacombe Common *Public Road B.*

54 Geo. III. *Commissioner's Award,* ch. lxxxvii.
Wallasey Inclosure.

aforesaid, leading from the last-mentioned road in a southwardly direction to a certain lane there called Whiteling Lane.

Public Road C.
One other public carriage road or highway marked with the letter C, on part of the said commons or waste lands on Poolton Common beginning at the end of the lane near the dwelling house occupied by Mr. Webster, in Poolton aforesaid, and running from thence in a westwardly direction to the south end of the before described public road on Wallasey Breck marked L.

Public Road D.
One other public carriage road and highway marked with the letter D on part of the said commons and waste lands on Poolton Common aforesaid, beginning at the premises held by Mr. William Garner and running from thence in a southwestwardly direction to the new embankment across Wallasey Pool.

Private Road a.
One private or occupation road marked with the letter a, on part of the said commons and waste lands on Seacombe Common aforesaid, of the width of six yards, commencing on the east side of the said public carriage road marked A, and running from thence in a northeastwardly direction to the southwest corner of an allotment E, by me sold to Thomas Lowry, and then turning off and running northwardly along the west side of other land part of the said commons and waste lands to an allotment of land marked A, by me sold to William Pendleton.

Private Road b.
Another private or occupation road marked with the letter b, on other part of the said commons and waste lands called Seacombe Common, of the width of three yards, commencing on the southwest side of the said public carriage road marked A, and running in a southwestwardly direction to a cottage and garden belonging to and in the occupation of Anne Bennett.

Private Road c.
Another private or occupation road marked with the letter c, on other part of the said commons and waste lands on Seacombe Common, of the width of three yards, commencing on the southwest side of the public carriage road marked A, and running from thence in a southwestwardly direction to a cottage and garden belonging to William Evans.

Private Road d.
Another private or occupation road marked with the letter d, on other part of the said commons and waste lands called Seacombe Common, of the width of eight yards, commencing on the west side of the public carriage road marked B, and running in a westwardly direction to land belonging to Richard Smith, Esquire, and then turning off and running in a southwestwardly direction to the northeast end of the private road e.

Private Road e.
Another private or occupation road marked with the letter e on other part of the said commons and waste lands called Seacombe Dale of the width of eight yards commencing at the southwest end of the private road marked d, and forming a continuance of the same and running from thence in a southwestwardly direction in an irregular line along and through the whole of Seacombe Dale to the track leading to the southeast end of a new road lately made by Mr. Quirk and to the Hooks Common.

Private Road f.
Another private or occupation road marked with the letter f on other part of the said commons and waste lands called Poolton Common of the width of seven yards commencing on the southwest

side of the before described road marked d, and running in a southwestwardly direction in an irregular line to the strand or shore of Wallasey Pool.

Another private or occupation road on part of the said commons and waste lands in the Township of Poolton-cum-Seacombe called the Hooks of the width of eight yards marked in the said map with the letters a b, commencing at the southwest end of a private road before described leading down Seacombe Dale and marked e, and running thence in a southwardly direction along the fences of ancient inclosed lands in the said township belonging to Richard Smith, Esquire, Mr. Samuel Smith and Mr. William Quirke to the strand of Wallasey Pool. *Private Road a b.*

Another private or occupation road on other part of the said commons and waste lands called the Hooks marked a c of the width of eight yards commencing at the southwest end of a new road lately made by Mr. Quirke through a field of his there called the Big Cock Butts in lieu of the old road round the fence of the said field and running thence in a westwardly direction to ancient lands belonging to the master or trustees of the Wallasey Grammar School, and thence turning off and running in a southwestwardly direction along the east fence of the said school lands and continuing to the strand of Wallasey Pool. *Private Road a c.*

Another private or occupation road other part of the said commons and waste lands called the Hooks of the width of eight yards marked a d, commencing at the southwest side of the last-mentioned road and running in a northwestwardly direction to an allotment No. 67, to Mr. Samuel Smith. *Private Road a d.*

Another private or occupation road other part of the said commons and waste lands called the Hooks marked a e, of the width of eight yards, commencing at the southeast corner of the ancient lane leading from the village of Poolton to the Hooks and running thence in a southeastwardly direction along the ancient inclosed lands belonging to James Mainwaring, Esquire, and Robert Vyner, Esquire, and along the allotments No. 63A and 63, to Robert Vyner, Esquire, to an allotment No. 64, to Richard Smith, Esquire. *Private Road a e.*

Another private or occupation road other part of the said commons and waste lands on Seacombe Dale, of the width of five yards, marked on the said map with the letters a f, commencing at the west side of the said private road marked e, and running northwardly to ancient inclosed lands belonging to Joseph Cooper. *Private Road a f.*

And I direct that the before described private or occupation roads by me set out as aforesaid marked f, shall be for ever hereafter maintained and kept in repair by and at the expense of owners or occupiers of land in the said Township of Poolton-cum-Seacombe, and that the before described private or occupation roads marked b c, and a f, shall be maintained and kept in repair by and at the expense of the owners or occupiers of the ancient inclosed lands to which the said roads lead and shall be solely used and enjoyed by them. And that all the other private or occupation roads by me set out as aforesaid shall be for ever hereafter maintained and kept in repair by the owners or occupiers of the lands adjoining to or abutting on the same and shall be solely used and enjoyed by them.

54 Geo. III.   Commissioner's Award,   ch. lxxxvii.
Wallasey Inclosure.

Footway No. 1.
A footway marked No. 1, across part of the said commons and waste lands called Seacombe Common, commencing on the southwest side of the said public road marked A, and running southwestwardly across the allotment No. 15 to Richard Smith, Esquire, to a stile and footway over ancient land belonging to the said Richard Smith.

Footway No. 2.
Another footway marked No. 2 across other part of the said commons and waste lands called Seacombe Dale and commencing at the southeast side of the private road marked c, running in a southeastwardly direction across an allotment No. 36 to a stile and footway leading over other lands belonging to the said Richard Smith.

Footway No. 3.
Another footway marked No. 3 across other part of the said commons and waste lands, commencing at the south side of Mill Lane, and running southeastwardly across an allotment No. 49, to the master or trustees of the Free Grammar School in Wallasey to a stile and footway over the lands belonging to the said trustees or master.

Footway No. 4.
A footway marked No. 4 in the said map over a part of the said commons and waste lands called the Hooks, commencing at the northwest corner of a field belonging to James Mainwaring, Esquire, and running northwestwardly across the allotment No. 81, to the master or trustees of Wallasey Grammar School to a stile and footway over ancient lands belonging to the said master or trustees.

And in the next place I have set out and allotted from and out of the said commons and waste lands in Poolton-cum-Seacombe aforesaid, several parcels of land hereinafter mentioned for sale towards defraying the charges and expenses incident to and attending the obtaining the said Act and of carrying the same into execution in the manner and as directed in the said Act and which parcels of land are described as follows :—

Sale allotment, William Pendleton, A, 1, 0, 6.
One part of the said commons and waste lands on Seacombe Common, containing one acre and six perches marked in the said map with the letter A, and by me sold to William Pendleton, bounded on the north side thereof by the ancient inclosed lands of Richard Smith, Esquire, on the east by the strand or shore of the River Mersey, on the south by the allotment by me in like manner sold to the said William Pendleton marked B, and on the west side by the allotment No. 19, to Richard Smith, Esquire, and I do direct the fences on the east, south and west sides thereof to be made and for ever afterwards kept in repair by the owner thereof.

Sale allotment, William Pendleton, B, 0, 3, 15.
One other part of the said commons and waste lands on Seacombe Common aforesaid, containing three roods and fifteen perches, marked upon the said map with the letter B, and by me sold in like manner to the said William Pendleton, bounded on the northwardly side by the last-mentioned allotment, on the east by the strand or shore of the River Mersey, and on the south by the allotment by me in like manner sold to George Skerritt, marked C, and on the west by the private road marked on the said map with the letter a. And I do direct that the fences on the east, south, and west sides thereof to be made and for ever afterwards kept in repair by the owner thereof.

Sale allotment, George Skerritt, C, 0, 3, 24.
One other part of the said commons and waste lands on Seacombe Common aforesaid, containing three roods and twenty-four perches,

marked upon the said map with the letter C, and by me sold in like manner to George Skerritt, bounded on the north side thereof by the last before-described allotment, on the east by the strand or shore of the River Mersey, on the south by another allotment, by me in like manner sold to Leigh Blundell, Esquire, marked D, and on the west by the said private road marked in the said map with the letter a. And I direct the fences on the east, south, and west sides thereof to be made and for ever afterwards kept in repair by the owner thereof.

One other part of the said commons and waste lands on Seacombe Common aforesaid, containing three roods and thirty-five perches marked upon the said map with the letter D, and by me in like manner sold to Leigh Blundell, Esquire, bounded on the north side thereof by the last described allotment, on the east by the strand or shore of the River Mersey, on the south by another allotment by me in like manner sold to Mr. Thomas Lowry marked E, and on the west by the said private road marked a. And I direct the fences on the east, south and west sides thereof to be made and for ever afterwards kept in repair by the owner thereof. — Sale allotment, Leigh Blundell, D, 0, 3, 35.

One other part of the said commons and waste lands on Seacombe Common aforesaid, containing one acre three roods and thirty-five perches, marked upon the said map with the letter E, and by me sold to Thomas Lowry, bounded on the north by the said last-mentioned allotment, on the east by the strand or shore of the River Mersey, on the south by the allotment No. 4 to Richard Smith, Esquire, and on the west by the said private road marked a. And I do direct the fences on the east, south, and west sides thereof to be made and for ever afterwards kept in repair by the owner thereof. — Sale allotment, Thomas Lowry, E, 1, 3, 35.

And I do also set out and allot unto Richard Smith, Esquire, his heirs and assigns, in respect of his royalty as the Lord of the Manor of Poolton-cum-Seacombe aforesaid, and in satisfaction of the claims upon the said commons or waste lands in the township of Poolton-cum-Seacombe as Lord of the said Manor the two pieces or parcels of land next hereinafter described and marked No. 1 and No. 65, in the said map which I estimate as equal to one-sixteenth part in value of the said commons and waste lands in the township of Poolton-cum-Seacombe aforesaid, that is to say a part of the said commons and waste lands called Seacombe Common marked on the said map No. 1, containing one acre two roods and thirty-eight perches, bounded northeastwardly by an allotment No. 4, to the said Richard Smith, southeastwardly in part by the strand or shore of the River Mersey in other part by an allotment No. 3, to Mrs. Wade's trustees in other part by an allotment No. 2, to Joseph Evans, and in other part by ancient inclosed lands belonging to the said Richard Smith, westwardly in part by the said ancient inclosed lands belonging to the said Richard Smith, and in other part by the said public road marked in the said map with the letter A, northwardly by the private road marked on the said map with the letter a. And I direct the fences on the southeastward, excepting so much thereof as adjoins the allotment No. 2 and No. 3 and the fences on the southwestward and northwestward sides thereof, to be made and for ever afterwards kept in repair by the owner thereof.

Richard Smith, Esquire (Royalty). No. 1 and 65.

No. 1—1 2 38
„ 65 —2 3 0
———
4 1 38

A piece or parcel of land part of the said commons and waste lands called the Hooks marked on the said map No 65, containing two

5-4 *Geo. III.* *Commissioner's Award,* ch. *lxxxvii.*
Wallasey Inclosure.

acres and three roods bounded northeastwardly by an allotment No. 66, to Robert Vyner, Esq., southeastwardly by an allotment No. 67, to Samuel Smith, southwestwardly by the strand or shore of Wallasey Pool, and northwestwardly by an allotment No. 64, to the said Richard Smith, and I direct the fences on the southeastward and southwestward sides thereof to be made and for ever afterwards kept in repair by the owner thereof.

And in further execution of the said Acts I do hereby set out and allot the remainder of the said commons and waste lands in the township of Poolton-cum-Seacombe aforesaid, by the said recited Act directed to be inclosed in manner following, that is to say :—

Richard Smith, Esq., No. 4, 0, 3, 21 — I set out and allot unto the said Richard Smith, Esquire, his heirs and assigns, in respect of his ancient inclosed lands within the township of Poolton-cum-Seacombe aforesaid, a piece or parcel of land other part of the said commons and waste lands on Seacombe Common aforesaid, marked upon the said map No. 4, containing three roods and twenty-one perches, bounded on the north side thereof by the allotment by me sold to Mr. Thomas Lowry marked with the letter E, eastwardly by the strand or shore of the River Mersey, and southwestwardly by an allotment No. 1, by me hereinbefore made to the said Richard Smith, Esquire, in respect of the royalty as Lord of the Manor of Poolton-cum-Seacombe aforesaid, and I direct the fences on the eastward and southwestward sides thereof to be made and for ever afterwards kept in repair by the owner thereof.

Richard Smith, Esq., No. 5, 0, 0, 10 — I also set out and allot unto the said Richard Smith, Esquire, his heirs and assigns in respect of his same ancient lands, a piece or parcel of land other part of the said commons and waste lands adjoining the strand or shore of the River Mersey, marked upon the said map No. 5, containing ten perches bounded northeastwardly by an allotment No. 6, to Joseph Cooper, southwardly by the strand or shore of the River Mersey, and westwardly by ancient inclosed lands belonging to the said Richard Smith, the same being an encroachment upon the said waste, and I direct the fences on the southerly side thereof to be kept in repair by the owner thereof.

Richard Smith, Esq., No. 8, 0, 0, 2. — I also set out and allot unto the said Richard Smith, Esquire, his heirs and assigns, in respect of his same ancient lands a piece or parcel of land other part of the said commons or waste lands upon Seacombe Common aforesaid, marked upon the said map No. 8, containing two perches, bounded on the northward side by an allotment No. 9, to Samuel Smith, eastwardly in part by the public road marked A, and in other part by a building now used as a coach-house belonging to the said Richard Smith, and southwestwardly by ancient inclosed lands belonging to Samuel Smith, and I direct the fences on the north side, and so much of the fence as adjoins the said road A, shall be kept in repair by the owner thereof.

Richard Smith, Esq., No. 10, 1, 1, 15 — I also set out and allot unto Richard Smith, Esquire, his heirs and assigns, in respect of his same ancient inclosed lands, a piece or parcel of land other part of the said commons and waste lands on Seacombe Common aforesaid, marked upon the said map No. 10, containing one acre one rood and fifteen perches, bounded northwestwardly by the aforesaid public road A, southwardly by an allotment No. 9 to Samuel Smith, westwardly in an irregular line by ancient inclosed lands belonging to the said Richard Smith and Anne Bennett, northwestwardly by the private road marked in the said map with the letter b. And I direct the fences on the northeastward and on the northwest sides thereof to be made and for ever afterwards kept in repair by the owner thereof.

I also set out and allot unto the said Richard Smith, his heirs and assigns, in respect of his said ancient lands, a piece or parcel of land other part of the said commons and waste lands on Seacombe Common aforesaid, marked upon the said map No. 15, containing one rood and ten perches, bounded northeastwardly in part by the public road marked A, and in other part by the allotment to Richard Smith No. 14, eastwardly in part by the said allotment No. 14, and in other part by an allotment No. 12 to Thomas Blackburne, southwardly by ancient inclosed lands belonging to the said Richard Smith, and westwardly in part by ancient lands belonging to William Evans, and in other part by the private road marked in the said map with the letter c. And I direct the fences on the northeastward and westward sides thereof to be made and for ever afterwards kept in repair by the owner thereof. *Richard Smith, Esq., No. 15, 0, 1, 10*

I also set out and allot unto the said Richard Smith, Esquire, his heirs and assigns, in respect of his same ancient lands, a piece or parcel of land other part of the said commons and waste lands on Seacombe Common aforesaid, marked on the said map No. 19, containing five acres two roods and three perches, bounded northwardly by ancient inclosed lands belonging to the said Richard Smith, eastwardly in part by an allotment sold by me to William Pendleton, marked with the letter A, and in other part by a private road marked a, southwestwardly by the said public road marked A, and northwestwardly by an allotment No. 20 to the master and trustees of the Free Grammar School of Wallasey. And I direct so much of the fences on the eastwardly side thereof as adjoins the said private road a, and the fences on the southwestwardly side of the said allotment to be made and for ever afterwards kept in repair by the owner thereof. *Richard Smith, Esq., No. 19, 5, 2, 3.*

I also set out and allot unto the said Richard Smith, Esquire, his heirs and assigns, in respect of his same ancient lands, a piece or parcel of land other part of the said commons and waste lands on Seacombe Common aforesaid, marked upon the said map No. 24, and containing ten acres three roods and thirty-nine perches, bounded on the northwardly side thereof by ancient inclosed lands belonging to the said Richard Smith, eastwardly in part by ancient lands belonging to the said Richard Smith, in other part by an allotment No. 23 to Messrs. Horne and Stackhouse, and on the southwestwardly side thereof by the said public road marked A, and northwestwardly by allotment No. 24A to John Orrell. And I direct so much of the fences as adjoins the said allotment No. 23, and the fences on the southwestwardly side thereof to be made and for ever afterwards kept in repair by the owner thereof. *Richard Smith, Esq., No. 24, 10, 3, 39.*

I also set out and allot unto the said Richard Smith, Esquire, his heirs and assigns, in respect of his same ancient lands in Poolton-cum-Seacombe, a piece or parcel of land, other part of the said commons and waste lands on Seacombe Common aforesaid, marked *Richard Smith, Esq., No. 29, 1, 0, 19* upon the said map No. 29, containing one acre and nineteen perches, bounded northwardly by an allotment No. 30 to James Mainwaring, Esquire, eastwardly by an allotment No. 28 to Mr. Samuel Smith, southwardly by the ancient inclosed lands of Richard Smith, and westwardly by the public road marked on the said map with the letter B. And I do direct the fences on the northward and westward sides thereof to be made and for ever afterwards kept in repair by the owner thereof.

Richard Smith, Esq., No. 35, 1, 0, 24

I also set out and allot to the said Richard Smith, Esquire, his heirs and assigns, in respect of his same ancient lands, a piece or parcel of land, other part of the said commons and waste lands in Seacombe Dale aforesaid, marked upon the said map No. 35, containing one acre and twenty-four perches, bounded eastwardly by a private road marked on the said map with the letter e, and westwardly in part by the private road a f, and in other part by the ancient inclosed lands of the said Richard Smith and Mr. Joseph Cooper. And I direct the fences on the eastward side thereof and so much of the fence on the westward side as adjoins the private road marked a f to Joseph Cooper's field to be made and for ever afterwards kept in repair by the owner thereof.

Richard Smith, Esq., No. 36, 0, 3, 10

I also set out and allot unto the said Richard Smith, Esquire, his heirs and assigns, in respect of his same ancient lands, a piece or parcel of land, other part of the said commons and waste lands in Seacombe Dale aforesaid, marked upon the said map No. 36, containing three roods and ten perches, bounded eastwardly by ancient inclosed lands belonging to the said Richard Smith, westwardly in part by the said private road marked e, and in other part by a private road over the Hooks marked a b. And I direct the fences on the westwardly side thereof to be made and for ever afterwards kept in repair by the owner thereof.

Richard Smith, Esq., No. 45, 0, 0, 15

I also set out and allot unto the said Richard Smith, his heirs and assigns, in respect of his same ancient lands, a piece or parcel of land, other part of the said commons and waste lands in Mill Lane, in the said Township of Poolton-cum-Seacombe, marked on the said map No. 45, containing fifteen perches, bounded southeastwardly by the said Mill Lane, and westwardly by ancient inclosed lands belonging to the said Richard Smith, Esquire. And I direct the fence on the southeastward side to be made and for ever afterwards kept in repair by the owner thereof.

Richard Smith, Esq., No. 47, 0, 1, 5

I also set out and allot unto the said Richard Smith, Esquire, his heirs and assigns, in respect of his same ancient lands, a piece or parcel of the said commons and waste lands in Mill Lane aforesaid, marked upon the said map No. 47, containing one rood and five perches, bounded southeastwardly by the said Mill Lane, and northwestwardly by ancient inclosed lands belonging to the said Richard Smith, the same being an encroachment made upon the said waste by the said Richard Smith, Esquire. And I direct the fences on the southeastwardly side thereof to be made and for ever afterwards kept in repair by the owner thereof.

Richard Smith, Esq., No. 53, 0, 1, 36

I also set out and allot unto the said Richard Smith, Esquire, his heirs and assigns, in respect of his said ancient inclosed lands in the said Township of Poolton-cum-Seacombe, a piece or parcel of land, other part of the said commons and waste lands

54 Geo. III.   Commissioner's Award,   ch. lxxcvii.
Wallasey Inclosure.

called the Hooks Common, marked on the said map No. 53, containing one rood and thirty-six perches, bounded northeastwardly in part by ancient inclosed land belonging to William Bird, and in other part by the private road marked on the said map with the letters a c, southwardly and southwestwardly by the strand or shore of Wallasey Pool, and northwestwardly by ancient inclosed lands belonging to the said Richard Smith. And I direct the fences on the northeastward side adjoining the said private road and the fences on the southward and southwestward sides thereof to be made and for ever afterwards kept in repair by the owner or owners thereof.

I also set out and allot unto the said Richard Smith, Esquire, his heirs and assigns, in respect of his same ancient lands, a piece or parcel of land other part of the said commons and waste lands called the Hooks Commons, marked in the said map No. 64, containing fifteen acres and twenty perches bounded northeastwardly in part by ancient inclosed lands belonging to the said Richard Smith, and in other part by an allotment No. 66 to Robert Vyner, Esquire, southeastwardly in part by the said allotment No. 66 to the said Robert Vyner, and in other part by an allotment No. 65 to the said Richard Smith, southwestwardly by the strand or shore of Wallasey Pool, and northwardly in part by an allotment No. 54 to James Mainwaring, Esquire, in other part by an allotment No. 62 to Sir John Tobin, in other part by the said private road a c, and in other part by an allotment No. 63 to the said Robert Vyner. And I direct the fences on the southeastwardly and southwestward sides and the fence on the northwestward side thereof, except so much as adjoins the allotment made to the said Robert Vyner, No. 63, to be made and for ever afterwards kept in repair by the owner thereof. *(Richard Smith, Esq., No. 64, 15, 0, 20.)*

And I do also set out and allot unto the said Richard Smith, his heirs and assigns, a piece or parcel of land other part of the said commons and waste lands, marked upon the said map No. 14, containing two perches, and bounded northeastwardly by the public road marked A, on the said map, southeastwardly by the allotment No. 13 to the devisees of William Smith, southwestwardly and northeastwardly by the allotment No. 15 to the said Richard Smith, and which said piece of land lastly hereinbefore allotted to the said Richard Smith, was originally set out by me unto Leigh Blundell, in respect of his ancient inclosed lands in the said Township of Poulton, and has been given in exchange by the said Leigh Blundell to the said Richard Smith for a piece or parcel of land marked in the said map "exchanged land No. 1," and by this my award hereinafter allotted to the said Leigh Blundell. And I direct the fences on the northeastward and northwestward sides thereof to be made and for ever afterwards kept in repair by the owner thereof. *(Richard Smith, Esq. No. 14, 0, 0, 2. Exchange with L. Blundell.)*

I also set out and allot unto John Orrell, his heirs and assigns, a piece or parcel of land other part of the said commons and waste lands called Seacombe Common, marked in the said map No. 24A, containing one rood and two perches, bounded northeastwardly by ancient inclosed land belonging to the said Richard Smith, southeastwardly by the allotment, marked No. 24, to the said Richard Smith, and southwestwardly by the public road marked A on the said map, the right to which said allotment, marked No. 24A, belonged to *(John Orrell, No. 24a, 0, 1, 2. Purchased from Richard Smith.)*

the said Richard Smith, who has sold and disposed of the same to the said John Orrell, to whom I have made this allotment in pursuance of the said Act. And I direct the fences on the south-eastward and southwestward sides thereof to be made and for ever afterwards kept in repair by the owner thereof.

James Mainwaring, Esq., No. 25, 4, 0, 32.

I also set out and allot unto James Mainwaring, Esquire, his heirs and assigns in right of his ancient lands within the Township of Poolton-cum-Seacombe aforesaid, a piece or parcel of land part of the said commons and waste lands on Seacombe Common aforesaid, marked upon the said map No. 25, containing four acres and thirty-two perches, bounded northeastwardly by the said public road A, southeastwardly by an allotment No. 18 to the devisees of Thomas Johnson, southwardly in part by ancient inclosed lands belonging to William Evans the said Richard Smith and the said James Mainwaring and in other part by an allotment No. 26 to the said James Mainwaring and westwardly in part by ancient inclosed lands of Mr. Samuel Smith and in other part by an allotment No. 27 to Sir John Tobin. And I direct the fences on the northeastward side and so much of the fences as adjoins the allotment No. 27 to the said Sir John Tobin to be made and for ever afterwards kept in repair by the owner thereof.

James Mainwaring, No. 26, 0, 0, 24

I also set out and allot to the said James Mainwaring, Esquire, his heirs and assigns in respect to his said ancient lands a piece or parcel of land, other part of the said commons and waste lands on Seacombe Common aforesaid, marked upon the said map No. 26, containing twenty-four perches, bounded northwardly and westwardly by the last mentioned allotment No. 25, southwardly by ancient inclosed lands of the said James Mainwaring, Esquire, in the said Township of Poolton-cum-Seacombe the same being an encroachment made by the said James Mainwaring upon the said waste. And I direct that the fences on the north and west sides shall be for ever hereafter kept in repair by the owner thereof.

James Mainwaring, No. 30, 1, 0, 18

I also set out and allot unto the said James Mainwaring, Esquire, his heirs and assigns in respect of his same ancient lands a piece or parcel of land part of the said commons and waste lands on Seacombe Common aforesaid, marked upon the said map No. 30, containing one acre and eighteen perches, bounded northwardly in part by the said public road A, and in other part by two several allotments marked No. 30A and No. 30B made to the said James Mainwaring, eastwardly by an allotment No. 28 to Mr. Samuel Smith, southwardly by the allotment No. 29 to the said Richard Smith and westwardly by the public road B. And I direct the fences on the northward and westward sides shall be made and for ever hereafter kept in repair by the owner or owners thereof.

James Mainwaring, No. 30a, 0, 0, 17.

I also set out and allot unto the said James Mainwaring, Esquire, his heirs and assigns in respect of his same ancient lands a piece or parcel of land, other part of the said commons and waste lands on Seacombe Common aforesaid, containing seventeen perches, marked in the said map No. 30A, bounded northwardly by the said public road A, eastwardly by the allotment to the said James Mainwaring No. 30B, southwardly and westwardly by the last described allotment No. 30, and in making this allotment it is meant and intended that James Wade who holds the lands in respect of which this allotment is made under a lease for three lives from the said James Mainwaring *Wade's Leasehold.* shall hold this allotment together with the other lands and tenements included in the said lease during the continuance thereof. And I direct the fences on the north and east sides thereof to be made and kept in repair by the said James Wade during the continuance of the said lease and afterwards to be kept in repair by the owners thereof.

I also set out and allot unto the said James Mainwaring, Esquire, *James Mainwaring, Esq., No. 30a, 0, 0, 11.* his heirs and assigns, in respect of his same ancient lands a piece or parcel of land other part of the said commons and waste lands on Seacombe Common aforesaid, containing eleven perches marked on the said map No. 33, bounded northwardly by the said public road A, eastwardly by the allotment No. 28 to Mr. Samuel Smith, southwardly by the said allotment to the said James Mainwaring, and westwardly by the last described allotment No. 30a. And in making this allotment it is meant and intended that William Bird who holds *Bird's Leasehold.* the lands in respect of which this allotment is made under a lease for three lives from the said James Mainwaring, shall hold and enjoy the same along with the other tenements included in the said lease during the continuance thereof. And I direct the fences on the northward and westward sides thereof shall be made and kept in repair by the said William Bird during the continuance of his lease, and afterwards kept in repair by the owners thereof.

I also set out and allot unto the said James Mainwaring, Esquire, *James Mainwaring, Esq., No. 31, 2, 0, 17* his heirs and assigns, in respect of his same ancient lands a piece or parcel of land other part of the said commons and waste lands on Seacombe Common aforesaid, marked in the said map No. 31, containing two acres and seventeen perches, bounded northwardly by the said public road A, eastwardly by the said public road B, southwardly by the private road d, and northwestwardly by ancient inclosed lands in the said township belonging to the said Richard Smith. And I direct the fences on the northward, eastward and southward sides thereof to be made and for ever afterwards kept in repair by the owners thereof.

I also set out and allot to the said James Mainwaring, Esquire, his *James Mainwaring, Esq., No. 46, 0, 0, 14* heirs and assigns, in respect of his same ancient lands a piece or parcel of land other part of the said commons or waste lands in Mill Lane marked on the said map No. 46, containing fourteen perches, bounded southeastwardly by ancient inclosed lands belonging to the said James Mainwaring in the said township, and northwestwardly by Mill Lane aforesaid. And I direct the fence on the northwestward side to be made and for ever afterwards kept in repair by the owner thereof.

I also set out and allot to the said James Mainwaring, his heirs and *James Mainwaring, Esq., No. 48, 0, 0, 12* assigns, in respect of his same ancient lands a piece or parcel of land other part of the commons and said waste lands in Mill Lane aforesaid, marked in the said map No. 48, containing twelve perches, bounded northeastwardly by an allotment No. 49 to the master or trustee of the Wallasey Grammar School, southeastwardly by buildings and ancient inclosed lands in the said township belonging to the said James Mainwaring, and northwestwardly by Mill Lane aforesaid. And I direct the fences on the northeast and northwestward sides to be made and for ever afterwards kept in repair by the owner thereof.

James Mainwaring, Esq., No. 54, 7, 2, 39.

I also set out and allot unto James Mainwaring, Esquire, his heirs and assigns, in right of his same ancient lands a piece or parcel of land other part of the said commons and waste lands called the Hooks Common marked on the said map No. 54, containing seven acres, two roods and thirty-nine perches, bounded northeastwardly in part by the said private road a e, in other part by two allotments No. 54A and No. 54B to the said James Mainwaring, in other part by allotment No. 55 to Richard Evans, in other part by an allotment No. 56 to Mrs. Jackson, in other part by an allotment No. 60, to William Bird, in other part by another allotment No. 61, to Leigh Blundell, and in other part by an allotment No. 62 to Sir John Tobin, southeastwardly in part by an allotment No. 54A, to the said James Mainwaring in part by an allotment No. 55, to Richard Evans, and in other part by an allotment No. 64, to Richard Smith, southwestwardly and northwestwardly by the strand or shore of Wallasey Pool. And I direct that so much of the fences on the northeastward side thereof as adjoins the said private road marked a e, the fences on the southeastward and northeastward sides thereof shall be made and for ever afterwards kept in repair by the owner thereof.

James Mainwaring, Esq., No. 54A, 0, 0, 16.

I also set out and allot to the said James Mainwaring, Esquire, his heirs and assigns, in respect of his same ancient lands a piece or parcel of land other part of the said commons and waste lands called the Hooks Common marked on the said map No. 54A, containing sixteen perches, bounded northeastwardly by the said private road a e, southeastwardly by an allotment No. 54B, to the said James Mainwaring, and southwestwardly and northwestwardly by an allotment No. 54 to the said James Mainwaring, but in making this allotment to the said James Mainwaring it is meant and intended that William Bird who holds the lands in respect of which this allotment is made under a lease for three lives from the said James Mainwaring shall hold and enjoy the same along with the said tenements included in the said lease during the continuance thereof. And I direct the fences on the northeastward, southwestward and northwestward sides thereof to be made and kept in repair by the said William Bird during the continuance of the said lease, and afterwards shall be kept in repair by the owner thereof.

Bird's Leasehold.

James Mainwaring, Esq., No. 54B, 0, 0, 20.

I also set out and allot unto the said James Mainwaring, Esquire, his heirs and assigns, in respect of his same ancient lands, a piece or parcel of land other part of the said commons and waste lands called the Hooks Common marked on the said map No. 54B, containing twenty perches, bounded northeastwardly by the said private road a e, southeastwardly by an allotment No. 55, to Richard Evans, southwestwardly by an allotment No. 54, to the said James Mainwaring, and northwestwardly by an allotment No. 54A, to the said James Mainwaring, but in making this allotment to the said James Mainwaring it is meant and understood that James Wade, who holds the land in respect of which this allotment is made under a lease for three lives from the said James Mainwaring, shall hold and enjoy the same during the continuance of the said lease. And I direct the fences on the northeastward, southwestward and northwestward sides thereof to be made and kept in repair by the said James Wade during the continuance of the said lease, and afterwards shall be kept in repair by the owner thereof.

James Wade's Leasehold.

I also set out and allot to Sir John Tobin, Knight, his heirs and assigns, in respect of his ancient inclosed lands in the said Township of Poolton-cum-Seacombe, a piece or parcel of land other part of the said commons and waste lands on Seacombe Common marked in the said map No. 27, containing two roods and thirty two perches, bounded northeastwardly by the said public road A, southeastwardly by the said allotment No. 25, to James Mainwaring, Esquire, southwardly by ancient inclosed lands in the said township belonging to Mr. James Smith, and northwestwardly by an allotment No. 28, to the said Samuel Smith. And I direct the fences on the northeastward and northwestward sides to be made and for ever afterwards kept in repair by the owner thereof.

Sir J. Tobin, Knight, No. 27, 0, 2, 32

I also set out and allot unto the said Sir John Tobin, Knight, his heirs and assigns, in respect of his same ancient lands, another piece or parcel of land part of the said commons and waste lands in Mill Lane aforesaid, marked in the said map No. 51, and containing eight perches, bounded northeastwardly by part of the commons in the Township of Liscard, lately allotted to the said Sir John Tobin, southeastwardly by Mill Lane aforesaid, and northwestwardly by ancient inclosed lands of the said Sir John Tobin, in the Township of Wallasey. And I direct the fences on the southeastward side shall be made and for ever thereafter kept in repair by the owner thereof.

Sir John Tobin, Kngt., No. 51, 0, 0, 8.

I also set out and allot unto Sir John Tobin, his heirs and assigns, in respect of his same ancient lands, a piece or parcel of land other part of the said commons and waste lands called the Hooks Common, marked in the said map No. 62, containing one acre one rood and nineteen perches, bounded northeastwardly by the private road a c, southeastwardly by the allotment No. 64 to Richard Smith, Esquire, southwestwardly by the allotment No. 54 to the said James Mainwaring, and northwestwardly by the allotment No. 61 to Leigh Blundell. And I direct the fences on the northeastward, southwestward and northwestward sides thereof to be made and for ever afterwards kept in repair by the owner thereof.

Sir John Tobin, Kngt., No. 62, 1, 1, 19

I also set out and allot unto Mary Antin Jackson, wife of the Reverend Roger Jackson, of Bebington, in the County of Chester, Clerk, in respect of her ancient inclosed lands in the said Township of Poolton-cum-Seacombe, devised to her separate use in and by the last will and testament of the Reverend George Briggs, deceased, or to such other uses as the same ancient lands are limited, a piece or parcel of land other part of the said commons and waste lands in Seacombe Common aforesaid, marked in the said map No. 21, containing two roods and thirty-six perches, bounded northeastwardly by ancient inclosed lands of the said Richard Smith in Poolton-cum-Seacombe, southeastwardly by an allotment No. 20 to the master or trustees of Wallasey Free Grammar School, southwestwardly by the public road A, northwestwardly by an allotment No. 22 to Mr. Richard Evans. And I direct the fences on the northeastward and southwestward sides to be made and for ever afterwards kept in repair by the owner thereof.

Mary Antin Jackson, No. 21, 0, 2, 36

I also set out and allot unto the said Mary Antin Jackson, in respect of the said ancient lands, and in manner and to the uses aforesaid, a piece or parcel of land other part of the said commons

Mary Antin Jackson, No. 56, 0, 3, 20

54 *Geo. III.* *Commissioner's Award,* ch. *lxxxvii.*
Wallasey Inclosure.

and waste lands called the Hooks Common, marked in the said map No. 56, containing three roods and twenty perches, bounded northeastwardly in part by the said private road a c, in other part by an allotment No. 57 to William Garner's assignees, and in other part by an allotment No. 58 to Thomas Molyneux, southeastwardly in part by an allotment No. 57 to the said William Garner's assignees, and in other part by an allotment No. 60 to William Bird, southwestwardly by an allotment No. 54 to James Mainwaring, and northwestwardly by an allotment No. 55 to Richard Evans. And I direct the fences on the northeastward, southwestward and northwestward sides thereof to be made and for ever afterwards kept in repair by the owner thereof.

Robert Vyner, Esq., No. 37, 0, 1, 7.

I also set out and allot unto Robert Vyner, Esquire, his heirs and assigns, in right of his ancient inclosed lands in the said Township of Poolton-cum-Seacombe, a piece or parcel of land part of the said commons and waste lands in Poolton Common, marked in the said map No. 37 containing one rood and seven perches, bounded northwardly by the public road D, southeastwardly by ancient inclosed lands in the said township belonging to the said Richard Smith, southwardly by the strand or shore of Wallasey Pool and northwestwardly by the private road f, but in making this allotment to the said Robert Vyner it is meant and intended that the said Richard Smith who holds the lands in right of which this allotment is made under a lease for three lives from the said Robert Vyner, Esquire, is to hold this allotment along with his other lands during the continuance of the said lease. And I direct the fences on the northward, southward and northwest sides to be made and kept in repair by the said Richard Smith during the said lease and for ever afterwards to be kept in repair by the owners thereof.

Richard Smith's Leasehold.

Robert Vyner, Esq., No. 38, 0, 1, 12.

I also set out and allot unto the said Robert Vyner, Esquire, his heirs and assigns in respect of his said ancient lands, another piece or parcel of land part of the said commons and waste lands in Poolton Common aforesaid, marked in the said map No. 38, containing one rood and twelve perches, bounded northwardly and northwestwardly by the said public road D, southeastwardly by the said private road f, and southwardly by the strand or shore of Wallasey Pool, but in making this allotment to the said Robert Vyner it is meant and intended that the said Richard Smith who holds the lands in right of which this allotment is made under a lease for three lives from the said Robert Vyner shall hold and enjoy the allotment along with the other lands in the said lease during the continuance of his said lease. And I direct the whole of the fences round the said allotment to be made and kept in repair by the said Richard Smith during the continuance of the said lease and for ever thereafter kept in repair by the owner thereof.

Richard Smith's Leasehold.

Robert Vyner, Esquire, No. 39, 1, 1, 5.

I also set out and allot unto the said Robert Vyner, Esquire, his heirs and assigns in respect of his said ancient lands, a piece or parcel of land, other part of the said commons and waste lands in Poolton Common, marked in the said map No. 39, containing one acre one rood and five perches, bounded northwardly in part by an allotment No. 40 to Leigh Blundell and in other part by another allotment No. 41 to Mr. William Bird, eastwardly by the allotment No. 39A to the said Robert Vyner, southwardly in part by the said public road

D, and in other part by the new embankment across Wallasey Pool, and in other part by the Watercourse running to the said embankment and northwestwardly by ancient inclosed lands in the Township of Wallasey, belonging to Mrs. Wade's trustees. And I direct the fences on the southward side to be made and for ever thereafter kept in repair by the owner thereof.

 I also set out and allot unto the said Robert Vyner, Esquire, his heirs and assigns in respect of his said ancient land, a piece or parcel of land, other part of the said commons and waste lands called Poolton Common, marked in the said map No. 39A, containing thirteen perches, bounded northeastwardly by an allotment No. 41 to William Bird, southwardly by the said public road D, northwestwardly by an allotment No. 39 to the said Robert Vyner, but in making this allotment to the said Robert Vyner it is meant and intended that Peter Wilson who holds the land in respect of which this allotment is made under a lease for three lives from the said Robert Vyner shall hold and enjoy this allotment with the other lands comprised in the said lease during the continuance thereof. And I direct the fences on the southward and northwestward sides thereof shall be made and kept in repair by the said Peter Wilson during the continuance of the said lease and afterwards shall be kept in repair by the owner thereof. *Robert Vyner, No. 39A, 0, 0, 13. Peter Wilson's Leasehold.*

 I also set out and allot unto Robert Vyner, Esquire, his heirs and assigns, in respect of his said ancient lands, a piece or parcel of land, other part of the said commons and waste lands in Poolton Common, marked in the said map No. 44, containing thirteen perches, bounded northeastwardly by ancient inclosed lands in the Township of Poolton-cum-Seacombe, southwestwardly by the public road C. And I direct the fences on the southwestward side to be made and for ever thereafter kept in repair by the owner thereof. *Robert Vyner, No. 44, 0, 0, 13*

 I also set out and allot unto Robert Vyner, Esquire, his heirs and assigns, in respect of his same ancient lands, a piece or parcel of land, other part of the said commons and waste lands called Hook Common, marked in the said map No. 63, containing thirty-four perches, bounded northwardly and northwestwardly by ancient inclosed land in the Township of Poolton belonging to the said Robert Vyner, southeastwardly by an allotment No. 63A to the said Robert Vyner, and southwestwardly by the said private road a c, but in making this allotment to the said Robert Vyner it is meant and intended that Richard Smith, Esquire, who holds the lands in right of which this allotment is made under the said lease, for three lives is to hold this allotment along with the other lands during the continuance of the said lease. And I direct the fences on the southeastward and southwestward sides thereof to be made and kept in repair by the said Richard Smith during the continuance of the said lease and for ever afterwards to be kept in repair by the owner thereof. *Robert Vyner, No. 63, 0, 0, 34. Richard Smith's Leasehold.*

 I also set out and allot unto the said Robert Vyner, Esquire, his heirs and assigns, in respect of his same ancient lands, a piece or parcel of land, other part of the said commons and waste lands called the Hooks, marked on the said map No. 63A, containing twenty-one perches, bounded northeastwardly by ancient inclosed lands belonging to the said Robert Vyner, southeastwardly in part by *Robert Vyner, No. 63A, 0, 0, 21.*

ancient inclosed lands belonging to Richard Smith, Esquire, and in other part by an allotment No. 64 to the said Richard Smith, southwestwardly by the said private road a c, and northwestwardly by an allotment No. 63 to the said Robert Vyner, but in making this allotment to the said Robert Vyner it is meant and intended that Peter Wilson, who holds the lands in respect of which this allotment is made under the said lease, for three lives shall hold and enjoy this allotment with the other lands comprised in such lease during the continuance thereof. And I direct the fences on the southeastward and southwestward sides thereof to be made and kept in repair by the said Peter Wilson during the continuance of such lease and afterwards shall be kept in repair by the owner thereof.

Peter Wilson's Leasehold.

Robert Vyner, No. 66, 2, 3, 32

I also set out and allot unto Robert Vyner, Esquire, his heirs and assigns, in respect of his said ancient lands, another piece or parcel of lands, other part of the said commons and waste lands called the Hook Commons, marked in the said map No. 66, containing two acres three roods and thirty-two perches, bounded northwardly by ancient inclosed lands belonging to the said Robert Vyner, eastwardly in part by ancient inclosed lands in the Township of Poolton, belonging to James Mainwaring, Esquire, and in other part by an allotment to Mr. Samuel Smith, No. 67, southwestwardly by allotments to the said Richard Smith, No. 65 and No. 64, and northwestwardly in part by the said allotment No. 64, and in other part by ancient inclosed lands belonging to the said Richard Smith, but in making this allotment to the said Robert Vyner it is meant and intended that the said Richard Smith, who holds the lands in right of which this allotment is made, under the said lease for three lives is to hold this allotment together with the said lands during the continuance of the said lease. And I direct the fences on the said allotments to be made and kept in repair by the said Richard Smith during the continuance of the said lease and afterwards to be kept in repair by the owner thereof.

Richard Smith's Leasehold.

Samuel Smith, No. 7, 0, 0, 34.

I also set out and allot to Mr. Samuel Smith, his heirs and assigns, in right of his ancient inclosed lands in the said Township of Poolton-cum-Seacombe, a piece or parcel of land part of the said commons and waste lands on Seacombe Common, marked in the said map No. 7, containing 34 perches, bounded on the north by another allotment No 9 to the said Samuel Smith, on the east by ancient inclosed lands used as a garden, belonging to the said Samuel Smith, on the south side by a private road leading from the strand or shore of the River Mersey to a field belonging to Richard Smith, Esquire, and on the west in part by the said field, and in other part by a garden belonging to the said Samuel Smith, the same being an encroachment on the said commons by the said Samuel Smith. And I direct the fences on the north and south sides to be made and for ever hereafter kept in repair by the owner thereof.

Samuel Smith, No. 9, 0, 1, 5.

I also set out and allot to the said Samuel Smith, his heirs and assigns, in respect of his said ancient lands, another piece or parcel of land other part of the said commons and waste lands on Seacombe Common, marked in the said map No. 9, containing one rood and five perches, bounded northwardly by the allotment No. 10 to Richard Smith, Esquire, and eastwardly by the public road A, southwardly in part by the allotment No. 8, to the said Richard Smith, and in other part by ancient inclosed land used as a garden belonging to the said Samuel Smith, and in other part by the encroachment No. 7 allotted to the said Samuel Smith, westwardly by other ancient inclosed lands used as a garden belonging to the said Samuel Smith. And I direct the fences on the northward and eastward sides of the said allotment to be made and for ever thereafter kept in repair by the owner thereof.

I also set out and allot to the said Samuel Smith, his heirs and assigns, in respect of his said ancient lands, another piece or parcel of land other part of the said commons and waste lands on Seacombe Common, marked in the said map No. 28, containing one acre, one rood, and twenty-six perches, bounded northeastwardly by the said public road A, southeastwardly by the allotment No. 27 to Sir John Tobin, southwardly by ancient inclosed land of the said Samuel Smith, and northwestwardly in part by the allotment No. 29, to Richard Smith, Esquire, and in other part by the allotments No. 30, and No. 30B to James Mainwaring, Esquire. And I direct the fences on the northeastward and northwestward sides thereof to be made and for ever thereafter kept in repair by the owners thereof.
Samuel Smith, No. 28, 1, 1, 26

I also set out and allot to the said Samuel Smith, his heirs and assigns, in respect of his said ancient lands another piece or parcel other part of the said commons and waste lands in Seacombe Dale, marked in the said map No. 34, containing eight perches, bounded southeastwardly by ancient inclosed lands in the said township belonging to the said Samuel Smith, northwestwardly by the private road c, and northwardly by an allotment No. 33 to Mr. William Quirk. And I direct the fences on the northwest side to be made and for ever thereafter kept in repair by the owner thereof.
Samuel Smith, No. 34, 0, 0, 8.

I also set out and allot unto the said Samuel Smith, his heirs and assigns, in respect of his said ancient lands a piece or parcel of land other part of the said commons and waste lands called the Hook Common marked in the said map No. 67, containing one acre, one rood and seventeen perches, bounded northeastwardly by ancient inclosed lands in the said township of Poolton-cum-Seacombe belonging to James Mainwaring, Esquire, southeastwardly by an allotment No. 76 to the Master or Trustees of the Wallasey Grammar School in part, in other part by the private road a d, and in other part by an allotment No. 68 to the devisees of Thomas Johnston deceased, southwestwardly by the strand of Wallasey Pool, and northwestwardly in part by an allotment No. 65 to Richard Smith, Esquire, and in other part by an allotment No. 66 to Robert Vyner, Esquire. And I direct the fences on the southeastward and southward sides thereof to be made and for ever afterwards kept in repair by the owner thereof.
Samuel Smith, No. 67, 1, 1, 17

I also set out and allot unto the said Samuel Smith, his heirs and assigns, in respect of his said ancient lands a piece or parcel of land other part of the said commons and waste lands called the Hook Common marked in the said map No. 77, containing one acre and two roods, bounded northwardly by a private road marked a c, southeastwardly by an allotment No. 78 to Mr. William Quirk, southwestwardly by the strand of Wallasey Pool, and northwestwardly by the private road a c. And I direct the fences on the northward and southwestward and northwestward sides thereof to be made and for ever afterwards kept in repair by the owner thereof.
Samuel Smith, No. 77, 1, 2, 0.

54 Geo. III. Commissioner's Award, ch. lxxxvii.
Wallasey Inclosure.

Mr. William Quirk, No. 32, 1, 2, 30.

I also set out and allot unto the said Mr. William Quirk, his heirs and assigns, in respect of his ancient inclosed lands in the said township of Poolton-cum-Seacombe a piece or parcel of land other part of the said commons and waste lands in Seacombe Common marked in the said map No. 32, containing one acre, two roods and thirty perches, bounded northeastwardly and northwestwardly by the private road d, southeastwardly by the public road B, and southwestwardly by ancient inclosed lands belonging to the said William Quirk. And I direct the fences on the northeastward and southeastward and northwestward sides thereof to be made and for ever thereafter kept in repair by the owner thereof.

William Quirk, No. 33, 0, 0, 18.

I also set out and allot unto the said William Quirk, his heirs and assigns, in respect of his said ancient lands another piece or parcel of land other part of the said commons and waste lands in Seacombe Dale aforesaid, marked in the said map No. 33, and containing eighteen perches, bounded eastwardly by ancient inclosed lands of the said William Quirk, southwardly by allotment No. 34 to Mr. Samuel Smith, and westwardly by the private road c. And I direct the fences on the westward and southward sides thereof to be made and for ever afterwards kept in repair by the owner thereof.

William Quirk, No. 78, 1, 3, 36.

I also set out and allot unto the said William Quirk, his heirs and assigns, in respect of his said ancient lands, a piece or parcel of land other part of the said commons and waste lands called the Hooks Common, marked in the said map No. 78, containing one acre, three roods and thirty-six perches, bounded northwardly by the said private road a c, eastwardly by lands running along the fence of the ancient inclosed lands of the said William Quirk, by me given in exchange for the private road lately made by him through his field called the Big Cock Butts, southwestwardly by the strand or shore of Wallasey Pool, and northwestwardly by an allotment No. 77 to Samuel Smith, and I direct the fences on the southwestward, northward and northwestward sides thereof to be made and for ever afterwards kept in repair by the owner thereof.

W. Quirk, No. 79, 2, 0, 18

I also set out and allot unto the said William Quirk, his heirs and assigns, in respect of his said ancient lands a piece or parcel of land other part of the said commons and waste lands called the Hooks Common, marked on the said map No. 79, containing two acres and eighteen perches, bounded northeastwardly and eastwardly by the said private road marked a b, southwardly by the strand or shore of the Wallasey Pool, and northwestwardly by the lands running along the fence of the ancient inclosed lands of the said William Quirk, by me given in exchange for the private road lately made by him through his field called the Big Cock Butts. And I direct the fences on the northeastward, southward and eastward sides thereof to be made and for ever afterwards kept in repair by the owner thereof.

W. Quirk, No. 80, 0, 0, 11

I also set out and allot unto the said William Quirk, his heirs and assigns in respect of his said ancient lands, a piece or parcel of land other part of the said commons and waste lands called the Hooks Common, marked on the said map No. 80, containing eleven perches bounded eastwardly by the private road marked on the said map with the letter c, southwardly by the said land by me given in exchange to the said William Quirk, and northwestwardly by ancient inclosed land belonging to the said William Quirk, and I direct the fences on the southward and eastward sides thereof to be made and for ever afterwards kept in repair by the owner thereof.

I also set out and allot unto the Devisees in Trust named in the last Will and Testament of Thomas Johnson late of Seacombe, aforesaid, sailmaker, deceased, their heirs and assigns, in right of the ancient inclosed lands in the said township of Poolton-cum-Seacombe vested in them as such Devisees as aforesaid, and to the uses upon which the same ancient lands are limited, a piece or parcel of land other part of the said commons and waste lands in Seacombe Common, aforesaid, marked upon the said map No. 18, containing one rood and twenty-five perches bounded northeastwardly by the said public road A, southeastwardly by the allotment No. 17 to Joseph Cooper, southwardly by ancient inclosed land belonging to Mr. William Evans, and northwestwardly by allotment No. 25 to James Mainwaring, Esquire, and I direct the fences on the northeastward and northwestward sides thereof to be made, and for ever afterwards kept in repair by the owner thereof.

<small>Devisees of T. Johnson, No. 18, 0, 1, 25</small>

I also set out and allot unto the said Devisees in trust under the said Will of the said Thomas Johnson deceased, in respect of the ancient lands so vested in them in trust in manner aforesaid, a piece or parcel of land other part of the said commons and waste lands called the Hook Common, marked in the said map No. 68, containing two roods bounded northeastwardly by the private road a d, southeastwardly by an allotment to Messrs. Horne and Stackhouse No. 69, and southwardly by the Strand of Wallasey Pool, and northwestwardly by an allotment No. 67 to Mr. Samuel Smith. And I direct the fences on the northeastward, southeastward, and southward sides thereof, to be made and for ever afterwards kept in repair by the owner thereof.

<small>Devisees of T. Johnson, No. 68, 0, 2, 0.</small>

I also set out and allot unto Joseph Cooper, his heirs and assigns, in right of his ancient inclosed lands in the township of Poolton-cum-Seacombe, a piece or parcel of land other part of the said commons and waste lands adjoining the strand or shore of the River Mersey marked in the said map No. 6, containing eleven perches, bounded northeastwardly by the private road leading from the said strand of the River Mersey to a field of Richard Smith, Esquire, southeastwardly to the said strand, southwestwardly by the allotment No. 5 to the said Richard Smith, and northwestwardly by ancient inclosed land belonging to the said Joseph Cooper, the same being an encroachment on the said commons by the said Joseph Cooper. And I direct the whole of the fences belonging to the said allotment to be made and for ever thereafter kept in repair by the owner thereof.

<small>Joseph Cooper, No. 6, 0, 0, 11.</small>

I also set out and allot unto the said Joseph Cooper, his heirs and assigns, in respect of his said ancient lands, another piece or parcel of land other part of the said commons and waste lands in Seacombe Common marked in the said map No. 17, containing seventeen perches, bounded northeastwardly by the public road A, southeastwardly by the allotment No. 16 to Mr. William Evans, southwardly by land belonging to the said William Evans, and northwestwardly by an allotment No. 18 to the devisees of the late Thomas Johnson. And I direct the fences on the southeastward and northwestward sides thereof to be made and for ever afterwards kept in repair by the owner thereof.

<small>Joseph Cooper, No. 17, 0, 0, 17</small>

54 *Geo. III.*   Commissioner's Award,   ch. lxxxvii.
Wallasey Inclosure.

Joseph Cooper, No. 70, 0, 0, 31

I also set out and allot unto the said Joseph Cooper, his heirs and assigns, in respect of his said ancient lands, a piece or parcel of land other part of the said commons and waste lands called the Hook Common marked in the said map No. 70, containing thirty-one perches, bounded northeastwardly by the private road a d, southeastwardly in part by an allotment No. 71 to Joseph Evans, and in other part by an allotment No. 72 to William Evans, southwardly by the strand of Wallasey Pool, and northwestwardly by the allotment No. 69 to Messrs. Horne and Stackhouse. And I direct the fences on the northeastward, southwestward, and southward sides thereof, to be made and for ever afterwards kept in repair by the owner thereof.

William Evans, No. 16, 0, 0, 13.

I also set out and allot unto William Evans, his heirs and assigns, in right of his ancient inclosed lands in the said township of Poolton-cum-Seacombe, a piece or parcel of land other part of the said commons and waste lands on Seacombe Common marked in the said map No. 16, containing thirteen perches, bounded northeastwardly by the said public road A, southeastwardly by the private road marked c, southwardly by ancient inclosed lands of the said William Evans, and northwestwardly by the allotment No. 17 to the said Joseph Cooper. And I direct the fences on the northeastward and northwestward sides thereof, shall be made and for ever afterwards kept in repair by the owner thereof.

William Evans, No. 72, 0, 0, 14.

I also set out and allot unto the said William Evans, his heirs and assigns, in respect of his said ancient lands, a piece or parcel of land other part of the said commons and waste lands called the Hooks marked in the said map No. 72, containing fourteen perches, bounded northeastwardly by the said private road a d, southeastwardly in part by an allotment to the devisees of the late William Smith No. 75, other part by an allotment to Leigh Blundell No. 74, and in other part by an allotment to Ann Bennett No. 73, southwardly by the strand of Wallasey Pool and northwestwardly in part by an allotment No. 70 to Joseph Cooper, and in other part by an allotment No. 71 to Joseph Evans, and I direct the fences on the northeastward and southward and southeastward sides thereof to be made and for ever afterwards kept in repair by the owner thereof.

Devisees in Trust of William Smith, No. 13, 0, 0, 1.

I also set out and allot unto the devisees in trust named in the last will and testament of William Smith, late of Seacombe aforesaid, innkeeper, deceased, their heirs and assigns, in right of the land and hereditaments in the said township of Poolton-cum-Seacombe, and formerly belonging to the said William Smith, and vested in them as such devisees as aforesaid, to the uses upon which the same lands are limited, a piece or parcel of land other part of the said commons and waste lands in Seacombe Common marked in the said map No. 13, containing one perch bounded northeastwardly by the said public road A, southeastwardly and southwestwardly by a part of an allotment No. 12 to Thomas Blackburne, and northwestwardly by an allotment No. 14, to Richard Smith, and I direct the fences on the northeastward and northwestward sides thereof shall be made and for ever thereafter kept in repair by the owners thereof.

Devisees in Trust of William Smith, No. 75, 0, 0, 2.

I also set out and allot unto the said devisees in trust under the said Will of the said William Smith, their heirs and assigns, in respect of their said ancient lands vested in them in trust as aforesaid, a piece or parcel of land on part of the said commons and waste lands called the Hook Common, marked in the said map No. 75, containing two perches, bounded northeastwardly by the private road a d, southeastwardly by the private road a c, southwestwardly by an allotment to Leigh Blundell No. 74, and northwestwardly by an allotment to William Evans No. 72, and I direct the fences on the northeastward, southeastward and southwestward sides thereof to be made and for ever afterwards kept in repair by the owners thereof.

I also set out and allot unto Thomas Blackburne, his heirs and assigns, a piece or parcel of land other part of the said commons and waste lands on Seacombe Common marked on the said map No. 12, containing thirty-four perches, bounded northeastwardly by the public road A, southeastwardly by the allotment No. 11A to Anne Bennett, southwardly in part by ancient inclosed lands of the said Anne Bennett, and in other part by ancient inclosed lands of Richard Smith, Esquire, and northwestwardly in part by an allotment No. 15 to Richard Smith, and in other part by the allotment No. 13 to the devisees of William Smith the right to which said allotment belonged to Thomas Molyneux, in respect of his ancient lands in the said township of Poolton-cum-Seacombe, and was sold and disposed of by them to the said Thomas Blackburne to whom I have made this allotment in pursuance of the said Act, and I direct the fences on the northeast and northwest sides thereof shall be made and for ever afterwards kept in repair by the owner thereof. *Thomas Blackburne, No. 12, 0, 0, 34 Purchase from T. Molyneux.*

I also set out and allot unto the said Thomas Molyneux, his heirs and assigns, in respect of his said ancient inclosed lands in the said township of Poolton-cum-Seacombe, a piece or parcel of land part of the said commons and waste lands in Liscard Lane in the said Township of Poolton-cum-Seacombe, marked in the said map No. 52, containing nine perches, bounded northeastwardly by ancient inclosed lands belonging to the said Thomas Molyneux, southwardly by ancient inclosed lands belonging to James Mainwaring, southwestwardly by Liscard Lane aforesaid and northwestwardly by lands in Liscard allotted to the said Thomas Molyneux, the same being an encroachment made by the said Thomas Molyneux on the said waste lands. And I direct the fences on the southwest side thereof to be made and for ever afterwards kept in repair by the owner thereof. *Thomas Molyneux, No. 52, 0, 0, 9.*

I also set out and allot unto the said Thomas Molyneux, his heirs and assigns in respect of his said ancient lands, a piece or parcel of land, other part of the said commons and waste lands called the Hook Commons, marked in the said map No. 58, containing thirty-nine perches, bounded northeastwardly by the said private road a, c, southeastwardly in part by the allotment No. 59 to Mr. Twist, in other part by the allotment No. 60 to William Bird and southwestwardly by the allotment No. 56 to Mrs. Jackson, northwestwardly by the allotment No. 57 to the assignees of William Garner. And I direct the fences on the northeastward, southwestward and northwestward sides thereof to be made and for ever after kept in repair by the owner thereof. *Thomas Molyneux, No. 58, 0, 0, 39*

I also set out and allot unto Anne Bennett, her heirs and assigns in respect of her ancient inclosed lands in the said Township of Poolton-cum-Seacombe, a piece or parcel of land, other part of the said commons and waste lands in Seacombe Common aforesaid, marked in the said map No. 11, containing five perches, bounded *Anne Bennett, No. 11, 0, 0, 5.*

northeastwardly by the said private road a, southeastwardly by the private road b, southwestwardly by a garden belonging to the said Anne Bennett and northwestwardly by the allotment No. 12 hereinbefore made to the said Thomas Blackburne. And I direct the fences on the northeastward and northwestward sides thereof to be made and for ever thereafter kept in repair by the owner thereof.

Anne Bennett, No. 73, 0, 0, 6.

I also set out and allot unto the said Anne Bennett, her heirs and assigns in respect of her said ancient lands, a piece or parcel of land, other part of the said commons and waste lands called the Hook Common, marked in the said map No. 73, containing six perches, bounded northeastwardly by an allotment No. 74 made to Leigh Blundell, southeastwardly by the private road a c, southwardly by the Strand of Wallasey Pool and northwestwardly by the allotment No. 72 to William Evans. And I direct the fences on the northeastward, southeastward and southward sides thereof to be made and for ever afterwards kept in repair by the owner thereof.

Master or Trustee of Wallasey Free Grammar School, No. 20, 1, 0, 21.

I also set out and allot unto the master or the trustee of the Free Grammar School at Wallasey in respect of their ancient inclosed lands in the said Township of Poolton-cum-Seacombe, a piece or parcel of land, other part of the said commons and waste lands on Seacombe Common aforesaid. marked upon the said map No. 20, containing one acre and twenty-one perches or thereabouts, bounded northeastwardly by ancient inclosed lands belonging to Richard Smith, Esquire, southeastwardly by an allotment No. 19 to the said Richard Smith, southwestwardly by the public road marked A, and northwestwardly by an allotment No. 21 to Mrs. Jackson. And I direct the fences on the southeastward and southwestward sides thereof to be made and for ever afterwards kept in repair by the owner thereof.

Master or Trustee of Wallasey Free Grammar School, No. 76, 0, 2, 21.

I also set out and allot unto the said master or trustee of the Free Grammar School at Wallasey, in respect of their said ancient lands, a piece or parcel of land, other part of the said commons and waste lands called the Hook Common, marked in the said map No. 76, containing two roods and twenty-one perches, bounded northeastwardly in part by ancient inclosed lands belonging to James Mainwaring, Esquire, in other part by ancient inclosed lands belonging to the said master or trustee, southeastwardly by the private road a c, southwestwardly by the private road a d, and northwestwardly by an allotment No. 67 to Samuel Smith. And I direct the fences on the southeastward and southwestwardly sides thereof to be made and for ever afterwards kept in repair by the owner thereof.

Same, No. 81, 0, 3, 19.

I also set out and allot unto the said master or trustee aforesaid, in respect of their said ancient lands, a piece or parcel of land, other part of the said commons and waste lands called the Hook Common, marked in the said map No. 81, containing three roods and nineteen perches, bounded northeastwardly by ancient inclosed lands belonging to Richard Smith, Esquire, southeastwardly by ancient inclosed lands belonging to Joseph Cooper and James Mainwaring, Esquire, southwestwardly by the said private road a c, and northwestwardly by ancient inclosed lands belonging to the said master or trustee. And I direct the fences on the southwestward sides thereof to be made and for ever afterwards kept in repair by the owner thereof.

I also set out and allot unto Richard Evans, his heirs and assigns, in respect of his ancient inclosed lands in the said Township of Poolton-cum-Seacombe, a piece or parcel of land, other part of the said commons and waste lands on Seacombe Common aforesaid, marked upon the said map No. 22, containing one rood and thirty-nine perches, bounded northwardly by ancient inclosed lands belonging to Richard Smith, Esquire, southeastwardly by an allotment No. 21 to the said Mrs. Jackson, southwestwardly by the public road A, and northwestwardly by an allotment No. 23 to Messrs. Horne and Stackhouse. And I direct the fences on the southeastward and southwestward sides thereof to be made and for ever afterwards kept in repair by the owner thereof.

Richard Evans, No. 22, 0, 1, 39.

I also set out and allot unto the said Richard Evans, his heirs and assigns, in respect of his said ancient lands, a piece or parcel of land, other part of the said commons and waste lands called the Hook Common, marked on the said map No. 55, containing two roods and ten perches, bounded northeastwardly by the said private road a e, southeastwardly by an allotment No. 66 to Mrs. Jackson, southwestwardly and northwestwardly by the said allotment No. 54 and No. 54B to James Mainwaring, Esquire. And I direct the fences on the northeastward, southwestward, and northwestward sides thereof to be made and for ever afterwards kept in repair by the owner thereof.

Richard Evans, No. 55, 0, 2, 10.

I also set out and allot unto William Horne and Jonathan Stackhouse, their heirs and assigns, or to the person or persons entitled to an allotment under this my Award in respect of a piece or parcel of ancient inclosed land called the Pool sand hey, according to his, her, or their estate and interest therein, a piece or parcel of land, other part of the said commons and waste lands on Seacombe Common, marked on the said map No. 23, containing one rood and four perches, bounded northwardly by ancient inclosed lands belonging to Richard Smith, Esquire, southeastwardly by an allotment No. 22, to Richard Evans, southwestwardly by the said public road marked A, and northeastwardly by an allotment No. 24 to the said Richard Smith, and I direct the fences on the southeastward and southwestward sides thereof to be made and for ever afterwards kept in repair by the owner thereof.

Wm. Horne and Jon. Stackhouse, No. 23, 0, 1, 4.

I also set out and allot unto the said William Horne and Jonathan Stackhouse, or to the person or persons entitled as aforesaid and in manner aforesaid their heirs and assigns, a piece or parcel of land other part of the said commons and waste lands called the Hook Common, marked on the said map No. 69, containing one rood and twelve perches bounded northeastwardly by the private road a, d, southeastwardly by an allotment to Joseph Cooper No. 70, and southwardly by the strand of Wallasey Pool and northwestwardly by the said allotment No. 68 to the Devisees of the late Thomas Johnson, and I direct the fences on the northeastward, southeastward and southward sides thereof to be made and for ever afterwards kept in repair by the owner thereof.

Wm. Horne and J. Stackhouse, No. 69, 0, 1, 12.

I also set out and allot unto Joseph Evans his heirs and assigns, in right of his ancient lands in the said township of Poolton-cum-Seacombe aforesaid a piece or parcel of land other part of the said commons and waste lands on Seacombe Common, marked on the said map No. 2, containing six perches bounded northeastwardly by an

Joseph Evans, No. 2, 0, 0, 6.

K

allotment No. 3 to Mrs. Wade's Trustees, southeastwardly by the messuages belonging to the said Joseph Evans, southwestwardly and northwestwardly by an allotment No. 1 to Richard Smith, Esquire, and I direct the fences on the southwestward and northwestward sides thereof to be made and for ever afterwards kept in repair by the owner thereof.

Joseph Evans, No. 71, 0, 0, 7.

I also set out and allot unto the said Joseph Evans his heirs and assigns, in respect of his said ancient lands, a piece or parcel of land other part of the said commons and waste lands called the Hook Common, marked in the said map No. 71, containing seven perches, bounded northeastwardly by the said private road a d, southeastwardly by an allotment No. 72 to William Evans, and southwestwardly and northwestwardly by an allotment No. 70 to Joseph Cooper, and I direct the fences on the northeastward and southeastward and southward sides thereof to be made and for ever afterwards kept in repair by the owners thereof.

Samuel Whitby, No. 42, 0, 1, 12

I also set out and allot unto Samuel Whitby his heirs and assigns, a piece or parcel of land part of the said commons and waste lands on Poolton Common, in the said Township of Poolton-cum-Seacombe marked in the said map No. 42, containing one rood and twelve perches bounded northwardly by the public road marked C, southeastwardly by ancient inclosed lands belonging to the assignees of William Garner, southwestwardly by an allotment No. 41 to William Bird, and northwestwardly by an allotment No. 43 to Joseph Twist, the right to which said allotment No. 42 belonged to the Assignees of the estate and effects of William Garner, in respect of his ancient inclosed lands in the said township of Poolton-cum-Seacombe has been sold and disposed of by them to the said Samuel Whitby, reserving to themselves the exclusive right of quay to whom I have made this allotment in pursuance of the said Act, and I direct the fences on the northward and southwestward sides thereof to be made and for ever afterwards kept in repair by the owner thereof.

Purchase from Garner's Assignees.

Assignees of Wm. Garner, No. 57, 0, 0, 31

I also set out and allot unto the said assignees of William Garner, their heirs and assigns, in respect of their said ancient lands, a piece or parcel of land other part of the said commons and waste lands called the Hook Common, marked in the said map No. 57, containing thirty-one perches, bounded northeastwardly by the private road a e, southeastwardly by an allotment No. 58, to Thomas Molyneux, southwestwardly and northwestwardly by an allotment No. 56 to Mrs. Jackson. And I direct the fences on the northeastward, southwestward, and northwestward sides thereof to be made and for ever afterwards kept in repair by the owner thereof.

Joseph Twist, No. 43, 0, 0, 13

I also set out and allot unto Joseph Twist, his heirs and assigns, in respect of his ancient inclosed lands in the said Township of Poolton-cum-Seacombe, a piece or parcel of land other part of the said commons and waste lands on Poolton Common, marked on the said map No. 43, containing thirteen perches, bounded northeastwardly by the public road C, southeastwardly by an allotment No. 42 to Samuel Whitby, southwestwardly and northwestwardly by an allotment No. 41 to William Bird. And I direct the fences on the northeastward, southeastward, and southwestward sides thereof to be made and for ever afterwards kept in repair by the owner thereof.

And I also set out and allot unto the said Joseph Twist, his heirs and assigns, in respect of his said ancient lands, a piece or parcel of land part of the said commons and waste lands in Mill Lane, marked on the said map No. 50, containing eighteen perches, bounded northeastwardly by a private road leading to a field belonging to Robert Vyner, southeastwardly by ancient inclosed lands belonging to the said Joseph Twist, southwestwardly by an allotment No. 49 to the said trustees of Wallasey School, and northwestwardly by Mill Lane aforesaid. And I direct the fences on the northeastward and northwestward sides thereof to be made and for ever afterwards kept in repair by the owner thereof. *Joseph Twist, No. 50, 0, 0, 18*

I also set out and allot unto the said Joseph Twist, his heirs and assigns, in respect of his said ancient lands, a piece or parcel of land other part of the said commons and waste lands called the Hook Common, marked in the said map No. 59, containing seventeen perches, bounded northeastwardly by the said private road a e, southeastwardly and southwestwardly by the allotment No. 60 to William Bird, northwestwardly by the allotment No. 58 to Thomas Molyneux. And I direct the fences on the northeastward, southwestward, and northwestward sides thereof to be made and for ever afterwards kept in repair by the owner thereof. *Joseph Twist, No. 59, 0, 0, 17*

I also set out and allot unto William Bird, his heirs and assigns, in respect of his ancient inclosed lands in the said Township of Poolton-cum-Seacombe, a piece or parcel of the said commons and waste lands on Poolton Common aforesaid, marked on the said map No. 41, containing three roods and thirty perches, bounded northeastwardly in part by the said public road C, in other part by an allotment No. 43, to Joseph Twist, and by an allotment No. 42 to Samuel Whitby, southeastwardly in part by an allotment No. 43, to the said Joseph Twist, in other part by the public road marked on the said map D, southwestwardly by allotments Nos. 39 and 39A to Robert Vyner, Esquire, and northwestwardly by an allotment No. 40 to Leigh Blundell. And I direct that so much of the fences as adjoins the public road C, and the fence on the southeastwardly side adjoining the allotment No. 43 to Joseph Twist, and also the fences to the public road D, and those on the southwestwardly side to be made and for ever afterwards kept in repair by the owner thereof. *William Bird, No. 41, 0, 3, 30.*

I also set out and allot unto the said William Bird, his heirs and assigns, in respect of his ancient lands a piece or parcel of land other part of the said commons and waste lands called the Hook Common marked on the said map No. 60, containing two roods and thirty-one perches, bounded northeastwardly in part by an allotment to Mr. Twist No. 59, and in other part by the said private road a e, southeastwardly by an allotment to Leigh Blundell No. 61, southwestwardly by an allotment No. 54 to James Mainwaring, Esquire, northwestwardly in part by an allotment No. 56 to Mrs. Jackson, in other part by an allotment No. 58 to Thomas Molyneux, and in other part by an allotment No. 59 to Joseph Twist. And I direct the fences on the northwestward and southwestward sides thereof, and as much of the fence on the northeastward side thereof as adjoins the private road marked a e to be made and for ever afterwards kept in repair by the owner thereof. *William Bird, No. 60, 0, 2, 31*

54 Geo. III.   Commissioner's Award,   ch. lxxxvii.
Wallasey Inclosure.

Leigh Blundell, Esq., No. 3, 0, 0, 13.

I also set out and allot unto Leigh Blundell, Esquire, his heirs and assigns a piece or parcel of land part of the said commons and waste lands on Seacombe Common marked on the said map No. 3, containing thirteen perches, bounded northeastwardly and northwestwardly by an allotment No. 1 to Richard Smith, Esquire, southeastwardly in part by the strand or shore of the River Mersey, and in other part by certain messuages belonging to John Davies and the said Leigh Blundell, and southwestwardly by an allotment No. 2 to Joseph Evans. And I direct the fences on the southwestward and northwestward sides thereof, and also the fences adjoining the strand or shore of the River Mersey to be made and for ever afterwards kept in repair by the owner thereof.

And I do hereby reserve unto the owner of the cottage now belonging to John Davies, full and free permission at all times hereafter to enter upon the said hereinbefore described allotment for the sole purpose of repairing the roof or walls of his said cottage.

Leigh Blundell, Esq., No. 40, 0, 2, 12.

Purchase from Wade's Trustees.

I also set out and allot unto the said Leigh Blundell, his heirs and assigns, a piece or parcel of land other part of the said commons and waste lands on Poolton Common marked on the said map No. 40, containing two roods and twelve perches, bounded northeastwardly by the public road C, southeastwardly by an allotment No. 41 to William Bird, southwardly by an allotment No. 39 to Robert Vyner, Esquire, and westwardly in part by ancient inclosed lands in the township of Wallasey belonging to the trustees of Margaret Wade, and in other part by the common land in the said township of Wallasey called Wallasey Brake, the right to which said two last hereinbefore described allotments belonged to the trustees of Mrs. Margaret Wade in respect of their ancient lands in the said township of Poolton-cum-Seacombe, who have sold and disposed of the same to the said Leigh Blundell to whom I have made the said allotments in pursuance of the said Act. And I direct all the fences on every side of the said allotment to be made and for ever afterwards kept in repair by the owner thereof.

Leigh Blundell, "Exchanged Land No. 1," 11 square yards.

I also set out and allot unto the said Leigh Blundell, his heirs and assigns, a piece or parcel of land in the said township of Poolton-cum-Seacombe marked on the said map "Exchanged Land No. 1," containing eleven square yards or thereabouts, adjoining to the shore of the River Mersey and the garden of the said Leigh Blundell, which said piece or parcel of land hereinbefore allotted to the said Leigh Blundell was part of the lands of Richard Smith, Esquire, in the said township of Poolton-cum-Seacombe, and has been taken in exchange by the said Leigh Blundell from the said Richard Smith, Esquire, for the allotment No. 14 to the said Richard Smith.

Leigh Blundell, No. 61, 0, 2, 7.

Purchased from Wade's Trustees.

I also set out and allot unto the said Leigh Blundell a piece or parcel of land other part of the said commons and waste lands called the Hook Common, marked on the said map No. 61, containing two roods and seven perches, bounded northeastwardly by the said private road a e, southeastwardly by an allotment No. 62 to Sir John Tobin, southwestwardly by an allotment No. 54 to James Mainwaring, Esquire, and northwestwardly by an allotment No. 60 to William Bird, the right to which said allotment No. 61 belonged to the trustees of Margaret Wade in respect of their said ancient lands, and was sold and disposed of by them to the said Leigh Blundell to whom I have made this allotment in pursuance of the said Act. And I direct the fences on the northeastward, southwestward and northwestward sides thereof to be made and for ever afterwards kept in repair by the owners thereof.

I also set out and allot unto Leigh Blundell, his heirs and assigns, in respect of his ancient inclosed lands in the said township of Poolton-cum-Seacombe, a piece or parcel of land other part of the said commons and waste lands called Hook Common marked in the said map No. 74, containing three perches, bounded northeastwardly by an allotment to the devisees of William Smith deceased No. 75, northeastwardly by the private road a c, and southwardly by an allotment to Ann Bennett No. 73, and northwestwardly by an allotment No. 72 to William Evans. And I direct the fences on the northeastward, southeastward, and southwestward sides thereof to be made and for ever after kept in repair by the owner thereof. *Leigh Blundell, No. 74, 0, 0, 3.*

And with respect to a certain other tract or parcel of common land within the parish of West Kirby in the said county called the Carr, I the said Commissioner do make my Award as follows, that is to say in the first place, I do hereby particularise and describe the roads and ways so set out by me through and over the same last mentioned tract or parcel of common land aforesaid in manner following, that is to say :—

One private occupation road marked with the letter a, in part of the said tract or parcel of common land called the Carr, of the width of eight yards commencing at the northeast corner of the ancient occupation road leading from the village of Grange to the Carr, and running from thence in a northeastwardly direction along the northwest side of a field belonging to John Leigh, Esquire, near to the gate leading into the said field and thence turning off and running northwardly as far as the southeast corner of an allotment No. 4 hereinafter allotted to the said John Leigh. *Private Road a.*

Another private occupation road marked in the said map with the letter b, of the width of eight yards, other part of the said Carr commencing at the east side of the last-mentioned road marked a, and running thence in an eastwardly direction to an allotment on the said Carr No. 10 to the said John Leigh. *Private Road b.*

One other private occupation road marked in the said map with the letter c, of the width of eight yards, other part of the said Carr commencing at the north end of the ancient occupation road leading from the village of Newton to the Carr, and running thence in a northwardly direction to an allotment No. 21 to the trustees of the Woodchurch Grammar School, and thence turning off and running in a westwardly direction to an allotment on the said Carr No. 13 to Sir Thomas Stanley Massey Stanley, Baronet. *Private Road c.*

One other private occupation road marked in the said map with the letter d, of the width of six yards, other part of the said Carr commencing at the north end of the said road from the village of Newton to the Carr, and branching from the south end of the last-mentioned road c, and running from thence in an eastwardly direction along ancient inclosed lands belonging to the Reverend Roger Jackson to a field in the township of Grange called the Holmes belonging to the said John Leigh. *Private Road d.*

Private Road e.	One other private occupation road other part of the said Carr marked on the said map with the letter e, of the width of eight yards, commencing on the east side of the before-mentioned road c, at the northwest corner of an allotment No. 23 to the Reverend Roger Jackson, and running from thence in an eastwardly direction to an allotment No. 24 to the trustees of the poor of West Kirby.
	And I the said Commissioner do direct that the before-described private or occupation road marked d, shall be for ever afterwards maintained and kept in repair by the owners or occupiers of the ancient inclosed lands to which the road leads, and shall be solely used and enjoyed by such owner or occupier, and that the other four private or occupation roads by me set out as aforesaid, shall be for ever afterwards maintained and kept in repair by the several owners or occupiers of the land adjoining to or abutting on the same, subject to the footway hereinafter described.
Private Road f.	One other private occupation road other part of the said Carr marked on the said map with the letter f, of the width of eight yards, commencing at the south end of the ancient occupation road leading from Little Meols to the Carr, and thence running in a southwardly direction to an allotment No. 12 to the said Sir Thomas Stanley Massey Stanley, Baronet, and thence turning off and running in an eastwardly direction as far as the northeast corner of an allotment No. 25, to the said trustees for the poor of West Kirby. And I the said Commissioner do direct that the said last-described private or occupation road shall be for ever afterwards maintained and kept in repair by the owner or occupier of the allotments Nos. 26 and 27 to the Reverend Edward Stanley and shall be solely used and enjoyed by him or them subject to the footway hereinafter described.
Footway No. 1.	A footway marked No. 1, over part of the said Carr commencing at the east end of the ancient occupation road, leading from the village of Grange along the private road marked a, to and along the private road b, and running from thence in a northeastwardly direction over the allotments No. 10 and No. 11 to the said John Leigh and over an allotment No. 12 to the said Sir Thomas Stanley Massey Stanley to the southwest corner of the said private road f, and thence continuing along part of the road f to the said south end of the ancient occupation road from Little Meols.
Footway No. 2.	One other footway marked No. 2 over part of the said Carr and commencing at the south end of the ancient occupation road leading from the village of Little Meols over and along part of the said road marked f, and thence to the southwest corner thereof and running from thence in a southeastwardly direction over allotment on the said Carr No. 12 to the said Sir Thomas Stanley Massey Stanley over the allotment No. 19 to the trustees of Witton School and over the allotment No. 21 to the trustees of the Woodchurch Grammar School to the northeast corner of the said private road c, and over and along the same road to the north end of the ancient occupation road leading from the said village of Newton, and I the said Commissioner do direct that the necessary platts over the public drain on the said Carr where the before described footways crossed, the said drain shall be laid over the same and for ever afterwards maintained and kept in repair by the owners or occupiers of the several allotments on the said Carr and all other platts and stiles for the said footways shall be made and for ever afterwards maintained and

kept in repair by the owners or occupiers of the allotments over which the said footways are before described to pass.

And in further execution of the said Act I have set out and made a certain public drain on the said Carr, marked on the said map with the words "Public Drain," commencing at the ancient ditch or water course between the ancient inclosed lands of the Reverend Edward Stanley and the said John Leigh and running in an irregular course in a southeastwardly and eastwardly direction across the said Carr to the ancient inclosed lands belonging to the Trustees for the Poor of West Kirby, and from thence running along the ancient fence in a northwardly direction to the fender or drain at Tornall Green. And I direct that the said public drain be from time to time for ever hereafter amended, cleansed and repaired by and at the expense of the owners or occupiers of the allotments on the said Carr in the proportions and according to a rate by me made for the same, and which is written in the margin of the said map of the Carr annexed to this my Award under the direction of a person or persons to be from time to time appointed by the major part in value of the owners of the several allotments upon the said Carr according to the said rates who shall attend at a meeting to be called for that purpose by any three of the said owners of which meeting notice shall be first given at least two Sundays in the Parish Church of West Kirby before the same shall be held. *Public drain.*

And in further execution of the said recited acts I allot and set out a piece or parcel of land, part of the said Carr for the purpose of getting marl for the use of the lord and landowners of the Township of Grange, and of the landowners of the Township of Newton-cum-Larton and Little Meols, that is to say a piece or parcel of land containing twenty-one perches, bounded northwardly and westwardly by an allotment No. 14 to the Trustees of the Poor of West Kirby, eastwardly by the private road marked on the said map with the letter c, and southwestwardly by ancient inclosed lands belonging the said Trustees of the Poor of West Kirby. *"Marl," 0, 0, 21.*

And in the next place I set out and allot unto the said John Leigh, his heirs and assigns, in respect of his royalty as Lord of the Manor of Grange aforesaid, the two pieces or parcels of land hereinafter described and respectively marked No. 1 and No. 1A, part of the said tract or parcel of common land called the Carr, the same containing together eleven acres, that is to say, a piece or parcel of land marked on the said map No. 1, containing five acres three roods and eight perches, bounded northwardly by an allotment No. 2 to the said Sir Thomas Stanley Massey Stanley, eastwardly and southeastwardly by a private road marked on the said map with the letter a, and southwestwardly in part by the ancient road there leading to Grange, and in other part ancient inclosed lands belonging to the said John Leigh. And I direct the fences on the northward, eastward, and southeastward sides thereof to be made and for ever afterwards kept in repair by the owner thereof. *John Leigh, Esq. (Royalty). No. 1, 5, 3, 8.*

Another piece or parcel of land, part of the said Carr, marked on the said map No. 1A, containing five acres and thirty-two perches, bounded northwardly in part by an allotment No. 8 to the said John Leigh, and in other part by the private road marked on the said map with the letter b, eastwardly by an allotment No. 9 to the said *No. 1a, 5, 0, 32*

John Leigh, southeastwardly by ancient inclosed lands belonging to the said John Leigh, and westwardly in part by the private road marked on the said map a, and in other part by the said allotment No. 8 to the said John Leigh. And I direct the fences on the northward, eastward, and westward sides thereof to be made and for ever afterwards kept in repair by the owner thereof.

John Leigh, Esq., No. 6, 12, 2, 23.

And in further execution of the said Acts I do hereby set out and allot the remainder of the said tract or parcel of common land called Newton Carr in manner following (that is to say), I set out and allot unto the said John Leigh, his heirs and assigns, in right of his ancient inclosed lands in the Township of Grange, a piece or parcel of land, other part of the said Carr, marked on the said map No. 6, containing twelve acres two roods and twenty-three perches, bounded northwardly by an allotment No. 27 to the Reverend Edward Stanley, eastwardly by an allotment No. 11 to the said John Leigh, southwardly and southwestwardly by the public drain marked on the said map "Public Drain" between this allotment and allotments No. 7 and No. 7A to the said John Leigh, and westwardly by an allotment No. 5 to the said John Leigh. And I direct the fences on the northward and eastward sides thereof to be made and for ever afterwards kept in repair by the owner thereof.

John Leigh, Esq., No. 7A, 12, 1, 19.

I also set out and allot unto the said John Leigh, his heirs and assigns, in respect of his same ancient inclosed lands, a piece or parcel of land, other part of the said Carr, and marked on the said map No. 7A, containing twelve acres one rood and nineteen perches, bounded northwardly by an allotment No. 6 to the said John Leigh, eastwardly by allotment No. 7 to the said John Leigh, southwardly by a private road marked on the said map b, and westwardly in part by a private road marked in the map a, and in other part by an allotment No. 4 to the said John Leigh. And I direct the fences on the eastward and southward sides thereof and so much of the fence on the westward side as adjoins the said private road a, to be made and for ever afterwards kept in repair by the owner thereof.

John Leigh. Esq., No. 9, 7, 3, 5.

I also set out and allot unto the said John Leigh, his heirs and assigns, in respect of his same ancient land, a piece or parcel of land other part of the said Carr, marked on the said map No. 9, containing seven acres three roods and five perches, bounded northwardly by the said private road b, eastwardly by an allotment No. 10 to the said John Leigh, southwardly by ancient inclosed lands belonging to the said John Leigh, and westwardly by an allotment No. 1A to the said John Leigh. And I direct the fences on the northward and eastward sides thereof to be made and for ever afterward kept in repair by the owner thereof.

John Leigh, Esq., No. 7, 0, 3, 39.

I also set out and allot unto the said John Leigh, his heirs and assigns, in respect of his ancient inclosed lands in the Township of Newton-cum-Larton, a piece or parcel of land other part of the said Carr, marked on the said map No. 7, containing three roods and thirty-nine perches, bounded northwardly by the said public drain between this allotment and the allotment No. 6 to the said John Leigh, eastwardly by an allotment No. 10 to the said John Leigh, southwardly by the said private road marked b, and westwardly by an allotment No. 7A, to the said John Leigh. And I direct the fences on the eastward and southward sides thereof to be made and for ever afterwards kept in repair by the owner thereof.

I also set out and allot unto the said John Leigh, his heirs and assigns, a piece or parcel of land other part of the said Carr, marked on the said map No. 8, containing fourteen perches, bounded northwardly by the said private road b, eastwardly and southwardly by an allotment No. 1A to the said John Leigh, and westwardly by the said private road a, the right to which said allotment, marked No. 8, belonged to Thomas Daulby, in respect of his ancient inclosed lands in the said Township of Grange, and was sold and disposed of by him to the said John Leigh to whom I have made this allotment in pursuance of this Act. And I direct the fences on the northward and westward sides thereof to be made and for ever afterwards kept in repair by the owner thereof.

John Leigh, Esq., No. 8, 0, 0, 14.

I also set out and allot unto the said John Leigh, his heirs and assigns, in right of certain closes or parcels of ancient inclosed land in the said Township of Grange, mentioned and contained in certain indentures of lease and release bearing date the sixth and seventh days of December, one thousand seven hundred and eighty-one, made or expressed to be made between William Glegg, Esquire, of the one part and Felix Doran, Esquire, of the other part, and in certain other indentures of lease and release, bearing date the twenty-ninth and thirtieth days of July, one thousand seven hundred and ninety-six and made between the said Felix Doran of the one part and the said John Leigh of the other part, a piece or parcel of land other part of the said Carr, marked on the said map No. 4, containing five acres, two roods, and thirty-nine perches, bounded northeastwardly by the said public drain between this allotment and an allotment No. 5 to the said John Leigh, eastwardly by an allotment No. 7A to the said John Leigh, southwardly in part by the said private road a, and in other part by an allotment to the Reverend Roger Jackson, No. 3, southeastwardly and southwestwardly by ancient inclosed lands in the said Township of Grange belonging to the said John Leigh. And I direct the fences on the eastward and southward sides thereof to be made and for ever afterwards kept in repair by the owner thereof.

John Leigh, Esq., No. 4, 5, 2, 39.

I also set out and allot unto the said John Leigh, his heirs and assigns, in right of the said closes or parcels of ancient land, a piece or parcel of land other part of the said Carr marked on the said map No. 5, containing three acres three roods and twenty-eight perches, bounded northeastwardly by an allotment No. 27 to the Reverend Edward Stanley, eastwardly by an allotment No. 6 to the said John Leigh, southwestwardly by an allotment No. 4 to the said John Leigh, and northwestwardly by ancient inclosed lands in the township of Little Meols belonging to the said Reverend Edward Stanley. And I direct the fences on the northwestward and eastward sides thereof, to be made and for ever afterwards kept in repair by the owner thereof.

John Leigh, Esq., No. 5, 3, 3, 28.

I also set out and allot unto the said John Leigh, his heirs and assigns, in right of the said closes or parcels of ancient land, a piece or parcel of land other part of the said Carr marked on the said map No. 10, containing twelve acres three roods and twenty-eight perches, bounded northwardly by the said public drain between this allotment and an allotment No. 11 to the said John Leigh, eastwardly by an allotment No. 13 to the said Sir Thomas Stanley Massey Stanley, southwardly by ancient inclosed lands in the said township of Grange

John Leigh, Esq., No. 10, 12, 3, 28.

belonging to the said John Leigh, and westwardly in part by an allotment No. 9 to the said John Leigh, in other part by a private road b, and in other part by an allotment No. 7 to the said John Leigh. And I direct the fences on the eastward side thereof to be made and for ever afterwards kept in repair by the owner thereof.

John Leigh, Esq., No. 11, 6, 3, 38.

I also set out and allot unto the said John Leigh, his heirs and assigns, in right of the before mentioned closes or parcels of ancient land other part of the said Carr marked on the said map No. 11, and containing six acres three roods and thirty-eight perches, bounded northwardly by an allotment No. 27 to the Reverend Edward Stanley, eastwardly by an allotment No. 12 to the said Sir Thomas Stanley Massey Stanley, southwardly by the said "Public Drain" between this allotment and an allotment No. 10 to the said John Leigh, and westwardly by an allotment No. 6 to the said John Leigh. And I direct the fences on the northward and eastward sides thereof to be made and for ever afterwards kept in repair by the owner thereof.

Sir Thomas Stanley, No. 2, 4, 1, 15.

I also set out and allot unto Sir Thomas Stanley Massey Stanley, baronet, in respect of his ancient inclosed land in the township of Newton-cum-Larton in the said parish of West Kirby, for his life or to the uses upon which the said ancient inclosed lands are limited, a piece or parcel of land other part of the said Carr marked on the said map No. 2, containing four acres one rood and fifteen perches, bounded northwardly in part by ancient inclosed lands belonging to the Reverend Roger Jackson, and in other part by an allotment No. 3 to the said Reverend Roger Jackson, eastwardly by the said private road a, southwardly by an allotment No. 1 to the said John Leigh, and westwardly in part by ancient inclosed lands belonging to the said Sir Thomas Stanley Massey Stanley, and in other part by ancient inclosed lands in the township of Grange belonging to the said John Leigh, and I direct the fences on the northward and eastward sides thereof, to be made and for ever afterwards kept in repair by the owner thereof.

Sir Thomas Stanley, No. 12, 6, 0, 24

I also set out and allot unto the said Sir Thomas Stanley Massey Stanley, Baronet, as aforesaid, in respect of his said ancient inclosed lands a piece or parcel of land other part of the said Carr marked on the said map No. 12, and containing six acres and twenty-four perches, bounded northwardly in part by an allotment No. 27 to the Reverend Edward Stanley, and in other part by a private road marked in the said map f, eastwardly by an allotment No. 19 to the trustees of the Witton School, southwardly by the said public drain between this allotment and allotment No. 13 to the said Sir Thomas Stanley Massey Stanley, and westwardly by an allotment No. 11 to the said John Leigh, and I direct that so much of the northward fence as adjoins the allotment No. 27 to the Reverend Edward Stanley, and the whole of the eastward fence thereof to be made and for ever afterwards kept in repair by the owner thereof.

Sir Thomas Stanley, No. 13, 10, 3, 15.

I also set out and allot unto the said Sir Thomas Stanley Massey Stanley as aforesaid, in right of his ancient inclosed lands a piece or parcel of land other part of the said Carr marked on the said map No. 13, containing ten acres three roods and fifteen perches, bounded northwardly by the said public drain between this allotment and an allotment No. 12 to the said Sir Thomas Stanley Massey Stanley eastwardly in part by an allotment No. 18 to the trustees of Witton School, in other part by a private road marked in the said map C, in

54 Geo. III.   Commissioner's Award,   ch. lxxvii.   139
                 Wallasey Inclosure.

other part by an allotment No. 16 to Josiah Day, in other part by an allotment No. 15 to Thomas Bloor, and in other part by an allotment No. 14 to the trustees of West Kirby School, southwardly in part by ancient inclosed lands belonging to the trustees for the poor of West Kirby, and in other part by ancient inclosed lands belonging to the said John Leigh, and westwardly by an allotment No. 10 to the said John Leigh, and I direct the fences on the eastward side thereof to be made and for ever afterwards kept in repair by the owner thereof.

I also set out and allot unto the trustees or trustee named and appointed in and by the last will and testament of Thomas Bennett, deceased, for the benefit of the poor of West Kirby or to the person or persons entitled thereto in respect of the ancient inclosed estates or lands in the said township of Grange called the Newbold and the Rakehouse to the uses upon which such ancient lands and estates are limited a piece or parcel of land other part of the said Carr marked on the said map No. 14, containing four acres one rood and twenty-three perches, bounded northwardly by an allotment No. 15 to Thomas Bloor, eastwardly in part by a private road marked in the said map C, and in other part by the allotment by me set out on the said Carr for the purpose of the inhabitants of the several townships of Grange, Little Meols and Newton-cum-Larton getting marl therein, southwardly by ancient inclosed lands belonging to the said trustees for the poor of West Kirby, and westwardly by an allotment No. 13 to Sir Thomas Stanley Massey Stanley, and I direct the fences on the northward and eastward sides thereof to be made and for ever afterwards kept in repair by the owner thereof.

Trustees of T. Bennett, No. 14, 4, 1, 23

I also set out and allot unto the said Trustees or persons aforesaid, and in manner aforesaid and in respect to the said ancient lands a piece or parcel of land other part of the said Carr marked in the said map No. 24, containing eleven acres and three perches bounded northwardly by the said public drain between this allotment and an allotment No. 25 to the said Trustees, and an allotment to the Reverend Edward Stanley marked No. 26, northeastwardly, southeastwardly and southwardly by ancient inclosed lands in the said township of Grange belonging to the said Trustees and the said John Leigh, and westwardly in part by the said allotment No. 23 to the Reverend Roger Jackson, in other part by the private road e, and in other part by an allotment No. 22 to the devisee of Newport Urmson, and I direct the fence on the westward side thereof to be made and for ever afterwards kept in repair by the owner thereof.

Trustees of T. Bennett, No. 24, 11, 0, 3

I also set out and allot unto the said Trustees or persons aforesaid, and in manner aforesaid in respect of the said ancient lands a piece or parcel of land, other part of the said Carr marked in the said map No. 25, containing twelve acres and sixteen perches, bounded northwardly by the private road f, eastwardly by the allotment No. 26 to the Reverend Edward Stanley, southwardly by the said "public drain" between this allotment and an allotment to the said Trustees, No. 24 and an allotment No. 22 to the devisee of Newport Urmson, and westwardly by the said allotment No. 20 to the trustees of the Free Grammar School at Woodchurch, and I direct the fences on the eastward side thereof to be made and for ever afterwards kept in repair by the owners thereof.

Trustees of T. Bennett, No. 25, 12, 0, 16.

54 Geo. III. Commissioner's Award, ch. lxxxvii.
Wallasey Inclosure.

Thomas Bloor, No. 15, 2, 1, 30.
I also set out and allot unto Thomas Bloor, his heirs and assigns, in right of his ancient inclosed land in the said township of Newton-cum-Larton, a piece or parcel of land, other part of the said Carr marked on the said map No. 15, and containing two acres, one rood and thirty perches bounded northwardly by an allotment No. 16 to Josiah Day, eastwardly by the said private road C, southwardly by an allotment No. 14 to the trustees for the poor of West Kirby, and westwardly by an allotment No. 13 to Sir Thomas Stanley Massey Stanley, and I direct the fences on the northward and eastward sides thereof to be made and for ever afterwards kept in repair by the owner thereof.

Josiah Day, No. 16, 4, 3, 33
I also set out and allot unto Josiah Day, his heirs and assigns, in right of his ancient inclosed lands in the said township of Newton-cum-Larton, a piece or parcel of land, other part of the said Carr marked on the said map No. 16, containing four acres, three roods and thirty-three perches bounded northwardly in part by the said private road C, and in other part by an allotment No. 17 to Daniel Daulby, and eastwardly in part by the said allotment No. 17 to Daniel Daulby, and in other part by the said private road C, southwardly by an allotment No. 15 to the said Thomas Bloor, and westwardly by an allotment No. 13 to Sir Thomas Stanley Massey Stanley, and I direct the fences on the northward and eastward sides thereof to be made and for ever afterwards kept in repair by the owner thereof.

Daniel Daulby, No. 17, 0, 1, 32
I also set out and allot unto Daniel Daulby, his heirs and assigns, in right of his ancient and inclosed lands in the township of Newton-cum-Larton a piece or parcel of land other part of the said Carr marked in the said map No. 17, containing one rood and thirty-two perches, bounded northwardly and eastwardly by the said private road C, southwardly and westwardly by an allotment No. 16 to the said Josiah Day. And I direct the fences on the northward and eastward sides thereof to be made and for ever afterwards kept in repair by the owner thereof.

Trustees of Witton School, No. 18, 2, 0, 20.
I also set out and allot unto the Feoffees or Trustees of Witton School, in the said County of Chester for the purposes of the said school in right of ancient inclosed land in the said township of Newton-cum-Larton a piece or parcel of land part of the said Carr marked on the said map No. 18, containing two acres and twenty perches, bounded northwardly by the said "Public Drain" between this allotment and the allotment No. 19 to the said Trustees or Feoffees, eastwardly by an allotment No. 21 to the Trustees of the Woodchurch Grammar School, southwardly by the said private road C, and westwardly by an allotment No. 13 to the said Sir Thomas Stanley Massey Stanley. And I direct the fences on the eastward and southward sides thereof to be made and for ever afterwards kept in repair by the owner thereof.

Trustees of Witton School, No. 19, 5, 1, 18.
I also set out and allot unto the said Trustees and Feoffees and for the purposes aforesaid, in right of their said ancient lands a piece or parcel of land other part of the said Carr marked on the said map No. 19, containing five acres, one rood and eighteen perches, bounded northwardly by the said private road f, eastwardly by an allotment No. 20 to the Trustees of Woodchurch Grammar School, southwardly by the said "Public Drain" between this allotment and the allotment No. 18 to the said Trustees or Feoffees, and westwardly by

No. 12 to the said Sir Thomas Stanley Massey Stanley. And I direct the fences on the eastward side thereof to be made and for ever afterwards kept in repair by the owner thereof.

I also set out and allot unto the Trustees of the Free Grammar School of Woodchurch, in respect of ancient inclosed lands in the said township of Newton-cum-Larton, and to the uses upon which the same ancient lands are limited a piece or parcel of land other part of the said Carr marked on the said map No. 20, containing four acres, one rood and seven perches, bounded northwardly by the private road marked f, eastwardly by an allotment to the Trustees for the Poor of West Kirby No. 25, southwardly by the said "Public Drain" between this allotment and the allotment No. 21 to the said Trustees, and westwardly by the said allotment No. 19 to the said Trustees or Feoffees of Witton School. And I direct the fences on the east side of the said allotment to be made and for ever afterwards kept in repair by the owner thereof. _{Trustees of Woodchurch Free Grammar School, No.20, 4, 1, 7.}

I also set out and allot unto the said Trustees, in respect to the said ancient lands and to the uses aforesaid, a piece or parcel of land other part of the said Carr marked on the said map No. 21, containing one acre, two roods and eighteen perches, bounded northwardly by the said "Public Drain" between this allotment and the allotment No. 20 last described, eastwardly by the allotment No. 22 to the devisee of Newport Urmson, southwardly by the said private road marked C on the said map, and westwardly by the allotment No. 18 to the Trustees or Feoffees of Witton School. And I direct the fences on the southward side thereof to be made and for ever afterwards kept in repair by the owners thereof. _{Trustees of Woodchurch Free Grammar School, No.21, 1, 2, 18.}

I also set out and allot unto the devisee in trust, named in the last will and testament of Newport Urmson, deceased, his heirs and assigns, in respect of ancient inclosed lands in the said Township of Newton-cum-Larton and upon the trusts in the said will, a piece or parcel of land, other part of the said Carr, marked in the said map No. 22, containing three acres three roods and eleven perches, bounded northwardly by the said public drain between this allotment and the allotment No. 25 to the said Trustees for the Poor of West Kirby, eastwardly by the allotment No. 24 to the same trustees, southwardly by the private road marked c, and westwardly in part by the said private road c, and in other part by the allotment No. 21 to the Trustees of Woodchurch Grammar School. And I direct the fences on the southward and westward sides thereof to be made and for ever afterwards kept in repair by the owner thereof. _{Devisees of N. Urmson, No. 22, 3, 3, 11}

I also set out and allot unto the Reverend Roger Jackson Clerk, his heirs and assigns, in right of his ancient inclosed lands in the Township of Newton-cum-Larton and Grange, a piece or parcel of land, other part of the said Carr, marked in the said map No. 3, containing two acres one rood and fifteen perches, bounded northwardly by the allotment No. 4 to the said John Leigh, eastwardly by a private road marked a, southwardly by allotment to the said Sir Thomas Stanley Massey Stanley, No. 2, and westwardly by ancient inclosed lands in the Township of Newton belonging to the said Reverend Roger Jackson. And I direct the fences on the eastward side to be made and for ever afterwards kept in repair by the owner thereof. _{Rev. R. Jackson, No. 3, 2, 1, 15}

Rev. R. Jackson, No. 23, 9, 3, 31

I also set out and allot unto the said Reverend Roger Jackson, in respect of his said ancient inclosed lands, his heirs and assigns, another piece or parcel of land, other part of the said Carr, marked on the said map No. 23, containing nine acres three roods and thirty-one perches, bounded northwardly by the private road marked c, eastwardly in part by the allotment No. 24 to the said Trustees for the Poor of West Kirby, and in other part by ancient inclosed lands in the Township of Grange belonging to the said John Leigh, southwardly by a private road marked a, and westwardly by the private road c. And I direct the fences on the northward, southward, and westward sides thereof to be made and for ever afterwards kept in repair by the owner thereof.

Rev. Edward Stanley, No. 26, 26, 2, 33.

I also set out and allot unto the Reverend Edward Stanley, Clerk, and his assigns for his life, in respect of his ancient inclosed lands in the Township of Little Meols and after his decease to Sir John Thomas Stanley, Baronet, and his heirs and assigns, a piece or parcel of land other part of the said Carr, marked in the said map No. 26, containing twenty-six acres, two roods, and thirty-three perches bounded northwardly and northeastwardly in part by ancient inclosed lands in the Township of Little Meols, belonging to the said Reverend Edward Stanley and in other part by ancient inclosed lands in the Townships of Hoose and Great Meols, and southeastwardly by ancient inclosed lands in the Township of Grange, belonging to the Trustees for the Poor of West Kirby, southwardly in part by an allotment to the same trustees, No. 24, and in other part by a private road f, and westwardly in part by allotment No. 25 to the same trustees, and in other part by the said private road f, and as it is not intended or meant that the said private road f, on the south side of this allotment, should be inclosed or fenced off, I direct that the owner or owners of this allotment shall in lieu thereof make and for ever afterwards keep in repair so much of the fence on the south side of the said road as adjoins the allotment No. 12 to Sir Thomas Stanley Massey Stanley, No. 19 to the trustees or feoffees of Witton School, No. 20 to the trustees of Woodchurch Grammar School, and No. 25 to the said trustees for the poor of West Kirby.

Rev. Edward Stanley, No. 27, 14, 1, 8

I also set out and allot unto the said Reverend Edward Stanley and his assigns, in respect of his said ancient lands and in manner aforesaid, a piece or parcel of land other part of the said Carr, marked on the said map No. 27, containing fourteen acres one rood and eight perches, bounded northwardly by ancient lands in the Township of Little Meols belonging to the said Reverend Edward Stanley, eastwardly by the private road f, southwardly and southwestwardly in part by an allotment No. 12 to the said Sir Thomas Stanley Massey Stanley, in other part by three several allotments to the said John Leigh No. 11, No. 6 and No. 5, and northwestwardly by ancient inclosed lands in the Township of Little Meols belonging to the said Reverend Edward Stanley. And I direct the fences on the eastward side of this allotment shall be made and for ever afterwards kept in repair by the owner or owners thereof.

In witness whereof I have hereunto set my hand and seal and have also signed the maps hereunto annexed, and do deliver this as my Award, in the presence of the proprietors now attending at a **special** general meeting, duly called by notice for that purpose this thirteenth day of May, in the year of our Lord one thousand eight hundred and twenty-three. James (L. S.) Boydell. Signed, sealed and delivered by the said James Boydell (the several interlineations, alterations and erasures opposite to which the initials of our names are written having been first made) in the presence of us the undersigned and in presence of the several proprietors interested then attending. JNO. PENNINGTON, Atty., Liv'l. WM. HY. ATHERTON.

This is to certify that this copy of the Award of James Boydell of Rossett in the County of Denbigh, gentleman, was on the thirteenth day of May, one thousand eight hundred and twenty-four, examined with the original Award, and afterwards enrolled amongst the records of the Court of General Quarter Sessions of the Peace for the County of Chester.

CHARLES POTTS,
Deputy Clerk of the Peace for the County of Chester.

I hereby certify that the foregoing is a true copy of an examined copy of an Award, purporting to bear date the thirteenth day of May, one thousand eight hundred and twenty-three, under the hand and seal of James Boydell, of Rossett, in the County of Denbigh, gentleman, the Commissioner named and appointed in and by the Act of Parliament therein referred to, deposited in the office of the Clerk of the Peace for the County of Chester.

Dated this third day of February, one thousand eight hundred and sixty-six.

THOMAS ROBERTS,
Deputy Clerk of the Peace for the County of Chester.

THE WALLASEY IMPROVEMENT ACT, 1845.

(8 Vict. c. 6.)

ARRANGEMENT OF SECTIONS.

	SECTION.
Preamble	
Repealed	1 to 5
Shareholders in Companies established under Act of Parliament not disqualified as Commissioners by reason of contracts	6
Repealed	7 to 16
Mode of supplying occasional vacancies	17
Repealed	18 to 83
Lands allotted under 49 Geo. III., c. 103, and 54 Geo. III., c. 87, for stone and marl when exhausted may be sold	84
Land covered with sand hills left as a protection against encroachment of the sea, to be under the control of the Commissioners	85
Saving of rights of Commissioners under the Leasowes Embankment Act, 10 Geo. IV., c. 16	85
Power to lease or purchase ferries	86
Power to provide steam-boats, &c.	87
Commissioners may provide a public Office, &c.	88
Limits of Act	89
Repealed	90 to 117
Commissioners to order land adjoining streets to be fenced in	118
Repealed	119 to 141
Cellars in courts not to be occupied as dwellings	142
Repealed	143 to 152
Penalty on persons hoisting in or delivering goods into warehouses without proper tackle	153
Penalty on occupiers of warehouses, &c., permitting goods to be so hoisted in, or delivered out of warehouses, &c.	154
Penalty for casting slates from roof	155
Public houses to be shut on the mornings of Sundays, &c.	156
Repealed	157 to 181

	SECTION.
Penalty on blacksmiths not shutting out the light of their forges from streets after sunset	182
Repealed	183 to 186
Dogs not to be used for drawing carts	187
Street musicians to depart when desired	188
Repealed	189 to 197
Commissioners empowered to provide market places	198
Repealed	199 to 235
Licensing porters plying for hire	236
Penalty on acting without such license	237
Repealed	238 & 239
Licenses may be suspended, and for certain offences revoked by Justices	240
Repealed	241
Order for overcharge by porters to be included in conviction and returned to aggrieved party	242
Recovery of fares of porters	243
Repealed	244
Commissioners may make bye-laws for the regulation of porters	245
Penalty for enforcing bye-laws	246
Repealed	247 to 250
Evidence of bye-laws	251
Repealed	252 to 255
Power to two Justices to dismiss constables	256
Regulations of the Commissioners to be observed under a penalty	257
Repealed	258 to 293
Unoccupied houses not rateable except to expenses of Act ...	294
Repealed	295 to 299
Persons letting lodgings, &c., to be rated as occupiers ...	300
Repealed	301 to 323
Saving the rights of the Crown	324
Repealed	325 & 326
Interpretation clause	327
Repealed	328

Sec. 1—17

AN ACT

for paving, lighting, watching, cleansing, and otherwise improving the Parish of Wallasey, in the County of Chester; and for establishing a Police, and also a Market, within the said Parish; and for other Purposes.

8TH MAY, 1845.

WHEREAS it is expedient that powers should be granted for paving, lighting, watching, cleansing, and repairing the streets, highways, and other public passages and places within the parish of Wallasey in the county of Chester, and for establishing an effective police, and also a public market and weighing machines, within the said parish; but the objects aforesaid cannot be effected without the authority of Parliament: May it therefore please your Majesty that it may be enacted; and be it enacted by the Queen's Most Excellent Majesty, by and with the advice and consent of the Lords Spiritual and Temporal, and Commons, in this present Parliament assembled and by the authority of the same.

[Sections 1 to 5 were repealed by The Wallasey Order, 1852. These sections provided for the election of twenty-one Commissioners to put this Act into execution, a residential and £35 rating qualification for Commissioners, and certain disqualifications for the office.]

* * *

Short Title.
21 & 22 Vic.
cap. lxiii.

In citing this Act for any purposes, it shall be sufficient to use the expression "The Wallasey Improvement Act, 1845."

[*Vide* "The Wallasey Improvement Act, 1858, sec. 2."]

* * *

Shareholders in companies established under Act of Parliament not disqualified by reason of contracts.

6. Provided always, and be it enacted, That no person, being a shareholder or member of any joint stock company established by Act of Parliament, shall be prevented from acting as a Commissioner by reason of any contract entered into between such company and the Commissioners; but no such Commissioner, being a member of such company, shall vote on any question relating to the execution of this Act in which such company may be interested.

[Sections 7 to 16 inclusive were repealed by the Wallasey Order, 1852. The 15th section provided a residential and £10 rating qualification for electors.]

* * *

Mode of supplying occasional vacancies.

17. And be it enacted, That if any Commissioner die, or resign, or be disqualified, or cease to be a Commissioner from any other cause than that of going out of office by rotation, it shall be lawful for the remaining Commissioners, if they think fit, to elect another Commissioner in his place; and every Commissioner so elected shall continue

8 *Vict.* *The Wallasey Improvement Act*, 1845. *ch. vi.* 147

in office only so long as the person in whose place he shall be elected **Sec. 18—85**
would have been entitled to continue had he remained in office:
Provided always, that all Acts of the Commissioners done during any
such vacancy shall be as valid and effectual as if such vacancy had
not existed.

[Secs. 18 to 62.—Repealed by The Wallasey Order, 1852.
    Sec. 63.—   ,,   ,,   ,,   ,,   1870, art. 4.
    Secs. 64 to 68.—   ,,   ,,   ,,   ,,   1852.
    Sec. 69.—   ,,   ,,   ,,   ,,   1870, art. 4.
    Secs. 70 to 83.—   ,,   ,,   ,,   ,,   1852.]

84. And whereas under and by virtue of an Act of Parliament *Lands*
passed in the forty-ninth year of the reign of His late Majesty King *allotted*
George the Third, intituled " An Act for Inclosing Waste Lands in *under 49*
the Township of Liscard in the Parish of Wallasey in the County *G. 3, c. 103,*
palatine of Chester," and of another Act passed in the fifty-fourth *c. 87, for*
year of the reign of His said late Majesty, intituled " An Act for *stone and*
Inclosing Waste Lands in the Parishes of Wallasey and West Kirby *marl, when*
in the County of Chester," several parcels of land, respectively situate *exhausted,*
in the said Township of Liscard and in the Township of Wallasey in *may be sold.*
the said Parish of Wallasey, have been allotted for the purpose of
getting stone and marl therefrom, and of a watering pit for the use
of the landowners within the said townships, and the stone, marl, and
water respectively in such parcels of land are or may become
exhausted and dried up; be it therefore enacted, That it shall be
lawful for the Commissioners to sell to the person whose lands adjoin
thereto, or if for the space of one month after an offer thereof made
to him he refuse or neglect to purchase, then to sell to any other
person the said parcels of land or any of them from which the stone
or marl or water shall have been so exhausted and dried up as aforesaid, at or for such price as the Commissioners may deem fair and
reasonable, and convey the same to the purchaser thereof by deed
under the hands and seals of any three or more of the Commissioners,
whose receipt shall be a sufficient discharge to the purchaser of any
such lands for the purchase money in such receipt expressed to be
received; and the money arising from any such sale shall be applied
by the Commissioners to the same purposes as the improvement rate
is hereby directed to be applied: Provided always, that it shall be
lawful for the Commissioners, if they shall think fit, instead of selling
and disposing of the said watering pit, to retain the same, and to
excavate, deepen, and improve the same for the use of the inhabitants
of the said parish, and also to manage, regulate, and protect for the
purposes for which they were appropriated the said parcels of land
allotted for stone and marl, until the same shall be sold under the
provisions of this Act.

[Extended by the Wallasey Improvement Act, 1858, sec. 68; the
Wallasey Improvement Act, 1864, sec. 20; and The Wallasey
Order (No. 1), 1877, art. 1.]

85. And whereas under and by virtue of the said recited Act *Land covered*
passed in the fifty-fourth year of the reign of His said late Majesty *with sand*
King George the Third, it was enacted that nothing therein contained *hills left as a*
should be construed to authorise the Commissioner therein named to *protection*
divide, set out, or allot any of the land covered with sand hills on *against encroachment*
the north-west side of the commons or waste lands in the township *of the sea to*
of Wallasey aforesaid beyond such line or extent of land as the said *be under the*
Commissioner might think fit for cultivation, but that the said sand *control of the Commissioners.*

Sec. 86	hills should remain uninclosed and open, for the better security and preservation of the land to the eastward and southward of the same from the encroachment of the sea, and for which purpose such land covered with sand hills was thereby appropriated: And whereas the said Commissioner left undivided and uninclosed for the purpose aforesaid so much of the said land covered with sand hills as is defined and delineated by the plan annexed to his award: and it is expedient, for the purpose of the better preservation thereof, that the same should be placed under the control of the Commissioners to be appointed under this Act; be it therefore enacted, That all the land covered with sand hills in the township of Wallasey left undivided and uninclosed under and by virtue of the said recited Act of the fifty-fourth year of the reign of His late Majesty King George the Third shall be under the control and management of the Commissioners to be appointed under this Act, in order to its more efficient appropriation for the purposes mentioned and intended by the said recited Act, but for no other use, intent, or purpose whatsoever, and it shall be lawful for the said Commissioners to plant star grass, and to prevent trespass and damage thereon, and to take such other ways and means as in their judgment may be proper and necessary for the protection, care, and due preservation of the same:
Saving of rights of Commissioners under the Leasowes Embankment Act 10 G. 4, c. 16.	Provided always, that nothing herein contained shall be construed to affect, alter, abridge, or take away any of the powers or authorities, rights or privileges, vested in the Commissioners appointed under and by virtue of an Act, passed in the tenth year of the reign of His Majesty King George the Fourth, intituled "An Act for making an Embankment on the north-west side of the Leasowes in the township of Wallasey and Great Meols in the County of Chester," to prevent the further encroachment of the sea, and the injury to arise therefrom to the lowlands contiguous, and to the port of Liverpool.

[*Vide* the Wallasey Inclosure Act, 1814 (54 Geo. III. c. 87) sec. 23 ; and the Wallasey Local Board Act, 1890, sec. 11]

Power to lease or purchase ferries ;	86. And whereas there is within the township of Poulton-cum-Seacombe a ferry known by the name of Seacombe Ferry, and there is within the township of Liscard aforesaid a ferry known by the name of the Egremont Ferry, and it would be of great public and local advantage if the said Commissioners were enabled to rent or purchase both or either of such ferries, or any other ferry which may be hereafter established within the said townships or either of them, together with the wharfs, landing places, and conveniences connected therewith : be it therefore enacted, That it shall be lawful for the Commissioners, subject to the provisions in this Act contained, to hire and take on lease, for any term not exceeding twenty-one years, and, if thought expedient, to purchase and take absolutely, by agreement with the several parties interested therein respectively, but not otherwise, and to hold and use the said two ferries or either of them, or any other ferry which may hereafter be established as aforesaid, with the wharfs, landing places, and conveniences connected therewith, or such of them or such part thereof respectively as the Commissioners shall think proper ; and it shall be lawful for all persons interested in any such ferries, land, and property respectively, including such persons as would be capacitated to sell lands under the provisions of this Act, to contract for a lease or the sale of and to demise or sell

8 Vict. *The Wallasey Improvement Act*, 1845. *ch. vi.* 149

and convey their respective interests in any such ferries, land, and property respectively to the Commissioners. **Sec. 87—89**

[*Vide* The Wallasey Improvement Act, 1858, sec. 36.]

87. And be it enacted, That it shall be lawful for the Commissioners from time to time to provide and purchase and maintain such steam and other boats, materials, and things, and employ and recompense such persons, as shall be necessary for the proper and efficient working of any such ferry as shall be so hired or purchased by the Commissioners. <small>And to provide steam boats, &c.</small>

[Power to Hire and Charter: The Wallasey Improvement Act, 1858, sec. 37.]

88. And be it enacted, that it shall be lawful for the Commissioners from time to time to provide and maintain a fit and convenient public office within the limits of this Act for holding the meetings and transacting the business of the Commissioners, and for the holding of such other public meetings and transacting such other public business relating to the said parish as the Commissioners shall, from time to time, direct or allow to be held or transacted therein, and also to provide land and buildings fit and convenient for the deposit of the dust, dung, ashes, and other filth to be swept and collected under the authority of this Act, for the depositing of stone and other materials for the highways, and for the accommodating of all horses, carts, fire engines, weighing machines, tools, implements, and other articles, matters, and things, and for any of such purposes to hire any lands, messuages, or buildings which shall by the Commissioners be considered necessary, of and from any person who shall be willing to let the same, or otherwise to cause any new erection or building to be made upon any land or ground which shall be purchased or hired under the provisions of this Act; and it shall be lawful for the Commissioners from time to time to make and establish such rules, orders, and provisions for the use and management of such public office, and of any such lands and buildings, and to make such allowance to the keeper of the same public office for his necessary attendance and trouble about the same, as shall from time to time appear expedient to the Commissioners. <small>Commissioners may provide a public office, &c.</small>

89. And be it enacted, That this Act shall extend to the townships of Liscard and Poulton-cum-Seacombe, and so much of the township of Wallasey as lies to the eastward and south-eastward of a straight line drawn from a point at high-water mark of the Irish Sea fifteen hundred and sixty yards distant, along such high-water mark, from the point where the township of Wallasey adjoins the township of Liscard, to and along the eastward boundary of an occupation road running from the high road leading from the village of Wallasey towards Leasowe Castle, to a field now or late belonging to Sir John Tobin, and thence across the western extremity of such field to a brook or watercourse dividing the township of Wallasey from the parish of Bidston; and all the powers and provisions in this Act contained shall and may be exercised and put in force within the limits aforesaid accordingly: Provided always, that nothing herein contained shall exclude or limit the jurisdiction or powers by this Act granted to the Commissioners over the land covered with sand hills in the township of Wallasey left as a protection against the encroachment of the sea, as hereinbefore mentioned. <small>Limits of Act.</small>

[The limits were by The Wallasey Order, 1852, art. 1, extended

8 Vict. *The Wallasey Improvement Act*, 1845. *ch. vi.*

S. 90—154

to an area constituted and called the Wallasey District for the purposes of the Public Health Act, 1848, the provisions of which statute (with the exceptions of secs. 50 and 109), were applied thereto. The district was further enlarged by the Wallasey Order (No. 2), 1877, which, with the Wallasey Order 1878, extended to it the unrepealed provisions of the local Acts. The Public Health Act, 1848, was repealed by the Public Health Act, 1875, sec. 343 and schedule. For substituted provisions vide sec. 313 of the Public Health Act, 1875 (38 and 39 Vict., ch. 55). The Wallasey Local Board Act, 1890, sec. 5, defines the sea and river boundary of the district.]

[Secs. 90 to 117, repealed by The Wallasey Order, 1852.]

* * * * *

Commissioners to order land adjoining streets to be fenced in.

118. And be it enacted, That with respect to all such land as is or may be the property of private persons which shall not be built upon, and shall lie next adjoining to any street within the limits of this Act, or land laid out or left for a street, so as to be dangerous to passengers, it shall be lawful for the Commissioners, if they shall think it necessary, to give notice in writing, to be signed by the clerk, to the owner of such land, to fence in the same in a proper and sufficient manner; and if such owner shall neglect or omit to fence in the same in manner aforesaid for the space of five days next after such notice, the Commissioners shall cause the same to be done in such manner as they shall think proper, and the expenses thereof shall be recovered from such owner by distress.

[*Vide* The Wallasey Local Board Act, 1890, sec. 24.]

[Secs. 119 to 141, repealed by The Wallasey Order, 1852.]

* * * * *

Cellars in courts not to be occupied as dwellings.

142. And be it enacted, That it shall not be lawful to let separately, except as a warehouse or storehouse, or to suffer to be occupied as a dwelling place, any cellar under any house in any court.

[Secs. 143 to 152, repealed by The Wallasey Order, 1852.]

* * * * *

Penalty on persons hoisting in or delivering goods into warehouses without proper tackle;

153. And be it enacted, That if any person shall hoist, lower, take in, or deliver any cask, puncheon, barrel, sack, bag, or other thing into or from any warehouse, building, cellar, or vault, within the limits of this Act, without proper and sufficient ropes and other tackle, in good order and condition, and fit for such hoisting, lowering, and taking in or delivering, and without slinging or otherwise effectually securing such cask, puncheon, barrel, sack, bag, or other thing, so as to prevent the same from slipping, breaking away, or falling, every person so offending shall for every such offence forfeit a sum not exceeding five pounds.

and on occupiers of warehouses, &c., permitting goods to be so hoisted in or delivered out of warehouses, &c.

154. And be it enacted, That if any owner or occupier of any warehouse or building or room therein respectively, cellar or vault, or master porter, shall wilfully or negligently permit or suffer any cask, puncheon, barrel, sack, bag, or other thing to be hoisted, lowered, taken in, or delivered out of any warehouse, building, cellar, or vault, without having proper and sufficient ropes and other tackle, in good order and condition, and fit for such hoisting, lowering, taking in, or delivering, every person so offending shall for every offence forfeit a sum not exceeding five pounds; provided that no person shall be liable to the said penalty other than the party whose duty it was to

8 Vict. The Wallasey Improvement Act, 1845. ch. vi. 151

provide and have or keep sufficient rope and tackle for any of the purposes aforesaid, and who shall be proved to have failed to provide or have or keep the same. **S 155—198**

155. And be it enacted, That if any person shall throw or cast from the roof or other part of any house or other building, into any street within the limits of this Act, any slate, brick, tile, wood, rubbish, or other material or thing, he shall for every offence forfeit a sum not exceeding twenty shillings. *Penalty for casting slates from roof.*

156. And be it enacted, That no licensed victualler or other person shall open his house within the limits of this Act, for the sale of wine, spirits, beer, or other fermented or distilled liquors, or permit the same to be sold therein, on Sundays or Christmas Day or Good Friday, before the hour of one in the afternoon, under a penalty not exceeding five pounds for each offence; provided that nothing herein contained shall extend to prevent refreshment to travellers. *Public houses to be shut on the mornings of Sundays, &c.*

[Secs. 157 to 165.—Repealed by The Wallasey Order, 1852.
Secs. 166 to 171.—   „   „   „   „   1870, art. 4.
Secs. 172 to 181.—   „   „   „   „   1852.]

182. And be it enacted, That if any blacksmith, whitesmith, anchor-smith, nailmaker, or other person using a forge, and having a door, window, or aperture fronting or opening into or towards any street within the limits of this Act, shall not close such door, or fasten the shutters or other fastenings of such windows, and close such aperture, every evening within one half-hour after sunset, so as effectually to prevent the light from shining through the doorway, window, or aperture into or upon such street, every person so offending shall for every offence forfeit a sum not exceeding twenty shillings; provided that nothing herein contained shall extend to forges below the pavement of the street. *Penalty on blacksmiths not shutting out the light of their forges from streets after sunset.*

[Secs. 183 to 186, repealed by The Wallasey Order, 1852.]

187. And be it enacted, That from and after the passing of this Act every person who within the limits of this Act shall use any dog or goat for the purpose of drawing or helping to draw any cart, carriage, truck, or barrow, shall be liable to a penalty of not more than forty shillings for each offence. *Dogs not to be used for drawing carts.*

188. And be it enacted, That it shall be lawful for any householder within the limits of this Act, personally, or by his servant or any of his family, or by the street keeper or a constable, to require any street musicians or singer to depart from the neighbourhood of the house of such householder, on account of the illness of any inmate of such house, or other reasonable cause; and every person who shall sound or play upon any musical instrument or sing in any street near any house, after being so required to depart, shall be liable to a penalty of not more than forty shillings. *Street musicians to depart when desired.*

[Secs. 189 to 191.—Repealed by The Wallasey Order, 1852.
Secs. 192 to 197.—   „   „   „   „   1870, art. 1.]

198. And be it enacted, That it shall be lawful for the Commissioners to build and provide upon the land to be purchased by them as herein mentioned, and for ever after to maintain and improve, as *Commissioners empowered to provide market places.*

S. 199—240 they shall think fit, one or more market place or market places for the sale of cattle, animals, and provisions and all other marketable commodities within the limits of this Act, together with all stalls, standings, and other conveniences and suitable approaches for all persons resorting thereto.

[Secs. 199 to 235, repealed by The Wallasey Order, 1852.]

*   *   *

Licensing porters plying for hire.

236. And whereas it is expedient that errand, message, and luggage porters plying for hire within the limits of this Act, should be licensed; be it therefore enacted, That every person shall be licensed by the Commissioners before he shall act as an errand, message, or luggage porter; and that every such licence shall, within seven days after the granting thereof, be registered at the clerk's office (a certificate of which registry shall be given to every such person upon payment of such sum as the Commissioners may determine, not exceeding the sum of one shilling and sixpence); and every person neglecting to register his licence shall forfeit for every such neglect a sum not exceeding twenty shillings.

[So much of sec. 236 as related to drivers of hackney carriages was repealed by The Wallasey Order, 1852. By art. 17 of that Order, the sections of the Town Police Clauses Act, 1847, with respect to hackney carriages, were incorporated with so much of this Act as remained unrepealed.]

Penalty on acting without such licence.

237. And be it enacted, That if any person shall act as such porter as aforesaid without having obtained such licence, or shall lend or part with his licence or badge, every such person shall for every offence respectively forfeit a sum not exceeding twenty shillings.

[So much of sec. 237 as related to drivers of hackney carriages, and secs. 238 and 239 were repealed by the Wallasey Order, 1852. As to penalties, *vide* note to sec. 246.]

Licences may be suspended, and for certain offences revoked by justices.

240. And be it enacted, That it shall be lawful for any Justice before whom any errand, message, or luggage porter shall be convicted of any offence under this Act, if such Justice, in his discretion, shall think proper to suspend, for any period not exceeding two months, the licence granted to such porter; and it shall also be lawful for any Justice, upon proof that any porter has been convicted of felony, or upon the conviction before him for a second offence of any porter, to revoke the licence granted to such porter; and whenever the licence of any porter shall be suspended or revoked as aforesaid, it shall be lawful for any Justice to require such porter to deliver up forthwith to such Justice his licence and badge; and if any porter shall, upon being so required, refuse or neglect to deliver up such licence or badge, or either of them, he shall forfeit any sum not exceeding five pounds; and every Justice to whom any licence or badge shall be delivered up shall forthwith transmit the same to the clerk, who shall, at the expiration of the period for which any such licence shall have been suspended, **re-deliver** such licence, with the badge, to the person to whom it shall have been granted.

[So much of sec. 240 as related to drivers of hackney carriages, and sec. 241 were repealed by The Wallasey Order, 1852.]

8 Vict. *The Wallasey Improvement Act*, 1845. *ch. ri.* 153

242. And be it enacted, That whenever any errand, message, or luggage porter shall be convicted of taking and receiving as and for a fare a greater sum than is or shall be authorized by any Bye-law made under and by virtue of this Act, it shall be lawful to include in the conviction of such porter an order for the payment of the sum so overcharged, over and above the penalty and costs which shall be imposed for every such offence, and upon payment or recovery of the said overcharge to cause the same to be returned to the party aggrieved, whose evidence shall be admissible in proof of the said offence. *S. 242—246 Order for overcharge by porters to be included in conviction and returned to aggrieved party.*

[So much of sec. 242 as related to drivers of hackney carriages was repealed by The Wallasey Order, 1852.]

243. And be it enacted, That if any person shall refuse to pay, on demand, to any errand, message, or luggage porter, such fare as shall be authorized to be taken and received by the Bye-laws to be made as herein directed, such fares or rates may, together with costs, be recovered as any penalty imposed by this Act. *Recovery of fares of porters.*

[So much of sec. 243 as related to drivers of hackney carriages and sec. 244 were repealed by The Wallasey Order, 1852.]

* * * *

245. And be it enacted, That it shall be lawful for the Commissioners from time to time to make such Bye-laws as they shall think fit for all or any of the purposes following (that is to say)— *Commissioners may make Bye-laws for the regulation of porters.*

For regulating all loads, rates, fares or prices which shall be allowed to be taken by errand, message, or luggage porters for hire, and in what manner errand, message, and luggage porters plying for hire shall behave and conduct themselves, and for punishing extortion, imposition, misconduct, or misbehaviour in such errand, message, and luggage porters respectively:

And it shall be lawful for the Commissioners from time to time as they shall think fit to repeal, alter, or amend any such Bye-laws, and make others in their stead, provided such Bye-laws be not repugnant to the laws of England or the provisions of this Act, and be reduced into writing, and signed by any three of the Commissioners, and if affecting other persons than the officers or servants of the Commissioners, be printed and published as herein provided.

[The other parts of sec. 245 relating to the regulation of markets, hackney carriages, &c., were repealed by The Wallasey Order, 1852.]

246. And be it enacted, That it shall be lawful for the Commissioners by the Bye-laws so to be made by them to impose such reasonable penalties as they shall think fit, not exceeding five pounds for each offence: Provided always, that such Bye-laws be so framed as to allow the Justices before whom any penalty imposed thereby is sought to be recovered to order the whole or part only of such penalty to be paid. *Penalty for enforcing Bye-laws.*

[The Wallasey Order, 1852 (sched.), repealed "so much of any unrepealed part" of the Wallasey Improvement Act, 1845, "as fixes the amount of any penalty for any offence under the said Act, wherever the penalty for such offence is fixed by the Public Health Act or any Act hereby incorporated therewith, or by any Bye-law of the Local Board of Health,

154　　8 *Vict. The Wallasey Improvement Act*, 1845.　*ch. ri.*

S. 247—299

at an amount other than that fixed by the said Local Act." By The Wallasey Order, 1888, art. 3, sub-sec. 2, the provisions contained in the Public Health Act, 1875, with respect to Bye-laws, and the penalties which may be imposed thereby, and the recovery and application of penalties, were applied to all Bye-laws under the Wallasey Improvement Act, 1845.]

[Secs. 247 to 250.—Repealed by The Wallasey Order, 1852.]

Evidence of Bye-laws.

251. And be it enacted, That the production of a written or printed copy of the Bye-laws of the Commissioners, authenticated by the signatures of three of the Commissioners or their clerk, shall be evidence of the existence and of the due making of such Bye-laws in all prosecutions under the same; and with respect to the proof of the publication it shall be sufficient that painted boards containing a copy thereof were affixed or continued in the manner by this Act directed, and in case of any such boards being afterwards destroyed or obliterated it shall be sufficient to prove that such board was replaced or restored as soon as conveniently might be, unless proof be adduced by the party complained against that such painted boards did not contain a copy of the Bye-law under which he shall be prosecuted, or that boards were not affixed or continued to be affixed as required by this Act.

[Secs. 252 to 255.—Repealed by The Wallasey Order, 1852.]

Power to two Justices to dismiss constables.

256. And be it enacted, That it shall be lawful for any two Justices to dismiss or suspend for neglect of duty any constable or officer appointed under this Act; and no person so suspended or dismissed shall be re-appointed, except with the consent of two Justices; and when any person shall be so dismissed or suspended all powers vested in him as a constable shall cease or be suspended.

Regulations of the Commissioners to be observed under a penalty.

257. And be it enacted, That it shall be lawful for the Commissioners to make such rules and orders as they shall think fit for regulating the conduct of the said constables and officers; and if any such constable or other officer shall not faithfully observe and perform such rules and orders he shall forfeit for every such offence any sum not exceeding forty shillings, and if the Commissioners shall think proper shall also be immediately discharged from his office or employment.

[As to penalties, *vide* note to sec. 246.
Secs. 258 to 277.—Repealed by The Wallasey Order, 1852.
Secs. 278 to 280.—Repealed by The Wallasey Order, 1870, art. 4.
Secs. 281 to 292.—　　　　　,,　　　　,,　　　　1852.
Sec. 293.—Repealed with proviso by The Wallasey Order, 1870, art. 1, such proviso being subsequently repealed by the Wallasey Improvement Act, 1872, sec. 20.]

Unoccupied houses not rateable except to expenses of Act.

294. And be it enacted, That no house or other property shall be rated under this Act whilst the same shall be unoccupied, save and except only to so much of the said improvement rate as shall be made for defraying the expenses of preparing, applying for, obtaining, and passing this Act, or in any way incident thereto.

[Secs. 295 to 299.—Repealed by The Wallasey Order, 1852.]

300. And be it enacted, That every person who shall let his house in separate apartments or ready furnished shall be rated as the occupier thereof. — *S. 300—327 Persons letting lodgings, &c., to be rated as occupiers.*

[Secs. 301 to 323.—Repealed by The Wallasey Order, 1852.]

* * * * *

324. And be it enacted, That nothing in this Act contained shall operate to vest in the said Commissioners, or to authorize them to rent, take, or use or have any control over any land, soil, foreshore, piers, ferries, or landing places belonging to Her Majesty in right of her crown, without the consent in writing of the Commissioners for the time being of Her Majesty's Woods, Forests, Land Revenues, Works, and Buildings, or any two of them, first had and obtained for that purpose, or to prejudice, diminish, alter, take away, or in any manner interfere with any of the rights, privileges, powers, or authorities vested in or enjoyed by Her Majesty, her heirs or successors. — *Saving the rights of the Crown.*

[Secs. 325 and 326.—Repealed by The Wallasey Order, 1852.]

327. And be it enacted, That in this Act the following words and expressions shall have the several meanings hereby assigned to them, unless there be something in the subject or context repugnant to such construction; that is to say, — *Interpretation Clause.*

> Words importing the singular number shall include the plural number, and words importing the plural number shall include the singular number.
>
> Words importing the masculine gender only shall include females:
>
> The word "month" shall mean calendar month:
>
> The word "person" or the word "persons" shall include corporation, whether aggregate or sole; and whenever any forfeiture, penalty, or damage is payable to a party aggrieved, it shall be payable to a body corporate in like manner as to an individual:
>
> The word "oath" shall include affirmation in the case of Quakers, or other declaration or solemnity lawfully substituted for an oath in case of any other persons exempted by law from the necessity of taking an oath:
>
> The expression "Superior Courts" shall mean Her Majesty's Superior Courts of Record at Westminster:
>
> The word "clerk" shall mean the clerk of the Commissioners:
>
> The word "Commissioners" shall mean the Commissioners for the improvement of the Parish of Wallasey for the time being, acting by virtue of this Act:
>
> The word "Justice" shall mean any justice of the peace for the county or place where the matter requiring the cognizance of any justice shall arise:
>
> The words "General or Quarter Sessions" shall mean the general or quarter sessions of the peace for the County of Chester:
>
> The word "street" shall include any square, street, court, or alley, highway, lane, road, thoroughfare, or public passage or place within the limits of this Act:

[*Vide* The Wallasey Local Board Act, 1890, Sec. 38.]

Sec. 327 The word "house" shall mean dwelling house within the limits of this Act:

The word "building" shall extend to and comprise all buildings of what nature and kind soever, not being buildings or structures wholly underground, or bridges, or walls to be used as fences only, now built or hereafter to be built, and every part of such building respectively, within the limits of this Act:

The word "lands" shall extend to messuages, lands, tenements, and hereditaments of any tenure:

The word "owner" shall mean the party in possession or receipt of the rents or profits of any tenement:

The word "Surveyor" or the word "Surveyors" shall mean the surveyor or surveyors of highways or buildings, as the case may be, to be appointed by the Commissioners in pursuance of this Act, and shall extend to any assistant surveyor or assistant surveyors to be appointed by the Commissioners:

The words "hackney carriage" shall include any coach, chariot, car, fly, cabriolet, sociable, lorry, or such like carriage:

The word "carriage" shall include any coach, chariot, car, fly, cabriolet, gig, sociable, lorry, waggon, timber carriage, float, dray, cart, shandrey, sledge, truck, hand cart, wheelbarrow or handbarrow:

The word "driver" shall include the driver, conductor, or carter of any such carriage:

[The words "hackney carriage" and "carriage" in this section included also "omnibus," but this provision was repealed by art. 4 of The Wallasey Order, 1888. For provisions relating to the regulation of hackney carriage and omnibuses, *vide* The Wallasey Order, 1852, Art. 17, and The Wallasey Order, 1888.]

[Sec. 328. which enacted that this Act should be a public Act, and judicially noticed as such, was repealed by The Wallasey Order, 1852.]

[The Wallasey Order, 1852, also repealed "so much of any unrepealed part" of the Wallasey Improvement Act, 1845, "as fixes the amount of any penalty for any offence under the said Act, wherever the penalty for such offence is fixed by the Public Health Act, or any Act hereby incorporated therewith, or by any Bye-law of the Local Board of Health, at an amount other than that fixed by the said Local Act." By art. 11 of the same Order the unrepealed parts of the Wallasey Improvement Act, 1845, were incorporated with the Public Health Act, 1848, and art. 17 incorporated certain sections of the Town Police Clauses Act, 1847; of the Town Improvement Clauses Act, 1847; and of the Markets and Fairs Clauses Act, 1847. As to the sections of the Town Police Clauses Act, 1847, so incorporated *vide* The Wallasey Order, 1888. By art. 3 (sub-sec. 2) of this Order the provisions contained in the Public Health Act, 1875, with respect to Bye-laws, and the penalties which may be imposed thereby, and the recovery and application of penalties, were applied to all Bye-laws under the Wallasey Improvement Act, 1845.

Sec. 327

The Commissioners appointed to put into execution and administer the provisions of The Wallasey Improvement Act, 1845, were superseded by a Local Board of Health created in pursuance of the Public Health Act, 1848, by The Wallasey Order, 1852. By this Order the powers of the Improvement Commissioners were transferred to the Local Board of Health. The Public Health Act, 1848, was repealed by the Public Health Act, 1875 (sec. 343 and sched.), which statute consolidated and amended the Acts relating to public health in England.]

Sec. 1—12

The Public Health Supplemental Act, 1853 (No. 1).

(*Confirms The Wallasey Order, 1852*).

AN

ACT

to confirm and extend certain Provisional Orders of the General Board of Health for the Towns of Wakefield, Elland, WALLASEY, Dudley, Barnsley, Dorchester, and Welshpool.

9TH MAY, 1853.

WHEREAS the General Board of Health have, in pursuance of the Public Health Act, 1848, made, published, and deposited, according to the Provisions of that Act, certain Provisional Orders mentioned in the Schedule to this Act annexed, and it is expedient that the said Orders should be confirmed, and further Provisions made in relation thereto: Be it therefore enacted by the Queen's most Excellent Majesty, by and with the advice and consent of the Lords Spiritual and Temporal, and Commons, in this present Parliament assembled, and by the authority of the same,

Certain Provisional Orders of the General Board of Health confirmed.

1. That the Provisional Orders of the General Board of Health referred to in the Schedule annexed shall, from and after the passing of this Act, so far as the same are authorized by the said Public Health Act, be absolute, and be as binding and of the like force and effect as if the Provisions of the same had been expressly enacted in this Act.

First Election of Local Board for Wallasey.

3. The First Election of the Local Board of Health for the District of Wallasey, for the purposes of the said Public Health Act, shall take place on the Twenty-eighth day of April, in the year of our Lord one thousand eight hundred and fifty-three.

[This date appears to have been altered to the 21st of June, by order of General Board of Health dated May 10th, 1853.]

Act incorporated with Public Health Act.

11. This Act shall be deemed to be incorporated with the Public Health Act, and shall be as if this Act and the Public Health Act were One Act.

Short Title.

12. That in citing this Act in any other Act of Parliament, or in any Proceeding, Instrument, or Document whatsoever, it shall be sufficient to use the words and figures "The Public Health Supplemental Act, 1853 (No. 1.)"

[The omitted Sections and Orders relate to districts other than Wallasey.]

SCHEDULE.

THE WALLASEY ORDER, 1852.

Provisional Order for the Application of the Public Health Act, 1848, to the District of Wallasey, in the County of Chester.

[This Order may be cited as The Wallasey Order, 1852.—*Vide* The Wallasey Order, 1896, art. II.]

GENERAL BOARD OF HEALTH.

Whereas in pursuance of the Public Health Act, 1848, the General Board of Health, upon the joint petition of not less than one tenth of the inhabitants rated to the relief of the poor of and within the Township of Poulton-cum-Seacombe, in the Parish of Wallasey, in the County of Chester (the number of the said petitioners exceeding thirty in the whole), directed Robert Rawlinson, one of their Superintending Inspectors, to visit the said Township, and to make public inquiry, and to examine witnesses as to the sewerage, drainage, and supply of water, the state of the burial grounds, the number and sanitary condition of the inhabitants, and as to any Local Acts of Parliament in force within the said Township for paving, lighting, cleansing, watching, regulating, supplying with water, or improving the said Township, or having relation to the purposes of the said Act; also, as to the natural drainage areas, and the existing parochial or other local boundaries, and the boundaries which might be most advantageously adopted for the purposes of the said Act.

And whereas the said Superintending Inspector, having previously given the notices required by the said Act, proceeded upon the said inquiry in the manner directed by the said Act, and hath reported in writing to the said General Board upon the several matters with respect to which he was so directed to inquire as aforesaid, and upon certain other matters in respect of which he deemed it expedient to report for the purposes of the said Act.

And whereas copies of the said Report, accompanied by a notice stating that within the time directed by the said Act, written statements might be forwarded to the said Board with respect to any matter contained in or omitted from the said Report, or any amendment proposed to be made therein, have been duly published and deposited as required by the said Act, and the time for forwarding such statements has now elapsed, and all such statements as have been received by the said Board have been duly deposited as required by that Act.

And whereas it having appeared to the said General Board that the boundaries which might be most advantageously adopted for the purposes of the said Act were not the same as those of the said Township with respect to which the said inquiry had been made, the said Board caused the said Robert Rawlinson to visit the parts within the boundaries proposed to be adopted for the purposes of the said Act.

Schedule.

And whereas the said Superintending Inspector, after having given such notice as is required by the said Act, did hear all persons desirous of being heard before him on the subject of the said Report, and did make further inquiry and report according to the directions of the said Board.

And whereas copies of such further Report, accompanied by a notice stating that, within the time directed by the said Act, written statements might be forwarded to the said Board with respect to any matter contained in or omitted from the said Report, or any amendment proposed to be made therein, have been duly published and deposited as required by the said Act, and the time for forwarding such statements has now elapsed, and all such statements as have been received by the said Board have been duly deposited as required by that Act.

And whereas it appears upon such Reports that there is a certain Local Act in force within the said Township having relation to the purposes of the said Public Health Act, that is to say,

> An Act passed in the Eighth Year of the Reign of Her present Majesty Queen Victoria, intituled "An Act for paving, "lighting, watching, cleansing, and otherwise improving the "Parish of Wallasey, in the County of Chester; and for "establishing a police, and also a market, within the said "parish; and for other purposes."

And whereas it appears to the said General Board to be expedient that the said Public Health Act should be applied to a district included within the same boundaries as those of the herein-before recited Local Act, subject to the extension hereafter mentioned, being the boundaries within which the said inquiry and further inquiry have been made, and that provision should be made in respect to the said Local Act of Parliament, and the repeal, alteration, extension, and future execution thereof, but the same cannot be done without the authority of Parliament.

Now, therefore, in pursuance of the powers vested in the said Board by the Public Health Act, 1848, We, the said General Board of Health, do, by this Provisional Order under our hands and official seal, direct, That from and after the day appointed for the first election of the Local Board of Health by any Act of Parliament confirming this Order :—

> 1.—The Public Health Act, and every part thereof, except the Sections numbered 50 and 109 in the copies of that Act printed by Her Majesty's Printers, shall apply to the area comprised within the jurisdiction of the Commissioners under the herein-before recited Local Act, and to the strand or shore between high and low water mark of the Irish Sea, bounding such part of the said area as in the Township of Wallasey, subject to any rights of the Crown therein ; and such area so extended shall constitute a district called the Wallasey District, for the purposes of the said Public Health Act.
>
> [The Wallasey Order (No. 2) 1877, declares "that all that part of the Parish of Wallasey which is comprised in the Rural Sanitary District of the Birkenhead Union shall be included in, and shall, for the purposes of the Public Health Act, 1875,

be deemed to form part of the Local Government District of Wallasey." The Wallasey Local Board Act, 1890, sec. 5, defines the sea and river boundary of the district.]

2.—The Local Board of Health shall consist of fifteen persons, of whom six shall be elected by the owners of and ratepayers in respect of property in the Township of Poulton-cum-Seacombe, six by the owners of and ratepayers in respect of property in the Township of Liscard, and the remaining three by owners of and ratepayers in respect of property in the Township of Wallasey.

3.—One third in number of the said Local Board shall go out of office on the day next after the expiration of a year from the day appointed by Parliament for the first election of the said Local Board, and so on annually ; so that two of the members elected for the Townships of Poulton-cum-Seacombe and Liscard respectively, and one of the members elected for the Township of Wallasey, shall go out every year.

4.—Every person shall, when elected, and while he continues a member of the said Local Board, be resident, as in the Public Health Act, 1848, is required, and be possessed of real or personal estate or both, to the amount of not less than one thousand pounds, or shall be so resident and rated to the relief of the poor of the said parish, or of some township or place of which some part is within the said district, upon an annual value of not less than thirty pounds.

5.—At the first election of the said Local Board, Isaac Penny, Esquire, of Poulton-cum-Seacombe, within the aforesaid district of Wallasey, shall perform the duties which it may be requisite for him to perform in conducting the said first election ; and in case the said Isaac Penny, from illness or other sufficient cause, shall be unable to discharge such duties, or shall be absent, or shall refuse to act, then Henry Pooley, Esquire, of Liscard, likewise within the district of Wallasey aforesaid, shall perform such of the said duties as then remain to be performed.

[Arts. 2 to 5.—The Public Health Act, 1875, which repealed the Public Health Act, 1848, contained in sec. 8 and Schedule II, provisions relating to the election of Local Boards, the number and qualifications of members, the qualification of electors, and the mode of election. These provisions were repealed by the Local Government Act, 1894 (56 and 57 Vict. ch. 73, sec. 89 and Schedule II). By the operation of the Local Government Act, 1894, Urban Sanitary Authorities (Local Boards), became Urban District Councils. The qualification and disqualifications of Councillors in Urban Districts, not boroughs, are contained in secs. 23 and 46 of that statute. Elections of District Councils are, subject to the provisions of the Local Government Act, 1894, conducted according to rules framed under the Act by the Local Government Board.

The voters are the "parochial electors" of the parishes in the district – *vide* secs. 23 and 44.]

6.—The fourteen days notice of qualification required by the Public Health Act, 1848, to be given by owners of property in order to entitle them to vote at the said first election shall be given to the said Isaac Penny, at his dwelling-house in Poulton-

Schedule.

cum-Seacombe, within the aforesaid district of Wallasey; or in case he shall refuse or be unable to receive the same, then to the said Henry Pooley, at his dwelling-house in Liscard, likewise within the district of Wallasey aforesaid.

7.—The parts of the said Local Act specified in the Schedule to this Order shall be repealed, except in so far as the same repeal any other Act or Acts of Parliament.

8.—All the powers of the Commissioners under the said Local Act shall cease, and those of their officers shall cease from the time appointed by order under the hands and seal of office of the said Local Board.

9.—Such of the said powers as are granted by the unrepealed parts of the said Local Act shall, so far as the same are not repugnant to or inconsistent with the said Public Health Act, or this Order, or any byelaw lawfully made under the said Public Health Act, be transferred to the said Local Board of Health, and the officers of the said Local Board, and shall be exercised in the same manner as if such powers had been granted by the said Public Health Act.

10.—The said Local Board shall be the Commissioners for executing the unrepealed parts of the said Local Acts. And they shall have the like powers of nominating and electing out of their own body persons to be trustees of the Birkenhead Docks, under the provisions of an Act of the 11th and 12th Vict. ch. 144, intituled " An Act to amend the several Acts relating " to the Birkenhead Commissioners Docks, and to transfer the " several powers of the said Commissioners to a Corporate " Body to be entitled the Trustees of the Birkenhead Docks " and for other purposes," as are thereby vested in the Commissioners under the said Local Act.

[The Act 11 and 12 Vict. ch. 144, was repealed by the Mersey Docks and Harbour Act, 1857, under which the Mersey Docks and Harbour Board was constituted. The powers of the trustees were by that Act vested in the Dock Board.]

11.—The provisions (except as aforesaid) of the said Public Health Act may, whenever practicable, be applied to anything which shall arise under the unrepealed parts of the said Local Act, and such unrepealed parts shall be incorporated with the said Public Health Act.

12.—All property and estate whatsoever of the Commissioners under the said Local Act shall be transferred to the said Local Board of Health, and shall be held by them upon the same trusts and for the same purposes as by such Commissioners.

13.—All debts, monies, and securities for money, contracted or payable by such Commissioners, shall be satisfied by the said Local Board out of such parts of the said transferred property and estate as would have been chargeable therewith if this Order had not been made, and shall be paid and satisfied by the said Local Board as by such Commissioners.

14.—Provided always, that if such property and estate be insufficient, the deficiency shall be charged upon the rates leviable under the said Public Health Act, in the parts only which would have been chargeable with such deficiency if this Order had not been made.

15.—Provided also, that if such property and estate be more than sufficient, the surplus shall be applied to the use of the same parts and to the same purposes as it would have been if this Order had not been made.

16.—All expenses which shall be incurred by the said Local Board of Health under the unrepealed parts of the said Local Act, and not defrayed out of the monies arising under that Local Act, shall be deemed to be expenses incurred under the said Public Health Act, and shall be defrayed out of the rates under that Act (as the nature of the case may require); and the monies necessary to be raised for the purposes of such Local Act may be raised as under the said Public Health Act.

Schedule.

17.—The sections of the Towns Police Clauses Act, 1847, with respect to—

The appointment and the powers, duties, and privileges of constables;

And obstructions and nuisances in the streets, and fires, and places of public resort, and [*Vide* The Wallasey Order, 1888.] hackney carriages;

And with respect to public bathing;

And the sections of the Towns Improvement Clauses Act, 1847, with respect to—

Naming the streets and numbering the houses, and improving the line of the streets and removing obstructions;

And ruinous or dangerous buildings;

And precautions during the construction and repair of sewers, streets, and houses;

And the section with respect to the prevention of nuisances, numbered 104;

And the sections with respect to the prevention of smoke;

And the sections with respect to the construction of houses for prevention of fire;

And the sections with respect to supplying buildings with fresh air, numbered 110 and 111;

And clocks;

And so much of the sections with respect to things to be done by the Commissioners by special order only, as relate to baths and wash-houses, except so much of the said last-mentioned sections as requires any special order in respect of the matters contained therein;

And the sections of the Markets and Fairs Clauses Act, 1847, with respect to the construction of the market or fair and the works connected therewith, except so much thereof as relates to lands taken compulsorily;

And the holding of the market or fair, and the protection thereof;

And slaughter-houses;

And with respect to weighing goods and carts;

And stallages, rents, and tolls;

And byelaws;

Shall be incorporated with so much of the said Local Act as remains unrepealed by this Order, and with the said Public Health Act, as applied to the said Town by this Order, and any Act of Parliament confirming the same; and the expression "The Special Act," used in the said sections, shall be con-

Schedule.

strued to mean the unrepealed part of the said Local Act, and the said Public Health Act so applied; and the expression "Limits of the Special Act," used in the same sections, shall be construed to mean the District constituted by this Order; and the expression "the Commissioners," used in the said sections, shall mean the said Local Board.

18.—The said Local Board may exercise with regard to horses, mules, or asses let for hire the same powers as to the licensing of the owners, drivers, or persons attending upon the same, and as to their regulation, and for imposing penalties upon such persons as they are empowered to exercise in the case of hackney carriages and the drivers thereof.

19.—Provided always, that this Order, and the repeal of the parts of the said local Act mentioned in the Schedule thereto shall not prejudicially affect anything done under that Act before the passing of any Act of Parliament confirming this Order, but notwithstanding this Order and the Schedule thereto, all such things shall be as valid, with reference to the said Local Board of Health, as if the same had been done with reference to that Board, and may be dealt with in the same manner in all respects as if they related to that Board instead of such Commissioners.

20.— Provided also, that this Order, and the repeal of the parts of the said Local Act mentioned in the Schedule thereto, shall be without prejudice to any penalties incurred under that Act, but all such penalties may be recovered by the said Local Board of Health, according to the provisions of this Order.

Given under our Hands and under the Seal of the General Board of Health, this Ninth day of November in the year of our Lord One thousand eight hundred and fifty-two,

(Signed)   SHAFTESBURY,
EDWIN CHADWICK.
T. SOUTHWOOD SMITH.

SCHEDULE to which this Order refers.

The parts of the Local Act referred to in this Order to be repealed are as follows; that is to say :—

The sections numbered respectively in the copies of the said Act printed by the Queen's Printers, 1 to 5, 7 to 16, all inclusive; 18 to 62, 64 to 68, 70 to 83, 90 to 117, 119 to 141, 143 to 152, 157 to 165, 172 to 181, 183 to 186, 189 to 191, and 199 to 235, all inclusive; so much of 236 and 237 as relates to drivers of hackney carriages; 238, 239, so much of 240, 242, and 243 as relates to drivers of hackney carriages; 241, 244, 245, except so much as provides for the regulation of loads, rates, fares, and prices of errand, message, or luggage porters, and their behaviour and conduct, and the punishment of the same; 247 to 250, 252 to 255, 258 to 277, 281 to 292, 295 to 299, 301 to 323, all inclusive. 325, 326 and 328.

And so much of any unrepealed part of the said Act as fixes the amount of any penalty for any offence under the said Act, wherever the penalty for such offence is fixed by the Public Health Act, or any Act hereby incorporated therewith, or by any Byelaw of the Local Board of Health, at an amount other than that fixed by the said Local Act.

THE
WALLASEY IMPROVEMENT ACT, 1858.

(21 and 22 Vict. ch. 63.)

ARRANGEMENT OF SECTIONS.

	SECTION.
Preamble.	
Commencement of Act	1
Short titles of the Wallasey Improvement Act, 1845, and of this Act	2
Limits of Act	3
Act to be executed by Local Board	4
8 and 9 Vict. ch. 18, and parts of 10 and 11 Vict. chs. 15 and 17 incorporated	5
Same meanings to words in Incorporated Acts as this Act ...	6
Power to construct Waterworks according to deposited plans..	7
Powers for compulsory purchases limited	8
Period for completion of Waterworks	9
Lands of Mersey Docks and Harbour Board, not to be taken without consent	10
Rates at which water is to be supplied for domestic purposes.	11
Local Board not to be bound to supply water unless apparatus approved by them	12
Supply of water for domestic purposes	13
Rates for waterclosets and baths	14
Supply of water for other than domestic purposes	15
Penalty for using water for other than domestic purposes, &c., without agreement	16
Power to construct Gasworks	17
Gas to be consumed by meter on request ...	18
Penalty for tampering with meters	19
Local Board may remove pipes from unoccupied premises on giving notice to owner	20
Penalties not cumulative... ...	21
Maximum price of gas	22
Quality of gas	23
Local Board to erect a meter to test purity of gas	24

	SECTION.
Power to Justices on requisition to authorise testing of gas ...	25
Cost of experiment to be paid according to the event... ...	26
Power to levy Wallasey Waterworks Rate	27
Monies received from Water Rents, &c., to be carried to Waterworks Account	28
Power to levy Wallasey Lighting Rate...	29
Monies received from Gas Rents, &c., to be carried to Lighting Account	30
Rates may be levied on separate districts ...	31
Rates for more or less than a year	32
Water and Lighting Rate, how to be made and recovered ..	33
Extending provisions of 11 and 12 Vict. ch. 63, as to compositions for and recovery of Rates, &c.	34
Act not to alter or affect the question of rating the docks, &c.	35
Power to lease or purchase New Brighton Ferry as well as other ferries	36
Power to provide steam-boats, &c.	37
Local Board to negotiate for lease or purchase of existing ferries before acquiring or establishing any new Ferry ...	38
Power to Local Board to levy Tolls for use of Ferries, &c. ...	39
Tolls to be charged equally	40
Ferries to be free on payment of Tolls	41
Taking and recovery of Tolls	42
Disputes as to the amount of Tolls chargeable	43
Differences as to weights...	44
Local Board to provide Weighing Machines, Weights, &c. ...	45
Penalty on Passengers practising frauds on the Local Board..	46
List of Tolls to be printed and exhibited	47
Tolls to be taken only while list exhibited	48
Penalties on Toll Collectors	49
Toll Collector to be liable for wrong detention of goods ...	50
Local Board to regulate the use of Ferries	51
Bye-laws may be repealed or altered from time to time	52
Bye-laws may be enforced by imposition of Penalties ...	53
No Bye-laws to come into operation until allowed in the manner prescribed	54
Notice of allowance of Bye-laws to be given in one or more Newspapers, &c.	55
A copy of proposed Bye-laws to be open for inspection	56
Publication of Bye-laws...	57
Bye-laws to be binding on all Parties	58
Proof of publication of Bye-laws	59
Power to borrow on Mortgage for purposes herein named— Waterworks, Gas, Ferries	60

21 & 22 *Vict.* *The Wallasey Improvement* *ch. liii.* 167
Act, 1858.

SECTION.

Provisions of 11 & 12 Vict., c. 63, to apply to Mortgages under this Act	61
Saving priority of existing Mortgages and future Mortgages under 11 & 12 Vict., c. 63	62
Application of Monies borrowed on Wallasey Waterworks Account, &c.	63
Application of Monies borrowed on Wallasey Lighting Account, &c.	64
Application of Wallasey Waterworks Account ...	65
Application of Wallasey Lighting Account	66
Application of Wallasey Ferries Account	67
Lands empowered to be sold by sec. 84 of 8 & 9 Vict., ch. vi., may be either sold, let or exchanged, 49 Geo. 3, ch. 103...	68
Repealed	69 to 79
Local Board may agree to execute Works at expense of Owners	80
Proof of debts in Bankruptcy	81
Authentication of Notices	82
Interest in Contract or Liability to Rates not to disqualify Justices	83
Recovery of Penalties	84
Application of Penalties	85
Saving rights of Birkenhead and Claughton Gas and Water Company	86
Saving Rights of Local Board ...	87
Expenses of Act	88

AN ACT

for enabling the Local Board of Health for the District of Wallasey to construct Works and supply their District with Water and Gas; for enlarging their Powers with respect to the Acquisition and Maintenance of Ferries; and for other Purposes.

28TH JUNE, 1858.

8 & 9 Vict. ch. vi.

WHEREAS the Act of the eighth and ninth years of Her present Majesty, chapter six (local), was passed for paving, lighting, watching, cleansing, and otherwise improving the Parish of Wallasey in the County of Chester, and for establishing a Police and also a Market within the said Parish, and for other purposes, whereby commissioners were appointed for carrying the said Act into execution: and whereas by "The Public Health Supplemental Act, 1853, No. 1," and the Provisional Order relating to Wallasey, set forth in the Schedule thereto, certain of the powers of the first-recited Act were repealed, and the powers thereof remaining unrepealed were transferred to and vested in the Local Board of Health for the District of Wallasey (herein-after called "The Local Board"), who were thereby appointed the commissioners for executing the unrepealed parts of the said first-recited Act: And whereas it is expedient that powers should be conferred on the Local Board for supplying the District of Wallasey with water and gas, and that they should be empowered to construct Waterworks and Gasworks, and to levy additional rates for such purposes: And whereas it is expedient that the powers granted by the first-recited Act for the taking on lease or purchase of Ferries within the said District, and the Wharfs, Landing Places, and conveniences connected therewith, and for providing, purchasing, and maintaining steam and other boats, materials, and things, and otherwise in relation to the working of any such Ferry, should be extended and enlarged, and that the Local Board should be empowered more efficiently to exercise these powers: And whereas the provisions of the said "Public Health Act, 1848," as applied to the said District of Wallasey, are as regards the construction and regulation of buildings and in other respects insufficient, and it is expedient to make other provisions in regard thereto: And whereas the purposes aforesaid cannot be effected without the authority of Parliament: May it therefore please Your Majesty that it may be enacted; and be it enacted by the Queen's most Excellent Majesty, by and with the advice and consent of the Lords Spiritual and Temporal, and Commons in this present Parliament assembled, and by the authority of the same, as follows; (that is to say,)

21 & 22 Vict.   The Wallasey Improvement Act, 1858.   ch. lviii.   169

Sec. 1—7

1. This Act shall commence and have effect on and from the first Thursday next after the passing thereof. *Commencement of Act.*

2. In citing the first-recited Act for any purpose it shall be sufficient to use the expression "The Wallasey Improvement Act, 1845," and in citing this Act for any purpose it shall be sufficient to use the expression "The Wallasey Improvement Act, 1858." *Short Titles of first-recited Act and this Act.*

3. This Act shall apply to the area comprised within the jurisdiction of the Local Board, as defined by "The Public Health Supplemental Act, 1853, No. 1," and the provisional order relating to Wallasey set forth in the Schedule thereto. *Limits of Act.*

4. This Act shall be executed by the Local Board according to the powers and provisions of "The Public Health Act, 1848," and of the several acts supplemental thereto, or otherwise relating to the public health, and from time to time in force within the limits of this Act. *Act to be executed by Local Board.*

5. "The Lands Clauses Consolidation Act, 1845," "The Waterworks Clauses Act, 1847," (except the Sections of the last-mentioned Act "with respect to the amount of profit to be received by the undertakers when the waterworks are carried on for their benefit," and "with respect to the yearly receipt and expenditure of the Undertakers," and which are numbered from 75 to 83, inclusive of both Numbers,) and "The Gasworks Clauses Act, 1847," (except the Sections of the last-mentioned Act "with respect to the amount of profit to be received by the undertakers when the gasworks are carried on for their benefit," and "with respect to the yearly receipt and expenditure of the undertakers," and which are numbered from 30 to 38, inclusive of both numbers,) shall be incorporated with and form part of this Act, except so far as the clauses and provisions of such Acts respectively are excepted or varied by this Act; and in construing those Acts in connexion with this Act the expression "the undertakers" and "the promoters of the undertaking" shall mean the Local Board. *8 & 9 Vict. ch. 18 and parts of 10 & 11 Vict. cc. 15-17, incorporated.*

6. The several words and expressions to which by the Acts wholly or partially incorporated with this Act meanings are respectively assigned shall have in this Act the same respective meanings, unless there be in the subject or context something repugnant to or inconsistent with such construction. *Same meanings to words in incorporated Acts as this Act.*

7. And whereas plans showing the line or situation of the waterworks intended to be constructed, and the lands proposed to be purchased or taken under the powers of this Act for the purposes of the proposed waterworks and gas works, and also a book of reference to such plans and sections, showing the levels of the proposed waterworks, have been deposited with the Clerk of the Peace for the County of Chester: Therefore, subject to the provisions in this Act, and in the Acts and parts of Acts incorporated herewith contained, the Local Board may make and maintain the said waterworks in the situation according to the levels and upon the lands delineated on the said plans and described in the said book of reference, and may enter upon, take, and use all or any of the said lands for the purposes of this Act. *Power to construct waterworks according to deposited plans.*

21 & 22 *Vict.* The *Wallasey Improvement* *ch. liii.*
Act, 1858.

Sec. 8—14

Powers for compulsory purchases limited.

8. The powers of the Local Board for the compulsory purchase of lands for the purposes of this Act shall not be exercised after the expiration of three years from the commencement of this Act.

Period for completion of waterworks.

9. The works by this Act authorised to be constructed for the supply of water, and shown on the deposited plans, shall be completed within five years from the commencement of this Act, and on the expiration of that period the powers of this Act granted to the Local Board for making those works, or otherwise in relation thereto, shall cease to be exercised except as to so much thereof as is then completed.

Lands of Mersey Docks and Harbour Board not to be taken without consent.

10. Nothing in this Act contained shall authorize or empower the Local Board to enter upon, take, or use any of the lands belonging to the Mersey Docks and Harbour Board without the consent of such Board.

Rates at which water is to be supplied for domestic purposes.

11. The Local Board shall from time to time, at the request of the owner or occupier of any house or part of a house in any street in which any pipe of the Local Board is within the distance of *twenty yards* from such house, or of any person who, under the provisions of this Act or "The Public Health Act, 1848," is entitled to demand a supply of water for domestic purposes, furnish to such owner or occupier or other person a sufficient supply of water for domestic purposes, for the annual rents hereinafter specified ; (that is to say,)

[The remainder of this section which prescribed the rents at which the Local Board should supply water for domestic purposes is repealed by the Wallasey Improvement Act, 1864, s. 18, " In lieu thereof the Local Board may demand for a supply of water for domestic purposes an annual rent not exceeding six pounds per centum on the annual value of the house in respect of which such supply of water is afforded." —*Vide* Wallasey Improvement Act, 1864, s. 18.]

Local Board not to be bound to supply water unless apparatus approved by them.

12. The Local Board shall not be bound to supply any watercloset, or the apparatus, cisterns, or pipes connected therewith, or any water for domestic purposes, unless the cisterns, pipes, and cocks necessary for such supply shall be constructed in manner approved by the Local Board.

Supply of water for domestic purposes.

13. A supply of water for domestic purposes shall in every case include a supply for private baths and waterclosets, not exceeding one bath and one watercloset, but shall not in any case include a supply for cattle or for horses, or for washing carriages, where such horses or carriages are kept for hire, or are the property of any dealer, or for any hotel, tavern, trade, manufacture, or business whatsoever, or for watering gardens, or for fountains, or for any ornamental purpose.

[*Vide* Waterworks Clauses Act, 1863, s.12, incorporated with the Wallasey Improvement Act, 1864, s. 3.]

Rates for waterclosets and Baths.

14. In addition to the rents for the supply for domestic purposes, the Local Board may demand and receive for every watercloset in any house (beyond the first) any yearly sum not exceeding four shillings ; and for every bath (beyond the first) any yearly sum not exceeding eight shillings.

15. The Local Board may use water for any public purpose, and may supply any person with water for other than domestic purposes, for such remuneration and upon such terms and conditions as may be agreed upon between the Local Board and such person. *Supply of water for other than domestic purposes.*

16. Every person using for other than domestic purposes any water supplied by the Local Board, and not having previously agreed with the Local Board for a supply for such other purpose, and every person having agreed with the Local Board for a supply of water for any other than domestic purposes, and using for any purposes other than the purposes so agreed for the water so supplied by the Local Board, shall respectively for every such offence forfeit and pay to the Local Board any sum not exceeding five pounds. *Penalty for using water for other than domestic purposes, &c., without agreement.*

17. Subject to the provisions contained in this Act and the Acts and parts of Acts incorporated herewith, the Local Board may from time to time construct and maintain upon all or any part of the lands numbered respectively 1, 2, 3, 4, 5, 6, 7, and 8 on the deposited plans but upon no other lands within the limits of this Act, gasworks, apparatus, and buildings, with approaches thereto, and may do all such other acts as they shall think necessary for manufacturing gas and supplying the inhabitants and lighting the streets within the limits of this Act; and the Local Board may supply such gas to such inhabitants upon such terms as shall be agreed upon between the Local Board and the persons supplied therewith, and may sell and dispose of the coke and other residuum arising from the materials used in the manufacture of gas, in such manner as the Local Board may think proper. *Power to construct gasworks.*

[The powers and provisions contained in sects. 17 to 26 of this Act apply also to the gasworks authorised by The Wallasey Improvement Act, 1867—*Vide* sec. 9 of that Act.]

18. Every consumer of gas supplied by the Local Board shall, on request in writing by the Local Board, consume the gas supplied to him by meter, and all such meters and all service pipes shall be provided by the Local Board at the expense of the consumer, or (at the option of the consumer) by the consumer and approved by the Local Board, and shall in each case be maintained to the satisfaction of the Local Board, and may from time to time be examined and tested by them. *Gas to be consumed by meter on request.*

19. Every person who shall knowingly and wilfully prevent any meter from duly registering the quantity of gas supplied shall for every such offence forfeit and pay to the Local Board any sum not exceeding five pounds; and the existence of artificial means for causing such prevention shall, where such meter shall be under the custody or control of the consumer, be *primâ facie* evidence that the same has been knowingly and wilfully caused by the consumer using such meter. *Penalty for tampering with meters.*

20. In all cases in which the Local Board are by "The Gasworks Clauses Act, 1847," incorporated with this Act, authorized to cut off and take away the supply of gas from any house, building, or premises, then, if such house, building, or premises, be unoccupied, the Local Board, their agents, servants, or workmen, after giving twenty-four hours previous notice to the owner, by serving the notice *Local Board may remove pipes from unoccupied premises, on giving notice to owner.*

Sec. 21—25 on him, or if the owner be not known to the Local Board by affixing the same for three days on some conspicuous part of such house, building, or premises, may enter into such building or premises between the hours of nine in the forenoon and four in the afternoon, and remove and carry away any pipe, meter, or fittings, or other works, the property of the Local Board.

Penalties not cumulative. **21.** Penalties imposed on the Local Board for one and the same offence by several Acts of Parliament shall not be cumulative, and for this purpose this Act and the Acts incorporated therewith shall be deemed several Acts.

Maximum price of gas. **22.** The maximum price at which gas shall be sold by the Local Board to all persons who shall burn the same by meter shall not exceed six shillings per thousand cubic feet.

[The Wallasey Improvement Act, 1867, s. 13, altered the maximum price of gas to five shillings and sixpence per thousand cubic feet.]

Quality of gas. **23.** All the gas supplied by the Local Board shall be of such quality as to produce, from an Argand burner having fifteen holes and a seven inch chimney, or other approved burner and chimney, and consuming five cubic feet of gas per hour, a light equal in intensity to the light produced by *ten sperm candles of six in the pound burning one hundred and twenty grains per hour.

[*Altered to *fourteen* by The Wallasey Improvement Act, 1867, s. 14.]

Local Board to erect a meter to test purity of gas. **24.** The Local Board shall within six months after they shall have commenced to supply gas under the provisions of this Act, cause to be erected in some convenient part of their works an experimental meter, furnished with an Argand fifteen hole burner and a seven inch chimney, or other approved burner and chimney capable of consuming five cubic feet of gas per hour, with other necessary apparatus for testing the illuminating power of gas.

Power to Justices on requisition to authorize testing of gas. **25.** It shall at any time be lawful for any two Justices of the Peace for the County of Chester not being members or officers of the Local Board, nor directors, shareholders, or officers of any company supplying gas within the district, on receiving a requisition signed by not less than five consumers of the gas supplied by the Local Board, complaining that the gas supplied to them is not in their judgment and belief of the full illuminating power prescribed in this Act, if they shall think fit by order in writing under their hands, to appoint some competent person to proceed to the works of the Local Board, and the person so appointed, on giving six hours previous notice in writing to the Local Board may at any reasonable hour in the daytime, on producing the said order, enter on the premises of the Local Board, and in the presence of the superintendent or other officer of the Local Board, make experiment of the illuminating power of the gas of the Local Board, by means of the experimental meter and other apparatus before mentioned; and the Local Board and their officers shall afford all reasonable facilities and assistance for making such experiment; and if it shall thereupon be proved to the satisfaction of the said two justices, after hearing the parties, that the illuminating power of the gas supplied by the Local Board did not, when so tested as aforesaid, equal the illuminating power by this Act prescribed, or that the Local Board or their officers refused to afford such reasonable facilities as aforesaid, or hindered or prevented the making of such experiment, in any such case the Local Board shall forfeit such sum, not exceeding twenty pounds, as the said justices shall determine.

Sec. 26—31

[*Vide* The Wallasey Improvement Act, 1867, s. 14.]

26. The costs of and attending such experiment, including the remuneration to be paid to the person making the same and the costs of the proceedings before the justices, shall be ascertained by such justices, and in the event of any penalty being imposed on the Local Board shall be paid, together with such penalty, by the Local Board; but in the event of the gas being found, when tested, to be of not less illuminating power than is by this Act prescribed, such costs shall be awarded to be paid to the Local Board by the body or persons making such requisition as aforesaid, as the case may be, and shall be paid or levied accordingly.

Cost of experiment to be paid according to the event.

[*Vide* The Wallasey Improvement Act, 1867, s. 14.]

27. The Local Board may from time to time make and levy a rate, to be called "The Wallasey Waterworks Rate," of such amount as they from time to time think fit, not exceeding in any year one shilling and threepence in the pound of the net annual value of the property included in such rate; and the monies arising therefrom shall be carried to an account to be called "The Wallasey Waterworks Account."

Power to levy Wallasey Waterworks Rate.

28. All monies which shall come to the hands of the Local Board from rents or payments made to them in respect of water supplied by them, or from any other source whatever connected with or relating to the Waterworks, or from any penalties recovered under the clauses of "The Waterworks Clauses Act, 1847," incorporated herewith, shall fall into and form part of the Wallasey Waterworks Account, and shall be applicable as part thereof.

Monies received from water rents, &c., to be carried to Waterworks Account.

29. The Local Board may from time to time make and levy a rate to be called "The Wallasey Lighting Rate," of such amount as they from time to time think fit, not exceeding in any year ninepence in the pound of the net annual value of the property included in such rate; and the monies arising therefrom shall be carried to an account to be called "The Wallasey Lighting Account."

Power to levy Wallasey Lighting Rate.

30. All monies which shall come to the hands of the Local Board in respect of gas supplied by them, or of coke or other residuum disposed of by them, and in respect of any penalties recovered under the clauses of "The Gasworks Clauses Act, 1847," incorporated herewith, shall fall into and form part of the Wallasey Lighting Account, and shall be applicable as part thereof.

Monies received from gas rents, &c., to be carried to Lighting Account.

31. The Local Board may (if they think fit) order the Wallasey Waterworks Rate and the Wallasey Lighting Rate, or either of them, to be levied by assessments to be made for separate and distinct districts, and may fix and determine such separate and distinct districts, and may from time to time vary such districts: provided always, that the Wallasey Waterworks Rate and the Wallasey Lighting Rate, as the case may be, shall not be levied within any

Rates may be levied on separate districts.

Sec. 32—36 part of the limits of this Act which shall not have been declared either a separate or distinct district, or be included in some district for water or lighting purposes under this Act; and the Local Board shall, subject to the provisions of this Act, supply water or gas (as the case may be) to all parts within the limits of this Act which shall be declared a separate and distinct district, or be included in some other district, as herein-before provided.

Rates for more or less than a year.

32. Any rate made under the authority of this Act may be made in respect of a period shorter or longer than a year, but not so as to increase the total amount payable in or for any year in respect of any rate.

Water and lighting Rate how to be made and recovered.

33. "The Wallasey Waterworks Rate," and "The Wallasey Lighting Rate," may be made upon the occupiers of all property within the limits of this Act, of whatever value, liable to be assessed under "The Public Health Act, 1848," and this Act, and may be assessed, levied, and recovered in the same manner as the special and general district rates are by that Act authorised to be levied and recovered; and such rates respectively shall from time to time be collected and paid in advance by yearly, half-yearly or quarterly payments as the Local Board shall think proper; and every such rate may be made and levied, either prospectively, in order to raise money for the payment of future expenses, or retrospectively, in order to raise money for the payment of expenses already incurred, or such rates may, at the option of the Board, be partly prospective and partly retrospective.

Extending provisions of 11 & 12 Vict. ch. 63 as to compositions for and recovery of rates, &c.

34. The provisions of "The Public Health Act, 1848," with respect to compositions for rates upon tenements under the annual value of ten pounds, and all the provisions of the same Act for the recovery of rates thereby authorized to be levied, and with respect to appeals against rates, shall extend and apply to and may be enforced with regard to all water rates and lighting rates made under the powers of this Act.

[The Public Health Act, 1848, was repealed by the Public Health Act, 1875. As to substituted provisions, *vide* sec. 313 of the latter Act (38 and 39 Vict. c. 55).]

Act not to alter or affect the question of rating the docks, &c.

35. Nothing in this Act contained shall alter or affect the question of the liability of any of the docks or works for the time being vested in the Mersey Docks and Harbour Board to the rates authorised to be levied under or by virtue of this Act, or to any other parochial or local rates, but the same shall in all respects be judged of and determined as if this Act had not been passed.

Power to lease or purchase New Brighton Ferry as well as other ferries;

36. Subject to the provisions of the first-recited Act and this Act contained, it shall be lawful for the Local Board to hire and take on lease, for any term not exceeding twenty-one years, and if thought expedient, to purchase and take absolutely by agreement with the several parties interested therein, but not otherwise, and to hold and use the ferry called "New Brighton Ferry," as well as the two ferries respectively called "Seacombe Ferry" and "Egremont Ferry," or any or either of them, and any other ferry which may hereinafter be established within the townships of Poulton-cum-Seacombe and Liscard, or either of them, with the wharfs, landing

places, and conveniences connected therewith, or such of them **Sec. 37—38**
such parts thereof as the Local Board may think proper; and it
shall be lawful for all persons interested in the said ferry called "New
Brighton Ferry," including such persons as would be capacitated to
sell lands under the provisions of "The Lands Clauses Consolidation
Act, 1845," to contract for a lease or the sale of, and to demise or
sell and convey their respective interests in, such last mentioned
ferry to the Local Board : provided always, that in case of a lease
granted by any party under any disability or incapacity the rent to
be reserved in such lease shall not be less than that which shall be
certified by a surveyor, to be appointed by two Justices of the Peace for
the County of Chester, to be a sufficient consideration for or in
respect of the premises demised by any such lease.

37. The Local Board may from time to time hire and charter, *and provide*
as well as provide, purchase, and maintain, such steam and other *steam boats,*
boats, materials, and things, and employ and recompense such *&c.*
persons as shall be necessary for the proper and efficient working of
any such ferry as shall be so hired or purchased by the Local Board
under the provisions of the first-recited Act or this Act.

[This is an extension of the powers conferred by sec. 87 of the
Wallasey Improvement Act, 1845.]

38. And whereas William Rushton Coulborn and Edward *Local Board*
Warburton Coulborn of New Brighton in the County of Chester are *to negotiate*
or claim to be lessees of the ferries known respectively as Seacombe *purchase of*
Ferry, Egremont Ferry, and New Brighton Ferry, all within the *existing*
district of the Local Board, and it is just and expedient, and has been *Ferries before*
agreed between the said William Rushton Coulborn and Edward *acquiring or*
Warburton Coulborn and the said Local Board that provision should *establishing*
be made as follows, as well for protecting the said William Rushton *Ferry.*
Coulborn and Edward Warburton Coulborn from injury by reason
of the exercise of the powers of the before-recited Acts or this Act in
relation to the acquisition of ferries by the Local Board as for
facilitating the acquisition of such ferries by the Local Board : Therefore it shall not be lawful for the Local Board to contract or negotiate
for the lease or purchase of any ferry, or to do any act to establish
any new ferry within the townships of Poulton-cum-Seacombe and
Liscard, or either of them, until they shall have given notice in
writing under the hand of their clerk, delivered to or at the place of
abode of the said William Rushton Coulborn and Edward Warburton
Coulborn, or the persons in whom their interest in the said ferries
may for the time being be vested (and which said William Rushton
Coulborn and Edward Warburton Coulborn and such persons aforesaid are hereinafter designated by the term "the Lessees"), requiring
the lessees to signify in writing, within three months from the
delivery as aforesaid of such notice, whether or not they the lessees
are willing to treat with the Local Board for a lease of, or (as the
case may be) for the sale of their interest in the said Seacombe Ferry
Egremont Ferry and New Brighton Ferry ; and if the lessees shall,
within three months after the delivery of such notice, signify in
writing, delivered at the office of the Local Board, or to the clerk or
one of the members of the Local Board, their willingness to grant a
lease of or (as the case may be) to sell their interest in the said
ferries, then the Local Board shall be bound to take a lease of or

Sec. 39—41 (as the case may be) to purchase the interest of the lessees in the said ferries, and in such case the rent to be reserved in, or other consideration to be paid for any such lease, or the consideration to be paid for any such purchase, and the terms and conditions of such lease or purchase, (as the case may be), shall in case the parties differ about the same, be settled by arbitration under and in the manner provided by the clauses of "The Lands Clauses Consolidation Act, 1845," numbered respectively 25 to 37, both inclusive: provided always, that if the lessees shall neglect or omit, for the space of three months after the delivery to them of such notice as aforesaid, to signify their willingness to grant a lease of or (as the case may be) to sell their interest in the said Ferries, then the restriction imposed on the Local Board by this section against negotiating or contracting for the lease or purchase of any other Ferry, or from doing any act for establishing a new Ferry in the said Townships or either of them, shall be null and void: provided also that if the lessees and the Local Board hereafter determine to grant and accept a lease or make a sale and purchase of one or two only of the said three Ferries instead of all the said three Ferries, it shall be lawful for them so to do by mutual agreement entered into between them; and in that case the rent or consideration and terms and conditions applicable to such lease or purchase of the said one or two of the said three Ferries shall (in case the parties differ about the same) be settled in the same manner as herein-before provided, applicable to the lease or purchase of the said three Ferries; and when the said lease or purchase of the said one or two of the said three Ferries shall have been carried into effect, the Local Board shall thenceforth stand discharged from liability to lease or purchase the other or others of the said three Ferries, as well as from the restriction imposed by this section against leasing or purchasing or establishing any other Ferry as aforesaid.

Power to Local Board to levy tolls for use of ferries, &c.

39. The Local Board may demand and receive for the use of any Ferry purchased or leased by them, and the conveyance of passengers, cattle, and goods in any steam or other boat purchased, hired, chartered, or provided by them under the authority of the first-recited Act or this Act, any tolls (in this Act called "Ferry Tolls") not exceeding the sums mentioned in the Schedule to this Act; and the monies arising therefrom shall be carried to an account to be called "The Wallasey Ferries Account."

[*Vide* The Wallasey Improvement Act, 1867, sec. 19, Tolls after January 1, 1868, The Wallasey Improvement Act, 1867, sec. 20 and sched. C.]

Tolls to be charged equally.

40. The Ferry tolls shall be at all times charged equally to all persons and after the same rate in respect of all passengers and goods, animals, or carriages of a like description conveyed under the like circumstances; and no reduction or advance in any such tolls shall be made either directly or indirectly in favour of or against any particular company or person using the said Ferry.

[*Vide* The Wallasey Improvement Act, 1864, sec. 16, and The Wallasey Improvement Act, 1867, sec. 21.]

Ferries to be free on payment of tolls.

41. The Local Board shall not at any time demand or take a greater ferry toll, or make any greater charge for ferryage, than the amounts specified in the schedule to this Act; and upon payment of the tolls from time to time demandable, all persons shall be entitled to use the ferry in respect of which such toll is demandable, subject nevertheless to the regulations to be from time to time made by the Local Board by virtue of the powers in that behalf herein conferred upon them.

42. Such Ferry tolls shall be paid to such persons and at such places upon or near to the Ferry, in respect of which the same are demandable, and in such manner and under such regulations as the Local Board shall by notice, to be annexed to the account or list of tolls appoint; and if, on demand, any person fail to pay the tolls due in respect of any goods, it shall be lawful for the collector to detain and sell all or any part of such goods, and out of the monies thence arising to retain the toll payable in respect of such goods, and all charges and expenses of such detention and sale; and such collector shall upon demand, render the overplus, if any, of the monies arising by such sale, and such of the goods as shall remain unsold, to the persons entitled thereto; and if such goods happen to be removed before the tolls payable in respect of the same be paid, then the Local Board may recover such tolls in a summary manner before a Justice or by action at law in any court of competent jurisdiction.

Taking and recovery of tolls.

[Incorporated with The Wallasey Improvement Act, 1867, by sec. 23 of that Act.]

43. If any Dispute arise concerning the amount of the Ferry Tolls due to the Local Board, or concerning the charges occasioned by any distress levied with reference thereto, the collector or person distraining may detain the goods distrained, or (if the case so require) the proceeds of the sale thereof, until the amount of the tolls due, or until such tolls and the amount of the costs of such distress have been ascertained by some justice; and upon application made to any such justice for that purpose, he shall examine the matter upon oath of the parties or witnesses, and determine the amount of the tolls due, and also the amount of the costs; and it shall be lawful for such justice to award such costs to be paid by either of the parties to the other of them as he shall think reasonable; and if, on demand thereof, such costs be not paid by the party ordered to pay the same, they shall be levied by distress, and such justice shall issue his warrant accordingly.

Disputes as to the amount of tolls chargeable.

[Incorporated with The Wallasey Improvement Act, 1867, by sec. 23 of that Act.]

44. If any difference arise between any toll collector or other officer or servant of the Local Board, and any owner of or person having the charge of any articles liable to Ferry tolls, respecting the weight, quantity, or nature of such articles, such collector or other officer may lawfully detain and examine, gauge, or otherwise measure all such articles conveyed thereby; and if, upon such measuring, such articles appear to be of greater weight or quantity, or of other nature than shall have been stated in the account given thereof, then the person who shall have given such account, or the respective owners of such articles, as the case may be, shall pay the costs of such measuring; but if such articles appear to be of the same or less weight or quantity than shall have been stated in such account, then the Local Board shall pay such costs, and they shall also pay to such owner of or person having charge of such articles such damage (if

Differences as to weights.

N

21 & 22 *Vict.* *The Wallasey Improvement Act*, 1858. *ch. lxiii.*

Sec. 45—49 any) as shall appear to any justice, on a summary application to him for that purpose, to have arisen from such detention.

[Incorporated with the Wallasey Improvement Act, 1867, by sec. 23 of that Act.]

Local Board to provide weighing machines, weights, &c.

45. The Local Board shall provide and maintain at each Ferry which may be leased or purchased by them weighing machines and weights and scales for weighing and measuring goods or articles liable to the Ferry tolls.

Penalty on passengers practising frauds on the Local Board.

46. If any person shall knowingly and wilfully refuse or neglect to pay his Ferry toll when the same shall be payable by virtue of this Act, every such person shall for every such offence forfeit a sum not exceeding forty shillings.

[This section is incorporated with the Wallasey Improvement Act, 1867, by sec. 23 of that Act. The powers conferred by this section are extended by sec. 26 of that Act and by sec. 15 of the Wallasey Improvement Act, 1872.]

List of tolls to be printed and exhibited.

47. A list of all the Ferry tolls from time to time appointed by the Local Board to be taken shall be published by the same being printed and exhibited in some conspicuous place on the toll gates or toll houses, or places where such tolls shall be payable, and also on some conspicuous part of the boats plying at the Ferry in respect of which such tolls are demanded.

[Incorporated with the Wallasey Improvement Act, 1867, by sec. 23 of that Act.]

Tolls to be taken only while list exhibited.

48. No Ferry tolls shall be demanded or taken by the Local Board for the use of any Ferry during any time at which the list of tolls hereinbefore directed to be exhibited in respect of such Ferry shall not be so exhibited; and if any person wilfully pull down, deface, or destroy any such list of tolls he shall forfeit a sum not exceeding five pounds for every such offence.

[Incorporated with the Wallasey Improvement Act, 1867, by sec. 23 of that Act.]

Penalties on toll collectors.

49. Every toll collector who shall commit any of the following offences shall forfeit a sum not exceeding ten pounds for each such offence; (that is to say,)

If he refuse to tell his Christian name and surname to any person demanding the same who shall have paid or tendered the tolls demanded of him, or if he give a false name to any such person:

If he demand or take a greater or less toll from any person than he shall be authorized to do by virtue of this Act, and of the orders of the Local Board made in pursuance thereof:

If, upon the legal toll being paid or tendered, he do unnecessarily detain or wilfully hinder any goods or any person from passing by the Ferry:

If he make use of any scurrilous or abusive language to any passenger or to any person lawfully using the Ferry.

[Incorporated with the Wallasey Improvement Act, 1867, by sec. 23 of that Act.]

50. If at any time it be made to appear to any justice that any such detention and measuring of any goods as hereinbefore mentioned was without reasonable ground, or that it was vexatious on the part of such collector or other officer, then the collector or other officer shall himself pay the costs of such detention and measuring, and the damage occasioned thereby ; and in default of immediate payment of any such costs or damage, the same may be recovered by distress of the goods of such collector, and such justice shall issue his warrant accordingly. *[Toll collector to be liable for wrong detention of goods.]*

[Incorporated with the Wallasey Improvement Act, 1867, by sec. 23 of that Act.]

51. It shall be lawful for the Local Board from time to time, subject to the provisions and restrictions in this Act contained, to make, in connexion with their Ferries or any of them, Byelaws for the following purposes ; (that is to say,) *[Local Board to regulate the use of Ferries.]*

- For regulating the times of the arrival and departure of boats using any such Ferry ;
- For regulating the embarking and discharging of passengers, and the loading and unloading of goods and carriages carried on board the boats using any such Ferry ;
- For regulating the delivery of goods and other things which are conveyed on board such boats ;
- For preventing the smoking of tobacco, and the commission of any other nuisance in or upon such boats, or in any of the premises occupied by the Local Board ;
- And generally for maintaining order and decorum on board the boats using any such Ferry, and for regulating the using or working of the Ferry and boats ;

But no such byelaw shall authorise the closing of any Ferry at reasonable hours, except at any time when in consequence of the state of the weather, or from any other sufficient cause, it shall be necessary to suspend the working of the Ferry boats.

52. The Local Board may from time to time, as they shall think fit, repeal or alter any such byelaws: provided always, that such byelaws shall not be repugnant to the laws of England or to the provisions of this Act or of any Act incorporated therewith, and such byelaws shall be in writing under the seal of the Local Board and the signatures of any five or more of their number, and if affecting other persons than the officers and servants of the Local Board shall be printed and published as herein provided. *[Byelaws may be repealed or altered from time to time.]*

[This and the following sections up to and inclusive of sec. 59 are applied to all byelaws under the Wallasey Improvement Act, 1867, by sec. 29 of that Act.]

53. The Local Board, by the byelaws so to be made by them, may impose such reasonable penalties as they shall think fit, not exceeding forty shillings for each breach of such byelaws ; provided that every such byelaw shall be so framed as to allow the justices before whom any penalty imposed thereby shall be sought to be recovered to order the whole or part only of such penalty to be paid. *[Byelaws may be enforced by imposition of penalties.]*

21 & 22 Vict. *The Wallasey Improvement* ch. lxiii.
Act, 1858.

Sec. 54—59

No byelaws to come into operation until allowed in the manner prescribed.

54. No byelaws made under the authority of this Act (except such as may relate solely to the officers or servants of the Local Board) shall come into operation until the same shall have been allowed by the Court of Quarter Sessions for the County of Chester, and it shall be incumbent on the Justices at Quarter Sessions, on the request of the Local Board, to examine into the byelaws which may be tendered to them for that purpose, and to allow of or disallow the same as to them may seem meet.

Notice of allowance of byelaws to be given in one or more newspapers, &c.

55. Provided always, That no such byelaw shall be allowed in manner herein mentioned unless notice of the intention to apply for an allowance of the same shall have been given in one or more newspapers of the County of Chester one month at least before the hearing of such application; and any party aggrieved by any such byelaw, on giving notice of the nature of his objection to the Local Board ten days before the hearing of the application for the allowance thereof, may, by himself or his counsel, attorney or agent, be heard thereon, but not so as to allow more than one party to be heard upon the same matter of objection.

A copy of proposed byelaws to be open for inspection.

56. For one month at least before any such application for allowance of any byelaw a copy of such proposed byelaws shall be kept at the office of the Local Board, and shall be put up in some conspicuous part of every toll house or building at which the ferry tolls are payable, and all persons at all reasonable times may inspect such copy without fee or reward, and the Local Board shall furnish every person who shall apply for the same with a copy thereof, or of any part thereof, on payment of sixpence for every one hundred words so to be copied.

Publication of byelaws.

57. The said byelaws shall be printed, and the Clerk of the Local Board shall give a printed copy thereof to every person applying for the same without charge, and a printed copy thereof shall be put up in some conspicuous part of the office of the Local Board and also in some conspicuous part of every toll house or building at which the Ferry tolls are payable, and the same shall be renewed from time to time as occasion shall require, and shall be open to inspection without fee or reward; and in case the said Clerk shall not permit the same to be inspected at all reasonable times he shall, for every such offence, be liable to a penalty not exceeding five pounds.

Byelaws to be binding on all parties.

58. All byelaws made and confirmed according to the provisions of this Act, when so published and put up, shall be binding upon and be observed by all parties, and shall be a sufficient warrant for all persons acting under the same.

Proof of Publication of byelaws.

59. The production of a written or printed copy of the byelaws requiring confirmation by the Court of Quarter Session, authenticated by the signature of the Chairman of the Court, who shall have approved of the same, and a written or printed copy of the byelaws not requiring such confirmation or approval, authenticated by the seal of the Local Board and the signatures of any five or more of their number, shall be evidence of the existence and making of such byelaws in all cases of prosecution, under the same, without proof of the signature of such Chairman or the seal or signature of the Local Board; and with respect to the proof of the publication of

21 & 22 Vict. *The Wallasey Improvement Act,* 1858. ch. lxiii. 181

any such byelaws it shall be sufficient to prove that a printed copy thereof was put up and continued in manner by this Act directed, and in case of its afterwards being displaced or damaged that the same was replaced or restored as soon as conveniently might be, unless proof be adduced by the party complained against that a printed copy of such byelaws was not duly put up or continued as directed by this Act.

Sec. 60

60. Subject to the provisions contained in this Act and the Acts and parts of Acts incorporated therewith, the Local Board may from time to time borrow on mortgage any sums not exceeding the respective amounts hereinafter mentioned ; (that is to say,)

Power to borrow on mortgage for purposes herein named.

> On mortgage of the " Wallasey Waterworks Account," and of the waterworks for the time being vested in or belonging to the Local Board, any sum not exceeding fifteen thousand pounds :

Waterworks.

> On mortgage of the " Wallasey Lighting Account " and of the gasworks for the time being vested in or belonging to the Local Board, any sum not exceeding ten thousand pounds :

Gas.

> On mortgage of the " Wallasey Ferries Account " and of the ferries for the time being belonging to or leased by the Local Board, and the steam and other boats, materials, and things connected therewith, and also (as a collateral security) of the general district rate authorized by " The Public Health Act, 1848," to be made and levied, any sums of money not exceeding seventy-five thousand pounds necessary for enabling the Local Board to carry out the purposes of this Act with reference to the acquisition of ferries and of steam and other boats in connexion therewith :

Ferries.

Provided always, that the monies which the Local Board are expressly authorised to borrow under this Act shall be in addition to the monies which they are authorised to borrow by " The Public Health Act, 1848," or any Act supplemental thereto or otherwise relating to the public health.

[FURTHER BORROWING POWERS :—

1. *Water :* Wallasey Improvement Act, 1861, sec. 3.
    Wallasey Order, 1863.
    　　　　　　　,,　　　,, 　　1870, art. 5.
    　　　　　　　,,　Improvement Act, 1872, sec. 17.
2. *Gas :* Wallasey Improvement Act, 1861, sec. 3.
    　　　　　,,　　　　　　,,　　　　,, 1867, sec. 30.
    　　　　　,,　Order (No. 1), 1877, art. 2.
    　　　　　,,　　　　,,　1883, art. 1.
    　　　　　,,　　　　,,　1892, art. 2.
    　　　　　,,　　　　,,　1896, art. 1.
    　　　　　,,　　　　,,　1898, art. 1.
3. *Ferries :* Wallasey Improvement Act, 1861, sec. 3
    　　　　　,,　　　　　　,,　　　　　　,,　1864, sec. 21
    　　　　　,,　　　　　　,,　　　　　　,,　1872, sec. 17
    　　　　　,,　Order (No. 1), 1877, art. 3.
    　　　　　,,　　　　,,　1881, art. 1.
    　　　　　,,　　　　,,　1883, art. 2.
    　　　　　,,　　　　,,　1895, art. 1.
    　　　　　,,　　　　,,　1897, art. 1.]

21 & 22 Vict. *The Wallasey Improvement Act,* 1858. *ch. lxiii.*

Sec. 61—65

Provisions of 11 & 12 Vict. ch. 63, to apply to mortgages under this Act.

61. The sections of "The Public Health Act, 1848," one hundred and ten to one hundred and fourteen, both inclusive, and the schedules (B.) and (C.) to that Act, shall be applicable to the mortgages to be executed by the Local Board under the authority of this Act.

[The Public Health Act, 1848, was repealed by the Public Health Act, 1875. As to substituted provisions, *vide* sec. 313 of the Public Health Act, 1875, 38 and 39 Vict. ch. 55.]

Saving Priority of existing mortgages and future mortgages under 11 & 12 Vict. ch. 63.

62. Provided always, that all mortgages granted by the Commissioners under the authority of the first-recited Act, and all mortgages granted by the Local Board under the authority of "The Public Health Act, 1848," and subsisting at the time of the passing of this Act, and all mortgages to be hereafter granted by the Local Board under the authority of "The Public Health Act, 1848," shall respectively have priority over all mortgages which may be granted under the authority of this Act on the collateral security of the general district rate, so far as relates to such collateral security.

[Altered and amended by the Wallasey Order, 1883, art 9. For provisions as to repayment of moneys borrowed and sinking fund, *vide* The Wallasey Order, 1883, arts. 4 and 7.]

Application of monies borrowed on Wallasey Waterworks Account, &c.

63. All monies from time to time borrowed by the Local Board under the authority of this Act on mortgage of the "Wallasey Waterworks Account" and of the waterworks for the time being vested in or belonging to the Local Board shall be applied as follows:

First, in payment of such part as the Local Board think fit of the expenses attending or incident to the obtaining and passing of this Act:

Secondly, in the construction of the waterworks, and in laying down, constructing, and erecting water mains, pipes, engines, wells, pumps and other works and conveniences connected therewith, and in the supply of water.

Application of monies borrowed on Wallasey Lighting Account, &c.

64. All monies from time to time borrowed by the Local Board, under the authority of this Act, on mortgage of the "Wallasey Lighting Account," and of the gas works for the time being vested in or belonging to the Local Board, shall be applied as follows:

First, in payment of such part as the Local Board think fit of the expenses attending or incident to the obtaining and passing of this Act:

Secondly, in the constructing of the gas works, and in laying down, fixing, and providing gas mains, pipes, lamps, lamp posts, lamp irons, and other works and conveniences connected therewith, and in the manufacture and supply of gas.

Application of Wallasey Waterworks Account.

65. The Wallasey Waterworks Account shall be applied and disposed of as follows:

First, in paying the interest of all monies borrowed or which shall from time to time be due and owing on the credit of the Wallasey Waterworks Account.

Secondly, in setting apart and appropriating the sum required to be set apart and appropriated for paying off the principal monies which shall have been borrowed or secured on the credit of the Wallasey Waterworks Account:

Thirdly, in paying the costs and expenses of maintaining the waterworks, and in laying down, constructing, erecting, maintaining, repairing, renewing, and altering water mains, pipes, engines, wells, pumps, and other works and conveniences connected therewith, and in otherwise carrying into effect the purposes of this Act, and of the Acts or parts of Acts incorporated herewith, so far as the same relate to the supply of water within the limits of this Act, or in any way incident thereto:

Fourthly, in paying off all monies due on the credit of the Wallasey Waterworks Account:

Lastly, any surplus which may remain shall be carried to the credit of and be applicable to the same purposes as the General District Rates under " The Public Health Act, 1848."

66. The Wallasey Lighting Account shall be applied and disposed of as follows: *Application of Wallasey Lighting Account.*

First, in paying the interest of all monies borrowed or which shall from time to time be due and owing on the credit of the Wallasey Lighting Account:

Secondly, in setting apart and appropriating the sum required to be set apart and appropriated for paying off the principal monies which shall have been borrowed or secured on the credit of the Wallasey Lighting Account.

Thirdly, in paying the costs and expenses of maintaining the gasworks, and in laying down, fixing, and providing, and from time to time repairing, renewing, and altering, the gas mains pipes, lamps, lamp posts, lamp irons, and other works and conveniences connected therewith, and in the manufacture and supply of gas, and in otherwise carrying the purposes of this Act and of the Acts or parts of Acts incorporated herewith into effect, so far as the same in any way relate to the lighting of the streets, and the manufacture and supply of gas, or in any way incident thereto:

Fourthly, in paying off all monies due on the credit of the Wallasey Lighting Account:

Lastly, any surplus which may remain shall be carried to the credit of and be applicable to the same purposes as the General District Rates under " The Public Health Act, 1848."

67. All monies which shall come to the hands of the Local Board from the Wallasey Ferries Account shall be applied and disposed of (so far as the same will extend) as follows: *Application of Wallasey Ferries Account.*

First, in paying the interest of all monies borrowed, or which shall from time to time be due and owing on the credit of the Wallasey Ferries Account, or on the joint credit of that account and the General District Rate:

Secondly, in setting apart and appropriating the sum required to be set apart and appropriated for paying off the principal monies which shall have been borrowed or secured on the

Sec. 68

credit of the Wallasey Ferries Account, or on the joint credit of that account and the General District Rate:

Thirdly, in defraying the costs, charges, and expenses incurred or to be incurred by the Local Board in and about the hiring leasing, or purchasing any ferry or ferries, or the providing, hiring, chartering, purchasing, and maintaining any steam or other boat, materials, or things, or the employing and recompensing persons for the working of any ferry or ferries which shall be hired, leased, or purchased by the Local Board under the authority of the first-recited Act or this Act, or in any manner connected therewith or incident thereto;

Fourthly, in paying off all monies due on the credit of the Wallasey Ferries Account, or on the joint credit of that account and the General District Rate:

Lastly, any surplus which may remain shall be carried to the credit of and be applicable to the same purposes as the General District Rates made under "The Public Health Act, 1848."

Lands empowered to be sold by sec. 84 of 8 & 9 Vict. ch. vi. may be either sold, let, or exchanged.

49 G. 3, ch. ciii.

68. And whereas under the first-recited Act, section eighty-four, the Local Board are empowered to sell in manner therein provided certain parcels of lands therein mentioned, and it is expedient that the Local Board should be empowered (if they shall think fit) to let or exchange the said several parcels of land, or to sell the same: And whereas there is a small piece of waste land situate on the north side of Mill Lane in the Township of Liscard, containing six hundred and ninety-four square yards or thereabouts, which was left unallotted and undisposed of by the Commissioner acting in the execution of an Act passed in the forty-ninth year of the reign of King George the Third, intituled an Act for inclosing Waste Lands in the Township of Liscard in the Parish of Wallasey in the County of Chester: And whereas the said piece of land is in its present state wholly useless and unproductive, and it is expedient that the Local Board should be empowered to sell, let exchange, or otherwise appropriate the same in manner hereinafter mentioned: Therefore the Local Board may sell or let to or exchange with the person whose lands adjoin thereto, or if for the space of one month after an offer made to him he refuse or neglect to purchase, or take on lease or in exchange, then the Local Board may sell or let to or exchange with any other person the before-mentioned parcel of land, or any part thereof; and in the case of a sale or lease at or for such price or rent as the Local Board may deem fair and reasonable; and in the case of an exchange for other land of equal value, as near as may be, to be conveyed to the Local Board; and the Local Board may convey and demise the same, or such part thereof as shall be so sold, leased, or exchanged, to the purchaser or lessee thereof, or the person with whom such exchange shall be made, by deed under their seal and the hands of five or more members of the Local Board, and the receipt of the Chairman and of any two or more members of the Local Board shall be a sufficient discharge to the purchaser or lessee of any such land, or other person as aforesaid, for the purchase money or rent, or for any money payable by way of equality of exchange in such receipt expressed to be received; and the money arising from any such sale or lease, or for equality of exchange, shall be applied by the Local Board to the same purposes as the general district rate is by "The Public Health Act, 1848," directed to be applied: Provided, that the Local Board may, until any such sale or lease or exchange of the said piece of land, or any part thereof, shall be made, enter into and take possession thereof, and manage, fence, and protect the same from trespass and injury in such manner as they shall think fit: Provided also, that in case of any such sale or lease or exchange being made to or with any person other than the owner of the adjoining land, it shall not be necessary to prove that any such offer has been made to such owner, or that he has refused or neglected to become such purchaser or lessee, or to make such exchange as herein-before mentioned: Provided also, that the Local Board may, instead of selling or leasing or exchanging the said piece of land, or in case a sale or lease or exchange upon fair and reasonable terms cannot be effected, retain the same absolutely, or for such period or length of time as they shall think fit; and the Local Board may at any time thereafter in manner aforesaid either sell or demise or exchange the said piece of land, or any part thereof, or may appropriate and dedicate the same, or any part thereof, to all or any of the purposes of this Act, except the erection of gasworks. {Sec. 69—81}

[The powers conferred by this section are extended by the Wallasey Improvement Act, 1864, sec. 20, and the Wallasey Order (No. 1) 1877, art. 1.]

[S.S. 69 to 79 inclusive—Repealed by the Wallasey Order, 1870, art. 3. These sections contained regulations with respect to buildings in this district.]

80. And whereas it would tend to insure greater efficiency and economy in the execution of works if the same were executed by persons under the immediate direction and control of the Local Board: therefore the Local Board and the owner of any land or building in respect of which such works may be required to be executed may agree that the same shall be constructed by the Local Board, and the expense thereof, as certified by the surveyor of the Local Board, shall be repaid on demand by such owner to the Local Board, and in default of payment the same may be recovered from him in a summary manner or by action in any court of competent jurisdiction, or may be declared to be private improvement expenses, and be recovered as such in the manner provided by "The Public Health Act, 1848." {Local Board may agree to execute works at expense of owners.}

[The Public Health Act, 1848, was repealed by the Public Health Act, 1875, which consolidated and amended the Acts relating to public health; as to substituted provisions, *vide* sec. 313 of the Public Health Act, 1875.]

81. If any person, against whom the Local Board shall have any claim or demand, become bankrupt or take the benefit of any Act for the relief of insolvent debtors, it shall be lawful for the clerk of the Local Board in all proceedings against the estate of such bankrupt or insolvent to represent the Local Board and act in their behalf in all respects as if such claim or demand had been the claim or demand of such clerk and not of the Local Board. {Proof of debts in bankruptcy.}

Sec. 82—88

Authentication of Notices.

82. Any summons, demand, or notice, or other such document under "The Public Health Act, 1848," or any supplemental Act or this Act, may be in writing or print, or partly in writing and partly in print, and if the same require authentication by the Local Board, the signature thereof by the Clerk to the Local Board shall be sufficient authentication.

Interest in contract or liability to rates not to disqualify Justices.

83. No person shall be incapable of acting as a justice in the execution in any respect of this Act by reason of his being interested in any contract under this Act for a supply of water or gas, or being liable under this Act to the payment of any rate or other money.

Recovery of penalties.

84. All penalties imposed by or under this Act, or any byelaw made under this Act, the recovery whereof is not otherwise expressly provided for, may be recovered in manner provided for the recovery of penalties by "The Public Health Act, 1848."

[The Public Health Act, 1848, was repealed by the Public Health Act, 1875, which consolidates and amends the Acts relating to public health.]

Application of penalties.

85. The justices by whom any penalty or forfeiture shall be imposed under this Act shall, where the application thereof is not otherwise provided for, award the same to be paid to the Local Board.

Saving rights of Birkenhead and Claughton Gas and Water Company.

86. Provided always, That nothing in this Act contained shall in any way prejudice or affect any right or power which the Birkenhead and Claughton Gas and Water Company are now entitled to so long as such right or power remains vested in the said Company.

[The property of the Birkenhead and Claughton Gas and Water Company was transferred to the Birkenhead Improvement Commissioners by the Birkenhead Commissioners' Gas and Water Act, 1858.]

Saving rights of Local Board.

87. Except as is by this Act expressly otherwise provided, this Act or anything therein contained shall not take away, lessen, prejudice, or alter any of the jurisdictions, estates, rights, powers or privileges of the Local Board.

Expenses of Act.

88. The costs, charges, and expenses attending or incident to the obtaining and passing of this Act shall be paid by the Local Board.

The SCHEDULE referred to in the foregoing Act.

[This Schedule contained the Ferry Tolls, leviable and payable under the Act. They remained in force until the 1st January, 1868, when they were altered by virtue of The Wallasey Improvement Act, 1867. *Vide* Secs. 19 and 20 and Sched. C. of that Act.]

THE WALLASEY IMPROVEMENT ACT, 1861.

(24 Vict. ch. 4.)

ARRANGEMENT OF SECTIONS.

	SECTION.
Preamble	
Short title	1
Act to be executed by Local Board ...	2
Power to borrow moneys on Mortgage as hereafter mentioned	3
Provisions of 11 and 12 Vict. ch. 63 to apply to Mortgages to be granted under this Act	4
Saving Priority of existing Mortgages, &c., and of future Mortgages granted under 11 and 12 Vict. ch. 63	5
Further power to Local Board for acquisition of Seacombe Ferry	6
Saving Rights of Messieurs Coulborn ...	7
Incorporation of Local Board ...	8
General saving of Rights under existing Acts ...	9
Actions not to abate, &c.	10
Expenses of Act	11

24 Vict. The Wallasey Improvement Act, 1861.

Sec. 1

AN

ACT

for conferring on the Local Board of Health for the District of WALLASEY further Powers for raising Money; for the Acquisition of Seacombe Ferry; and for incorporating the said Board; and for other Purposes.

17TH MAY, 1861.

21 & 22 Vict. c. 63.

WHEREAS by "The Wallasey Improvement Act, 1858," the Local Board of Health for the District of Wallasey (in this Act called the "Local Board") were empowered to supply the District of Wallasey with Water and Gas, and to raise money for such purposes, and also for carrying into effect the purposes of the said Act with respect to the acquisition of Ferries, and otherwise in relation thereto: And whereas it is expedient that the Local Board should be empowered to raise further monies for carrying the purposes aforesaid and the purposes of this Act into effect: And whereas by the said Act the Local Board were empowered, subject to the restrictions and conditions therein contained, to acquire the rights and interests of the then lessees, William Rushton Coulborn and Edward Warburton Coulborn, in the Ferry called Seacombe Ferry, and in other Ferries called Egremont Ferry and New Brighton Ferry: And whereas in pursuance of the said Act, and of an award duly made thereunder, dated the thirtieth day of April, one thousand eight hundred and sixty, the Local Board have contracted to purchase the interest of the said William Rushton Coulborn and Edward Warburton Coulborn in the said three Ferries for the price of sixty thousand and two pounds: and whereas it is expedient that the Local Board be empowered to acquire the reversion in the said Ferry called Seacombe Ferry, and in certain lands and property held or used in connexion therewith, which are shown on certain plans, and described in a book of reference thereto, which have been deposited with the Clerk of the Peace for the County of Chester: And whereas it is expedient that the Local Board should be incorporated: And whereas the purposes aforesaid cannot be effected without the authority of Parliament: May it therefore please Your Majesty that it may be enacted; and be it enacted by the Queen's most Excellent Majesty, by and with the advice and consent of the Lords Spiritual and Temporal, and Commons, in this present Parliament assembled, and by the authority of the same, as follows; (that is to say,)

Short Title.

1. In citing this Act for any purpose it shall be sufficient to use the expression "The Wallasey Improvement Act, 1861."

The Wallasey Improvement Act, 1861.

Sec. 2—3

2. This Act shall be executed by the Local Board, according to the powers and provisions of "The Public Health Act, 1848," and of the several Acts supplemental thereto, and of "The Local Government Act, 1858," and of any other Act relating to the Public Health, and from time to time in force within the District of Wallasey.

Act to be executed by Local Board.

[The Public Health Act, 1848, and the Local Government Act, 1858, were repealed by the Public Health Act, 1875, which consolidated and amended the Acts relating to Public Health. Its provisions were substituted for those of the repealed Acts by sec. 313.]

3. In addition to the monies which the Local Board are empowered to borrow under the provisions of "The Wallasey Improvement Act, 1858," and "The Public Health Act, 1848," or any Act supplemental thereto or otherwise relating to the Public Health, they may from time to time borrow on mortgage any sums not exceeding the respective amounts herein-after mentioned; (that is to say,)

Power to borrow Monies on Mortgage as hereafter mentioned.

On mortgage of the security mentioned and referred to in "The Wallasey Improvement Act, 1858," as the Wallasey Waterworks Account, and of the Waterworks for the time being vested in or belonging to the Local Board, any sum not exceeding twenty thousand pounds, which sum shall be applied, first, in payment of such part as the Local Board think fit of the expenses attending or incident to the obtaining and passing of this Act, and, secondly, to the purposes to which by the said Act the monies to be borrowed under the authority of that Act on the above-mentioned securities are thereby directed to be secondly applied;

On mortgage of the security mentioned or referred to in the same Act as the "Wallasey Lighting Account," and of the gasworks for the time being vested in or belonging to the Local Board, any sum not exceeding ten thousand pounds, which sum shall be applied, first, in payment of such part as the Local Board think fit of the expenses attending or incident to the obtaining and passing of this Act, and secondly, to the purposes to which by the said Act the monies to be borrowed under the authority of that Act on the above-mentioned securities are thereby directed to be secondly applied;

On mortgage of the security mentioned or referred to in the same Act as the "Wallasey Ferries Account," and of the Ferries for the time being belonging to or leased by the Local Board and the steam and other boats, materials, and things connected therewith and also (as a collateral security) of the general district rate authorized by "The Public Health Act, 1848," to be made and levied, any sums not exceeding fifty thousand pounds, which sum shall be applied to the acquisition under this Act of the reversion in Seacombe Ferry and the said lands and property held or used in connexion therewith, and to the improvement of the said Ferry, and of any other Ferries from time to time belonging to or leased by the Local Board, and to the several other purposes to which by "The Wallasey Improvement Act, 1858," monies coming to the hands of the

Sec. 4–5

Local Board from the "Wallasey Ferries Account" are thereby directed to be applied, but so that of the said sum of fifty thousand pounds the sum of thirty thousand pounds shall not be raised or applied otherwise than for acquiring the reversion in Seacombe Ferry and the lands and property held and used in connexion therewith, as aforesaid.

[BORROWING POWERS EXTENDED:—

1. *Water:*—The Wallasey Order, 1863.
 „   „   „   1870, art. 6.
 The Wallasey Improvement Act, 1872, sec. 17.
2. *Gas:*—The Wallasey Improvement Act, 1867, sec. 30.
 The Wallasey Order (No. 1,) 1877, art. 2.
 „   „   „   1883, art. 1,
 „   „   „   1892, art. 2.
 „   „   „   1896, art. 1.
 „   „   „   1898, art. 1.
3. *Ferries:*—The Wallasey Improvement Act, 1864, sec. 21.
 „   „   „   „   1872, sec. 17.
 The Wallasey Order (No. 1.) 1877, art. 4.
 „   „   „   1881, art. 1.
 „   „   „   1883, art. 2.
 „   „   „   1895, art. 1.
 „   „   „   1897, art. 1.

Vide also The Wallasey Improvement Act, 1858, sec. 60].

Provisions of 11 & 12 Vict. ch. 63 to apply to Mortgages to be granted under this Act.

4. The sections of "The Public Health Act, 1848," One hundred and ten to One hundred and fourteen, both inclusive, and the Schedules (B.) and (C.) to that Act, shall be applicable to the Mortgages to be executed by the Local Board under the Authority of this Act.

["The Public Health Act, 1848," was repealed by "The Public Health Act, 1875," which consolidated and amended the Acts relating to Public Health in England.]

Saving priority of existing Mortgages, &c., and of future Mortgages granted under 11 & 12 Vict. ch. 63.

5. Provided always, That all Mortgages granted by the Commissioners under the authority of "The Wallasey Improvement Act, 1845," and all Mortgages granted by the Local Board under the authority of "The Public Health Act, 1848," or "The Wallasey Improvement Act, 1858," (and thereby charged upon the General District Rate,) and subsisting at the time of the passing of this Act, and all Mortgages to be hereafter granted by the Local Board under the authority of "The Public Health Act, 1848," shall respectively have priority over all Mortgages which may be granted under the authority of this Act on the collateral security of the General District Rate, so far as relates to such collateral security; and all Mortgages granted by the Local Board prior to the passing of this Act, under the authority of "The Wallasey Improvement Act, 1858," on the security of "The Wallasey Waterworks Account" and the Wallasey Waterworks, or on the security of the "Wallasey Lighting Account" and the Wallasey Gasworks, or on the security of the "Wallasey

Ferries Account," and the Ferries for the time being belonging to or leased by the Local Board, and the steam and other boats, materials, and things connected therewith, shall respectively during their continuance have priority over all Mortgages granted on those respective securities, under the provisions of this Act.

Sec. 6—9

[Altered and amended by the Wallasey Order, 1883, art. 9. *Vide* also arts. 4 and 7 of the same Order for Provisions for Re-payment and Sinking Fund.]

6. The Local Board may purchase and acquire the Reversion and any other interest for the purchase of which they have not already contracted in the Ferry called Seacombe Ferry, and in the Slip, Landing Stage, Quays, Wharf, and other Works, and all other the Lands and Property shown on the deposited plans and described in the books of reference thereto, upon such terms and conditions as shall be agreed on between the Local Board and the persons for the time being entitled to such reversion or other interest in such Ferry, Works, and Lands as aforesaid.

Further power to Local Board for acquisition of Seacombe Ferry.

7. This Act and everything herein contained or referred to shall be without prejudice to the Award dated the thirtieth day of April one thousand eight hundred and sixty, herein-before mentioned, and to all the rights, interests, powers and remedies of the said William Rushton Coulborn and Edward Warburton Coulborn under the same Award, and under any Act of Parliament, or otherwise howsoever, all which rights, interests, powers, and remedies are hereby expressly saved and reserved.

Saving rights of Messieurs Coulborn.

8. The Local Board and their successors to be from time to time elected under the provisions of "The Public Health Act, 1848," or any other Act or Acts for the time being in force with relation to the Local Board, shall, for the purposes of "The Wallasey Improvement Act, 1845," so far as the provisions thereof are or may be still unrepealed, "The Wallasey Improvement Act, 1858," and this Act, and any other Act for the time being in force with relation to the said Local Board, be incorporated by the name of "The Wallasey Local Board," and by that name shall be a body corporate and have a common seal, with perpetual succession, and shall have power to purchase and hold and sell and dispose of lands, within the restrictions in the said Acts and this Act contained, for the purposes thereof.

Incorporation of Local Board.

9. Notwithstanding the passing of this Act, and the Incorporation of the Local Board, and except only as is by this Act otherwise expressly provided, everything before the passing of this Act done, suffered, and confirmed respectively under or by any Act relating to the Local Board shall be as valid as if this Act were not passed, and the Incorporation of the Local Board and this Act respectively shall accordingly be subject and without prejudice to everything so done, suffered, and confirmed respectively, and to all rights, liabilities, claims, and demands, both present and future, which if the Local Board had not been incorporated and this Act were not passed would be incident to or consequent on any and every thing so done, suffered, and confirmed respectively; and with respect to all such things so done, suffered, and confirmed respectively, and all such rights, liabilities, claims, and demands, the Local Board

General Saving of rights under existing Acts.

24 Vict. *The Wallasey Improvement Act*, 1861.

Sec. 10—11 incorporated shall to all intents represent the Local Board prior to their incorporation: Provided always, that the generality of this provision shall not be restricted by any other of the sections and provisions of this Act.

Actions not to abate, &c.

10. Notwithstanding the Incorporation of the Local Board, and except only as is by this Act otherwise expressly provided, any action, suit, prosecution, or other proceeding commenced either by or against the Local Board or their Clerk before the passing of this Act shall not abate or be discontinued or prejudicially affected by this Act, but, on the contrary, shall continue and take effect both in favour of and against the Local Board incorporated by this Act, in the same manner, to all intents, as if this Act were not passed, save only that the Local Board so incorporated shall be substituted therein for the Local Board before their incorporation or their Clerk.

Expenses of Act.

11. The costs, charges, and expenses attending or incident to the obtaining and passing of this Act shall be paid by the Local Board.

The Local Government Supplemental Act, 1863 (No. 2).

(Confirming The Wallasey Order of 1863.)

AN ACT

to confirm certain Provisional Orders under the Local Government Act (1858), relating to the Districts of Plymouth, Holywell, Llanelly, West Ham, Worthing, Aberavon, and WALLASEY.

21st JULY, 1863.

WHEREAS the Secretary of State for the Home Department, being one of Her Majesty's Principal Secretaries of State, has under the provisions of the Local Government Act, 1858, duly made certain Provisional Orders which are contained in the Schedule to this Act annexed, and it is provided by the aforesaid Local Government Act that no such Orders shall be of any validity whatever until they shall have been confirmed by Parliament; and it is expedient that the said Orders should be so confirmed, and further provision made in relation thereto: Be it therefore enacted by the Queen's most Excellent Majesty, by and with the advice and consent of the Lords Spiritual and Temporal, and Commons, in this present Parliament assembled, and by the authority of the same, as follows:

1. The Provisional Orders contained in the Schedule hereunto annexed shall from and after the passing of this Act be absolute, and be as binding and of the like force and effect as if the provisions of the same had been expressly enacted in this Act. *Provisional Orders in Schedule.*

2. This Act shall be deemed to be incorporated with the Local Government Act, 1858, and shall be as if this Act and the said Local Government Act were one Act. *This Act incorporated with 21 & 22 Vict. ch. 98.*

3. In citing this Act in any other Act, or in any proceeding, instrument, or document whatsoever, it shall be sufficient to use the words and figures "The Local Government Supplemental Act, 1863 (No. 2)." *Short Title.*

SCHEDULE of Provisional Orders referred to in the preceding Act.

[The omitted orders relate to Districts other than Wallasey.]

* * * * * *

8. WALLASEY.—Extending the Borrowing Powers of the Board.

WALLASEY.

Provisional Order for extending the Borrowing Powers of the Wallasey Local Board of Health,—Local Government Act, 1858.

Whereas the Local Board of Health for the District of Wallasey in the County of Chester (now called "The Wallasey Local Board") have duly borrowed under the provisions of the Public Health Act, 1848, the Wallasey Improvement Act, 1858, the Wallasey Improvement Act, 1861, and of the Local Government Act, 1858, sums amounting altogether to forty-eight thousand pounds, to defray the expense of works for the sewerage of and supply of water to the said district, being works of a permanent nature under the aforesaid Acts; and whereas there is now owing of that amount a sum of forty-two thousand five hundred and twenty-five pounds, and a further sum will be required to carry out and complete the said works, but such further sum, with the hereinbefore mentioned £42,525, will exceed the assessable value for one year of the premises assessable under the said Acts within such district, constituted as aforesaid.

And whereas the said Board have now, under the authority of the 78th Section of the Local Government Act, 1858, petitioned me, as one of Her Majesty's Principal Secretaries of State, for powers to borrow for such works, on mortgage of the rates leviable by the aforesaid Local Board of Health under the powers of the aforesaid Acts, a sum or sums which, with the amount already borrowed, shall not exceed in the whole two years' assessable value of the premises assessable within the district in respect of which such sum or sums may be borrowed.

And whereas after due enquiry and report by William Ranger, Esquire, the Inspector appointed by me for the purpose, I am of opinion that the prayer of such petition should be granted; but the same cannot be done without the consent of Parliament.

Now, therefore, in pursuance of the power now vested in me as one of Her Majesty's Principal Secretaries of State as aforesaid, I do hereby, by this Provisional Order under my hand, direct as follows:—

That from and after the passing of any Act of Parliament confirming this present Order—

The Local Government Supplemental Act, 1863 (No. 2).

1. The Local Board of Health for the district of Wallasey in the County of Chester (now called "The Wallasey Local Board") shall have power and authority to borrow or reborrow, for the execution and completion of the aforesaid works of a permanent nature within such district, and on mortgage of the rates leviable by them under the aforesaid Acts, a further sum, not exceeding thirteen thousand pounds, which, together with the sums already sanctioned to be borrowed by the Local Board aforesaid, will not exceed in the whole two years' assessable value of the premises assessable under such Acts within the aforesaid district; the several aforesaid sums already borrowed and to be further borrowed under the authority of this present Order, and of the Act confirming the same, to be repaid, with interest thereon, within a period of fifty years from the date of the borrowing thereof.

Given under my hand this 9th day of June, 1863.

(Signed) G. GREY.

[The Board empowered to mortgage the works and water rents as well as rates, *vide* The Wallasey Improvement Act, 1864, s. 28.

The limitation of borrowing powers in this Order was removed by The Wallasey Order, 1870, Article 6, which authorised the Local Board to borrow for permanent works to the amount of twice the assessable value of the premises assessable under the Local Government Act in the district. Article 6 of The Wallasey Order, 1870, was repealed by The Wallasey Order, 1894, Article 1.

Further borrowing powers for water purposes were conferred by The Wallasey Improvement Act, 1872, s. 17.]

THE WALLASEY IMPROVEMENT ACT, 1864.

(27 & 28 Vict., ch. cxvii.)

ARRANGEMENT OF SECTIONS.

	SECTION.
Preamble.	
Short Title	1
Act to be executed by Local Board	2
8 & 9 Vict. ch. 18, 10 & 11 Vict. ch. 17, and 23 & 24 Vict. ch. 106 incorporated	3
Same Meanings to Words in incorporated Acts as in this Act	4
Interpretation of Terms	5
Power to take Lands	6
Power to construct Works	7
Before Pier or Landing Stage commenced, Plans, &c., to be deposited at Admiralty	8
Lights to be exhibited during Execution of Works	9
Exemption from Rates in certain cases	10
Power to Admiralty to order Local Survey at Expense of Local Board	11
Works affecting Tidal Waters abandoned, &c., may be removed by Admiralty at Expense of Local Board	12
Powers for compulsory Purchases limited	13
Period for Completion of Works	14
Power to deviate	15
Power to alter Ferry Rates	16
Power to sell or let Steam Vessels	17
Alterations as to Supply of Water for domestic purposes	18
Power to Local Board to Contract for Supply of Fittings for Gas and Water	19
Sec. 68 of 21 and 22 Vict. c. 63 extended to other lands herein specified, 49 G. 3, c. ciii. 54 G. 3, c. 87	20
Power to raise further Money on Mortgage of "The Wallasey Ferries Account"	21

	SECTION.
Certain parts of 11 and 12 Vict. c. 63, and 21 and 22 Vict. c. 98 to apply to Mortgages...	22
Saving Priority of existing Mortgages ...	23
Power to apply to Purposes of Reservoir, &c., Funds applicable to Waterwork Purposes ...	24
Power to Re-borrow ...	25
Power to accept Surrender of Mortgages ...	26
Time within which borrowed Money shall be paid off ...	27
Power to Board to Mortgage Works as well as Rates for raising Money under a Provisional Order ..	28
Courts and Passages to be flagged and channelled	29
Vaults under Streets to be repaired by owners...	30
Local Board to put in Branch Drains at the Expense of Owners of Houses. ...	31
Power to Local Boards to order Removal and Construction of Urinals by Innkeepers and Beersellers ...	32
Power to Local Board to agree with Owners of projecting Buildings, and of Houses at Corners of Streets, to alter and round-off same ...	33
As to Purchase of Lands for opening new Streets ...	34
For preventing the filling up or Embankment upon Ground with offensive or unwholesome matter ...	35
Repealed ...	36
Power to repeal Bye-laws ...	37
Power to grant Superannuation Allowances ...	38
Recovery of Penalties ..	39
Power to Local Board to order Costs of Prosecutions..	40
Assessments to different rates may be in one Rate Book ...	41
Power to charge Salaries to particular Account ...	42
Agreement set forth in Schedule confirmed	43
Saving Rights of the Crown ...	44
Expenses of Act ...	45
Schedule.	

27 & 28 Vict. *The Wallasey Improvement Act, 1864.* ch. cxvii.

AN

ACT

to confer further Powers on the WALLASEY Local Board; and for other Purposes.

[23RD JUNE, 1864.]

21 & 22 Vict. c. 63.

24 & 25 Vict. c. 4.

WHEREAS under the Provisions of The "Wallasey Improvement Act, 1858," (in this Act called "the Act of 1858,") and of "The Wallasey Improvement Act, 1861," (in this Act called "The Act of 1861") certain Ferries, called respectively New Brighton Ferry, Egremont Ferry, and Seacombe Ferry, with the landing stages, piers, jetties, slips, and accommodations connected therewith, are vested in and worked and managed by the Wallasey Local Board (in this Act called "the Local Board"): And whereas it is expedient that the Local Board be empowered to construct a pier or landing stage at New Brighton in the Township of Liscard and Parish of Wallasey in the County of Chester, in connexion with their existing ferry at New Brighton, and that further powers should be conferred upon them in relation to their ferries, landing stages, and steamboats, and with respect to the tolls and rates leviable in respect thereof: And whereas by the Act of 1858 the Local Board are empowered to supply the District of Wallasey with water, and it is expedient that they should be empowered to construct an additional reservoir and other works connected therewith: And whereas plans and sections of the proposed pier or landing stage and reservoir, and showing the lands on which the same respectively are to be constructed, and a book of reference to such plans, have been deposited with the Clerk of the Peace for the County of Chester: And whereas it is expedient that the Local Board should be empowered to raise a further sum in connexion with and for the purposes of their ferries, landing stages, and piers, and that further provision should be made with reference to the borrowing, reborrowing, and paying off of monies borrowed by the Local Board: And whereas it is also expedient to alter the qualification of persons entitled to vote in the election of members of the Local Board: And whereas it is also expedient to make provision for superannuation, or other allowances to officers, servants, workmen, and other persons appointed or employed by the Local Board: And whereas it is also expedient to confer further powers on the Local Board, in relation to the good government and sanitary condition of the district and otherwise: And whereas the purposes aforesaid cannot be effected without the authority of Parliament: May it therefore please your Majesty that it may be enacted; and be it enacted by the Queen's most Excellent Majesty, by and with the advice and consent of the Lords Spiritual and Temporal, and Commons, in this present Parliament assembled, and by the authority of the same, as follows; (that is to say,)

27 & 28 Vict.   *The Wallasey Improvement*   ch. cxvii.   199
                        Act, 1864.

                                                                Sec. 1—7

1. In citing this Act for any purpose it shall be sufficient to use   Short Title.
the expression "The Wallasey Improvement Act, 1864."

2. This Act shall be executed by the Local Board, subject to the   Act to be
powers and provisions of "The Public Health Act, 1848," and of   executed by
the several Acts supplemental thereto, and of "the Local Govern-   Local Board.
ment Act, 1858," and of any other Act relating to the Public Health,
and from time to time in force within the district of Wallasey.

> [The Public Health Act, 1848, and the Local Government Act,
> 1858, were repealed by the Public Health Act, 1875, which
> consolidated and amended the Acts relating to Public Health.
> Its provisions were substituted for those of the repealed Acts
> by sec. 313.]

3. "The Lands Clauses Consolidation Act, 1845," "The Lands   8 & 9 Vict.
Clauses Consolidation Acts Amendment Act, 1860," "The Water-   c. 18,
works Clauses Act, 1847," and "The Waterworks Clauses Act,   10 & 11 Vict.
1863," shall, so far as the same respectively are applicable to the   c. 17, and
purposes of this Act, and are not expressly altered or varied by this   23 & 24 Vict.
Act, be incorporated with this Act.   c. 106,
                                                                   incorporated.

4. The several words and expressions to which by the Acts   Same mean-
wholly or partially incorporated with this Act meanings are respec-   ings to
tively assigned shall have in this Act the same respective meanings,   words in
unless there be something in the subject or context repugnant to or   incorporated
inconsistent with such construction.   Acts as in
                                                                    this Act.

5. The expression "Superior Courts," or "Court of Competent   Interpreta-
Jurisdiction," or any other like expression, when used in this Act, or   tion of Terms
in any Act incorporated herewith, shall be read and have effect as if
the debt or demand with respect to which the expression is used
were a common simple contract debt, and not a debt or demand
created by statute.

6. The Local Board (subject to the provisions of this Act, and of   Power to
the Acts wholly or partially incorporated with this Act), may enter   take Lands.
upon, take, use, and hold, and appropriate to the purposes of this Act
all or any of the lands defined on the deposited plans and described
in the books of reference thereto, or any estate, or interest, or easement
in or over all or any of the said lands.

7. The Local Board, subject to the provisions in this Act and in   Power to
the Acts wholly or partially incorporated with this Act, may make   construct
and maintain, in the line or situation, and according to the levels   Works.
defined on the deposited plans and sections, and upon the lands delineated on the said plans and described in the books of reference
thereto, the following works ; (that is to say,)

> A pier or landing stage at New Brighton aforesaid, from a point at
> or near the east end of Victoria Road, together with all such
> jetties, esplanades, landing places, toll gates or bars, and other
> works and conveniences in connection therewith, as the Local
> Board shall from time to time think fit :
>
> A reservoir in the said Township of Liscard, together with all such
> mains, pipes, and other apparatus in connection therewith, as the
> Local Board shall from time to time think fit ; and the said
> reservoir and works shall for all purposes be deemed part of
> the waterworks of the Local Board.

27 & 28 Vict. *The Wallasey Improvement Act*, 1864. ch. cxvii.

Sec. 8—10

Before Pier or Landing Stage commenced Plans, &c., to be deposited at Admiralty.

8. Previously to commencing the pier or landing stage or the works connected therewith, the Local Board shall deposit at the Admiralty office plans, sections, and working drawings of the said pier or landing stage and works connected therewith for the approval of the Lord High Admiral of the United Kingdom of Great Britain and Ireland, or the Commissioners for executing the office of Lord High Admiral aforesaid, such approval to be signified in writing under the hand of the secretary of the Admiralty, and such pier or landing stage and works shall be constructed only in accordance with such approval; and when any such pier or landing stage or works shall have been commenced or constructed it shall not be lawful for the Local Board at any time to alter or extend the same without obtaining, previously to making any such alteration or extension, the like consent or approval; and if any such pier or landing stage or works shall be commenced or completed, or be altered, extended, or constructed contrary to the provisions of this Act, it shall be lawful for the said Lord High Admiral, or the said Commissioners for executing the office of Lord High Admiral, to abate, alter, and remove the same, and to restore the site thereof to its former condition, at the cost and charge of the Local Board, and the amount thereof shall be a debt due from the Local Board to the Crown, and be recoverable accordingly with costs of suit, or may be recovered with costs as a penalty is or may be recoverable from the Local Board.

Lights to be exhibited during execution of Works.

9. During the construction of the pier or landing stage, and works connected therewith, the Local Board shall cause to be hung out or exhibited every night from sunset to sunrise lights to be kept burning by and at the expense of the Local Board for the navigation and safe guidance of vessels, and for ever after the completion of the pier or landing stage the Local Board shall cause to be hung out or exhibited thereon every night from sunset to sunrise good and sufficient lights to be kept burning by and at the expense of the Local Board, for the navigation and safe guidance of vessels, and which lights shall be from time to time altered by the Local Board in such manner, and be of such description, and be so used and placed, as the Lord High Admiral or the Commissioners for executing the office of Lord High Admiral shall by writing under the hand of the secretary of the Admiralty approve of; and in case the Local Board shall neglect to exhibit and keep either of such lights burning as aforesaid, they shall forfeit and pay for every such neglect the sum of ten pounds.

Exemption from Rates in certain Cases.

10. Nothing in this Act contained shall extend to charge with rates or duties, or to regulate or subject to any control, any vessel or boat belonging to or employed in the service of Her Majesty, her heirs and successors, or any member of the Royal Family, or in the service of the Admiralty, Coast Guard, Customs, or Excise, or of the Corporation of Trinity House of Deptford Strond, or the Commissioners of Northern Lights, using the pier or landing stage, and not conveying goods for hire; or any packet boat or post office packet, being a packet boat or post office packet, as defined under the provisions of any Act relating to the post office, or any post office bag of letters conveyed by any such packet boat or packet, or by any other vessel whatsoever, or any of the officers or persons belonging to Her

27 & 28 Vict.   *The Wallasey Improvement*   ch. cxvii.   201
                    Act, 1864.

Majesty's Navy, or employed in the service of the Admiralty, Coast **Sec. 11—15**
Guard, Ordnance, Customs, Excise, or Post Office, or their baggage,
or any vessel or goods being under seizure by the officers of the
revenue, or any naval, victualling, or ordnance stores, or other
stores, goods, or supplies for the service of or being the property
of Her Majesty, or any marines or troops landed upon, or delivered,
or disembarked from the pier or landing stage, or their baggage; but
all such vessels, officers, or persons aforesaid shall have the free use
of the pier or landing stage without any charge or rate being made
for using the same; provided always, that if any person claim and
take the benefit of any such exemption as aforesaid, without being
entitled thereto, he shall for every such offence be liable to a
penalty not exceeding ten pounds.

11. If at any time or times it shall be deemed expedient by the Power to
Lord High Admiral of the United Kingdom, or the Commissioners Admiralty
for executing the office of Lord High Admiral, to order a local survey to order
and examination of any works of the Local Board, in, over, or Local Survey
affecting any tidal or navigable water or river, or of the intended at expense of
site thereof, the Local Board shall defray the costs of every such Local Board.
local survey and examination, and the amount thereof shall be a debt
due to Her Majesty from the Local Board; and if not paid upon
demand, may be recovered as a debt due to the Crown, with the
costs of suit, or may be recovered with costs as a penalty is or may
be recoverable from the Local Board.

12. If any work to be constructed by the Local Board in, under, Works
over, through, or across any tidal water or navigable river, or if any affecting
portion of any work which affects or may affect any such water or tidal Waters
river, or access thereto, shall be abandoned or suffered to fall into abandoned,
disuse or decay, it shall be lawful for the Lord High Admiral, or the removed by
Commissioners for executing the office of Lord High Admiral, to Admiralty at
abate and remove the same, or such part or parts thereof as he or Expense of
they may at any time or times deem fit and proper, and to restore Local Board.
the site thereof to its former condition, at the cost and charge of the
Local Board; and the amount thereof shall be a debt due from the
Local Board to the Crown, and if not paid upon demand may be
recovered as a debt due to the Crown with the costs of suit, or may
be recovered with costs as a penalty is or may be recoverable from
the Local Board.

13. The powers of the Local Board for the purchase of lands by Powers for
compulsion, for the purposes of this Act, shall not be exercised after compulsory
the expiration of three years from the passing of this Act. Purchases
                                                              limited.

14. The pier or landing stage and reservoir by this Act authorized Period for
shall be completed within five years from the passing of this Act, Completion
and on the expiration of that period the powers granted to the Local of Works.
Board for making those respective works, or otherwise in relation
thereto, shall cease to be exercised, except as to so much thereof as
is then completed.

15. The Local Board in the construction of the pier or landing Power to
stage and reservoir may deviate laterally from the line or situation deviate.
thereof shown on the deposited plans to the extent of the limits of
deviation shown on those plans, and may deviate from the levels

Sec. 16—18 shown on the deposited sections to the extent following ; (that is to say,) as regards the pier or landing stage, not exceeding five feet; and as regards the reservoir, not exceeding three feet.

Power to alter Ferry Rates.

16. Notwithstanding anything in the Act of 1858 contained, the Local Board may from time to time exercise the following powers in relation to the tolls or rates receivable at their ferries, piers, and landing stages, and in respect of their steamboats :

They may contract for any shorter period than six months with any person or family, provided that no preference be shown to any particular person or family :

They may contract for the conveyance at reduced tolls or rates of any body of persons, such as schools, charitable institutions, benefit societies, pleasure parties, and the like :

They may charge increased tolls or rates (not in any case exceeding sixpence) in respect of every person, whether a contractor or non-contractor, conveyed to or from their ferries, or any of them, between half-past eleven o'clock in the evening and five o'clock in the morning, but they shall not be compellable to run steam vessels to or from their ferries, or any of them, between those hours :

They may demand and receive such reasonable tolls or rates as they may from time to time think fit from persons using their piers and landing stages, or any of them, for purposes of exercise or recreation, but not desiring to embark or disembark thereat, and may compound with any person or family for the payment of such tolls or rates for such period as may be mutually agreed upon ; but such tolls and rates shall be charged equally to all persons and families under the like circumstances :

They may permit persons to land at or depart from their piers and landing stages, or any of them, from or into any steam vessels or other boats or vessels not belonging to the Local Board upon payment of such tolls or rates as the Local Board shall from time to time prescribe.

[*Vide* The Wallasey Improvement Act, 1858, Secs. 40, 41 ; also Sec. 23 of The Wallasey Improvement Act, 1867, with which the above section is incorporated.]

Power to sell or let Steam Vessels.

17. The Local Board may from time to time, as they think fit, sell and dispose of any of their steamboats, and provide others in lieu thereof, if required for the purposes of their ferries, or any of them ; and the Local Board may also from time to time, as they think fit, let to hire for any special purpose, or by the day, or for a longer term, all or any of their steamboats which may not for the time being be required for the efficient management and working of their ferries, and may demand and receive for the hire thereof such sums of money or other consideration as may be agreed upon between the Local Board and the company or person hiring the same.

Alterations as to Supply of Water for domestic Purposes.

18. From and after the passing of this Act so much of the eleventh section of the Act of 1858 as prescribes the rents at which the Local Board shall supply water for domestic purposes shall be

27 & 28 *Vict.*   *The Wallasey Improvement*   *ch. cxvii.*   203
                          Act, 1864.

repealed, and in lieu thereof the Local Board may demand for a **Sec. 19—21**
supply of water for domestic purposes :

    An annual rent not exceeding six pounds per centum on the
    annual value of the house in respect of which such supply of
    water is afforded :

And the Act of 1858 shall henceforth be read and construed accordingly.

19. The Local Board may from time to time contract with any *Power to* person, or with any company or body, for providing such person, *Local Board* company, or body with pipes, meters, burners, lamps, cisterns, *to contract* fittings, and apparatus connected with the supply of gas or water, *Fittings for* and for the repair thereof, in such manner and upon such terms as *Gas and* may be agreed upon between the Local Board and any such person, *Water.* company, or body.

20. And whereas by the sixty-eighth section of the Act of 1858 *Sec. 68 of* provision is made for enabling the Local Board to sell or grant on *21 & 22 Vict.* lease or exchange a certain piece or parcel of land in the said *ch. lxiii.* section mentioned, and being situate on the north side of Mill Lane *extended to* in the Township of Liscard : And whereas under and by virtue of *herein* an Act passed in the forty-ninth year of the reign of King George *specified.* the Third, intituled An Act for inclosing Waste Lands in the *49 G. 3,* Township of Liscard in the Parish of Wallasey in the County *ch. ciii.* Palatine of Chester ; and of another Act passed in the fifty-fourth *54 G. 3,* year of the reign of his said Majesty, intituled An Act for inclosing *ch. lxxxvii.* Waste Lands in the Parishes of Wallasey and West Kirby in the County of Chester, several parcels of land respectively situate in the said Townships of Liscard and Wallasey were allotted for the purpose of getting stone or marl therefrom, and of a watering pit for the use of the landowners within the said townships, and the stone, marl, and water respectively in such parcels of land are or may become exhausted, and it is expedient that provision be made in relation thereto : Therefore, the sixty-eighth section of the Act of 1858 shall extend and apply to and shall be in force and effect in relation to the said parcels of land to the same extent and in the same manner as the said section extends and applies to the said parcel of land therein mentioned situate on the north side of Mill Lane in the Township of Liscard, and the Local Board may sell, lease, or exchange, and otherwise deal with the said parcels of land accordingly.

    [*Vide* also The Wallasey Order (No. 1), 1877, art. 1.]

21. In addition to the monies which the Local Board are *Power to* empowered to borrow under the provisions of the Act of 1858 and the *raise further* Act of 1861, or either of them, in connexion with and for the purposes *Money on* of their ferries, they may from time to time borrow on mortgage of *Mortgage of* "The Wallasey Ferries Account," and of the ferries for the time *lasey Ferries* being belonging to or leased by the Local Board, and the steam and *Account."* other boats, materials, and things connected therewith, and also (as a collateral security) of the general district rate authorized by " The Public Health Act, 1848," to be made and levied, any sums not exceeding in the whole forty-five thousand pounds, of which the Board may apply a sum not exceeding fifteen thousand pounds in and towards the erection and construction of the pier or landing

Sec. 22—23 stage at New Brighton by this Act authorized, and the jetties, esplanades, toll gates, toll houses, works, and conveniences connected therewith; and a sum not exceeding twelve thousand pounds, for the purchase of or otherwise in connection with their steamboats; and if any surplus of the said sums of fifteen thousand pounds and twelve thousand pounds respectively remains after fulfilling the purposes for which they are made specially applicable, such surplus of the one of such sums may be in the first instance applied in making good the deficiency (if any) which may exist in the other of such sums; and the residue of the said sum of forty-five thousand pounds, and also any surplus of the aggregate of the said sums of fifteen thousand pounds and twelve thousand pounds respectively, which may remain after fulfilling the purposes to which they are specially made applicable, shall from time to time be applied for the purposes of the ferries of Seacombe and Egremont respectively: Provided always, that the monies which the Local Board are by this Act expressly authorized to borrow shall be in addition to the monies which they are authorized to borrow by "The Public Health Act, 1848," or any Act supplemental thereto, or otherwise relating to the public health.

[FURTHER BORROWING POWERS:—

Ferries:—The Wallasey Improvement Act, 1872, sec. 17.
The Wallasey Order (No. 1), 1877, art. 3.
,, ,, ,, 1881, art. 1.
,, ,, ,, 1883, art. 2.
,, ,, ,, 1895, art. 1.
,, ,, ,, 1897, art. 1.

The provision as to the application of the moneys borrowed under this section is in effect repealed by the Wallasey Improvement Act, 1867, sec. 37.]

Certain parts of 11 & 12 Vict. ch. 63, and 21 & 22 Vict. ch. 98, to apply to Mortgages.

22. The sections of "The Public Health Act," 1848, 111, 112, and 114, and the schedules (B.) and (C.) to that Act, and section 57 of "The Local Government Act, 1858," shall be applicable to the mortgages to be executed by the Local Board under this Act.

[The Public Health Act, 1848, and the Local Government Act, 1858, were repealed by the Public Health Act, 1875, which consolidated and amended the Acts relating to public health. As to provisions substituted, *vide* sec. 313 of that Act.]

Saving Priority of existing Mortgages.

23. Provided that all mortgages granted by the Local Board on the security of "The Wallasey Ferries Account," and subsisting at the time of the passing of this Act, shall have priority of any mortgage granted under this Act on the security of that account, and all mortgages then subsisting or to be hereafter granted on the security of "The General District Rate," shall respectively have priority over all mortgages which may be granted under the authority of this Act on the collateral security of "The General District Rate," so far as relates to such collateral security.

[Altered and amended by The Wallasey Order, 1883, Article 9.]

24. The Local Board may from time to time apply to the construction and maintenance of the reservoir and the works connected therewith by this Act authorized any of the monies applicable to waterworks purposes which from time to time may be in their hands.

Power to apply to Purposes of Reservoir, &c., Funds applicable to Waterworks Purposes.

25. The Local Board may from time to time re-borrow, at such rate of interest as may be necessary, such sums of money as may be necessary for paying off the whole or any part of any principal monies from time to time outstanding on mortgage, on whatever account such monies may have been borrowed; and if having re-borrowed any such sums, they pay off the same, they may again re-borrow the amount so paid off, and so from time to time; provided that all mortgages granted by the Local Board for the purpose of paying off any principal monies from time to time outstanding on mortgage shall be granted, and be chargeable on the same securities as the principal monies for the paying off of which such mortgages are granted were secured.

Power to re-borrow.

> [This section also applied to mortgages under the Wallasey Improvement Act, 1867; *vide* sec. 33, of that Act. As to priority, *vide* The Wallasey Order, 1883, art. 9.]

26. The Local Board may at any time after the passing of this Act, by agreement with the holders of any outstanding mortgages, accept and take a surrender of such mortgages, and grant other mortgages on the like securities in lieu thereof, at such rate of interest as may be agreed upon, and the mortgages so granted shall be subject to the same provisions as if the sums thereby secured were re-borrowed under the authority of this Act.

Power to accept Surrender of Mortgages.

> [This section also applied to Mortgages under the Wallasey Improvement Act, 1867; *vide* sec. 33, of that Act.]

27. Notwithstanding anything in "The Public Health Act, 1848," or "The Local Government Act, 1858," the Act of 1858, the Act of 1861, or in any other Act authorizing the Local Board to raise money to the contrary contained, the whole of the sums to be borrowed by the Local Board under the powers of any such Act or of this Act shall be repaid within fifty years from the time of borrowing the same; and in the case of monies already borrowed by the Local Board, the period limited by "The Public Health Act, 1848," or "The Local Government Act, 1858," or any such other Act as aforesaid, for the repayment of the same may, with the consent of the mortgagees, but not otherwise, be extended to the like period of fifty years from the time of borrowing the same.

Time within which borrowed Money shall be paid off.

> [This section also applied to mortgages under the Wallasey Improvement Act, 1867; *vide* sec. 33 of that Act. By The Wallasey Order (No. 1) 1877, art. 4, "section 27 of the Wallasey Improvement Act, 1864, shall be wholly repealed except so far as the same may have been acted upon, and in lieu thereof it shall be provided that all the provisions of the Public Health Act, 1875, with respect to borrowing powers (except sub-sections 2 and 3 of sec. 234) shall apply to all moneys to be hereafter borrowed, &c." (*Vide* The Wallasey Order (No. 1) 1877). Amended provisions for repayment of moneys borrowed and sinking fund are contained in The Wallasey Order 1883, arts. 4 to 8.]

Sec. 28—31

Power to Board to mortgage Works as well as Rates for raising money under a Provisional Order

28. And whereas by "The Local Government Supplemental Act, 1863 (No. 2,)" a Provisional Order for extending the borrowing powers of the Board was confirmed, by which Provisional Order the Board are empowered to borrow and re-borrow for the execution and completion of the works of a permanent nature in the said Provisional Order mentioned, a further sum, not exceeding thirteen thousand pounds, on mortgage of the rates leviable by them under the Acts in the said Provisional Order mentioned, but the said Provisional Order does not empower the Board to mortgage the works in respect of which such rates are leviable, and the rents for supply of water, and it would facilitate the borrowing of the said money if the Board were empowered to mortgage the said works and rents: therefore, in addition to the rates which, by the said Provisional Order, the Board may mortgage for raising the said sum of thirteen thousand pounds, the Board may also mortgage the works in respect of which the said rates are leviable, and the said rents.

Courts and Passages to be flagged and channelled.

29. Every court and passage within the district shall be well and sufficiently paved or flagged, channelled, and sewered, and (except as herein-after mentioned, and unless the same shall be a public thoroughfare) shall be kept in good repair to the satisfaction of the Local Board by the owners of the houses, buildings and lands abutting thereon and having the right to the use thereof; and if at any time any such court or passage shall not be well and sufficiently paved or flagged, channelled, and sewered, and kept in good repair to their satisfaction, the Local Board may cause the same to be paved, flagged, channelled, and sewered to their satisfaction; and the whole of the costs, charges, and expenses attending the same shall be paid and reimbursed to the Local Board by, and may be recovered in any court of competent jurisdiction from the owners of the houses, buildings, and lands abutting on such court or passage, and having the use thereof, in such proportions as the Local Board or their surveyor shall determine; and any court or passage being sufficiently paved, flagged, channelled and sewered, and in good repair, to the satisfaction of the Local Board, may be dedicated to the public use by the owners thereof; and after notice in writing under the hands of such owners given to the Local Board, the court or passage, being then also in such good repair as aforesaid, shall, if the Local Board shall be of opinion that the same can be beneficially used as a public thoroughfare, be kept in repair by the Local Board.

Vaults under Streets to be repaired by Owners.

30. The owner of any vault, arch, or cellar, at any time existing under any street within the district, shall keep the same in substantial repair, so as not to occasion any injury to the street; and in default of his so doing, the Local Board may cause such vault, arch, or cellar to be substantially repaired, and may recover the expenses thereof as damages from the owner of such vault, arch, or cellar.

[*Vide* The Wallasey Local Board Act, 1890, Sec. 26.]

Local Board to put in Branch Drains at the Expense of Owners of Houses.

31. When and so soon as a main or other sewer shall have been constructed by the Local Board for the general sewerage or drainage of the houses, privies, ashpits, cesspools, and other premises in any street within the district (whether or not the same shall be a highway), it shall be lawful for the Local Board or their surveyor to construct and lay branch drains of such size, at such level, and with such fall as they or he shall think proper, from such houses, privies, ashpits, cesspools, and other premises, into the main or other sewer of such street, or to divert any present drain so that the same may discharge its contents into such main or other sewer for the drainage of such houses, privies, ashpits, cesspools, and other premises; and the owners of such houses, privies, ashpits, cesspools, and other premises shall repay to the Local Board such expenses as they shall incur, each owner contributing in proportion to the length of drain laid down for him, such proportion to be ascertained by the surveyor of the Local Board, and the expenses aforesaid shall be recovered from the owner or occupier of such premises as damages.

[*Vide* The Wallasey Local Board Act, 1890, Sec. 35.]

32. The Local Board may from time to time, by notice in writing under the hand of their clerk, order the owner or occupier of any inn, public house, or beershop within the district to remove any urinal now or hereafter adjoining such inn, public house, beershop, or place, and may from time to time order the owner or occupier of any inn, public house, or beershop to construct or place adjoining such inn, public house, or beershop an urinal, in such position and according to such plan as the Local Board or their surveyor may approve; and if any such owner or occupier fail for fourteen days after the time allowed by the Local Board for the removal, or the construction, or placing of any such urinal, to remove, or construct, or place the same according to such order, every person so offending shall for every such offence be liable to a penalty not exceeding five shillings for every day after the expiration of fourteen days during which such order is not complied with.

Sec. 32--35

Power to Local Board to order Removal and Construction of Urinals by Inn-keepers and Beer-sellers.

33. In every case in which the Local Board shall deem it expedient that the whole or any part of any house or building projecting beyond the regular line of any house or street, or beyond the front of the house or building on either side thereof, in any street, or at the corner of any street, or opposite to or projecting across the end of any street, should be taken down, for the purpose of straightening the line of any street, or of rounding off the corner of any street, or improving the entrance or approach thereto, or to any adjoining street, it shall be lawful for the Local Board to agree with the owner and occupier of such house or building to pull down, set back, or alter the same in such manner as the Local Board shall require, and to pay to such owner and occupier such compensation as shall be agreed upon between them and the Local Board; and it shall be lawful for the Local Board to add to the street so much of the site of any house or building so pulled down, set back, or altered, as shall be agreed upon between the Local Board and such owner and occupier.

Power to Local Board to agree with Owners of Projecting Buildings, and of Houses at Corners of Streets, to alter and round off same.

34. The Local Board may agree with the owners of any houses or lands within the district for the absolute purchase thereof or of any part thereof, for the purpose of opening new streets or passages or making any other convenient communications, or of straightening, widening, or diverting any existing streets, ways, or passages.

As to Purchase of Lands for opening new Streets.

Sec. 35—43

For preventing the filling up or Embankment upon Ground with offensive or unwholesome matter.

35. It shall not be lawful to raise, fill up, or embank upon any ground within the district with any offensive, noxious, or unwholesome matter, and every person who shall offend contrary to this enactment shall, for every such offence, forfeit and pay a sum not exceeding five pounds, and a further sum not exceeding forty shillings, for every day during which such offensive or unwholesome matter shall continue unremoved, after notice shall have been given by the surveyor of the Local Board for the removal thereof.

[Sec. 36.—This section, which required a rating qualification and prior payments of rates by voters at elections of the Local Board, was repealed by the Wallasey Order, 1870, art. 5.]

Power to repeal Byelaws.

37. The Local Board from time to time, as they shall think fit, may repeal any byelaws, rules, or orders made by them, without its being obligatory on them to make others in lieu thereof.

Power to grant Superannuation Allowances.

38. The Local Board may from time to time grant such superannuation or other allowances to officers, servants, workmen, and other persons appointed or employed by them, as they shall think fit.

Recovery of Penalties.

39. All damages and penalties by or under this Act, the recovery whereof is not otherwise expressly provided for, may be recovered in manner provided for the recovery of penalties by "The Public Health Act, 1848," and the Justices by whom any penalty or forfeiture for any offence under this Act shall be imposed shall, where the application thereof is not otherwise provided for, award the same to be paid to the Local Board.

[The Public Health Act, 1875, repealed the Public Health Act, 1848, as to substituted provisions, *vide* sec. 313 of the former Act.]

Power to Local Board to order costs of prosecutions.

40. It shall be lawful for the Local Board, except as is by this Act otherwise expressly provided, to direct any prosecution for any public nuisance whatever which shall be committed or suffered within the limits of this Act, and to order proceedings to be taken for the recovery of any penalties, and for the punishment of any persons offending against the provisions of this Act or any other Act relating to the district, and to direct and order the expenses of such prosecution or other proceedings to be paid and borne by and out of the General District Rate.

Assessments to different rates may be in one rate book.

41. The Local Board may include in one Rate Book the Assessments to all or any of the rates which they are authorized to levy.

Power to charge salaries to particular account.

42. The Local Board may from time to time, as they think fit, direct to what particular or special account the salaries or wages of all or any of their officers or servants shall be charged, and may, if they think fit, direct that the salary or wages of any officer or servant may be charged partly to one account and partly to another account; and such salaries and wages shall be charged to and paid out of such accounts accordingly.

Agreement set forth in Schedule confirmed.

43. The agreement between the Local Board of the first part, the honourable Charles Alexander Gore, a Commissioner of Her Majesty's Woods, Forests, and Land Revenues, of the second part, and the Queen's most Excellent Majesty of the third part, a copy whereof is contained in the Schedule to this Act, is hereby confirmed.

44. Nothing contained in this Act, or in any of the Acts herein referred to, shall authorise the said Local Board to take, use, or in any manner interfere with any land, soil, tenements, or hereditaments, or any rights of whatsoever nature belonging to or enjoyed or exerciseable by the Queen's most Excellent Majesty in right of her Crown, without the consent in writing of the Commissioners for the time being of Her Majesty's Woods, Forests, and Land Revenues, or one of them, on behalf of Her Majesty, first had and obtained for that purpose (which consent such Commissioners are hereby respectively authorised to give), neither shall anything in the said Act or Acts contained divest, take away, prejudice, diminish, or alter any estate, right, privilege, power, or authority vested in or enjoyed or exerciseable by the Queen's Majesty, her heirs or successors. *Saving rights of the Crown.*

45. All the costs, charges, and expenses of and incident to the preparing, obtaining, and passing this Act, or incident thereto, shall be paid by the Local Board. *Expenses of Act.*

The SCHEDULE referred to in the foregoing Act.

AN AGREEMENT made the twenty-seventh day of May, one thousand eight hundred and sixty-four, between the Wallasey Local Board, of the first part; the Honourable Charles Alexander Gore, the Commissioner of Her Majesty's Woods, Forests, and Land Revenues in charge of the Land Revenues of the Crown in the County of Chester, of the second part; and the Queen's most Excellent Majesty of the third part.

Whereas the said Wallasey Local Board are promoting a Bill in Parliament to enable them to erect a pier or landing stage, in substitution of the present pier or landing stage, on certain lands, including a portion of the foreshore of the River Mersey, at New Brighton, in the County of Chester, belonging to Her Majesty in right of her Crown: And whereas the said Board have applied to the said Charles Alexander Gore, as such Commissioner as aforesaid, for the grant of a new lease of a part of the foreshore aforesaid, for the purposes contemplated by the said Bill: Now, therefore, it is hereby agreed between the Wallasey Local Board and the Queen's most Excellent Majesty, and between the said Charles Alexander Gore, as such Commissioner as aforesaid, and the Wallasey Local Board, as follows:

1. The said Wallasey Local Board, in consideration of the grant of a lease by the Crown, as in this agreement provided, shall with

27 & 28 Vict. *The Wallasey Improvement Act, 1864.* ch. cxvii.

Schedule.

the consent of the Commissioners of Her Majesty's Treasury surrender to Her Majesty on or before the tenth day of October next the Crown lease of the Pier at New Brighton in the County of Chester, granted to Messieurs William Rushton Coulborn and Edward Warburton Coulborn, and dated the Twenty-ninth day of December, one thousand eight hundred and fifty-one, and the entirety of the hereditaments comprised in such lease; and also such part or parts of the several pieces of land, parts of the foreshore of the said River Mersey, held by the Board under an agreement between the Crown and the said William Rushton Coulborn and Edward Warburton Coulborn, and dated the fourth day of October, one thousand eight hundred and fifty-nine, and under a lease from the crown, dated the third day of July, one thousand eight hundred and sixty-two, as may be wanted for the purpose of being included in the lease hereinafter agreed to be granted to the Wallasey Local Board.

2. The said Charles Alexander Gore, as such Commissioner as aforesaid, or other the Commissioner or Commissioners of Her Majesty's Woods, Forests, and Land Revenues for the time being in charge of the land revenues of the crown in Chester, hereinafter called the said Commissioner or Commissioners, with the consent of the Commissioners of Her Majesty's Treasury will grant, and the Wallasey Local Board will accept, a lease from the crown of such part of the foreshore of the River Mersey as may in the opinion of the said Commissioner or Commissioners be necessary for the purpose of enabling the said Board to construct the pier or landing stage aforesaid wherever the same may be placed, within the limits of deviation as set down in the plans deposited by the said Board in connexion with the said bill, and which limits of deviation are shown by the dotted lines in the plan drawn in the margin of this agreement, and also such portion of the said foreshore between high-water to low-water mark on the south side of the proposed pier or landing stage as shall measure fifty yards in breadth therefrom, and also such portion of the said foreshore between high and low water mark on the north side of the said proposed pier or landing stage as shall measure fifty yards in breadth therefrom, the last-mentioned piece of land to be limited however by the southern boundary of that part of the said foreshore which is under lease from the crown to William Rowson, now deceased; the said lease shall also include the rights of ferry or passage between New Brighton and the Lancashire shore now enjoyed by the Local Board.

3. The said lease so to be granted by the said Commissioner or Commissioners as aforesaid shall be for a term of seventy-five years from the tenth day of October next at an annual rent of fifty-four pounds: provided always, that if the land included in the said lease shall be larger in quantity than what is included in the area bounded by the limits of deviation, a corresponding and proportionate addition shall be made in the rent to be reserved under the said lease, the amount of such proportionate addition to be settled by John Stewart, Esquire, of Liverpool, if he shall then be alive and willing to act, or otherwise by a surveyor to be named by the said Commissioner or Commissioners.

27 & 28 Vict. *The Wallasey Improvement   ch. cxvii.   211
                        Act, 1864.*

4. The said Board shall be allowed five years from the commence- **Schedule.**
ment of the said term to remove the present pier and landing stage
at New Brighton, and shall enter into a covenant to construct, after
such removal, and within the same period, a new pier or landing
stage, according to plans to be previously approved of by the said
Commissioner or Commissioners.

5. The lease shall contain covenants binding the lessees to maintain the pier or landing stage, and such other covenants and clauses as are usually inserted in crown leases of a similar nature.

6. The rents reserved by the agreement of the fourth October one thousand eight hundred and fifty-nine and the lease of the third July one thousand eight hundred and sixty-two are not to be reduced, nor are the covenants, provisoes, or agreements therein respectively contained to be affected, although portions of the land demised by them respectively may be surrendered.

7. The surrenders and new lease are to be prepared by the solicitor to the said Commissioner or Commissioners, at the expense of the said Wallasey Local Board, who are also to pay the costs of this agreement.

8. The Local Board shall not call for the production of any title to the land to be included in the said lease.

9. This agreement to be subject to the said Bill so promoted by the said Local Board passing into an Act, otherwise to be void and have no effect: and the said Charles Alexander Gore doth hereby direct that this deed shall be deemed to be fully and sufficiently enrolled by the deposit of a duplicate thereof in the office of the land revenue records and enrolments, and the filing or making an entry of such deposit by the keeper of the said records and enrolments. In witness, &c.

The common seal of the said Board was affixed }
   in the presence of   }   (L.S.)
                        H. A. Ewer,
            Law Clerk to the said Board, pro tem.

                        Charles A. Gore,

Signed, sealed, and delivered by the within-named }
   Charles Alexander Gore, in the presence of   }
                        Horace Watson,
                Office of Woods, London.

THE WALLASEY IMPROVEMENT ACT, 1867.

(30 & 31 Vict. ch. 132.)

ARRANGEMENT OF SECTIONS.

	SECTION.
Preamble.	
Short title	1
Interpretation	2
Incorporation of general Acts	3
Same meanings	4
Act to be executed by Local Board	5
Power to lay down street tramways	6
For securing communication over the permanent embankment across the eastern end of the Great Float	7
Power to sewer into marginal sewer of Mersey Docks and Harbour Board	8
Extension of gas works	9
Moneys received under this Act for gas rents, &c., to be carried to Wallasey Lighting Account	10
Security for payment of gas and water rates and charges	11
Justice may determine nature of security	12
Maximum price of gas	13
Quality of gas	14
Power to make regulations as to supplying water and gas	15
Power to compel owners of houses to take and pay for supply of water to houses if not otherwise supplied	16
Gas and water rents to be paid quarterly	17
Power to compound with owners for water rents	18
Cessor on 1st January, 1868, of ferry tolls under Act of 1858	19
Ferry tolls after 1st January, 1868	20
Ferry tolls to be charged equally	21
Ferries to be free on payment of tolls	22

	SECTION.
Sections of the Acts of 1858 and 1864 applicable to ferry tolls	23
Power to provide goods accommodation in connexion with ferries	24
Time and place for payment of ferry tolls	25
Penalty on persons using steam-boats without paying toll	26
Persons may be prevented from using ferry on refusal to pay toll	27
Bye-laws as to tramways and ferries	28
Provisions of Act of 1858 to relate to bye-laws under this Act	29
Power to borrow for purposes of Act	30
Priority of former mortgages	31
Provisions of 11 and 12 Vict., c. 63, and 21 and 22 Vict., c. 98, to apply to mortgages	32
Certain sections of Act of 1864 to apply to mortgages under this Act	33
Power to issue coupons for interest on mortgages, and to invest moneys in hands of Local Board	34
Payment of Coupons	35
Estimates for General District Rates to include sums charged thereon	36
Repeal of Act of 1864, section 21, as to application of moneys borrowed under that section	37
Rates to be parochial rates within section 156 of "Bankruptcy Act, 1861."	38
Power for inspector of nuisances to certify under the "Nuisances Removal Act, 1855," as to overcrowding of houses	39
Interest in contract or liability to rates not to disqualify justices	40
Power to pay police officers in connection with ferries, &c.	41
Payment of expenses of legal proceedings against Local Board, &c.	42
Recovery and application of penalties	43
Penalties not cumulative	44
Saving rights of Local Board	45
Expenses of Act	46
Schedules.	

AN

ACT

for making further Provision with respect to the Ferries of the Wallasey Local Board, and to empower them to extend their Gasworks and to raise further Monies; and for other Purposes.

[15TH JULY, 1867.]

8 & 9 Vict. ch. vi.
WHEREAS by "The Wallasey Improvement Act, 1845," (in this Act called "the Act of 1845,") Commissioners were appointed, and provision was made for the paving, lighting, watching, cleansing, and otherwise improving so much of the Parish of Wallasey as was

16 & 17 Vict. ch. 24. (Public)
within the limits of that Act: And whereas by "The Public Health Supplemental Act, 1853, No. 1," and the Provisional Order relating to Wallasey, parts of the Act of 1845 were repealed, and the unrepealed powers thereof were transferred to and vested in the Local Board of Health for the District of Wallasey (who were afterwards incorporated under the name of the Wallasey Local Board, and are in this Act called "The Local Board"), and "The Public Health Act, 1848," and the unrepealed powers of the Act of 1845, were applied to the District of Wallasey as defined by the Provisional Order: And whereas by "The Wallasey Improvement

21 & 22 Vict. ch. lxiii.
Act, 1858," (in this Act called the Act of 1858,) the Local Board were empowered to construct waterworks and gasworks for the supply of their district with water and gas, and powers were conferred on the Local Board for the leasing or purchasing of the Ferries called respectively "New Brighton Ferry," "Seacombe Ferry," and "Egremont Ferry," and for the providing of steamboats and other things necessary for the working of the Ferries: And

24 & 25 Vict. ch. iv.
whereas by "The Wallasey Improvement Act, 1861," (in this Act called "the Act of 1861,") and "The Wallasey Improvement Act, 1864," (in this Act called "the Act of 1864,") further powers were conferred on the Local Board, and by the Acts of 1858, 1861, and 1864, or some or one of them, New Brighton, Seacombe, and Egremont Ferries, and the works connected therewith respectively, are worked and managed by the Local Board: And whereas it is expedient that the rates and tolls with respect to Ferries be altered and amended: And whereas it is expedient that section 52 of "The Mersey Docks and Harbour (Works) Act, 1858," relating to the levying of tolls by the Mersey Docks and Harbour Board at the Duke Street Bridge, be temporarily repealed: And whereas, under the Act of 1858 the Local Board have constructed gasworks, and are now supplying gas within their district, and the demand for gas there is greatly increasing, and the present gas works are insufficient,

30 & 31 Vict. *The Wallasey Improvement Act,* 1867. ch. cxxvii. 215

and it is expedient that the Local Board be authorized to extend their present gasworks, and for that purpose to purchase lands and to borrow further monies: And whereas the amount owing by the Local Board on mortgage of the Wallasey Lighting Account is eighteen thousand five hundred pounds or thereabouts: And whereas by the Act of 1864 (section 21) the Local Board were authorised to borrow on mortgage of "The Wallasey Ferries Account," and of the Ferries and other property therein mentioned, and also (as a collateral security) of the General District Rate, any sums not exceeding in the whole forty-five thousand pounds, of which not exceeding fifteen thousand pounds was to be applied towards the New Brighton Pier, and not exceeding twelve thousand pounds for the purchase of steamboats, and the surplus of either sum was to be applied in making good any deficiency in the other sum, and the residue of the said sum of forty-five thousand pounds, and any surplus of the aggregate of the said sums of fifteen thousand pounds and twelve thousand pounds which might remain, was to be applied for the purposes of Seacombe and Egremont Ferries: And whereas the Local Board have constructed and opened the new Pier at New Brighton, but the same is not yet completed, and the amount already expended thereon by the Local Board (being part of the said sum of forty-five thousand pounds) is about twenty-one thousand pounds, and a further expenditure will be requisite for the completion of the Pier and works connected therewith, and it is expedient that section 21 of the Act of 1864 be amended and the Local Board be authorized to expend on the New Brighton Pier and Works, and for steamboats in connexion with all or any of their Ferries, so much of the residue of the forty-five thousand pounds as they deem expedient: And whereas the objects of this Act cannot be attained without the authority of Parliament; May it therefore please your Majesty that it may be enacted; and be it enacted by the Queen's most Excellent Majesty, by and with the advice and consent of the Lords Spiritual and Temporal, and Commons, in this present Parliament assembled, and by the authority of the same, as follows; (that is to say,)

Sec. 1—2

1. This Act may for all purposes be cited as "The Wallasey Improvement Act, 1867."

Short Title

2. In the Act the following words and expressions have the meanings hereby assigned to them, unless there be something in the subject or context repugnant to such construction, that is to say,

Interpretation of Terms.

The expression "the Local Board" means the Wallasey Local Board:

The expression "the district" means the district of the Local Board:

The expression "the Public Health Acts" means and includes "the Public Health Act, 1848," and "the Local Government Act, 1858," and "the Local Government Act, 1858, Amendment Act, 1861," and the several present and future Acts supplemental to or amending those Acts respectively, and which from time to time are in force and applied to the Local Board or the district

216   30 & 31 Vict.   *The Wallasey Improvement*   ch. cxxxii.
Act, 1867.

Sec. 3—7

8 & 9 Vict. ch. 18., 10 & 11 Vict. ch. 15, and 23 & 24 Vict. ch. 106, incorporated.

3. "The Lands Clauses Consolidation Act, 1845," and "The Lands Clauses Consolidation Acts Amendment Act, 1860," and "The Gasworks Clauses Act, 1847," (except the provisions thereof with respect to the amount of profit to be received by the undertakers when the gasworks are carried on for their benefit,) shall (except where expressly excepted or varied by this Act) be incorporated with and form part of this Act, and in construing those Acts in connexion with this Act the expressions "the undertakers" and "the promoters of the undertaking" mean respectively the Local Board.

Same meanings to words in incorporated Acts as in this Act.

4. In this Act the several words and expressions to which meanings are assigned by the Acts wholly or partially incorporated with this Act have the same respective meanings, unless there be something in the subject or context repugnant to such construction: Provided always, that the expression "Superior Courts" or "Court of competent Jurisdiction," or any other like expression in this Act or any Act wholly or partially incorporated with this Act, shall be read and have effect as if the debt or demand with respect to which the expression is used were a common simple contract debt, and not a debt or demand created by statute.

Act to be executed by Local Board.

5. This Act shall be executed by the Local Board, with the powers and indemnities and according to the provisions of "The Public Health Acts," and those Acts shall, in relation to the Local Board, and the several objects and purposes of this Act, be read and construed as if the purposes and provisions of this Act were purposes and provisions of the Public Health Acts, so far as the same shall be applicable thereto, and except so far as any of the provisions of the Public Health Acts are expressly varied, altered, or otherwise provided for by this Act.

Power to lay down street tramways.

6. The Local Board may from time to time lay down, maintain, and renew in and upon such streets or roads within the district as they may think fit (not being streets or roads vested in the Mersey Docks and Harbour Board) iron or other rails, plates, or trams for the passage of carriages or waggons to be moved by horse power, and may remove the same when they think fit: Provided always, that any such rails, plates, or trams shall be laid along the middle of the street, and so that the upper surface of the rail, plate, or tram shall be even with the upper surface of the roadway, and shall offer no obstruction to the passage across or along the same of ordinary carriage traffic.

For securing communication over the permanent embankment across the eastern end of the Great Float.

7. Notwithstanding anything in "The Mersey Docks and Harbour (Works) Act, 1858," contained, it shall not be lawful for the Mersey Docks and Harbour Board henceforth to demand or receive any toll for the use of the Duke Street bridge, and the road through the Docks and Works of the Mersey Docks and Harbour Board, over the Duke Street embankment, unless and until the said Mersey Docks and Harbour Board shall have completed and opened for the passage of passengers, carts, carriages, vehicles, and animals a road or public thoroughfare over the embankment by that Act authorized, and therein described as a "permanent Embankment across the eastern end of the Great Float," (including the bridges connecting the various portions of such embankment,) and arrangements have been made for establishing the same communication over such embankment as

aforesaid, for the passage between Seacombe and Birkenhead of such traffic as aforesaid, as the communication for the public over the quays at Liverpool, so far as the circumstances of the case will permit ; and if any difference arise between the Local Board and the Mersey Docks and Harbour Board as to the sufficiency of the communication and accommodation from time to time provided and maintained by the Mersey Docks and Harbour Board in pursuance of this section, such difference shall be determined by an arbitrator to be agreed upon between the parties, or, in default of agreement, to be, on the application of either party, appointed by the Board of Trade, and his decision may be made a rule of any of the superior Courts, on the application of either party.

8. And whereas the Mersey Docks and Harbour Board have constructed in the district of the Local Board a marginal sewer on the northern side of the Great Float, for the purpose of receiving the drainage which would otherwise have flowed into the pool converted into a dock, and now called the Great Float: Therefore the Local Board from time to time, under the superintendence of the Engineer of the Mersey Docks and Harbour Board, at their own expense, may cause to branch into and to communicate with the said marginal sewer, at such points or places as the Local Board from time to time require, any one or more sewer or sewers for the purpose of discharging the sewerage of all or any part of the district into the said marginal sewer : Provided always, that the Local Board shall not interfere with the road along which the said marginal sewer is carried further or otherwise than may be necessary for the purposes of this present enactment ; and every such interference shall be under the superintendence aforesaid ; and the Local Board shall, at their own expense, make good and restore any damage or disturbance occasioned to the said road or the surface thereof.

Power to sewer into marginal sewer of Mersey Docks and Harbour Board.

9. Subject to the provisions of this Act, the Local Board may from time to time acquire by agreement, for the purposes of the gasworks, all or any part of the lands described in schedule (A) to this Act, and may from time to time, on all or any part of such lands, make and maintain all such gasworks, buildings, gasometers, and apparatus, with approaches thereto, for the manufacture, storage, and supply of gas, and may do all such other acts as they think necessary for manufacturing and storing gas ; and the Local Board from time to time may, by means of the gasworks to be made and maintained by them under this Act, and also of the gasworks authorized by the Act of 1858, supply gas within the limits of the Act of 1858 ; and the powers and provisions of the Act of 1858 contained in sections 17 to 26, both inclusive, of that Act, shall apply to the gasworks authorized by this Act, as well as the gasworks authorized by the Act of 1858 : Provided always, that the Local Board shall not make or store gas on any lands other than the lands which are described in the said schedule (A), or the lands on which the Local Board are now authorized to make or store gas, and which are described in schedule (B) to this Act.

Extension of Gasworks.

[This section is altered and amended by The Wallasey Order (No. 1), 1877, art. 5, and The Wallasey Order, 1892, art. 1, which confer powers for further extensions.]

30 & 31 Vict. *The Wallasey Improvement Act*, 1867. ch. cxxxii.

Sec. 10—14

Monies received under this Act for gas rents, &c., to be carried to Wallasey Lighting Account.

10. All monies which shall come to the hands of the Local Board in respect of gas supplied by them from or by means of the gasworks by this Act authorised, or of coke, or of other residuum arising from those gasworks, and disposed of by the Local Board, and in respect of any penalties recovered under this Act, or under the "Gasworks Clauses Act, 1847," with reference to those gasworks or the gas so supplied, shall form part and be applicable as part of the "Wallasey Lighting Account" mentioned in the Act of 1858.

[*Vide* The Wallasey Improvement Act, 1858, secs. 29 and 30.]

Security for payment of gas and water rates and charges.

11. Any person having or requesting to have a supply of gas or water from the Local Board, and any person having or requesting to have gas or water fittings and pipes provided or let on hire by the Local Board, shall, if and when so required by the Local Board or their Treasurer, and before such person is entitled to have the fittings or pipes provided and laid, or to have a supply of gas or water provided or let on hire or continued, give to the Local Board such security for the payment of the rate or charge for the gas or water to be supplied to him, and for the fittings and pipes, as he and the Local Board or such Treasurer shall agree on, or as, failing agreement, shall be determined in the manner by this Act provided; but the Local Board shall not at any time be entitled to discontinue the supply of gas or water to any such person then having a supply, or to discontinue the letting on hire of such fittings or pipes to any such person, unless otherwise expressly authorized by the Act of 1858, or this Act, or any Act wholly or partially incorporated with those Acts, or either of them, until such person shall have failed to give the security for seven days after the same shall have been agreed on or determined as aforesaid.

Justice may determine nature of security.

12. Where any such person and the Local Board do not agree on the security to be given, the same shall be determined by a Justice; and any single Justice shall, on the application of the person and the Local Board, or either of them, determine the nature and amount of the security to be given, and the security may be the deposit with the Local Board of a sum of money or any other security which the Justice thinks sufficient and reasonable, and the determination of the Justice shall be binding on all parties.

Maximum price of gas.

13. Notwithstanding anything in the Act of 1858, the maximum price at which gas shall be sold by the Local Board to all persons who shall burn the same by meter shall not exceed five shillings and sixpence per thousand cubic feet.

[*Vide* The Wallasey Improvement Act, 1858, sec. 22.]

Quality of gas.

14. Notwithstanding anything in the Act of 1858, all the Gas supplied by the Local Board shall be of such quality as to produce from an argand burner having fifteen holes and a seven-inch chimney, or other approved burner and chimney, and consuming five cubic feet of gas per hour, a light equal in intensity to the light produced by fourteen sperm candles of six to the pound, burning one hundred and twenty grains per hour; and the 25th and 26th sections of the Act of 1858 shall be read and have effect as if the illuminating power prescribed by that Act had been such as is prescribed by this Act.

[*Vide* The Wallasey Improvement Act, 1858, ss. 23, 25 and 26.]

30 & 31 *Vict.* *The Wallasey Improvement Act*, 1867. *ch. cxxcii.* 219

Sec. 15—18

15. Subject to the provisions of this Act, the Local Board from time to time may make and enforce such reasonable bye-laws or regulations as they think proper, with respect to the inspection and control by them or their officers, of the laying down or fixing of water and gas pipes and fittings in or in connexion with all present and future houses or buildings within the district, and also for the more effectually preventing, controlling, or regulating all interference with the pipes, plugs, stopcocks, and other apparatus connected with their waterworks and gasworks respectively, or their water or gas mains or pipes, for the supply by the Local Board of water and gas respectively, or the mode or duration of such supply, and if and whenever any of those regulations are not observed by any person having or requiring a supply of water or gas, the Local Board may cut off the water or gas supplied by them, or refuse to supply water or gas to him, unless and until the regulations be complied with.

Power to make regulations as to supplying water and gas.

[*Vide* The Wallasey Local Board Act, 1890, sec. 70.]

16. If it shall appear to the Local Board, on the report of their Inspector of Nuisances, that any house within the district is without a proper supply of water, they may give notice in writing to the owner of such house requiring him within one month to do all such work as may be necessary for obtaining such supply from the works of the Local Board; and if such notice be not complied with the Local Board may, if they think fit, do such works, and recover the expenses thereof from the owner of the premises in like manner as water rate or rents are recoverable under the Act of 1858 and this Act respectively; provided no owner shall be compelled to carry his pipes to any main where the same shall be more than twenty yards distant from the house to be supplied; and the water rent for the supply of water to any such house, not exceeding the annual value of thirteen pounds, shall be due and payable by the owner, or, at the the option of the Local Board, the occupier thereof, and may be recovered by the Local Board as if such owner or occupier had contracted with the Local Board for the supply of such water.

Power to compel owners of houses to take and pay for supply of water to houses, if not otherwise supplied.

17. All the rates, rents, and monies payable to the Local Board for the supply of water shall be payable in advance quarterly on the first day of January, the first day of April, the first day of July, and the first day of October in every year, and the first payment of such rates, rents, or monies under this Act shall be made on such one of the said quarterly days as shall first happen after the passing of this Act, and shall be payable in respect of the quarter commencing with that quarterly day: Provided always, that all rates, rents, and monies for the supply of water by the Local Board up to that quarterly day shall be payable to and recoverable by them as if this Act were not passed.

Gas and water rents to be paid quarterly.

[This section refers to *Water* only, although the marginal heading includes *Gas*.]

18. Where the annual value of any house supplied with water by the Local Board does not exceed the sum of thirteen pounds, the Local Board from time to time may compound with the owner of such house for the payment of all or any of the water rates or rents for the time being payable for the supply of water to such house, and to any other houses of the same owner not exceeding the annual

Power to compound with owners for water rents.

Sec. 19—23 value of thirteen pounds each, upon such reduced estimate of the annual value of the house or houses so supplied as the Local Board deem reasonable, not being less than two thirds or more than four fifths of such annual value.

[*Vide* The Wallasey Local Board Act, 1890, sec. 72.]

Cessor on 1st January, 1868, of ferry tolls under Act of 1858.

19. The several ferry tolls leviable and payable under the Act of 1858 shall continue and be leviable and payable until the first of January one thousand eight hundred and sixty-eight, and shall then cease to be levied, but without prejudice to the recovery by the Local Board of any tolls theretofore payable.

Ferry tolls after 1st January, 1868.

20. On and after the first day of January one thousand eight hundred and sixty-eight, the Local Board from time to time may demand and receive, for the use of any ferry for the time being purchased or leased by or belonging to the Local Board, and for the conveyance of passengers, animals, and goods in any steam or other boat for the time being belonging to or provided by the Local Board, any tolls (in this Act called "Ferry Tolls,") not exceeding the sums mentioned in schedule (C) to this Act annexed, and the monies arising therefrom shall be carried to the Account mentioned or referred to in the Act of 1858 as the "Wallasey Ferry Account."

Ferry tolls to be charged equally.

21. The ferry tolls shall be at all times charged equally to all persons and after the same rate in respect of all passengers and goods, animals, or carriages of a like description conveyed in the same class of steamboats, and under the like circumstances, and no reduction or advance in any such tolls shall be made, either directly or indirectly, in favour of or against any particular company or person using the ferry.

[*Vide* The Wallasey Improvement Act, 1858, sec. 40; and the Wallasey Improvement Act, 1864, sec. 16.]

Ferries to be free on payment of tolls.

22. The Local Board shall not at any time demand or take a greater Ferry toll or make any greater charge for ferryage than the amounts specified in the schedule (C) to this Act; and upon payment of the tolls from time to time demandable all persons shall be entitled to use the Ferry in respect of which such toll is demandable, subject nevertheless to the regulations to be from time to time made by the Local Board by virtue of the powers in that behalf conferred upon them by the Acts of 1858, 1861, and 1864, and this Act respectively.

[*Vide* The Wallasey Improvement Act, 1858, sec. 41; as to Regulations, secs. 51 to 59 of the same Act, power to alter Ferry tolls: The Wallasey Improvement Act, 1864, sec. 16.]

Sections of the Acts of 1858 and 1864 applicable to ferry tolls.

23. Sections 42 to 44, both inclusive, and 46 to 50, both inclusive, of the Act of 1858, with respect to the levying, recovery, and collection of Ferry tolls, and section 16 of the Act of 1864 relating to the alteration of Ferry tolls, shall be incorporated with this Act, and shall be applicable to the Ferry tolls authorized to be levied under this Act, and as if the same were Ferry tolls authorized to be levied under the Acts of 1858 and 1864, or either of them.

24. In connexion with their Ferries, the Local Board from time to time may erect and provide such warehouses, sheds, and other buildings, works and conveniences as they think necessary for the storage and accommodation of animals and goods, and for the loading and unloading of animals and goods, and may provide and employ carts, waggons, and vehicles, and horses, for the cartage and carriage of animals and goods to and from their Ferries, from and to any part of the district, and may make such reasonable charges as they think fit for all or any of the accommodation and services so provided or performed, and the amount of such charges shall be recoverable in like manner as Ferry tolls.

Power to provide goods accommodation in connexion with ferries.

25. The Local Board may demand and take the Ferry tolls on either side of the River Mersey at such times, either before using the Ferry or entering the steam or other boat, or during the user of the Ferry or the conveyance on the steam or other boat, or immediately thereafter, as the Local Board from time to time direct, and, subject to the consent of the Mersey Docks and Harbour Board, may erect a bar, box, or other suitable building for the reception of such tolls on any land or property of the said Board which they may be willing to allocate for that purpose.

Time and place for payment of ferry tolls.

26. If any person travel or attempt to travel in any steam or other boat provided by the Local Board in connexion with their Ferries without having previously paid the Ferry toll which shall have been demanded from him, and be payable by him under this Act, every such person shall for every such offence forfeit a sum not exceeding forty shillings.

Penalty on persons using steamboats without paying tolls.

[*Vide* also The Wallasey Improvement Act, 1858, sec. 46, and The Wallasey Improvement Act, 1872, sec. 15.]

27. If the Ferry toll payable by any person desirous of using the Ferry, or of being conveyed on any steam or other boat provided by the Local Board, be demanded from him before using the Ferry or entering the steam or other boat, and such person shall, after demand from him of the Ferry toll payable for such user or conveyance, (such demand being made by any collector or other person appointed to receive the same toll,) knowingly and wilfully refuse or neglect to pay the same or any part thereof, the collector or other person so appointed may refuse to permit the person so in default to use the Ferry or enter the steam or other boat in respect of which the toll ought to be or to have been paid, and may by himself, or with such assistance as he shall think necessary, stop and prevent the person so in default from using the Ferry or entering the steam or other boat; and every person who, having been so refused, shall use the Ferry or enter the steam or other boat, and shall refuse or neglect to pay his Ferry toll or any part thereof, shall for every such offence forfeit a sum not exceeding forty shillings, in addition to any penalty or forfeiture to which he may be otherwise liable under the Acts of 1858 and 1864 and this Act respectively for nonpayment of Ferry toll.

Persons may be prevented from using ferry on refusal to pay toll.

[Extended and applied to persons refusing to produce contract or season tickets—The Wallasey Local Board Act, 1890, sec. 74.]

30 & 31 Vict. *The Wallasey Improvement Act,* 1867. ch. cxxxii.

Sec. 28—31

Byelaws as to tramways and ferries.

28. The Local Board from time to time may make, alter, and repeal such byelaws as they think expedient for all or any of the purposes and objects following; (that is to say,)

For regulating the mode by which and the speed at which carriages using the tramways by this Act authorized are to be moved or propelled, and generally for regulating the travelling upon or the using and working of the same tramways:

For regulating and controlling or preventing, if thought fit, the fastening or mooring of vessels or boats of every description to any of the piers, landing stages, stairs or works of the Local Board:

For regulating and controlling the mooring and anchoring of vessels and boats of every description in the River Mersey within one hundred yards of any of the piers, landing stages, stairs, or works of the Local Board, and for prescribing the limits within which and the particular places within the said one hundred yards at which such vessels or boats shall be moored or anchored.

[Application to Seacombe Ferry—*The Wallasey Improvement Act,* 1872, sec. 14.]

Secs. 52 to 59 of Act of 1858 to apply.

29. Sections 52 to 59 both inclusive, of the Act of 1858, shall apply to all byelaws under this Act.

Power to borrow on mortgage for purposes of Act.

30. In addition to the monies which the Local Board are empowered to borrow under the recited Acts or any of them, and the Public Health Acts or any of them, they may from time to time borrow on mortgage of the security mentioned in the Act of 1858 as "The Wallasey Lighting Account," and of the gasworks for the time being vested in or belonging to the Local Board under the Act of 1858 or this Act, and also, if the Local Board think fit, (as a collateral security,) of the General District Rate to be made and levied under the Public Health Acts or any of them, any sums not exceeding in the whole twenty thousand pounds, which sums shall be applied, first, in payment of such part as the Local Board think fit of the costs, charges, and expenses of and incident to the preparing, obtaining, and passing this Act, or otherwise in relation thereto, secondly, in the construction, alterations, and extension of the gasworks, and the pipes, works, and conveniences connected therewith authorized by the Act of 1858 and this Act, or either of them.

[*Vide* The Wallasey Improvement Act, 1858, sec. 29.

For FURTHER BORROWING POWERS—

Gas: *Vide* The Wallasey Order (No. 1,) 1877, art. 2.
The Wallasey Order, 1883, art. 1.
The Wallasey Order, 1892, art. 2.
The Wallasey Order, 1896, art. 1.
The Wallasey Order, 1898, art. 1.]

Priority of former mortgages.

31. All mortgages granted under the Acts of 1858, 1861, and 1864 respectively, and subsisting at the time of the passing of this Act, shall during the continuance thereof respectively have, with respect to the rates, properties, and securities comprised therein respectively, priority over all mortgages granted under this Act on the same rates, properties, and securities respectively; and all mortgages granted and to be hereafter granted by the Local Board under the authority of the Public Health Acts or any of them shall respectively have priority over all mortgages granted under this Act on the collateral security of the General District Rate, so far as relates to such collateral security.

[Altered and amended by The Wallasey Order, 1883, art. 9.]

32. The sections of the "Public Health Act, 1848," 111, 112, and 114, and the schedules (B.) and (C.) to that Act, and section 57 of the "Local Government Act, 1858," shall be applicable to the mortgages to be made by the Local Board under this Act. *Provisions of 11 & 12 Vict. ch. 63, and 21 & 22 Vict. ch. 98 to apply to mortgages.*

[The "Public Health Act, 1848," and the "Local Government Act, 1858," were repealed by the "Public Health Act, 1875," sec. 313 of which relates to substituted sections.]

33. Sections 25, 26, and 27 of the Act of 1864 with respect to the reborrowing of money, the surrender of mortgages, and the time for paying off borrowed money, shall be applicable to the mortgages to be made by the Local Board under this Act, and to the monies to be borrowed under this Act. *Certain sections of Act of 1864 to apply to mortgages under this Act.*

[As to priority *vide* The Wallasey Order, 1883, art. 9. Provisions for repayment and sinking fund in the Wallasey Order, 1883, arts. 4 and 7.]

34. The Local Board from time to time, if and when they think fit, may issue to the mortgagees from time to time of the Local Board under the recited Acts and this Act or any of them, or under the Public Health Acts or any of them, coupons for the interest from time to time to fall due on their respective mortgages, and the coupons may be in such form as the Local Board from time to time think fit, so as every coupon refer to the mortgage to which it relates, and specifies the amount and time of payment of one half year's interest to fall due on the principal monies secured by the mortgage and be authenticated by the signatures of two persons thereunto expressly authorized by the Local Board, and the Local Board from time to time may invest in government or parliamentary securities, or in deposit accounts with their bankers, any monies from time to time in their hands under the recited Acts, and this Act respectively, or the Public Health Acts. *Power to issue coupons for interest on mortgages, and to invest monies in hands of Local Board.*

35. On the presentation to the treasurer or the bankers for the time being of the Local Board of any coupon issued under this Act, he or they may pay to the person presenting the coupon the amount of interest thereon expressed and appearing by the coupon to be then due and payable (after deducting the income or property tax then payable,) and on the audit of the treasurer's or bankers' accounts the coupon shall be accepted as a sufficient warrant for such payment by him or them: Provided always that the treasurer or bankers shall not be bound, unless he or they think fit, to make any payment of *Payment of coupons.*

Sec. 36—38 interest beyond the amount of the monies of the Local Board then in his or their hands, and applicable in that behalf.

Estimates for General District Rates to include sums charged thereon.

36. The deficiency (if any) from time to time in the Wallasey Waterworks Account, the Wallasey Lighting Account, and the Wallasey Ferries Account, respectively referred to in the Act of 1858, whether under that Act or the Acts of 1861 and 1864, or either of them, or this Act, shall be borne and paid by the Local Board out of the General District Rate, and the amount of the General District Rates, and of the estimates of the money required for the purposes of the General District Rates, shall respectively include all monies required for payment of any such deficiency, and also of any monies from time to time due or accruing due for principal, interest, or sinking fund in respect of mortgages under the recited Acts and this Act, or any of them charged on the General District Rate as a collateral security, and for the payment of which the other securities (if any) comprised in such mortgages respectively shall be insufficient.

Repeal of Act of 1864, sec. 21, as to application of monies borrowed under that section.

37. Notwithstanding anything contained in the 21st section of the Act of 1864 with respect to the application of the forty-five thousand pounds by that section authorized to be borrowed, the Local Board may, if they think fit, apply the whole or any part of the said sum of forty-five thousand pounds in or towards the erection, construction, or maintenance of the pier or landing stage at New Brighton authorised by the Act of 1864, and the jetties, esplanades, toll gates, toll houses, works, and conveniences connected therewith, and in payment of such part as the Local Board think fit of the costs, charges, and expenses of and incident to the preparing, obtaining, and passing of this Act, or otherwise in relation thereto, and in the purchase or otherwise in connexion with the steam or other boats to be purchased or provided by them for the purposes of their ferries or any of them; and the surplus not so applied shall from time to time be applied for the purposes of the Seacombe and Egremont Ferries respectively; and the expenditure of the Local Board before the passing of this Act, on or in connexion with the New Brighton Pier and Works, in excess of the amount by section 21 of the Act of 1864 authorized to be expended in that behalf, is by this Act confirmed.

Rates to be parochial rates within sec. 156 of "Bankruptcy Act, 1861."

38. All rates and rents leviable by or payable to the Local Board under the recited Acts or any of them, or this Act, or the Public Health Acts or any of them, shall be deemed parochial rates within the meaning of section 156 of "The Bankruptcy Act, 1861."

[The Bankruptcy Act, 1861, was repealed by the Bankruptcy Repeal and Insolvent Court Act, 1869 (32 & 33 Vict, ch. 83, sec. 201), which was in its turn repealed by the Statute Law Revision (No. 2) Act, 1893 (56 & 57 Vict. ch. 54, sec. 1 and sched). For the present law relating to the priority of rates in the distribution of the property of a bankrupt or of the assets of a company being wound up, *vide* the Preferential Payments in Bankruptcy Act, 1888, sec. 1 (51 & 52 Vict. (ch. 62), and 1897, sec. 1 (60 & 61 Vict. ch. 19.)]

39. Whenever the Inspector of Nuisances of the Local Board shall certify to the Local Board that any house in the district is so overcrowded as to be dangerous or prejudicial to the health of the inhabitants, the certificate of such inspector shall, with respect to section 29 of "The Nuisances Removal Act, 1855," have the like effect, and the like proceedings shall be had under that section, as if the same were a certificate of the Medical Officer of Health, or of two qualified medical practitioners referred to in that section. *Power for Inspector of Nuisances to certify under the "Nuisances Removal Act, 1855," as to overcrowding of houses.*

> [The Nuisance Removal Act. 1855, was repealed (except as to London) by the Public Health Act, 1875, sec. 343 and sched v.; *vide* sec. 313 of the latter Act as to substituted provisions.]

40. No person shall be incapable of acting as a Justice in the execution in any respect of this Act by reason of his being interested in any contract under this Act for a supply of gas, or being liable under this Act to the payment of any rate, toll, or other money. *Interest in contract or liability to rates not to disqualify Justices.*

41. The Local Board from time to time may employ and may pay monies to the Treasurer, Chief Constable, or other proper officer of the County of Chester in respect of the employment of such police constables as the Local Board think requisite in connexion with and for the protection and for the preservation of order in the ferries, waterworks, and gasworks, and other property of the Local Board, and the expenses and monies so incurred or paid by the Local Board shall be paid by them, and be debited by them to the proper account. *Power to pay police officers in connexion with ferries, &c.*

42. All monies and expenses incurred by or imposed upon the Local Board, or any member, officer, or servant of the Local Board, in legal proceedings brought against the Local Board, or any such member acting in his capacity of member of the Local Board, or any such officer or servant acting under the direction or in the service of the Local Board, may be paid by the Local Board, and if so paid shall be debited by them to the proper account. *Payment of expenses of legal proceedings against Local Board, &c.*

43. All damages and penalties by or under this Act, or any byelaw made under this Act, the recovery whereof is not otherwise expressly provided for, may be recovered in manner provided for the recovery of penalties by "The Public Health Act, 1848;" and the Justices by whom any penalty or forfeiture for any offence under this Act shall be imposed shall (except where the Local Board shall be the party by whom the penalty has to be paid) award the same to be paid to the Local Board. *Recovery and application of penalties.*

> [The Public Health Act, 1848, repealed by the Public Health Act, 1875, and its provisions substituted by sec. 313 of that Act.]

44. Penalties imposed on the Local Board for one and the same offence by several Acts of Parliament shall not be cumulative, and for this purpose this Act and the Acts wholly or partially incorporated therewith shall be deemed several Acts. *Penalties not cumulative.*

45. Except as is by this Act otherwise expressly provided, this Act or anything therein contained shall not take away, lessen, prejudice, or alter any of the jurisdictions, estates, rights, powers, or privileges of the Local Board. *Saving rights of Local Board.*

Sec. 46
xpenses of Act.

46. All the costs, charges, and expenses of and incident to the preparing, obtaining, and passing this Act, or otherwise in relation thereto, shall be paid by the Local Board.

SCHEDULES referred to in the foregoing Act.

SCHEDULE (A.)

All that field in the Township of Poulton-cum-Seacombe bounded on the south by the existing gasworks and waterworks of the Local Board, on the south-west by Dock Road, on the north in part by an occupation road, and in other part by a field, and on the east by a field.

SCHEDULE (B.)

All that piece or parcel of land in the Township of Poulton-cum-Seacombe, in the Parish of Wallasey, on which the existing Gasworks of the Local Board are constructed, lying on the north-east side of and adjoining the Dock Road near the junction therewith of Lime Kiln Lane, and bounded on the other three sides by land belonging or reputed to belong to and in the occupation of Salusbury Kynaston Mainwaring, Esquire, and containing by admeasurement 5,400 square yards or thereabouts.

SCHEDULE (C.)

FERRY TOLLS.

For each person, not being a contractor, any sum or sums not exceeding as follows; that is to say,

	d.
New Brighton to Liverpool, or vice versâ	3
Egremont to ,, ,,	2
Seacombe to ,, ,,	1

RATES FOR CONTRACTORS.

	12 Months.			6 Months.			3 Months.		
	£	s.	d.	£	s.	d.	£	s.	d.
Not exceeding as follows:— For any One Person from New Brighton to Liverpool or vice versâ	3	13	6	2	12	6	1	11	6
For every additional Person of the same Family, and dwelling together, including Servants (Domestic or otherwise), but not Lodgers	1	11	6	1	1	0	0	15	0

30 & 31 *Vict.* *The Wallasey Improvement* *ch. cxxvii.*
Act, 1867.

RATES FOR CONTRACTORS—*Continued.*

	12 Months.	6 Months.	3 Months.
	£ s. d.	£ s. d.	£ s. d.
For any One Person from Egremont to Liverpool, or vice versâ	2 12 6	1 11 6	1 1 0
For every additional Person of the same Family, and dwelling together, including Servants (Domestic or otherwise), but not Lodgers	1 1 0	0 15 0	0 10 6
For any One Person from Seacombe to Liverpool, or vice versâ	1 11 6	0 19 0	0 12 6
For every additional Person of the same Family, and dwelling together, including Servants (Domestic or otherwise), but not Lodgers	0 15 0	0 9 0	0 6 6

SPECIAL BOATS.

For Every Person, whether a Contractor or not, to or from each Ferry, any sum not exceeding 1s.

RATES FOR CARRIAGES, CATTLE, GOODS, AND MERCHANDISE.

	New Brighton.	Egremont and Seacombe.
	s. d.	s. d.
Not exceeding as follows :—		
Carriage, with 2 Horses	12 0	10 0
Ditto, with 1 Horse	8 0	6 0
Light 4-wheeled Phaeton, with 2 Horses ...	8 0	6 0
Ditto. with 1 Horse ...	6 0	4 0
Pony Phaeton, small	4 0	3 0
Hearse, with 2 Horses	15 0	12 0
Ditto, ditto, returning same day	5 0	4 0
Gig and Horse	3 0	2 0
Cab or Car, and Horse	4 0	3 0
Cart and Horse, loaded	10 0	8 0
Ditto, empty	5 0	4 0
Hand Cart, large, loaded, and 1 Man	1 6	1 0
Ditto, small, ditto	1 0	0 9
Ditto, empty ditto	0 9	0 6
Handbarrow, loaded, and 2 men ...	1 3	1 0
Ditto empty, ditto ...	0 9	0 6
Wheelbarrow, loaded, and 1 man ...	0 10	0 8
Ditto, empty, ditto .	0 6	0 4
Coffin, empty	1 3	1 0
Corpse, and 4 Men	6 0	5 0
Horse, and 1 Man	1 6	1 0

RATES FOR CARRIAGES, &c.—Continued.

	New Brighton.		Egremont and Seacombe.	
	s.	d.	s.	d.
Donkey, and 1 ditto	0	10	0	8
Sheep, dead, each	0	2	0	2
Ditto alive,	0	1½	0	1
Ditto, ditto, per score	1	8	1	6
Geese, alive or dead, per score	0	11	0	10
Cows or Oxen, each,	1	3	1	0
Calves, Pigs, and Goats, each	0	4	0	3
Tables, large, each	1	3	1	0
Ditto, small, each	0	7	0	6
Beds, each	1	3	1	0
Wardrobes	0	9	0	6
Chest of Drawers, large	0	9	0	6
Ditto, small	0	6	0	4
Chairs, parlour or common, each	0	1½	0	1
Ditto, light bedroom, per dozen	0	7	0	6
Ditto, easy or rocking, each	0	2	0	1½
Hay, per truss or sack	0	3	0	2
Ditto, per ton	4	0	3	0
Sugar, per loaf	0	1	0	1
Ditto, per cask, not exceeding 10 cwt.	1	2	1	0
Ditto, ditto, exceeding 10 cwt.	2	4	2	0
Soap, per box, 1 cwt.	0	3	0	2
Ditto, ditto, 2 to 3 cwt.	0	4	0	3
Spirits or Wine, hamper, large	0	9	0	6
Ditto, ditto, small	0	4	0	3
Ditto, quarter cask	0	6	0	4
Ditto, hogshead	1	0	0	8
Ditto, pipe, puncheon or tierce	2	0	1	4
Ale or Porter, per barrel	0	9	0	6
Ditto, half barrel	0	6	0	4
Ditto, quarter barrel	0	4	0	3
Vitriol, per bottle	0	3	0	2
Oil and Tar, per bottle	0	3	0	2
Molasses, per cask	0	9	0	6
Ditto, per puncheon	1	6	1	0
Cement or Lime, per barrel or cwt	0	3	0	2
Nails, per bag or keg, ½ cwt.	0	4	0	3
Ditto, 1 to 2 cwt.	0	6	0	4
Ditto, 2 to 3 cwt.	0	9	0	6
Basket of Fruit, Eggs, Fish, &c.	0	3	0	2
Cockles or Mussels, per bag	0	1½	0	1
Chips or Wood, per bag	0	3	0	2
Paint, Lead, or Iron, per cwt.	0	3	0	2
Ditto, per ton	3	0	2	6
Oil Paint, per can	0	3	0	2
Ditto, per cask	0	9	0	6
Wool, per cwt.	0	9	0	6
Wool, per bale	1	3	1	0
Bricks, Flags, Slates, Tiles, &c., per cwt.	0	3	0	2
Ditto, per ton	2	9	2	6

30 & 31 Vict. *The Wallasey Improvement Act,* 1867.   ch. cxxvii.

RATES FOR CARRIAGES, &c.—*Continued.*

	New Brighton.		Egremont and Seacombe.	
	s.	d.	s.	d.
Sofas or Ottomans, each	0	9	0	6
Pianofortes, grand	3	0	2	0
Ditto, upright	2	0	1	6
Ditto, cottage	1	6	1	0
Parcels, large, each	0	2½	0	2
Ditto, small, each	0	1½	0	1
Baskets, large	0	3	0	2
Ditto, small	0	1½	0	1
Portmanteaus or Carpet Bags, large	0	2½	0	2
Ditto, ditto, small	0	1½	0	1
Boxes, large, each	0	4	0	3
Ditto, small, each	0	2½	0	2
Hamper, large	0	4	0	3
Ditto, small	0	2½	0	2
Bacon, per flitch	0	1½	0	1
Ditto, per side	0	3	0	2
Ditto, per bale, large	0	9	0	6
Ditto, ditto, small	0	4½	0	3
Hams, each	0	1½	0	1
Cheese, each	0	1½	0	1
Salt, per bag, 12 lumps	0	4½	0	3
Ditto, 6 ditto	0	2½	0	2
Ditto, per lump	0	0¾	0	0½
Butter, per keg, per 56 lbs.	0	2½	0	2
Ditto, per keg, per cwt.	0	5	0	4
Ditto, per firkin	0	5	0	4
Candles, per box, under 30 lbs.	0	1½	0	1
Ditto, 30 lbs. and under 60 lbs	0	3	0	2
Ditto, 60 lbs. and under 1 cwt	0	4½	0	3
Glass, small box	0	3	0	2
Ditto, small crate	0	6	0	4
Ditto, large crate	0	10	0	8
Tea, per box	0	3	0	2
Ditto, half box	0	2	0	1
Coffee, per bag, under ½ cwt	0	2	0	1
Ditto, above ditto	0	3	0	2
Pocket of Hops	0	8	0	6
Sack of Flour, Wheat, Barley, Oats, or other Grain	0	3	0	2
Potatoes, per sack or measure	0	1½	0	1
Earthenware or Hollow-ware, per crate or Hogshead	1	0	0	9
Skins, each	0	1½	0	1
Skins, in lots	1	6	1	0
Yeast, small tub	0	1½	0	1
Yeast, large tub	0	2	0	1½
Laths, per bundle	0	1½	0	1
Cargo Boats, per tide	12	0	10	0
Iron ditto per tide	20	0	15	0

Articles not particularly enumerated as per Agreement.

Sec. 1—7 # THE LOCAL GOVERNMENT SUPPLEMENTAL ACT, 1870.

(*Confirming The Wallasey Order*, 1870.)

AN

ACT

to confirm certain Provisional Orders under "The Local Government Act, 1858," relating to the districts of Blackpool, Bristol, Eton, Heckmondwike, Kidderminster, Lincoln, Nottingham, Plymouth, South Molton, WALLASEY, and Ware; and for other purposes relative to certain districts under the said Act.

14th JULY, 1870.

WHEREAS the Secretary of State for the Home Department, being one of Her Majesty's Principal Secretaries of State, has, under the provisions of the Local Government Act, 1858, duly made certain Provisional Orders, which are contained in the schedule to this Act annexed; and it is provided by the aforesaid Local Government Act that no such orders shall be of any validity whatever until they shall have been confirmed by Parliament; and it is expedient that the said orders should be so confirmed, and other provisions made with respect to certain districts under the Local Government Act aforesaid:

Be it therefore enacted by the Queen's most Excellent Majesty, by and with the advice and consent of the Lords Spiritual and Temporal, and Commons, in this present Parliament assembled, and by the authority of the same, as follows:—

Provisional Orders in schedule confirmed.

1. The Provisional Orders contained in the schedule hereunto annexed shall, from and after the passing of this Act, be absolute, and be as binding and of like force and effect as if the provisions of the same had been expressly enacted in this Act.

[The omitted sections and orders relate to districts other than Wallasey.]

Act incorporated with 21 & 22 Vict. ch. 98.

6. This Act shall be deemed to be incorporated with the Local Government Act, 1858, and shall be as if this Act and the said Local Government Act were one Act.

Short title.

7. In citing this Act in any other Act of Parliament, or in any proceeding, instrument, or document whatever, it shall be sufficient to use the words and figures "the Local Government Supplemental Act, 1870."

SCHEDULE of Provisional Orders referred to in the preceding Act.

Schedule.

11. WALLASEY.—Alteration and partial repeal of Local Act.

THE WALLASEY ORDER, 1870.

[This Order may be cited as The Wallasey Order, 1870.— *Vide* The Wallasey Order, 1896, art. II.]

Provisional Order repealing and altering parts of Local Acts in force within the District of the Wallasey Local Board.

Whereas petitions have been presented to me as one of Her Majesty's Principal Secretaries of State, under the 77th section of the Local Government Act, 1858, from the Wallasey Local Board, in the County of Chester, praying for the partial repeal and alteration of certain Local Acts in force within the said district; viz.,

An Act passed in the eighth year of the reign of Her Majesty Queen Victoria, intituled "An Act for paving, lighting, watching, " cleansing, and otherwise improving the Parish of Wallasey in the " County of Chester, and for establishing a police, and also a market, " within such parish; and for other purposes;" [The Wallasey Improvement Act, 1845.]

An Act passed in the twenty-first and twenty-second years of the reign of Her Majesty Queen Victoria, intituled " An Act for enabling " the Local Board of Health for the District of Wallasey to construct " works and supply their district with water and gas; for enlarging " their powers with respect to the acquisition and maintenance of " ferries; and for other purposes;" and [The Wallasey Improvement Act, 1858.]

An Act passed in the twenty-seventh and twenty-eighth years of the reign of Her Majesty Queen Victoria, intituled " An Act to confer " further powers on the Wallasey Local Board; and for other " purposes:" [The Wallasey Improvement Act, 1864.]

And whereas, in pursuance of the said Local Government Act, inquiry has been directed and made in the said district in respect of the several matters mentioned in the said petitions, and report duly made to me thereon by Arnold Taylor, Esquire, the Inspector appointed for the purpose:

And whereas it is desirable that authority should be given to the said Local Board to exercise the power conferred by the Local Government Act, in certain cases of borrowing, up to twice the assessable value of their district, and for this purpose it is necessary that the limitation to thirteen thousand pounds, of the power to borrow conferred by a Provisional Order bearing date the ninth day of June, one thousand eight hundred and sixty-three, and confirmed by the Local Government Supplemental Act, 1863, (No. 2,) be removed, but no Provisional Order for such purpose can be valid without confirmation by Parliament:

Now, therefore, in pursuance of the powers vested in me by the said Local Government Act, I, as one of Her Majesty's Principal Secretaries of State, do, by this Provisional Order under my hand,

Schedule. direct, that from and after the passing of any Act of Parliament confirming this Order,—

1. The two hundred and ninety-third section of the said firstly herein-before recited Act, which provides, "that no person " shall be liable to be rated under this Act to the said " Improvement Rate in respect of his being the owner or " occupier only of any property under the actual annual value " of ten pounds, such value to be ascertained either according " to the amount of rent actually paid for such property, or in " such other manner as the Commissioners may determine, " and that in respect of any such property the said Lighting " Rate shall be chargeable upon the owner, and not upon the " occupier thereof," shall be repealed.

[*Vide* The Wallasey Improvement Act, 1845, note to sec. 293.]
[2.—Repealed by the Wallasey Improvement Act, 1872, sec. 20.]

3. The sections of the said secondly herein-before recited Local Act, numbered respectively 69 to 79, both inclusive, containing regulations with respect to buildings in the said district, shall be repealed.

4. The sections in the said firstly herein-before recited Local Act providing for matters now provided for by Acts in force within the said district and numbered respectively 63, 69, 166 to 171, both inclusive, 192 to 197, both inclusive, 278, 279, and 280, shall be repealed.

5. The section in the said thirdly herein-before recited Local Act numbered 36, and enacting that "after the passing of this " Act no person shall be qualified to vote at any election of " members of the Local Board unless he shall for at least " twelve months prior to the day of election have been rated " to the amount of at least ten pounds to the rate for the " relief of the poor within the district, or to some rate leviable " by the Local Board, and unless he shall, prior to the day of " election, have paid all rates then due from him to the Local " Board, except such as shall have been made or become due " within six months immediately preceding the day of tendering " his vote," shall be repealed.

[*Vide* note to arts. 2 to 5 in The Wallasey Order, 1852.]

6. So much of the herein-before recited Provisional Order as limits the powers of the said Local Board thereby given to borrow for the purposes therein described to the amount of thirteen thousand pounds shall be repealed, and the Local Board shall be authorized from time to time to borrow for permanent works to the amount of twice the assessable value of the premises assessable under the Local Government Act in the said district; all sums so borrowed to be borrowed with the sanction of one of Her Majesty's Principal Secretaries of State, and to be repaid, with interest thereon, within a period of fifty years from the borrowing thereof.

[Art. 6 was repealed (except so far as it may have been acted upon, or so far as relates to the repayment of money borrowed in pursuance thereof) by The Wallasey Order, 1894, art. 1.]

Given under my hand, this ninth day of May in the year one thousand eight hundred and seventy

(Signed)   H A. BRUCE.

THE WALLASEY IMPROVEMENT ACT, 1872.

(35 & 36 Vict. ch. 125.)

ARRANGEMENT OF SECTIONS.

Preamble.

	SECTION.
Short Title...	1
Interpretation of terms ...	2
Provisions of general Acts herein named incorporated ...	3
Same meanings to words in incorporated Acts as in this Act .	4
Act to be executed by Local Board	5
Power for Local Board to make works according to Plans ...	6
Works authorized...	7
Power to deviate ...	8
Saving Rights of the Crown	9
Saving Rights of the Crown in the Foreshore ...	10
Power to appropriate slip or road opposite Victoria Road	11
Period for completion of works ...	12
Confirmation of agreement in schedule and borrowing powers of Mersey Docks and Harbour Board ...	13
Bye-laws as to Ferries ...	14
Penalty on persons using steam boats without paying toll	15
New Wells, &c.	16
Power to borrow for purposes of Act ...	17
Provisions of Public Health Acts to apply to mortgages	18
Priority of former mortgages	19
Rating of Houses under £10, &c.	20
Rates to be parochial rates within section 32 of Bankruptcy Act, 1869	21
Depreciation and renewal fund ...	22
Expenses of Act ...	23

Schedule—Agreement between Wallasey Local Board and Mersey Docks and Harbour Board.

AN ACT

for authorising the Wallasey Local Board to make and maintain works in connexion with their Seacombe and Egremont ferries, and to extend their waterworks, and to raise further moneys; and for other purposes.

18th July, 1872.

21 & 22 Vict. ch. lxiii.

WHEREAS by "The Wallasey Improvement Act, 1858," (in this Act, called the Act of 1858,) the Wallasey Local Board (in this Act called the Local Board) were empowered to construct waterworks for the supply of their district with water, and powers were conferred on the Local Board in relation to the ferries called respectively "New Brighton Ferry, Seacombe Ferry, and Egremont Ferry," and the providing of steamboats and other things necessary for the working of the ferries:

And whereas under the Act of 1858 the Local Board have constructed waterworks on a piece of land near the Great Float in the township of Poulton-cum-Seacombe in the county of Chester, and are now supplying water within their district, and the demand for water there is greatly increasing, and the present waterworks are insufficient, and it is expedient that the Local Board be authorized to extend their present waterworks, and for that purpose to borrow further moneys:

24 & 25 Vict. ch. iv.

And whereas by "The Wallasey Improvement Act, 1861," (in this Act called the Act of 1861,) further provision was made with respect to the Seacombe Ferry:

And whereas under or by virtue of the Acts of 1858 and 1861, or one of them, the Seacombe Ferry and Egremont Ferry, with the landing stages, piers, jetties, slips, and works connected therewith respectively, are vested in and worked and managed by the Local Board, and the foreshore between ordinary high and low watermark contiguous to such ferries is demised to the Local Board by leases from the Commissioners of Her Majesty's Woods, Forests, and Land Revenues:

27 & 28 Vict. ch. cxvii.

And whereas by "The Wallasey Improvement Act, 1864," the Local Board were empowered to construct a pier or landing stage at New Brighton, and to execute other works therein mentioned:

30 & 31 Vict. ch. xxxii.

And whereas by "The Wallasey Improvement Act, 1867," the Local Board were empowered to levy certain rates and tolls in connexion with their said ferries, and to do other things therein mentioned:

The Wallasey Improvement Act, 1872.

35 & 36 Vict. ch. ccxv. 235

Sec. 1—2

And whereas by "The Local Government Supplemental Act, 1870," a provisional order under "The Local Government Act, 1858," was confirmed, repealing and altering parts of the local Acts in force within the district of the Local Board: *33 & 34 Vict. ch. cxiv.*

And whereas it is expedient that the Local Board be authorized to make and maintain in connexion with their Seacombe Ferry the embankment, pier, roads, and other works by this Act authorized, and to extend the pier at their Egremont Ferry as by this Act authorized, and to borrow further moneys for the purposes of their ferries, and to enter into contracts with the Mersey Docks and Harbour Board with respect to the Seacombe Ferry and the works connected therewith:

And whereas the amount owing by the Local Board on mortgage of the Wallasey ferries account is one hundred and sixty-eight thousand four hundred and twenty-seven pounds or thereabouts, and on mortgage of the Wallasey waterworks account the sum of thirty-nine thousand two hundred and six pounds or thereabouts:

And whereas it is expedient that some of the provisions of the recited Acts be altered or repealed as by this Act provided:

And whereas plans and sections of the embankment, piers, roads, and other works by this Act authorized (not including the waterworks), showing the lines and levels thereof, and the plans showing also the lands to be taken for the purposes of those works, and a book of reference to the plans containing the names of the owners or reputed owners, lessees, or reputed lessees, and occupiers of the lands, have been deposited with the clerk of the peace for the county of Chester, and those plans and sections and book of reference are in this Act referred to as the deposited plans, sections, and book of reference:

And whereas the objects of this Act cannot be attained without the authority of Parliament:

May it therefore please Your Majesty that it may be enacted; and be it enacted by the Queen's most Excellent Majesty, by and with the advice and consent of the Lords Spiritual and Temporal, and Commons, in this present Parliament assembled, and by the authority of the same as follows; (that is to say,)

1. This Act may for all purposes be cited as the Wallasey Improvement Act, 1872. *Short title.*

2. In this Act the following words and expressions have the meanings hereby assigned to them, unless there be something in the subject or context repugnant to such construction; that is to say, *Interpretation of terms.*

The expression "the Local Board" means the Wallasey Local Board:

The expression "the district" means the district of the Wallasey Local Board:

The expression "the Public Health Acts" means and includes the Public Health Act, 1848, and the Local Government Act, 1858, and the Local Government Act, 1858, Amendment Act,

236   35 & 36 Vict.   *The Wallasey Improvement*   *ch. cxxv.*
Act, 1872.

Sec. 3–6   1861, and the several present and future Acts supplemental to or amending those Acts respectively, and which from time to time are and shall be in force and applied to the Local Board or the district:

The expression "local Acts" means and includes the Wallasey Improvement Act, 1858, the Wallasey Improvement Act, 1861, the Wallasey Improvement Act, 1864, and the Wallasey Improvement Act, 1867.

[The Public Health Act, 1848, the Local Government Act, 1858, and the Local Government Act, 1858, Amendment Act, 1861, were all repealed by the Public Health Act, 1875, sec. 343 and sched. For substituted provisions *vide* sec. 313 of the Public Health Act, 1875.]

Provisions of general Acts herein named incorporated.

3. The Lands Clauses Consolidation Acts, 1845, 1860, and 1869, and the Waterworks Clauses Act, 1847, (except the sections of the last-mentioned Act with respect to the amount of profit to be received by the undertakers when the waterworks are carried on for their benefit, and with respect to the yearly receipt and expenditure of the undertakers,) and the Waterworks Clauses Act, 1863, and the Harbours, Docks, and Piers Clauses Act, 1847, shall be incorporated with and form part of this Act, (except where expressly excepted or varied by this Act), but it shall not be necessary for the Local Board to provide any lifeboat, tide or weather gauge, or barometer, unless and until they are required by the Board of Trade to do so, and for the purposes of the last-mentioned Act, the prescribed limits shall be deemed to be one hundred yards in every direction beyond the piers and works.

Same meanings to words in incorporated Acts as in this Act.

4. In this Act the several words and expressions to which meanings are assigned by the Acts wholly or partially incorporated with this Act have the same respective meanings, unless there be something in the subject or context repugnant to such construction: Provided always, that the expressions "superior courts" or "court of competent jurisdiction," or any other like expression in this Act or any Act wholly or partially incorporated with this Act, shall be read and have effect as if the debt or demand with respect to which the expression is used were a common simple contract debt, and not a debt or demand created by statute.

Act to be executed by Local Board.

5. This Act and the Local Acts shall have effect together as one Act, and shall be executed by the Local Board with the powers and indemnities, and according to the provisions of the Public Health Acts, and those Acts shall, in relation to the Local Board and the several objects and purposes of this Act and the local Acts, be read and construed as if the purposes and provisions of this Act were purposes and provisions of the Public Health Acts, so far as the same shall be applicable thereto, and except so far as any of the provisions of the Public Health Acts are expressly varied, altered, or otherwise provided for by this Act, and penalties under this Act shall be recoverable and applicable as penalties under the Public Health Acts.

Power for Local Board to make works according to plans.

6. Subject to the provisions of this Act, the Local Board may from time to time make and may maintain the embankment, piers, roads, and other works connected therewith shown on the deposited plans, with all necessary and proper approaches, works, and conveniences, and, so far as the lines and levels of those works are shown on the deposited plans and sections respectively, may make and maintain the works in the lines and in accordance with the levels shown thereon, and in the lands shown on the plans and specified in the deposited book of reference, and may enter, upon, take, and use such of those lands as they require for that purpose.

7. The works authorised by this Act comprise the following works, with all such incidental ways, approaches, stairs, jetties, landing places, walls, works and conveniences, and things connected therewith, as the Local Board think fit ; (that is to say,) *Works authorised.*

Sea Wall.

An embankment or river wall in connexion with the existing ferry of the Local Board at Seacombe, to commence from and out of the northern end of the existing river wall of the Birkenhead Docks at the point marked C on the deposited plans, and to terminate at or near Seacombe Point by a junction with the existing river wall at the point marked D on the deposited plans ;

The reclamation by means of the said embankment of so much of the foreshore of the River Mersey as will be situate to the west of the said intended embankment or river wall.

Pier.

A pier or jetty commencing at the said intended embankment at about two hundred yards from the south end thereof, and extending for a distance of twenty-five yards or thereabouts into the River Mersey, together with a floating landing stage to be connected at or near its northern end with the said intended pier by means of a bridge, and to be connected at or near its southern end with the said intended embankment by means of a bridge, and which said landing stage will be moored in the said river at a distance of ninety-five yards or thereabouts from the said intended embankment.

Road.

A road to commence at and by a junction with the Birkenhead Road at the north-east end thereof at the junction thereof with Victoria Road near the Seacombe Hotel, and to terminate on the said embankment.

Egremont Pier.

An extension of the pier at Egremont Ferry from the eastern extremity thereof for a distance of eighty yards or thereabouts in an easterly direction.

8. The Local Board in the construction of the aforesaid works shown on the deposited plans may deviate from the levels shown on the deposited sections to any extent not exceeding five feet. *Power to deviate.*

Sec. 9—12

Saving rights of the Crown.

9. Nothing contained in this Act or in any of the Acts herein referred to shall authorise the Local Board to take, use, or in any manner interfere with (otherwise than in accordance with the said leases) any land, soil, tenements, or hereditaments, or any rights of whatsoever nature belonging to or enjoyed or exerciseable by the Queen's most Excellent Majesty in right of her Crown, and under the management of the Commissioners of Her Majesty's Woods, Forests, and Land Revenues, or either of them, without the previous consent in writing of the same Commissioners, or one of them, on behalf of Her Majesty first had and obtained for that purpose (which consent such Commissioners are hereby respectively authorised to give); and as incidental to any such consent as aforesaid the Local Board may enter into any agreement with the Commissioners of Her Majesty's Woods, Forests, and Land Revenues, or either of them, who respectively may, with the approval of the Commissioners of Her Majesty's Treasury, join in every such agreement; and the said Commissioners of Her Majesty's Woods, Forests, and Land Revenues, with the like approval, and the Local Board may respectively execute all necessary conveyances, leases, licenses, or other deeds of or relating to any land, hereditaments, or rights belonging to Her Majesty in right of her Crown, and under the management of the same Commissioners, and every agreement so entered into as aforesaid shall be performed by the same Commissioners and the Local Board respectively; and nothing in the said Act or Acts contained shall divest, take away, prejudice, diminish, or alter any estate, right, privilege, power, or authority now or from time to time vested in or enjoyed or exerciseable by the Queen's Majesty, her heirs or successors.

Saving rights of the Crown in the foreshore.

10. Nothing contained in this Act or any of the Acts herein referred to shall authorise the Local Board to take, use, or in any manner interfere with any portion of the shore or bed of the sea or of the River Mersey, or any right in respect thereof, belonging to the Queen's most Excellent Majesty in right of her Crown, and under the management of the Board of Trade, without the previous consent in writing of the Board of Trade on behalf of Her Majesty (which consent the Board of Trade may give); neither shall anything in the said Act or Acts contained extend to take away, prejudice, diminish, or alter any of the estates, rights privileges, powers, or authorities vested in or enjoyed or exerciseable by the Queen's Majesty, her heirs or successors.

Power to appropriate slip or road opposite Victoria Road.

11. Subject to the provisions of this Act the Local Board may stop up and discontinue as a public slip or road the existing public slip or road in the Township of Poulton-cum-Seacombe, extending from the east side of the Birkenhead Road, nearly opposite to the Victoria Road, on to the foreshore, or any part thereof, and may appropriate the site of the same or of the part thereof stopped up.

Period for completion of works.

12. If the aforesaid works shown on the deposited plans and authorised by this Act are not completed within seven years from the passing of the Act, then on the expiration of that period the powers of this Act granted to the Local Board for making those works or otherwise in relation thereto shall cease to be exercised, except as to so much thereof as is then completed.

35 & 36 Vict.   The Wallasey Improvement   ch. cxxx.   239
                         Act, 1872.
                                                        Sec. 13—17

13. The agreement between the Local Board and the Mersey   Confirmation
Docks and Harbour Board set forth in the schedule to this Act, of agreement
is hereby confirmed, and for the purposes of that agreement the in schedule,
Mersey Docks and Harbour Board may from time to time apply any and borrowing powers
funds, money, rates, or rents which belong to them, or which they of Mersey
are at the passing of this Act authorised to raise or levy under any Docks and
Act, and which are not required for the purposes (if any) to which Harbour
the same are by any Act made specially applicable, and may borrow Board.
at interest on the security of the rates at the passing of this Act
belonging to them such further money, not exceeding in the whole
the sum of twenty thousand pounds, as they think necessary, and
they may apply all money so borrowed for the purposes of the said
agreement or some of them.

14. The powers conferred upon the Local Board by the Wallasey Byelaws as to
Improvement Act, 1867, section 28, with respect to the making of ferries.
bye-laws, regulating the fastening, mooring, or anchoring of vessels,
shall apply to the pier, landing stage, and works at Seacombe Ferry
authorised by this Act.

15. If any person travels or attempts to travel in any steam or Penalty on
other boat provided by the Local Board in connexion with their   persons using
ferries, without payment of the ferry toll payable by him, or evades steamboats
or attempts to evade payment of such toll, every such person shall without
for every such offence be liable to a penalty not exceeding forty paying toll.
shillings.

   [*Vide* also the Wallasey Improvement Act, 1858, sec. 46; the
   Wallasey Improvement Act, 1867, secs. 26 and 27; and the
   Wallasey Local Board Act, 1890, sec. 74; Recovery of
   Penalties, sec. 5 of this Act.]

16. Subject to the provisions of this Act the Local Board may, New wells,
from time to time, on lands belonging to them at the passing of this &c.
Act, sink, bore, and make, and may maintain, and from time to time
improve and enlarge all such wells and apparatus, with approaches
thereto, for the pumping and supply of water, and may do all such
other acts as they may think necessary for obtaining and storing
water, and may from time to time, by means thereof, and also
of the waterworks authorised by the Act of 1858, supply water
according to and within the limits of the Act of 1858.

17. In addition to the moneys which the Local Board are em- Power to
powered to borrow under the local Acts, or any of them, and the borrow for
Public Health Acts, or any of them, they may from time to time purposes of
borrow on mortgage any sums not exceeding the respective amounts Act.
herein-after mentioned; that is to say,

   On mortgage of the security mentioned in the Act of 1858 as the
   Wallasey waterworks account, and of the waterworks for the
   time being vested in or belonging to the Local Board, and also, if
   the Local Board think fit (as a collateral security), of the general
   district rate to be made and levied under the Public Health
   Acts, or any of them, any sums not exceeding in the whole
   fifteen thousand pounds, which sums shall be applied, first, in
   payment of such part as the Local Board think fit of the costs,
   charges, and expenses of and incident to the preparing, obtaining and passing of this Act or incident thereto; secondly, in the
   execution of the powers of this Act and of the local Acts in
   relation to water;

Sec. 18—21 On mortgage of the security mentioned in the Act of 1858 as the Wallasey ferries account, and on the ferries for the time being belonging to or leased by the Local Board, and the steam and other boats, materials, and things connected therewith, and also (as a collateral security) of the general district rate authorised to be made and levied by the Public Health Acts, or any of them, any sums not exceeding in the whole seventy-four thousand pounds, which sum shall be applied, first, in payment of such part as the Local Board think fit of the costs, charges, and expenses of and incident to the preparing, obtaining, and passing this Act or incident thereto; secondly, in the construction of the embankment, piers, roads, and works connected therewith by this Act authorised; and, thirdly, in carrying into execution the several purposes of the local Acts respectively and this Act with reference to the acquisition of ferries, or to the construction of works in connection therewith, and as to the purchasing and providing of steam or other boats in connexion therewith.

[*Vide* The Wallasey Improvement Act, 1858, secs. 27 and 39.

FURTHER BORROWING POWERS—
Ferries: The Wallasey Order (No. 1,) 1877, art. 3.
The Wallasey Order, 1881, art. 1.
The Wallasey Order, 1883, art. 2.
The Wallasey Order, 1895, art. 1.
The Wallasey Order, 1897, art. 1.]

Provisions of Public Health Acts to apply to mortgages. **18.** The provisions of the Public Health Acts relating to mortgages shall be applicable to the mortgages to be made by the Local Board under this Act.

[*Vide* The Wallasey Order, 1881, art. 1; also art. 2 as to annual return to Local Government Board; and further see The Wallasey Order, 1883, art. 2 and arts. 4 to 8.]

Priority of former mortgages. **19.** All mortgages granted under the local Acts respectively, and subsisting at the time of the passing of this Act, shall, during the continuance thereof respectively, have, with respect to the rates, properties, and securities comprised therein respectively, priority over all mortgages granted under this Act on the same rates, properties and securities respectively; and all mortgages granted and to be hereafter granted by the Local Board, under the authority of the Public Health Acts, or any of them, shall respectively have priority over all mortgages granted under this Act, on the collateral security of the general district rate so far as relates to such collateral security.

[Altered and amended by The Wallasey Order, 1883, art. 9.]

Rating of houses under £10, &c. **20.** The provisional order relating to Wallasey, scheduled to and confirmed by the Local Government Supplemental Act, 1870, shall have effect as if the proviso contained in the paragraph numbered 2 therein had not been inserted in that order.

[*Vide* The Wallasey Order, 1870.]

Rates to be parochial rates within section 32 of Bankruptcy Act, 1869. **21.** All rates and rents leviable by or payable to the Local Board under the local Acts, or any of them, or this Act, or the Public Health Acts, or any of them, shall be deemed parochial rates within the meaning of section thirty-two of the Bankruptcy Act, 1869.

[The Bankruptcy Act, 1869, was repealed by the Bankruptcy Act, 1883 (46 and 47 Vict. ch. 52, sec. 169,) as to priority of "parochial or other local rates" in the distribution of the property of a bankrupt or of the assets of a company being wound up. *Vide* the preferential payments in Bankruptcy Act, 1888 (51 and 52 Vict. ch. 62,) sec. 1, and the Preferential Payments in Bankruptcy Amendment Act, 1897 (60 and 61 Vict. ch. 19. sec. 1.)]

Sec. 22—23

22. The Local Board may, from time to time, out of any rates, rents, tolls, or duties leviable or receivable by them, set aside any money, not exceeding four thousand pounds in any year, for the purpose of forming a depreciation fund and providing for the renewal, repair, reconstruction, or extension of their waterworks, gasworks, ferries, and steamboats, and the plant connected therewith respectively, and may from time to time apply the same accordingly.

Depreciation and renewal fund.

[Altered and amended by substituting "eight thousand pounds" for "four thousand pounds."—The Wallasey Order, 1883, art. **3.**]

23. All the costs, charges, and expenses of and incident to the preparing, obtaining, and passing of this Act, or incident thereto, shall be paid by the Local Board.

Expenses of Act.

SCHEDULE referred to in the foregoing Act.

AGREEMENT BETWEEN LOCAL BOARD AND MERSEY DOCKS AND HARBOUR BOARD.

The Wallasey Local Board, (herein-after called the "Local Board") of the one part, and the Mersey Docks and Harbour Board (hereinafter called "the Mersey Board") of the other part, hereby agree with each as follows, videlicet:

Schedule.

1. The Local Board will expunge from the Wallasey Improvement Bill now before Parliament clause 12 of the Bill as now printed, a copy whereof is hereunto annexed.

2. The Mersey Board shall not oppose the preamble of the Wallasey Improvement Bill or the clauses of that Bill as now printed, clause 12 being expunged.

3. The Local Board shall not, either before or after the passing of the Bill, conclude any agreement for the purchase of the foreshore to be reclaimed as mentioned in clause 7 of the Bill, except at a price to be approved by the Mersey Board.

4. If the Bill should pass, and if an agreement should before or after the passing of the Bill be entered into for the purchase of the foreshore to be reclaimed, the Mersey Board shall have the option (to be exercised by written notice, to be given within three months after the passing of the Bill or after an agreement for the purchase of the foreshore shall have been entered into, whichever shall last happen) of acquiring, and the Local Board shall, if such option be exercised, convey or concur in such acts and conveyances as may

Schedule. be requisite for vesting in the Mersey Board that portion of the foreshore to be reclaimed which is coloured pink in the plan hereto annexed, and which contains about eight thousand and thirty square yards, on the following terms:—

(a) The Mersey Board are to pay for such portion of foreshore the price agreed to be paid for the same by the Local Board.

(b) On the completion of embankment or river wall mentioned in clause 7 of the Bill, the Mersey Board are to pay to the Local Board the same proportion of the cost of such embankment or river wall, and of filling up the foreshore to be reclaimed to the level of the top of such embankment or river wall as the area of that portion of such foreshore which is to be so taken by the Mersey Board shall bear to the area of the whole of the foreshore to be reclaimed as above mentioned.

5 If the Mersey Board shall exercise the option provided for by clause 4 of this agreement, then on the completion in a proper and substantial manner (to the approval of the engineer for the time being of the Mersey Board) of the said embankment or river wall, the Mersey Board and the Local Board shall, at their joint cost, at all times thereafter maintain and keep in good repair such river wall, extending from the point marked C to the point marked D on the said plan, and the cost of such maintenance and repairs shall be borne from time to time, as follows, videlicet: The Mersey Board shall contribute in respect thereof an amount which shall bear the same proportion to the entire cost of such maintenance and repairs as the area of the foreshore to be conveyed to the Mersey Board, as above mentioned, shall bear to the area of the whole of the foreshore to be reclaimed by such river wall, and the remainder of such entire cost of such maintenance and repairs shall be contributed by the Local Board: Provided that no repairs shall be undertaken without the sanction of the Mersey Board and the Local Board respectively, and that all repairs sanctioned by the Mersey Board shall be executed to their satisfaction.

6. If required by either party a formal agreement for carrying out this arrangement, to be settled in case of difference by J. H. Lloyd, Esquire, barrister-at-law, shall be prepared at the joint expense of the parties hereto and executed, and when executed shall be regarded as a contract or arrangement within the meaning of the 13th section of the said Bill.

7. This Agreement shall be confirmed by a clause to be inserted in the Bill for that purpose.

[*Vide* sec. 13.]

Dated the twelfth day of April, 1872.

Passed under the common seal of the Mersey Docks and Harbour Board, in the presence of
    W. LANGTON,
        Chairman.

Passed under the common seal of the Wallasey Local Board in the presence of
    T. SOMERVILLE JONES,
  Clerk to the said Local Board.

Local Government Board's Provisional Orders Confirmation (Birmingham, &c.) Act, 1876.

Confirming The Wallasey Order of 1876.

AN

ACT

to confirm certain Provisional Orders of the Local Government Board relating to the Borough of Birmingham, the Rural Sanitary District of the Chesterfield Union, the Districts of Dawlish and Keswick, the Rural Sanitary District of the Leek Union, the Borough of Maidstone, the Districts of Mistley, Moss Side, and Southend, the Rural Sanitary District of the Tadcaster Union, and the Districts of WALLASEY and Weston-super-Mare.

11TH AUGUST, 1876.

WHEREAS the Local Government Board have, as regards the boroughs and districts herein mentioned, made the Provisional Orders set forth in the schedule hereunto annexed, under the provisions of the Public Health Act, 1875:

And whereas it is requisite that the said Orders should be confirmed by Parliament, and that the provisions herein contained should be enacted in reference to the borough of Birmingham and certain of the said districts:

Be it therefore enacted by the Queen's most Excellent Majesty, by and with the advice and consent of the Lords Spiritual and Temporal, and Commons, in this present Parliament assembled, and by the authority of the same, as follows:

244   **38 & 40 Vict.**   *Local Government*   *ch. ccii.*
Board's Provisional Orders Confirmation
Sec. 1—6   *(Birmingham, &c.) Act, 1876.*

The Provisional Orders in schedule confirmed.
1. The Orders set out in the schedule hereunto annexed shall be and the same are hereby confirmed, and all the provisions thereof shall, from and after the passing of this Act, have full validity and force.

Short title.
6. This Act may be cited as the Local Government Board's Provisional Orders Confirmation (Birmingham, &c.) Act, 1876.

[The omitted Sections and orders relate to districts other than Wallasey.]

THE WALLASEY ORDER OF 1876.

DISTRICT OF WALLASEY.

Provisional Order to enable the Urban Sanitary Authority for the District of Wallasey to put in force the Compulsory Clauses of the Lands Clauses Consolidation Acts, 1845, 1860, and 1869.

To the Wallasey Local Board, being the Sanitary Authority for the Urban Sanitary District of Wallasey, in the County of Chester;—

And to all others whom it may concern.

Whereas the Wallasey Local Board, as the Sanitary Authority for the Urban Sanitary District of Wallasey, in the County of Chester, require to purchase and take certain lands and premises, which are described in the Schedule to this Order, for the purposes of widening and improving the approaches to Seacombe Ferry in their district;

And whereas the said Local Board have made due publication in the newspaper, and served the several notices as required by the Public Health Act, 1875, and have presented a Petition to the Local Government Board, stating as required by that Act, and praying, with reference to the said lands and premises, to be allowed to put in force the powers of the Lands Clauses Consolidation Acts, with respect to the purchase and taking of lands otherwise than by agreement;

And whereas upon receipt of such Petition, the Local Government Board directed a Local Inquiry to be held as to the propriety of assenting to the prayer thereof, which Inquiry was held after due notice, and report has been made to them thereon:

Now therefore, We, the Local Government Board, in pursuance of the powers given by the Statutes in that behalf, do hereby empower the Wallasey Local Board, from and after the date of the Act of Parliament confirming this Order, to put in force, with reference to the lands and premises described in the Schedule hereto, the powers of the Lands Clauses Consolidation Acts, 1845, 1860, and 1869, with respect to the purchase and taking of lands otherwise than by agreement, or any of them.

39 & 40 Vict.   Local Government   ch. ccii.   245
Board's Provisional Orders Confirmation
(Birmingham, &c.) Act, 1876.

The SCHEDULE above referred to.

Township of POULTON-CUM-SEACOMBE, in the Parish of WALLASEY, in the County of CHESTER.

No. on deposited Plan.	Description of Property.	Owners.	Occupiers.
1	Hotel, vaults, and part of yard.	Isaac Penny, Thomas Ridgway Bridson, and Henry Smith, trustees of Richard Smith, deceased.	Eliza Stokes.
2	Cottage and yard.	Ditto	Bernard Floyd.
3	Cottage, with garden in front.	Ditto	Robert Gregory.
4	Cottage, with garden in front, and yard behind.	Ditto	John Pemberton.
5	Cottage, with garden in front, and part of yard behind.	Ditto	Frederick Guy.
6	Part of dwelling-house and garden.	George Smith ...	James McArdle.
7	Ditto ...	Ditto	Joseph White.
8	Ditto ...	Isaac Penny, Thomas Ridgway Bridson, and Henry Smith, trustees of Richard Smith, deceased.	James Jones.
9	Ditto	Ditto	John Henry Irving.
10	Cottage ...	George Smith ...	Emily Norman.
11	Ditto	Ditto	William Watson.
12	Bowling-green	Isaac Penny, Thomas Ridgway Bridson, and Henry Smith, trustees of Richard Smith, deceased.	Eliza Stokes.

Given under the Seal of Office of the Local Government Board, this Seventh day of June, in the year one thousand eight hundred and seventy-six.

G. SCLATER-BOOTH, President.
JOHN LAMBERT, Secretary.

Local Government Board's Provisional Orders Confirmation (Caistor Union, &c.) Act, 1877.

Confirming The Wallasey Order (No. 1), 1877, and The Wallasey Order (No. 2), 1877.

AN

ACT

to confirm certain Provisional Orders of the Local Government Board relating to the Rural Sanitary District of the Caistor Union, the Borough of Chesterfield, the Local Government Districts of Cleckheaton and Ebbw Vale, the Boroughs of Honiton and King's Lynn (two) the Rural Sanitary District of the Maldon Union, the Local Government Districts of New Sleaford, Redcar, and Sandown, the Town of Southampton (Poor Law), the Local Government Districts of WALLASEY (two), Wallingfen, Wellingborough and Ystradyfodwg.

10th August, 1877.

WHEREAS the Local Government Board have, as regards the town of Southampton, made the Provisional Order set forth in the schedule hereunto annexed, under the provisions of the Poor Law Amendment Act, 1867, and as regards the other districts and boroughs herein mentioned, made the Provisional Orders set forth in the schedule hereunto annexed, under the provisions of the Public Health Act, 1875:

And whereas it is requisite that the said Orders should be confirmed by Parliament, and that the provisions herein contained should be enacted in reference thereto:

Be it therefore enacted by the Queen's most Excellent Majesty, by and with the advice and consent of the Lords Spiritual and Temporal, and Commons, in this present Parliament assembled, and by the authority of the same, as follows:

1. The Orders set out in the schedule hereunto annexed shall, subject to the provisions of this Act, be and the same are hereby confirmed, and all the provisions thereof shall, from and after the passing of this Act, have full validity and force. *The Provisional Orders in schedule confirmed.*

8. This Act may be cited as the Local Government Board's Provisional Orders Confirmation (Caistor Union, &c.) Act, 1877. *Short title.*

[The omitted sections and orders relate to districts other than Wallasey.]

THE WALLASEY ORDER (No. 1), 1877.

LOCAL GOVERNMENT DISTRICT OF WALLASEY.

Provisional Order for altering, amending, and partially repealing certain Local Acts.

[This Order may be cited as The Wallasey Order (No. 1), 1877— *Vide* The Wallasey Order, 1896, art. ii.]

To the Wallasey Local Board, being the Sanitary Authority for the Urban Sanitary District of Wallasey, in the County of Chester;—

And to all others whom it may concern.

Whereas the Local Government District of Wallasey, in the County of Chester, is an Urban Sanitary District, of which the Local Board are the Urban Sanitary Authority;

And whereas by section 303 of the Public Health Act, 1875, the Local Government Board are empowered, on the application of the Sanitary Authority of any Sanitary District, by Provisional Order, wholly or partially to repeal, alter, or amend any Local Act, other than an Act for the conservancy of rivers, which is in force in any area comprising the whole or part of any such district, and not conferring powers or privileges on any persons or person for their or his own pecuniary benefit, which relates to the same subject-matters as the Public Health Act, 1875;

And whereas certain Local Acts of Parliament, intituled respectively "The Wallasey Improvement Act, 1858," "The Wallasey Improvement Act, 1861," "The Wallasey Improvement Act, 1864," "The Wallasey Improvement Act, 1867," and "The Wallasey Improvement Act, 1872," are in force in the said Urban Sanitary District;

And whereas under the provisions of section 68 of the Wallasey Improvement Act, 1858, the Wallasey Local Board are empowered to sell, let, or exchange, or otherwise appropriate certain land therein mentioned ;

And whereas under the provisions of section 60 of the Wallasey Improvement Act, 1858, of section 3 of the Wallasey Improvement Act, 1861, and of section 30 of the Wallasey Improvement Act, 1867, the said Local Board were authorised to borrow on mortgage of the Wallasey Lighting Account, and of the gasworks for the time being vested in or belonging to the said Local Board, and in addition to the moneys which they were authorised to borrow under the Public Health Acts, the several sums of ten thousand pounds, ten thousand pounds, and twenty thousand pounds respectively ;

And whereas under the provisions of section 60 of the Wallasey Improvement Act, 1858, of section 3 of the Wallasey Improvement Act, 1861, of section 21 of the Wallasey Improvement Act, 1864, and of section 17 of the Wallasey Improvement Act, 1872, the Wallasey Local Board were authorised to borrow on mortgage of the Wallasey Ferries Account, and of the ferries for the time being belonging to or leased by the Local Board, and the steam and other boats, materials, and things connected therewith, and also (as a collateral security) of their General District Rate, and in addition to the moneys which they were authorised to borrow under the Public Health Acts, the several sums of seventy-five thousand pounds, fifty thousand pounds, forty-five thousand pounds, and seventy-four thousand pounds respectively ;

And whereas under the provisions of section 9 of the Wallasey Improvement Act, 1867, the Wallasey Local Board are empowered, subject to the provisions of that Act, to acquire, by agreement, for the purposes of their gasworks, the lands described in schedule A to that Act ;

And whereas the said local Acts are local Acts within the meaning of, and relate to the same subject-matters as, the Public Health Act, 1875, and the said Urban Sanitary Authority have applied to the Local Government Board to alter and amend the same as hereinafter mentioned ;

And whereas the Local Government Board, on receipt of such application, directed a local inquiry to be held on the subject, and the same was held, after due public notice, and report has been made to them thereon :

Now, therefore, we, the Local Government Board, in pursuance of the powers given by the statutes in that behalf, do hereby order that, from and after the twenty-ninth day of September, one thousand eight hundred and seventy-seven, the following provisions shall take effect, viz. :—

I. Section 68 of the Wallasey Improvement Act, 1858, shall be amended, and shall provide that the provisions as to selling, letting, exchanging, or otherwise appropriating the land therein mentioned, shall extend to any land acquired by the said Local Board for the purposes of constructing new piers or landing-stages, or widening and improving the approaches thereto.

II. Section 30 of the Wallasey Improvement Act, 1867, shall be altered and amended as follows; viz. :—

The said Local Board may borrow in accordance with and under and subject to the provisions of that Act, and subject to the sanction of the Local Government Board, any sum or sums not exceeding in the whole the sum of twenty-five thousand pounds, in addition to the sum of twenty thousand pounds therein mentioned, such additional sum or sums to be repaid in the manner provided by section 234 of the Public Health Act, 1875, and to be applied towards the construction, alterations, and extensions of their gasworks, and the pipes, works, and conveniences connected therewith.

[FURTHER BORROWING POWERS :—
Gas : The Wallasey Order, 1883, art. 1.
,, ,, ,, 1892, art. 2.
,, ,, ,, 1896, art. 1.
,, ,, ,, 1898, art. 1.]

III. Section 17 of the Wallasey Improvement Act, 1872, shall be altered and amended as follows; viz. : —

The said Local Board may borrow, in accordance with and under and subject to the provisions of that Act, and subject to the sanction of the Local Government Board, any sum or sums not exceeding in the whole the sum of one hundred and two thousand five hundred pounds, in addition to the sum of seventy-four thousand pounds therein mentioned, such additional sum or sums to be repaid in the manner provided by section 234 of the Public Health Act, 1875, and to be applied towards the construction of the piers, landing-stages, and approaches at Seacombe Ferry, and the provision of new boats for the ferries between Liverpool and Wallasey.

[FURTHER BORROWING POWERS :—
Ferries : The Wallasey Order, 1881, art 1.
,, ,, ,, 1883, art. 2.
,, ,, ,, 1895, art. 1.
,, ,, ,, 1897, art. 1.]

IV. Section 27 of the Wallasey Improvement Act, 1864, shall be wholly repealed, except so far as the same may have been acted upon, and in lieu thereof it shall be provided that all the provisions of the Public Health Act, 1875, with respect to borrowing powers (except sub-sections 2 and 3 of section 231) shall apply to all moneys to be hereafter borrowed under the hereinbefore mentioned Local Acts as hereby altered, as if they were loans contracted under the said Public Health Act, 1875.

[As to provisions for repayment and sinking fund, *vide* art. 2 of The Wallasey Order, 1881, and arts. iv. to viii. of The Wallasey Order, 1883.]

V. Section 9 of The Wallasey Improvement Act, 1867, shall be altered and amended as follows; viz. :—

The Local Board may acquire by agreement, for the purposes of their gasworks, the land described in the schedule hereto, and may make and maintain thereon gasworks, buildings, gasometers, and apparatus, with approaches thereto, for the manufacture, storage, and supply of gas, and may on such land do all such other acts as they think necessary for manufacturing and storing gas.

Provided that no gasworks or building or apparatus connected therewith shall be constructed on such land at a greater distance than one hundred and twenty yards from the northern boundary of the existing gasworks.

[This article is altered by The Wallasey Order, 1892, art. 1, which confers powers for further extension.]

The SCHEDULE above referred to.

All that piece of land in the Township of Poulton-cum-Seacombe, in the County of Chester, situate, adjoining, and to the north of the Gasworks of the Wallasey Local Board, and to the north-east of the Dock Road and Limekiln Lane.

Given under the Seal of Office of the Local Government Board, this fourth day of June, in the year one thousand eight hundred and seventy-seven.

(L.S.)

G. SCLATER-BOOTH, President.
JOHN LAMBERT, Secretary.

THE WALLASEY ORDER (No. 2), 1877.

LOCAL GOVERNMENT DISTRICT OF WALLASEY.

Provisional Order for extending the Wallasey Local Government District, and of the provisions of certain Local Acts

[This Order may be cited as The Wallasey Order (No. 2), 1877—*Vide* The Wallasey Order, 1896, art. ii.]

To the Wallasey Local Board, being the Sanitary Authority for the Urban Sanitary District of Wallasey, in the County of Chester;—

To the Guardians of the Poor of the Birkenhead Union, in the County of Chester, being the Sanitary Authority for the Rural Sanitary District of that Union;—

Board's Provisional Orders Confirmation (Caistor Union, &c.) Act, 1877.

To the inhabitants of that part of the Parish of Wallasey which is situate in the said Rural Sanitary District ;—

And to all others whom it may concern.

Whereas by section 270 of the Public Health Act, 1875, the Local Government Board are empowered, by Provisional Order, to declare the whole or any portion of a Rural Sanitary District immediately adjoining a Local Government District to be included in such last-mentioned district, and it is enacted that thereupon the included area shall, for the purposes of that Act, be deemed to form part of the district in which it is included by such Order ;

And whereas by section 275 of the same Act it is enacted that every Order made by the Local Government Board under Part VIII. of that Act, which includes section 270 above recited, shall specify the day on which such Order shall come into operation (in that Act referred to as the commencement of the Order) ; and that where any Local Government District is increased in extent under that part of the Act, the Order shall prescribe the number of members to be elected for the District when altered ;

And whereas by section 303 of the same Act, the Local Government Board are empowered, on the application of the Sanitary Authority of any sanitary district, by Provisional Order, wholly or partially to repeal, alter, or amend any local Act, other than an Act for the conservancy of rivers, which is in force in any area comprising the whole or part of any such district, and not conferring powers or privileges on any persons or person for their or his own pecuniary benefit, which relates to the same subject-matters as the Public Health Act, 1875 ;

And whereas by the same section it is enacted that any such Provisional Order may provide for the extension of the provisions of the Local Act referred to therein beyond the district or districts within the limits of such Act, or for the exclusion of the whole or a portion of any such district from the application of such Act ; and may provide what Sanitary Authority shall have jurisdiction for the purposes of the Public Health Act, 1875, in any area which is by such Order included in, or excluded from, such district ;

And whereas the Local Government District of Wallasey, in the County of Chester, is an Urban Sanitary District, of which the Wallasey Local Board are the Urban Sanitary Authority, and certain local Acts of Parliament, intituled respectively the Wallasey Improvement Act, 1845, the Wallasey Improvement Act, 1861, the Wallasey Improvement Act, 1864, the Wallasey Improvement Act, 1867, and the Wallasey Improvement Act, 1872, are in force in the said district ;

And whereas parts of the said local Acts were altered and partially repealed by certain provisional orders of the General Board of Health and of one of Her Majesty's Principal Secretaries of State respectively, which were duly confirmed by the Public Health Supplemental Act, 1853 (No. 1), and the Local Government Supplemental Act, 1870 ;

And whereas the said local Acts are local Acts within the meaning of, and relate to the same subject-matter as, the Public Health Act, 1875;

And whereas part of the Parish of Wallasey is situated in that part of the Rural Sanitary District of the Birkenhead Union, in the County of Chester, which immediately adjoins the said Local Government District of Wallasey, and the Wallasey Local Board have applied to the Local Government Board to issue a Provisional Order to include the said part of the Parish of Wallasey in their district, and to provide for the extension of the provisions of the said local Acts beyond the district within the limits of such Acts;

And whereas the Local Government Board, upon receipt of such application, directed local inquiry to be held on the subject thereof, and the same was held, after due public notice thereof, and report has been made to them thereon:

Now therefore, we, the Local Government Board, in pursuance of the powers given by the statutes in that behalf, do hereby declare that all that part of the Parish of Wallasey which is comprised in the Rural Sanitary District of the Birkenhead Union shall be included in, and shall, for the purposes of the Public Health Act, 1875, be deemed to form part of, the Local Government District of Wallasey.

[*Vide* The Wallasey Order, 1852, art. 1. The Wallasey Local Board Act, 1890, sec. 5, defines the sea and river boundary of the district.]

And we do hereby order as follows; viz.:—

I. This Order shall come into operation on the twenty-ninth day of September, one thousand eight hundred and seventy-seven.

II. The number of members constituting the Wallasey Local Board shall, from and after the said twenty-ninth day of September, remain and be the same as before the date of this Order.

III. The provisions of the above-mentioned Local Acts, as altered and partially repealed by the above-mentioned Provisional Orders and by a Provisional Order of the Local Government Board dated the fourth day of June, one thousand eight hundred and seventy-seven, shall be extended beyond the district heretofore within the limits of such Local Acts, and shall apply to and be in force within the Local Government District of Wallasey as hereby extended, and the Wallasey Local Board shall have jurisdiction for the purposes of the Public Health Act, 1875, in such extended district.

[The Wallasey Improvement Act, 1858, also extended and applied by the Wallasey Order, 1878, having been accidentally omitted from this Order.]

Given under the Seal of Office of the Local Government Board, this fifth day of June, in the year one thousand eight hundred and seventy-seven.

(L.S.)

G. SCLATER-BOOTH, President.
JOHN LAMBERT, Secretary.

Local Government Board's Provisional Orders Confirmation (Bristol, &c.) Act, 1878.

Confirming The Wallasey Order, 1878.

AN ACT

to confirm certain Provisional Orders of the Local Government Board relating to the City of Bristol the Rural Sanitary District of Chester-le-Street Union, the Local Government District of Finchley, the Rural Sanitary District of the Newbury Union, and the Local Government Districts of WALLASEY and West Derby.

16TH APRIL, 1878.

WHEREAS the Local Government Board have, as regards the districts herein mentioned, made the Provisional Orders set forth in the schedule hereunto annexed, under the provisions of the Public Health Act, 1875: [38 & 39 Vict. ch. 55.]

And whereas it is requisite that the said Orders should be confirmed by Parliament:

Be it therefore enacted by the Queen's most Excellent Majesty, by and with the advice and consent of the Lords Spiritual and Temporal, and Commons, in this present Parliament assembled, and by the authority of the same, as follows:

1. The Orders as set out in the schedule hereunto annexed shall be and the same are hereby confirmed, and all the provisions thereof shall, from and after the passing of this Act, have full validity and force. *[The Provisional Orders in schedule confirmed]*

2. This Act may be cited as the Local Government Board's Provisional Orders Confirmation (Bristol, &c.) Act, 1878. *[Short title.]*

[The omitted Orders relate to districts other than Wallasey.]

THE WALLASEY ORDER, 1878.

LOCAL GOVERNMENT DISTRICT OF WALLASEY.

Provisional Order for extending the provisions of a Local Act.

[This Order may be cited as The Wallasey Order, 1878.—*Vide* The Wallasey Order, 1896, art. II.]

To the Wallasey Local Board, being the Sanitary Authority for the Urban Sanitary District of Wallasey, in the County of Chester;—

And to all others whom it may concern.

Whereas by section 303 of the Public Health Act, 1875, the Local Government Board are empowered, on the application of the Sanitary Authority of any Sanitary District, by Provisional Order, wholly or partially to repeal, alter, or amend any Local Act, other than an Act for the conservancy of rivers, which is in force in any area comprising the whole or part of any such district, and not conferring powers or privileges on any persons or person for their or his own pecuniary benefit, which relates to the same subject-matters as the Public Health Act, 1875;

And whereas by the same section it is enacted that any such Provisional Order may provide for the extension of the provisions of the Local Act referred to therein beyond the district or districts within the limits of such Act, or for the exclusion of the whole or a portion of any such district from the application of such Act; and may provide what Sanitary Authority shall have jurisdiction for the purposes of the Public Health Act, 1875, in any area which is by such order included in, or excluded from such district;

And whereas the Local Government District of Wallasey, in the County of Chester, is an Urban Sanitary District, of which the Wallasey Local Board are the Urban Sanitary Authority;

And whereas in the month of January, 1877, the Wallasey Local Board applied to the Local Government Board to issue a Provisional Order to include in their district the part of the Parish of Wallasey which was situated in that part of the rural sanitary district of the Birkenhead Union, in the County of Chester, which immediately adjoined the said Local Government District of Wallasey, and to provide for the extension of the provisions of the Local Acts hereinafter mentioned to the extended area of the said district;

And whereas at the time of such application certain Local Acts of Parliament, intituled respectively the Wallasey Improvement Act, 1845, the Wallasey Improvement Act, 1858, the Wallasey Improvement Act, 1861, the Wallasey Improvement Act, 1864, the Wallasey Improvement Act, 1867, and the Wallasey Improvement Act, 1872, were in force in the area then comprised in the said district;

And whereas parts of the said Local Acts were altered and partially repealed by certain Provisional Orders of the General Board of

Health and of one of Her Majesty's Principal Secretaries of State respectively, which were duly confirmed by the Public Health Supplemental Act, 1853 (No. 1), and the Local Government Supplemental Act, 1870;

And whereas the said Local Acts are Local Acts within the meaning of, and relate to the same subject-matters as, the Public Health Act, 1875;

And whereas the Local Government Board, upon receipt of such application, directed local inquiry to be held on the subject thereof, and the same was held, after due public notice thereof, and report was made to them thereon;

And whereas by a Provisional Order dated the fifth day of June, one thousand eight hundred and seventy-seven, and duly confirmed by the Local Government Board's Provisional Orders Confirmation (Caistor Union, &c.) Act, 1877, the Local Government Board declared the part of the Parish of Wallasey which was comprised in the Rural Sanitary District of the Birkenhead Union to be included in the Local Government District of Wallasey, and ordered that that order should come into operation on the twenty-ninth day of September, one thousand eight hundred and seventy-seven, and that the provisions of the Wallasey Improvement Act, 1845, the Wallasey Improvement Act, 1861, the Wallasey Improvement Act, 1864, the Wallasey Improvement Act, 1867, and the Wallasey Improvement Act, 1872, as altered and partially repealed by the above-mentioned Provisional Orders and by a further Provisional Order of the Local Government Board dated the fourth day of June, one thousand eight hundred and seventy-seven, likewise confirmed by the said Act of 1877, should be extended beyond the district theretofore within the limits of such Local Acts, and should apply to and be in force within the Local Government District of Wallasey as thereby extended, and that the Wallasey Local Board should have jurisdiction for the purposes of the Public Health Act, 1875, in such extended district;

And whereas it is expedient that the provisions of the Wallasey Improvement Act, 1858, which was accidentally omitted from the operative part of the said Provisional Order of the fifth day of June, one thousand eight hundred and seventy-seven, should be extended beyond the district within the limits of such Act:

Now therefore We, the Local Government Board, in pursuance of the powers given by the statutes in that behalf, do hereby order that, from and after the twenty-ninth day of September, one thousand eight hundred and seventy-eight, the provisions of the Wallasey Improvement Act, 1858, as altered and partially repealed by the aforesaid Provisional Orders, shall be altered so as to extend beyond the district heretofore within the limits of such Act, and shall apply to and be in force within the Local Government District of Wallasey as extended by the aforesaid Provisional Order dated the fifth day of June, one thousand eight hundred and seventy-seven.

  Given under the Seal of Office of the Local Government
   Board, this twenty-second day of January, in the year
   one thousand eight hundred and seventy-eight.

       G. SCLATER-BOOTH. President.
     JOHN LAMBERT, Secretary.

Sec. 1—5

LOCAL GOVERNMENT BOARD'S PROVISIONAL ORDERS CONFIRMATION (ACTON, &c.) ACT, 1881.

Confirming the Wallasey Order, 1881.

AN

ACT

to confirm certain Provisional Orders of the Local Government Board relating to the Local Government Districts of Acton, Buxton, and Crompton, the Port of Harwich, the Improvement Act District of Llandudno, the Borough of Monmouth, the Local Government District of Normanton, the Borough of Pontefract, the Local Government District of WALLASEY, the Borough of Walsall, the Improvement Act District of Wath-upon-Dearne, and the Local Board of Health District of Woolwich.

11TH AUGUST, 1881.

WHEREAS the Local Government Board have, as regards the districts, port, and boroughs herein mentioned, made the Provisional Orders set forth in the schedule hereto under the provisions of the Public Health Act, 1875 :

38 & 39 Vict. ch. 55.

And whereas it is requisite that the said Orders as amended should be confirmed by Parliament, and that the provisions herein contained should be enacted in reference to certain of such Orders :

Be it therefore enacted by the Queen's most Excellent Majesty, by and with the advice and consent of the Lords Spiritual and Temporal, and Commons, in this present Parliament assembled and by the authority of the same as follows :

The Orders in schedule confirmed.

1. The Orders as set out in the schedule hereto shall be and the same are hereby confirmed, and all the provisions thereof shall, from and after the passing of this Act, have full validity and force :

Short title.

5. This Act may be cited as the Local Government Board's Provisional Orders Confirmation (Acton, &c.) Act, 1881.

[The omitted Sections and Orders relate to districts other than Wallasey.]

THE WALLASEY ORDER, 1881.

LOCAL GOVERNMENT DISTRICT OF WALLASEY.

Provisional Order for altering and amending certain Local Acts and a Confirming Act.

[This Order may be cited as the Wallasey Order, 1881—*Vide* The Wallasey Order, 1896, Art. II.]

To the Wallasey Local Board being the Sanitary Authority for the Urban Sanitary District of Wallasey, in the County of Chester ;—

And to all others whom it may concern.

Whereas the Local Government District of Wallasey, in the County of Chester, is an Urban Sanitary District, of which the Wallasey Local Board (herein-after referred to as " the Local Board ") are the Urban Sanitary Authority, and certain Local Acts of Parliament, intituled respectively " The Wallasey Improvement Act, 1858," " The Wallasey Improvement Act, 1861," " The Wallasey Improvement Act, 1864," and " The Wallasey Improvement Act, 1872," are in force in the said Urban Sanitary District ;

And whereas under the provisions of section 60 of the Wallasey Improvement Act, 1858, of section 3 of the Wallasey Improvement Act, 1861, of section 21 of the Wallasey Improvement Act, 1864, and of section 17 of the Wallasey Improvement Act, 1872, the Local Board were authorised to borrow on mortgage of the Wallasey Ferries Account, and of the ferries for the time being belonging to or leased by the Local Board, and the steam and other boats, materials, and things connected therewith, and also (as a collateral security) of their General District Rate, and in addition to the moneys which they were authorised to borrow under the Public Health Acts, the several sums of seventy-five thousand pounds, fifty thousand pounds, forty-five thousand pounds, and seventy-four thousand pounds respectively ;

And whereas by section 303 of the Public Health Act, 1875, the Local Government Board are empowered, on the application of the Sanitary Authority of any Sanitary District, by Provisional Order, wholly or partially to repeal, alter, or amend any Local Act, other than an Act for the conservancy of rivers, which is in force in any area comprising the whole or part of any such District, and not conferring powers or privileges on any persons or person for their or his own pecuniary benefit, which relates to the same subject-matters as the Public Health Act, 1875 ;

And whereas by a Provisional Order of the Local Government Board dated the fourth day of June, One thousand eight hundred and seventy-seven, and duly confirmed by the Local Government Board's Provisional Orders Confirmation (Caistor Union, &c.) Act,

44 & 45 Vict. *Local Government* ch. clxii.
Board's Provisional Orders Confirmation
(Acton, &c.) Act, 1881.

1877 (which Order and Act are herein-after respectively referred to as "the Order of 1877," and "the Confirming Act of 1877," Section 17 of the Wallasey Improvement Act, 1872, was altered so as to enable the Local Board to borrow, in accordance with and under and subject to the provisions of that Act, and subject to the sanction of the Local Government Board, any sum or sums not exceeding in the whole the sum of one hundred and two thousand five hundred pounds, in addition to the sum of seventy-four thousand pounds therein mentioned, such additional sum or sums to be repaid in the manner provided by section 234 of the Public Health Act, 1875, and to be applied towards the construction of the piers, landing stages, and approaches at Seacombe Ferry, and the provision of new boats for the ferries between Liverpool and Wallasey;

And whereas by the Order of 1877 section 27 of the Wallasey Improvement Act, 1864 was wholly repealed, except so far as the same had been acted upon, and in lieu thereof it was provided that all the provisions of the Public Health Act, 1875, with respect to borrowing powers (except sub-sections 2 and 3 of section 234) should apply to all moneys to be thereafter borrowed under the Local Acts mentioned in the Order of 1877, as thereby altered, as if they were loans contracted under the said Public Health Act, 1875;

And whereas the said Local Acts are Local Acts within the meaning of section 303 of the Public Health Act, 1875, and the Local Board, as such Urban Sanitary Authority as aforesaid, have applied to the Local Government Board to alter and amend the same;

And whereas the Local Government Board upon receipt of such application, directed local inquiry to be held on the subject, which inquiry was held, after due public notice, and report has been made to them thereon:

Now therefore, We, the Local Government Board, in pursuance of the powers given to us by the statutes in that behalf, do hereby order that, from and after the date of the Act of Parliament confirming this order, the following provisions shall take effect, viz. :—

Art. 1. Section 17 of the Wallasey Improvement Act, 1872, shall be further altered and amended so as to provide that the Local Board may, subject to the sanction of the Local Government Board, borrow, in accordance with and under and subject to the provisions of that Act as amended by the Confirming Act of 1877, and in addition to the sums of seventy-four thousand pounds and one hundred and two thousand five hundred pounds which they are empowered to borrow upon the security of the Wallasey Ferries Accounts under that section as amended by the Confirming Act of 1877, any sum or sums not exceeding in the whole the sum of twenty-two thousand pounds, such additional sum or sums to be repaid in the manner provided by section 234 of the Public Health Act, 1875, and to be applied towards the execution and completion of works at the New Brighton and Seacombe Ferries.

Provided that all the provisions of the Public Health Act, 1875, with respect to borrowing powers (except sub-sections 2 and 3 of section 234) shall apply to moneys borrowed under the powers hereby conferred as if they were loans contracted under the said Public Health Act, 1875.

[*Vide* the Wallasey Order 1883, arts. 4 to 8: provisions for repayment and sinking fund.

FURTHER BORROWING POWERS:—
Ferries—The Wallasey Order, 1883, art. 2.
  „   „   1895, art. 1.
  „   „   1897, art. 1.]

Art. II. The Wallasey Improvement Act, 1872, as altered by the Confirming Act of 1877, shall be further altered and amended so as to provide as follows :

(*a*) The Clerk of the Local Board, shall, within twenty-one days after the Twenty-fifth day of March in every year during which any sum is required to be paid as an instalment, or to be set apart for a sinking fund, in respect of moneys borrowed under the powers conferred by this Order, or in respect of moneys re-borrowed for the repayment of moneys so borrowed, transmit to the Local Government Board a return in such form as may be prescribed by that Board, and verified by statutory declaration, if so required by them, showing the amounts which have been paid as instalments, and the amounts which have been invested or applied for the purposes of such sinking fund during the year next preceding the making of such return, and the description of the securities upon which any investment has been made, and the purposes to which any portion of the sinking fund or investment, or of the sums accumulated by way of interest, has been applied during the same period, and the total amounts (if any) remaining invested at the end of the year; and in the event of any wilful default in making such return, such Clerk shall be liable to a penalty not exceeding twenty pounds, which shall be paid to the Local Government Board, and shall be recoverable by that Board in the same manner as penalties recoverable under the Public Health Act, 1875, in a summary manner, may be recovered by parties aggrieved within the meaning of that Act.

(*b*) If it appears to the Local Government Board, by that return or otherwise, that the Local Board have failed to pay any instalment required to be paid, or to set apart any sum required for such sinking fund, or have applied any portion of the money set apart for such sinking fund, or of the sums accumulated by way of interest, to any purposes other than those authorised, they may, by Order, direct that a sum not exceeding double the amount in respect of which default has been made shall be paid by way of instalment, or be set apart and invested, or applied as part of such sinking fund; and any such Order shall be enforceable by writ of mandamus, to be obtained by the Local Government Board out of Her Majesty's High Court of Justice.

Given under the Seal of Office of the Local Government Board, this Seventh day of May, in the year One thousand eight hundred and eighty-one.

J. G. DODSON, President.
JOHN LAMBERT, Secretary.

Sec. 1—4

LOCAL GOVERNMENT BOARD'S PROVISIONAL ORDERS CONFIRMATION (No. 7) ACT, 1883.

Confirming the Wallasey Order, 1883.

AN

ACT

to confirm certain Provisional Orders of the Local Government Board relating to the Local Government District of Bognor, the Borough of Cheltenham, the Improvement Act District of Chiswick, the Borough of Plymouth, the Local Government District of Skipton, the Borough of Stockton and the Local Government District of South Stockton, and the Local Government Districts of Stroud and WALLASEY.

2nd August, 1883.

WHEREAS the Local Government Board have, as regards the boroughs and districts herein mentioned, made the Provisional Orders set forth in the schedule hereto, under the provisions of the Public Health Act, 1875:

And whereas it is requisite that the said Orders should be confirmed by Parliament, and that the provisions herein contained should be enacted with reference to two of such Orders:

Be it therefore enacted by the Queen's most Excellent Majesty, by and with the advice and consent of the Lords Spiritual and Temporal, and Commons, in this present Parliament assembled, and by the authority of the same, as follows:

The Orders in schedule confirmed.

1. The orders set out in the schedule hereto shall be and the same are hereby confirmed, and all the provisions thereof shall, from and after the passing of this Act, have full validity and force.

Short title.

4. This Act may be cited as the Local Government Board's Provisional Orders Confirmation (No. 7) Act, 1883.

[The omitted sections and orders relate to districts other than Wallasey.]

THE WALLASEY ORDER, 1883.

LOCAL GOVERNMENT DISTRICT OF WALLASEY.

Provisional Order for altering and amending certain Local Acts and Confirming Acts.

[This order may be cited as The Wallasey Order, 1883. *Vide* The Wallasey Order, 1896, art. 2.]

To the Wallasey Local Board, being the sanitary authority for the Urban Sanitary District of Wallasey in the county of Chester.

And to all others whom it may concern.

Whereas the Local Government District of Wallasey, in the county of Chester, is an Urban Sanitary District, of which the Wallasey Local Board (herein-after referred to as "the Local Board") are the Urban Sanitary Authority;

And whereas by section 17 of the Wallasey Improvement Act, 1858 (herein-after referred to as "the Act of 1858,") the Local Board were empowered to construct gasworks, apparatus, and buildings, with approaches thereto, and to do all such other acts as they should think necessary for manufacturing gas and supplying the inhabitants and lighting the streets within the limits of that Act;

And whereas by section 60 of the Act of 1858, the Local Board were empowered from time to time, to borrow on mortgage of the Wallasey Lighting Account and of the gasworks for the time being vested in or belonging to them any sum not exceeding ten thousand pounds.

And whereas by section 3 of the Wallasey Improvement Act, 1861 (herein-after referred to as "the Act of 1861,") an additional sum not exceeding ten thousand pounds, and by section 30 of the Wallasey Improvement Act, 1867 (hereinafter referred to as "the Act of 1867,") additional sums not exceeding in the whole twenty thousand pounds were authorised to be borrowed for gasworks purposes;

And whereas by article 11. of a provisional order of the Local Government Board, dated the fourth day of June, one thousand eight hundred and seventy-seven, and confirmed by the Local Government Board's Provisional Orders Confirmation (Caistor Union, &c.) Act, 1877 (which Order and Act are respectively hereinafter referred to as "the Order of 1877" and "the Confirming Act of 1877,") the Local Board were empowered to borrow for gasworks purposes in accordance with and under and subject to the provisions of the Act of 1867, and subject to the sanction of the Local Government Board, an additional sum or sums not exceeding in the whole the sum of twenty-five thousand pounds;

46 & 47 Vict.　　　*Local Government*　　　*ch. cxxxvii.*
*Board's Provisional Orders Confirmation
(No. 7) Act*, 1883.

And whereas by sections 36 and 37 of the Act of 1858 the Local Board were empowered to purchase, hold, and use certain ferries, and from time to time to hire, charter, provide, purchase, and maintain such steam and other boats, materials, and things, and to employ and recompense such persons as should be necessary for the proper and efficient working of any such ferry ;

And whereas by section 60 of the Act of 1858 the Local Board were empowered from time to time to borrow for ferry purposes on the security therein mentioned sums not exceeding seventy-five thousand pounds ;

And whereas by section 3 of the Act of 1861 the Local Board were empowered to borrow for the like purposes additional sums not exceeding fifty thousand pounds ;

And whereas by section 21 of the Wallasey Improvement Act, 1864, hereinafter referred to as "the Act of 1864," the Local Board were empowered to borrow for the like purposes additional sums not exceeding in the whole forty-five thousand pounds ;

And whereas by section 17 of the Wallasey Improvement Act, 1872 (herein-after referred to as "the Act of 1872,") the Local Board were empowered to borrow for the like purposes additional sums not exceeding in the whole seventy-four thousand pounds ;

And whereas by article III. of the order of 1877 as confirmed by the Confirming Act of 1877, the Local Board were for the like purposes empowered to borrow in accordance with and under and subject to the provisions of the Act of 1872, and subject to the sanction of the Local Government Board additional sums not exceeding in the whole one hundred and two thousand five hundred pounds ;

And whereas by article 1. of a provisional order of the Local Government Board, dated the seventh day of May, one thousand eight hundred and eighty-one, and confirmed by the Local Government Board's Provisional Orders Confirmation (Acton, &c.) Act. 1881 (which Order and Act are hereinafter respectively referred to as "the Order of 1881" and "the Confirming Act of 1881,") the Local Board were for the like purposes empowered, subject to the sanction of the Local Government Board, to borrow in accordance with and subject to the provisions of the Act of 1872 as amended by the Confirming Act of 1877, additional sums not exceeding in the whole the sum of twenty-two thousand pounds ;

And whereas by section 22 of the Act of 1872 the Local Board were authorised from time to time out of any rates, rents, tolls, or duties leviable or receivable by them to set aside any money, not exceeding four thousand pounds in any year, for the purpose of forming a depreciation fund, and providing for the renewal, repair, re-construction or extension of their waterworks, gasworks, ferries, and steamboats and the plant connected therewith respectively, and from time to time to apply the same accordingly ;

And whereas by section 61 of the Act of 1858 certain provisions of the Public Health Act, 1848, including the requirements of section 113 of that Act with regard to the appropriation and setting apart and investment of the sinking fund therein mentioned, were rendered applicable to the mortgages of the Local Board under the Act of 1858 ;

Local Government Board's Provisional Orders Confirmation (No. 7) Act, 1883.

And whereas an enactment to the like effect was contained in section 4 of the Act of 1861;

And whereas by section 22 of the Act of 1864, the provisions of section 57 of the Local Government Act, 1858, instead of section 113 of the Public Health Act, 1848, were rendered applicable to the mortgages of the Local Board under the Act of 1864, but subject to the provisions of section 27 of that Act with regard to the period assigned for the re-payment of borrowed moneys;

And whereas provisions to the like effect were contained in the Act of 1867;

And whereas by section 18 of the Act of 1872 it was enacted that the provisions of the Public Health Acts relating to mortgages should be applicable to the mortgages of the Local Board under the Act of 1872;

And whereas by section 313 of the Public Health Act, 1875, it was enacted that where in any Act in force at the time of the passing of the Public Health Act, 1875, any provisions of any of the Sanitary Acts repealed by that Act are mentioned or referred to such Act should be read as if the provisions of the Public Health Act, 1875, applicable to purposes the same as or similar to those of the repealed provisions were therein mentioned or referred to instead of such repealed provisions, and were substituted for the same, but that nevertheless those substituted provisions should have effect, subject to any modification or restriction in such Act expressed in relation to the repealed provisions therein mentioned or referred to;

And whereas by Articles II. and III. of the Order of 1877, as confirmed by the Confirming Act of 1877, the provisions of section 234 of the Public Health Act, 1875, were rendered applicable to the loans thereby authorised;

And whereas by Article IV. of the Order of 1877, as confirmed by the Confirming Act of 1877, it was enacted that section 27 of the Act of 1864 should be wholly repealed, except so far as the same might have been acted upon, and that in lieu thereof all the provisions of the Public Health Act, 1875, with respect to borrowing powers (except sub-sections 2 and 3 of section 234), should apply to all moneys to be thereafter borrowed under the therein-before mentioned Local Acts as thereby altered, as if they were loans contracted under the Public Health Act, 1875;

And whereas by Article 1. of the Order of 1881, as confirmed by the Confirming Act of 1881, it was provided that all the provisions of the Public Health Act, 1875, with respect to borrowing powers (except sub-sections 2 and 3 of section 234), should apply to moneys borrowed under the powers thereby conferred as if they were loans contracted under the said Public Health Act, 1875;

And whereas the sums set apart by the Local Board as sinking funds in respect of moneys borrowed under the several Acts hereinbefore recited, are less than the sums which should have been set apart in accordance with the requirements of the statutory provisions applicable to such sinking funds;

And whereas by section 62 of the Act of 1858, section 5 of the Act of 1861, section 23 of the Act of 1864, section 31 of the Act of 1867, and section 19 of the Act of 1872, provision was made with regard to the priority of certain mortgages;

And whereas the Act of 1858, the Act of 1861, the Act of 1864, the Act of 1867, and the Act of 1872, are Local Acts within the meaning of section 303 of the Public Health Act, 1875;

And whereas the Confirming Act of 1877 and the Confirming Act of 1881 are Acts which under section 297 of the Public Health Act, 1875, may be repealed, altered, or amended by any Provisional Order made by the Local Government Board and confirmed by Parliament;

And whereas the Local Board have applied to the Local Government Board to issue a Provisional Order to alter and amend the said Local Acts and Confirming Acts:

Now therefore, We, the Local Government Board, in pursuance of the powers given to Us by sections 297 and 303 of the Public Health Act, 1875, and by any other Statutes in that behalf, do hereby Order that from and after the date of the Act of Parliament confirming this Order (herein-after referred to as "the commencement of this Order"), the following provisions shall take effect; namely,—

Art. 1. The Confirming Act of 1877 so far as it confirms Article II. of the Order of 1877 shall be altered and amended, and section 30 of the Act of 1867 shall be further altered and amended so as to provide as follows:

In addition to the sums of twenty thousand pounds and twenty-five thousand pounds which the Local Board were empowered under section 30 of the Act of 1867, as amended by the Confirming Act of 1877, to borrow, the Local Board may, subject to the sanction of the Local Government Board, borrow from time to time, on mortgage of the securities mentioned in the said section, any sum or sums not exceeding in the whole the sum of twenty thousand pounds, to be applied to the extension of the works of the Local Board for the manufacture and storage of gas, to the conversion of the residual products arising from their gasworks, to the extension of their mains and of service pipes and lamps, and to the provision of meters, or to any one or more of such purposes.

All the provisions of the Public Health Act, 1875, with respect to borrowing powers (except sub-sections 2 and 3 of section 234, and subject to so much of Article IV. of this Order as relates to the investment of the sinking fund), shall apply to all moneys to be borrowed by the Local Board in the exercise of the powers conferred by this Article, as if they were loans contracted under the said Public Health Act, 1875.

[FURTHER BORROWING POWERS—

Gas.—The Wallasey Order, 1892, Art. 2,
,, ,, 1896, ,, 1,
,, ,, 1898, ,, 1.]

Art. II. The Confirming Act of 1877, so far as it confirms Article III. of the Order of 1877, and the Confirming Act of 1881, so far as it confirms Article I. of the Order of 1881, shall be altered and amended, and section 17 of the Act of 1872 shall be further altered and amended so as to provide as follows:

Local Government Board's Provisional Orders Confirmation (No. 7) Act, 1883.

In addition to the sums of seventy-four thousand pounds, one hundred and two thousand five hundred pounds, and twenty-two thousand pounds, which the Local Board were empowered to borrow under section 17 of the Act of 1872 as amended by the Confirming Act of 1877 and the Confirming Act of 1881, the Local Board may, subject to the sanction of the Local Government Board, borrow from time to time, on mortgage of the securities mentioned in the said section, any sum or sums not exceeding in the whole the sum of *thirty thousand pounds*, to be applied towards the payment of the cost of providing new steamboats for the ferries for the time being belonging to or leased by the Local Board.

All moneys borrowed by the Local Board in pursuance of the powers conferred by this Article shall be repaid within such period, not exceeding ten years from the date of borrowing, as the Local Government Board may, by their sanction, determine.

All the provisions of the Public Health Act, 1875, with respect to borrowing powers (except sub-sections 2 and 3 of section 234, and so much of sub-section 4 of that section as prescribes the period for which money may be borrowed, and subject to so much of Article IV. of this Order as relates to the investment of the sinking fund) shall apply to all moneys to be borrowed by the Local Board in the exercise of the powers conferred by this Article as if they were loans contracted under the said Public Health Act, 1875.

> [*Altered to *fifty-five thousand pounds* by art. 1 of the Wallasey Order, 1895, money borrowed under the additional powers to be repaid within such period not exceeding 20 years as the Local Government Board may by their sanction determine. By art. 1 of the Wallasey Order, 1897, power is given to borrow a further sum of £10,600 for the purposes of a dredger in connection with the ferry undertaking.]

Art. III. Section 22 of the Act of 1872 shall be altered and amended by the substitution of the words "eight thousand pounds" for the words "four thousand pounds."

Art. IV. The Act of 1858, the Act of 1861, the Act of 1864, the Act of 1867, and the Act of 1872, and so much of the Confirming Acts of 1877 and 1881 as confirm the Orders of 1877 and 1881, shall be altered and amended so as to provide that notwithstanding anything therein contained all moneys borrowed by the Local Board under the said Acts or Orders, or under either of them, shall, except as to so much of the moneys so borrowed as shall have been repaid before the commencement of this Order, and as will be repaid by means of the amounts required to be appropriated and set apart under Article VII. of this Order, be repaid by the Local Board either by equal annual instalments of principal, or of principal and interest, or by setting apart in every year as a sinking fund such a sum or sums as will, according to a reasonable calculation for the time being, with accumulations in the way of compound interest, be sufficient after payment of all expenses to pay off the money so borrowed within the unexpired part of the period prescribed for the repayment of the money so borrowed.

If the repayment be by means of a sinking fund, the Local Board shall invest the same in the purchase of exchequer bills or other government securities or in securities in which trustees are by law for the time being authorised to invest, or in mortgages, debentures, debenture stock, or other securities issued by any local authority as defined by section 34 of the Local Loans Act, 1875, other than the Local Board, with liberty from time to time to vary and transpose such investments and at any time to apply the whole or any part of the sinking fund in or towards the discharge of the money for the repayment of which the fund is established: Provided that the Local Board pay into the fund each year and accumulate until the whole of the money borrowed is discharged a sum equivalent to the interest which would have been produced by the sinking fund or the part of the sinking fund so applied.

Art. V. So much of the Confirming Act of 1877 as confirms Article IV. of the Order of 1877, and so much of the Confirming Act of 1881 as confirms Article I. of the Order of 1881 shall be altered and amended so as to provide that so much of Article IV. of this Order as relates to the investment of the sinking fund therein mentioned shall extend to any sinking fund which, in pursuance of Article IV. of the order of 1877 and of Article I. of the Order of 1881, and of such of the provisions of the Public Health Act, 1875, with respect to borrowing powers as are mentioned in those Articles may have been or may hereafter be set aside for securing the repayment of any borrowed moneys to which the said Articles apply.

Art. VI. The Local Board shall apply all sums appropriated and set apart under Article VII. of this Order and all sums standing to the credit of sinking funds at the commencement of this Order in respect of moneys borrowed by the Local Board under the said Acts or under either of them or under the provisions of the Order of 1877 and the Order of 1881 in the repayment of the principal moneys in respect of which such sums were respectively appropriated and set apart as sinking funds, and pending such application shall invest such sums in any of the securities in which sinking funds may be invested under Article IV. of this Order.

Art. VII. The Act of 1858, the Act of 1861, the Act of 1864, the Act of 1867, and the Act of 1872 shall be altered and amended so as to provide that the Local Board shall, within twenty years from the commencement of this Order, out of the rates, funds, and revenues out of which the same should have been appropriated and set apart, appropriate and set apart as sinking funds the amounts which before the commencement of this Order should have been so appropriated and set apart in accordance with the requirements in that behalf contained in the said Acts and which have not been so appropriated and set apart, and the amounts to be annually appropriated and set apart under this Article shall be such as the Local Board with the approval of the Local Government Board determine.

Art. VIII. The Clerk of the Local Board shall within twenty-one days after the Twenty-fifth day of March in every year during which any sum is required to be paid as an instalment or to be set apart for a sinking fund under Articles I., II., IV., and VII., of this Order, transmit to the Local Government Board a return in such form as may be prescribed by that Board and verified by statutory declaration, if so required by them, showing the amounts which have been paid

46 & 47 *Vict.*   *Local Government*   *ch. cxxxvii.*
Board's Provisional Orders Confirmation
(No. 7) Act, 1883.

as instalments and the amounts which have been invested or applied for the purposes of such sinking fund during the year next preceding the making of such return, and the description of the securities upon which any investment has been made, and the purposes to which any portion of the sinking fund, or investment or of the sums accumulated by way of interest has been applied during the same period, and the total amounts (if any) remaining invested at the end of the year; and in the event of any wilful default in making such return, such Clerk shall be liable to a penalty not exceeding twenty pounds, which shall be paid to the Local Government Board, and shall be recoverable by that Board in the same manner as penalties recoverable under the Public Health Act, 1875, in a summary manner may be recovered by parties aggrieved within the meaning of that Act.

If it appears to the Local Government Board by that return or otherwise that the Local Board have failed to pay any instalment required to be paid or to set apart any sum required for such sinking fund, or have applied any portion of the money set apart for such sinking fund, or of the sums accumulated by way of interest, to any purposes other than those authorised, they may, by order, direct that a sum not exceeding double the amount in respect of which default has been made shall be paid by way of instalment, or be set apart and invested or applied as part of such sinking fund; and any such Order shall be enforceable by writ of mandamus to be obtained by the Local Government Board out of Her Majesty's High Court of Justice.

Art. IX. section 62 of the Act of 1858, section 5 of the Act of 1861, section 23 of the Act of 1864, section 31 of the Act of 1867, and section 19 of the Act of 1872 shall be altered and amended so as to provide that nothing in the said sections contained shall be deemed to apply to any mortgages hereafter to be granted by the Local Board in the exercise of the powers conferred by section 25 of the Act of 1864 and by section 33 of the Act of 1867 with respect to the reborrowing of moneys, so as to assign to any such mortgage priority over any other mortgage to be granted in the exercise of the said powers.

       Given under the Seal of Office of the Local Government Board, this twenty-second day of May, one thousand eight hundred and eighty-three.

L.S.

           CHARLES W. DILKE, President.
           HUGH OWEN, Secretary.

Sec. 1—3

LOCAL GOVERNMENT BOARD'S
PROVISIONAL ORDERS CONFIRMATION
(No. 4) ACT, 1888.

Confirming The Wallasey Order, 1888.

AN

ACT

to confirm certain Provisional Orders of the Local Government Board relating to the Boroughs of Birkenhead and Stockton-on-Tees, the Local Government Districts of Cleckheaton, Pickering, Rawmarsh, and WALLASEY, and the Wirral Joint Hospital District.

28TH JUNE, 1888.

38 & 39 Vict. ch. 55.

WHEREAS the Local Government Board have made the Provisional Orders set forth in the schedule hereto, under the provisions of the Public Health Act, 1875:

And whereas it is requisite that the said Orders should be confirmed by Parliament, and that the provisions herein contained should be enacted with reference to two of such Orders:

Be it therefore enacted by the Queen's most Excellent Majesty, by and with the advice and consent of the Lords Spiritual and Temporal, and Commons, in this present Parliament assembled, and by the authority of the same, as follows:

Orders in schedule confirmed

1. The Orders set out in the schedule hereto shall be and the same are hereby confirmed, and all the provisions thereof shall, from and after the dates therein respectively mentioned, have full validity and force.

Short title.

3. This Act may be cited as the Local Government Board's Provisional Orders Confirmation (No. 4) Act, 1888.

[The omitted Section and Orders apply to districts other than Wallasey.]

51 & 52 Vict. Local Government ch. lvii.
Board's Provisional Orders Confirmation
(No. 4) Act, 1888.

THE WALLASEY ORDER, 1888.

LOCAL GOVERNMENT DISTRICT OF WALLASEY.

Provisional Order for altering a Local Act and a Confirming Act.

[This Order may be cited as The Wallasey Order, 1888.— *Vide* The Wallasey Order, 1896, Art. II.]

To the Wallasey Local Board, being the Sanitary Authority for the Urban Sanitary District of Wallasey, in the County of Chester ;—

And to all others whom it may concern.

Whereas the Local Government District of Wallasey, in the County of Chester (herein-after referred to as "the District"), is an Urban Sanitary District, of which the Wallasey Local Board (herein-after referred to as "the Local Board") are the Urban Sanitary Authority, and the Wallasey Improvement Act, 1845 (herein-after referred to as "the Local Act,") as partially repealed and altered by the Provisional Orders herein-after mentioned is in force in the District ;

And whereas the Local Act has been partially repealed and altered by the following Provisional Orders ; viz. :

(1.) A Provisional Order of the General Board of Health dated the Ninth day of November, One thousand eight hundred and fifty-two, and duly confirmed by the Public Health Supplemental Act, 1853 (No. 1) (which Order and Act are herein-after respectively referred to as "the Order" and "the Confirming Act") ;

(2.) A Provisional Order of one of Her Majesty's Principal Secretaries of State dated the Ninth day of May, One thousand eight hundred and seventy, and duly confirmed by the Local Government Supplemental Act, 1870 ;

(3.) A Provisional Order of the Local Government Board dated the Fifth day of June, One thousand eight hundred and seventy-seven, and duly confirmed by the Local Government Board's Provisional Orders Confirmation (Caistor Union, &c.) Act, 1877 ;

And whereas by Section 327 of the Local Act it was enacted that in that Act the words " hackney carriage " should include any coach, omnibus, chariot, car, fly, cabriolet, sociable, lorry, or such like carriage ;

And whereas by Article 17 of the Order it was ordered that the sections of the Town Police Clauses Act, 1847, with respect (inter alia) to hackney carriages should be incorporated with so much of the Local Act as remained unrepealed by the Order, and with the Public Health Act, 1848, as applied to the town of Wallasey by the Order and the Confirming Act :

Now therefore, We, the Local Government Board, in pursuance of the powers given to Us by Sections 297 and 303 of the Public Health Act, 1875, and by any other statutes in that behalf, do hereby Order that, from and after the date of the Act of Parliament confirming this Order, the Local Act and the Confirming Act, so far as it relates to the Order, shall be altered to as to provide as follows :—

51 & 52 Vict. *Local Government Board's Provisional Orders Confirmation (No. 4) Act,* 1888.

Art. I.—(1.) The terms "hackney coaches," "hackney carriages," "hackney carriage," "carriages," or "carriage," whenever used in such of the provisions of the Town Police Clauses Act, 1847, incorporated with the Local Act by the Order, as are referred to in subdivision (2) of this Article, shall, anything in section 38 of the Town Police Clauses Act, 1847, notwithstanding, be deemed to include every omnibus; and such provisions shall apply to the owners and drivers of every omnibus; and the provisions of section 39 of the last-mentioned Act shall apply to omnibus licenses.

(2.) The following are the provisions of the Town Police Clauses Act, 1847, to which reference is made in subdivision (1) of this Article, viz., sections 37, 40 to 52, both inclusive, 54, 58, and 60 to 67, both inclusive, and so much of section 68 as enables the Local Board from time to time to make byelaws for all or any of the following purposes; that is to say,—

> For regulating the conduct of the proprietors and drivers of hackney carriages plying within the prescribed distance in their several employments, and determining whether such drivers shall wear any and what badges:
>
> For regulating the manner in which the number of each carriage, corresponding with the number of its license, shall be displayed:
>
> For regulating the number of persons to be carried by such hackney carriages, and in what manner such number is to be shown on such carriage:
>
> For fixing the stands for such hackney carriages:
>
> For securing the safe custody and re-delivery of any property accidentally left in hackney carriages, and fixing the charges to be made in respect thereof.

Provided that the expression "within the prescribed distance" in sections 37, 45, 46, 51, and 68 of the Town Police Clauses Act, 1847, shall, for the purposes of the Local Act, as hereby altered, mean within the district, and whenever the word "driver" or "drivers" occurs in any of the sections of the Town Police Clauses Act, 1847, mentioned in this Article, it shall be deemed to include every conductor of any omnibus.

Provided further, that, for the purposes of sections 54, 58, and 66 of the Town Police Clauses Act, 1847, as incorporated with the Local Act by the Order, the fare, according to the statement of fares exhibited on any omnibus, shall be deemed to be the fare allowed by the special Act, or the fare authorised by a byelaw under the special Act.

Provided also, that nothing in this Order contained shall empower the Local Board to fix the site of the stand of any omnibus in any railway station, or in any yard adjoining or connected therewith, except with the consent of the railway company owning such site.

(3) A license granted to a driver or conductor under the Local Act, as hereby altered, shall only authorise the holder thereof to act as driver or conductor of the class or description of carriage specified in such license, and shall be in force for one year only from the date thereof, or until the next general licensing meeting, in case any annual licensing day be appointed, and shall be subject to the power

of suspension or revocation provided for by section 50 of the Town Police Clauses Act, 1847.

Art. II. The Local Board may make byelaws for all or any of the following purposes; viz.:—

(1.) To provide for the exhibition on some conspicuous part of any omnibus of a statement, in legible letters and figures, of fares to be demanded and received from the persons using, or carried for hire, in such omnibus:

(2.) To prevent within the District—

(a.) The owner, driver, or conductor of any omnibus, or any other person on their behalf, by touting, calling out, or otherwise, from importuning any person to use, or to be carried for hire in, such omnibus, to the annoyance of such person, or of any other person,

(b.) The blowing of, or playing upon, horns or other musical instruments, or the ringing of bells, by the driver or conductor of any omnibus, or by any person travelling on or using any such omnibus:

(3.) To fix the points within the District at which any omnibus shall or may take up and set down passengers.

Art. III.—(1.) For the purposes of the Local Act, as altered by this Order, the term "omnibus" shall mean every omnibus, char-à-banc, waggonette, stage coach, and other carriage, plying or standing for hire by, or used to carry, passengers at separate fares to or from any part of the District (except tramway cars and carriages licensed by the Local Board under the provisions of the Tramways Act, 1870, or of any Provisional Order made thereunder and confirmed by Parliament), but nothing in this Order contained shall affect any omnibus bringing into the District passengers carried at separate fares, but not plying or standing for hire in the District, or the owner, driver, and conductor of any such last-mentioned omnibus.

(2.) The provisions contained in the Public Health Act, 1875, with respect to byelaws, and the penalties which may be imposed thereby, and the recovery and application of penalties, shall apply to all byelaws made, altered or repealed by the Local Board under the provisions of the Local Act as hereby altered, or of this Order, and to all penalties imposed thereby, and to all penalties imposed by any of the sections of the Town Police Clauses Act, 1847, mentioned in Article I. of this Order, so far as they are by this Order, rendered applicable to omnibuses, and their owners, drivers, and conductors.

[*Vide* the Public Health Act, 1875, s. 182, *et seq.*]

Art. IV. So much of section 327 of the Local Act as provides that the expressions "hackney carriage" and "carriage" shall include "omnibus" shall be repealed.

Given under the Seal of Office of the Local Government Board, this Thirtieth day of April, One thousand eight hundred and eighty-eight.

CHAS. T. RITCHIE, President.

HUGH OWEN, Secretary.

THE WALLASEY LOCAL BOARD ACT, 1890.

(53 and 54 Vict. c. 121.)

ARRANGEMENT OF SECTIONS.

Preamble.

PART I.—Preliminary.

	SECTION
Short Title...	1
Division of Act into parts	2
Interpretation	3
Execution and limits of Act	4

PART II.—Foreshore.

Defining sea and river boundary of district	5
Foreshore and vacant land to be street for certain purposes	6
Board may make bye-laws as to user of foreshore	7
Provisions as to bathing	8
Power to annex conditions to licenses of bathing machine proprietors	9
Protection of bathers	10
Saving for Wallasey Embankment Commissioners	11
Part II. not to apply to enclosed lands...	12

PART III.—Streets, Buildings, and Sewers.

Deposit of plan to be void after certain interval	13
Powers to vary position or direction of new streets	14
Protection of footways	15
Power to name or alter names of streets and names to be put up and houses to be numbered, &c.	16
What to be deemed new buildings	17
Height of buildings	18
Height of rooms	19
Certificate that houses fulfil certain requirements	20
Power of inspection	21
Power of surveyor on inspecting	22
Hoards to be set up during progress of buildings, &c...	23
Fencing in of vacant land	24
Prevention of lock-up shops and other places of business being improperly used for purposes of habitation	25

53 & 54 Vict.   The Wallasey Local Board   ch. cxvi.   273
Act, 1890.

	SECTION.
As to repair of vaults, &c., under streets	26
Back yards to be paved, &c.	27
Penalty for not keeping common courts and passages clean ...	28
Power to make bye-laws for sanitary purposes ...	29
Cesspools	30
Public waterclosets, urinals, and lavatories ...	31
Undertakings to bind successive owners	32
Placing matters in sewers so as to affect run of water	33
Steam, &c., not to be turned into sewers	34
Board may make communication between private drains and their sewers on payment, &c.	35
Extension of section 41 of the Public Health Act, 1875 ...	36
Exemption in respect of Her Majesty's buildings	37

PART IV.—PRIVATE STREET WORKS.

Definition of street	38
Definition of paving, metalling and flagging ...	39
Private street works	40
Objections to proposed works	41
Hearing and determination of objections	42
Incidental works	43
Apportionment of expenses ...	44
Amendment of plans, &c.	45
Final apportionment and recovery of expenses	46
Charge on premises	47
Recovery of expenses summarily or by action ..	48
Contribution by Board to expenses	49
Exemption from expenses of Incumbent of church	50
Power for limited owners to borrow for expenses	51
Power of Board to borrow for private street works	52
Adoption of private streets	53
On street being paved, &c., Board to declare same public highway	54
Separate accounts of expenses of works ...	55

PART V.—SANITARY PROVISIONS.

Cowkeepers and others to furnish lists of customers in certain cases	56
Medical Officer may inspect dairies, &c., beyond district in certain cases	57
Persons engaged in washing or mangling clothes to furnish lists of owners of clothes in certain cases	58
Further powers in relation to disinfection of premises	59

T

53 & 54 Vict. The *Wallasey Local Board* ch. cxxi.
Act, 1890.

SECTION.

Penalty on persons ceasing to occupy houses without previous disinfection, or giving notice to owner, or making false answers	60
Prohibiting the retention of dead bodies in certain cases	61
Bodies of persons dying in hospital, &c., of infectious diseases to be removed only for burial	62
Justices may in certain cases order dead bodies to be buried..	63
Corpses not to be carried in public conveyances	64
Detention of infected persons without proper lodging in hospital by order of Justice...	65
Temporary shelter and nurses	66
Extension of sections 116 to 119 (inclusive) of Public Health Act, 1875	67
Powers of entry for purposes of sections 49, 120, and 121 of Public Health Act, 1875	68
Saving for Acts relating to animals, &c.	69

PART VI.—WATER AND GAS.

Bye-laws for testing and stamping water fittings	70
Forging stamps or marks	71
Rate payable by owner for small houses	72
Power to supply gas or water to local authorities and others...	73

PART VII.—MISCELLANEOUS PROVISIONS.

Section 27 of Act of 1867 extended to persons refusing to produce their contract tickets	74
Passenger ferry steamers plying during fog	75
Cheshire Justices to have jurisdiction in respect of offences in river	76
Further powers as to slaughter houses	77
Power to close pleasure grounds, &c., on special occasions, &c.	78
Bye-laws	79
Expenses of Execution of Act	80
As to appeal	81
Penalties	82
Recovery of penalties, &c.	83
Authentication and service of notices	84
General provisions as to bye-laws	85
Saving rights of the Crown	86
Saving rights of the Crown in the foreshore	87
Saving in favour of R. C. De Grey Vyner	88
Saving for Mersey Docks and Harbour Board	89
Saving for Mersey Commissioners	90
Costs of Act	91
Schedule.	

AN ACT

to make better provision for the Improvement and Health of the Local Government District of Wallasey in the County of Chester and for other purposes.

25TH JULY, 1890.

WHEREAS the local government district of Wallasey in the County of Chester (in this act called the district) is under the government of the Wallasey Local Board (in this Act called the Board) who are the urban sanitary authority of the district:

And whereas the unrepealed provisions of the following local Acts (besides various orders confirmed by Parliament) are in force within the district (that is to say) :—

The Wallasey Improvement Act, 1845;
The Wallasey Improvement Act, 1858;
The Wallasey Improvement Act, 1861;
The Wallasey Improvement Act, 1864;
The Wallasey Improvement Act, 1867;
The Wallasey Improvement Act, 1872;

Which Acts with the said orders are in this Act collectively referred to as the recited Acts and each of the said Acts is separately referred to as the Act of the year in which it was passed :

And whereas it is expedient that the Board should be invested with further powers of control over the foreshore and seashore of their district, and that better provision should be made with reference to streets, buildings, and sewers within the district :

And whereas the Seacombe Ferry, Egremont Ferry, and New Brighton Ferry with the works connected therewith are vested in and worked and managed by the Board, and it is expedient that further powers be conferred upon the Board in relation to those undertakings :

And whereas the Board are the owners of the waterworks and gasworks which respectively supply the district with water and gas, and it is expedient that further powers in relation to those undertakings should be conferred upon the Board :

Sec. 1 -2

And whereas it is expedient that the powers of the Board in relation to the health and improvement of the district should be enlarged and that the recited Acts should be in divers respects amended :

And whereas the objects aforesaid cannot be effected without the authority of Parliament :

And whereas an absolute majority of the whole number of the Board at a meeting held on the first day of November, one thousand eight hundred and eighty-nine, after ten clear days' notice by public advertisement of the meeting and of the purpose thereof in the " Wallasey and Wirral Chronicle," a local newspaper published and circulating in the district, such notice being in addition to the ordinary notices required for summoning that meeting resolved that the expense in relation to promoting the Bill for this Act should be charged on the district fund and general district rate :

And whereas that resolution was published twice in the said " Wallasey and Wirral Chronicle " and has received the approval of the Local Government Board :

And whereas the propriety of the promotion of the Bill for this Act was confirmed by an absolute majority of the whole number of the Board at a further special meeting held in pursuance of a similar notice on the second day of January, one thousand eight hundred and ninety, being no less than fourteen days after the deposit of the Bill for this Act in the offices of the Houses of Parliament :

And whereas the owners and ratepayers of the district by resolution passed in the manner prescribed by the Public Health Act, 1875 (Schedule III.), have consented to the promotion of the Bill for this Act :

May it, therefore, please your Majesty that it may be enacted and be it enacted by the Queen's most Excellent Majesty by and with the advice and consent of the Lords Spiritual and Temporal and Commons in this present Parliament assembled, and by the authority of the same as follows (that is to say) :—

PART I.—PRELIMINARY.

Short title.

1. This Act may be cited as the Wallasey Local Board Act, 1890.

Division of Act into parts.

2. This Act is divided into parts as follows :—

PART I.—Preliminary.
PART II.—Foreshore.
PART III.—Streets, Buildings and Sewers.
PART IV.—Private Street Works.
PART V.—Sanitary Provisions.
PART VI.—Water and Gas.
PART VII.—Miscellaneous Provisions.

3. In this Act the following words and expressions have the meanings hereby assigned to them unless the subject or context otherwise requires:— *Interpretation.*

"The district" means the local government district of Wallasey in the county of Chester as defined by this Act:

"The Board" means the Wallasey Local Board:

"The foreshore" means and includes the seashore and the foreshore of the River Mersey within the district:

"Infectious disease" means any infectious disease to which the Infectious Disease (Notification) Act, 1889, for the time being applies within the district:

[*Vide* the Infectious Disease (Notification) Act, 1889, sec. 6 (52 & 53 Vict. c. 72.)]

"The clerk," "the surveyor," "the medical officer of health" and "the inspector of nuisances" mean respectively the clerk, the surveyor, the medical officer of health and the inspector of nuisances to the Board:

"The district fund" and "general district rate" mean the district fund and general district rate of the district:

"Daily penalty" means a penalty for each day on which any offence is continued after conviction:

"The Public Health Acts" means the Public Health Act, 1875, and all Acts for the time being in force amending the same:

Subject to the provisions of this Act words and expressions to which meanings are assigned by the Public Health Act, 1875, have in this Act the same respective meanings unless the subject or context otherwise requires:

Provided that the expression "superior courts" or "court of competent jurisdiction" shall have effect as if the debt or demand with respect to which it is used were a simple contract debt and not a debt or demand created by statute.

4. This Act shall be carried into execution by the Board with all the powers, privileges, duties, obligations, and indemnities of the Board as an urban sanitary authority. And this Act shall unless otherwise expressed or implied apply only to the district. *Execution and limits of Act.*

PART II.—FORESHORE.

5. The boundary of the district on the northern or seaward side is hereby declared to be the line of low water of the lowest spring tide of the Irish sea, and on the eastern side the River Mersey to the middle of the stream. *Defining sea and river boundary of district.*

[*Vide* The Wallasey Improvement Act, 1845, sec. 89; The Wallasey Order, 1852, art. 1; and the Wallasey Order (No. 2), 1877.]

53 & 54 Vict. *The Wallasey Local Board Act,* 1890. ch. cxri.

Sec. 6—9

Foreshore and vacant land to be street for certain purposes.
5 Geo. 4, c. 83.

6. The foreshore on the northern and eastern boundaries of the district, and any unfenced ground adjoining or abutting upon such foreshore or on any street, shall for the purposes of sections 28 and 29 of the Town Police Clauses Act, 1847, be deemed to be a street, and shall for the purposes of the Act passed in the fifth year of the reign of King George the Fourth intituled "An Act for the punishment of "idle and disorderly persons, rogues, and vagabonds, in that part of "Great Britain called England" so far as such Act is unrepealed, and any Act altering, affecting, or amending the same, and for the time being in force be deemed to be a public place. Nothing in this Act shall interfere with any right now possessed by the owners of unfenced private land in front of houses or shops to display their wares or merchandise on such private land.

Board may make byelaws as to user of foreshore.

7. The Board may from time to time make byelaws for all or any of the following purposes (that is to say):—

For regulating the erection, or placing, or continuance on the foreshore, or the approaches thereto, or any part or parts thereof, of any booths, tents, sheds, stands, stalls, shows, exhibitions, performances, swings, roundabouts, fishing stakes, wreckage, or other like erections or things, vans, photographic carts, or other vehicles, whether drawn or propelled by animals or persons, or steam, or other motive power, and the playing of any games on the foreshore, or any part thereof:

For regulating the selling and hawking of any article, commodity, or thing on the foreshore:

For regulating the user of the foreshore, or any part thereof for riding and driving.

Provisions as to bathing.

8.—(1.)—The Board may by resolution, from time to time, fix and determine, and alter the hours during which bathing may take place from those parts of the foreshore within the district, which are not comprised in any public bathing place, or any stand for bathing machines.

(2.) And any person who shall undress on the foreshore, or bathe in the sea or river Mersey within the district, except from a bathing machine, or from a public bathing place, or from a boat distant from the shore not less than one hundred yards, and from any stand for ladies' bathing machines not less than two hundred yards at any other time than between the hours so appointed, shall for every such offence be liable to a penalty not exceeding forty shillings.

(3.) And the Board may, from time to time, make byelaws for the preservation of decency and order at public bathing stations on the foreshore and for regulating the hours during which bathing may take place therefrom and may by such byelaws prescribe the use of decent and sufficient bathing garments.

Power to annex conditions to licenses of bathing machine proprietors.

9. The Board may from time to time annex to any license granted to the owner or lessee of any bathing machine such conditions as to the employment of boats boatmen and attendants for the purpose of ensuring the safety of bathers as the Board may think fit and as to the qualifications of such boatmen and attendants, and any owner or lessee of any bathing machine, who or any of whose boatmen attendants or servants shall commit a breach of any

such conditions shall be liable to a penalty not exceeding five pounds and the Board may in the event of conviction suspend or revoke the license of any such owner or lessee.

10. The Board may employ and pay boatmen for the purpose of protecting persons whilst bathing. *Protection of bathers.*

11. Provided always that nothing herein contained shall be construed to affect alter abridge or take away any of the powers or authorities rights or privileges vested in the commissioners appointed under and by virtue of the following Acts of Parliament or either of them, namely an Act passed in the tenth year of the reign of His Majesty King George the Fourth, intituled "An Act for making an "embankment on the north-west side of the Leasowes in the town- "ship of Wallasey and Great Meols in the county of Chester, to "prevent the further encroachment of the sea, and the injury to "arise therefrom to the low lands contiguous and to the Port "of Liverpool," and an Act passed in the seventeenth and eighteenth years of the reign of Her Majesty Queen Victoria, intituled "An "Act to make further provision for the maintenance and repair of "the Wallasey embankment, and for other purposes." *Saving for Wallasey Embankment Commissioners.*

[*Vide* The Wallasey Improvement Act, 1845, sec. 85.]

12. This part of this Act shall not apply to so much of the foreshore and open land as shall for the time being be lawfully inclosed, and nothing in this Act shall take away alter or abridge any right of any owner of property abutting on the foreshore or open lands to the same, or to inclose or (except as otherwise expressly provided by this Act or by any bye-law made under this Act) otherwise deal with the foreshore or open lands or any portion thereof respectively. *Part II. not to apply to inclosed lands.*

PART III.—STREETS, BUILDINGS AND SEWERS.

13. The deposit with the Board of any plan of any street or building shall be null and void, if the execution of the work specified in such plan be not commenced within the following periods (that is to say):— *Deposit of plan to be void after certain interval.*

As to plans deposited after the passing of this Act within three years from the date of such deposit: and

As to plans deposited before the passing of this Act within three years from the passing of this Act:

And at the expiration of those respective periods fresh notice and deposits shall, unless the Board otherwise determine, be requisite.

14. The Board may by order vary or alter the intended position or direction of any intended new street for the purpose of causing it to communicate in a direct line with any other street adjoining or leading thereto. The Board shall make compensation to all persons injuriously affected by the exercise of the powers of this section. *Powers to vary position or direction of new streets.*

15.—(1.) Every person desirous of forming a communication for horses or vehicles across any footway so as to afford access to any premises from any street, shall first give at least fourteen days' notice in writing to the Board of his intention to do so, and shall *Protection of footways.*

Sec 16—18 before permitting the use of such communication construct a sufficient crossing over the footway of the street of such materials and in such manner as shall be satisfactory to the surveyor of the Board. Any person who makes default in complying with the provisions of this enactment shall be liable to a penalty not exceeding five pounds and to a daily penalty not exceeding one pound.

(2.) Any person who drives or permits or causes to be driven any horse or vehicle across any footway (whether paved or not) except over such part thereof on which a sufficient communication has been made, shall for each such offence be liable to a penalty not exceeding one pound, and to pay in addition any damage thereby occasioned.

Power to name or alter names of streets and names to be put up and houses to be numbered, &c.

16. The Board may name any street or any part of a street which is without a name or which bears two names, and may from time to time alter the name of any street or of any part of a street, and may from time to time paint engrave or otherwise describe and place the name of any street or of any part of a street on a conspicuous part of any building or other erection at or near each end corner or entrance thereof, and number every building or other erection therein on the door thereof or otherwise as they think proper, and if any person wilfully or without sufficient reason destroys obliterates defaces removes or without the consent of the Board alters any such name or number or any part thereof, he shall be liable to a penalty not exceeding forty shillings.

17. From and after the passing of this Act—

What to be deemed new buildings.

The re-erection wholly or partially on the same site of any building of which the outer wall is pulled down, to or within ten feet of the surface of the adjoining ground, and of any frame building so far pulled down as to leave only the framework of the ground floor storey thereof;

The making of any addition to an existing building by raising any part thereof, or making any projection therefrom but so far as regards such addition only; and

The roofing or covering over of an open space between walls or buildings;

shall for all the purposes of this part of this Act, and of the Public Health Acts, and of any bye-law made thereunder respectively be deemed to be the erection of a "new building," and the word "building" shall for all such purposes include an erection or building of a permanent character of whatever material constructed.

Height of buildings.

18. No new building shall without the approval of the Board be erected on the side of any street not existing at the commencement of this Act, which shall exceed in height the distance from the front of such building to the opposite side of such street nor shall the height of any building at any time erected on the side of any street be at any time subsequently increased without such approval as aforesaid so as to exceed such distance. In determining the height of a building the measurement shall be taken from the level of the centre of the street immediately opposite to the centre of the front of the building up to the top of the parapet or to the eaves of the roof as the case may be. In case of a gable facing the street the measurement shall be to a point half way between the level of the eaves and the ridge. In the case of a roof which slopes away from the street at any greater angle to the horizon than fifty degrees, the measurement shall be to the ridge of the roof and not to the eaves.

19. In every new building every room used as a dwelling or sleeping room shall be in every part thereof eight feet six inches in height at least from the floor to the ceiling except rooms in the roof and every room in the roof so used shall be at least eight feet in height from the floor to the ceiling above one-fourth of the area of the floor, and shall have vertical walls at least five feet in height.

Height of rooms.

20. No building which was not at any time before the passing of this Act occupied as a dwelling-house shall be so occupied until the drainage thereof shall have been made and completed and a proper water supply shall have been laid on thereto nor until a certificate shall have been granted by the surveyor to the owner that such house is in every respect in accordance with the byelaws and requirements for the time being in force. Provided that if the surveyor shall fail to give such certificate within seven days after a written application for it shall have been made to him by the owner of such building, and shall not in the meantime have specified to the owner which of the aforesaid byelaws and requirements have not been complied with with respect to such building, then such building shall be thenceforth deemed to be in every respect in accordance with the aforesaid byelaws and requirements and may be occupied as a dwelling-house. And if any building shall be occupied contrary to the provisions of this section the owner of such building if he shall occupy or shall allow to be occupied, and every person who shall wilfully and knowingly occupy such building as a dwelling-house shall be deemed to have committed an offence against the provisions of this section and shall be liable to a penalty not exceeding five pounds and to a daily penalty not exceeding forty shillings.

Certificate that houses fulfil certain requirements.

21. The surveyor and his assistants may at any reasonable times inspect any building in progress of construction or any work connected therewith and for such inspection he and they shall have from the builder free of expense all reasonable use and assistance of ladders, scaffolding and plant in and about the building or works inspected. The owner or his agent or the builder shall give forty-eight hours' notice in writing to the surveyor before the commencement of the building and before any foundation of a new building or any sewer or drain is covered up and the like notice after any work required by the Board to be done in amendment of any irregularity has been completed and before the same is covered up.

Power of inspection.

22. If the surveyor on inspecting any building or work finds that the same is so far advanced that he cannot ascertain whether anything has been done contrary to any enactments or byelaws in force in the district or to the plans and sections approved by the Board in pursuance of any such byelaws or whether anything required by any such enactments, byelaws or plans and sections has been omitted to be done the surveyor shall within twenty-four hours after such inspection give to the owner or his agent or to the builder or person engaged in erecting such building or doing such work

Power of surveyor on inspecting

282   53 & 54 *Vict.*   *The Wallasey Local Board*   ch. c.c.ci.
Act, 1890.

Sec. 23—25   notice in writing requiring such builder or person within forty-eight hours from the service of such notice to cause so much of any building or work as prevents such surveyor from ascertaining whether anything has been done or omitted to be done as aforesaid to be to a sufficient extent cut into laid open or pulled down and such builder or other person shall forthwith comply with the notice so given. Provided always that the expense of cutting into, laying open or pulling down as the case may be any such building or work and of reinstating the same and a reasonable sum for the delay occasioned thereby shall be borne and paid by the Board if it shall appear on inspection that such enactments, byelaws, plans and sections have not been infringed.

Hoards to be set up during progress of buildings, &c.

23. Before commencing the removal, or taking down, or the erection or repair of any building abutting on, or within six feet of any street being a highway, or any other operations whereby any part of any such street may be obstructed or rendered inconvenient or dangerous, the contractor or other person having control of the work shall cause to be put up a hoard or fence, and also if required by the surveyor an overhead covering or hood and a convenient platform and hand-rail to serve as a footway for passengers in such position and of such dimensions and for such period and subject to such conditions as the surveyor may approve on application being made to him, and shall maintain the same respectively in good condition to the satisfaction of the surveyor, and such contractor or other person shall, on receiving permission from the surveyor and before putting up such hoard or fence, pay to the Board a sum equal to one halfpenny per month for every superficial yard of land enclosed from the street during the period for which permission is granted.

The said erections shall be removed by such contractor or other person within the period limited by the surveyor, and on the removal of such erection the pavement or flagging of the street shall be restored or made good by the Board and the cost thereof shall be paid by such contractor or other person.

Fencing in of vacant land.

24. If any vacant or waste land is in the opinion of the Board, from want of sufficient protection or enclosure, dangerous to the passengers along any street, the Board may by notice require the owner or occupier of such land to enclose the same so as to prevent any danger therefrom, and if within fourteen days from the service of such notice, such owner or occupier shall fail to comply with the requirements thereof, the Board may cause such land to be enclosed in such manner as they may think fit, and the expense thereby incurred shall be recoverable from such owner or occupier summarily, or as a debt in any court of competent jurisdiction.

[*Vide* the Wallasey Improvement Act, 1845, sec. 118.]

Prevention of lock-up shops and other places of business being improperly used for purposes of habitation.

25. (1) Where on the plan of any building whether built before or after the passing of this Act as deposited with and approved by the Board, a part of such building is described or shown as or appears to be intended to be separated from the remainder of such building for the purpose of being used as a lock-up shop, workshop, shed, or place of business, and not a dwelling-house the use of such part of such building for the purposes of human habitation shall be an offence, and every person who shall wilfully so use or knowingly suffer to be so used such part of such building shall for every such offence be liable to a penalty not exceeding forty shillings, and to a daily penalty not exceeding twenty shillings.

(2) Provided that if such part of such building has in the rear thereof and adjoining and exclusively belonging thereto such an open space as is required by any Act or byelaw for the time being in force with respect to buildings intended to be used as dwelling-houses, and if such part of such building has undergone the structural alterations (if any) necessary in the opinion of the Board for converting it into a dwelling-house, the Board may on the application of the owner thereof authorise the same to be used as a dwelling-house.

(3.) Any justice of the peace by warrant under his hand may authorise any officer of the Board at any time to enter upon and examine any building suspected of being used in contravention of this section.

(4) Every person who shall prevent or obstruct any such officer so authorised (and producing such authority if required) from or in making such inspection shall be liable to a penalty not exceeding forty shillings, and to a daily penalty not exceeding the like sum.

26. All vaults, arches, and cellars at any time subsisting under any street, and all openings into such vaults, arches, or cellars in the surface of any such street, and all cellar heads, gratings, lights, and coal holes existing in the surface of any such street, and all landings, flags, or stones of the path or street supporting the same respectively shall be by the owners or occupiers of the same, or of the houses or buildings to which the same respectively belong kept in substantial repair, and in good and proper condition, and so as not to occasion any injury to the street or passengers therein, and in default thereof the Board may after twenty-four hours' notice in that behalf cause the same respectively to be repaired and put in good order, and the expenses of so doing may be recovered summarily from the owner or occupier in default. *As to repair of vaults, &c., under streets.*

[*Vide* The Wallasey Improvement Act, 1864, sec. 30.]

27. The back yards of all houses which shall be built after the passing of this Act shall be formed with such fall, and shall for the space of at least one hundred and fifty square feet be flagged or asphalted or paved with such materials as shall be satisfactory to the Board for the purpose of carrying off the surface water to the drains of such houses, and if the back yard of any house erected before or after the passing of this Act shall not be so formed flagged, asphalted or paved so as to allow of the surface water being carried off as aforesaid, the Board may give to the owner of such house notice in writing requiring him within seven days after such notice shall have been so given to proceed to form and to flag, asphalte or pave such back yard so as to allow of the surface water being carried off to the drain of such house and within twenty-one days after such notice shall have been so given to complete such several works to the satisfaction of the Board, and if such owner shall make default in complying with any of such requirements to the satisfaction of the Board within the respective times aforesaid the Board may if they think fit execute the works necessary for carrying out such requirements and the *Back yards to be paved, &c.*

Sec. 28—31	expenses incurred by them in so doing shall be paid to the Board by such owner and shall be recoverable as a penalty under this Act is recoverable or shall be deemed private improvement expenses and be recoverable accordingly.
Penalty for not keeping common courts and passages clean.	**28.** If any court or passage leading to the back of several buildings in separate occupations (such court or passage not being a public highway) be not regularly and effectually swept and kept clean and free from rubbish or other accumulation to the satisfaction of the Board the Board may if they think fit (after twenty-four hours' notice to the occupiers of such buildings of their intention to exercise the powers of this section) sweep and clean such court or passage, and the expense thereby incurred may be recovered in a summary manner in equal proportions from the occupiers of the buildings in the court or to the back of which the passage leads.
Power to make bye-laws for sanitary purposes.	**29.** The Board may from time to time make and enforce bye-laws for all or any of the following purposes (that is to say) For prescribing the times for the removal or carriage through the streets of any fœcal or offensive or noxious matter or liquid whether such matter or liquid shall be in course of removal or carriage from within or without or through the district and that the vessel, receptacle, cart or carriage used therefor shall be properly constructed so as to prevent the escape of any such matter or liquid and for compelling the cleansing of any place whereon such matter or liquid shall have been dropped or spilt in such removal or carriage.
Cesspools.	**30.** No cesspool shall be made or continued on any premises if there is a sewer belonging to the Board within one hundred feet of any part of such premises fit to receive the drainage thereof except when in the opinion of the Board the making or continuance of such cesspool shall be unavoidable and when any cesspool shall be allowed to be made it shall be constructed in such situation and in such manner as the Board shall direct. Every person who shall make a new cesspool contrary to the provisions of this section or who shall continue an existing cesspool for two months after notice in writing from the Board to discontinue the same shall be liable to a penalty not exceeding five pounds and to a daily penalty not exceeding forty shillings.
Public water-closets, urinals and lavatories.	**31.** The Board may erect and maintain or permit to be erected and maintained in any street or on land belonging to them or on land belonging to any person with the consent of the owner, lessee or occupier thereof for the time being, waterclosets, urinals, and lavatories for the use of the public and may charge for the use of such waterclosets and lavatories erected or maintained by them, such sums as they may think proper, and the Board may make byelaws for the management of such waterclosets urinals and lavatories and for the conduct of the persons using the same. Every watercloset, urinal or lavatory erected by permission of the Board under this section, shall be subject to such terms and conditions as the Board may prescribe with respect to the charges, if any, to be made for the use thereof and for repairing and keeping the same in proper order and for closing or removing the same if and when required by the Board, but nothing herein shall be held to authorise a charge for the use of a public urinal.

32. Every undertaking or agreement in writing given by or to the Board to or by or on behalf of any owner of property on the passing of plans or for the removal of obstructions or otherwise in connexion with the property of such owner shall be binding upon the owner of the property for the time being and upon his successors in title and upon the Board, and may be enforced by either party in any court of summary jurisdiction by a penalty not exceeding five pounds for each breach of such undertaking or agreement and a daily penalty not exceeding twenty shillings for each such breach and such owner shall be entitled to require from the Board a copy of such undertaking or agreement and any intending owner of property shall be entitled to information from the Board as to the existence of any such undertaking or agreement affecting the property and the terms of the undertaking or agreement if any such exist. *Undertakings to bind successive owners.*

33. It shall not be lawful for any person to throw or to suffer or permit to be thrown or to pass into any drain or sewer any matter or substance which would interfere with the free flow of the sewage or surface or storm water, or which would be injurious to the drains or sewers, and every person offending against this enactment shall for every such offence be liable to a penalty not exceeding five pounds. *Placing matters in sewers so as to affect run of water.*

34. Every person who having had notice from the Board of the provisions of this section, shall at any time after the expiration of seven days from the service of such notice, turn or knowingly permit to enter into any sewer or drain communicating therewith, any waste steam condensing water or heated water from any boiler or other receptacle used with any steam engine, or for any manufacturing or trade purpose (such water being of a higher temperature than one hundred and ten degrees of Fahrenheit), shall be liable for every such offence to a penalty not exceeding ten pounds and to a daily penalty not exceeding five pounds. The Board or any of their officers duly authorised in this behalf, by writing under the hand of the Clerk to the Board, and producing such authority if required, may enter into any premises for the purpose of examining whether the provisions of this section are being contravened, and if such admission be refused, any justice, on complaint thereof on oath by any officer of the Board (made after reasonable notice in writing, of such intended complaint, has been given to the person having custody of the premises), may by order under his hand require such person to admit the officer of the Board into the premises, and any such order shall continue in force until the offence shall have ceased, or the works necessary to prevent the recurrence thereof shall have been executed. *Steam, &c., not to be turned into sewers.*

35. If the owner or occupier of any premises within the district desires that the sewer or drain from such premises shall be made to communicate with any sewer of the Board, the Board may and shall make so much of such sewer or drain as is to be constructed under any public highway, and also the junction of such sewer or drain with the sewer of the Board, and may and shall execute all necessary works for those purposes upon the reasonable cost or estimated cost thereof being paid to the Board, or the payment thereof to them being secured to their satisfaction. *Board may make communications between private drains and their sewers on payment, &c.*

[*Vide* The Wallasey Improvement Act, 1864, sec. 31.]

Sec. 36—40

Extension of section 41 of the Public Health Act, 1875.

36. In cases where two or more houses erected after the passing of this Act are connected with a single private drain which conveys their drainage into a public sewer, the Board shall have all the powers conferred by section 41 of the Public Health Act, 1875.

[The powers conferred by sec. 41 of the Public Health Act, 1875, relate to the examination of drains, privies, &c., on complaint of nuisance.]

Exemption in respect of Her Majesty's buildings.

37. There shall be exempted from so much of the provisions of this Act as relates to buildings and structures, every building structure or work vested in or in the occupation of Her Majesty, Her heirs and successors either beneficially or as part of the hereditary revenues of the crown, or in trust for the public service or for public services, also any building structure or work vested in or in the occupation of any department of Her Majesty's Government for public purposes or for the public service.

PART IV.—PRIVATE STREET WORKS.

Definition of street.

38. "Street" in this part of this Act means (unless the context otherwise requires) a street as defined by the Public Health Act, 1875, and not being a highway repairable by the inhabitants at large.

[*Vide* Public Health Act, 1875, 38 & 39 Vict. c. 55, sec. 4. The definition there given is as follows:—"Street includes any highway (not being a turnpike Road) and any public bridge (not being a county bridge) and any road, lane, footway, square, court, alley or passage, whether a thoroughfare or not."]

Definition of paving, metalling and flagging.

39. The expression "paving, metalling and flagging" used in this part of this Act shall include macadamising asphalting, gravelling, kerbing, and every method of making a carriageway or footway, and words referring to paving, metalling and flagging shall be construed accordingly.

Private street works.

40.—(1). Where any street or part of a street is not sewered, levelled, paved, metalled, flagged, kerbed, channelled, made good and lighted to the satisfaction of the Board, the Board may from time to time resolve with respect to such street or part of a street, to do any one or more of the following works (in this Act called private street works) (that is to say) To sewer, level, pave, metal, flag, kerb, channel, or make good, or to provide proper means for lighting such street or part of a street, and the expenses incurred by the Board in executing private street works shall be apportioned (subject as in this Act mentioned) on the premises fronting, adjoining or abutting on such street or part of a street. Any such resolution may include several streets or parts of streets or may be limited to any part or parts of a street.

(2) The Surveyor shall prepare as respects each street or part of a street—

(*a*) A specification of the private street works referred to in the resolution with plans and sections (if applicable):

(b) An estimate of the probable expenses of the works:

(c) A provisional apportionment of the estimated expenses among the premises liable to be charged therewith under this Act:

Such specifications, plans, sections, estimates, and provisional apportionments shall comprise the particulars prescribed in Part I. of the Schedule to this Act, and shall be submitted to the Board, who may by resolution approve the same respectively with or without modification or addition as they think fit.

(3.) The resolution approving the specifications, plans and sections (if any), estimates and provisional apportionments shall be published in the manner prescribed in Part II. of the Schedule to this Act and copies thereof shall be served on the owners of the premises shown as liable to be charged in the provisional apportionment. During one month from the date of the first publication, the approved specifications, plans and sections (if any), estimates and provisional apportionments (or copies thereof certified by the surveyor) shall be kept deposited at the offices of the Board and shall be open to inspection at all reasonable times.

41. During the said month any owner of any premises shown in a provisional apportionment as liable to be charged with any part of the expenses of executing the works may, by written notice served on the Board, object to the proposals of the Board on any of the following grounds (that is to say):— *Objections to proposed works.*

(a) That an alleged street or part of a street is not or does not form part of a street within the meaning of this Act:

(b) That a street or part of a street is (in whole or in part) a highway repairable by the inhabitants at large:

(c) That there has been some material informality, defect or error in or in respect of the resolution, notice, plans, sections or estimate:

(d) That the proposed works are insufficient, unreasonable or unnecessary, or that the estimated expenses are excessive:

(e) That any premises ought to be excluded from or inserted in the provisional apportionment:

(f) That the provisional apportionment is incorrect in respect of some matter of fact to be specified in the objection or (where the provisional apportionment is made with regard to other considerations than frontage as hereinafter provided) in respect of the degree of benefit to be derived by any persons or the amount or value of any work already done by the owner or occupier of any premises.

For the purposes of this Act joint tenants or tenants in common may object through one of their number authorised in writing under the hands of the majority of such joint tenants or tenants in common.

42.—(1) The Board at any time after the expiration of the said month may apply to a court of summary jurisdiction to appoint a time for determining the matter of all objections made as in this Act mentioned and shall publish a notice of the time and place appointed, and copies of such notice shall be served upon the objectors, and at the time and place so appointed any such court *Hearing and determination of objections.*

Sec. 43—44 may proceed to hear and determine the matter of all such objections in the same manner as nearly as may be and with the same powers and subject to the same provisions with respect to stating a case as if the Board were proceeding summarily against the objectors to enforce payment of a sum of money summarily recoverable. The court may quash in whole or in part, or may amend the resolution, plans, sections, estimates and provisional apportionments, or any of them on the application either of any objector or of the Board. The court may also, if it thinks fit, adjourn the hearing and direct any further notices to be given.

(2) No objection which could be made under this Act shall be otherwise made or allowed in any court proceeding or manner whatsoever.

(3) The costs of any proceedings before a court of summary jurisdiction in relation to objections under this Act shall be in the discretion of the court and the court shall have power, if it thinks fit, to direct that the whole or any part of such costs ordered to be paid by an objector or objectors shall be paid in the first instance by the Board and charged as part of the expenses of the works on the premises of the objector or objectors in such proportions as may appear just.

Incidental works.

43.—(1) The Board may include in any works to be done under this Act with respect to any street or part of a street any works which they think necessary for bringing the street or part of a street as regards sewerage, drainage, level or other matters into conformity with any other streets (whether repairable or not by the inhabitants at large), including the provision of separate sewers for the reception of sewage and of surface water respectively.

(2) The Board in any estimate of the expenses of private street works may include a commission not exceeding two pounds ten shillings per centum (in addition to the estimated actual cost) in respect of surveys and superintendence.

Apportionment of expenses.

44. In a provisional apportionment of expenses of private street works the apportionment of expenses against the premises fronting, adjoining or abutting on the street or part of a street in respect of which the expenses are to be incurred shall, unless the Board otherwise resolve, be apportioned according to the frontage of the respective premises, but the Board may if they think just resolve that in settling the apportionment regard shall be had to the following considerations (that is to say):—

(a) The greater or less degree of benefit to be derived by any premises from such works:

(b) The amount and value of any work already done by the owners or occupiers of any such premises.

They may also if they think just include any premises which do not front adjoin or abut on the street or part of a street but which in their opinion will be benefited by the works and may fix the sum or proportion to be charged against any such premises accordingly. But no premises which do not front adjoin or abut on such street or part of a street as aforesaid shall be included unless there is an access thereto from the street in respect of which the expenses are to be incurred or from an immediately adjoining street.

Sec. 45—47

45. The Board may from time to time amend the specifications plans and sections (if any) estimates and provisional apportionments for any private street works but if the total amount of the estimate in respect of any street or part of a street is increased such estimate and the provisional apportionment shall be published in the manner prescribed in Part II. of the Schedule to this Act and shall be open to inspection at the Board Offices at all reasonable times and copies thereof shall be served on the owners of the premises affected thereby and objections may be made to the increase and apportionment and if made shall be dealt with and determined in like manner as objections to the original estimate and apportionment. *Amendment of plans, &c.*

46. (1) When any private street works have been completed and the expenses thereof ascertained the surveyor shall make a final apportionment by dividing the expenses in the same proportions in which the estimated expenses were divided in the original or amended provisional apportionment (as the case may be) and such final apportionment shall be conclusive for all purposes and notice of such final apportionment shall be served upon the owners of the premises affected thereby and the sums apportioned thereby shall be recoverable in manner provided by this Act or in the same manner as private improvement expenses are recoverable under the Public Health Act 1875 including the power to declare any such expenses to be payable by instalments. *Final apportionment and recovery of expenses.*

(2) Within one month after such notice the owner of any premises charged with any expenses under such apportionment may by a written notice to the Board object to such final apportionment on the following grounds or any of them :—

(*a*) That the actual expenses have without sufficient reason exceeded the estimated expenses by more than fifteen per cent. :

(*b*) That the final apportionment has not been made in accordance with this section :

(*c*) That there has been an unreasonable departure from the specification plans and sections :

(*d*) That the interest has been increased by unreasonable delay in ascertaining the expenses or making the apportionment.

(3.) Objections under this section shall be determined in the same manner as objections to the provisional apportionment.

[*Vide* sec. 42.]

47. (1) Any premises included in the final apportionment and all estates and interests from time to time therein shall stand and remain charged (to the like extent and effect as under section 257 of the Public Health Act, 1875) with the sum finally apportioned on them or if objection has been made against the final apportionment with the sum determined to be due as from the date of the final apportionment with interest at the rate of five pounds per centum per annum and the Board shall for the recovery of such sum and interest have all the same powers and remedies under the Conveyancing and Law of Property Act 1881 and otherwise as if they were mortgagees having powers of sale and lease and of appointing a receiver. *Charge on premises.*

U

Sec. 49—53

(2) The Board shall keep a register of charges under this Act and of the payments made in satisfaction thereof and the register shall be open to inspection to all persons at all reasonable times on payment of not exceeding one shilling in respect of each name or property searched for and the Board shall furnish copies of any part of such register to any person applying for the same on payment of such reasonable sum as may be fixed by the Board.

Recovery of expenses summarily or by action.

48. The Board if they think fit may from time to time (in addition and without prejudice to any other remedy) recover summarily in a court of summary jurisdiction or as a simple contract debt by action in any court of competent jurisdiction from the owner for the time being of any premises in respect of which any sum is due for expenses of private street works the whole or any portion of such sum together with interest at a rate not exceeding five pounds per centum per annum from the date of the final apportionment till payment thereof.

Contribution by Board to expenses.

49. The Board if they think fit may at any time resolve to contribute the whole or a portion of the expenses of any private street works and may pay the same out of the district fund or general district rate.

Exemption from expenses of incumbent of church.

50. The incumbent or minister or trustee of any church chapel or place appropriated to public religious worship which is for the time being by law exempt from rates for the relief of the poor shall not be liable to any expenses of private street works as the owner of such church chapel or place or of any churchyard or burial ground attached thereto nor shall any such expenses be deemed to be a charge on such church chapel or other place or on such churchyard or burial ground or to subject the same to distress execution or other legal process, but the proportion of expenses in respect of which an exemption is allowed under this section, shall be borne and paid by the Board.

Power for limited owners to borrow for expenses.

51. All owners of buildings or lands being persons who under the Lands Clauses Consolidation Act 1845 are empowered to sell and convey or release lands, may charge such buildings or lands with such sum as may be necessary to defray the whole or any part of any expenses which the owners of, or any persons in respect of such buildings or lands for the time being are liable to pay under this part of this Act and the expenses of making such charge and for securing the repayment of such sum with interest, may mortgage such buildings or lands to any person advancing such sum but so that the principal due on any such mortgage shall be repaid by equal yearly or half-yearly payments within twenty years

Power of Board to borrow for private street works.

52. The Board may from time to time with the sanction of the Local Government Board borrow on the security of the district fund and general district rate, moneys for the purpose of temporarily providing for expenses of private street works and the powers of the Board to borrow under the Public Health Act 1875 shall be available as if the execution of private street works under this Act were one of the purposes of the Public Health Act 1875.

Adoption of private streets.

53. Whenever all or any of the private street works in this Act mentioned have been executed in a street or part of a street by the

53 & 54 Vict.   *The Wallasey Local Board*   ch. cxxi.   291
Act, 1890.

Board and the Board are of opinion that such street or part of a **Sec. 54—56**
street ought to become a highway repairable by the inhabitants at
large, they may by notice to be fixed up in such street or part of a
street, declare the whole of such street or part of a street to be a
highway repairable by the inhabitants at large, and thereupon such
street or part of a street as defined in the notice shall become a
highway repairable by the inhabitants at large :

Provided that no such street shall become a highway so repairable if within one month after such notice has been put up the
owner or the majority in number or value of owners of such street,
by notice in writing to the Board, object thereto, and in ascertaining
such majority joint owners shall be reckoned as one owner.

54. If any street is now or shall hereafter be sewered, levelled, On street
paved, metalled, flagged, kerbed, channelled and made good (all such being paved,
works being done to the satisfaction of the Board) then on the declare same
application in writing of the greater part in value of the owners of public
the houses and land in such street the Board shall within three highway.
months from the time of such application by notice put up in such
street declare the same to be a highway repairable by the inhabitants
at large, and thereupon such street shall become a highway
repairable by the inhabitants at large.

55. The Board shall keep separate accounts of all moneys Separate
expended and recovered by them in the execution of the provisions accounts of
of this Act relating to private street works. All moneys recovered expenses
by the Board under this part of this Act in respect of street works of works.
shall be applied in the execution of other private street works or in
repayment of moneys borrowed for the purpose of executing private
street works.

[The foregoing sections relating to private street works are in
 general similar to the provisions contained in the adoptive
 Private Street Works Act, 1892, ss. 5 to 21. (55 & 56 Vict.
 c. 57).]

PART V.—SANITARY PROVISIONS.

56. Whenever it shall be certified to the Board by the medical Cowkeepers
officer of health or by any other registered medical practitioner, and others
that the outbreak or spread of infectious disease is in the opinion of to furnish
such medical officer of health or medical practitioner, attributable to customers
the milk supplied by any cowkeeper, purveyor of milk, or occupier in certain
of a dairy, milkstore, or milkshop, the Board may require such cases.
cowkeeper purveyor of milk or occupier to furnish to them within
a time to be fixed by them a full and complete list of the names and
addresses of all his customers within the district and such cowkeeper, purveyor of milk, or occupier shall furnish such list accordingly and the Board shall pay to him for every such list the sum of
sixpence, and after the rate of sixpence for every twenty-five names
contained therein, but no such payment shall exceed three shillings,
and every person who shall wilfully or knowingly offend against
this enactment shall for each such offence be liable to a penalty not
exceeding five pounds and to a daily penalty not exceeding forty
shillings.

Sec. 57—59

Medical officer may inspect dairies, &c., beyond district in certain cases.

57. In case the medical officer of health shall have reasonable cause to believe that any person in the district is suffering from infectious disease attributable to milk supplied within the district from any farmhouse, dairy, cowshed, milkshop, or place situate beyond the boundary of the district or that the consumption of milk from such farmhouse, dairy, cowshed, milkshop, or place, is likely to cause infectious disease to any person residing in the district, such medical officer shall if authorised in that behalf by any order of a justice having jurisdiction in the place where such farmhouse, dairy, cowshed, milkshop, or place is situate, have power to inspect such farmhouse, dairy, cowshed, milkshop, or place, and if on such inspection he shall be of opinion that infectious disease is caused or is likely to arise from consumption of the milk supplied therefrom he shall report thereon to the Board who may thereupon give notice to the occupier of such farmhouse, dairy, cowshed, milkshop, or place not to supply any milk therefrom within the district until such notice has been withdrawn by the Board, and the Board shall forthwith give notice of the facts to the sanitary authority of the district acting in execution of the Contagious Diseases (Animals) Acts 1878 to 1886, in which such farmhouse, dairy, cowshed, milkshop or place is situate, and also to the Local Government Board in order that such further measures may be adopted in relation thereto as may be considered proper, and as may be within the provinces of such authorities respectively. Any person refusing to permit the medical officer of health on the production of such order as aforesaid to inspect any such farmhouse, dairy, cowshed, milkshop, or place, or after any such notice by the Board has been given, supplying any milk therefrom within the district, or selling it for consumption therein until such notice has been withdrawn shall be deemed guilty of an offence against this Act, and shall on summary conviction be liable to a penalty not exceeding five pounds for such offence, and to a daily penalty not exceeding forty shillings. Provided always that proceedings for the recovery of any penalty under this enactment shall be taken before the justices of the peace having jurisdiction in the place where the said farmhouse, dairy, cowshed, milkshop, or place is situate.

Persons engaged in washing or mangling clothes to furnish lists of owners of clothes in certain cases.

58. Whenever it shall be certified to the Board by the medical officer of health that it is desirable with a view to prevent the spread of infectious disease, that they should be furnished with a list of the customers of any person or company earning a livelihood or deriving gain by the washing or mangling of clothes, the Board may require such person or company to furnish to them a full and complete list of the names and addresses of the owners of clothes, for whom such persons or company washes or mangles, or has washed or mangled during the past six weeks, and such person or company shall furnish such list accordingly, and the Board shall pay to him, her, or them for every such list the sum of sixpence, and at the rate of sixpence for every twenty-five names contained therein, but no such payment shall exceed three shillings, and every person who shall wilfully or knowingly offend against this enactment shall for each such offence be liable to a penalty not exceeding five pounds, and to a daily penalty not exceeding forty shillings.

Further powers in relation to disinfection of premises.

59. Where the Board are of opinion on the certificate of their medical officer of health, or of any other registered medical practitioner that the cleansing and disinfecting of any house or part thereof, and of any articles therein likely to communicate any infectious disease or to retain infection, would tend to prevent or to check infectious disease, and that such cleansing and disinfection would more effectually be carried out by the Board than by the owner or occupier of such house or part thereof, the Board without requiring such owner or occupier to carry out such cleansing and disinfection as aforesaid, may if they think fit, but at their own cost themselves cleanse and disinfect such house or part thereof and articles, and may for that purpose remove any such articles, and shall make compensation to such owners or occupiers for all property or articles destroyed or injured by the exercise of the provisions of this section. And any person who shall obstruct any duly authorised officer of the Board in carrying out the provisions of this section shall be liable to a penalty not exceeding five pounds, and to a daily penalty not exceeding forty shillings.

60. Every person who shall cease to occupy any house, room, or part of a house in which any person has within six weeks previously been suffering from any infectious disease without having such house, room, or part of a house, and all articles therein liable to retain infection disinfected to the satisfaction of a registered medical practitioner as testified by a certificate signed by him, or without first giving to the owner of such house, room, or part of a house notice of the previous existence of such disease, and every person ceasing to occupy any house, room, or part of a house, and who on being questioned by the owner thereof, or by any person negotiating for the hire of such house, room, or part of a house as to the fact of there having within six weeks previously been therein any person suffering from any infectious disease, knowingly makes a false answer to such question shall be liable to a penalty not exceeding ten pounds. *[Penalty on persons ceasing to occupy houses without previous disinfection or giving notice to owner or making false answers.]*

61. No person shall, without the sanction in writing of the medical officer of health, or other registered medical practitioner retain unburied elsewhere than in a mortuary for more than forty-eight hours the dead body of any person who has died of any infectious disease, and any person offending against this enactment shall be liable to a penalty not exceeding ten pounds, and to a daily penalty not exceeding forty shillings. *[Prohibiting the retention of dead bodies in certain cases.]*

62. If any person shall die from any infectious disease in any hospital, or place of temporary accommodation, and the medical officer of health, or any other registered medical practitioner certifies that in his opinion it is desirable in order to prevent the risk of communicating any infectious disease, or of spreading infection that the dead body shall not be removed from such hospital or place except for the purpose of being forthwith buried, it shall not be lawful for any person or persons to remove such dead body from such hospital or place, except for the last-mentioned purpose and when the dead body is taken out of such hospital or place for that purpose it shall be forthwith carried or taken directly to some cemetery or place of burial and shall be forthwith there buried, and any person wilfully offending against this section shall be liable to a penalty not exceeding fifty pounds. But nothing in this section shall prevent the removal of any dead body from any such hospital or place of temporary accommodation to any public *[Bodies of persons dying in hospital, &c., of infectious diseases to be removed only for burial.]*

Sec. 63—65

Justices may in certain cases order dead bodies to be buried.

mortuary, and such mortuary shall for the purposes of this section be deemed part of such hospital or place of temporary accommodation.

63. Where the body of any person who has died of any infectious disease remains unburied elsewhere than in a mortuary for more than forty-eight hours after death without the sanction of the medical officer of health or other registered medical practitioner, or is retained in a room in which persons live or sleep, or where the dead body of any person is retained in any house or building so as to endanger the health of the inmates of such house or building, or of any adjoining or neighbouring house or building, any justice may on the application of the medical officer of health order the body to be removed at the cost of the Board to any mortuary provided by the Board, and may direct the same to be buried within a time to be limited in the order, or such justice may in the case of the body of any person who has died from any infectious disease or in any case in which he shall consider immediate burial necessary, direct such body to be so buried, without requiring the same to be removed to a mortuary, and unless the friends or relatives of the deceased undertake to bury and do bury the body within the time limited by such order, it shall be the duty of the relieving officer to bury such body at the expense of the poor rate, but any expense so incurred may be recovered by the relieving officer in a summary manner from any person legally liable to pay the expense of such burial. Any person obstructing the execution of an order made by a justice under this section shall be liable to a penalty not exceeding five pounds.

Corpses not to be carried in public conveyances.

64. Any person who hires or uses a public conveyance other than a hearse for the conveyance of the corpse of a person who has died from any infectious disease without previously notifying to the owner or driver of such public conveyance that the person whose corpse is or is intended to be so conveyed has died from infectious disease, and any owner or driver of a public conveyance other than a hearse which has been used for conveying the corpse of a person who has died from infectious disease, who shall not immediately afterwards provide for the disinfection of such conveyance shall be liable to a penalty not exceeding five pounds.

Detention of infected person without proper lodging in hospital by order of justice.

65. The provisions of the Public Health Act, 1875, respecting infectious diseases and hospitals, shall be and are hereby extended so as to authorise any court of summary jurisdiction having jurisdiction in the district, upon certificate of the Medical Officer of Health, to make an order directing the detention in hospital at the cost of the sanitary authority of any person in the district suffering from any infectious disease and not provided with lodging or accommodation in which proper precautions can be taken to prevent the spreading of the disorder by such person. Any order so to be made by any such court shall be limited to some specific time not exceeding one month, but with full power to any such court if it shall seem necessary to enlarge such time as often as may be shown to be necessary by certificate of the said medical officer. It shall be lawful for any sanitary officer or inspector of police on any such order being made to take all necessary measures and do all necessary acts for enforcing the execution thereof.

66. The Board shall, from time to time, provide temporary shelter or house accommodation for the members of any family in which any infectious disease has appeared, and who have been compelled to leave their dwellings for the purpose of enabling such dwellings to be disinfected, and shall also provide or contract with some person or persons to provide nurses for attendance upon the members of any family suffering from any infectious disease within the district, or upon children who may have been compelled to leave their dwellings as aforesaid, and may charge a reasonable sum for the service of any nurse provided by them.

Temporary shelter and nurses.

67. The provisions contained in sections 116 to 119 (both inclusive) of the Public Health Act, 1875, shall extend and apply to all articles intended for the food of man, sold or exposed for sale or deposited in any place for the purpose of sale or of preparation for sale within the district.

Extension of sections 116 to 119 (inclusive) of Public Health Act, 1875.

[Secs. 116 to 119 of the Public Health Act, 1875, relate to the inspection and destruction of unsound meat, &c.]

68. For the purpose of carrying into effect the provisions of sections 49, 120 or 121 of the Public Health Act, 1875, the Board may by any officer appointed in that behalf, and producing his authority if required, enter on any premises between the hours of ten o'clock in the forenoon and six o'clock in the afternoon.

Powers of entry for purposes of sections 49, 120 and 121 of Public Health Act, 1875.

[Secs. 49, 120 & 121 of the Public Health Act, 1875, relate to the removal of filth on the certificate of the Inspector of Nuisances; the cleansing and disinfecting of premises, and the destruction of infected bedding, &c.]

69. Nothing in or done under this Act shall interfere with the operation or effect of the Contagious Diseases (Animals) Acts, 1878 to 1886, or of any Act amending the same, or of any order, license, or act of the Board of Agriculture, made, granted or done, or to be made, granted or done thereunder, or of any order, regulation, license or act of a local authority made, granted or done, or to be made, granted or done under any such order of the Board of Agriculture, or exempt the slaughter-houses or knackers' yards to which this Act relates or any building or thing whatsoever or any body or person from the provisions of any general Act relating to animals already passed or to be passed in this or any future session of Parliament.

Saving for Acts relating to animals, &c.

PART VI.—WATER AND GAS.

70. It shall be lawful for the Board from time to time to make byelaws for the testing and stamping of water fittings, and for requiring any person employed in or about the erection, alteration, or repair of any water pipes or fittings to give notice thereof to the Board as soon as practicable, specifying also the premises affected by such work:

Byelaws for testing and stamping water fittings.

No byelaws made under this section shall have any retrospective operation with regard to work done prior to such byelaws coming into force:

Sec. 71—73

Provided that any such byelaws shall apply only in the case of premises to which the Board are bound to afford and do in fact afford or are prepared to afford a constant supply of water:

The provisions of this section shall be in addition to and not in derogation of any other powers relating to the matters aforesaid vested in the Board.

[*Vide* The Wallasey Improvement Act, 1867, s. 15.]

Forging stamps or marks.

71. If any person forges or counterfeits any stamp or mark used by the Board or by authority of the Board, for any of the purposes of this Act, or uses, or supplies anything marked with any such stamp or mark which he knows to be forged or counterfeited or abets the commission of any offence against this section he shall be liable on summary conviction to a fine not exceeding twenty pounds.

Rate payable by owner for small houses.

72. Where a house supplied with water is let to monthly or weekly tenants or tenants holding for any other period less than a quarter of a year the owner instead of the occupier shall pay the rate for the supply, but the rate may be recovered in the first instance from the occupier and may be deducted by him from any rent from time to time due from him to the owner.

[Power to compound for water rents with owners of houses not exceeding £13 annual value.—*Vide* The Wallasey Improvement Act, 1867, s. 18.]

Power to supply gas or water to local authorities and others.

73.—(1.) It shall be lawful for the Board to supply gas or water by agreement to any local or sanitary authority, company or person beyond the district, on such terms and conditions in all respects and for such periods as the Board and such local or sanitary authority company or person may from time to time agree, but no such supply shall be furnished to any company or person except with the consent in writing of the sanitary authority in whose district the premises of such company or person are situate, which consent may be determinable by a six months' notice in writing. Provided that in regard to the supply of water under this section no such supply shall interfere with the Board giving a proper supply for all purposes to persons within their district.

(2.) For the purposes of affording a supply of gas or water under this section the Board may exercise the powers of the Gasworks Clauses Act, 1847, or the Waterworks Clauses Act, 1847 (as the case may be) with respect to the breaking up of streets for the purpose of laying pipes within the district of any sanitary authority immediately adjacent to the district. Provided that no such power shall be exercised without the consent in writing of the road authority and of the sanitary authority and subject to any conditions as to affording or discontinuing the supply of gas or water as such sanitary authority may impose.

(3.) At any time after the laying down of any gas or water mains, pipes or apparatus under this section the Board shall if required by the sanitary authority of the district within which such mains, pipes or apparatus are situate sell to that authority all such gas mains, pipes and apparatus, or water mains, pipes and apparatus at such price and on such terms and conditions as may be settled by agreement between the Board and the sanitary authority, or failing agreement as may be determined by an arbitrator to be appointed for that purpose by the Local Government Board on the application of either party, and from and after such sale the powers of the Board to supply gas or water (as the case may be) under this section shall in regard to the district to which such sale relates cease and the purposes of this sub-section shall be deemed to be purposes of the Public Health Acts.

Sec. 74—77

PART VII.—MISCELLANEOUS PROVISIONS.

74. Section 27 (persons may be prevented from using ferry on refusal to pay toll) of the Act of 1867 shall extend and apply to persons refusing to produce on demand their contract or season tickets.

Section 27 of Act of 1867 extended to persons refusing to produce their contract tickets.

[*Vide* also The Wallasey Improvement Act, 1858, s. 46
„ „ „ 1867, ss. 26 and 27
„ „ „ 1872, s. 15.]

75. If any of the events mentioned in sub-sections 1, 2, 3, and 4 of section 54 of the Merchant Shipping Act Amendment Act, 1862, shall occur in relation to any passenger ferry steamer of the Board whilst plying to or from any of their ferries at Seacombe and Liverpool during fog such event shall for the purposes of that section or any statutory modification thereof for the time being in force so far only as regards the plying of any such passenger ferry steamers during fog be deemed to have occurred without the actual fault or privity of the Board.

Passenger ferry steamers plying during fog.

[The Merchant Shipping Act Amendment Act, 1862, was repealed by the Merchant Shipping Act, 1894, sec. 54 of the earlier statute provided for the limitation of the shipowner's liability in certain events and the corresponding enactment in the later statute is s. 503 (57 and 58 Vict. c. 60).]

76. The Cheshire justices of the peace for the petty sessional division of Wirral shall have jurisdiction over the ferry boats of the Board and over all persons on board of or embarking or disembarking on or from any such ferry boats in respect of any offence committed against any local Act or byelaw of the Board notwithstanding that the offence charged may have been committed in the River Mersey:

Cheshire justices to have jurisdiction in respect of offences in river.

Provided that nothing herein contained shall in any way prejudice or affect the jurisdiction of the stipendiary magistrate or justices of the peace or of the police of the city of Liverpool or the borough of Bootle or of the justices of the peace or police of the counties of Lancaster and Cheshire or either of them.

77. With respect to slaughter-houses the following provisions shall have effect:—

Further powers as to slaughter-houses.

(1) Licenses granted after the passing of this Act for the use and occupation of places as slaughter-houses or knackers' yards shall be in force for such time or times only as the Board shall think fit to specify in such licenses:

Sec. 78—84

(2) The Board may require any slaughter-house existing at the passing of this Act which by reason of its surroundings or otherwise is a nuisance or prejudicial to health or decency to be discontinued as such on payment to the owner and occupier thereof of such compensation as shall be agreed or as in default of agreement shall be determined by arbitration in manner provided by the Public Health Acts.

Power to close pleasure grounds, &c., on special occasions, &c.

78. The Board may on any special occasion but not exceeding twelve days in any one year nor more than four consecutive days on any one occasion close any public park garden pleasure ground or recreation ground against the public and may on such occasions admit thereto the members of any society or of any public or private institution or persons being attendants at or supported by any public or private institution or such other persons as the Board may think fit and the admission of every individual to any such park garden or ground on such occasions may be either with or without payment as directed by the Board. Provided that the powers conferred by this section shall only be exercised in respect of one park garden pleasure ground or recreation ground at the same time.

Byelaws.

79. The Board may from time to time make byelaws for all or any of the following purposes (that is to say):—

For the preservation of order and good conduct among persons frequenting the promenades and foreshore:

For regulating the erection of hoardings the exhibition thereon of advertisements and the maintenance repair and removal of such hoardings.

Expenses of execution of Act.

80. Any expenses of the execution by the Board of this Act with respect to which no other provision is made may be defrayed by the Board out of the district fund and general district rate.

As to appeal.

81. Any person deeming himself aggrieved by any order, judgment, determination or requirement or the withholding of any order certificate, consent or approval of or by the Board or of or by any officer of the Board or by any conviction or order made by a court of summary jurisdiction under any provision of this Act may appeal to the next practicable court of quarter sessions under and according to the provisions of the Summary Jurisdiction Acts.

Penalties.

82. Every person offending against any of the provisions of Parts III. and V. of this Act shall except as otherwise provided be liable to a penalty not exceeding five pounds for every such offence and to a daily penalty not exceeding forty shillings.

Recovery of penalties, &c.

83. Offences against this Act and penalties, forfeitures, costs and expenses imposed or recoverable under this Act or any byelaw made in pursuance thereof may be prosecuted and recovered in a summary manner.

Authentication and service of notices.

84. Any notice or other such document under this Act may be in writing or print or partly in writing and partly in print and if the same require authentication by the Board the signature of the clerk or other duly authorised officer of the Board shall be sufficient authentication. Notices, orders and any other documents required or authorised to be served under this Act may be served in the same manner as notices under the Public Health Act are by section 267 of that Act authorised to be served, provided always that in the case of any company any such notice or document shall be delivered or sent by post addressed to the secretary of the company at their principal office or place of business.

Sec. 85—91

85. All the provisions with respect to byelaws contained in sections 182 to 186 (both included) of the Public Health Act, 1875 (except so much thereof as relates to byelaws of a rural sanitary authority) shall apply to all byelaws from time to time made by the Board under the powers of this Act.

General provisions as to byelaws.

[Sections 182 to 186 of the Public Health Act, 1875 relate to the authentication, alteration and repeal of byelaws, power to impose penalties for breach thereof; confirmation, printing and evidence of the same.]

86. Nothing contained in this Act or in any byelaw made thereunder shall extend to take away prejudice diminish or alter any of the estates, rights, privileges, powers or authorities vested in or exerciseable by the Queen's Majesty Her heirs or successors.

Saving rights of the Crown.

87. Nothing contained in this Act shall authorise the Board to take, use, or in any manner interfere with any portion of the shore or bed of the sea, or of any river, channel, creek, bay, or estuary, or any right in respect thereof belonging to the Queen's most Excellent Majesty in right of Her Crown, and under the management of the Board of Trade without the previous consent in writing of the Board of Trade on behalf of Her Majesty (which consent the Board of Trade may give), neither shall anything in this Act contained extend to take away prejudice, diminish, or alter any of the estates, rights, privileges, powers, or authorities vested in or enjoyed, or exerciseable by the Queen's Majesty, Her heirs, or successors.

Saving rights of the Crown in the foreshore.

88. Nothing in this Act shall be deemed or taken to prejudice, or affect any question which may hereafter arise between Robert Charles De Grey Vyner and the Board in respect of any right, estate, or interest which he may claim to or in any part or parts of the open land and foreshore.

Saving in favour of R. C. De Grey Vyner.

89. Provided always that nothing in this Act contained shall be deemed to extend or apply to any part of the estate for the time being of the Mersey Docks and Harbour Board within the district, or to any works or buildings (except dwelling-houses), now or hereafter to be executed, constructed, or carried out on the said estate, and used or intended to be used for, or in connexion with the business or purposes of the Mersey Docks and Harbour Board under any power vested in them, or prejudice, or affect any of the rights, powers, or privileges of that Board.

Saving for Mersey Docks and Harbour Board.

90. Nothing in this Act or in any byelaw made under this Act contained shall in any way prejudice, affect, or alter any of the rights or powers of the Commissioners for the conservancy of the River Mersey.

Saving for Mersey Commissioners.

91. All the costs, charges, and expenses preliminary to and of, and incidental to the preparing, applying for, obtaining, and passing

Costs of Act.

Schedule. of this Act as taxed by the taxing officer of the House of Lords, or of the House of Commons shall be paid by the Board out of the district fund and general district rate, or out of moneys to be borrowed on the security of that fund and rate, and which moneys the Board are hereby authorised to borrow and required to repay in accordance with the provisions of the Public Health Acts.

THE SCHEDULE.

Private Street Works.

PART I.

Particulars to be stated in Specifications, Plans and Sections, Estimates and Provisional Apportionments.

Specifications.—These shall describe generally the works and things to be done, and in the case of structural works shall specify as far as may be the foundation, form, material, and dimensions thereof.

Plans and Sections.—These shall show the constructive character of the works and the connexions (if any), with existing streets, sewers, or other works, and the lines and levels of the works, subject to such limits of deviation (if any), as shall be indicated on the plans and sections respectively.

Estimates.—These shall show the particulars of the probable cost of the whole works including the commission provided for by this Act.

Provisional Apportionments.—These shall state the amounts charged on the respective premises, and the names of the respective owners or reputed owners, and shall also state whether the apportionment is made according to the frontage of the respective premises or not, and the measurements of the frontages and the other considerations (if any), on which the apportionment is based.

PART II.

Publication of Notice.

Any resolution, notice, or other document required by this Act to be published in the manner prescribed by this schedule shall be published once in each of two successive weeks in some local newspaper circulating within the district, and shall be publicly posted in or near the street to which it relates, once at least in each of three successive weeks.

LOCAL GOVERNMENT BOARD'S
PROVISIONAL ORDERS CONFIRMATION
(No. 12) ACT, 1892.

(*Confirming the Wallasey Order, 1892.*)

AN
ACT
to confirm certain Provisional Orders of the Local Government Board relating to the Urban Sanitary Districts of Bath, Cheltenham, Louth, Nottingham and West Bridgeford, Portsmouth, Salford, and WALLASEY.

28TH JUNE, 1892.

WHEREAS the Local Government Board have made the Provisional Orders set forth in the schedule hereto under the provisions of the Public Health Act, 1875; [*38 & 39 Vict. c. 55.*]

And whereas it is requisite that the said Orders should be confirmed by Parliament, and that the provision herein contained should be enacted with reference to two of such orders:

Be it therefore enacted by the Queen's most Excellent Majesty, by and with the advice and consent of the Lords Spiritual and Temporal, and Commons, in this present Parliament assembled, and by the authority of the same, as follows:

1. The Orders as altered and set out in the schedule hereto shall be and the same are hereby confirmed, and all the provisions thereof shall have full validity and force. [*Orders in schedule confirmed.*]

2. The Sanitary Authorities mentioned in the Orders relating to the Urban Sanitary Districts of Cheltenham and Wallasey shall not, without the consent of the Local Government Board, purchase or acquire, either compulsorily or by agreement, in any city, borough, or other urban sanitary district or in any parish or part of a parish not being within an urban sanitary district, ten or more houses included in the schedules to those Orders hereby confirmed which, [*Special provision as to houses of labouring class in Cheltenham and Wallasey.*]

55 & 56 Vict. *Local Government Board's* **ch. ccxriii**
Provisional Orders Confirmation
(No. 12) Act, 1892.

Sec. 3
after the passing of this Act have been, or on the fifteenth day of December last were, occupied either wholly or partially by persons belonging to the labouring class as tenants or lodgers.

For the purposes of this section the expression "labouring class" includes mechanics, artisans, labourers, and others working for wages, hawkers, costermongers, persons not working for wages but working at some trade or handicraft without employing others, except members of their own family, and persons, other than domestic servants, whose income does not exceed an average of thirty shillings a week and the families of any of such persons who may be residing with them.

Short title
3. This Act may be cited as the Local Government Board's Provisional Orders Confirmation (No. 12) Act, 1892.

[The omitted Orders relate to districts other than Wallasey.]

THE WALLASEY ORDER, 1892.

LOCAL GOVERNMENT DISTRICT OF WALLASEY.

Provisional Order for altering certain Local Acts and Confirming Acts.

[This Order may be cited as The Wallasey Order, 1892.—*Vide* The Wallasey Order, 1896, art. ii.]

To the Wallasey Local Board, being the Sanitary Authority for the Urban Sanitary District of Wallasey, in the County of Chester;

And to all others whom it may concern.

Whereas the Local Government District of Wallasey, in the County of Chester (herein-after referred to as "the District"), is an Urban Sanitary District, of which the Wallasey Local Board (hereinafter referred to as "the Local Board") are the Urban Sanitary Authority;

21 & 22 Vict. c. lxiii.
24 Vict. c. iv.
30 & 31 Vict. c. cxxxii.
40 & 41 Vict. c. ccxxvii.

And whereas the unrepealed provisions of the Wallasey Improvement Act, 1858, the Wallasey Improvement Act, 1861, and the Wallasey Improvement Act, 1867 (which Acts are herein-after together referred to as "the Local Acts," and each of which Acts is herein-after referred to as the Act of the year in which it was passed), as altered by a Provisional Order of the Local Government Board dated the 4th day of June, 1877, and duly confirmed by the Local Government Board's Provisional Orders Confirmation (Caistor Union, &c.) Act, 1877 (which Order and Act are herein-after respectively referred to as "the Order of 1877" and "the Confirming Act of 1877"), and by another Provisional Order of the Local Government Board dated the 22nd day of May, 1883, and duly confirmed by the

Local Government Board's Provisional Orders Confirmation (No. 12) Act, 1892.

Local Government Board's Provisional Orders Confirmation (No. 7) Act, 1883 (which Order and Act are herein-after respectively referred to as "the Order of 1883" and "the Confirming Act of 1883"), and by certain other Local Acts and Provisional Orders which do not affect the subject-matter of this Order, are in force in the District; *46 & 47 Vict. c. cxxxvii.*

And whereas by section 9 of the Act of 1867, the Local Board were empowered, subject to the provisions of that Act, to acquire by agreement for the purposes of their gasworks the lands described in Schedule A. to that Act, but it was provided that the Local Board should not make or store gas on any lands other than the lands which were described in the said Schedule A., or the lands on which they were then authorised to make or store gas, and which were described in Schedule B. to the Act of 1867;

And whereas by Article V. of the Order of 1877 section 9 of the Act of 1867 was altered so as to enable the Local Board to acquire by agreement for the purposes of their gasworks, the land described in the Schedule to that Order, and, subject as therein provided, to make and maintain works for the manufacture, storage, and supply of gas, and to do all such other acts as they might think necessary for manufacturing and storing gas;

And whereas by section 60 of the Act of 1858, section 3 of the Act of 1861, section 30 of the Act of 1867, Article II. of the Order of 1877, and Article I. of the Order of 1883, the Local Board have been empowered to borrow for the purposes of their gas undertaking, sums amounting in the whole to the sum of eighty-five thousand pounds:

Now therefore, We, the Local Government Board, in pursuance of the powers given to Us by sections 297 and 303 of the Public Health Act, 1875, and by any other Statutes in that behalf, do hereby Order that, from and after the date of the Act of Parliament confirming this Order, the following provisions shall take effect, viz.,— *38 & 39 Vict. c. 55.*

Art I. section 9 of the Act of 1867 and the Confirming Act of 1877, so far as it relates to Article V. of the Order of 1877, shall be further altered so as to provide as follows:—

(1.) The Local Board may acquire by agreement the land described in the Schedule hereto.

(2.) The Local Board may, on the land described in the Schedule hereto, if and when the same shall have been acquired by them, construct, alter, enlarge, or, when necessary, remove buildings, apparatus, and works for the manufacture and storage of gas, and of coke, culm, asphaltum, pitch, coal-tar, oil, ammoniacal liquor, and other refuse or residual products arising from the manufacture of gas and any matters producible therefrom, and they may, on the said land, make and store gas.

(3.) The Local Board may, with the consent of the Local Government Board, appropriate part of the said land for electric lighting purposes, or as a site for a refuse destructor, or for any other purpose which the Local Government Board may approve.

Art. II. The Act of 1867 and the Confirming Act of 1877, so far as it relates to the Order of 1877, and the Confirming Act of 1883, so far as it relates to the Order of 1883, shall be altered so as to provide as follows:—

(1.) The Local Board may with the sanction of the Local Government Board, and subject to the provisions of this Order, borrow on the security of the "Wallasey Lighting Account," as mentioned in the Act of 1858, and of the district fund and general district rates of the District, or upon either of such securities, such sum or sums as they may from time to time think necessary for the purposes of their gas undertaking, not exceeding in the whole the sum of *fifty thousand pounds in addition to the said sum of eighty-five thousand pounds.

[*Altered to seventy-two thousand pounds by the Wallasey Order, 1896, Art. 1, and further altered to one hundred and twelve thousand pounds by the Wallasey Order, 1898, art. 1.]

38 & 39 Vict. c. 83.

38 & 39 Vict. c. 55.

(2.) For the purpose of raising money under this Order the provisions of the Local Loans Act, 1875 (including the power of creating debenture stock), shall be available to the Local Board, and sections 236 to 239, both inclusive, of the Public Health Act, 1875, shall apply to all money raised and borrowed under this Order, other than money borrowed under the provisions of the Local Loans Act, 1875.

(3.) The moneys borrowed under subdivision (1) of this Article shall be repaid within the following periods, viz.:—

(a) The moneys borrowed for the purposes of purchasing the land described in the Schedule to this Order within such period, not exceeding fifty years from the date of borrowing, as the Local Board, with the sanction of the Local Government Board, may determine ;

(b) The other moneys borrowed within such period, not exceeding thirty years from the date of borrowing, as the Local Board, with the sanction of the Local Government Board, shall determine ;

and the period so determined and sanctioned in each case shall be deemed to be the prescribed period within the meaning of the Local Loans Act, 1875, and is hereinafter referred to as "The prescribed period."

(4.) The Local Board shall repay the moneys borrowed under this Order, other than money borrowed under the provisions of the Local Loans Act, 1875, either by equal annual instalments of principal, or of principal and interest, or by setting apart in every year as a sinking fund such a sum or sums as will, according to a reasonable calculation for the time being, with accumulations in the way of compound interest, be sufficient, after payment of all expenses, to pay off the moneys so borrowed within the prescribed period.

(5.) The Local Board shall invest any sinking fund so set apart, and the interest on and the sums paid into the fund, in the

55 & 56 *Vict.* *Local Government Board's* ch. ccxviii. 305
Provisional Orders Confirmation
(No. 12) *Act,* 1892.

purchase of Exchequer bills or other Government securities, or in securities in which trustees are by law authorised to invest, or in mortgages, debentures, debenture stock, or other securities issued by any Local Authority, as defined by Section 34 of the Local Loans Act, 1875, other than the Local Board, the Local Board being at liberty from time to time to vary and transpose such investments.

(6.) The Local Board may at any time apply the whole or any part of any such sinking fund in or towards the discharge of the money for the repayment of which the fund is established: provided that the Local Board pay into such fund each year, and accumulate until the whole of the money borrowed is discharged, a sum equivalent to the interest which would have been produced by such sinking fund or the part of such sinking fund so applied, at the rate per cent. on which the annual payments to the sinking fund are based.

(7) The Local Board may re-borrow for the purpose of paying off moneys borrowed under this order, and not paid off by means of any sinking fund set apart for their repayment, or by instalments, or out of the proceeds of the sale or disposition of land, or out of other moneys received on capital account (not being borrowed moneys): provided that all moneys so re-borrowed shall be repaid within the prescribed period; and any moneys from time to time re-borrowed shall be deemed to form the same loan as the money in lieu of which such re-borrowing has been made, and the obligations of the Local Board with respect to the repayment of such moneys shall not be in any way affected by such re-borrowing.

(8,) The clerk to the Local Board shall, within twenty-one days after the twenty-fifth day of March in each year in which any sum is required to be paid as an instalment, or to be appropriated, or to be set apart for a sinking fund, in pursuance of the provisions of this order, or in respect of any money raised thereunder, transmit to the Local Government Board a return in such form as may be prescribed by that Board, and verified by statutory declaration if so required by them, showing for the year next preceding the making of such return, the amounts which have been paid as instalments and the amounts which have been appropriated and the amounts which have been invested or applied for the purpose of such sinking fund, and the description of the securities upon which any investment has been made, and the purposes to which any portion of the sinking fund or investment or of the sums accumulated by way of interest has been applied during the same period, and the total amount (if any) remaining invested at the end of the year: and, in the event of any wilful default in making such return such clerk shall be liable to a penalty not exceeding twenty pounds which shall be paid to the Local Government Board, and shall be recoverable by that Board in the same manner as penalties recoverable under the Public Health Act, 1875, in a summary manner may be recovered by parties aggrieved within the meaning of that Act.

w

(9.) If it appears to the Local Government Board by that return, or otherwise, that the Local Board have failed to pay any instalment required to be paid, or to appropriate any sum required to be appropriated, or to set apart any sum required for any sinking fund, or have applied any portion of the moneys set apart for any sinking fund or of the sums accumulated by way of interest to any purpose other than those authorised, the Local Government Board may, by order, direct that the sum in such order mentioned, not exceeding double the amount in respect of which default has been made, shall be paid by way of instalment, or be appropriated, or be set apart and invested or applied as part of the sinking fund; and any such order shall be enforceable by writ of mandamus to be obtained by the Local Government Board out of the High Court.

(10.) Where the Local Government Board cause local inquiry to be held with reference to any of the purposes of the Local Acts the above-mentioned Provisional Orders or this order, the costs incurred by that Board in relation to such inquiry (including such reasonable sum, not exceeding three guineas a day, as that Board may determine, for the services of any inspector or officer of the Board engaged in such inquiry, and including the expenses of any witness summoned by such inspector or officer) shall be paid by the Local Board, and the Local Government Board may certify the amount of the costs so incurred and any sum so certified and directed by that Board to be paid by the Local Board shall be a debt due to the Crown from the Local Board.

The SCHEDULE above referred to.

All that piece of land situate in the Township of Poulton-cum-Seacombe, in the Parish of Wallasey, in the County of Chester, containing by admeasurement fifty-seven thousand five hundred and fifty-seven square yards or thereabouts, and bounded on the north by Cinder Lane, on the east by Gorsey Lane, on the south partly by land belonging or reputed to belong to the Midland Railway Company and partly by the existing gasworks of the Local Board, and on the west partly by the said works and partly by land belonging or reputed to belong to Robert Clare de Vyner.

Given under the Seal of Office of the Local Government Board, this Fifth day of May, One thousand eight hundred and ninety-two.

CHAS. T. RITCHIE, President.
HUGH OWEN, Secretary.

Local Government Board's Provisional Orders Confirmation (No. 2) Act, 1894.

(*Confirming the Wallasey Order, 1894.*)

AN ACT

to confirm certain Provisional Orders of the Local Government Board relating to the Urban Sanitary Districts of Accrington, Ashton-under-Lyne, Berwick-upon-Tweed, Bolton, Hexham, Knaresborough, and Tentergate, Llandilo, Merthyr Tydfil, Penrith, Southport, WALLASEY, Widnes, and Workington.

18th JUNE, 1894.

WHEREAS the Local Government Board have made the Provisional Orders set forth in the schedule hereto, under the provisions of the Public Health Act, 1875: [38 & 39 Vict. c. 55.]

And whereas it is requisite that the said Orders should be confirmed by Parliament:

Be it therefore enacted by the Queen's most Excellent Majesty, by and with the advice and consent of the Lords Spiritual and Temporal, and Commons, in this present Parliament assembled, and by the authority of the same, as follows:—

1. The Orders set out in the schedule hereto shall be and the same are hereby confirmed, and all the provisions thereof shall have full validity and force. *Orders in schedule confirmed.*

2. This Act may be cited as the Local Government Board's Provisional Orders Confirmation (No. 2) Act, 1894. *Short title.*

[The omitted Orders relate to Districts other than Wallasey.]

Provisional Orders Confirmation (No. 2) Act, 1894.

THE WALLASEY ORDER, 1894.

LOCAL GOVERNMENT DISTRICT OF WALLASEY.

Provisional Order for partially repealing a Confirming Act.

To the Wallasey Local Board, being the Sanitary Authority for the Urban Sanitary District of Wallasey, in the County of Chester :—

And to all others whom it may concern.

Whereas the Local Government District of Wallasey, in the County of Chester (herein-after referred to as "the District"), is an Urban Sanitary District, of which the Wallasey Local Board (hereinafter referred to as "the Local Board") are the Urban Sanitary Authority.

33 & 34 Vict. c. cxiv.

And whereas by Article 6 of a Provisional Order of one of Her Majesty's Principal Secretaries of State, dated the Ninth day of May, One thousand eight hundred and seventy, and duly confirmed by the Local Government Supplemental Act, 1870 (which Order and Act are herein-after respectively referred to as "the Order" and "the Confirming Act"), it was (inter alia) ordered that the Local Board should be authorised from time to time to borrow for permanent works to the amount of twice the assessable value of the premises assessable under the Local Government Act, 1858, in the District; and it was provided that all sums so borrowed should be borrowed with the sanction of one of Her Majesty's Principal Secretaries of State, and should be repaid, with interest thereon, within a period of fifty years from the borrowing thereof :

38 & 39 Vict. c. lv.

Now therefore, We, the Local Government Board, in pursuance of the powers given to Us by section 297 of the Public Health Act, 1875, and by any other Statutes in that behalf, do hereby Order that, from and after the date of the Act of Parliament confirming this Order, the following provisions shall have effect ; viz.,—

Art. I. So much of the Confirming Act as relates to the above-recited provisions of Article 6 of the Order shall be repealed, except so far as it may have been acted upon, so that the said part of the Order shall, except as aforesaid, cease to have any effect :

Provided that nothing herein contained shall be deemed to alter or affect the repayment of any money borrowed in pursuance of the said Article.

Art. II. This Order may be cited as the Wallasey Order, 1894.

Given under the Seal of Office of the Local Government Board, this Twenty-second day of January, One thousand eight hundred and ninety-four.

HENRY H. FOWLER, President.
HUGH OWEN, Secretary.

Local Government Board's Provisional Orders Confirmation (No. 1) Act, 1895.

(Confirming the Wallasey Order, 1895.)

AN ACT

to confirm certain Provisional Orders of the Local Government Board relating to Battle, Dorchester, Eton, Fareham, Ilfracombe, Leicester, Ryde, Sandgate, Southampton, Torquay, Ulverston, WALLASEY, West Cowes, and Wilton.

20TH JUNE, 1895.

WHEREAS the Local Government Board have made the Provisional Orders set forth in the schedule hereto under the provisions of the Public Health Act, 1875: [38 & 39 Vict. c. 55.]

And whereas it is requisite that the said Orders should be confirmed by Parliament:

Be it therefore enacted by the Queen's most Excellent Majesty, by and with the advice and consent of the Lords Spiritual and Temporal and Commons in this present Parliament assembled, and by the authority of the same, as follows:—

1. The Orders as altered and set out in the schedule hereto shall be and the same are hereby confirmed, and all the provisions thereof shall have full validity and force. *Orders in schedule confirmed.*

2. This Act may be cited as the Local Government Board's Provisional Orders Confirmation (No. 1) Act, 1895. *Short title.*

[The omitted Orders have relation to districts other than Wallasey.]

58 & 59 Vict. *Local Government Board's Provisional Orders Confirmation (No. 1) Act*, 1895.

THE WALLASEY ORDER, 1895.

URBAN DISTRICT OF WALLASEY.

Provisional Order for altering a Confirming Act.

To the Urban District Council of Wallasey;—

And to all others whom it may concern.

Whereas the Urban District Council of Wallasey (hereinafter referred to as "the Urban District Council") are the Local Authority within the meaning of the Public Health Act, 1875, for the Urban District of Wallasey (hereinafter referred to as "the District"), and the unrepealed provisions of the Wallasey Improvement Act, 1872 (hereinafter referred to as "the Local Act"), as altered by the Provisional Orders hereinafter mentioned are in force in the District;

[35 & 36 Vict. c. cxxv.]

And whereas by Section 17 of the Local Act, the Wallasey Local Board (hereinafter referred to as "the Local Board,") were empowered to borrow for ferry purposes sums not exceeding in the whole seventy-four thousand pounds in addition to the sums already authorised for those purposes;

And whereas by Article III. of a Provisional Order of the Local Government Board, dated the Fourth day of June, One thousand eight hundred and seventy-seven, and confirmed by the Local Government Board's Provisional Orders Confirmation (Caistor Union, &c.) Act, 1877 (which Order and Act are respectively hereinafter referred to as "the Order of 1877" and "the Confirming Act of 1877"), and by Article I. of another Provisional Order of the Local Government Board, dated the Seventh day of May, One thousand eight hundred and eighty-one, and confirmed by the Local Government Board's Provisional Orders Confirmation (Acton, &c.) Act, 1881 (which Order and Act are hereinafter respectively referred to as "the Order of 1881" and "the Confirming Act of 1881"), the Local Board were for the like purposes empowered to borrow additional sums not exceeding in the whole the respective sums of one hundred and two thousand five hundred pounds and twenty-two thousand pounds;

[40 & 41 Vict. c. ccxxvii.]

[44 & 45 Vict. c. clxii.]

And whereas by Article II. of another Provisional Order of the Local Government Board, dated the Twenty-second day of May, One thousand eight hundred and eighty-three, and duly confirmed by the Local Government Board's Provisional Orders Confirmation (No. 7) Act, 1883 (which Order and Act are hereinafter respectively referred to as "the Order of 1883" and "the Confirming Act of 1883"), the Confirming Act of 1877 so far as it confirms Article III. of the Order of 1877, and the Confirming Act of 1881 so far as it confirms Article I. of the Order of 1881, were altered and amended, and Section 17 of the Act of 1872 was further altered and amended so as to provide as follows :—

[46 & 47 Vict. c. cxxxvii.]

"In addition to the sums of seventy-four thousand pounds, one hundred and two thousand five hundred pounds, and twenty-two thousand pounds, which the Local Board were empowered to borrow under Section 17 of the Act of 1872 as amended by the Confirming Act of 1877 and the Confirming Act of 1881, the Local Board may, subject to the sanction of the Local Government Board, borrow from time to time on mortgage of the securities mentioned in the said section, any sum or sums not exceeding in the whole the sum of thirty thousand pounds, to be applied towards the payment of the cost of providing new steamboats for the ferries for the time being belonging to or leased by the Local Board :"

Now therefore, We, the Local Government Board, in pursuance of the powers given to Us by Section 297 of the Public Health Act, 1875, and by any other Statutes in that behalf, do hereby order that from and after the date of the Act of Parliament confirming this Order, the following provisions shall take effect, viz. :— 38 & 39 Vict. c. 55.

Art. 1. The Confirming Act of 1883 shall be altered by the insertion in Article II. of the Order of 1883 of the words "fifty-five thousand pounds" in lieu of the words "thirty thousand pounds :"

Provided that any money borrowed under the additional powers of borrowing conferred by this Order shall be repaid within such period, not exceeding twenty years from the date of borrowing, as the Local Government Board may, by their sanction, determine.

[By Art. I. of the Wallasey Order, 1897, power is given to borrow a further sum of £10,600 for the purposes of a dredger in connection with the ferry undertaking.]

Art. II. This Order may be cited as the Wallasey Order, 1895.

Given under the Seal of Office of the Local Government Board, this Sixth day of March, One thousand eight hundred and ninety-five.

(L.S.)

G. SHAW-LEFEVRE, President.

S. B. PROVIS, Assistant Secretary.

Sec. 1—2

LOCAL GOVERNMENT BOARD'S PROVISIONAL ORDERS CONFIRMATION (No. 4) ACT, 1896.

(*Confirming the Wallasey Order, 1896.*)

AN

ACT

to confirm certain Provisional Orders of the Local Government Board relating to Clitheroe, Goole, Halifax, Llandudno, Plymouth, Stratford-upon-Avon, Swansea and Wallasey.

21st MAY, 1896.

38 & 39 Vict. c. lv.

WHEREAS the Local Government Board have made the Provisional Orders set forth in the schedule hereto, under the provisions of the Public Health Act, 1875:

And whereas it is requisite that the said Orders should be confirmed by Parliament:

Be it therefore enacted by the Queen's most Excellent Majesty by and with the advice and consent of the Lords Spiritual and Temporal and Commons in this present Parliament assembled and by the authority of the same as follows:—

Orders in schedule confirmed.

1. The Orders set out in the schedule hereto shall be and the same are hereby confirmed and all the provisions thereof shall have full validity and force.

Short title.

2. This Act may be cited as the Local Government Board's Provisional Orders Confirmation (No. 4) Act, 1896.

[The omitted Orders have relation to districts other than Wallasey.]

THE WALLASEY ORDER, 1896.

URBAN DISTRICT OF WALLASEY.

Provisional Order for altering a Confirming Act.

To the Urban District Council of Wallasey; —

And to all others whom it may concern.

Whereas the Urban District Council of Wallasey (herein-after referred to as "the District Council") are the Local Authority within the meaning of the Public Health Act, 1875, for the Urban District of Wallasey (herein-after referred to as "the District");

And whereas the unrepealed provisions of the Wallasey Improvement Act, 1858, the Wallasey Improvement Act, 1861, and the Wallasey Improvement Act, 1867 (which Acts are herein-after together referred to as "the Local Acts," and each of which Acts is herein-after referred to as the Act of the year in which it was passed) as altered by a Provisional Order of the Local Government Board, dated the Fourth day of June, One thousand eight hundred and seventy-seven, and duly confirmed by the Local Government Board's Provisional Orders Confirmation (Caistor Union, &c.) Act, 1877, (which Order and Act are herein-after respectively referred to as "the Order of 1877" and "the Confirming Act of 1877,") by another Provisional Order of the Local Government Board dated the Twenty-second day of May, One thousand eight hundred and eighty-three, and duly confirmed by the Local Government Board's Provisional Orders Confirmation (No. 7) Act, 1883 (which Order and Act are herein-after respectively referred to as "the Order of 1883" and "the Confirming Act of 1883"), and by another Provisional Order of the Local Government Board dated the Fifth day of May, One thousand eight hundred and ninety-two, and confirmed by the Local Government Board's Provisional Orders Confirmation (No. 12) Act, 1892 (which Order and Act are herein-after respectively referred to as "the Order of 1892" and "the Confirming Act of 1892") and by certain other Local Acts and Provisional Orders which do not affect the subject-matter of this Order, are in force in the District;

21 & 22 Vict. c. lxiii.
24 Vict. c. lv.
30 & 31 Vict. c. cxxxii.

40 & 41 Vict. c. ccxxvii.

46 & 47 Vict. c. cxxxvii.

55 & 56 Vict. c. ccxxiii.

And whereas by section 60 of the Act of 1858, section 3 of the Act of 1861, section 30 of the Act of 1867, Article II. of the Order of 1877, and Article I. of the Order of 1883, the Wallasey Local Board were empowered to borrow for the purposes of their gas undertaking, sums amounting in the whole to the sum of eighty-five thousand pounds;

And whereas by subdivision (1) of Article II. of the Order of 1892, the Act of 1867, and the Confirming Acts of 1877 and 1883, so far as they respectively related to the Orders of 1877 and 1883, were

Local Government Board's Provisional Orders Confirmation (No. 4) Act, 1896.

altered so as to enable the Local Board with the sanction of the Local Government Board and subject to the provisions of the Order of 1892 to borrow on the security of the "Wallasey Lighting Account" as mentioned in the Act of 1858, and of the district fund and general district rates of the District or upon either of such securities such sum or sums as they might from time to time think necessary for the purposes of their gas undertaking not exceeding in the whole the sum of fifty thousand pounds in addition to the said sum of eighty-five thousand pounds:

38 & 39 Vict. c. 55.

Now therefore We, the Local Government Board, in pursuance of the powers given to Us by section 297 of the Public Health Act, 1875, and by any other Statutes in that behalf do hereby order that from and after the date of the Act of Parliament confirming this Order the following provisions shall take effect:—

Art. I. The Confirming Act of 1892 shall be altered by the insertion in subdivision (1) of Article II. of the Order of 1892 of the words "seventy-two thousand pounds" in lieu of the words "fifty thousand pounds."

[Further altered to "one hundred and twelve thousand pounds" by the Wallasey Order, 1898, Art. I.]

Art. II. Each of the Provisional Orders relating to Wallasey the dates whereof are mentioned in column 1 of the Schedule hereto, may be cited by the short title mentioned in column 2 of that Schedule, this Order may be cited as the Wallasey Order, 1896, and all of the said Orders and the Wallasey Order, 1894, may be cited together as the Wallasey Orders, 1852 to 1896.

The SCHEDULE above referred to.

Date of Order.	Short Title of Order.
9th November, 1852	The Wallasey Order, 1852.
9th May, 1870	The Wallasey Order, 1870.
4th June, 1877	The Wallasey Order (No. 1), 1877
5th June, 1877	The Wallasey Order (No. 2), 1877.
22nd January, 1878	The Wallasey Order, 1878.
7th May, 1881	The Wallasey Order, 1881.
22nd May, 1883	The Wallasey Order, 1883.
30th April, 1888	The Wallasey Order, 1888.
5th May, 1892	The Wallasey Order, 1892.

Given under the Seal of Office of the Local Government Board this Nineteenth day of February, One thousand eight hundred and ninety-six.

(L.S.)

HENRY CHAPLIN, President.

HUGH OWEN, Secretary.

THE
Wallasey Urban District Council
(Promenade) Act, 1896.

(59 & 60 Vict. ch. ccix.)

ARRANGEMENT OF SECTIONS.

	SECTION.
Preamble	
Short title	1
Incorporation of Lands Clauses Acts	2
Interpretation	3
Execution of Act	4
Power to take lands shown on deposited Plans	5
Correction of errors, &c., in deposited Plans, and book of reference	6
Owners required to sell parts only of lands	7
Period for compulsory purchase of lands	8
Purchase of additional lands by agreement	9
Restriction on taking houses of labouring class	10
Power to grant easements, &c.	11
Power to Council to sell lands	12
Power to construct promenade	13
Power to deviate	14
Period for completion of works	15
Power to make subsidiary works	16
Alteration of position of mains and pipes	17
Promenade to be a public highway, and repairable as such	18
Bye-laws for regulating promenade	19
Power to erect shelters, &c., on promenade	20
Provisions as to laying out, &c., of open lands	21
Matters to be taken into account by arbitrators	22
Power to borrow	23
Mode of raising money	24
Certain regulations of Public Health Act not to apply	25
Application of provisions of Public Health Act as to mortgages	26
Periods for discharge of loans	27

	SECTION.
Mode of repayment of money borrowed on mortgage	28
Regulations as to sinking fund	29
Saving for existing charges	30
Council not to regard trusts	31
Appointment of Receiver	32
Power to re-borrow	33
Annual return to Local Government Board	34
Proceeds of sale of surplus lands to be treated as capital	35
Application of money borrowed	36
Protection of lender from inquiry	37
Inquiries by Local Government Board	38
Expenses of execution of Act	39
Audit of Accounts	40
As to lands of the devisees of Charles Holland	41
As to lands of Edgar Swinton Holland	42
As to lands of Philip Michael Vaughan	43
For protection of the Rock Point Estate	44
For protection of the Mersey Conservancy Commissioners	45
Saving rights of Her Majesty's Principal Secretary of State for the War Department	46
Saving rights of the Crown	47
Costs of Act	48

AN ACT

to authorise the Wallasey Urban District Council to construct a Promenade and other Works to acquire certain Lands and for other purposes.

7th August, 1896.

WHEREAS the urban district of Wallasey in the county of Chester (in this Act called the district) is under the government of the Wallasey Urban District Council (in this Act called the Council) :

> [By virtue of the Local Government Act, 1894, Urban Sanitary Authorities became "Urban District Councils" (56 and 57 Vict. c. 73, sec. 21).]

And whereas the Council (under their former name of the Wallasey Local Board) constructed a promenade along part of the shore of the estuary of the River Mersey on the east side of the district :

And whereas there is certain unenclosed ground adjoining or abutting on the foreshore of the estuary of the River Mersey between the northern end of the said promenade and New Brighton Pier and public rights of way or rights of user are claimed to exist over the said ground but the owners of the lands adjoining or abutting on such ground claim to be the absolute owners thereof :

And whereas the construction of a promenade in extension of the existing promenade to New Brighton Pier and the laying out or planting in ornamental manner of the part of the said unenclosed ground situate on the landward side of such extended promenade would be a great improvement to the district and would greatly increase the value of the lands abutting on the said ground and it is expedient that the Council should be authorised to construct the said extension of the said existing promenade and to acquire the said ground accordingly for the purposes aforesaid and that all public or other rights over the said ground save as by this Act provided should be extinguished :

And whereas it is expedient that the borrowing powers of the Council be extended :

And whereas an estimate has been prepared by the Council for the purchase of land and the execution of the works by this Act authorised and for other the purposes of this Act and such estimate amounts to fifty thousand pounds :

And whereas the works included in such estimate are permanent works within the meaning of section 234 of the Public Health Act, 1875 :

And whereas a plan and sections showing the lines and levels of the works authorised by this Act and the lands and property to be taken under the powers thereof and a book of reference containing the names of the owners and lessees or reputed owners and lessees and of the occupiers of all such lands were duly deposited with the clerk of the peace for the county of Chester and are herein-after respectively referred to as the deposited plan sections and book of reference :

And whereas the purposes of this Act cannot be effected without the authority of Parliament :

And whereas an absolute majority of the whole number of the Council at a meeting held on the first day of August one thousand eight hundred and ninety-five after ten clear days' notice by public advertisement of the meeting and of the purpose thereof in the Wallasey and Wirral Chronicle a local newspaper published and circulating in the district such notice being in addition to the ordinary notices required for summoning that meeting resolved that the expense in relation to promoting the Bill for this Act should be charged on the district fund and general district rate :

And whereas that resolution was published twice in the said Wallasey and Wirral Chronicle and has received the approval of the Local Government Board :

And whereas the propriety of the promotion of the Bill for this Act was confirmed by an absolute majority of the whole number of the Council at a further special meeting held in pursuance of a similar notice on the second day of January one thousand eight hundred and ninety-six being not less than fourteen days after the deposit of the Bill for this Act in the Offices of the Houses of Parliament :

And whereas the owners and ratepayers of the district by resolution passed in the manner prescribed by the Public Health Act, 1875 (Schedule III.) have consented to the promotion of the Bill for this Act :

May it therefore please Your Majesty that it may be enacted and be it enacted by the Queen's most Excellent Majesty by and with the advice and consent of the Lords Spiritual and Temporal and Commons in this present Parliament assembled and by the authority of the same as follows (that is to say) :—

Short title.

1. This Act may be cited as the Wallasey Urban District Council (Promenade) Act, 1896.

Incorporation of Lands Clauses Acts.

2. The Lands Clauses Acts so far as the same are applicable for the purposes of, and are not varied by or inconsistent with this Act are incorporated with, and form part of this Act.

Interpretation.

3. In this Act the words and expressions following shall have the several meanings hereby assigned to them, unless there be something in the subject or context repugnant to such construction (that is to say) :—

"The Council" means the Wallasey Urban District Council;

"The district" means the district of the Council;

"The clerk" means the clerk of the Council;

"The district fund" and "general district rate" mean the district fund and general district rate of the district;

"The open lands" means the unfenced ground adjoining or abutting on the foreshore between the termination of the existing promenade and the New Brighton Pier, which the Council are authorised to acquire under the powers of this Act;

"The enclosed lands" means the lands adjoining or abutting on the western side of the open lands, or on the foreshore between the points aforesaid;

"The frontagers" means the owners, lessees, and occupiers of the enclosed lands:

For the purposes of this Act in the Acts incorporated with this Act the expression "superior courts" or "court of competent jurisdiction" shall have effect, as if the debt or demand with respect to which it is used were a simple contract debt, and not a debt or demand created by statute.

4. This Act shall be carried into execution by the Council. *Execution of Act.*

5. Subject to the provisions of this Act the Council may enter upon, take and use such of the lands shown on the deposited plan and described in the deposited book of reference as may be required for any of the purposes of this Act. *Power to take lands shown on deposited plan.*

6. If any omission or misstatement or erroneous description is found to have been made of any lands or of any owners, lessees, or occupiers of any lands shown or described or intended to be shown or described on the deposited plan, or in the deposited book of reference, the Council may apply to two justices for the correction thereof after giving ten days' notice to the owners, lessees, and occupiers of the lands affected by the proposed correction, and if it appears to the justices that the omission, misstatement, or erroneous description arose from mistake they shall certify the same accordingly, stating the particulars of the omission, misstatement, or erroneous description, and such certificate shall be deposited with the clerk of the peace for the county of Chester, and shall be kept by him with the other documents to which it relates, and subject, and according to the same enactments and provisions as apply to those other documents, and thereupon the deposited plan, or book of reference (as the case requires), shall be deemed to be corrected according to the certificate, and the Council may enter on, take hold, and use those lands accordingly. *Correction of errors, &c., in deposited plans and book of reference.*

7. And whereas in the construction of the works hereby authorised, or otherwise in the exercise of the powers of this Act, it may happen that portions only of the lands, houses, or other buildings shown on the deposited plan may be sufficient for the purposes of the same, and that such portions may be severed from the remainder of the said properties without material detriment thereto. Therefore, notwithstanding section ninety-two of the Lands Clauses Consolidation Act, 1845, the owners of, and other persons interested *Owners required to sell parts only of lands.*

Sec. 8—12 in the lands, houses, or other buildings numbered respectively three and four on the deposited plan, whereof portions only are required for the purposes of this Act, may if such portions can in the opinion of the arbitrators, jury, or other authority to whom the question of disputed compensation shall be submitted be severed from the remainder of such properties without material detriment thereto, be required to sell and convey to the Council the portions only of the premises so required, without the Council being obliged or compellable to purchase the whole or any greater portion thereof, the Council paying for the portions required by them, and making compensation for any damage sustained by the owners thereof, and other parties interested therein by severance or otherwise.

Period for compulsory purchase of lands.

8. The powers of the Council for the compulsory purchase of lands for the purposes of this Act shall cease after the expiration of three years from the passing of this Act.

Purchase of additional lands by agreement.

9. The Council may from time to time for the purposes of this Act purchase by agreement any lands not exceeding twenty acres in addition to the lands which they are authorised to take by compulsion, but the Council shall not create, or permit the creation or continuance of any nuisance on any lands purchased under the provisions of this section.

Restriction on taking houses of labouring class.

10.—(1) The Council shall not under the powers of this Act purchase or acquire ten or more houses, which on the fifteenth day of December last were occupied either wholly or partially by persons belonging to the labouring class as tenants or lodgers or, except with the consent of the Local Government Board, ten or more houses which were not so occupied on the said fifteenth day of December, but have been or shall be subsequently so occupied.

(2) For the purpose of this section the expression "labouring class" means and includes mechanics, artisans, labourers, and others working for wages, hawkers, costermongers, persons not working for wages, but working at some trade or handicraft without employing others except members of their own family, and persons, other than domestic servants, whose income does not exceed an average of thirty shillings a week, and the families of any such persons who may be residing with them.

Power to grant easements, &c.

11. Persons empowered by the Lands Clauses Acts to sell and convey or release lands, may if they think fit, subject to the provisions of those Acts and of this Act, grant to the Council any easement, right or privilege (not being an easement, right or privilege of water, in which others than parties to the agreement have an interest) required for the purposes of this Act in over or affecting any such lands, and the provisions of the Lands Clauses Acts with respect to lands and rentcharges, so far as the same are applicable in this behalf, shall extend and apply to such grants, easements, rights and privileges as aforesaid.

Power to Council to sell lands.

12. The Council may, from time to time, sell and dispose of any lands acquired by them under this Act (other than the open lands) and not for the time being required for the purposes thereof.

59 & 60 Vict.   The *Wallasey Urban*   ch. ccix.
              District Council (Promenade) Act, 1896.

Sec. 13—19

13. Subject to the provisions of this Act, the Council may make and maintain in the Parish of Wallasey, in the county of Chester, in the line and according to the levels shown on the deposited plan and sections, a promenade and embankment or river wall (in this Act called the promenade) commencing at or near to the northern termination of the existing promenade, and terminating at or near to the New Brighton Pier, together with all such footways, carriage-ways, approaches, landing places, slipways, steps, sewers, drains, works and conveniences, as may be necessary or convenient.

Power to construct promenade.

14. In constructing the promenade by this Act authorised, the Council may, subject to the provisions of this Act, deviate from the line thereof as shown on the deposited plan to any extent not exceeding the limits of deviation shown on that plan, and they may deviate from the levels thereof as shown on the deposited sections to any extent not exceeding one foot upwards and one foot downwards.

Power to deviate.

15. If the works by this Act authorised and shown on the deposited plan and sections, are not completed within five years after the passing of this Act, then on the expiration of that period the powers by this Act granted for the making thereof or otherwise in relation thereto shall cease, except with respect to so much thereof as is then completed.

Period for completion of works.

16. Subject to the provisions of this Act, and within the limits of deviation defined on the deposited plan, the Council in connexion with and for the purposes of the promenade, may make junctions and communications with the existing promenade and any existing streets which may be interfered with by or contiguous to the promenade, and may make diversions, widenings or alterations of the lines or levels of the existing promenade, and of any existing streets for the purpose of connecting the same with the promenade. Provided that the Council shall make to the owners, lessees, and occupiers of and all other parties interested in any lands or houses injuriously affected by any such interference or alteration, compensation for all damage sustained by them or any of them by the exercise of the powers of this section.

Power to make subsidiary works.

17. The Council may for the purposes of, or in connexion with the promenade, and within the limits of deviation raise, sink, or otherwise alter the position of any sewer or drain and gas or water main or pipe, and may remove any other obstruction, making in case of alterations proper substituted works in the meantime, and causing as little detriment and inconvenience as circumstances admit, and making compensation to any person who suffers damage by any such alteration.

Alteration of position of mains and pipes.

18. Subject to the provisions of this Act, the promenade when completed shall be a public highway, and shall be repaired, maintained, lighted, and kept in order in the same way as the highways in the district repairable by the inhabitants at large shall for the time being be by law repaired, maintained, lighted, and kept in order.

Promenade to be a public highway and repairable as such.

19. - (1.) The Council may make bye-laws for the regulation of the promenade for prescribing the nature of traffic for which it may be used, and for the preservation of order and good conduct among persons frequenting the promenade. The bye-laws in force at the

Byelaws for regulating promenade.

x

Sec. 20—21 commencement of this Act relating to the promenade within the district, shall until altered or repealed, or until bye-laws are made under the provisions of this section apply to the promenade.

(2.) The provisions with respect to byelaws contained in sections 182 to 186 of the Public Health Act, 1875 (except so much thereof as relates exclusively to the byelaws of a rural sanitary authority) shall apply to all byelaws from time to time made by the Council under the powers of this Act.

[Secs. 182 to 186 of the Public Health Act, 1875, relate to the authentication and alteration of byelaws; power to impose penalties for breach thereof; confirmation, printing, and evidence of the same.]

Power to erect shelters, &c., on promenade
20. The Council may provide and maintain on the promenade such seats, shelters, steps, stands for bands of music and other conveniences as they may deem expedient.

Provisions as to laying out, &c., of open lands.
21. The following provisions shall apply with respect to the open lands (other than the lands referred to in the sections of this Act whereof the marginal notes are respectively " As to lands of the devisees of Charles Holland " " As to lands of Edgar Swinton Holland " and " As to lands of Philip Michael Vaughan ") lying to the westward of the promenade (that is to say):—

(1.) The Council, when they shall have acquired the said open lands, shall make and maintain, through, along, or across the same such footways, not less than four feet in width as hereinafter mentioned and shall connect the same with the promenade at convenient intervals, so as to give a convenient access to the promenade and thence to the foreshore from the enclosed lands:

(2.) The Council shall before taking any of the said open lands deposit for public inspection at the office of the Council a plan showing the footways which they propose to make under the provisions of this section and shall give notice of such deposit by advertisement in some newspaper published or circulating in the district. Within one month from the date of the publication of such advertisement any frontager may object to the said plan by notice in writing stating the grounds of his objection, and delivered at the office of the Council. If no such objection is made within the period aforesaid or if all such objections are subsequently withdrawn by the persons respectively making the same, the said plans shall thereupon become binding on all parties interested, and the footway shall be made as shown thereon. If any such objection is made within the period aforesaid and not withdrawn the questions in difference shall stand referred to an arbitrator being a practical surveyor, to be appointed for that purpose by the Local Government Board, who shall determine the position of the said footways and any other incidental matters, and his decision shall be binding on all parties, and the footways shall be made in the position determined by him and the reasonable remuneration of such surveyor to be settled in case of difference by the Local Government Board shall be borne as he shall direct:

(3.) The Council may from time to time deposit for public inspection at their office a plan showing any alterations in regard to any footways made or required to be made in pursuance of this section, and may give notice of such deposit by advertisement in some newspaper published or circulating in the district and if no frontager affected by the proposed alteration shall object thereto by notice in writing delivered at the office of the Council within one month from the publication of the notice, or if all such frontagers who shall so object shall withdraw their objections, the Council may make the alteration shown on the said plan :

(4.) The frontagers and their sequels in estate shall at all times be entitled to use the said footways and to have access thereby to the promenade and foreshore :

(5.) The residue of the said open lands not required for the said footways shall be levelled planted and laid out by the Council in an ornamental manner and for ever kept unbuilt on and the Council may, if they think fit, permit the same or any part or parts thereof to be used as public pleasure grounds and the provisions of the Public Health Acts relating to parks and pleasure grounds shall apply accordingly :

(6.) Except as aforesaid all public and private rights of way or other rights over the said open lands shall on the acquisition thereof by the Council be extinguished.

22. In determining any question of disputed compensation under this Act the arbitrators jury or other authority shall take into account the provisions of the last preceding section and any public rights of way or other rights over or on the open lands and any permanent increase in value of the enclosed lands of the person claiming compensation, which, in the opinion of such authority, will result from or be caused by the construction of the promenade and other works by this Act authorised and generally all the other circumstances of the case which it is equitable to consider. *Matters to be taken into account by arbitrators.*

23. The Council may from time to time borrow at interest on the security of the district fund and general district rate and for the following purposes such sums as they see fit, not exceeding the following (that is to say) : — *Power to borrow.*

(1.) For the purchase of land and the execution of the works by this Act authorised and other the purposes of this Act fifty thousand pounds :

(2) For payment of the costs, charges and expenses of this Act as herein-after provided such sums as may be required :

And with the approval of the Local Government Board such further moneys as the Council may require for any of the purposes of this Act.

24. The Council may raise all or any moneys which they are authorised to borrow under this Act by mortgage or by the issue of debentures or annuity certificates under and subject to the provisions of the Local Loans Act, 1875, or by the issue of stock if and when they shall be authorised to issue stock or partly in one way and partly in another or others. *Mode of raising money.*

Sec. 25—29

Certain regulations of Public Health Act not to apply.

25. The powers of borrowing money by this Act given shall not be restricted by any of the regulations contained in section 234 of the Public Health Act, 1875, and in calculating the amount which the Council may borrow under that Act, any sums which they may borrow under this Act shall not be reckoned.

Application of provisions of Public Health Act as to mortgages.

26. The following sections of the Public Health Act, 1875, shall extend and apply to mortgages granted under this Act (that is to say):—

Section 236. Form of mortgage.
Section 237. Register of mortgages.
Section 238. Transfer of mortgages.

Periods for discharge of loans.

27. The Council shall pay off all moneys borrowed by them under this Act within the respective periods (in this Act referred to as the prescribed periods) following (that is to say):—

As to moneys borrowed for the purposes (1) mentioned in the section of this Act the marginal note whereof is "Power to borrow" within the limit there prescribed within fifty years from the date or dates of the borrowing of the same;

As to moneys borrowed for the purpose (2) in the said section mentioned within ten years from the date or dates of the borrowing of the same;

As to moneys borrowed with the approval of the Local Government Board within such period as they may think fit to sanction.

Mode of repayment of money borrowed on mortgage.

28. The Council shall pay off all moneys borrowed by them on mortgage under the powers of this Act either by equal yearly or half-yearly instalments of principal or of principal and interest combined or by means of a sinking fund or partly by one of these methods and partly by another or others of them.

Regulations as to sinking fund.

29. The following provisions shall apply to the repayment by means of a sinking fund of any moneys borrowed by virtue of this Act:—

(1) The sinking fund shall be formed and maintained either—

(*a*) By payment to the fund throughout the prescribed period of such equal annual sums as will together amount to the moneys for the repayment of which the sinking fund is formed. A sinking fund so formed is herein-after called a non-accumulating sinking fund; or

(*b*) By payment to the fund throughout the prescribed period of such annual sums as with accumulations at a rate not exceeding three per centum per annum will be sufficient to pay off within the prescribed period the moneys for the repayment of which such sinking fund is formed. A sinking fund so formed is herein-after called an accumulating sinking fund:

(2) Every sum paid to a sinking fund and in the case of an accumulating sinking fund the interest on the investments of the sinking fund shall unless applied in repayment of the loan in respect of which the sinking fund is formed be immediately

invested in securities in which trustees are by law for the time being authorised to invest or in mortgages, bonds, debentures, debenture stock, stock or other securities (not being annuity certificates or securities payable to bearer) duly issued by any local authority as defined by section 34 of the Local Loans Act, 1875, other than the Council, the Council being at liberty from time to time to vary and transpose such investments:

(3) In the case of a non-accumulating sinking fund the interest on the investments of the fund may be applied by the Council towards the equal annual payments to the fund:

(4) The Council may at any time apply the whole or any part of any sinking fund in or towards the discharge of the money for the repayment of which the fund is formed provided that in case of an accumulating sinking fund the Council shall pay into the fund each year and accumulate during the residue of the prescribed period a sum equal to the interest which would have been produced by such sinking fund or the part of such sinking fund so applied if invested at the rate per centum per annum on which the annual payments to the sinking fund are based:

(5) (a) If and so often as the income of an accumulating sinking fund is not equal to the income which would be derived from the amount invested if the same were invested at the rate per centum per annum on which the annual payments to the fund are based, any deficiency shall be made good by the Council out of the district fund or general district rate:

(b) If and so often as the income of an accumulating sinking fund is in excess of the income which would be derived from the amount invested if the same were invested at the rate per centum per annum on which the equal annual payments to the fund are based, any such excess may be applied towards such equal annual payments:

(6) The provisions of section 15 of the Local Loans Act, 1875, shall not apply to the creation of any sinking fund for the repayment of moneys borrowed by virtue of this Act.

[Sec. 15 of the Local Loans Act, 1875, contains provisions for the discharge of Loan by sinking fund.]

30. Nothing in this Act shall prejudicially affect any charge on the revenue and rates or the estates and property of the Council subsisting at the passing of this Act, and every mortgagee or person for the time being entitled to the benefit of any such charge shall have the same priority of charge and all the like rights and remedies in respect of the revenue rate and property subject to his charge as if this Act had not passed, and all such charges created before the passing of this Act shall, during the subsistence thereof, have priority over any mortgage or charge granted under this Act on the same revenue rate and property. *Saving for existing charges.*

31. The Council shall not be bound to see to the execution of any trust whether expressed or implied or constructive to which any loan or security for loan given by them may be subject, but the receipt of the person in whose name any loan or security for loan stands in the register of mortgages, debentures, annuity, certificates *Council not to regard trusts.*

Sec. 32—34. or stock of the Council shall, from time to time, be sufficient discharge to the Council in respect thereof, notwithstanding any trust to which such loan or security may be subject and whether or not the Council have had express or implied notice of any such trust or of any charge or incumbrance upon or the transfer of such loan or security or any part thereof or interest thereon not entered in their register.

Appointment of receiver.

32.—(1) The mortgagees of the Council by virtue of this Act may enforce the payment of arrears of interest or of principal or of principal and interest by the appointment of a receiver. The amount of arrears to authorise the appointment of a receiver shall not be less than five hundred pounds in the whole.

(2) The application for the appointment of a receiver shall be made to the High Court, and the court if it thinks fit may appoint a receiver on such terms as it thinks fit, and may at any time discharge the receiver and otherwise exercise full jurisdiction over him.

Power to re-borrow.

33. If the Council pay off any moneys borrowed by them under this Act otherwise than by instalments or by means of a sinking fund or out of the proceeds of the sale of land or other property or out of fines or premiums on leases or out of other moneys received on capital account not being borrowed moneys, they may, from time to time, re-borrow the same, but all moneys so re-borrowed shall be repaid within the prescribed period, and shall be deemed to form the same loan as the moneys originally borrowed, and the obligations of the Council with respect to the repayment of the loan and to the provision to be made for such repayment shall not be diminished by reason of such re-borrowing.

Annual return to Local Government Board.

34.—(1) The Clerk shall, within twenty-one days after the thirty-first day of March, in each year during which any sum is required to be paid as an instalment or annual payment or to be appropriated or to be paid to a sinking fund in pursuance of the provisions of this Act, transmit to the Local Government Board a return in such form as may, from time to time, be prescribed by that Board, and if required by that Board verified by statutory declaration, showing for the year next preceding the making of such return or for such other period as the Board may prescribe, the amounts which have been paid as instalments or annual payments, and the amounts which have been appropriated, and the amounts which have been paid to or invested or applied for the purpose of the sinking fund, and the description of the securities upon which any investment has been made, and the purposes to which any portion of the sinking fund or investment of the sum accumulated by way of compound interest has been applied during the same period, and the total amount (if any) remaining invested at the end of the year, and in the event of any wilful default in making such return, the clerk shall be liable to a penalty not exceeding twenty pounds to be recovered by action on behalf of the Crown in the High Court.

(2) If it appear to the Local Government Board by that return or otherwise that the Council have failed to pay any instalment or annual payment required to be paid or to appropriate any sum required to be appropriated or to set apart any sum required by this

Act for any sinking fund or have applied any portion of any sinking fund or any interest thereon to any purpose other than those authorised, the Local Government Board may by order direct that the sum in such order mentioned not exceeding double the amount in respect of which default shall have been made shall be paid or applied as in such order mentioned, and any such order shall be enforceable by writ of Mandamus to be obtained by the Local Government Board out of the High Court.

35. The proceeds of the sale of any lands of the Council under the powers of this Act shall be distinguished as capital in the accounts of the Council, and shall be applied in discharge of any moneys borrowed by the Council under this Act, but shall not be applied to the payments of instalments or annuities, or to payments into the sinking fund, except to such extent and upon such terms as may be approved by the Local Government Board. Provided that borrowed money discharged by the application of such moneys shall not be re-borrowed.

Proceeds of sale of surplus lands to be treated as capital.

36. All moneys borrowed by the Council under the powers of this Act shall be applied only to the purposes of this Act for which they are authorised to be borrowed, and to which capital is properly applicable.

Application of money borrowed.

37. A person lending money to the Council under this Act shall not be bound to inquire as to the observance by the Council of any provisions of this Act, or be bound to see to the application or be answerable for any loss, misapplication, or non-application of the money lent, or of any part thereof.

Protection of lender from inquiry.

38.—(1.) The Local Government Board may direct any inquiries to be held by their inspectors which they may deem necessary in regard to the exercise of any powers conferred upon them or the giving of any consents under this Act, and the inspectors of the Local Government Board shall for the purposes of any such inquiry have all such powers as they have for the purposes of inquiries directed by that Board under the Public Health Act, 1875.

Inquiries by Local Government Board.

(2.) The Council shall pay to the Local Government Board any expenses incurred by that Board in relation to any inquiries referred to in this section, including the expenses of any witnesses summoned by the inspector holding the inquiry, and a sum to be fixed by that Board not exceeding three guineas a day for the services of such inspector.

39. Any expenses of the execution by the Council of this Act with respect to which no other provision is made may be defrayed by the Council out of the district fund and general district rate.

Expenses of execution of Act.

40. Section 58 of the Local Government Act, 1894, shall apply to the accounts of the Council, and of their committees and officers under this Act.

Audit of accounts.

[Sec. 58 of the Local Government Act, 1894 (56 and 57 Vict. c. 73), relates to the Audit of Accounts of District Councils].

41. The following provisions shall apply to the taking and use under the powers of this Act of the lands and property of, or claimed by Charles Menzies Holland, Walter Holland, and Arthur Holland,

As to lands of the devisees of Charles Holland.

Sec. 41 devisees in trust under the will of Charles Holland, deceased (who and the survivors and survivor of whom, and the heirs and assigns of such survivor are in this section referred to as and included in the expression "the devisees"), and shall be binding upon the devisees and the Council (that is to say) :—

(1) The property of the devisees affected by this Act includes the freehold dwelling-house and the grounds attached thereto called Liscard Vale, in the parish of Wallasey (in this section referred to as "the enclosed grounds"), and the devisees claim to be absolutely entitled to the land (in this section referred to as "the open land") lying between the enclosed grounds and the River Mersey, in fee simple free from any public or other rights of way or other rights over or affecting the same, but the Council do not admit such claim:

(2) The promenade where it passes through the open land shall, unless otherwise agreed between the devisees and the Council, be so constructed that its western boundary shall be in the exact position shown on the deposited plan, so that if the promenade be made of greater width than is shown on the deposited plan the widening shall be exclusively on the eastern side:

(3) The promenade where it passes through the open land shall be fenced in on its western side by the Council by an unclimbable iron fence six feet high, above the level of the footpath on the western side of the promenade, founded upon a stone sill not less than fifteen inches high, but the devisees shall all times be at liberty to make gates or entrances through the said fence for the use of persons resorting to any house or houses on their property facing the promenade;

(4) Two slipways each at least six feet wide shall be made and maintained by the Council from the promenade to the shore of the River Mersey, one opposite Magazine Lane and the other opposite Holland Road, and both facing in a southerly direction.

(5) A flight of stone or concrete steps shall be made and maintained by the Council from the promenade to the shore of the River Mersey opposite the enclosed grounds at the point marked C upon the plan signed by James Willcox Alsop and William Danger:

(6) The Council shall not take or use under the powers of this Act without the consent in writing of the devisees any of the open land shown on the deposited plan as lying between the western side of the promenade and the enclosed grounds or between the western side of the promenade and the eastern boundary of the houses belonging to the devisees known as 1 and 2 River View in the district of Magazines:

(7) The devisees shall have the right of access from the enclosed grounds to the promenade by not more than three roads of such width as the devisees may think fit not being less than the minimum width prescribed by the byelaws of the Council and being respectively of uniform width with any roads on the devisees' property of which the roads respectively shall form extensions. Suitable provision shall be made by the Council during the construction of the promenade and until the roads

provided for by this subsection are made and available for securing access at all times from the enclosed grounds to the shore of the River Mersey :

(8) The Council shall when constructing the promenade lay a sewer longitudinally under the same and the devisees shall thereafter have the right to discharge sewage and drainage into the said sewer and in the meantime any existing sewers and drains from the enclosed grounds to the River Mersey shall be preserved :

(9) The devisees and all persons claiming under or through them shall be at liberty to build to within but not nearer than thirty feet from the western boundary of the promenade :

(10) The council shall not (notwithstanding anything in the section of this Act of which the marginal note is " Power to erect shelters, &c., on promenade ") erect or permit to be erected or continued, any building or erection of any description upon the promenade between a point opposite the north-eastern corner of Kirkdale Cottage grounds and a point opposite the south-eastern corner of the College grounds :

(11) All the estate right, title and interest (if any) of the devisees in and in respect of the land required for the construction of the promenade in exact accordance with the deposited plan so far as regards the western side of the promenade but with any widening of the promenade eastward beyond the line shown on the said plan which the Council may think necessary or expedient within the limits of deviation and in and in respect of the land situate within the district of Wallasey and lying east of the site of the promenade but not including in either case any mines or minerals under any such land and being more than five feet below the surface are hereby vested in the Council and any land so vested in the Council lying to the eastward of the promenade as actually constructed shall unless revested as herein-after provided remain and be for ever open and unbuilt upon. Provided that if the works by this Act authorised to be constructed on the said lands and shown on the deposited plan and sections are not constructed within the period limited by this Act in that behalf the estate right title and interest (if any) by this section vested in the Council shall be by this Act revested in the devisees :

(12) Except as by this section provided the Council shall not purchase, take or interfere with any land or property of or claimed by the devisees.

42. The following provisions shall apply to the taking and use under the powers of this Act of the lands and property of, or claimed by Edgar Swinton Holland of Liscard in the parish of Wallasey in the county of Chester (who and whose heirs and assigns are in this section referred to as and included in the expression "the owner") and shall be binding upon the owner and the Council (that is to say) :—

(1) The property of the owner affected by this Act includes the freehold house and grounds called the College in the parish of Wallasey (in this section referred to as "the enclosed

Sec. 42

As to lands of Edgar Swinton Holland.

Sec. 42 grounds") and the owner claims to be absolutely entitled to the land (in this section referred to as "the open land") lying between the enclosed grounds and the River Mersey in fee simple free from any public or other rights of way or other rights over or affecting the same but the Council do not admit such claim:

(2) The promenade where it passes through the open land shall unless otherwise agreed between the owner and the Council be so constructed that its western boundary shall be in the exact position shown on the deposited plan so that if the promenade be made of greater width than shown on the deposited plan the widening shall be exclusively on the eastern side:

(3) The promenade where it passes through the open land shall be fenced in on its western side by the Council by an unclimbable iron fence six feet high above the level of the footpath on the western side of the promenade founded upon a stone sill not less than fifteen inches high but the owner shall at all times be at liberty to make gates or entrances through the said fence for the use of persons resorting to any house or houses on his property facing the promenade:

(4) Two slipways each at least six feet wide shall be made and maintained by the Council from the promenade to the shore of the River Mersey one opposite Magazine Lane and the other opposite Holland Road and both facing in a southerly direction:

(5) The owner shall have the right of access from the enclosed grounds to the promenade by not more than one road of such width as the owner may think fit, not being less than the minimum width prescribed by the byelaws of the Council, and being of uniform width with any road on the owner's property of which it shall form an extension. Suitable provision shall be made by the Council during the construction of the promenade and until the road provided for by this subsection is made and available for securing access at all times from the enclosed grounds to the shore of the River Mersey:

(6) The Council shall when constructing the promenade, lay a sewer longitudinally under the same and the owner shall thereafter have the right to discharge sewage and drainage into the said sewer and in the meantime any existing sewer or drain from the enclosed grounds to the River Mersey shall be preserved:

(7) The owner and all persons claiming under or through him shall be at liberty to build to within but not nearer than thirty feet from the western boundary of the promenade:

(8) The Council shall not (notwithstanding anything in the section of this Act of which the marginal note is "Power to erect shelters, &c., on promenade") erect or permit to be erected or continued any building or erection of any description upon the promenade between a point opposite the north-eastern corner of Kirkdale Cottage grounds and a point opposite the south-eastern corner of the College grounds:

(9) All the estate, right, title and interest (if any) of the owner in and in respect of the land required for the construction of the promenade in exact accordance with the deposited plan so far as regards the western side of the promenade but with any widening of the promenade eastward beyond the line shown on the said plan which the Council may think necessary or expedient within the limits of deviation and in and in respect of the land situate within the district of Wallasey and lying east of the site of the promenade but not including in either case any mines or minerals under any such land and being more than five feet below the surface are hereby vested in the Council and any land so vested in the Council lying to the eastward of the promenade as actually constructed shall unless revested as herein-after provided remain for ever open and unbuilt upon. Provided that if the works by this Act authorised to be constructed on the said lands and shown on the deposited plan and sections are not constructed within the period limited by this Act in that behalf the estate, right, title and interest (if any) by this section vested in the Council shall be by this Act revested in the owner :

(10) Except as by this section provided the Council shall not purchase, take, or interfere with any land or property of or claimed by the owner.

43. The following provisions shall apply to the taking and use under the powers of this Act of the lands and property of or claimed by Philip Michael Vaughan of Kirkdale Cottage in the township of Liscard and in the parish of Wallasey in the county of Chester (who and whose heirs and assigns are in this section referred to as and included in the expression "the owner") and shall be binding upon the owner and the Council (that is to say) :—

Sec. 43

As to lands of Philip Michael Vaughan.

(1) The property of the owner affected by this Act includes the house and the grounds attached thereto called Kirkdale Cottage in the parish of Wallasey (in this section referred to as "the enclosed grounds") and the owner claims to be absolutely entitled to the land (in this section referred to as "the open land") lying between the enclosed grounds and the River Mersey in fee simple, free from any public or other rights of way or other rights over or affecting the same but the Council do not admit such claim :

(2) The promenade where it passes through the open land shall unless otherwise agreed between the owner and the Council be so constructed that its western boundary shall be in the exact position shown on the deposited plan so that if the promenade be made of greater width than shown on the deposited plan the widening shall be on the eastern side :

(3) The promenade where it passes through the open land shall be fenced in on its western side by the Council by an unclimbable iron fence six feet high above the level of the footpath on the western side of the promenade founded upon a stone sill not less than fifteen inches high but the owner shall at all times until the roads mentioned in subsection (6) of this section shall have been made have free access through the said fence to the River Mersey :

Sec. 43

(4) A slipway at least six feet wide shall be made and maintained by the Council from the promenade to the shore of the River Mersey opposite the road along the northern boundary of the enclosed grounds and facing in a northerly direction :

(5) Two flights of stone or concrete steps shall be made and maintained by the Council from the promenade to the shore of the River Mersey, opposite the enclosed grounds at the points marked A and B upon the plan signed by James Willcox Alsop and William Danger:

(6) The owner shall have the right of access from the enclosed grounds to the promenade by not more than four roads of such width as the owner may think fit, not being less than the minimum width prescribed by the byelaws of the Council and being respectively of uniform width with any roads on the owner's property, of which the roads respectively shall be extensions. Suitable provisions shall be made by the Council during the construction of the promenade and until the roads provided for by this subsection are made and available for securing access at all times from the enclosed grounds to the shore of the River Mersey :

(7) The Council shall, when constructing the promenade, lay a sewer longitudinally under the same, and the owner shall thereafter have the right to discharge sewage and drainage into the said sewer and for that purpose to carry pipes under and through the strip of land to be vested in the Council as aforesaid :

(8) The owner and all persons claiming under or through him shall be at liberty to build to within but not nearer than seventy feet from the western boundary of the promenade :

(9) The Council shall not (notwithstanding anything in the section of this Act of which the marginal note is "Power to erect shelters, &c., on promenade") erect or permit to be erected or continued any building or erection of any description upon the promenade between a point opposite the north-eastern corner of Kirkdale Cottage grounds and a point opposite the south-eastern corner of the College grounds.

(10) All the estate right title and interest (if any) of the owner in and in respect of the land required for the construction of the promenade in exact accordance with the deposited plan so far as regards the western side of the promenade, but with any widening of the promenade eastward beyond the line shown on the said plan which the Council may think necessary or expedient within the limits of deviation and in and in respect of the land situate within the district of Wallasey and lying east of the site of the promenade and in and in respect of the land lying on the west side of the promenade and extending for a distance therefrom of forty feet or (where less than that distance will intervene between the western side of the promenade and the enclosed grounds of Kirkdale Cottage) of such less distance but not including in any case any mines or minerals under any such land and being more than five feet below the surface are hereby vested in the Council, and any land so vested in the Council lying to the eastward of the promenade as actually constructed shall, unless revested as

hereinafter provided, remain and be for ever open and unbuilt upon. Provided that if the works by this Act authorised to be constructed on the said lands and shown on the deposited plan and sections are not constructed within the period limited by this Act in that behalf the estate, right, title and interest (if any) by this section vested in the Council shall be by this Act revested in the owner.

Sec. 44—46

(11) The land lying on the west side of the promenade and vested in the Council by the preceding subsection shall be fenced by the Council on all sides with a fence of the same description as that provided for by subsection (3) of this section and shall be for ever kept and maintained by the Council as an ornamental enclosure or as ornamental enclosures and planted with suitable trees and shrubs.

(12) Except as by this section provided the Council shall not purchase, take or interfere with any land or property of or claimed by the owner.

44.—(1) Except with the consent of the owner for the time being of the Rock Point Estate so much of the promenade as abuts upon the said estate shall not be so constructed that any part thereof shall be west of the river wall constructed for the protection of the said estate or of the site of such wall.

For protection of the Rock Point Estate.

(2) No lands forming part of the Rock Point Estate shall be acquired under the provisions of this Act otherwise than by agreement west of the lands required for the construction of the promenade.

(3) Except with the consent of the Council no hotel, stable, shop, dwelling-house or other similar structure shall be erected upon the Rock Point Estate within forty feet of the western side of the promenade.

(4) The owner for the time being of the said estate and his agents shall at all times be entitled to access at any point or points from the said estate to the promenade and thence by such approaches as the Council may be reasonably required to construct over the promenade to the lands lying east thereof and the river.

(5) The section of this Act the marginal note whereof is "Power to Council to sell lands" shall not apply to the said estate.

45. The Council shall not execute any works or conduct any operations under the powers of this Act within the jurisdiction of the Mersey Conservancy Commissioners except in accordance with plans and sections first submitted to and approved of in writing by the acting conservator for the time being appointed by the said Commissioners under the Mersey Conservancy Act, 1842, and the provisions of that Act shall apply to the works under this Act.

For protection of the Mersey Conservancy Commissioners.

46. And whereas it is necessary that the lands hereditaments and works belonging to Her Majesty or vested in Her Majesty's Principal Secretary of State for the War Department for the public service should be preserved intact and free from all intrusion or obstruction. Be it therefore enacted as follows (that is to say):—

Saving rights of Her Majesty's Principal Secretary of State for the War Department.

(1) Nothing in this Act contained shall authorise the Council to enter upon use or interfere with any land soil or water or

Sec. 47—48

any right in respect thereof vested in or exercised by the said Principal Secretary for the time being, or to take away lessen prejudice or alter any of the rights privileges or powers vested in or exercised by the said Principal Secretary for the time being without his previous consent signified in writing under his hand, and which consent the said Principal Secretary for the time being is hereby authorised to give subject to such special or other conditions as he shall see fit to impose on the Council:

(2) The said Principal Secretary for the time being shall at all times for himself his officers agents servants and workmen have full rights of way over the promenade to and from the Liscard Battery and rights of firing across the promenade from the Liscard Battery:

(3) So much of the promenade as abuts upon or is opposite to the Liscard Battery shall at all times be kept free from buildings and other obstructions:

(4) Provided that the Council shall be at liberty with the previous assent of the said Principal Secretary for the time being to level plant and lay out the open land lying between the west side of the promenade and the said battery, except so much thereof as lies within six feet of the wall of the said battery, such levelling planting and laying out being executed subject to the approval of the general officer commanding the district.

Saving rights of the Crown.   **47.** Nothing contained in this Act shall authorise the Council to take use or in any manner interfere with any land or hereditaments or any rights of whatsoever description belonging to the Queen's most Excellent Majesty in right of Her Crown and under the management of the Commissioners of Woods without the consent in writing of the Commissioners of Woods on behalf of Her Majesty first had and obtained for that purpose (which consent such Commissioners are hereby authorised to give) neither shall anything in this Act contained extend to take away prejudice diminish or alter any of the estates rights privileges powers or authorities vested in or enjoyed or exerciseable by the Queen's Majesty Her heirs or successors.

Costs of Act.   **48.** All the costs charges and expenses preliminary to and of and incidental to the preparing applying for obtaining and passing of this Act, as taxed by the taxing officer of the House of Lords or of the House of Commons shall be paid by the Council, and may be paid in the first instance out of any moneys in their hands, but shall be charged to and recouped by the moneys which the Council are authorised to borrow under the powers of this Act.

60 & 61 Vict.   Session 1897.   ch. lxvi.   335

ELECTRIC LIGHTING ORDERS CONFIRMATION (No. 6) ACT, 1897.

(Confirming The Wallasey Electric Lighting Order, 1897.)

AN ACT

to confirm certain Provisional Orders made by the Board of Trade under the Electric Lighting Acts, 1882 and 1888, relating to Barking Town, Morecambe, Ramsbottom, Swadlincote, and WALLASEY.

15th JULY, 1897.

WHEREAS under the authority of the Electric Lighting Acts, 1882 and 1888, the Board of Trade have made the several Provisional Orders set out in the schedule to this Act: [45 & 46 Vict. c. lvi. 51 & 52 Vict. c. xii.]

And whereas a Provisional Order made by the Board of Trade under the authority of the said Acts is not of any validity or force whatever until the confirmation thereof by Act of Parliament:

And whereas it is expedient that the several Provisional Orders made by the Board of Trade under the authority of the said Acts as set out in the schedule to this Act be confirmed by Act of Parliament:

Be it therefore enacted by the Queen's most Excellent Majesty, by and with the advice and consent of the Lords Spiritual and Temporal, and Commons in this present Parliament assembled, and by the authority of the same as follows:—

1. This Act may be cited as the Electric Lighting Orders Confirmation (No. 6) Act, 1897. *[Short title.]*

2. The several Orders as set out in the schedule to this Act shall be, and the same are hereby confirmed, and all the provisions thereof in manner and form as they are set out in the said schedule shall from and after the passing of this Act have full validity and effect. *[Orders in schedule confirmed.]*

[The omitted Orders relate to Districts other than Wallasey.]

Schedule.

SCHEDULE.

5. WALLASEY.—Provisional Order granted by the Board of Trade under the Electric Lighting Acts, 1882 and 1888, to the Wallasey Urban District Council.

THE WALLASEY ELECTRIC LIGHTING ORDER, 1897.

WALLASEY ELECTRIC LIGHTING.

Provisional Order granted by the Board of Trade under the Electric Lighting Acts, 1882 and 1888, to the Wallasey Urban District Council in respect of the Urban District of Wallasey.

PRELIMINARY.

Short title. 1. This Order may be cited as the Wallasey Electric Lighting Order, 1897.

Interpretation. 2. This order is to be read and construed subject in all respects to the provisions of the Electric Lighting Acts, 1882 and 1888, and of any other Acts or parts of Acts incorporated therewith which said Acts and parts of Acts are in this Order collectively referred to as "the principal Act" and the several words terms and expressions to which by the principal Act meanings are assigned shall have in this Order the same respective meanings provided that in this Order—

The expression "energy" shall mean electrical energy and for the purposes of applying the provisions of the principal Act to this Order electrical energy shall be deemed to be an agency within the meaning of electricity as defined in the Electric Lighting Act, 1882:

The expression "power" shall mean electrical power or the rate per unit of time at which energy is supplied:

The expression "main" shall mean any electric line which may be laid down by the Undertakers in any street or public place and through which energy may be supplied or intended to be supplied by the Undertakers for the purposes of general supply:

The expression "service line" shall mean any electric line through which energy may be supplied or intended to be supplied by the Undertakers to a consumer either from any main or directly from the premises of the Undertakers:

The expression "distributing main" shall mean the portion of any main which is used for the purpose of giving origin to service lines for the purposes of general supply:

The expression "general supply" shall mean the general supply of energy to ordinary consumers but shall not include the supply of energy to any one or more particular consumers under special agreement:

The expression "area of supply" shall mean the area within which the Undertakers are for the time being authorised to supply energy under the provisions of this Order:

The expression "consumer" shall mean any body or person supplied or entitled to be supplied with energy by the Undertakers:

The expression "consumer's terminals" shall mean the ends of the electric lines situate upon any consumer's premises and belonging to him at which the supply of energy is delivered from the service lines:

The expression "telegraphic line" when used with respect to any telegraphic line of the Postmaster-General shall have the same meaning as in the Telegraph Act, 1878, and any such telegraphic line shall be deemed to be injuriously affected where telegraphic communication by means of such line is whether through induction or otherwise in any manner affected:

The expression "railway" shall include any tramroad that is to say any tramway other than a tramway as herein-after defined:

The expression "tramway" shall mean any tramway laid along any street:

The expression "daily penalty" shall mean a penalty for each day on which any offence is continued after conviction thereof:

The expression "Board of Trade regulations" shall mean any regulations or conditions affecting the Undertaking made by the Board of Trade under the principal Act or this Order for securing the safety of the public or for insuring a proper and sufficient supply of energy:

The expressions "First Schedule" "Second Schedule" "Third Schedule" and "Fourth Schedule" shall mean the First Second Third and Fourth Schedules to this Order annexed respectively:

The expression "deposited map" shall mean the map of the area of supply deposited at the Board of Trade by the Undertakers together with this Order and signed by an assistant secretary to the Board of Trade:

The expression "plan" shall mean a plan drawn to a horizontal scale of at least one inch to eighty-eight feet and where possible a section drawn to the same horizontal scale as the plan and to a vertical scale of at least one inch to eleven feet or to such other scale as the Board of Trade may approve of for both plan and section together with such detail plan and sections as may be necessary.

3. This Order shall come into force and have effect upon the day when the Act confirming this Order is passed which date is in this Order referred to as "the commencement of this Order."

Commencement of Order.

Description of the Undertakers.

Description of Undertakers.

4. Subject to the provisions of this Order the Undertakers for the purposes of this Order shall be the Wallasey Urban District Council.

Area of Supply.

Area of supply

5. Subject to the provisions of this Order the area of supply shall be the whole of the area included in the First Schedule which said area is more particularly delineated upon the deposited map and thereon coloured red.

Nature and Mode of Supply.

Systems and mode of supply.

6. Subject to the provisions of this Order and the principal Act the Undertakers may supply energy within the area of supply for all public and private purposes as defined by the said Act provided as follows:—

(1) Such energy shall be supplied only by means of some system which shall be approved in writing by the Board of Trade and subject to the Board of Trade regulations, and

(2) The Undertakers shall not without the express consent of the Board of Trade place any electric line above ground, except within premises in the sole occupation or control of the Undertakers, and except so much of any service line as is necessarily so placed for the purpose of supply ; and

(3) The Undertakers shall not permit any part of any circuit to be connected with earth, except so far as may be necessary for carrying out the provisions of the Board of Trade regulations, unless such connexion is for the time being approved of by the Board of Trade with the concurrence of the Postmaster-General, and is made in accordance with the conditions (if any) of such approval.

Lands.

Purchase and use of lands.

7. Subject to the provisions of this Order and the principal Act, the Undertakers may acquire by purchase or on lease and use any lands for the purposes of this Order, and may also for such purposes use any other lands for the time being vested in or leased by them, but subject as to such last mentioned lands to the approval of the Local Government Board, and may dispose of any lands acquired by them under the provisions of this section which may not for the time being be required for the purposes of this Order. Provided that the amount of land so used by them shall not at any one time exceed in the whole five acres, except with the consent of the Board of Trade.

Provided also that the Undertakers shall not purchase or acquire for the purposes of this Order ten or more houses which, on the fifteenth day of December last, were occupied either wholly or partially by persons belonging to the labouring class as tenants or lodgers or except with the consent of the Local Government Board ten or more houses which were not so occupied on the said fifteenth day of December, but have been or shall be subsequently so occupied.

For the purposes of this section the expression " labouring class " means and includes mechanics, artizans, labourers, and others working for wages, hawkers, costermongers, persons not working for wages, but working at some trade or handicraft without employing others except members of their own family, and persons other than domestic servants, whose income does not exceed an average of thirty shillings a week, and the families of any such persons who may be residing with them.

Works.

8. Subject to the provisions of this Order and the principal Act, the Undertakers may exercise all or any of the powers conferred on them by this Order and the principal Act, and may break up such streets not repairable by the local authority, and such railways and tramways (if any) as are specified in the Third Schedule, so far as such streets railways and tramways may for the time being be included in the area of supply, and be or be upon land dedicated to public use. Provided, however, as respects any such railway, that the powers hereby granted shall extend only to such parts thereof as pass across or along any highway on the level. *Powers for execution of works.*

Nothing in this order shall authorise or empower the Undertakers to break up or interfere with any street or part of a street not repairable by the local authority, or any railway or tramway except such streets railways or tramways (if any) or such parts thereof as are specified in the said schedule without the consent of the authority, company or person by whom such street railway or tramway is repairable, or of the Board of Trade under section thirteen of the Electric Lighting Act, 1882, and where the Board of Trade give such consent the provisions of this Order shall apply to the street railway or tramway to which the consent relates as if it had been specified in the said schedule.

[Sec. 13 of the Electric Lighting Act, 1882, contains restrictions on breaking up of private streets, railways and tramways.]

9. Subject to the provisions of this Order and the principal Act and the Board of Trade regulations, the Undertakers may construct in any street such boxes as may be necessary for purposes in connexion with the supply of energy, including apparatus for the proper ventilation of such boxes. *Street boxes*

Every such box shall be for the exclusive use of the Undertakers and under their sole control, except so far as the Board of Trade may otherwise order, and shall be used by the Undertakers only for the purpose of leading off service lines and other distributing conductors, or for examining, testing, regulating, measuring, directing or controlling the supply of energy, or for examining or testing the condition of the mains or other portions of the works, or for other like purposes connected with the undertaking, and the Undertakers may place therein meters, switches and any other suitable and proper apparatus for any of the above purposes.

Every such box, including the upper surface or covering thereof, shall be constructed of such materials and shall be constructed and maintained by the Undertakers in such manner as not to be a source of danger whether by reason of inequality of surface or otherwise.

Notice of works with plan to be served on the Postmaster-General.

10. Where the exercise of any of the powers of the Undertakers in relation to the execution of any works (including the construction of boxes) will involve the placing of any works in, under, along, or across any street or public bridge, the following provisions shall have effect :—

(*a*.) One month before commencing the execution of such works (not being the repairs, renewals or amendments of existing works, of which the character and position are not altered) the Undertakers shall serve a notice upon the Postmaster-General describing the proposed works, together with a plan of the works, showing the mode and position in which such works are intended to be executed and the manner in which it is intended that such street or bridge is to be interfered with, and shall, upon being required to do so by the Postmaster-General, give him any such further information in relation thereto as he may desire.

(*b*.) The Postmaster-General may in his discretion approve of any such works or plan subject to such amendments or conditions as may seem fit or may disapprove of the same, and may give notice of such approval or disapproval to the Undertakers.

(*c*.) Where the Postmaster-General approves any such works or plan subject to any amendments or conditions with which the Undertakers are dissatisfied or disapprove of any such works or plan the Undertakers may appeal to the Board of Trade, and the Board of Trade may inquire into the matter and allow or disallow such appeal, and approve any such works or plan subject to such amendments or conditions as may seem fit or may disapprove the same.

(*d*.) If the Postmaster-General fail to give any such notice of approval or disapproval to the Undertakers within one month after the service of the notice upon him he shall be deemed to have approved such works and plan.

(*e*.) Notwithstanding anything in this Order or the principal Act the Undertakers shall not be entitled to execute any such works as above specified, except so far as the same may be of a description and in accordance with a plan which has been approved or is to be deemed to have been approved by the Postmaster-General or by the Board of Trade as above mentioned, but where any such works description and plan are so approved or to be deemed to be approved the Undertakers may cause such works to be executed in accordance with such description and plan, subject in all respects to the provisions of this Order and the principal Act.

(*f*.) If the Undertakers make default in complying with any of the requirements or restrictions of this section they shall (in addition to any other compensation which they may be liable to make under the provisions of this Order or the principal Act) make full compensation to the Postmaster-General for any loss or damage which he may incur by reason thereof, and in addition thereto they shall be liable to a penalty not exceeding ten pounds for every such default and to a daily penalty not exceeding five pounds. Provided that the Undertakers shall not be subject to any such penalties as aforesaid if the court having cognizance of the case shall be of opinion that the case was one of emergency, and that the Undertakers complied with the requirements of this section so far as was reasonable under the circumstances.

Where any street or public bridge is repairable by the county council the Undertakers shall serve a like notice and plan upon the county council in addition to those served upon the Postmaster-General, and the foregoing provisions of this section shall with the necessary modifications apply to the county council in like manner as to the Postmaster-General.

Nothing in this section shall exempt the Undertakers from any penalty or obligation to which they may be liable under this Order or otherwise by law in the event of any telegraphic line of the Postmaster-General being at any time injuriously affected by the Undertakers' works or their supply of energy.

11. Where the exercise of the powers of the Undertakers in relation to the execution of any works will involve the placing of any works in under along or across any street or part of a street not repairable by the local authority or county council or over or under any railway tramway or canal, the following provisions shall have effect unless otherwise agreed between the parties interested :— *As to streets not repairable by local authority or county council, railways, tramways, and canals.*

(a.) One month before commencing the execution of any such works (not being the repairs renewals or amendments of existing works of which the character and position are not altered), the Undertakers shall in addition to any other notices which they may be required to give under this Order or the Principal Act, serve a notice upon the body or person liable to repair such street or part of a street, or the body or person for the time being entitled to work such railway or tramway, or the owners of such canal (as the case may be) in this section referred to as the "owners" describing the proposed works together with a plan of the works, showing the mode and position in which such works are intended to be executed and placed, and shall upon being required to do so by any such owners give them any such further information in relation thereto as they may desire.

(b.) Every such notice shall contain a reference to this section and direct the attention of the owners to whom it is given to the provisions thereof.

(c.) Within three weeks after the service of any such notice and plan upon any owners, such owners may if they think fit serve a requisition upon the Undertakers requiring that any question in relation to such works or to compensation in respect thereof, and any other question arising upon such notice or plan as aforesaid shall be settled by arbitration, and thereupon such question unless settled by agreement shall be settled by arbitration accordingly.

(d.) In settling any question under this section an arbitrator shall have regard to any duties or obligations which the owners may be under in respect of such street railway tramway or canal, and may if he thinks fit require the Undertakers to execute any temporary or other works so as to avoid any interference with any traffic so far as may be possible.

(e.) Where no such requisition as in this section mentioned is served upon the Undertakers or where after any such requisition has been served upon them, any question required to be settled by arbitration has been so settled, the Undertakers may upon paying or securing any compensation which they may be required to pay or secure cause to be executed the works specified in such notice and plan as aforesaid and may repair renew and amend the same (provided that their character and position are not altered), but subject in all respects to the provisions of this Order and the principal Act, and only in accordance with the notice and plan so served by them as aforesaid or such modifications thereof respectively as may have been settled by arbitration as herein-before mentioned, or as may be agreed upon between the parties.

(f.) All works to be executed by the Undertakers under this section shall be carried out to the reasonable satisfaction of the owners who shall have the right to be present during the execution of such works.

(g.) Where the repair, renewal, or amendment of any existing works of which the character or position is not altered will involve any interference with any railway, level crossing, or any tramway over or under which such works have been placed, the Undertakers shall unless otherwise agreed between the parties, or in cases of emergency give to the owners not less than twenty-four hours' notice before commencing to effect such repair, renewal, or amendment, and the owners shall be entitled by their officer to superintend the work, and the Undertakers shall conform to such reasonable requirements as may be made by the owners or such officer. The said notice shall be in addition to any other notices which the Undertakers may be required to give under this Order or the principal Act.

(h.) If the Undertakers make default in complying with any of the requirements or restrictions of this section they shall (in addition to any other compensation which they may be liable to make under the provisions of this Order or the principal Act), make full compensation to the owners affected thereby for any loss or damage which they may incur by reason thereof, and in addition thereto they shall be liable to a penalty not exceeding ten pounds for every such default, and to a daily penalty not exceeding five pounds. Provided that the Undertakers shall not be subject to any such penalties as aforesaid, if the court having cognizance of the case shall be of opinion that the case was one of emergency and that the Undertakers complied with the requirements of this section so far as was reasonable under the circumstances.

Street authority, &c., may give notice of desire to break up streets, &c., on behalf of Undertakers.

12. Any body or person for the time being liable to repair any street or part of a street, or entitled to work any railway or tramway which the Undertakers may be empowered to break up for the purposes of this Order, may if they think fit serve a notice upon the Undertakers stating that they desire to exercise or discharge all or any part of any of the powers or duties of the Undertakers as therein specified in relation to the breaking up, filling in, reinstating, or making good any streets, bridges, sewers, drains, tunnels, or other works vested in, or under the control or management of such

body or person, and may amend, or revoke any such notice by another notice similarly served. Where such body or person as aforesaid (in this section referred to as the "givers of the notice,") have given notice that they desire to exercise or discharge any such specified powers and duties of the Undertakers, then so long as such notice remains in force, the following provisions shall have effect unless otherwise agreed between the parties interested:—

(*a*.) The Undertakers shall not be entitled to proceed themselves to exercise or discharge any such specified powers or duties as aforesaid, except where they have required the givers of the notice to exercise or discharge such powers or duties, and the givers of the notice have refused or neglected to comply with such requisition as herein-after provided or in cases of emergency.

(*b*.) In addition to any other notices which they may be required to give under the provisions of this Order or the principal Act, the Undertakers shall not more than four days and not less than two days before the exercise or discharge of any such powers or duties so specified as aforesaid is required to be commenced, serve a requisition upon the givers of the notice stating the time when such exercise or discharge is required to be commenced, and the manner in which any such powers or duties are required to be exercised or discharged.

(*c*.) Upon receipt of any such requisition as last aforesaid the givers of the notice may proceed to exercise or discharge any such powers or duties as required by the Undertakers, subject to the like restrictions and conditions as the Undertakers would themselves be subject to in such exercise or discharge so far as the same may be applicable.

(*d*.) If the givers of the notice decline or for twenty-four hours after the time when any such exercise or discharge of any powers or duties is by any requisition required to be commenced neglect to comply with such requisition, the Undertakers may themselves proceed to exercise or discharge the powers or duties therein specified in like manner as they might have done if such notice as aforesaid had not been given to them by the givers of the notice.

(*e*.) In any case of emergency the Undertakers may themselves proceed to at once exercise or discharge so much of any such specified powers or duties as aforesaid, as may be necessary for the actual remedying of any defect from which the emergency arises without serving any requisition on the givers of the notice but in such case the Undertakers shall within twelve hours after they begin to exercise or discharge such powers or duties as aforesaid, give information thereof in writing to the givers of the notice.

(*f*.) If the Undertakers exercise or discharge any such specified powers or duties as aforesaid, otherwise than in accordance with the provisions of this section they shall be liable to a penalty not exceeding ten pounds for every such offence, and to a daily penalty not exceeding five pounds. Provided that the Undertakers shall not be subject to any such penalties as aforesaid, if the court having cognizance of the case shall be of opinion that the case was one of emergency, and that the Undertakers complied with the requirements of this section so far as was reasonable under the circumstances.

(*g.*) All expenses properly incurred by the givers of the notice in complying with any requisition of the Undertakers under this section shall be repaid to them by the Undertakers, and may be recovered summarily.

Provided that nothing in this section shall in any way affect the rights of the Undertakers to exercise or discharge any powers or duties conferred or imposed upon them by this Order or the principal Act in relation to the execution of any works beyond the actual breaking up, filling in, reinstating, or making good any such street or part of a street or any such bridges, sewers, drains, tunnels, or other works, or railway, or tramway as in this section mentioned.

As to alteration of pipes, wires, &c., under streets.

13. The Undertakers may alter the position of any pipes or wires being under any street or place authorised to be broken up by them which may interfere with the exercise of their powers under the principal Act or this Order and any body or person may in like manner alter the position of any electric lines or works of the Undertakers being under any such street or place as aforesaid which may interfere with the lawful exercise of any powers vested in such body or person in relation to such street or place subject to the following provisions unless otherwise agreed between the parties interested:—

(*a.*) One month before commencing any such alterations the Undertakers or such body or person (as the case may be) in this section referred to as the "operators" shall serve a notice upon the body or person for the time being entitled to such pipes, wires, electric lines, or works (as the case may be) in this section referred to as the "owners" describing the proposed alterations together with a plan showing the manner in which it is intended that such alterations shall be made and shall upon being required to do so by any such owners give them any such further information in relation thereto as they may desire.

(*b.*) Within three weeks after the service of any such notice and plan upon any owners such owners may if they think fit serve a requisition upon the operators requiring that any question in relation to such works or to compensation in respect thereof or any other question arising upon such notice or plan as aforesaid shall be settled by arbitration and thereupon such question unless settled by agreement shall be settled by arbitration accordingly.

(*c.*) In settling any question under this section an arbitrator shall have regard to any duties or obligations which the owners may be under in respect of such pipes, wires, electric lines or works, and may if he thinks fit require the operators to execute any temporary or other works so as to avoid interference with any purpose for which such pipes, wires, electric lines or works are used so far as may be possible.

(*d.*) Where no such requisition as in this section mentioned is served upon the operators, the owners shall be held to have agreed to the notice or plan served on them as aforesaid and in such case or where after any such requisition has been served upon them any question required to be settled by arbitration has been so settled the operators upon paying or securing any compensation which they may be required to pay or secure may cause the alterations specified in such notice and plan as aforesaid to be made but subject in all respects to the provisions of this Order and the principal Act and only in accordance with the notice and plan so served by them as aforesaid or such modifications thereof respectively as may have been settled by arbitration as herein-before mentioned or as may be agreed upon between the parties.

(e.) At any time before any operators are entitled to commence any such alterations as aforesaid the owners may serve a statement upon the operators stating that they desire to execute such alterations themselves and where any such statement has been served upon the operators they shall not be entitled to proceed themselves to execute such alterations except where they have notified to such owners that they require them to execute such alterations and such owners have refused or neglected to comply with such notification as herein-after provided.

(f.) Where any such statement as last aforesaid has been served upon the operators they shall not more than forty-eight hours and not less than twenty-four hours before the execution of such alterations is required to be commenced, serve a notification upon the owners stating the time when such alterations are required to be commenced and the manner in which such alterations are required to be made.

(g.) Upon receipt of any such notification as last aforesaid the owners may proceed to execute such alterations as required by the operators subject to the like restrictions and conditions as the operators would themselves be subject to in executing such alterations so far as the same may be applicable.

(h.) If the owners decline or for twenty-four hours after the time when any such alterations are required to be commenced neglect to comply with such notification the operators may themselves proceed to execute such alterations in like manner as they might have done if no such statement as aforesaid had been served upon them.

(i.) All expenses properly incurred by any owners in complying with any notification of any operators under this section shall be repaid to them by such operators and may be recovered summarily.

(j.) Any owners may if they think fit by any statement served by them under this section upon any operators not being a local authority require the said operators to give them such security for the repayment to them of any expenses to be incurred by them in executing any alterations as above mentioned as may be determined in manner provided by this Order and where any operators have been so required to give security they shall not be entitled to serve a notification upon the owners requiring them to execute such alterations until such security has been duly given.

(k.) If the operators make default in complying with any of the requirements or restrictions of this section they shall (in addition to any other compensation which they may be liable to make under the provisions of this Order or the principal Act) make full compensation to the owners affected thereby for any loss, damage or penalty which they may incur by reason thereof and in addition thereto they shall be liable to a penalty not exceeding ten pounds for every such default and to a daily penalty not exceeding five pounds. Provided that the operators shall not be subject to any such penalties as aforesaid if the court having cognizance of the case shall be of opinion that the case was one of emergency and that the operators complied with the requirements of this section so far as was reasonable under the circumstances.

Laying of electric lines, &c., near gas or water pipes, or other electric lines.

14. Where the Undertakers require to dig or sink any trench for laying down or constructing any new electric lines (other than service lines) or other works near to which any main pipe syphon electric line or other work belonging to any gas electric supply or water company has been lawfully placed or where any gas or water company require to dig or sink any trench for laying down or constructing any new mains or pipes (other than service pipes) or other works near to which any lines or works of the Undertakers have been lawfully placed, the Undertakers or such gas or water company (as the case may be) in this section referred to as the "operators" shall unless otherwise agreed between the parties interested or in case of sudden emergency give to such gas electric supply or water company or to the Undertakers (as the case may be) in this section referred to as the "owners" not less than three days' notice before commencing to dig or sink such trench as aforesaid, and such owners shall be entitled by their officer to superintend the work and the operators shall conform with such reasonable requirements as may be made by the owners or such officer for protecting from injury every such main pipe syphon electric line or work, and for securing access thereto and they shall also if required to do so by the owner thereof, repair any damage that may be done thereto.

Where the operators find it necessary to undermine but not alter the position of any pipe electric line or work they shall temporarily support the same in position during the execution of their works and before completion provide a suitable and proper foundation for the same where so undermined.

Where the operators (being the Undertakers) lay any electric line crossing or liable to touch any mains pipes lines or services belonging to any gas electric supply or water company, the conducting portion of such electric line shall be effectively insulated in a manner approved by the Board of Trade and the Undertakers shall not except with the consent of the gas electric supply or water company as the case may be and of the Board of Trade lay their electric lines so as to come into contact with any such mains pipes lines or services, or except with the like consent employ any such mains pipes lines or services as conductors for the purposes of their supply of energy.

Any question or difference which may arise under this section shall be determined by arbitration.

If the operators make default in complying with any of the requirements or restrictions of this section they shall make full compensation to all owners affected thereby for any loss damage penalty or costs which they may incur by reason thereof, and in addition thereto they shall be liable to a penalty not exceeding ten pounds for every such default, and to a daily penalty not exceeding five pounds. Provided that the operators shall not be subject to any such penalty if the court having cognizance of the case shall be of opinion that the case was one of emergency and that the operators complied with the requirements and restrictions of this section so far as was reasonable under the circumstances, or that the default in question was due to the fact that the operators were ignorant of the position of the main pipe syphon electric line or work affected thereby, and that such ignorance was not owing to any negligence on the part of the operators.

For the purposes of this section the expression "gas company" shall mean any body or person lawfully supplying gas the expression "water company," shall mean any body or person lawfully supplying water or water power and the expression "electric supply company" shall mean any body or person supplying energy under the principal Act but not under this Order.

15. In the exercise of any of the powers of this Order relating to the execution of works the Undertakers shall not in any way injure the railways tunnels arches works or conveniences belonging to any railway or canal company, nor obstruct or interfere with the working of the traffic passing along any railway or canal. *For protection of railway and canal companies.*

16.—(1.) The Undertakers shall take all reasonable precautions in constructing laying down and placing their electric lines and other works of all descriptions, and in working their undertaking so as not injuriously to affect whether by induction or otherwise the working of any wire or line from time to time used for the purpose of telegraphic telephonic or electric signalling communication or the currents in such wire or line whether such wire or line be or be not in existence at the time of the laying down or placing of such electric lines or other works. If any question arises between the Undertakers and the owner of any such wire or line as to whether the Undertakers have constructed laid down or placed their electric lines or other works or worked their undertaking in contravention of this sub-section and as to whether the working of such wire or line or the current therein is or is not injuriously affected thereby such question shall be determined by arbitration and the arbitrator (unless he is of opinion that such wire or line not having been so in existence at such time as aforesaid has been placed in unreasonable proximity to the electric lines or works of the Undertakers) may direct the Undertakers to make any alterations in or additions to their system so as to comply with the provisions of this section and the Undertakers shall make such alterations or additions accordingly, *For protection of telegraphic and telephonic wires.*

(2.) Seven days before commencing to lay down or place any electric line or to use any electric line in any manner, whereby the work of telegraphic or telephonic or electric signalling communication through any wire or line lawfully laid down or placed in any position may be injuriously affected the Undertakers shall unless otherwise agreed between the parties interested give to the owner of such wire or line notice in writing specifying the course nature and gauge of such electric line, and the manner in which such electric line is intended to be used and the amount and nature of the currents intended to be transmitted thereby and the extent to and manner in which (if at all) earth returns are proposed to be used and any owner entitled to receive such notice may from time to time serve a requisition on the Undertakers requiring them to adopt such precautions as may be therein specified in regard to the laying placing or user of such electric line for the purpose of preventing such injurious affection and the undertakers shall conform with such reasonable requirements as may be made by such owner for the purpose of preventing the communication through such wire or line from being injuriously affected as aforesaid.

If any difference arises between any such owner and the undertakers with respect to the reasonableness of any requirements so made such difference shall be determined by arbitration.

Provided that nothing in this sub-section shall apply to repairs or renewals of any electric line so long as the course nature and gauge of such electric line and the amount and nature of the current transmitted thereby are not altered.

(3.) If in any case the Undertakers make default in complying with the requirements of this section they shall make full compensation to every such owner as aforesaid for any loss or damage which he may incur by reason thereof, and in addition thereto they shall be liable to a penalty not exceeding five pounds for every such default and to a daily penalty not exceeding forty shillings. Provided that the Undertakers shall not be subject to any such penalties as aforesaid if the court having cognizance of the case shall be of opinion that the case was one of emergency and that the Undertakers complied with the requirements of this section so far as was reasonable under the circumstances or that the default in question was due to the fact that the Undertakers were ignorant of the position of the wire or line affected thereby and that such ignorance was not owing to any negligence on the part of the Undertakers.

(4.) Nothing in this section contained shall be held to deprive any owner of any existing rights to proceed against the Undertakers by indictment action or otherwise in relation to any of the matters aforesaid.

COMPULSORY WORKS.

Mains, &c., to be laid down in streets specified in Second Schedule and in remainder of area of supply.

17.—(1.) The Undertakers shall within a period of two years after the commencement of this Order lay down suitable and sufficient distributing mains for the purposes of general supply throughout every street or part of a street specified in that behalf in the Second Schedule and shall thereafter maintain the same.

(2.) In addition to the mains hereinbefore specified the Undertakers shall at any time after the expiration of six months after the commencement of this Order lay down suitable and sufficient distributing mains for the purposes of general supply throughout every other street or part of a street within the area of supply upon being required to do so in manner by this Order provided.

All such mains as last abovementioned (unless already laid down) shall be laid down by the Undertakers within six months after any requisition in that behalf served upon them in accordance with the provisions of this Order has become binding upon them or such further time as may in any case be approved of by the Board of Trade.

(3.) When any such requisition is made in respect of any street not repairable by the local authority which is not mentioned in the Third Schedule, the Undertakers shall (unless the authority or person by whom such street is repairable consent to the breaking up thereof) forthwith apply to the Board of Trade under section thirteen of the Electric Lighting Act 1882, for the written consent of the Board authorising and empowering the Undertakers to break up such street, and the requisition shall not be binding upon them if the Board of Trade refuse their consent in that behalf.

18. If the Undertakers make default in laying down any distributing mains in accordance with the provisions of this Order within the periods prescribed in that behalf respectively the Board of Trade may after considering any representations of the Undertakers, either revoke this Order as to the whole or any part of the area of supply or if the Undertakers so desire suffer the same to remain in force as to such area or part thereof subject to such conditions as they may think fit to impose, and any conditions so imposed shall be binding on and observed by the Undertakers and shall be of the like force and effect in every respect as though they were contained in this Order. Provided that the Board of Trade shall not revoke this Order as to part of the area of supply where the Undertakers make a representation that they desire to be relieved of their liabilities as respects the rest of the area of supply and in such case the Board of Trade shall not under this section revoke this Order otherwise than as to the whole of the area of supply. *If Undertakers fail to lay down mains, &c., Order may be revoked.*

19. Any requisition requiring the Undertakers to lay down distributing mains for the purposes of general supply throughout any street or part of a street may be made by six or more owners or occupiers of premises along such street or part of a street. *Manner in which requisition is to be made.*

Every such requisition shall be signed by the persons making the same and shall be served upon the Undertakers.

Forms of requisition shall be kept by the Undertakers at their office and a copy shall be supplied free of charge to any owner or occupier of premises within the area of supply on application for the same and any requisition so supplied shall be deemed valid in point of form.

20. Where any such requisition is made by any such owners or occupiers as aforesaid, the Undertakers (if they think fit) may within fourteen days after the service of the requisition upon them serve a notice on all the persons by whom the requisition is signed, stating that they decline to be bound by such requisition unless such persons or some of them will bind themselves to take or will guarantee that there shall be taken a supply of energy for three years of such amount in the aggregate (to be specified by the Undertakers in such notice) as will at the rates of charge for the time being charged by the Undertakers for a supply of energy from distributing mains to *Provisions on requisition by owners or occupiers.*

ordinary consumers within the area of supply produce annually such reasonable sum as shall be specified by the Undertakers in such notice. Provided that in such notice the Undertakers shall not without the authority of the Board of Trade specify any sum exceeding twenty per centum upon the expense of providing and laying down the required distributing mains and any other mains or additions to existing mains which may be necessary for the purpose of connecting such distributing mains with the nearest available source of supply.

Where such notice is served the requisition shall not be binding on the Undertakers unless within fourteen days after the service of such notice on all the persons signing the requisition has been effected or in case of difference the delivery of the arbitrator's award there be tendered to the Undertakers an agreement severally executed by such persons or some of them binding them to take or guaranteeing that there shall be taken for a period of three years at the least such specified amounts of energy respectively as will in the aggregate at the rates of charge above specified produce an annual sum amounting to the sum specified in the notice or determined by arbitration under this section nor unless sufficient security for the payment to the Undertakers of all moneys which may become due to them from such persons under such agreement is offered to the Undertakers (if required by them by such notice as aforesaid) within the period limited for the tender of the agreement as aforesaid.

If the Undertakers consider that the requisition is unreasonable or that under the circumstances of the case the provisions of this section ought to be varied they may within fourteen days after the service of the requisition upon them appeal to the Board of Trade, who after such inquiry (if any) as they shall think fit may by order either determine that the requisition is unreasonable and shall not be binding upon the Undertakers, or may authorise the Undertakers by their notice to require a supply of energy to be taken for such longer period than three years and to specify such sum or percentage whether calculated as herein-before provided or otherwise as shall be fixed or directed by the Order and the terms of the above-mentioned agreement shall be varied accordingly.

In case of any such appeal to the Board of Trade any notice by the Undertakers under this section may be served by them within fourteen days after the decision of the Board of Trade.

If any difference arises between the Undertakers and any persons signing any such requisition as to any such notice or agreement such difference shall subject to the provisions of this section and to the decision of the Board of Trade upon any such appeal as aforesaid be determined by arbitration.

SUPPLY.

Undertakers to furnish sufficient supply of energy to owners and occupiers within the area of supply.

21. The Undertakers shall upon being required to do so by the owner or occupier of any premises situate within fifty yards from any distributing main of the Undertakers in which they are for the time being required to maintain or are maintaining a supply of energy for the purposes of general supply to private consumers under this Order or the Board of Trade regulations give and continue to give a supply of energy for such premises in accordance with the provisions of this

Order and of the said regulations and they shall furnish and lay any electric lines that may be necessary for the purpose of supplying the maximum power with which any such owner or occupier may be entitled to be supplied under this Order subject to the conditions following (that is to say) :

> The cost of so much of any electric line for the supply of energy to any owner or occupier as may be laid upon the property of such owner or in the possession of such occupier and of so much of any such electric lines as it may be necessary to lay for a greater distance than sixty feet from any distributing main of the Undertakers although not on such property, shall if the Undertakers so require be defrayed by such owner or occupier.
>
> Every owner or occupier of premises requiring a supply of energy shall—
>
> Serve a notice upon the Undertakers specifying the premises in respect of which such supply is required and the maximum power required to be supplied and the day (not being an earlier day than a reasonable time after the date of the service of such notice) upon which such supply is required to commence ; and
>
> Enter into a written contract with the Undertakers (if required by them so to do) to continue to receive and pay for a supply of energy for a period of at least two years of such an amount that the payment to be made for the same at the rate of charge for the time being charged by the Undertakers for a supply of energy to ordinary consumers within the area of supply shall not be less than twenty per centum per annum on the outlay incurred by the Undertakers in providing any electric lines required under this section to be provided by them for the purpose of such supply, and give to the Undertakers (if required by them so to do) security for the payment to them of all moneys which may become due to them by such owner or occupier in respect of any electric lines to be furnished by the Undertakers and in respect of energy to be supplied by them.

Provided always that the Undertakers may after they have given a supply of energy for any premises by notice in writing require the owner or occupier of such premises within seven days after the date of the service of such notice to give to them security for the payment of all moneys which may become due to them in respect of such supply in case such owner or occupier has not already given such security or in case any security given has become invalid or is insufficient and in case any such owner or occupier fail to comply with the terms of such notice the Undertakers may if they think fit discontinue to supply energy for such premises so long as such failure continues.

Provided also that if the owner or occupier of any such premises as aforesaid uses any form of lamp or burner or uses the energy supplied to him by the Undertakers for any purposes or deals with it in any manner so as to unduly or improperly interfere with the efficient supply of energy to any other body or person by the Undertakers, the Undertakers may if they think fit discontinue to supply energy to such premises so long as such user continues.

Provided also that the Undertakers shall not be compelled to give a supply of energy to any premises unless they are reasonably satisfied that the electric lines fittings and apparatus therein are in good order and condition and not calculated to affect injuriously the use of energy by the Undertakers or by other persons.

If any difference arises under this section as to any improper use of energy or as to any alleged defect in any electric lines, fittings or apparatus, such difference shall be determined by arbitration.

Maximum power.

22. The maximum power with which any consumer shall be entitled to be supplied, shall be of such amount as he may require to be supplied with, not exceeding what may be reasonably anticipated as the maximum consumption on his premises. Provided that where any consumer has required the Undertakers to supply him with a maximum power of any specified amount he shall not be entitled to alter that maximum, except upon one month's notice to the Undertakers, and any expenses reasonably incurred by the Undertakers in respect of the service lines by which energy is supplied to the premises of such consumer, or any fittings or apparatus of the Undertakers upon such premises consequent upon such alteration shall be paid by him to the Undertakers, and may be recovered summarily as a civil debt.

If any difference arises between any such owner or occupier and the Undertakers as to what may be reasonably anticipated as the consumption on his premises or as to the reasonableness of any expenses under this section, such difference shall be determined by arbitration.

Penalty for failure to supply.

23. Whenever the Undertakers make default in supplying energy to any owner or occupier of premises to whom they may be and are required to supply energy under this Order, they shall be liable to a penalty not exceeding forty shillings in respect of every such default for each day upon which any such default occurs.

Whenever the Undertakers make default in supplying energy in accordance with the terms of the Board of Trade regulations, they shall be liable to such penalties as may by the said regulations be prescribed in that behalf.

Provided that the penalties to be inflicted on the Undertakers under this section shall in no case exceed in the aggregate the sum of fifty pounds in respect of any defaults not being wilful defaults on the part of the Undertakers for any one day, and provided also that in no case shall any penalty be inflicted in respect of any default if the court having cognisance of the case shall be of opinion that such default was caused by inevitable accident or force majeure or was of so slight or unimportant a character as not materially to affect the value of the supply.

PRICE.

Methods of charging.

24. The Undertakers may charge for energy supplied by them to any ordinary consumer (otherwise than by agreement)—

(1) By the actual amount of energy so supplied; or

(2) By the electrical quantity contained in such supply; or

(3) By such other method as may, for the time being, be approved by the Board of Trade.

Electric Lighting Orders Confirmation (No. 6) Act, 1897.

Provided that where the Undertakers charge by any method so approved by the Board of Trade any consumer who objects to that method may by one month's notice in writing require the Undertakers to charge him at their option by the actual amount of energy supplied to him or by the electrical quantity contained in such supply and thereafter the Undertakers shall not except with the consumer's consent charge him by any other method.

Provided also that before commencing to supply energy through any distributing main for the purposes of general supply the Undertakers shall by public advertisement give notice by what method they propose to charge for energy supplied through such main and where the undertakers have given any such notice they shall not be entitled to change such method of charging except after one month's notice of such change has been given by them to every consumer who is supplied by them from such main.

25. The prices to be charged by the Undertakers for energy supplied by them shall not exceed those stated in that behalf in the Fourth Schedule in the first and second sections thereof respectively, or in the case of a method of charge approved by the Board of Trade such price as the Board shall on approving such method determine. *Maximum prices.*

26. Subject to the provisions of this Order and of the principal Act and to the right of the consumer to require that he shall be charged according to some one or other of the methods above mentioned, the Undertakers may make any agreement with a consumer as to the price to be charged for energy and the mode in which such charges are to be ascertained and may charge accordingly. *Other charges by agreement.*

Electric Inspectors.

27. The Board of Trade, on the application of any consumer or of the Undertakers, may appoint and keep appointed one or more competent and impartial person or persons to be electric inspectors under this Order. *Appointment of electric inspectors.*

The duties of an Electric Inspector under this Order shall be as follows:—

(a) The inspection and testing periodically and in special cases of the Undertakers' electric lines and works and the supply of energy given by them;

(b) The certifying and examination of meters; and

(c) Such other duties in the relation to the undertaking as may be required of him under the provisions of this Order or of the Board of Trade regulations.

The Board of Trade may prescribe the fees to be taken by an electric inspector and the manner in which and the times at which his duties are to be performed.

28. The Undertakers shall pay to every electric inspector appointed under this Order such reasonable remuneration (if any) as may be determined by the Board of Trade and such remuneration may be in addition to or in substitution for any fees which are directed to be paid to electric inspectors for services rendered by them under *Remuneration of electric inspectors.*

this Order or the Board of Trade regulations as may be settled by such Board and where any such remuneration is settled to be in substitution for fees any fees payable by any party other than the Undertakers shall in lieu of being paid to such electric inspector for his own use be due and paid to him on behalf and for the use of the Undertakers and shall be carried by them to the credit of the local rate.

Notice of accidents and inquiries by Board of Trade.

29.—(1.) The Undertakers shall send to the Board of Trade notice of any accident by explosion or fire and also of any other accident of such kind as to have caused or to be likely to have caused loss of life or personal injury which has occurred in any part of the Undertakers' works or their circuits or in connexion with the same and also notice of any loss of life or personal injury (if any) occasioned by any such accident. Such notice shall be sent by the earliest practicable post after the accident occurs or as the case may be after the loss of life or personal injury becomes known to the Undertakers.

If the Undertakers fail to comply with the provisions of this subsection they shall be liable for each offence to a penalty not exceeding twenty pounds.

(2.) The Board of Trade may if they deem it necessary appoint any electric inspector or other fit person or persons to inquire and report as to the cause of any accident affecting the safety of the public which may have been occasioned by or in connexion with the Undertakers' works whether notice of the accident has or has not been received from the Undertakers or as to the manner and extent in and to which the provisions of this Order and the principal Act and of the Board of Trade regulations so far as such provisions affect the safety of the public have been complied with by the Undertakers and any person appointed under this section not being an electric inspector shall for the purposes of his appointment have all the powers of an electric inspector under this Order.

TESTING AND INSPECTION.

Testing of mains.

30. On the occasion of the testing of any main of the Undertakers reasonable notice thereof shall be given to the Undertakers by the electric inspector and such testing shall be carried out at such suitable hours as in the opinion of the inspector will least interfere with the supply of energy by the Undertakers and in such manner as the inspector may think expedient, but except under the provisions of a special order in that behalf made by the Board of Trade he shall not be entitled to have access to or interfere with the mains of the Undertakers at any points other than those at which the Undertakers have reserved for themselves access to the said mains. Provided that the Undertakers shall not be held responsible for any interruption in the supply of energy which may be occasioned by or required by such inspector for the purpose of any such testing as aforesaid. Provided also that such testings shall not be made in regard to any particular portion of a main oftener than once in any three months, unless in pursuance of a special order in that behalf made by the Board of Trade.

31. An electric inspector if and when required to do so by any consumer shall on payment by such consumer of the prescribed fee test the variation of electric pressure at the consumer's terminals or make such other inspection and testing of the service lines apparatus and works of the Undertakers upon the consumer's premises as may be necessary for the purpose of determining whether the Undertakers have complied with the provisions of this Order and the Board of Trade regulations. *Testing of works and supply on consumer's premises.*

32. A court of summary jurisdiction may upon the application of any ten consumers direct the Undertakers at their own cost to establish at such places within a reasonable distance from a distributing main and keep in proper condition such reasonable number of testing stations as the court shall deem proper and sufficient for testing the supply of energy by the Undertakers through such main, and thereupon the Undertakers shall establish such testing places and provide thereat such proper and suitable instruments of a pattern to be approved by the Board of Trade as the court may direct and they shall connect such stations by means of proper and sufficient electric lines with such mains and supply energy thereto for the purpose of such testing. *Undertakers to establish testing stations.*

33. The Undertakers shall set up and keep upon all premises from which they supply energy by any distributing mains such suitable and proper instruments of such pattern and construction as may be approved of or prescribed by the Board of Trade, and shall take and record and keep recorded such observations as the Board of Trade may from time to time prescribe and any observations so recorded shall be receivable in evidence. *Undertakers to keep instruments on their premises.*

34. The Undertakers shall keep in efficient working order all instruments which they are required by or under this Order to place set up or keep at any testing station or on their own premises and any electric inspector appointed under this Order may examine and record the readings of such instruments and any readings so recorded shall be receivable in evidence. *Readings of instruments to be taken.*

35. Any electric inspector appointed under this Order shall have the right to have access at all reasonable hours to the testing stations and premises of the Undertakers for the purpose of testing the electric lines and instruments of the Undertakers and ascertaining if the same are in order and in case the same are not in order he may require the Undertakers forthwith to have the same put in order. *Electric inspector may test Undertakers' instruments.*

36. The Undertakers may if they think fit on each occasion of the testing of any main or service line or the testing or inspection of any instruments of the Undertakers by any electric inspector be represented by some officer or other agent but such officer or agent shall not interfere with the testing or inspection. *Representation of Undertakers at testings.*

37. The Undertakers shall afford all facilities for the proper execution of this Order with respect to inspection and testing and the readings and inspection of instruments and shall comply with all the requirements of or under this Order in that behalf and in case the Undertakers make default in complying with any of the provisions of this section they shall be liable in respect of each default to a penalty not exceeding five pounds and to a daily penalty not exceeding one pound. *Undertakers to give facilities for testing.*

Report of results of testing.

38. Every electric inspector shall on the day immediately following that on which any testing has been completed by him under this Order make and deliver a report of the results of his testing to the authority or person by whom he was required to make such testing and also to the Undertakers and such report shall be receivable in evidence.

If the Undertakers or any such authority or person are or is dissatisfied with any report of any electric inspector, they or he may appeal to the Board of Trade against such report, and thereupon the Board of Trade shall inquire into and decide upon the matter of any such appeal and their decision shall be final and binding on all parties.

Expenses of electric inspector.

39. Save as otherwise provided by this Order or by the Board of Trade regulations all fees and reasonable expenses of an electric inspector shall unless agreed be ascertained by the Board of Trade, and shall be paid by the Undertakers and may be recovered summarily as a civil debt.

Provided that where the report of an electric inspector or the decision of the Board of Trade shows that any consumer was guilty of any default or negligence, such fees and expenses shall on being ascertained as above mentioned be paid by such consumer or consumers as the Board of Trade having regard to such report or decision shall direct and may be recovered summarily as a civil debt.

Provided also that in any proceedings for penalties under this Order any such fees and expenses incurred in connexion with such proceedings shall be payable by the complainant or defendant as the court may direct.

METERS.

Meters to be used except by agreement.

40. The amount of energy supplied by the Undertakers to any ordinary consumer under this Order or the electrical quantity contained in such supply (according to the method by which the Undertakers elect to charge) in this Order referred to as "the value of the supply" shall except as otherwise agreed between such consumer and the Undertakers be ascertained by means of an appropriate meter duly certified under the provisions of this Order.

Meters to be certified.

41. A meter shall be considered to be duly certified under the provisions of this Order if it be certified by an electric inspector appointed under this Order to be a correct meter and to be of some construction and pattern and to have been fixed and to have been connected with the service lines in some manner approved of by the Board of Trade, and every such meter is in this Order referred to as a "certified meter." Provided that where any alteration is made in any certified meter or where any such meter is unfixed or disconnected from the service lines, such meter shall cease to be a certified meter unless and until it be again certified as a certified meter under the provisions of this Order.

Inspector to certify meters.

42. Every electric inspector on being required to do so by the Undertakers or by any consumer and on payment of the prescribed fee by the party so requiring him shall examine any meter intended for ascertaining the value of the supply, and shall certify the same as a certified meter if he considers it entitled to be so certified.

43. Where the value of the supply is under this Order required to be ascertained by means of an appropriate meter the Undertakers shall if required so to do by any consumer supply him with an appropriate meter and shall if required so to do fix the same upon the premises of the consumer and connect the service lines therewith and procure such meter to be duly certified under the provisions of this Order and for such purposes may authorise and empower any officer or person to enter upon such premises at all reasonable times and execute all necessary works and do all necessary acts. Provided that previously to supplying any such meter the Undertakers may require such consumer to pay to them a reasonable sum in respect of the price of such meter or to give security therefor or (if he desires to hire such meter) may require him to enter into an agreement for the hire of such meter as herein-after provided.

Undertakers to supply meters if required to do so.

44. No consumer shall connect any meter used or to be used under this Order for ascertaining the value of the supply with any electric line through which energy is supplied by the Undertakers or disconnect any such meter from any such electric line unless he has given to the Undertakers not less than forty-eight hours' notice in writing of his intention so to do, and if any person acts in contravention of this section he shall be liable for each offence to a penalty not exceeding forty shillings.

Meters not to be connected or disconnected without notice.

45. Every consumer shall at all times at his own expense keep all meters belonging to him whereby the value of the supply is to be ascertained in proper order for correctly registering such value and in default of his so doing the Undertakers may cease to supply energy through such meter.

Consumer to keep his meter in proper order.

The Undertakers shall have access to and be at liberty to take off remove test inspect and replace any such meter at all reasonable times Provided that all reasonable expenses of and incident to any such taking off removing testing inspecting and replacing and the procuring such meter to be again duly certified where such re-certifying is thereby rendered necessary shall if the meter be found to be not in proper order be paid by the consumer but if the same be in proper order all expenses connected therewith shall be paid by the Undertakers.

46. The Undertakers may let for hire any meter for ascertaining the value of the supply and any fittings thereto for such remuneration in money and on such terms with respect to the repair of such meter and fittings and for securing the safety and return to the Undertakers of such meter and fittings as may be agreed upon between the hirer and the Undertakers or in case of difference decided by the Board of Trade and such remuneration shall be recoverable by the Undertakers summarily as a civil debt.

Power to the Undertakers to let meters.

47. The Undertakers shall unless the agreement for hire otherwise provides at all times at their own expense keep all meters let for hire by them to any consumer whereby the value of the supply is ascertained in proper order for correctly registering such value and in default of their so doing the consumer shall not be liable to pay rent for the same during such time as such default continues. The Undertakers shall for the purposes aforesaid have access to and be at liberty to remove test inspect and replace any such meter at all

Undertakers to keep meters let for hire in repair.

reasonable times. Provided that the expenses of procuring any such meter to be again duly certified where such re-certifying is thereby rendered necessary shall be paid by the Undertakers.

Differences as to correctness of meter to be settled by inspector.

48. If any difference arises between any consumer and the Undertakers as to whether any meter whereby the value of the supply is ascertained (whether belonging to such consumer or the Undertakers) is or is not in proper order for correctly registering such value or as to whether such value has been correctly registered in any case by any meter such difference shall be determined upon the application of either party by an electric inspector who shall also order by which of the parties the costs of and incidental to the proceedings before him shall be paid, and the decision of such inspector shall be final and binding on all parties. Subject as aforesaid the register of the meter shall be conclusive evidence in the absence of fraud of the value of the supply.

Undertakers to pay expenses of providing new meters where method of charge altered.

49. Where any consumer who is supplied with energy by the Undertakers from any distributing main is provided with a certified meter for the purpose of ascertaining the value of the supply and the Undertakers change the method of charging for energy supplied by them from such main, the Undertakers shall pay to such consumer the reasonable expenses to which he may be put in providing a new meter for the purpose of ascertaining the value of the supply according to such new method of charging and such expenses may be recovered by the consumer from the Undertakers summarily as a civil debt.

Undertakers may place meters to measure supply or to check measurement thereof.

50. In addition to any meter which may be placed upon the premises of any consumer to ascertain the value of the supply, the Undertakers may place upon his premises such meter or other apparatus as they may desire for the purpose of ascertaining or regulating either the amount of energy supplied to such consumer or the number of hours during which such supply is given or the maximum power taken by such consumer or any other quantity or time connected with the supply. Provided that such meter or apparatus shall be of some construction and pattern and shall be fixed and connected with the service lines in some manner approved by the Board of Trade and shall be supplied and maintained entirely at the cost of the Undertakers and shall not except by agreement be placed otherwise than between the mains of the Undertakers and the consumer's terminals.

MAPS.

Map of area of supply to be made.

51. The Undertakers shall forthwith after commencing to supply energy under this Order cause a map to be made of the area of supply and shall cause to be marked thereon the line and the depth below the surface of all their then existing mains service lines and other underground works and street boxes, and shall once in every year cause such map to be duly corrected so as to show the then existing lines. The Undertakers shall also if so required by the Board of Trade or the Postmaster-General cause to be made sections showing the level of all their existing mains and underground works other than service lines. The said map and sections shall be on such scale or scales as the Board of Trade shall prescribe.

Every map and section so made or corrected or a copy thereof marked with the date when it was so made or last corrected shall be kept by the Undertakers at their principal office within the area of supply and shall at all reasonable times be open to the inspection of all applicants and such applicants may take copies of the same or any part thereof. The Undertakers may demand and take from every such applicant as aforesaid, such fee not exceeding one shilling for each inspection of such map section or copy, and such further fee not exceeding five shillings for each copy of the same or any part thereof taken by such applicant as they may prescribe.

The Undertakers shall if so required by the Board of Trade or the Postmaster-General supply to them or him a copy of any such map or section and cause such copy to be duly corrected so as to agree with the original or originals thereof as kept for the time being at the office of the Undertakers.

If the Undertakers fail to comply with any of the requirements of this section they shall for every such offence be liable to a penalty not exceeding ten pounds and to a daily penalty not exceeding two pounds.

Application of Moneys Received.

52. All moneys received by the Undertakers in respect of the undertaking except (A) borrowed money and (B) money arising from the disposal of lands acquired for the purposes of this Order and (C) money not in the nature of rent received by them in respect of any transfer under the provisions of this Order shall be applied by them as follows: — *Application of revenue.*

(1.) In payment of the working and establishment expenses and cost of maintenance of the undertaking including all costs, expenses, penalties and damages incurred or payable by the Undertakers consequent upon any proceedings by or against the Undertakers, their officers or servants, in relation to the undertaking.

(2.) In payment of the interest or dividend on any mortgages stock or other securities granted and issued by the Undertakers in respect of money borrowed for electricity purposes.

(3.) In providing any instalments or sinking fund required to be provided in respect of moneys borrowed for electricity purposes.

(4.) In payment of all other their expenses of executing this Order not being expenses properly chargeable to capital.

(5) In providing a reserve fund if they think fit by setting aside such money as they may from time to time think reasonable and investing the same and the resulting income thereof in Government securities or in any other securities in which trustees are by law for the time being authorised to invest other than stock or securities of the Undertakers and accumulating the same at compound interest until the fund so formed amounts to one-tenth of the aggregate capital expenditure on the undertaking which fund shall be applicable to answer any deficiency at any time happening in the income of the Undertakers from the undertaking or to meet any extraordinary claim or demand at any time arising against the Undertakers in respect of the undertaking and so that if that fund is at any time reduced it may thereafter be again restored to the prescribed limit, and so from time to time as often as such reduction happens.

The Undertakers shall carry the net surplus remaining in any year and the annual proceeds of the reserve fund when amounting to the prescribed limit to the credit of the local rate as defined by the principal Act, or at their option shall apply such surplus or any part thereof to the improvement of the district for which they are the local authority, or in reduction of the capital moneys borrowed for electricity purposes.

Provided always that if the surplus in any year exceed five per centum per annum upon the aggregate capital expenditure on the undertaking, the Underwriters shall make such a rateable reduction in the charge for the supply of energy as in their judgment will reduce the surplus to the said maximum rate of profit, but this proviso shall only apply to so much of the undertaking as shall for the time being remain in the hands of the Undertakers.

Any deficiency of income in any year not answered out of the reserve fund shall be charged upon and payable out of the local rate.

Application of capital moneys.

53. All moneys arising from the disposal of lands acquired by the Undertakers for the purposes of this Order, and all moneys not of the nature of rent received by them in respect of any transfer of the undertaking under the provisions of this Order and all other capital moneys received by them in respect of the undertaking shall be applied by them as follows :—

(1) In the reduction of the capital moneys borrowed by them for electricity purposes.

(2) In the reduction of the capital moneys borrowed by them for other than electricity purposes.

NOTICES, &c.

Notices, &c., may be printed or written.

54. Notices, orders and other documents under this Order may be in writing or in print or partly in writing and partly in print, and where any notice, order or document requires authentication by the Undertakers, the signature thereof by their Clerk or Surveyor shall be sufficient authentication.

Service of notices, &c.

55. Any notice, order or document required or authorised to be served upon any body or person under this Order or the principal Act may be served by the same being addressed to such body or person and being left at or transmitted through the post to the following addresses respectively :—

(A) In the case of the Board of Trade, the office of the Board of Trade ;

(B) In the case of the Postmaster-General, the General Post Office ;

(C) In the case of any county council, the office of such council ;

(D) In the case of any local authority, the office of such local authority ;

(E) In the case of any company having a registered office, the registered office of such company ;

(F) In the case of a company having an office or offices, but no registered office, the principal office of such company ;

(G) In the case of any other person, the usual or last known place of abode of such person.

A notice, order or document by this Order required or authorised to be served on the owner or occupier of any premises shall be deemed to be properly addressed if addressed by the description of the "owner" or "occupier" of the premises (naming the premises) without further name or description.

A notice, order or document by this Order required or authorised to be served on the owner or occupier of premises, may be served by delivering the same or a true copy thereof to some person on the premises or, if there is no person on the premises to whom the same can with reasonable diligence be delivered, by fixing it on some conspicuous part of the premises.

Subject to the provisions of this Order as to cases of emergency where the interval of time between the service of any notice or document under the provisions of this Order, and the execution of any works or the performance of any duty or act is less than seven days, the following days shall not be reckoned in the computation of such time (that is to say) Sunday, Christmas Day, Good Friday, any bank holiday under and within the meaning of the Bank Holiday Act 1871, and any act amending that Act and any day appointed for public fast, humiliation or thanksgiving.

REVOCATION OF ORDER.

56. If at any time after the commencement of this Order, the Board of Trade have reason to believe that the Undertakers have made default in executing works or supplying energy in accordance with the provisions of this Order, the Board of Trade may, after such inquiry as they may think necessary, revoke this order as to the whole or with the consent of the Undertakers any part of the area of supply upon such terms as to the Board of Trade may seem just. *Revocation where works not executed.*

57. In addition to any powers which the Board of Trade may have in that behalf they may revoke this Order at any time with the consent and concurrence of the Undertakers upon such terms as the Board of Trade may think fit. *Revocation of Order with consent.*

58. If the Board of Trade at any time revoke this Order as to the whole or any part of the area of supply, any persons who may be liable to repair any street or part of a street within such area or part thereof in which any works of the Undertakers may have been placed may forthwith remove such works with all reasonable care, and the Undertakers shall pay to such persons such reasonable costs of such removal as may be specified in a notice to be served on the Undertakers by such persons or if so required by the Undertakers within one week after the service of such notice upon them as may be settled by arbitration. *Provisions where Order revoked.*

If the Undertakers fail to pay such reasonable costs as aforesaid within one month after the service upon them of such notice or the delivery of the award of the arbitrator (as the case may be) such persons, as aforesaid, may without any previous notice to the Undertakers (but without prejudice to any other remedy which they may have for the recovery of the amount) sell and dispose of any such works, as aforesaid, either by public auction or private sale, and for such sum or sums and to such person or persons as they may think fit and may out of the proceeds of such sale pay and reimburse themselves the amount of the costs so specified or settled as aforesaid and of the costs of sale and the balance (if any) of the proceeds of the sale shall be paid over by them to the Undertakers.

Transfers of Powers, &c.

Transfer of powers, &c.

59.—(1.) At any time after the commencement of this Order the Undertakers may with the consent of the Board of Trade by deed to be approved by the Board of Trade transfer their powers, duties, liabilities and works to any company or person subject to such exceptions and modifications (if any), and for such period and upon such terms as may be specified therein and either as to the whole or any part or parts of the area of supply and during the said period but subject to the provisions of this Order such Company or person shall to the extent of the powers, duties and liabilities so transferred be the Undertakers for the purposes of this Order.

(2.) One month at least before any draft deed is submitted to the Board of Trade for their approval under this section, notice of the intention to make such transfer shall be published by the Undertakers by advertisement, and a copy of the said draft deed shall be deposited for public inspection during office hours at the principal office of the Undertakers within the area of supply, and printed copies thereof shall be supplied to every person demanding the same at a price not exceeding sixpence for each copy.

(3.) Every such advertisement shall contain the following particulars:—

(A) The area in respect of which the transfer is proposed to be made;

(B) The period for which the transfer is proposed to be made;

(C) The rent or other pecuniary consideration in respect of the transfer;

(D) A general description of the powers, duties or liabilities of the Undertakers proposed to be excepted or modified, and of the terms upon which the transfer is proposed to be made; and

(E) The address of the office at which the copy of the said draft deed is deposited for public inspection and at which printed copies of the same are on sale:

And such advertisement shall be inserted once at least in each of two successive weeks in one and the same newspaper circulating within the area of supply, and once at least in the London Gazette.

(4.) The Undertakers may with the consent of the Board of Trade by deed to be approved in like manner renew or continue any such transfer for such period and subject to such variations or modifications (if any) as may be specified therein, and the above provisions as to advertisements and particulars shall apply to such matters as are hereby required to be specified in such last-mentioned deed.

(5.) Where in relation to any powers, duties or liabilities so transferred such company or person have in the opinion of the Board of Trade been guilty of any act or default in respect of which the Board of Trade are empowered to revoke this Order, the Board of Trade if they think fit in lieu of revoking this Order may by order permit the Undertakers to resume the undertaking as from such day as may be fixed by the order and from and after the said day the powers, duties and liabilities of the said company or person as Undertakers shall cease and determine but without prejudice to anything done or suffered during the period of transfer.

(6.) Any questions arising between the Undertakers and the said company or person respecting the resumption of the undertaking by the Undertakers shall be determined on the application of either party by the Board of Trade, regard being had to the deed of transfer so far as applicable and the decision of the Board of Trade shall be final and conclusive.

(7.) As soon as practicable after any such deed is approved by the Board of Trade printed copies thereof shall be kept by the Undertakers for public inspection at their principal office within the area of supply, and supplied to any person demanding the same at a price not exceeding sixpence for each copy, and in case of any default herein the Undertakers shall be liable to a penalty not exceeding five pounds and to a daily penalty not exceeding five pounds.

(8) Nothing in this section shall affect any powers, duties or liabilities of the Undertakers which shall not be transferred by any such deed and the Undertakers shall continue to have and be subject to such powers duties and liabilities (if any).

GENERAL.

60. If at any time it is established to the satisfaction of the Board of Trade (A) that the Undertakers are supplying energy otherwise than by means of a system which has been approved by the Board of Trade or (except in accordance with the provisions of this Order) have permitted any part of their circuits to be connected with earth or have placed any electric line above ground or (B) that any electric lines or works of the Undertakers are defective so as not to be in accordance with the provisions of this Order or the Board of Trade regulations or (C) that any work of the Undertakers or their supply of energy is attended with danger to the public safety or injuriously affects any telegraphic line of the Postmaster-General, the Board of Trade may by order specify the matter complained of and require the Undertakers to abate or discontinue the same within such period as may be therein limited in that behalf, and if the Undertakers make default in complying with such order they shall be liable to a penalty not exceeding twenty pounds for every day during which such default continues. *Remedying of system and works.*

The Board of Trade may also if they think fit by the same or any other order forbid the use of any electric line or work as from such date as may be specified in that behalf until the order is complied with or for such time as may be so specified and if the Undertakers make use of any such electric line or work while the use thereof is so forbidden they shall be liable to a penalty not exceeding one hundred pounds for every day during which such user continues.

In any case of non-compliance with an order under this section whether a pecuniary penalty has been recovered or not the Board of Trade if in their opinion the public interest so requires may revoke this Order on such terms as they may think just.

61. The Board of Trade regulations for the time being in force shall within one month after the same as made or last altered have come into force be printed at the expense of the Undertakers and true copies thereof certified by or on behalf of the Undertakers shall be kept by them at their principal office within the area of supply and supplied to any person demanding the same at a price not exceeding sixpence for each copy. *Publication of regulations*

If the Undertakers make default in complying with the provisions of this section they shall be liable to a penalty not exceeding five pounds and to a daily penalty not exceeding five pounds.

Nature and amount of security.

62. Where any security is required under this Order to be given to or by the Undertakers such security may be by way of deposit or otherwise and of such amount as may be agreed upon between the parties or as in default of agreement may be determined on the application of either party by a court of summary jurisdiction who may also order by which of the parties the costs of the proceedings before them shall be paid and the decision of the said court shall be final and binding on all parties. Provided that where any such security is given by way of deposit the party to whom such security is given shall pay interest at the rate of four per centum per annum on every sum of ten shillings so deposited for every six months during which the same remains in their hands.

Proceedings of Board of Trade.

63. All things required or authorised under this Order to be done by, to, or before the Board of Trade may be done by, to, or before the President or a secretary or an assistant secretary of the Board.

All documents purporting to be orders made by the Board of Trade and to be sealed with the seal of the Board or to be signed by a secretary or assistant secretary of the Board or by any person authorised in that behalf by the President of the Board shall be received in evidence and shall be deemed to be such orders without further proof unless the contrary is shown.

A certificate signed by the President of the Board of Trade that any order made or act done is the order or act of the Board shall be conclusive evidence of the order or act so certified.

As to approval or consent of Board of Trade.

64. Where this Order provides for any consent or approval of the Board of Trade the Board may give such consent or approval subject to terms or conditions or may withhold their consent or approval as in their discretion they may think fit.

All costs and expenses of or incident to any approval, consent, certificate, or order of the Board of Trade or of any inspector or person appointed by the Board of Trade including the cost of any inquiry or tests which may be required to be made by the Board of Trade for the purpose of determining whether the same should be given or made to such an amount as the Board of Trade shall certify to be due shall be borne and paid by the applicant or applicants therefor. Provided always that where any approval is given by the Board of Trade to any plan, pattern, or specification, they may require such copies of the same as they may think fit to be prepared and deposited at their office at the expense of the said applicant or applicants and may as they think fit revoke any approval so given or permit such approval to be continued subject to such modifications as they may think necessary.

Notice of approval of Board of Trade, &c., to be given by advertisement.

65. Where the Board of Trade upon the application of the Undertakers give any approval or grant any extension of any time limited for the performance of any duties by the Undertakers or revoke this Order as to the whole or any part of the area of supply notice that such approval has been given or such extension of time

granted or such revocation made shall if the Board of Trade so direct be published by public advertisement once at least in each of two successive weeks in some one and the same local newspaper by the Undertakers.

66. All penalties, fees, expenses, and other moneys recoverable under this Order or under the Board of Trade regulations the recovery of which is not otherwise specially provided for may be recovered summarily in manner provided by the Summary Jurisdiction Acts. *Recovery and application of penalties.*

Any penalty recovered on prosecution by any body or person or any part thereof may if the court shall so direct be paid to such body or person.

67. The Undertakers shall be answerable for all accidents, damages, and injuries happening through the act or default of the Undertakers or of any person in their employment by reason of or in consequence of any of the Undertakers' works and shall save harmless all authorities bodies and persons by whom any street is repairable and all other authorities companies and bodies collectively and individually and their officers and servants from all damages and costs in respect of such accidents, damages, and injuries. *Undertakers to be responsible for all damages.*

68. Section two hundred and sixty-five of the Public Health Act, 1875, shall be incorporated with this Order and in the construction of that section for the purposes of this Order "this Act" means this Order and the principal Act and the "local authority" means the Undertakers. *Incorporation of section 265 of Public Health Act, 1875.*

[Sec. 265 of the Public Health Act, 1875, protects local authorities and their officers from personal liability in the *bonâ fide* execution of their powers.]

69. Nothing in this Order shall affect any right or remedy of the Postmaster-General under the principal Act or the Telegraph Acts, 1863 to 1892, and all provisions contained in this Order in favour of the Postmaster-General shall be construed to be in addition to and not in modification of the provisions of those Acts. *Saving for Postmaster-General.*

70. Nothing in this Order shall exonerate the Undertakers from any indictment action or other proceedings for nuisance in the event of any nuisance being caused or permitted by them. *Undertakers not exempted from proceedings for nuisance.*

71. Nothing in this Order shall exempt the Undertakers or their undertaking from the provisions of or deprive the Undertakers of the benefits of any general Act relating to electricity or to the supply of or price to be charged for energy which may be passed after the commencement of this Order. *Provision as to general Acts.*

72. The Wallasey Electric Lighting License, 1896, is hereby revoked as from the commencement of this Order but this revocation shall not affect anything done or suffered or any right obligation or liability acquired accrued or incurred under the said License, and any legal proceeding may be taken in respect thereof as if the said License had not been revoked. *Revocation of License.*

SCHEDULES.

FIRST SCHEDULE.

AREA OF SUPPLY.

The Urban District of Wallasey as the same is constituted at the commencement of this Order.

SECOND SCHEDULE.

List of streets and parts of streets throughout which the Undertakers are to lay distributing mains within a period of two years after the commencement of this Order:—

Sea View Road, Liscard.
Liscard Village, Liscard.
Manor Road, Liscard.
Sea Bank Road, New Brighton, Liscard and Egremont.
Rowson Street, New Brighton.
Victoria Road, New Brighton.
King Street, Egremont.
Brighton Street, Seacombe.
Church Road, Seacombe.
Tobin Street, Egremont.

THIRD SCHEDULE.

List of streets not repairable by the local authority railways and tramways which may be broken up by the Undertakers in pursuance of the special powers granted by this Order:—

(*a*.) STREETS.

Sea View Road, Liscard.
Claremont Road, Wallasey.

(*b*.) RAILWAYS.

None.

(*c*.) TRAMWAYS.

The tramways of the Wirral Tramway Company, Limited.

FOURTH SCHEDULE.

In this schedule the expression "unit" shall mean the energy contained in a current of 1,000 ampères flowing under an electromotive force of one volt during one hour.

Schedules.

SECTION 1.

Where the Undertakers charge any consumer by the actual amount of energy supplied to him they shall be entitled to charge him at the following rates per quarter. For any amount up to twenty units thirteen shillings and fourpence and for each unit over twenty units eightpence.

SECTION 2.

Where the Undertakers charge any consumer by the electrical quantity contained in the supply given to him they shall be entitled to charge him according to the rates set forth in section 1 of this schedule the amount of energy supplied to him being taken to be the product of such electrical quantity and the declared pressure at the consumer's terminals (that is to say) such a constant pressure at those terminals as may declared by the Undertakers under the Board of Trade regulations.

Sec. 1—2

Local Government Board's Provisional Orders Confirmation (No. 2) Act, 1897.

(*Confirming the Wallasey Order, 1897.*)

AN

ACT

to confirm certain Provisional Orders of the Local Government Board relating to Buxton, Kingston-upon-Hull, Plymouth, Ramsgate (two), Southampton, Southend-on-Sea, WALLASEY, and West Ham.

15TH JULY, 1897.

38 & 39 Vict. c. 55. WHEREAS the Local Government Board have made the Provisional Orders set forth in the schedule hereto under the provisions of the Public Health Act, 1875.

And whereas it is requisite that the said Orders should be confirmed by Parliament.

Be it therefore enacted by the Queen's Most Excellent Majesty by and with the advice and consent of the Lords Spiritual and Temporal and Commons in this present Parliament assembled and by the authority of the same as follows:—

Orders in schedule confirmed.
1. The Orders as altered and set out in the schedule hereto shall be and the same are hereby confirmed and all the provisions thereof shall have full validity and force.

Short title.
2. This Act may be cited as the Local Government Board's Provisional Orders Confirmation (No. 2) Act, 1897.

[The omitted Orders relate to districts other than Wallasey.]

60 & 61 Vict.   Local Government Board's   ch. lxviii.
          Provisional Orders Confirmation
                  (No. 2) Act, 1897.

THE WALLASEY ORDER, 1897.

URBAN DISTRICT OF WALLASEY.

Provisional Order for altering a Local Act and certain Confirming Acts.

To the Urban District Council of Wallasey :—

And to all others whom it may concern.

Whereas the Urban District Council of Wallasey (hereinafter referred to as "the District Council") are the local authority within the meaning of the Public Health Act, 1875, for the Urban District of Wallasey (hereinafter referred to as "the District") and the unrepealed provisions of the Wallasey Improvement Act, 1872 (hereinafter referred to as "the Local Act") as altered by the Provisional Orders hereinafter recited and by certain other Provisional Orders made by the Local Government Board and duly confirmed by Parliament, but which last-mentioned Orders do not affect the subject-matter of this Order are in force in the district. — 35 & 36 Vict. c. cxxv.

And whereas by section 17 of the Local Act as altered by the Wallasey Order (No. 1), 1877, which was confirmed by the Local Government Board's Provisional Orders Confirmation (Caistor Union, &c.) Act, 1877, by the Wallasey Order, 1881, which was confirmed by the Local Government Board's Provisional Orders Confirmation (Acton, &c.) Act, 1881, by the Wallasey Order 1883, which was confirmed by the Local Government Board's Provisional Orders Confirmation (No. 7) Act, 1883, and by the Wallasey Order, 1895, which was confirmed by the Local Government Board's Provisional Orders Confirmation (No. 1) Act, 1895, the District Council or their predecessors were empowered to borrow for ferry purposes sums amounting in the whole to the sum of two hundred and fifty-three thousand five hundred pounds; — 40 & 41 Vict. c. ccxxvii. 14 & 45 Vict. c. clxii. 46 & 47 Vict. c. cxxxvii. 58 & 59 Vict. c. xl.

And whereas it is expedient that the District Council should be empowered to borrow further moneys for the purposes hereinafter mentioned;

Now therefore we the Local Government Board in pursuance of the powers given to us by sections 297 and 303 of the Public Health Act, 1875, and by any other Statutes in that behalf do hereby order that from and after the date of the Act of Parliament confirming this Order the Local Act and the Confirming Acts above mentioned so far as they respectively relate to the Orders above mentioned shall be altered so as to provide as follows, viz. :— 38 & 39 Vict. c. 55.

Art. I. The District Council may with the sanction of the Local Government Board and subject to the provisions of this Order borrow upon the security of the Wallasey Ferries Account and of the district fund and general district rate of the District or upon either of such securities either together or separately such sums not exceeding in the whole the sum of ten thousand and six hundred pounds as may from time to time be necessary for the purposes of a dredger in connection with their ferry undertaking in addition to the said sum of two hundred and fifty-three thousand five hundred pounds.

A A

Art. II. For the purpose of raising money by virtue of this Order the provisions of the Local Loans Act, 1875, shall be available to the District Council and sections 236 to 238 both inclusive of the Public Health Act, 1875, shall apply to all moneys raised and borrowed on mortgage by virtue of this Order.

Art. III. The moneys borrowed by virtue of this Order shall be repaid within such period not exceeding twenty years from the date of borrowing as the District Council with the sanction of the Local Government Board shall determine and the period so determined and sanctioned is hereinafter referred to as "the prescribed period" and shall be the prescribed period for the purpose of the Local Loans Act, 1875.

Art. IV.—(1.) The District Council shall repay the moneys borrowed by virtue of this Order other than moneys borrowed under the provisions of the Local Loans Act, 1875 by equal annual instalments of principal or by equal annual instalments of principal and interest combined or by means of a sinking fund or partly by one of these methods and partly by another or the others of them.

(2.) Subject to the provisions of Article V. of this Order if the District Council determine to repay by means of a sinking fund any moneys borrowed by virtue of this Order such sinking fund shall be formed and maintained either:—

(a) by payment to the fund throughout the prescribed period of such equal annual sums as will together amount to the moneys for the repayment of which the sinking fund is formed. A sinking fund so formed is herein-after called a non-accumulating sinking fund; or

(b) by payment to the fund throughout the prescribed period of such equal annual sums as with accumulations at a rate not exceeding three pounds per centum per annum will be sufficient to pay off within the prescribed period the moneys for the repayment of which such sinking fund is formed. A sinking fund so formed is herein-after called an accumulating sinking fund.

(3.) Every sum paid to a sinking fund and in the case of an accumulating sinking fund the interest on the investments of the sinking fund shall unless applied in repayment of the loan in respect of which the sinking fund is formed be immediately invested in securities in which trustees are by law for the time being authorised to invest or in mortgages, bonds, debentures, debenture stock, stock or other securities (not being annuity certificates or securities payable to bearer) duly issued by any local authority as defined by section 34 of the Local Loans Act 1875 other than the District Council the District Council being at liberty from time to time to vary and transpose such investments.

(4.) In the case of a non-accumulating sinking fund the interest on the investments of the fund may be applied by the District Council towards the equal annual payments to the fund.

(5.) The District Council may at any time apply the whole or any part of any sinking fund in or towards the discharge of the money for the repayment of which the fund is formed. Provided that in the case of an accumulating sinking fund the District Council shall pay into the fund each year and accumulate during the residue of the prescribed period a sum equal to the interest which would have been produced by such sinking fund or part of a sinking fund so applied if invested at the rate per centum per annum on which the annual payments to the sinking fund are based.

(6.)—(a.) If and so often as the income of an accumulating sinking fund is not equal to the income which would be derived from the amount invested if the same were invested at the rate per centum per annum on which the equal annual payments to the fund are based any deficiency shall be made good by the District Council.

(b.) If and so often as the income of an accumulating sinking fund is in excess of the income which would be derived from the amount invested if the same were invested at the rate per centum per annum on which the equal annual payments to the fund are based any such excess may be applied towards such equal annual payments.

(7.) Any expenses connected with the formation, maintenance, investment, application, management or otherwise of any sinking fund under this Order shall be paid by the District Council in addition to the payments provided for by this Order.

Art. V.—(1.) If it appears to the District Council at any time that the amount in the sinking fund with the future payments thereto in accordance with the provisions of this Order together with the accumulations thereon (in the case of an accumulating sinking fund) will probably not be sufficient to repay within the prescribed period the moneys for the repayment of which the sinking fund is formed it shall be the duty of the District Council to make such increased payments to the sinking fund as will cause the sinking fund to be sufficient for that purpose. Provided that if it appears to the Local Government Board that any such increase is necessary the District Council shall increase the payments to such extent as the Board may direct.

(2.) If the District Council desire to accelerate the repayment of any loan they may increase the amounts payable to any sinking fund.

(3.) If the amount in any sinking fund with the future payments thereto in accordance with the provisions of this Order together with the probable accumulations thereon (in the case of an accumulating sinking fund) will in the opinion of the Local Government Board be more than sufficient to repay within the prescribed period the moneys for the repayment of which the sinking fund is formed the District Council may reduce the payments to be made to the sinking fund either temporarily or permanently to such an extent as that Board shall approve.

(4.) If the amount in any sinking fund at any time together with the probable accumulations thereon (in the case of an accumulating sinking fund) will in the opinion of the Local Government Board be sufficient to repay the loan in respect of which it is formed within the prescribed period the District Council may with the consent of that Board discontinue the equal annual payments to such sinking fund until the Local Government Board shall otherwise direct.

(5.) Any surplus of any sinking fund remaining after the discharge of the whole of the moneys for the repayment of which it was formed shall be applied to such purpose or purposes as the District Council with the consent of the Local Government Board may determine.

Art. VI. The District Council shall except as herein-after provided have power to re-borrow for the purpose of paying off moneys borrowed or re-borrowed by virtue of this Order which have not been repaid and are intended to be forthwith repaid or in respect of any moneys which have been repaid by the temporary application of funds at the disposal of the District Council within twelve months before the re-borrowing and which at the time of the repayment it was intended to re-borrow:

Provided that the District Council shall not have power to reborrow for the purpose of paying off any moneys repaid by instalments or annual payments or by means of a sinking fund or out of moneys derived from the sale of land or out of any capital moneys properly applicable to the purpose of such repayment other than moneys borrowed for that purpose:

Provided also that any moneys re-borrowed shall be deemed to form the same loan as the money for the repayment of which the re-borrowing has been made and shall be repaid within the prescribed period.

Art. VII. All moneys from time to time borrowed by virtue of this Order shall be applied by the District Council only for the purposes for which the same are respectively authorised to be borrowed excepting that moneys which may have been borrowed in excess of the amount required shall be applied in such manner as the District Council with the approval of the Local Government Board determine.

Art. VIII.—(1.) Any mortgagee of the District Council by virtue of this Order may enforce the payment of arrears of interest or of principal or of principal and interest by the appointment of a receiver. The amount of arrears due to such mortgagee, or in the case of a joint application by two or more mortgagees to such mortgagees collectively to authorise the appointment of a receiver shall not be less than five hundred pounds in the whole.

(2.) The application for the appointment of a receiver shall be made to the High Court and the Court if it thinks fit may appoint a receiver on such terms as it thinks fit and may at any time discharge the receiver and otherwise exercise full jurisdiction over him.

Art. IX.—(1.) The clerk to the District Council shall within twenty-one days after the Thirty-first day of March in each year if during the twelve months next preceding the said Thirty-first day of March any sum is required to be paid as an instalment or annual payment or to be appropriated or to be paid to a sinking fund in pursuance of the provisions of this Order or in respect of any money raised thereunder and at any other time when the Local Government Board may require such a return to be made transmit to the Local Government Board a return in such form as may from time to time be prescribed by that Board and if required by that

60 & 61 Vict.   Local Government Board's   ch. lxviii.
            Provisional Orders Confirmation
                  (No. 2) Act, 1897.

Board verified by statutory declaration of such clerk showing for the year next preceding the making of such return or for such other period as the Board may prescribe, the amounts which have been paid as instalments or annual payments and the amounts which have been appropriated and the amounts which have been paid to or invested or applied for the purpose of the sinking fund and the description of the securities upon which any investment has been made and the purposes to which any portion of the sinking fund or investment or of the sums accumulated by way of compound interest has been applied during the same period and the total amount (if any) remaining invested at the end of the year and in the event of his failing to make such return the said clerk shall for each offence be liable to a penalty not exceeding twenty pounds to be recovered by action on behalf of the Crown in the High Court and notwithstanding the recovery of such penalty the making of the return shall be enforceable by writ of mandamus to be obtained by the Local Government Board out of the High Court.

(2.) If it appears to the Local Government Board by that return or otherwise that the District Council have failed to pay any instalment or annual payment required to be paid or to appropriate any sum required to be appropriated or to set apart any sum required for any sinking fund (whether such instalment or annual payment or sum is required by this Order or by the Local Government Board in virtue thereof to be paid appropriated or set apart) or have applied any portion of any sinking fund to any purpose other than those authorised the Local Government Board may by Order direct that the sum in such Order mentioned not exceeding double the amount in respect of which default has been made shall be paid or applied as in such Order mentioned and any such Order shall be enforceable by writ of mandamus to be obtained by the Local Government Board out of the High Court.

Art. X. Where the Local Government Board cause any local inquiry to be held with reference to any of the purposes of this Order the costs incurred by that Board in relation to such inquiry (including such reasonable sum not exceeding three guineas a day as that Board may determine for the services of any inspector or officer of the Board engaged in such inquiry) shall be paid by the District Council and the Local Government Board may certify the amount of the costs so incurred and any sum so certified and directed by that Board to be paid by the District Council shall be a debt due to the Crown from the District Council.

Art. XI. This Order may be cited as the Wallasey Order 1897, and the Wallasey Orders 1852 to 1896, the Wallasey Order 1895, and this Order may be cited together as the Wallasey Orders 1852 to 1897.

          Given under the Seal of Office of the Local Government
              Board this Eighth day of April, One thousand eight
              hundred and ninety-seven.

                              HENRY CHAPLIN, President.
                              HUGH OWEN, Secretary.

Sec. 1—2

LOCAL GOVERNMENT BOARD'S PROVISIONAL ORDERS CONFIRMATION (No. 2) ACT, 1898.

(*Confirming the Wallasey Order, 1898.*)

AN

ACT

to confirm certain Provisional Orders of the Local Government Board relating to Eastbourne, Oswaldtwistle, Oswestry and WALLASEY, and to the Oakwell and Staines Joint Hospital Districts.

23RD MAY, 1898.

38 & 39 Vict. c. 55.

WHEREAS the Local Government Board have made the Provisional Orders set forth in the schedule hereto under the provisions of the Public Health Act, 1875:

And whereas it is requisite that the said Orders should be confirmed by Parliament:

Be it therefore enacted by the Queen's most Excellent Majesty by and with the advice and consent of the Lords Spiritual and Temporal and Commons in this present Parliament assembled and by the authority of the same as follows:—

Orders in schedule confirmed.

1. The Orders set out in the schedule hereto shall be and the same are hereby confirmed and all the provisions thereof shall have full validity and force.

Short title.

2. This Act may be cited as the Local Government Board's Provisional Orders Confirmation (No. 2) Act 1898.

[The Orders omitted relate to Districts other than Wallasey.]

THE WALLASEY ORDER, 1898.

URBAN DISTRICT OF WALLASEY.

Provisional Order for altering a Confirming Act.

To the Urban District Council of Wallasey :—

And to all others whom it may concern.

Whereas the Urban District Council of Wallasey (herein-after referred to as "the District Council") are the local authority within the meaning of the Public Health Act, 1875, for the Urban District of Wallasey (herein-after referred to as "the District");

And whereas the unrepealed provisions of the Wallasey Improvement Act 1858, the Wallasey Improvement Act 1861, and the Wallasey Improvement Act 1867 (each of which Acts is herein-after referred to as the Act of the year in which it was passed), as altered by the Wallasey Order (No. 1) 1877, which was confirmed by the Local Government Board's Provisional Orders Confirmation (Caistor Union &c.) Act 1877, by the Wallasey Order 1883, which was confirmed by the Local Government Board's Provisional Orders Confirmation (No. 7) Act 1883, by the Wallasey Order 1892, which was confirmed by the Local Government Board's Provisional Orders Confirmation (No. 12) Act 1892, by the Wallasey Order 1896, which was confirmed by the Local Government Board's Provisional Orders Confirmation (No. 4) Act 1896 (each of which Provisional Orders and Confirming Acts is herein-after referred to as the Order of the year in which it was made or the Confirming Act of the year in which it was passed as the case may be) and by certain other Local Acts and Provisional Orders which do not affect the subject-matter of this Order are in force in the District;

21 & 22 Vict. c. lxiii.
21 Vict. c. iv.
30 & 31 Vict. c. cxxxii.
40 & 41 Vict. c. ccxxvii.
46 & 47 Vict. c. cxxxvii.
55 & 56 Vict. c. ccxxiii.
59 Vict. c. xxix.

And whereas by Section 60 of the Act of 1858, Section 3 of the Act of 1861, Section 30 of the Act of 1867, Article II. of the Order of 1877, and Article I. of the Order of 1883, the Wallasey Local Board were empowered to borrow for the purposes of their gas undertaking sums amounting in the whole to the sum of eighty-five thousand pounds;

And whereas by subdivision (1) of Article II. of the Order of 1892, the Act of 1867, and the Confirming Acts of 1877 and 1883, so far as they respectively related to the Orders of 1877 and 1883, were altered so as to enable the Local Board, with the sanction of the Local Government Board, and subject to the provisions of the Order of 1892, to borrow on the security of the "Wallasey Lighting Account," as mentioned in the Act of 1858, and of the district fund and general district rates of the district or upon any such securities such sum or sums as they might from time to time think necessary for the purposes of their gas undertaking not exceeding in the whole the sum of fifty thousand pounds in addition to the said sum of eighty-five thousand pounds;

And whereas by Article I. of the Order of 1896 the Confirming Act of 1892 was altered by the insertion in subdivision (1) of Article II. of the order of 1892 of the words "seventy-two thousand pounds" in lieu of the words "fifty thousand pounds":

Now therefore We the Local Government Board in pursuance of the powers given to Us by Section 297 of the Public Health Act 1875 and by any other Statutes in that behalf do hereby order that from and after the date of the Act of Parliament confirming this Order the following provisions shall take effect:—

38 & 39 Vict. c. 55.

Art. I. The Confirming Act of 1892 as altered by Article I. of the Order of 1896 shall be further altered by the insertion in subdivision (1) of Article II. of the order of 1892 of the words "one hundred and twelve thousand pounds" in lieu of the words "seventy-two thousand pounds."

Art. II. This Order may be cited as the Wallasey Order 1898, and the Wallasey Orders 1852 to 1897, and this Order may be cited together as the Wallasey Orders 1852 to 1898.

Given under the Seal of Office of the Local Government Board this Second day of February, One thousand eight hundred and ninety-eight.

(L.S.)

HENRY CHAPLIN, President.
S. B. PROVIS, Assistant Secretary.

WALLASEY TRAMWAYS AND IMPROVEMENTS ACT, 1899.

(62 & 63 Vict. ch. 15.)

ARRANGEMENT OF SECTIONS.

Preamble.

PRELIMINARY.

	SECTION.
Short title	1
Incorporation of Acts	2
Interpretation of terms	3
Execution of Act	4

LANDS.

Power to take lands	5
Correction of errors in deposited plans and book of reference	6
Period for compulsory purchase of lands	7
Owners may be required to sell parts only of certain lands and buildings	8
Matters to be taken into account by arbitrators	9
Persons under disability may grant easements	10
Power to purchase additional lands by agreement	11
As to houses of labouring class	12
Power to retain, sell, &c., lands	13
Proceeds of sale of surplus lands	14
Saving rights of the Crown	15

TRAMWAYS.

Power to make Tramways	16
For protection of certain owners in Seabank Road	17
Inspection by Board of Trade	18
Tramways to be kept on level of surface of road	19
Plan of proposed mode of construction	20
Gauge of tramways	21
Rails of tramways	22
Penalty for not maintaining rails and roads	23

	SECTION.
Additional crossings	24
Alteration of tramways	25
Temporary tramways may be made where necessary	26
Application of road materials excavated in construction of works	27
Period for completion of works	28
Rates for passengers	29
Passengers' luggage	30
Rates for goods	31
Council not bound to carry animals and goods	32
As to fares on Sundays or holidays	33
Cheap fares for labouring classes	34
Periodical revision of rates and charges	35
Amendment of the Tramways Act, 1870, as to byelaws by local authority	36
Motive power	37
Alteration of tramways and construction of electric works	38
Special provisions as to use of electrical power	39
For the protection of the Postmaster-General	40
Mechanical power works to be subject to section 30 of Tramways Act, 1870	41
Byelaws	42
Power to work tramways	43
Regulations	44
Existing tramways not to be interfered with until acquired	45
Repeal of certain provisions of Tramway Acts	46
Power to acquire patent rights	47
Application of Conveyance of Mails Act, 1893	48
For the protection of the Wirral Railway Company	49

STREET IMPROVEMENTS.

Power to make street works	50
As to removal of human remains	51
Period for completion of works	52
Deviation	53
Subsidiary works	54

PROMENADES.

Power to construct promenades	55
Application of provisions of Act of 1896 as to promenade	56
For protection of the Mersey Conservancy Commissioners	57
For protection of John Edward Rayner	58
For the protection of the New Brighton Pier Company	59

Miscellaneous.

	SECTION.
Power to borrow	60
Periods for repayment of money borrowed ...	61
Application of financial provisions of Act of 1896	62
Application of revenue of tramway undertaking and deficiency of receipts	63
Power to supply electric fittings...	64
Byelaws with respect to electric fittings	65
Altering the date for filling up annual accounts for electric lighting	66
Authentication and service of notices	67
Orders, &c., of the Board of Trade	68
Recovery of penalties	69
Incorporation of s. 265 of Public Health Act, 1875	70
Costs of Act	71

Schedules.

AN ACT

to authorise the Wallasey Urban District Council to construct Tramways Street Improvements and Promenades and for other purposes.

JUNE 6TH, 1899.

WHEREAS the urban district of Wallasey, in the county of Chester is under the government of the Wallasey Urban District Council (in this Act called "the Council"):

And whereas by the Wallasey Tramways Act, 1878 the Wallasey Tramways Company were incorporated and empowered to construct the tramways therein described in the parish of Wallasey, and by the Wallasey Tramways Act, 1886 further provision was made in regard to their undertaking:

And whereas by section 43 of the Tramways Act, 1870 which is incorporated with the said Act of 1878 the council are empowered within six months after the expiration of the period of twenty-one years from the passing of the last mentioned Act with the approval of the Board of Trade to purchase the undertaking authorised by that Act:

And whereas it is expedient to empower the Council to construct and maintain the additional tramways in this Act described to work such tramways and the existing tramways when purchased by them and to make further provision in regard to the tramways of the district:

And whereas it is expedient to empower the Council to construct the street improvements and new street authorised by this Act:

And whereas by the Wallasey Urban District Council (Promenade) Act, 1896 the Council were empowered to construct the promenade and embankment or river wall therein described, and it is expedient to empower them to construct further promenades in extension thereof:

And whereas by the Wallasey Electric Lighting Order, 1897 the Council were empowered to supply electrical energy for public and private purposes within the district, and it is expedient to make further provision in regard to their electric lighting undertaking:

And whereas it is expedient that the borrowing powers of the Council be extended;

And whereas the purposes of this Act cannot be effected without the authority of Parliament.

And whereas estimates have been prepared by the Council for the purchase of lands for and the execution of the various works authorised by this Act and such estimates are as follows :—

	£
For the construction of the tramways authorised by this Act the re-construction of the existing tramways adapting the tramways for working by mechanical power and the provision of plant	87,000
For the purchase of lands for and the construction of the street improvements and new street authorised by this Act	92,000
For the purchase of the land for and the construction of the promenades authorised by this Act	90,000

And whereas the several works included in such estimates respectively are permanent works within the meaning of section 234 of the Public Health Act, 1875.

And whereas an absolute majority of the whole number of the Council, at a meeting held on the nineteenth day of October, one thousand eight hundred and ninety-eight, after ten clear days' notice by public advertisement of such meeting and of the purpose thereof in the Wallasey and Wirral Chronicle, a local newspaper published and circulating in the district, such notice being in addition to the ordinary notices required for summoning such meeting, resolved that the expense in relation to promoting the Bill for this Act should be charged on the district fund and general district rate :

And whereas such resolution was published twice in the said Wallasey and Wirral Chronicle, and has received the approval of the Local Government Board :

And whereas the propriety of the promotion of the Bill for this Act was confirmed by an absolute majority of the whole number of the Council at a further special meeting, held in pursuance of a similar notice on the eleventh day of January, one thousand eight hundred and ninety-nine, being not less than fourteen days after the deposit of the bill for this Act in Parliament :

And whereas the owners and ratepayers of the district by resolution in the manner provided in the third schedule of the Public Health Act, 1875, consented to the promotion of the Bill for this Act :

And whereas plans and sections showing the lines and levels of the works authorised by this Act, and also a book of reference containing the names of the owners and lessees or reputed owners and lessees and of the occupiers of the lands required or which may be taken for the purposes or under the powers of this Act were duly deposited with the clerk of the peace for the county of Chester, and are in this Act respectively referred to as the deposited plans, sections, and book of reference.

62 & 63 Vict. *Wallasey Tramways and Improvements Act,* 1899. ch. xv.

Sec. 1—6

MAY IT THEREFORE PLEASE YOUR MAJESTY

That it may be enacted and be it enacted by the Queen's Most Excellent Majesty by and with the advice and consent of the Lords Spiritual and Temporal and Commons in this present Parliament assembled and by the authority of the same as follows (that is to say):—

PRELIMINARY.

Short title.

1. This Act may be cited as the Wallasey Tramways and Improvements Act 1899.

Incorporation of Acts.

2. The following Acts and parts of Acts so far as they are applicable for the purposes and are not inconsistent with the provisions of this Act are hereby incorporated with and form part of this Act namely:—

The Lands Clauses Acts (except section 127 of the Lands Clauses Consolidation Act, 1845);

Section 3 (interpretation of terms) section 19 (local authority may lease or take tolls) and parts II and III of the Tramways Act, 1870.

Interpretation of terms.

3. In this Act the several words and expressions to which meanings are assigned by the Acts wholly or partially incorporated herewith have the same respective meanings, unless there be something in the subject or context repugnant to such construction, and in this Act unless the subject or context otherwise requires:—

"The Council" means the Wallasey Urban District Council;

"The district" means the urban district of Wallasey;

"The Act of 1878," "the Act of 1886," and the "Act of 1896" mean respectively the Wallasey Tramways Act, 1878, the Wallasey Tramways Act, 1886, and the Wallasey Urban District Council (Promenade) Act, 1896;

"The tramways" means the tramways authorised by the Act of 1878, when they shall have been acquired by the Council, and the tramways authorised by this Act;

"Mechanical power" includes steam, electric, and every other motive power not being animal power;

"Engine" includes motor.

Execution of Act.

4. This Act shall be carried into execution by the Council.

LANDS.

Power to take lands.

5. Subject to the provisions and for the purposes of this Act the Council may enter on, take, and use all or any of the lands delineated on the deposited plans and described in the deposited book of reference.

Correction of errors in deposited plans and book of reference.

6. If there be any omission, mis-statement or wrong description of any lands, or of the owners, lessees or occupiers of any lands shown on the deposited plans or specified in the deposited book of reference the Council after giving ten days' notice to the owners, lessees and occupiers of the lands in question may apply to two justices acting for the county of Chester for the correction thereof, and if it appear to the justices that the omission, mis-statement or wrong description arose from mistake they shall certify the same accordingly and they shall in their certificate state the particulars of the omission and in what respect any such matter is mis-stated or wrongly described and such certificate shall be deposited with the clerk of the peace for the county of Chester and a duplicate thereof shall also be deposited with the clerk to the Council and such certificate and duplicate respectively shall be kept by such clerk of the peace and clerk to the Council respectively with the other documents to which the same relate and thereupon the deposited plans and book of reference shall be deemed to be corrected according to such certificate and it shall be lawful for the Council to take the lands and execute the works in accordance with such certificate.

7. The powers of the Council for the compulsory purchase of lands under this Act shall not be exercised after the expiration of five years from the passing of this Act. *Period for compulsory purchase of lands.*

8. (1.) And whereas in the construction of the works by this Act authorised or otherwise in the exercise by the Council of the powers of this Act it may happen that portions only of certain properties shown or partly shown on the deposited plans will be sufficient for the purposes of the Council and that such portions or some other portions less than the whole can be severed from the remainder of the said properties without material detriment thereto, therefore the following provisions shall have effect:— *Owners may be required to sell parts only of certain lands and buildings.*

(a) The owner of and persons interested in any of the properties whereof the whole or part is described in the first schedule and whereof a portion only is required for the purposes of the Council or each or any of them are hereinafter included in the term "the owner" and the said properties are hereinafter referred to as "the scheduled properties";

(b) If for twenty-one days after the service of notice to treat in respect of a specified portion of any of the scheduled properties the owner shall fail to notify in writing to the Council that he alleges that such portion cannot be severed from the remainder of the property without material detriment thereto he may be required to sell and convey to the Council such portion only without the Council being obliged or compellable to purchase the whole the Council paying for the portion so taken and making compensation for any damage sustained by the owner by severance or otherwise;

(c) If within such twenty-one days the owner shall by notice in writing to the Council allege that such portion cannot be so severed the jury arbitrators or other authority to whom the question of disputed compensation shall be submitted (in this section referred to as "the tribunal") shall in addition to the other questions required to be determined by them determine whether the portion of the scheduled property specified in the notice to treat can be severed from the remainder without material detriment thereto, and if not whether any and what other portion less than the whole (but not exceeding the portion over which the Council have compulsory powers of purchase) can be so severed;

(*d*) If the tribunal determine that the portion of the scheduled property specified in the notice to treat or any such other portion as aforesaid can be severed from the remainder without material detriment thereto, the owner may be required to sell and convey to the Council the portion which the tribunal shall have determined to be so severable without the Council being obliged or compellable to purchase the whole the Council paying such sum for the portion taken by them including compensation for any damage sustained by the owner by severance or otherwise as shall be awarded by the tribunal;

(*e*) If the tribunal determine that the portion of the scheduled property specified in the notice to treat can notwithstanding the allegation of the owner be severed from the remainder without material detriment thereto the tribunal may in its absolute discretion determine and order that the costs charges and expenses incurred by the owner incident to the arbitration or inquiry shall be borne and paid by the owner;

(*f*) If the tribunal determine that the portion of the scheduled property specified in the notice to treat cannot be severed from the remainder without material detriment thereto (and whether or not they shall determine that any other portion can be so severed) the Council may withdraw their notice to treat and thereupon they shall pay to the owner all costs charges and expenses reasonably and properly incurred by him in consequence of such notice;

(*g*) If the tribunal determine that the portion of the scheduled property specified in the notice to treat cannot be severed from the remainder without material detriment thereto but that any other such portion as aforesaid can be so severed the Council in case they shall not withdraw the notice to treat shall pay to the owner all costs charges and expenses reasonably and properly incurred by him in consequence of such notice or such portion thereof as the tribunal shall having regard to the circumstances of the case and their final determination think fit.

(2.) The provisions of this section shall be in force notwithstanding anything in the Lands Clauses Consolidation Act, 1845, contained and nothing contained in or done under this section shall be held as determining, or as being or implying an admission that any of the scheduled properties or any part thereof, is or is not or but for this section would or would not be subject to the provisions of section 92 of the Lands Clauses Consolidation Act, 1845.

(3.) The provisions of this section shall be stated in every notice given thereunder to sell and convey any premises.

Sec. 9—12

9. In determining any question of disputed compensation to be paid by the Council for the acquisition of any land required for the construction of either of the promenades authorised by this Act the jury arbitrators or other authority to whom the question shall be referred, shall take into account any public rights of way or other rights over or on the lands to be acquired, and any permanent increase in value of any lands fronting or abutting upon the proposed promenade and retained by or belonging to the person claiming compensation which in the opinion of such authority will result from or be caused by the construction of the promenade, and generally all the other circumstances of the case which it is equitable to consider. *Matters to be taken into account by arbitrators.*

10. Persons empowered by the Lands Clauses Acts to sell and convey or release lands may if they think fit subject to the provisions of those Acts and of this Act grant to the Council any easement right or privilege (not being an easement right or privilege of water in which persons other than the grantors have an interest) required for the purposes of this Act in over or affecting any such lands and the provisions of the said Acts with respect to lands and rent-charges so far as the same are applicable in this behalf shall extend and apply to such grants and to such easements rights and privileges as aforesaid respectively. *Persons under disability may grant easements.*

11. The Council in addition to any other lands which they are by this Act authorised to acquire, may by agreement purchase, take on lease, acquire and hold for the purposes of this Act, any lands not exceeding in the whole five acres, and with the consent of the Local Government Board may appropriate to such purposes lands vested in the Council and not wanted for the purposes for which they were acquired : Provided that the Council shall not create or permit the creation or continuance of any nuisance on any lands acquired or appropriated in pursuance of this section, nor erect any buildings thereon except for the purposes of this Act. *Power to purchase additional lands by agreement.*

12. (1.) The Council shall not under the powers of this Act purchase or acquire ten or more houses which on the fifteenth day of December last were occupied either wholly or partially by persons belonging to the labouring class as tenants or lodgers, or except with the consent of the Local Government Board ten or more houses which were not so occupied on the said fifteenth day of December, but have been or shall be subsequently so occupied. *As to houses of labouring class.*

(2.) If the Council acquire or appropriate any house or houses under the powers by this Act granted in contravention of the provisions of this section, they shall be liable to a penalty of five hundred pounds in respect of every such house, which penalty shall be recoverable by the Local Government Board by action in the High Court, and shall be carried to and form part of the Consolidated Fund of the United Kingdom : Provided that the Court may if it think fit reduce such penalty.

(3.) For the purposes of this section the expression " labouring class " means mechanics, artisans, labourers and others working for wages, hawkers, costermongers, persons not working for wages, but

Sec. 13—16 working at some trade or handicraft without employing others except members of their own family and persons other than domestic servants whose income does not exceed an average of thirty shillings a week and the families of any of such persons who may be residing with them.

Power to retain sell &c. lands.

13. Notwithstanding anything in the Lands Clauses Acts or in any other Act or Acts to the contrary, the Council may retain hold and use for such time as they may think fit or may sell, lease, exchange or otherwise dispose of in such manner and for such consideration and purpose and on such terms and conditions as they may think fit and in case of sale either in consideration of the execution of works or of the payment of a gross sum or of an annual rent or of any payment in any other form any lands or any interest therein acquired by them under this Act, and may sell, exchange or dispose of any rents reserved on the sale, exchange, lease or disposition of such lands, and may make, do and execute any deed, act or thing proper for effectuating any such sale, lease, exchange or other disposition, and on any exchange may give or take any money for equality of exchange.

Proceeds of sale of surplus lands.

14. So long as any lands remain to be acquired by the Council under the authority of this Act, they may so far as they consider necessary, apply any capital moneys received by them on resale or exchange or by leasing as aforesaid in the purchase of lands so remaining to be acquired but as to capital moneys so received and not so applied the Council shall apply the same in or towards the extinguishment of any loan raised by them under the powers of this Act, and such application shall be in addition to and not in substitution for any other mode of extinguishment by this Act provided, except to such extent and upon such terms as may be approved by the Local Government Board: Provided that the amount to be applied in the purchase of land under this section shall not exceed the amount for the time being unexhausted of the borrowing powers conferred by this Act: Provided further that the borrowing powers by this Act authorised shall be reduced to the extent of the amount applied in the purchase of lands under the provisions of this section.

Saving rights of the Crown.

15. Nothing contained in this Act shall authorise the Council to take use or in any manner interfere with any land or hereditaments or any rights of whatsoever description belonging to the Queen's Most Excellent Majesty in right of her Crown and under the management of the Commissioners of Woods without the consent in writing of the Commissioners of Woods on behalf of Her Majesty first had and obtained for that purpose (which consent such Commissioners are hereby authorised to give) neither shall anything in this Act contained extend to take away prejudice diminish or alter any of the estates rights, privileges, powers, or authorities vested in or enjoyed or exercisable by the Queen's Majesty.

TRAMWAYS.

Power to make tramways.

16. Subject to the provisions of this Act the Council may make form lay down use and maintain the tramways hereinafter described in the lines and according to the levels shown on the deposited plans and sections and in all respects in accordance with those plans and

62 & 63 *Vict.*   *Wallasey Tramways and*   *ch. xv.*   387
                 Improvements Act, 1899.

sections with all proper rails, plates, junctions, turntables, turnouts,   **Sec. 16**
crossings, passing-places, posts, poles, brackets, wires, waiting-rooms,
stables, carriage-houses, sheds, buildings, engines, works, and conveniences connected therewith.

    The tramways hereinbefore referred to and authorised by this Act
will be situate within the district and are as follows:—

    Tramway No. 1 (2 miles 5 furlongs 5·2 chains in length, whereof
        2 miles 1 furlong 5·1 chains will be single line and 4 furlongs
        0·1 chain will be double line) commencing on the north side
        of Victoria Place, Seacombe, passing along Victoria Place,
        Church Road, Brighton Street, King Street, Trafalgar Road,
        Seabank Road, Rowson Street, and Victoria Road, New
        Brighton, and terminating in the last-named road.

    Tramway No. 2 (2 miles 4 furlongs 8·2 chains in length, whereof
        1 mile 5 furlongs 3·8 chains will be single line and 7 furlongs
        4·4 chains will be double line) commencing in Church Road
        by a junction with Tramway No. 1 passing along Church
        Road, St. Paul's Road, Wheatland Lane, intended new road
        between Wheatland Lane and Liscard Road, in continuation
        of Wheatland Lane, Liscard Road, Liscard Village, Rake
        Lane, Mount Pleasant Road, Upper Brighton, and Rowson
        Street, and terminating in the last-named street by a
        junction with Tramway No. 1.

    Tramway No. 3 (1 mile 7 furlongs 5·9 chains in length, whereof
        1 mile 3 furlongs 1·8 chains will be single line and 4 furlongs
        4·1 chains will be double line) commencing in Liscard Road
        by a junction with Tramway No. 2 passing along Liscard
        Road, Seaview Road, Hose Side Road, Grove Road, Warren
        Drive, and Victoria Road, New Brighton, and terminating
        in the last-named road by a junction with Tramway No. 1.

    Tramway No. 4 (single line 3 furlongs 2·3 chains in length) com-
        mencing on the north side of Victoria Place by a junction
        with Tramway No. 1, passing along Victoria Place, Victoria
        Road, Seacombe, Demesne Street, Brougham Road, and
        Brighton Street, and terminating in the last-named street
        by a junction with Tramway No. 1.

    Tramway No. 5 (single line 2 furlongs 4·5 chains in length) com-
        mencing in Brighton Street by a junction with Tramway No.
        1 passing along Brighton Street, Church Street, and Liscard
        Road, and terminating in the last-named road by a junction
        with Tramway No. 2.

    Tramway No. 6 (single line 3 furlongs 1·7 chains in length) com-
        mencing in Victoria Road, New Brighton, by a junction with
        Tramway No. 1 passing along Victoria Road, New Brighton,
        Virginia Road, Waterloo Road, Wellington Road, and
        Rowson Street, and terminating in the last-named street by
        a junction with Tramway No. 1.

    Tramway No. 1A (single line 8·5 chains in length) commencing
        in Church Road by a junction with Tramway No 1 passing

Sec. 17

along Church Road and Victoria Place, and terminating on the north side of Victoria Place, Seacombe, by a junction with Tramway No. 1.

Tramway No. 3A (single line 0·9 chain in length) commencing in Seaview Road by a junction with Tramway No. 3 passing along Seaview Road and terminating at the western boundary of that road.

Tramway No. 3B (single line 0·9 chain in length) commencing in Seaview Road by a junction with Tramway No. 3 passing along Seaview Road and terminating at the western boundary of that road.

Tramway No. 6A (single line 1·4 chains in length) commencing in Rowson Street by a junction with Tramway No. 6 passing along Rowson Street and Victoria Road, New Brighton and terminating in the last-named road by a junction with Tramway No. 3 at a point 0·5 chain west from the west side of Rowson Street.

For protection of certain owners in Seabank Road.

17. Notwithstanding anything shown upon the deposited plans and sections the following provisions for the benefit and protection of the owners of lands and property abutting upon Seabank Road shall apply (that is to say):—

(1.) So much of Tramway No. 1 authorised by this Act as will be situate between the points marked respectively A and B on the plan signed in triplicate by Sir Lewis M'Iver, Baronet, the Chairman of the Committee of the House of Commons to whom the Bill for this Act was referred shall not be constructed as double line unless and until the road shall have been widened on the easterly side thereof so that a space of not less than 9 feet 6 inches shall intervene between the outside of the footpath on that side of the road and the nearest rail of the tramway.

(2.) Provided that the restriction contained in sub-section (1) of this section shall not apply unless the owners of and other persons interested in the land required for widening the road shall agree with the Council to convey such land to them at such prices as may be agreed upon or as in default of agreement may be determined by arbitration under the Arbitration Act 1889.

(3.) So much of the said tramway No. 1 as will be situate between the points marked respectively B and C on the plan signed as aforesaid shall be laid as single line in such a situation that a space of not less than 9 feet 6 inches will intervene between the outside of the footpath on each side of the road and the nearest rail of the tramway.

(4.) The plans signed as aforesaid shall respectively within six months after the passing of this Act be deposited in the Parliament Office of the House of Lords the Private Bill Office of the House of Commons and with the clerk to the Council.

18. The tramways authorised by this Act shall not be opened for public traffic until they have been inspected and certified to be fit for such traffic by the Board of Trade. *Inspection by Board of Trade.*

19. If and whenever after the passing of this Act any road authority alters the level of any road along or across which any part of the tramways is laid or authorised to be laid the Council may and shall alter or (as the case may be) lay their rails so that the uppermost surface thereof shall be on a level with the surface of the road as altered. *Tramways to be kept on level of surface of road.*

20. In addition to the requirements of section 26 of the Tramways Act 1870 the Council shall before they open or break up any road for the purpose of constructing, laying down, maintaining and renewing any of the tramways, lay before the Board of Trade a plan showing the proposed mode of constructing, laying down, maintaining and renewing such tramways and a statement of the materials intended to be used therein and the Council shall not commence the construction, laying down, maintenance and renewal of any of the tramways or part of any of the tramways respectively until such plan and statement have been approved by the Board of Trade and after such approval the works shall be executed in accordance in all respects with such plan and statement. *Plan of proposed mode of construction.*

21. (1.) The tramways authorised by this Act shall be constructed on a gauge of four feet and eight and a-half inches or such other gauge as may from time to time be determined by the Council with the assent of the Board of Trade and the Council may alter the gauge of the existing tramways when acquired by them to such gauge as they may with the assent of the Board of Trade determine: Provided that when the gauge is less than 4 feet 8½ inches so much of section 34 of the Tramways Act, 1870 as limits the extent of the carriages used on any tramways beyond the outer edge of the wheels of such carriages shall not apply to carriages used on the tramways but no engine or carriage used on the tramways shall exceed six feet six inches in width or such other width as may from time to time be prescribed by the Board of Trade. *Gauge of tramways.*

(2.) No carriages or trucks adapted for use upon railways shall be used upon the tramways.

22. The rails of the tramways shall be such as the Board of Trade may approve. *Rails of tramways.*

23. (1.) The Council shall at all times maintain and keep in good condition and repair and so as not to be a danger or annoyance to the ordinary traffic the rails of the tramways and the sub-structure upon which the same rest and if the Council at any time fail to comply with this provision or with the provisions of section 28 of the Tramways Act, 1870, they shall be subject to a penalty not exceeding five pounds and to a further penalty not exceeding five pounds for every day on which such non-compliance continues after conviction thereof. *Penalty for not maintaining rails and roads.*

(2.) In case it is represented in writing to the Board of Trade by twenty inhabitant ratepayers of the district that the Council have made default in complying with the provisions in this section con-

Sec. 24—27 tained or with any of the requirements of section 28 of the Tramways Act, 1870, the Board of Trade may if they think fit direct an inspection by an officer to be appointed by the said Board and if such officer report that the default mentioned in such representation has been proved to his satisfaction then and in every such case a copy of such report certified by a secretary or an assistant secretary of the Board of Trade may be adduced as evidence of such default and of the liability of the Council to such penalty or penalties in respect thereof as is or are by this section imposed.

Additional crossings.

24. The Council may subject to the provisions of this Act make, maintain, alter and remove such crossings, passing-places, sidings, junctions and other works in addition to those particularly specified in and authorised by this Act as they find necessary or convenient for the efficient working of the tramways or for providing access to any warehouses, stables or carriage-houses or works of the Council: Provided that in the construction of any such works no rail shall be so laid that a less space than nine feet six inches shall intervene between it and the outside of the footpath on either side of the road if one-third of the owners or one-third of the occupiers of the premises abutting on the place where such less space shall intervene shall by writing under their hands addressed and delivered to the Council within three weeks after receiving from the Council notice in writing of their intention express their objection thereto.

Alteration of tramways.

25. The Council may with the consent of the Board of Trade lay down double lines in lieu of single lines or single lines in lieu of double lines or interlacing lines in lieu of double or single lines on any of the tramways, and if at any time after the construction of any of the tramways the road in which the same or any part thereof is laid has been or shall be altered or widened the Council may take up and remove such tramway or part thereof, and reconstruct the same in such position as they may think fit: Provided that in the exercise of the powers of this section no rail shall be so laid that a less space than nine feet six inches shall intervene between it and the outside of the footpath on either side of the road if one-third of the owners or one-third of the occupiers of the premises abutting on the place where such less space shall intervene shall by writing under their hands addressed and delivered to the Council within three weeks after receiving from the Council notice in writing of their intention express their objection thereto.

Temporary tramways may be made where necessary.

26. Where by reason of the execution of any work affecting the surface or soil of any road along which any of the tramways is laid it is in the opinion of the Council necessary or expedient temporarily to remove or discontinue the use of such tramway or any part thereof the Council may construct in the same or any adjacent road and maintain so long as occasion may require a temporary tramway or temporary tramways in lieu of the tramway or part of a tramway so removed or discontinued.

Application of road materials excavated in construction of works.

27. Any paving metalling or material excavated by the Council in the construction of any works under the authority of this Act from any road under their jurisdiction or control shall absolutely vest in and belong to the Council and may be dealt with removed and disposed of by them in such manner as they may think fit.

28. The tramways specified in and authorised by this Act shall be completed within seven years from the passing of this Act and on the expiration of that period the powers by this Act granted to the Council for executing the same or otherwise in relation thereto shall cease except as to so much thereof as shall then be completed. *Period for completion of works.*

29. The Council may demand and take for every passenger travelling upon the tramways or any part or parts thereof including every expense incidental to such conveyance, any rates or charges not exceeding one penny per mile, and in computing the said rates and charges the fraction of a mile shall be deemed a mile, but in no case shall the Council be bound to charge a less sum than two-pence. *Rates for passengers.*

30. Every passenger travelling upon the tramways may take with him his personal luggage not exceeding twenty-eight pounds in weight without any charge being made for the carriage thereof, provided that such luggage be carried by hand and at the responsibility of the passenger and do not occupy any part of a seat nor be of a form or description to annoy or inconvenience other passengers. *Passengers' luggage.*

31. The Council may demand and take in respect of animals goods and parcels conveyed by them on the tramways, including every expense incidental to the conveyance, any rates or charges not exceeding those specified in the second schedule to this Act, subject to the regulations in that behalf therein contained. *Rates for goods.*

32. The Council shall not be bound, unless they think fit, to carry on the tramways any goods, animals or other things other than passengers and passengers' luggage under and subject to the foregoing provisions of this Act. *Council not bound to carry animals and goods.*

33. The Council shall not take or demand on Sunday or any public holiday any higher tolls or charges than those levied by them on ordinary week days. *As to fares on Sundays or holidays.*

34. The Council at all times after the opening of the tramways for public traffic shall, and they are hereby required to, run at least two carriages each way every morning in the week and every evening in the week (Sundays, Christmas Day and Good Friday always excepted) at such hours not being later than seven in the morning nor earlier than six in the evening respectively as the Council think most convenient for artizans, mechanics and daily labourers at fares not exceeding one halfpenny per mile (the Council nevertheless not being required to take any fare less than one penny): Provided that in case of any complaint made to the Board of Trade of the hours appointed by the Council for the running of such carriages the said Board shall have power to fix and regulate the same. *Cheap fares for labouring classes.*

35. If at any time after three years from the opening for public traffic of the tramways or any portion thereof or after three years from the date of any order made in pursuance of this section in respect of the tramways or any portion thereof, it is represented in writing to the Board of Trade by twenty inhabitant ratepayers of the district or by the Council, that under the circumstances then existing all or any of the rates and charges demanded and taken in respect of the traffic on the tramways or on such portion should be revised, *Periodical revision of rates and charges.*

Sec. 36—37 the Board of Trade may (if they think fit) direct an enquiry by a referee to be appointed by the said Board in accordance with the provisions of the Tramways Act, 1870, and if the referee reports that it has been proved to his satisfaction that all or any of the rates and charges should be revised, the said Board may make an order in writing altering, modifying, reducing or increasing all or any of the rates and charges to be demanded and taken in respect of the traffic on the tramways or on such portion of the tramways in such manner as they think fit, and thenceforth such order shall be observed until the same is revoked or modified by an order of the Board of Trade made in pursuance of this section: Provided always that the rates and charges prescribed by any such order shall not exceed in amount the rates and charges authorised by this Act.

Amendment of the Tramways Act, 1870, as to byelaws by local authority.

36. The provisions of the Tramways Act, 1870, relating to the making of byelaws by the local authority with respect to the rate of speed to be observed in travelling on the tramways, shall not authorise the local authority to make any byelaws sanctioning a higher rate of speed than that authorised by the Board of Trade regulations, at which carriages are to be driven or propelled on the tramways under the authority of this Act, but the byelaws of the local authority may restrict the rate of speed to a lower rate than that so authorised.

Motive power.

37. The carriages used on the tramways may be moved by animal power or subject to the following provisions by mechanical power, that is to say:—

(1.) The mechanical power shall not be used except with the consent of and according to a system approved by the Board of Trade;

(2) The Board of Trade shall make regulations (in this Act referred to as "the Board of Trade regulations") for securing to the public all reasonable protection against danger arising from the use under this Act of mechanical power on the tramways and for regulating the use of electrical power;

(3.) The Council or any person using any mechanical power on the tramways contrary to the provisions of this Act, or of the Board of Trade regulations, shall for every such offence be liable to a penalty not exceeding ten pounds, and also in the case of a continuing offence to a further penalty not exceeding five pounds for every day during which such offence is continued after conviction thereof;

(4.) The Board of Trade if they are of opinion—

   (*a*) That the Council or such person have or has made default in complying with the provisions of this Act, or of the Board of Trade regulations whether a penalty in respect of such non-compliance has or has not been recovered; or—

   (*b*) That the use of mechanical power as authorised under this Act is a danger to the passengers or the public;

may by order either direct the Council or such person to cease to use such mechanical power or permit the same to be continued only subject to such conditions as the Board of Trade may impose and the Council or such person shall comply with every such order. In every such case the Board of Trade shall make a special report to Parliament notifying the making of such order.

Sec. 38—39

38. The Council may reconstruct any tramways for the time being belonging to them, and make such alterations thereof as may be necessary or expedient for working the same by mechanical power and for the purpose of working any of the tramways by mechanical power the Council may erect, construct, maintain and use engines, works, buildings, machinery and apparatus, and may place, construct, erect, lay down, make and maintain on, above or below the surface of any streets or roads posts, brackets, electric conductors, wires, apparatus, conduits, cables, tubes, and openings and may with the consent of the owners and occupiers of any houses or buildings affix to such houses or buildings and maintain posts, brackets, electric conductors, wires, and apparatus, and may supply electrical energy from any generating station constructed under powers conferred or to be conferred upon the Council, but the Council shall not construct a generating station under the powers of this Act.

Alteration of tramways and construction of electric works

39. The following provisions shall apply to the use of electrical power under this Act unless such power is entirely contained in and carried along with the carriages :—

Special provisions as to use of electrical power.

(1.) The Council shall employ either insulated returns or uninsulated metallic returns of low resistance.

(2) The Council shall take all reasonable precautions in constructing, placing and maintaining their electric lines and circuits and other works of all descriptions and also in working their undertaking so as not injuriously to affect by fusion or electrolytic action any gas or water pipes, or other metallic pipes, structures, or substances, or to interfere with the working of any wire, line or apparatus from time to time used for the purpose of transmitting electrical power or of telegraphic, telephonic, or electric signalling communication or the currents in such wire, line or apparatus.

(3) The electrical power shall be used only in accordance with the Board of Trade regulations, and in such regulations provisions shall be made for preventing fusion or injurious electrolytic action of or on gas or water pipes or other metallic pipes, structures, or substances, and for minimising as far as is reasonably practicable injurious interference with the electric wires, lines and apparatus of other parties and the currents therein, whether such lines do or do not use the earth as a return.

(4.) The Council shall be deemed to take all reasonable precautions against interference with the working of any wire line or apparatus if and so long as they adopt and employ at

Sec. 40 the option of the Council either such insulated returns or such uninsulated metallic returns of low resistance and such other means of preventing injurious interference with the electric wires lines and apparatus of other parties and the currents therein as may be prescribed by the Board of Trade regulations and in prescribing such means the Board shall have regard to the expense involved and to the effect thereof upon the commercial prospects of the undertaking.

(5.) At the expiration of two years from the passing of this Act the provisions of this section shall not operate to give any right of action in respect of injurious interference with any electric wire line or apparatus or the currents therein unless in the construction, erection, maintaining, and working of such wire line and apparatus all reasonable precautions including the use of an insulated return have been taken to prevent injurious interference therewith and with the currents therein by or from other electric currents.

(6.) If any difference arises between the Council and any other party with respect to anything hereinbefore in this section contained such difference shall unless the parties otherwise agree be determined by the Board of Trade or at the option of the Board by an arbitrator to be appointed by the Board and the costs of such determination shall be in the discretion of the Board or of the arbitrator as the case may be.

(7) The expression "Council" in this section shall include lessees licensees and any person owning, working, or running carriages over any tramway of the Council.

For protection of the Postmaster-General.

40. (1.) Notwithstanding anything in this Act contained if any of the works authorised to be executed by this Act involves or is likely to involve any alteration of any telegraphic line belonging to or used by the Postmaster-General the provisions of section 7 of the Telegraph Act, 1878, shall apply (instead of the provisions of section 30 of the Tramways Act, 1870), to any such alteration.

(2.) In the event of any tramways of the Council being worked by electricity the following provisions shall have effect:—

(a) The Council shall construct their electric lines and other works of all descriptions and shall work their undertaking in all respects with due regard to the telegraphic lines from time to time used or intended to be used by Her Majesty's Postmaster-General and the currents in such telegraphic lines and shall use every reasonable means in the construction of their electric lines and other works of all descriptions and the working of their undertaking to prevent injurious affection whether by induction or otherwise to such telegraphic lines or the currents therein. If any question arises as to whether the Council have constructed their electric lines or other works or work their undertaking in contravention of this sub-section such question shall be determined by arbitration and the Council shall be bound to make any alterations in or additions to their system which may be directed by the arbitrator.

(b) If any telegraphic line of the Postmaster-General is injuriously affected by the construction by the Council of their electric lines and works or by the working of the undertaking of the Council, the Council shall pay the expense of all such alterations in the telegraphic lines of the Postmaster-General as may be necessary to remedy such injurious affection.

Sec. 40

(c) (i.) Before any electric line is laid down or any act or work for working the tramways by electricity is done within ten yards of any part of a telegraphic line of the Postmaster-General (other than repairs or the laying of lines crossing the line of the Postmaster-General at right angles at the point of shortest distance and so continuing for a distance of six feet on each side of such point) the Council or their agents not more than twenty-eight nor less than fourteen days before commencing the work shall give written notice to the Postmaster-General specifying the course of the line and the nature of the work including the gauge of any wire and the Council and their agents shall conform with such reasonable requirements (either general or special) as may from time to time be made by the Postmaster-General for the purpose of preventing any telegraphic line of the Postmaster-General from being injuriously affected by the said act or work.

(ii.) Any difference which arises between the Postmaster-General and the Council or their Agents with respect to any requirements so made shall be determined by arbitration.

(d) In the event of any contravention of or wilful non-compliance with this section by the Council or their Agents the Council shall be liable to a fine not exceeding ten pounds for every day during which such contravention or non-compliance continues or if the telegraphic communication is wilfully interrupted not exceeding fifty pounds for every day on which such interruption continues.

(e) Provided that nothing in this section shall subject the Council or their agents to a fine under this section if they satisfy the court having cognisance of the case that the immediate doing of the act or execution of the work was required to avoid an accident or otherwise was a work of emergency and that they forthwith served on the postmaster or sub-postmaster of the postal telegraph office nearest to the place where the act or work was done a notice of the execution thereof stating the reason for doing or executing the same without previous notice.

(f) For the purposes of this section a telegraphic line of the Postmaster-General shall be deemed to be injuriously affected by an act or work if telegraphic communication by means of such line is whether through induction or otherwise in any way affected by such act or work or by any use made of such work.

Sec. 41—42

(g) For the purposes of this section and subject as therein provided sections two ten eleven and twelve of the Telegraph Act, 1878, shall be deemed to be incorporated with this Act.

(h) The expression "electric line" has the same meaning in this section as in the Electric Lighting Act, 1882.

(i) Any question or difference arising under this section which is directed to be determined by arbitration, shall be determined by an arbitrator appointed by the Board of Trade on the application of either party whose decision shall be final, and sections thirty to thirty-two both inclusive of the Regulation of Railways Act, 1868, shall apply in like manner as if the Council or their agents were a company with the meaning of that Act.

(j) Nothing in this section contained shall be held to deprive the Postmaster-General of any existing right to proceed against the Council by indictment, action, or otherwise in relation to any of the matters aforesaid.

(k) In this section the expression "the Council" includes their lessees and any person owning, working or running carriages on any of the tramways of the Council.

Mechanical power works to be subject to section 30 of Tramways Act, 1870.

41. All works to be executed by the Council in any street or road for working the tramways by mechanical power in pursuance of the powers of this Act shall be deemed to be works of a tramway, subject in all respects to the provisions of section 30 of the Tramways Act, 1870, as if they had been therein expressly mentioned.

Bye-laws.

42.—(1.) Subject to the provisions of this Act the Board of Trade may make bye-laws with regard to any of the tramways upon which mechanical power may be used for all or any of the following purposes, that is to say:—

For regulating the use of any bell, whistle, or other warning apparatus fixed to the engine or carriages:

For regulating the emission of smoke or steam from engines used on the tramways:

For providing that engines and carriages shall be brought to a stand at the intersection of cross streets and at such places and in such cases of horses being frightened or of impending danger as the Board of Trade may deem proper for securing safety:

For regulating the entrance to exit from and accommodation in the carriages used on the tramways and the protection of passengers from the machinery of any engine used for drawing or propelling such carriages:

For providing for the due publicity of all bye-laws and Board of Trade regulations in force for the time being in relation to the tramways by exhibition of the same in conspicuous places on the carriages and elsewhere.

(2.) Any person offending against or committing a breach of any of the bye-laws made by the Board of Trade under the authority of this Act shall be liable to a penalty not exceeding forty shillings.

43. Notwithstanding anything in the Tramways Act, 1870 to the contrary the Council may place and run carriages on and may work and may demand and take tolls and charges in respect of the tramways and in respect of the use of such carriages and may provide such stables, buildings, carriages, trucks, harness, engines, machinery, apparatus, horses, steam, cable, electric and other plant appliances and conveniences as may be requisite or expedient for the convenient working or user of the tramways by animal or mechanical power and may sell or dispose of such of the last mentioned articles and things as from time to time may no longer be required. *Power to work tramways.*

44. The regulations authorised by the Tramways Act, 1870 to be made by the promoters of any tramway and their lessees may with respect to any tramways or portions of tramways for the time being belonging to and worked by the Council be made by the Council alone. *Regulations.*

45. Notwithstanding anything contained in this Act the tramways thereby authorised shall not be opened for public traffic nor shall the tramways constructed under the powers of the Act of 1878 be interfered with in pursuance of this Act (except with the consent of the owners of such last-mentioned tramways) until such last-mentioned tramways have been acquired by the Council. *Existing tramways not to be interfered with until acquired.*

46. Upon the acquisition by the Council of the tramways constructed under the powers of the Act of 1878 the provisions of sections 8, 10 to 17, and 37 to 48 of that Act and the schedule thereto and section 6 of the Act of 1886 shall be by virtue of this Act repealed. *Repeal of certain provisions of Tramway Acts.*

47. For the purpose of using mechanical power the Council may acquire, hold and exercise patent and other rights or licenses relating to motive power or otherwise but not so as to acquire any exclusive right therein. *Power to acquire patent rights.*

48. The Conveyance of Mails Act 1893 shall extend and apply to all the tramways of the Council as if the same had been authorised by an Act of Parliament passed after the first day of January one thousand eight hundred and ninety-three. *Application of Conveyance of Mails Act, 1893.*

49. For the protection of the Wirral Railway Company (in this section called "the Company") the following provisions shall have effect (that is to say):— *For the protection of the Wirral Railway Company*

(1.) Before commencing to reconstruct the Tramway No. 1 in Church Road over the bridge of the Company and before commencing to construct the Tramway No. 2 in Wheatland Lane over the bridge of the Company the Council shall give 14 days' previous notice in writing to the Company of their intention to commence the same and such notice shall be accompanied by a plan and sections and all necessary particulars of the proposed works so far as they extend to the roadways over the said bridges and such works shall not be commenced until the Company have signified their

Sec. 50 approval of the same but if the Company do not signify their approval or disapproval thereof within fourteen days from the service of the said notice plan sections and particulars they shall be deemed to have approval of the same: Provided that if there shall be any difference between the Council and the Company with reference to the matters aforesaid the same shall be determined by the Board of Trade.

(2.) The Council shall comply with and conform to all reasonable directions and regulations of the Company in the execution of the said works and shall provide by new altered or substituted works in such manner as the Company shall reasonably require for the protection of and for preventing injury to the property and works of the Company by reason of the said tramways and shall save harmless the Company against all and every expense to be incurred thereby and any difference which may arise between the Council and the Company as to the reasonableness of the requirements of the Company shall be referred to the Board of Trade on the application of either party.

(3.) All such works shall be done under the inspection and to the reasonable satisfaction of the engineer of the Company if after service upon the engineer of not less than forty-eight hours' notice such engineer thinks fit to attend. Provided that if any question arises between the Company and the Council under this sub-section the same shall be determined by the Board of Trade.

(4.) In constructing Tramway No. 4 in Victoria Road between the junctions of that road with Victoria Place and Fell Street, the Council shall not construct any works at a greater depth than two feet three inches from the upper surface of Victoria Road as altered in pursuance of the Wirral Railway Act, 1898.

STREET IMPROVEMENTS.

Power to make street works. **50.** Subject to the provisions of this Act the Council may make and maintain in the lines and according to the levels shown on the deposited plans and sections the street works hereinafter mentioned together with all necessary works and conveniences connected therewith or incident thereto.

The street works hereinbefore referred to and authorised by this Act will be situate in the district and are as follows:—

Work No. 11.—A widening of Victoria Road, Seacombe, on the east side.

Work No. 12.—A widening of Victoria Road, Seacombe, on the west side.

Work No. 13.—A widening of Brougham Road on the south side.

Work No. 14.—A widening of Brighton Street on the east side.

Work No. 15.—A widening of Brighton Street on the west side.

Work No. 16.—A widening of Brougham Road and Brighton Street on the north side of Brougham Road and on the east side of Brighton Street.

Work No. 17.—A widening of King Street on the west side.

Work No. 18.—A widening of King Street on the east side.

Work No. 19.—A widening of Trafalgar Road and Seabank Road on the north side of Trafalgar Road and on the west side of Seabank Road.

Work No. 20.—A further widening of Seabank Road on the west side.

Work No. 21.—A widening of Wheatland Lane on the east side.

Work No. 22.—A further widening of Wheatland Lane on the east side.

Work No. 23.—A widening of Wheatland Lane on the west side.

Work No. 24.—A widening of Poulton Road and Liscard Road on the north side of Poulton Road and on the west side of Liscard Road.

Work No. 25.—A new road 180 yards in length between Poulton Road and Liscard Road commencing on the north side of Poulton Road at its junction with Wheatland Lane and terminating on the south-west side of Liscard Road at its junction with Rappart Road.

Work No. 26.—A widening of Liscard Road on the north-east side.

Work No. 27.—A widening of Liscard Road on the south-west side.

Work No. 28.—A further widening of Liscard Road on the north-east side.

Work No. 29.—A further widening of Liscard Road on the north-east side.

Work No. 30.—A further widening of Liscard Road on the north-east side.

Work No. 31.—A further widening of Liscard Road on the south-west side.

Work No. 32.—A widening of Liscard Village and Rake Lane on the north-west side of Liscard Village and on the west side of Rake Lane.

Work No. 33.—A widening of Liscard Village on the south-east side.

Work No. 34.—A widening of Rake Lane on the east side.

Work No. 35.—A further widening of Rake Lane on the east side.

Sec. 51

Work No. 36.—A widening of Rake Lane on the west side.

Work No. 37.—A further widening of Rake Lane on the east side.

Work No. 38.—A widening of Upper Brighton on the south-west side.

Work No. 39.—A widening of Rowson Street and Seabank Road on the south side of Rowson Street and on the west side of Seabank Road.

Work No. 40.— A widening of Liscard Village and Seaview Road on the north-west side of Liscard Village and on the north-east side of Seaview Road.

Work No. 41.—A widening of Seaview Road on the south-west side.

Work No. 42.—A further widening of Seaview Road on the south-west side.

Work No. 43.—A widening of Seaview Road on the south-west and north-west sides.

Work No. 44.— A widening of Seaview Road on the north-east and south-east sides.

Work No. 45.—A widening of Hose Side Road on the north-east side.

Work No. 46.—A widening of Grove Road and Warren Drive on the north side of Grove Road and on the north-east side of Warren Drive.

Work No. 47—A widening of Victoria Road, New Brighton, and Rowson Street on the north side of Victoria Road, and on the west side of Rowson Street.

Work No. 48.—A widening of Victoria Road, New Brighton, and Rowson Street on the south side of Victoria Road, and on the west side of Rowson Street.

Work No. 49.—A further widening of Victoria Road, New Brighton, on the south side.

Work No. 50.—A further widening of Victoria Road, New Brighton, on the north side.

Work No. 51.—A widening of Rowson Street and Wellington Road on the east side of Rowson Street and on the south side of Wellington road.

As to removal of human remains.

51. (1.) Before the Council in connection with the widening of Rake Lane, use or apply any part of the Congregational churchyard there for any purpose other than as an open space or ornamental ground or garden, they shall remove or cause to be removed the remains of any deceased person interred in the said churchyard : Provided that a Secretary of State on the application of the Council, and on being satisfied that such removal is not necessary or desirable, may dispense with all or any of the requirements of this section on such conditions (if any) as he thinks fit.

(2.) Before proceeding to remove any such remains, the Council shall publish a notice for two successive weeks in a local newspaper circulating in the Urban District of Wallasey, to the effect that it is intended to remove such remains and such notice shall have embodied in it the substance of the conditions of such removal provided in sub-sections (3) (4) (5) and (6) of this section.

(3.) At any time within two months after the first publication of such notice any person who is an heir executor or administrator or relative of any such deceased person may give notice in writing to the Council of his intention to undertake the removal of the remains of such deceased person, and thereupon he shall be at liberty to cause such remains to be removed to and re-interred in the Rake Lane Cemetery of the Council.

(4.) If any person giving such notice as aforesaid shall fail to satisfy the Council that he is such heir executor administrator or relative as he claims to be the question shall be determined on the application of either party in a summary manner by the Registrar of the Birkenhead County Court who shall have power to make an order specifying who shall remove the remains.

(5.) The expense of such removal and re-interment not exceeding in respect of remains removed from any one grave the sum of ten pounds shall be defrayed by the Council such sum to be apportioned equally if necessary according to the number of remains in such grave.

(6.) If within the aforesaid period of two months no such notice as aforesaid shall have been given to the Council in respect of the remains in any grave, or if after such notice has been given the person giving the same shall fail in any respect to comply with the provisions of this section the Council may remove the remains of the deceased person and cause them to be interred in the Rake Lane Cemetery of the Council.

(7.) All monuments and tombstones relating to the remains of any deceased person removed under this section shall at the expense of the Council be removed and re-erected at the place of re-interment of such remains, or at such places within the urban district of Wallasey as the Registrar of the Birkenhead County Court on the application (if any) of such heir or executor or administrator or relative as aforesaid of the deceased person may direct.

(8.) The removal of the remains of any deceased person shall be carried out under the supervision and to the satisfaction of the medical officer of health for the said district.

52. If the street works authorised by this Act are not completed within ten years from the passing of this Act then on the expiration of that period, the powers by this Act granted to the Council for executing those works or otherwise in relation thereto shall cease except as to such of them, or so much thereof respectively, as shall then be completed. *Period for completion of works.*

53. In the construction of the street works by this Act authorised, the Council may deviate vertically from the levels shown *Deviation.*

Sec. 54—56

on the deposited sections to any extent not exceeding two feet upwards and two feet downwards, and they may deviate laterally within the limits of deviation shown on the deposited plans.

Subsidiary works.

54. Subject to the provisions of this Act and within the limits of deviation defined on the deposited plans the Council in connection with the street improvements authorised by this Act, and for the purposes thereof may make junctions and communications with any existing streets which may be intersected or interfered with by or be contiguous to the street improvements or any of them and may make diversions widenings or alterations of lines or levels of any existing streets for the purpose of connecting the same with the street improvements or any of them, or of crossing under or over the same or otherwise, and may alter divert or stop up all or any part of any drain sewer channel or gas or water main or pipe within the said limits, the Council providing a proper substitute before interrupting the flow of sewage in any drain or sewer or of any gas or water in any main or pipe and making compensation for any damage done by them in the execution of the powers of this section.

PROMENADES.

Power to construct promenades.

55. Subject to the provisions of this Act the Council may make and maintain the following works in the lines and according to the levels shown upon the deposited plans and sections together with all such footways carriage-ways approaches landing-places slipways steps sewers drains works and conveniences as may be necessary or convenient (that is to say):—

> A promenade and embankment commencing at the north side of Seacombe Ferry Station and terminating at the junction of Sandon Road and the existing promenade.
>
> A promenade and embankment commencing at the north-east side of Victoria Road, New Brighton, and terminating at Rowson Street.

Application of provisions of Act of 1896 as to promenade.

56. The following sections of the Act of 1896 (that is to say):—

Section 14 (Power to deviate);

Section 15 (Period for completion of works);

Section 16 (Power to make subsidiary works);

Section 17 (Alteration of position of mains and pipes);

Section 18 (Promenade to be a public highway and repairable as such);

Section 19 (Bye-laws for regulating promenade); and

Section 20 (Power to erect shelters, &c. on promenade); shall, so far as the same are applicable in that behalf and are not inconsistent with the provisions of this Act, extend and apply mutatis mutandis to and in relation to the promenades authorised by this Act as if the same were re-enacted in this Act.

57. The Council shall not execute any works or conduct any operations under the powers of this Act within the jurisdiction of the Mersey Conservancy Commissioners, except in accordance with plans and sections first submitted to and approved of in writing by the acting Conservator for the time being appointed by the Mersey Conservancy Commissioners under the Mersey Conservancy Act, 1842, and the provisions of that Act shall apply to the works under this Act.

For protection of the Mersey Conservancy Commissioners.

58. For the protection and benefit of John Edward Rayner or other the owner for the time being of the lands numbered 31 to 35 on the deposited plans (in this section called "the owner)" the following provisions shall apply and have effect (that is to say):—

For protection of John Edward Rayner.

(1) The promenade from Seacombe Ferry Station to Sandon Road authorised by this Act (in this section called "the promenade") so far as it will abut upon the lands, numbered 31, on the deposited plans shall be completed within eighteen months from the passing of this Act.

(2.) The Council shall not without the consent of the owner acquire a greater part of the said land, numbered 31, than they shall require for constructing the promenade of a width of 50 feet measured from the east side of the river wall, together with such additional land as they shall require for constructing a fence in pursuance of this section, and for providing retaining walls where necessary.

(3) In constructing the promenade where the same will abut upon the said land, numbered 31, the Council shall not deviate from the levels shown on the deposited sections, and the Council shall, where necessary, raise the level of the said land, numbered 31, to the level of the promenade when completed.

(4.) The Council shall construct on the westerly side of the promenade an unclimbable fence six feet six inches high above the level of the promenade, founded upon a stone sill not less than two feet high, but the owner shall at all times be at liberty to make gates and entrances for the use of persons resorting to any house or houses on the property facing the promenade.

(5.) The owner shall at all times hereafter have the right of access to the promenade from so much of the said land, numbered 31, as shall be retained by him by not more than four roads of such width as the owner shall think fit, not being less than the minimum width prescribed by the bye-laws for the time being in force in the district.

(6) The Council shall when constructing so much of the promenade as will abut upon the said lands of the owner lay a sewer longitudinally under the same so far as such sewer has not already been laid, and the owner shall have the right to discharge sewage and drainage into the said sewer.

404   62 & 63 Vict.   *Wallasey Tramways and*   ch. xv.
Improvements Act, 1899.

Sec. 59

(7.) The provisions of the section of this Act whereof the marginal note is "matters to be taken into account by arbitrators" shall not apply in determining any question of disputed compensation to be paid by the Council to the owner for the acquisition of the said lands numbered 31 to 35 or any part thereof.

For the protection of the New Brighton Pier Company

59. For the protection of the New Brighton Pier Company (in this section referred to as the Pier Company), the following provisions shall (unless otherwise agreed between the Council and the Pier Company), be observed and have effect (that is to say):—

(1.) The Council shall before commencing to construct the New Brighton Promenade authorised by this Act make and complete subject to the consent of the Board of Trade Mersey Conservancy Commissioners and Mersey Docks and Harbour Board being obtained if and so far as such consent is necessary and to the reasonable satisfaction of the Pier Company's engineer or in case of dispute to the satisfaction of the President of the Institution of Civil Engineers or of an engineer to be nominated by him an alternative access to the Company's Pier from and on to the existing promenade at its nearest point to the said pier with the deck at the same level as that of the Company's pier and of a width of at least 30 feet or of such greater width not exceeding 60 feet as the Pier Company may desire to a point not exceeding 73 feet from the western end of the Company's pier and from that point by a sloping approach or steps to a point on the new promenade already constructed lineable with the western front of the proposed lavatories as shewn on the plan signed by Walter Henry Travers on behalf of the Council and Albert Tomlinson Wright on behalf of the Pier Company such sloping approach or steps to be of a clear width of 18 feet inside measurement and the Council shall grant to the Pier Company a sub-lease of the ground covered by such extension for a period expiring at the same time as the term granted by the sub-lease of the ground on which the Company's pier is constructed and at the same rent per superficial square yard and under the same conditions as the Pier Company now pay and are subject to under their present sub-lease and the Pier Company will in part consideration therefor grant and pay to the Council one-eighth of all tolls received by them for admission to the pier whether in cash or by sale of contract tickets.

(2.) The Pier Company shall pay to the Council the cost of the construction of the new access to and from their pier from and to the promenade.

(3.) No structure shall be erected by the Pier Company upon the new access except in accordance with plans and elevations submitted to and approved by the Council.

(4.) The Council shall at all reasonable times have access to the Pier Register and Toll Account Books of the Pier Company to enable them to check the amount of the Company's tolls whether in cash or contract tickets.

(5.) Before commencing the works provided for by this section the Council shall be entitled to require from the Pier Company a satisfactory guarantee for the payment of the cost thereof.

MISCELLANEOUS.

60. (1.) The Council may independently of any other borrowing power borrow at interest money for the following purposes (that is to say):— *Power to borrow.*

(a) For the construction of the tramways authorised by this Act the re-construction of the existing tramways adapting the tramways for working by mechanical power and for plant the sum of eighty-seven thousand pounds;

(b) For the purchase of lands for and the construction of the street improvements and new street authorised by this Act the sum of ninety-two thousand pounds;

(c) For the purchase of the land for and the construction of the promenades authorised by this Act the sum of ninety thousand pounds;

(d) For the payment of the costs, charges and expenses of this Act as hereinafter provided, such sum as may be necessary for the purpose.

(2.) The Council may, with the consent of the Board of Trade, borrow such further moneys as may be necessary for the purposes of the tramway undertaking of the Council, and with the consent of the Local Government Board, such further moneys as may be necessary for any of the other purposes of this Act.

(3.) In order to secure the repayment of the moneys borrowed under this section, and the payment of the interest thereon, the Council may charge the district fund and general district rate of the district, and as regards moneys borrowed for the purposes of the tramway undertaking of the Council, the revenue of that undertaking.

61. The Council shall pay off all moneys borrowed by them under this Act within the respective periods (in this Act referred to as "the prescribed periods") following (that is to say):— *Periods for repayment of money borrowed.*

As to moneys borrowed for the purposes (a) mentioned in the section of this Act the marginal note whereof is "Power to borrow" within forty years from the date or dates of the borrowing of the same;

As to moneys borrowed for the purposes (b) and (c) in the said section mentioned within sixty years from the date or dates of the borrowing of the same;

As to money borrowed for the purpose (d) in the said section mentioned within ten years from the date or dates of the borrowing of the same.

As to moneys borrowed with the consent of the Board of Trade or the Local Government Board within such period as the respective Board may sanction.

Sec. 62 - 63

Application of financial provisions of Act of 1896.

62. The following provisions of the Act of 1896 shall apply to the exercise of the powers of this Act as if the same were re-enacted in this Act namely:—

> Section 24 (Mode of raising money).
>
> Section 25 (Certain regulations of Public Health Act not to apply).
>
> Section 26 (Application of provisions of Public Health Act as to mortgages.)
>
> Section 28 (Mode of repayment of money borrowed on mortgage).
>
> Section 29 (Regulations as to sinking fund).
>
> Section 30 (Saving for existing charges).
>
> Section 31 (Council not to regard trusts).
>
> Section 32 (Appointment of Receiver).
>
> Section 33 (Power to re-borrow).
>
> Section 34 (Annual return to Local Government Board).
>
> Section 35 (Proceeds of sale of surplus lands to be treated as capital).
>
> Section 36 (Application of money borrowed).
>
> Section 37 (Protection of lender from inquiry).
>
> Section 38 (Inquiries by Local Government Board).
>
> Section 39 (Expenses of execution of Act).
>
> Section 40 (Audit of Accounts).

Provided that the provisions contained in section 29 of the Act of 1896 shall apply to the formation of sinking funds for the repayment of moneys borrowed under the Local Loans Act, 1875, instead of section 15 of the last mentioned Act.

Application of revenue of tramway undertaking and deficiency of receipts.

63. The council shall apply all money received by them on account of revenue in respect of their tramway undertaking in manner and in the order following (that is to say)—

> First.—In payment of the working and establishment expenses and cost of maintenance of the undertaking (including the maintenance of so much of the roads in which the tramways are laid as is required to be maintained and kept in good repair and condition by the promoters of tramways by section 28 of the Tramways Act, 1870).
>
> Secondly.—In payment of the interest on moneys borrowed by the Council for the purposes of the undertaking;
>
> Thirdly.—In providing the requisite appropriations instalments or sinking fund payments for the purposes of the undertaking;

62 & 63 Vict. *Wallasey Tramways and Improvements Act,* 1899. ch. xv. 407

Fourthly.—In extending and improving (if the Council think fit) any works for the purposes of the undertaking; {Sec. 64—65}

Fifthly.—In providing a reserve fund (if the Council think fit by setting aside such money as they think reasonable and investing the same and the resulting income thereof in securities in which the Council are authorised by the Act of 1896 to invest sinking funds and accumulating the same at compound interest until the fund so formed amounts to the maximum reserve fund for the time being prescribed by the Council not exceeding a sum equal to one-fifth of the aggregate capital expenditure for the time being by the Council upon the undertaking which fund shall be applicable to answer any deficiency at any time happening in the income of the Council from the undertaking or to meet any extraordinary claim or demand at any time arising against the Council in respect of the undertaking or for payment of the cost of renewing any part of the tramways of the Council or of the works connected therewith and so that if that fund be at any time reduced it may thereafter be again restored to the prescribed maximum and so from time to time as often as such reduction happens: Provided that resort may be had to the reserve fund under the foregoing provisions although such fund may not at the time have reached or may have been reduced below the prescribed maximum;

And the Council shall carry to the district fund so much of any balance remaining in any year of the income of their tramway undertaking (including the interest on the reserve fund when such fund amounts to the prescribed maximum) as may in the opinion of the Council not be required for carrying on the undertaking and paying the current expenses connected therewith.

(2.) Any deficiency in the revenue of the tramway undertaking of the Council shall be from time to time made good out of the district fund.

64. The Council may provide, sell, let for hire and fix, set up, alter, repair and remove lamps, meters, electric lines, fittings, apparatus and things for lighting and motive power and for all other purposes for which electric energy can or may be used or otherwise necessary or proper for the supply, distribution, consumption or use of electric energy and may provide all materials and do all works necessary or proper in that behalf and may require and take such remuneration in money or such rents and charges for and make such terms and conditions with respect to the sale, letting, fixing, setting up, altering, repairing or removing of such lamps, meters, electric lines, fittings, apparatus and things as aforesaid and for securing their safety and return to the Council as the Council may think fit or as may be agreed upon between them and the person to or for whom the same are sold, supplied, let, fixed, set up, altered, repaired or removed. {Power to supply electric fittings.}

65.—(1.) Any wires, apparatus and fittings in any building or premises supplied with electric energy by the Council shall be subject to such bye-laws for securing the safety of the inhabitants and for the prevention of fire as the Council may reasonably require. {Bye-laws with respect to electric fittings.}

Sec. 66 71	(2.) The provisions with respect to bye-laws contained in sections 182 to 186 of the Public Health Act, 1875 (except so much thereof as relates exclusively to bye-laws of a rural sanitary authority) shall apply to bye-laws made by the Council under this section: Provided that in the application of such provisions the Board of Trade shall be substituted for the Local Government Board.
Altering the date for filling up annual accounts for electric lighting.	**66.** Notwithstanding anything in section 9 of the Electric Lighting Act, 1882, contained the annual statement of accounts of the electric lighting undertaking of the Council shall after the passing of this Act be filled up on or before the twenty-fourth day of June in every year and shall be made up to the thirty-first day of March next preceding and section 9 of the Electric Lighting Act, 1882, shall as from the passing of this Act be read and have effect as regards the undertaking of the Council as if the twenty-fourth day of June and the thirty-first day of March were therein mentioned instead of the twenty-fifth day of March and the thirty-first day of December.
Authentication and service of notices.	**67.** Where any notice, summons or other document (except a conveyance contract or security) under this Act requires authentication by the Council, the signature thereof by their clerk shall be a sufficient authentication, and any notices, summonses and other documents required or authorised to be served under this Act may be served in manner prescribed by section 267 of the Public Health Act, 1875.
Orders, &c., of the Board of Trade.	**68.** All orders, regulations and bye-laws made by the Board of Trade under the authority of this Act shall be signed by a secretary or an assistant secretary of the Board.
Recovery of penalties.	**69.** Any penalty under this Act or under any bye-laws or regulations made under this Act may be recovered in manner provided by the Summary Jurisdiction Acts.
Incorporation of s. 265 of Public Health Act, 1875.	**70.** Section 265 (Protection of local authority and their officers from personal liability) of the Public Health Act, 1875, is hereby incorporated with and shall form part of this Act.
Costs of Act.	**71.** All the costs, charges and expenses preliminary to and of and incidental to the preparing, applying for, obtaining and passing of this Act, as taxed by the taxing officer of the House of Lords or of the House of Commons shall be paid by the Council out of the district fund or out of moneys to be borrowed under this Act.

SCHEDULES.

THE FIRST SCHEDULE.

Premises of which Portions only are Required.

Works for which properties are authorised to be taken.	Number on Deposited Plans.
Street improvements and new street referred to in the section of this Act whereof the marginal note is "Power to make street works."	8 to 12, 22, 48 to 66, 68 to 78, 120, 136, 144, 145, 153, 229 to 231, 233, 240, 248, 249, 252 to 258, 267, 280, 283, 287 to 289, 291, 294 to 316, 321 to 327, 352, 354, 355, 360, 368 to 371, 375 to 378, 381, 388, 390 to 394, 401 to 403, 417 to 422, 440, 441, 443, 444, 457 to 462, 464, 465, 467 to 470, 472 to 475, 560.
Promenade from Seacombe Ferry Station to Sandon Road referred to in the section of this Act whereof the marginal note is "Power to construct promenades."	5 to 16, 29, 36 to 39.

THE SECOND SCHEDULE.

Rates for Animals and Goods.

Animals.	Per mile
	s. d.
For every horse mule or other beast of draught or burden	0 4
For every ox cow bull or head of cattle	0 3
For every calf pig sheep or small animal ...	0 1½

Goods.

	Per mile
	s. d.
For all coals coke culm charcoal cannel limestone chalk lime salt sand fireclay cinders dung compost and all sorts of manure and all undressed materials for the repair of public roads or highways, per ton	0 2
For all iron ironstone iron ore pig iron bar iron rod iron sheet iron hoop iron plates of iron slabs billets and rolled iron bricks slag and stone stones for building pitching and paving tiles slates and clay (except fireclay) and for wrought iron not otherwise specially classed herein and for heavy iron castings including railway chairs ... per ton	0 2½
For all sugar grain corn flour hides dyewoods earthenware timber staves deals and metals (except iron) nails anvils vices and chains and for light iron castings ... per ton	0 3
For cotton wools drugs manufactured goods and all other wares merchandise fish articles matters or things not otherwise specially classed herein, per ton	0 4
For every carriage of whatever description	1 0

Parcels.

	Any distance
	s. d.
For any parcel not exceeding 7 lbs. in weight	0 3
For any parcel exceeding 7 lbs. and not exceeding 14 lbs. in weight ...	0 5
For any parcel exceeding 14 lbs. and not exceeding 28 lbs. in weight ...	0 7
For any parcel exceeding 28 lbs. and not exceeding 56 lbs. in weight ...	0 9
For any parcel exceeding 56 lbs. such sum as the Council may think fit:	

Provided always that articles sent in large aggregate quantities although made up in separate parcels such as bags of sugar coffee meal and the like shall not be deemed small parcels but that term shall apply only to single parcels in separate packages.

For the carriage of single articles of great weight.

	Per mile
	s. d.
For the carriage of any iron boiler cylinder or single piece of machinery or single piece of timber or stone or other single article the weight of which including the carriage shall exceed four tons but shall not exceed eight tons such sum as the Council may think fit not exceeding ... per ton	2 0
For the carriage of any single piece of timber stone machinery or other single article the weight of which with the carriage shall exceed eight tons such sum as the Council may think fit	

Regulations as to Rates.

For articles or animals conveyed on the tramways for a less distance than three miles the Council may demand rates and charges as for three miles ;

A fraction of a mile beyond an integral number of miles shall be deemed a mile ;

For the fraction of a ton the Council may demand rates according to the number of quarters of a ton in such fraction, and if there be a fraction of a quarter of a ton such fraction shall be deemed a quarter of a ton :

With respect to all articles except stone and timber the weight shall be determined according to Imperial avoirdupois weight ;

With respect to stone and timber fourteen cubic feet of stone forty cubic feet of oak, mahogany, teak, beech, or ash, and fifty cubic feet of any other timber shall be deemed one ton weight and so in proportion for any smaller quantity.

In addition to the foregoing rates the Council may demand such charges as are reasonable for loading and unloading the animals and goods and if any difference shall arise as to the reasonableness of any such charge the matter in difference shall be settled by the Board of Trade.

Schedules.

INDEX
TO
LOCAL ACTS.

INDEX.

In this Index the Statutes and Provisional Orders are denoted by their dates, accompanied by distinguishing letters, *e.g.* :—

    A.—Act.
    C.A.—Confirming Act.
    E.L.O.—Electric Lighting Order.
    O.—Provisional Order.

	ACT.	PAGE.
ACCIDENTS		
Notice of, and enquiries by Board of Trade	E.L.O. 1897 art. 29	354
ACCOUNTS		
Audit of, under	A. 1896 s. 40	327
	A. 1899 s. 62	406
Salaries may be charged to particular or special	A. 1864 s. 42	208
Sec. 9 of Electric Lighting Act, 1882, varied as to Electric Lighting	A. 1899 s. 66	408
Separate, of expenses of private street works	A. 1890 s. 55	291
"Wallasey Ferries Account"	A. 1858 s. 39	176
„ Lighting „	A. 1858 s. 29	173
„ Waterworks „	A. 1858 ss. 27-28	173
ADMIRALTY		
Approval of piers or landing stage, by	A. 1864 s. 8	200
Exemptions from pier rates or duties	A. 1864 s. 10	200
May order local survey	A. 1864 s. 11	201
May remove abandoned works affecting tidal waters	A. 1864 s. 12	201
ADOPTION		
Of private streets	A. 1890 ss. 53-54	290, 291
ADVERTISEMENTS		
Exhibited on hoardings	A. 1890 s. 79	298
Of charges for electrical energy	E.L.O. 1897 art. 24	352
Of notices of approval, &c., of the Board of Trade	E.L.O. 1897 art. 65	364

INDEX.

	ACT.	PAGE.
AGREEMENTS		
For lease of Foreshore	A. 1864 s. 43 & sched	208, 209
For supply of electrical energy	E.L.O. 1897 arts. 20 & 26	349, 353
To purchase additional lands	A. 1896 s. 9 / A. 1899 s. 11	320 / 385
To sell mains and pipes to sanitary authorities	A. 1890 s. 73 (ss. 3)	296
To supply gas and water to outside authorities and others	A. 1890 s. 73	296
With Mersey Docks and Harbour Board as to river wall	A. 1872 sched.	241
With owners of property to bind successors	A. 1890 s. 32	285
ALLOWANCES		
To officers and servants	A. 1864 s. 38	208
ANCHORING		
Of vessels, bye-laws regulating	A. 1867 s. 28 / A. 1872 s. 14	222 / 239
ANIMALS		
Accommodation at Ferries for	A. 1867 s. 24	221
Council not bound to carry, upon tramways	A. 1899 s. 32	391
Ferry Tolls for	A. 1858 s. 39 / A. 1867 ss. 19-20 and sched. C.	176 / 220 / 226
Power to sell, used for tramways	A. 1899 s. 43	397
APPEAL		
Under	A. 1890 s. 81	298
,, Electric Lighting Order to Board of Trade,	E.L.O. 1897 art. 10 (c)	340
APPORTIONMENT		
Of expenses of private street works, provisional	A. 1890 s. 40	286
,, ,, ,, final	A. 1890 s. 46	289
ARBITRATION		
Matters to be considered in	A. 1896 s. 22 / A. 1899 ss. 8-9	323 / 383-385
With frontages as to footways	A. 1896 s. 21 (2)	322
Under Electric Lighting Order, 1897	arts. 11, 13, 14, 16, 21, 22, 58	341, 344, 346, 347, 350, 352, 361

INDEX. v.

	ACT.	PAGE.
ARCH		
Under street, repair of	A. 1864 s. 30 A. 1890 s. 26	206 283
ASSES		
Power to license owners, or drivers of	O. 1852 art. 18	164
ASSESSMENTS		
To different Rates may be in one Rate Book...	A. 1864 s. 41	208
AUDIT		
Of accounts under Act of 1896	A. 1896 s. 40	327
BAND		
Stands on Promenade for	A. 1896 s. 20	322
BANKRUPTCY		
Priority of Rates in	A. 1867 s. 38 and note; A. 1872 s. 21	224 240
Proof of claims by clerk ...	A. 1858 s. 81	185
BATHING		
From Foreshore ...	A. 1890 s. 8	278
Power to make bye-laws regulating	A. 1890 s. 8 s.s. (3)	278
Provisions for protection of bathers	A. 1890 ss. 9-10	278 279
Sections of Town Police Clauses Act, 1847, applied	O. 1852 art. 17	163
BATHS		
Towns Improvement Clauses Act, 1847, respecting, applied ...	O. 1852 art. 17	163
Water Rents for additional	A. 1858 s. 14	170
BIRKENHEAD		
Communication with Seacombe...	A. 1867 s. 7	216
BLACKSMITHS		
To shut-out light of forges from streets	A. 1845 s. 182	151
BOARD OF TRADE		
Appeal from Postmaster-General to, re electrical works in streets ...	E.L.O. 1897 art. 10 (c)	340
Approval of systems and mode of supply of electrical energy by	E.L.O. 1897 art. 6	338
Approval of electrical works in streets by	E.L.O. 1897 art. 10 (c)	340
,, ,, rails of tramways ...	A. 1899 s. 22	389
Consent of, to break up private streets, etc. ...	E.L.O. 1897 art. 8	339
Inspection of tramways ...	A. 1899 ss. 18-23	389
Inquiries by, as to accidents	E.L.O. 1897 art. 29	354

	ACT.	PAGE.
Board of Trade—*Continued.*		
Notice of accidents in electrical works, etc., to	E.L.O. 1897 art. 29	... 354
Orders, &c., of, to be signed by Secretary	A. 1899 s. 68	... 408
Plan of proposed mode of construction of tramways to be laid before ...	A. 1899 s. 20	.. 389
Proceedings under Electric Lighting Order of	E.L.O. 1897 art. 63	... 364
Terms of approval or consent of	E.L.O. 1897 art. 64	... 364
BOATMEN		
Employment and payment of, protection of bathers	A. 1890 s. 10	... 279
Employment of, by bathing machine proprietors	A. 1890 s. 9	... 278
BOATS		
Power to make bye-laws regulating traffic ...	A. 1858 s. 51	.. 179
Preservation of order and decorum on ...	A. 1858 s. 51	... 179
BORROWING POWERS		
For construction of tramways ...	A. 1899 s. 60	... 405
For *Ferries*	A. 1858 s. 60; A. 1861 s. 3; A. 1864 s. 21; A. 1872 s. 17; O. (No. 1) 1877 art. 3 O. 1881 art. 1; O. 1883 art. 2; O. 1895 art. 1; and O. 1897 art. 1.	181 189 203 239 249 258 264 311 369
„ *Gas*	A. 1858 s. 60; A. 1861 s. 3; A. 1867 s. 30; O. (No. 1) 1877 art. 2 O. 1883 art. 1; O. 1892 art. 2; O. 1896 art. 1; and O. 1898 art. 1.	181 189 222 249 264 303 314 376
„ Private street works ...	A. 1890 ss. 51-52	... 290
„ Street works ...	A. 1899 s. 60	... 405
„ Purchase of land, etc., Promenade	A. 1896 ss. 23 & 33 A. 1899 s. 60	323 326 ... 405
„ *Water* ...	A. 1858 s. 60; A. 1861 s. 3; O. 1863; A. 1864 s. 28; O. 1870 art. 6; A. 1872 s. 17; O. 1894 art. 1.	181 189 194 206 232 239 308

INDEX. VII.

	ACT.	PAGE.
Borrowing Powers—*Continued.*		
Local Loans Act, 1875, available	O. 1892 art. 2 (s.s 2)	304
	A. 1896 s. 24 ;	323
	O. 1897 art. 2 ;	370
	A. 1899 s. 62.	406
Provisions of Public Health Act to apply	A. 1858 s. 61 ;	182
	A. 1861 s. 4 ;	190
	A. 1864 s. 22 ;	204
	A. 1867 s. 32 ;	223
	O.(No.1)1877 art. 4 ;	249
	O. 1881 art. 1 ;	258
	O. 1883 arts 1 & 2 ;	264
	O. 1892 art. 2 (s.s. 2),	304
	O. 1897 art. 2.	370
S. 234 of Public Health Act not to apply to Promenade loans ...	A. 1896 s. 25	324
	A. 1899 s. 62	406

BOUNDARIES

Of Improvement Commissioners' jurisdiction	A. 1845 s. 89	... 149
Of Liscard Commissioners' Award ...	—	22 / 61
Of Wallasey District	O. 1852 art. 1 ;	160
	O. (No. 1) 1877 ;	247
	and A. 1890 s. 5.	277

BRIDGES

Restrictions on breaking up public bridges, E.L.O. 1897 arts. 10-12 340 / 342

BUILDING

Compulsory purchase of portions only ...	A. 1896 s. 7	319
	A. 1899 s. 8	383
Deposit of plan, void after certain interval	A. 1890 s. 13	... 279
Drainage and water supply before occupation	A. 1890 s. 20	... 281
Entering for disinfecting	A. 1890 s. 68	... 295
Exemption of Crown or public	A. 1890 s. 37	... 286
Expense of pulling down for inspection, how borne	A. 1890 s. 22	... 281
Height, how determined ...	A. 1890 s. 18	... 280
Height of rooms ...	A. 1890 s. 19	... 281
Height prescribed...	A. 1890 s. 18	... 280
Hoards to be erected during progress of	A. 1890 s. 23	... 282
Improperly used for habitation ..	A. 1890 ss. 20 & 25	281 / 282
Inspection of	A. 1890 s. 21	... 281
Meaning under Act of 1845 s. 327	A. 1845 s. 327	156
"New Building" described ...	A. 1890 s. 17	... 280
Notice of commencement, &c. ...	A. 1890 s. 21	... 281
Numbering buildings ...	A. 1890 s 16	... 280

INDEX.

	ACT.	PAGE.
Building—*Continued.*		
Power of surveyor—inspecting ...	A. 1890 s. 22	... 281
Removal of projecting ...	A. 1864 s. 33	... 207
Ruinous or dangerous, Towns Improvement Clauses Act, 1847, applied ...	O. 1852 art. 17	... 163
Street names on ...	A. 1890 s. 16	... 280
Supplying with fresh air, sections 110 & 111 Towns Improvement Clauses Act, 1847, applied ...	O. 1852 art. 17	... 163
To be certified before occupation as dwellings ...	A. 1890 s. 20	... 281
BURIAL		
Of Infected body ...	A. 1890 s. 63	... 294
BYE-LAWS		
Advertisements, regulating exhibition of	A. 1890 s. 79	... 298
Alteration and authentication of...	O. 1888 art. 3 ; A. 1890 s. 85 (Note)	271 299
Bathing, regulating ...	A. 1890 s. 8 (s.s. 3)	278
Buildings to comply with	A. 1890 s. 20	... 281
Confirmation of ...	A. 1890 s. 85 (Note)	299
Drivers and conductors, regulating	O. 1888 arts. 1 to 3	270
Electric fittings, regulating ...	A. 1899 s. 65	... 407
Evidence of	A. 1845 s. 251 ; A. 1858 s. 59 ; A. 1867 s. 29 ; A. 1890 s. 85 (Note)	154 180 222 299
Ferries, regulating	A. 1858 ss. 51 to 59 ; A. 1867 s. 29	179 180 222
Foreshore, regulating ...	A. 1890 ss. 7 & 79	278 298
Gas fittings, regulating inspection and control of ...	A. 1867 s. 15 ; A. 1890 s. 70	219 295
Gas fittings, regulating supply of ...	A. 1867 s. 15	... 219
Hackney carriages and omnibuses, regulating ...	O. 1888 arts. 1 to 3	270
Hoardings, regulating erection and removal of ...	A. 1890 s. 79	... 298
Inspection of ...	A. 1858 s. 57	... 180
Jurisdiction of Wirral Justices in Ferry...	A. 1890 s. 76	... 297
Mooring and anchoring of vessels, regulating ...	A. 1867 s. 28 ; A. 1872 s. 14	222 239
Penalties for enforcing ...	A. 1845 s. 246 ; A. 1858 s. 53 ; A. 1867 s. 29 ; A. 1890 s. 85	153 179 222 299

	ACT.	PAGE.
Bye-Laws—*Continued*.		
Porters, regulating	A. 1845 s. 245	... 153
Promenades, preserving order	A. 1890 s. 79 ; A. 1896 s. 19 ; A. 1899 s. 56	298 321 402
Publication of	A. 1858 s. 57 ; A. 1867 s. 29 ; A. 1890 s. 85	180 222 299
Public Health Act to apply to	O. 1888 art. 3 (s.s. 2) ; A. 1890 s. 85 ; A. 1899 s. 65 (2)	271 299 407
Public lavatories, &c., regulating	A. 1890 s. 31	... 284
Speed of trams, regulating	A. 1899 s. 36	... 392
Tramways, relating to	A. 1899 ss. 36 & 42	392 396
Quarter Sessions to allow	A. 1858 s. 54 ; A. 1867 s. 29	180 222
Repeal of	A. 1858 s. 52 ; A. 1864 s. 37 ; A. 1867 s. 29 ; A. 1890 s. 85	179 208 222 299
Sanitary purposes for	A. 1890 s. 29	... 284
Water fittings, regulating inspection and control of	A. 1867 s. 15 ; A. 1890 s. 70	219 295
Water, regulating supply of	A. 1867 s. 15	... 219
Water fittings, testing and stamping	A. 1890 s. 70	... 295
CARRIAGE		
Meaning under Act of 1845, s. 327	A. 1845 s. 327	... 156
Power to provide, for tramways	A. 1899 ss. 16 & 43	386 397
Railway, not to be used upon tramways	A. 1899 s. 21 (2)	... 389
Regulation of hackney	O. 1852 art 17 ; O. 1888 arts 1 to 3	163 270 271
Width of	A. 1899 s. 21 (1)	... 389
CARTS		
Dogs or goats not to be used for drawing	A. 1845 s. 187	... 151
Weighing, Markets and Fairs' Clauses Act, 1847, applied	O. 1852, art 17	... 163
CELLARS		
In courts not to be occupied as dwellings	A. 1845 s. 142	... 150
Repair of	A. 1864 s. 30 ; A. 1890 s. 26	206 283
CERTIFICATE		
Of compliance with bye-laws	A. 1890 s. 20	... 281
„ Medical Officer as to cleansing and disinfecting	A. 1890 s. 59	... 292

	ACT.	PAGE.

Certificate—*Continued.*
    Of Medical Officer as to detention of infected persons ... A. 1890 s. 65 ... 294
    ,, Medical Officer as to outbreak of infectious disease due to milk ... A. 1890 s. 56 ... 291
    ,, Medical Officer as to removal of body for burial ... A. 1890 s. 62 ... 293
    ,, Medical Officer as to retention of infected body ... A. 1890 s. 61 ... 293

CESSPOOL
    Construction or continuance of ... A. 1890 s. 30 ... 284

CHARGE
    Private street expenses, a charge on premises ... A. 1890 s. 47 ... 289
    Protection of existing charges on mortgages ... A. 1896 s. 30 ... 325
    Register of charges to be kept ... A. 1890 s. 47 (2) ... 290

CISTERNS
    Approval of ... A. 1858 s. 12 ... 170

CLOCKS
    Power to provide public ... O. 1852 art. 17 ... 163

COAST GUARD
    Exemptions from pier rates or duties ... A. 1864 s. 10 ... 200

COKE
    Power to sell and dispose of ... A. 1858 s. 17 ... 171

COMMISSIONERS
    Definition of ... A. 1845 s. 327 ... 155
    Electors' qualifications ... A. 1845 (Note) ... 146
    Mode of supplying occasional vacancies A. 1845 s. 17 ... 146
    Powers, property and liabilities transferred to Local Board ... O. 1852 art 9, 12 & 13 162
    Qualification ... A. 1845 (Note) ... 146
    Shareholders not disqualified by contracts A. 1845 s. 6 ... 146
    Superseded by Local Board of Health ... A. 1845 s.327(Note) 157

COMMONS
    Allotment and division of commons and waste lands in Liscard ... Award ... 22
    Allotment and division of commons and waste lands in Wallasey and Poolton-cum-Seacombe ... Award ... 61
    Contents of, Wallasey and Poolton-cum Seacombe ... Award ... 61

INDEX. xi.

	ACT.	PAGE.
Commons—*Continued*.		
Highways and roads over, set out ...	Award	62 93 107
Lands sold by Commissioners under Inclosure Act, 1814	Award	61
Rights of commons extinguished, Inclosure Act, 1809, s. 21	A. 1814 s. 29	58
Roads over commons to be not less than 30 feet wide	A. 1809 s. 26	20

COMPANIES
Priority of rates in winding up ...	A. 1867 s. 38 (Note) A. 1872 s. 21	224 240

COMPENSATION
Matters to be considered by arbitrator in determining	A. 1896 s. 22; A. 1899 s. 9	323 385
On compulsory purchase of part of land, &c.	A. 1896 s. 7; A. 1899 ss.8(1)&9	319 383 384
To persons damaged by alteration of mains or pipes	A. 1896 s. 17	... 321
To owners affected by subsidiary works...	A. 1896 s. 16	... 321
To owners and occupiers of projecting buildings removed	A. 1864 s. 33	... 207
To Postmaster-General under electric lighting order	E.L.O. 1897 art. 10 (*f*)	340
Under electric lighting order ...	E.L.O. 1897 art. 10 (*f*) arts. 11, 13, 14, 16	340 341 347

CONDUCTORS
Regulation of ...	O. 1852 art. 17 O. 1888 arts. 1-3	163 270 271

CONSTABLES
Dismissal or suspension of ...	A. 1845 s. 256	... 154
Power to employ	A. 1867 s. 41	... 225
Power to make rules and orders for ...	A. 1845 s. 257	... 154
Town Police Clauses Act, 1847, applied...	O. 1852 art. 17	... 163

CONVEYANCE
Carrying infected body in public	A. 1890 s. 64	... 294
Disinfection of public ...	A. 1890 s. 64	... 294

CONVEYANCE OF MAILS ACT, 1893
To apply to all Tramways of Council ...	A. 1899 s. 48	... 397

CONVEYANCING AND LAW OF PROPERTY ACT, 1881
Remedies under, available for recovery of private street expenses	A. 1890 s. 47	... 289

	ACT.	PAGE.
COSTS		
Arbitration proceedings under notice to treat ...	A. 1899 s. 8	... 383
Of legal proceedings	A. 1867 s. 42	... 225
Local Government inquiries ...	O. 1892 art. 2 (10) A. 1896 s. 38 (2) O. 1897 art. 10 A. 1899 s. 62	306 327 373 406
Private street works proceedings	A. 1890 s. 42 (3) ...	288
Prosecutions	A. 1864 s. 40	... 208
Testing gas	A. 1858 s. 26	... 173
Recovery of	A. 1890 s. 83	... 298
Under electric lighting order	E.L.O. 1897 arts. 39, 64	356 364
COULBORN		
Purchase of Messrs. Coulborn's ferry rights	A. 1861 Preamble and s. 7	188 191
COUNTY COUNCIL		
Notification and approval of electrical work in streets or bridges repairable by	E.L.O. 1897 art. 10 (*f*) ...	340
Restrictions on breaking up streets or bridges repairable by	E.L.O. 1897 art. 10	... 340
COURTS		
Cellars in, not to be occupied as dwellings	A. 1845 s. 142	... 150
Cleaning of	A. 1890 s. 28	... 284
Dedication of	A. 1864 s. 29	... 206
To be flagged, sewered, &c.	A. 1864 s. 29	... 206
COWKEEPERS		
To furnish list of customers in certain cases	A. 1890 s. 56	... 291
COWSHEDS		
Inspection of ...	A. 1890 s. 57	... 292
CROSSINGS		
Power to make additional, for tramways	A. 1899 s. 24	... 390
CROWN		
Exemptions from pier rates or duties ...	A. 1864 s. 10	... 200
Protection of Rights of	A. 1845 s. 324; A. 1864 s. 44; A. 1872 ss. 9 & 10; A. 1890 ss. 86 & 87 A. 1896 ss. 46 & 47 A. 1899 s. 15	155 209 238 299 333 334 386
CUSTOMS		
Service exempted from pier rates or duties	A. 1864 s. 10	... 200

	ACT.	PAGE.
DAIRY		
Customers' list to be furnished ...	A. 1890 s. 56	... 291
Inspection of dairies, &c.	A. 1890 s. 57	... 292
Supplying milk prohibited in certain cases	A. 1890 s. 57	... 292
DEAD		
Dying of infectious disease, retention of body prohibited	A. 1890 s. 61	... 293
Justices may order removal and burial of infected body	A. 1890 s. 62	.. 293
Infected body not to be carried in public conveyance	A. 1890 s. 64	... 294
Removal of infected body from hospital for burial only	A. 1890 s. 62	.. 293
Vide "Human Remains."		
DEFINITIONS		
Buildings	A. 1845 s. 327	... 156
Carriage	A. 1845 s. 327	... 156
Clerk ... {	A. 1890 s. 3 A. 1896 s. 3	} 277 319
Council ... {	A. 1896 s. 3 A. 1899 ss. 3&39(7)	{ 318 382 394
Daily Penalty ...	A. 1890 s. 3	... 277
District ... {	A. 1890 s. 3 ; A. 1896 s. 3 ; A. 1899 s. 3	} 277 319 382
Driver	A. 1845 s. 327	... 156
Electric Line	A 1899 s. 40 (h)	.. 396
Electric Lighting Order, in ...	...E.L.O. 1897 art. 2	... 336
Enclosed lands	A. 1896 s. 3	... 319
Engine	A. 1899 s. 3	... 382
Foreshore	A. 1890 s. 3	... 277
Frontagers	A. 1896 s. 3	... 319
General or Quarter Sessions ...	A. 1845 s. 327	... 156
Hackney Carriage	A. 1845 s. 327	... 156
House	A. 1845 s. 327	... 156
Infectious Disease	A. 1890 s. 3	... 277
Justice	A. 1845 s. 327	... 156
Labouring Class ... {	C.A. 1892 s. 2 ; A. 1896 s. 10(2) E.L.O. 1897 art. 7 A. 1899 s. 12 (3)	} 302 320 338 385
Lands	A. 1845 s. 327	... 156
Mechanical Power	A. 1899 s. 3	... 382
Month	A. 1845 s. 327	... 156

		ACT.	PAGE.
Definitions—*Continued.*			
Omnibus		O. 1888 arts. 1 & 3	270 / 271
Open lands		A. 1896 s. 3	319
Owner		A. 1845 s. 327	156
Paving, metalling and flagging		A. 1890 s. 39	286
Person		A. 1845 s. 327	155
Street		A. 1845 s. 327; A. 1890 s. 38	155 / 286
Surveyor		A. 1845 s. 327; A. 1890 s. 3	156 / 277
Tramways		A. 1899 s. 3	382
DEMAND			
Authentication of summons, notice, or		A. 1858 s. 82	186
DEPRECIATION FUND			
Creation of Depreciation and Renewal Fund		A. 1872 s. 22; O. 1883 art. 3	241 / 265
DETENTION			
In hospital of infected person without lodging		A. 1890 s. 65	294
Of goods by Toll collectors		A. 1858 ss. 42, 43, 49, 50	177 / 178 / 179
DISINFECTION			
Entering houses for		A. 1890 s. 68	295
Of houses, &c.		A. 1890 ss. 59 & 60	292 / 293
Shelter during		A. 1890 s. 66	295
DISTRICT COUNCILS			
Supersede Local Boards		O. 1852, note to arts. 2 to 5 A. 1896 preamble (Note)	161 / 317
DISTRICT FUND AND RATE			
Contribution to private st. works expenses		A. 1890 s. 49	290
Security for land purchase, &c.		A. 1896 s. 23; A. 1899 s. 60	323 / 405
Security for mortgages		A. 1867 s. 36; A. 1890 s. 52; A. 1896 s. 23	224 / 290 / 323
DOCKS			
Communication across		A. 1867 s. 7	216
Liability to rates		A. 1858 s. 35	174
Protection of Mersey Docks and Harbour Board		A. 1867 s. 6; A. 1890 s. 89	216 / 299
River Wall, agreement with Dock Board		A. 1872 s. 13 and sched.	239 / 241

	ACT.	PAGE.
DOGS		
Not to be used for drawing carts	A. 1845 s. 187	151
DRAINS		
Altering position of	A. 1896 s. 17	321
Commissioner empowered to make drains, &c	Incl. A. 1814 s. 15	53
Connection with sewers	A. 1864 s. 31; A. 1890 s. 35	206 285
Construction or continuance of cesspools	A. 1890 s. 30	284
Examination of	A. 1890 s. 36	286
In private street works	A. 1890 s. 43	288
Inspection of	A. 1890 s. 36	286
Maintenance of public drains set out by Commissioner	Award	61
Notice of covering up	A. 1890 s. 21	284
Obstruction of	A. 1890 s. 33	285
Public drains set out by Commissioner	Award	61
To be made before houses occupied	A. 1890 s. 20	284
Turning steam, &c. into	A. 1890 s. 34	285
DREDGER		
Borrowing powers for	O. 1897 art. 1	369
DRIVERS		
Crossing footways	A. 1890 s. 15	279
Meaning	A. 1845 s. 327	155
Regulation of	O. 1852 art. 17; O. 1888 arts 1-3	163 270 271
DUKE STREET BRIDGE AND EMBANKMENT		
Communication secured	A. 1867 s. 7	216
EASEMENTS		
Power to grant	A. 1896 s. 11 A. 1899 s. 10	320 385
EGREMONT FERRY		
Lease or purchase of powers granted	A. 1845 s. 86	148
Pier extension	A. 1872 s. 7	237
ELECTORS		
Qualification of	A. 1845 note to repealed s. 15	116
Qualification of	O. 1852 note to arts. 2 to 5	161
ELECTRIC FITTINGS		
Bye-laws with respect to	A. 1899 s. 65	407
Power to supply	A. 1899 s. 64	407

ELECTRIC LIGHTING

	ACT.	PAGE.
Acquisition and use of lands for...	E.L.O. 1897 art. 7	338
Appropriation of land for purposes of	O. 1892 art. 1 (3)	303

ELECTRIC LIGHTING ORDER, 1897 (Wallasey)

Agreements for supply under	E.L.O. 1897 arts. 20 & 26	349, 353
Alteration of pipes, wires, &c., under street	,, ,, art. 13	344
Application of moneys under	,, ,, arts. 52 & 53	359, 360
Appointment and duties of electric inspectors	,, ,, art. 27	353
Approval of street works by Postmaster-General or Board of Trade	,, ,, art. 10	340
Arbitration under Electric Lighting Order	,, ,, arts. 11, 13, 14, 16, 58	341, 344, 347, 361
Area of supply	,, ,, art. 5 and sched. 1	338, 366
Compensation under order	,, ,, arts. 10, 11, 13, 14, 16	341, 347
Conditions of supply	,, ,, arts. 20 & 21	349, 350
Definitions in order	,, ,, art. 2	336
Distributing mains to be laid in specified streets	,, ,, art. 17 and sched. 2	348, 366
Expenses of electric inspector	,, ,, art. 39	356
Laying electric lines near gas or water pipes	,, ,, art. 14	346
Maps of area of supply	,, ,, art. 51	358
Maximum power	,, ,, art. 22	352
Maximum prices	,, ,, art. 25 and sched. IV.	353, 366
Methods of charging for	,, ,, art. 24	352
Mode and system of supply to be approved by Board of Trade	,, ,, art. 6	338
Nature and amount of security under	,, ,, art. 62	364
Notice of accidents and inquiries by Board of Trade	,, ,, art. 29	354
Order may be revoked on failure to lay mains	,, ,, art. 18	349
Penalties under Order	,, ,, arts. 10 to 14; 23; 51; 60 and 61	340, 346, 352, 358, 363

	ACT.	PAGE.
Electric Lighting Order, 1897 (Wallasey)—*Continued*.		
Postmaster-General to have notice of works	E.L.O. 1897 art. 10	340
Power to break up streets, railways and tramways	,, ,, art. 8	339
Proper instruments to be kept	,, ,, art. 33	355
Protection of members and officers of local authority from personal liability	,, ,, art. 68	365
Protection of telegraphic and telephonic wires	,, ,, art. 16	347
Purchase and use of lands for purposes of	,, ,, art. 7	338
Readings of instruments as evidence	,, ,, art. 34	355
Regulations as to meters	,, ,, arts. 40 to 50	356 / 358
Remedying of system of supply, &c.	,, ,, art. 60	363
Remuneration of electric inspectors	,, ,, art. 28	353
Requisition to lay distributing mains	,, ,, art. 19	349
Responsibility for damages	,, ,, art. 67	365
Restrictions on breaking up streets, bridges, railway, tramway, &c.	,, ,, arts. 10, 11, 12	340 342
Revocation of order	,, ,, arts. 56 to 58	361
Revocation of Wallasey Electric Lighting Licence, 1896	,, ,, art. 72	365
Street boxes for electrical purposes	,, ,, art. 9	339
Testing of instruments	,, ,, arts. 35 to 38	355 / 356
Testing of mains	,, ,, art. 30	354
Testing stations may be ordered by Court of Summary Jurisdiction	,, ,, art. 33	355
Testing supply at consumers' premises	,, ,, art. 31	355
Text of order	—	336
Transfer of powers, &c.	,, ,, art. 59	362
Undertakers for purposes of	,, ,, art. 4	338

ELECTRIC POWER
For Tramways, provisions relating to	A 1899 ss. 37 to 41	392 396

EMBANKMENT
Agreement with Dock Board respecting	A. 1872 (Sched.)	241
At Seacombe authorised	A. 1872 s. 7	237
Cost, maintenance, and repair	A. 1872 (Sched.)	242
Protection of Wallasey Embankment Commissioner	A. 1845 s. 85; A. 1890 s. 11	147 279
Promenade and embankment to New Brighton	A. 1896 s. 13	321
Road over Duke Street embankment	A. 1867 s. 7	216

	ACT.	PAGE.
ENGINE		
Definition of	A. 1899 s. 3	382
Power to provide, for tramways	,, ss. 16 & 43	386, 397
Width of, for tramways	,, s. 21 (1)	389
ESTIMATES		
For General District Rates	A. 1867 s. 36	224
Of expenses of private street works	A. 1890 ss. 40 & 43 (2)	286, 288
Particulars to be stated in street works	A. 1890 (Sched. I.)	300
EVIDENCE		
Of bye-laws	A. 1845 s. 251;	154
	A. 1858 s. 59	180
	A. 1867 s. 29	222
	A. 1890 s. 85 (Note)	299
Orders of Board of Trade in	E.L.O. 1897 art. 63	364
Readings of electric instruments receivable in	E.L.O. 1897 s. 34	355
EXEMPTIONS		
From Pier rates or duties	A. 1864 s. 10	200
Improperly claiming, from Pier rates, &c., penalty	A. 1864 s. 10	200
Of incumbent, minister, &c., from private street work expenses	A. 1890 s. 50	290
EXPENSES		
Of Electric Inspector	E.L.O. 1897 art 39	356
,, legal proceedings	A. 1864 s. 40;	208
	A. 1867 s. 42;	225
	A. 1890 s. 83	298
,, Local Government inquiries	A. 1896 s. 38 (2)	327
,, Objections to private street works	A. 1890 s. 42 (3)	288
,, Pulling down buildings for inspection	A. 1890 s. 22	281
,, Private street works, apportionment	A. 1890 s. 44	288
,, Private street works, a charge on premises	A. 1890 s. 47	289
,, Private street works, contribution out of district fund or rate	A. 1890 s. 49	290
,, Private street works, estimate	A. 1890 ss. 40 & 43 (2)	286, 288
,, Private street works, exemption of incumbent, &c.	A. 1890 s. 50	290
,, Private street works, power for limited owner to borrow	A. 1890 s. 51	290
,, Private street works, power for Urban Authority to borrow	A. 1890 s. 52	290

	ACT.	PAGE.
Expenses—*Continued.*		
Of Private street works recovery	A. 1890 ss. 46, 47, 48	289 290
,, Private street works, separate accounts	A. 1890 s. 55	... 291
,, Removal and reinterment of human remains	A. 1899 s. 51 (5)	... 400
,, Removal of monuments & tombstones	A. 1899 s. 51 (7)	... 400

FARMHOUSE

  Inspection of, supplying milk to district   A. 1890 s. 57   ... 292

FENCING

	ACT.	PAGE.
During progress of building	A. 1890 s. 23	... 282
Fencing of allotments under Inclosure Acts	A. 1809 s. 19 ; A. 1814 s. 27	18 57
,, Glebe Lands ...	Incl. A. 1814 s. 24	... 56
,, Lands on Promenade	A. 1896 s. 41 (3) ; s. 42 (3) ; s. 43 (3&11)	328 330 331 333
,, Lands on adjoining streets ...	A. 1845 s. 118 ; A. 1890 s. 24	150 282
Unfenced ground a " street " and " public place "...	A. 1890 s. 6	.. 278
Use of unfenced land for display of wares	A. 1890 s. 6	... 278

FERRIES

	ACT.	PAGE.
Accommodation for goods and animals at	A. 1867 s. 24	... 221
Borrowing powers for	A. 1858 s. 60 ; A. 1861 s. 3 ; A. 1864 s. 21 ; A. 1872 s. 17 ; O. (No. 1) 1877 art. 3 ; O. 1881 art. 1 ; O. 1883 art. 2 ; O. 1895 art. 1 ; O. 1897 art. 1	181 189 203 239 249 258 264 311 369
Bye-laws for regulating of	A. 1858 ss. 51 to 59 A. 1867 ss. 28 & 29 A. 1872 s. 14	179 180 222 239
Depreciation and renewal fund ...	A. 1872 s. 22 ; O. 1883 art. 3	241 265
Disputes as to tolls and weight ...	A. 1858 ss. 43 & 44	177
Jurisdiction of Wirral Justices over ferry boats, &c.	A. 1890 s. 76	... 297
Mooring at Ferry Works...	A. 1867 s. 28 ; A. 1872 s. 14	222 239

INDEX.

	ACT.	PAGE.
Ferries—*Continued.*		
Passengers evading tolls	A. 1858 s. 46; A. 1867 s. 26; A. 1872 s. 15	178 221 239
Passengers refusing toll	A. 1867 s. 27	... 221
Passengers refusing to produce tickets	A. 1890 s. 74	... 297
Plying of passenger ferry during fog	A. 1890 s. 75	... 297
Power to hire and charter steam-boats	A. 1858 s. 37	... 175
Power to lease or purchase	A. 1845 s. 86; A. 1858 s. 36	148 174
Power to levy tolls	A. 1858 s. 39; A. 1867 s. 20	176 220
Power to negotiate for existing ferries	A. 1858 s. 38	. 175
Power to provide steam-boats, &c.	A. 1845 s. 87; A. 1858 s. 37; A. 1864 s. 17	149 175 202
Power to sell or let steam-boats	A. 1864 s. 17	... 202
Purchase of Messrs. Coulborn's interest, preamble, and	A. 1861 s. 7	... 191
Purchase of reversion of Seacombe Ferry	A. 1861 s. 6	... 191
Recovery of tolls	A. 1858 s. 42; A. 1867 s. 23	177 220
Specified tolls not to be exceeded	A. 1858 s. 41; A. 1867 s. 22	176 220
Tolls after January 1st, 1868	A. 1867 s. 20; and sched. C	220 226
Tolls or rates may be altered	A. 1864 s. 16; A. 1867 s. 23	202 220
Tolls to be charged equally	A. 1858 s. 40; A. 1867 s. 21	176 220
Wallasey Ferries account	A. 1858 s. 39	... 176
FIRE		
Application of Town Police Clauses Act, 1847, respecting	O. 1852 art. 17	... 163
Construction of houses for prevention of, Towns Improvement Clauses Act, 1847, applied	O. 1852 art. 17	... 163
FLOATING STAGE		
At Seacombe authorised	A. 1872 s. 7	... 237
FOG		
Seacombe Ferry steamers plying during	A. 1890 s. 75	... 297
FOOD		
Inspection and destruction of unsound	A. 1890 s. 67	... 295

	ACT.	PAGE.

FOOTWAYS

Across open lands to promenade and Foreshore	A. 1896 s. 21	... 322
Alterations of, to promenade	A. 1896 s. 21 (3)...	323
Arbitration as to	A. 1896 s. 21 (2)...	322
Deposit of plan showing	A. 1896 s. 21 (2)...	322
Distance between tramway rails and ...	A. 1899 s. 25	... 390
Penalty for driving across	A. 1890 s. 15	... 279
Protection of	A. 1890 s. 15	... 279
Provision for Horses and vehicles crossing	A. 1890 s. 15	... 279
Set out by Commissioner ... ... Award		22 / 61

FORESHORE

Access by frontagers to	A. 1896 s. 21; A. 1896 s. 41; A. 1896 s. 42; A. 1896 s. 43; A. 1896 s. 44	322 / 327 / 329 / 331 / 333
Agreement for lease at New Brighton ...	A. 1864 s. 43 & sched.	208 / 209
A "street" and "public place"	A. 1890 s. 6	... 278
Bathing from	A. 1890 s. 8	.. 278
Crown Rights in, reserved	A. 1872 s. 10 / A. 1890 s. 87	238 / 299
Footways to promenade and	A. 1896 s. 21	... 322
Meaning of	A. 1890 s. 3	... 277
Protection of owners of land abutting on.	A. 1890 s. 12	... 279
Provisions relating to	A. 1890 ss. 5 to 12	277 / 279
Purchase of (agreement with Dock Board.)	A. 1872 (Sched.) .	241
Reclamation of, at Seacombe	A. 1872 s. 7	... 237
Regulation of user of	A. 1890 s. 7	... 278
Rights of R. C. De Grey Vyner in	A. 1890 s. 88	... 299

FORGERY

Of stamps or marks of Urban authority...	A. 1890 s. 71	... 296

FRONTAGERS

Access of, to promenade	A. 1896 s. 21; and ss. 41 to 44	322 / 327 / 333
Arbitration re footways with ...	A. 1896 s. 21 (2)...	322
Meaning of	A. 1896 s. 3	... 318
Objections by, to footways to promenade	A. 1896 s. 21 (2)...	322

GAS

	Act	Page
Altering position of mains or pipes	A. 1896 s. 17	321
Borrowing powers for	A. 1858 s. 60;	181
	A. 1861 s. 3;	189
	A. 1867 s. 30;	222
	O. (No. 1) 1877, art. 2;	249
	O. 1883 art. 1;	264
	O. 1892 art. 2;	303
	O. 1896 art. 1;	314
	O. 1898 art. 1	376
Breaking up streets adjacent to district to lay pipes	A. 1890 s. 73 (s. 2)	296
Bye-laws and regulations as to supply	A. 1867 s. 15	219
Consumption by meter	A. 1858 s. 18	171
Costs of testing	A. 1858 s. 26	173
Fittings, inspection and control of	A. 1867 s. 15;	219
	A. 1890 s. 70	295
Fittings, supply of..	A. 1864 s. 19;	203
	A. 1867 s. 15	219
Justices may order testing of	A. 1858 s. 25	172
Laying electric lines near gas pipes	E.L.O. 1897 art. 14	346
Maximum price of..	A. 1858 s. 22;	172
	A. 1867 s. 13	218
Meter to test power of	A. 1858 s. 24	172
Power to manufacture and supply	A. 1858 s. 17	171
Quality of	A. 1858 s. 23;	172
	A. 1867 s. 14	218
Removal of pipes and fittings from unoccupied houses	A. 1858 s. 20	171
Rents to form part of Wallasey Lighting Account	A. 1858 s. 30;	173
	A. 1867 s. 10	218
Sale of mains or pipes to outside authorities	A. 1890 s. 73 (s.s. 3)	296
Security for payment of	A. 1867 ss. 11 & 12	218
Service pipes, how provided	A. 1858 s. 18	171
Supply of, to outside authorities and others	A. 1890 s. 73	296
Tampering with meters	A. 1858 s. 19	171

GASWORKS

	Act	Page
Acquisition of land for	A. 1867 s. 9;	217
	O. (No. 1) 1877 art. 5;	250
	O. 1892 art. 1	303
Application of Gasworks Clauses Act, 1847	A. 1858 s. 5;	169
	A. 1867 s. 3;	216
	A. 1890 s. 73	296
Construction of, authorised	A. 1858 s. 17	171

INDEX.   XXIII.

	ACT.	PAGE.
Gasworks—*Continued.*		
Depreciation and renewal Fund...	A. 1872 s. 22 ; O. 1883 art. 3	241 265
Extension of	A. 1867 s. 9 ; O. (No. 1) 1877 art. 5 ; O. 1892 art. 1	217 250 303
Mortgage of	A. 1858 s. 60 ; A. 1861 s. 3 ; A. 1867 s. 30 ; O. (No. 1) 1877 art. 2 ; O. 1883 art. 1 ; O. 1892 art. 2 ; O. 1896 art. 1 ; O. 1898 art. 1	181 189 222 249 264 303 314 376
GAUGE		
Of tramways	A. 1899 s. 21 (1)	389
Power to alter	A. 1899 s. 21 (1)	389
GOATS		
Not to be used for drawing carts	A. 1845 s. 187	151
GOODS		
Accommodation for, at Ferries	A. 1867 s. 24	221
Bye-laws as to loading, &c.	A. 1858 s. 51	179
Carriage of, upon tramways	A. 1899 s. 32	391
Detention of	A. 1858 ss. 43, 44, 49 & 50	177 178 179
Ferry tolls for	A. 1858 s. 39 ; A. 1867 s. 20 ; and sched. C.	176 220 226
Weighing and measuring	A. 1858 ss. 44 and 45	177 178
GREAT FLOAT		
Communication across	A. 1867 s. 7	216
HABITATION		
Buildings improperly used for, penalty	A. 1890 s. 24 and s. 25	282
Cellars in courts not to be used for	A. 1845 s. 142	150
HACKNEY CARRIAGES		
Include "omnibus"	O. 1888 art. 1	270
Meaning of	A. 1845 s. 327	155
Regulation of	O. 1852 art. 17 ; O. 1888 art. 1 to 3	163 270 271

	ACT.	PAGE.
HARBOURS, DOCKS, AND PIERS CLAUSES ACT, 1847.		
Incorporated with local act	A. 1872 s. 3	... 236
HEIGHT		
Of buildings	A. 1890 s. 18	... 280
,, rooms ...	A. 1890 s. 19	... 281
HIGHWAYS		
Adoption of private streets, as ...	A. 1890 ss. 53 and 54	290 291
Highways and roads over commons and waste lands set out—Award ...	—	22 61
Public Carriage roads and highways in Liscard set out—Award	—	22 61
Public, over commons, to be not less than 30 feet wide	A. 1809 s. 26	... 20
HOARDINGS		
Bye-laws for erection and removal of	A. 1890 s. 79	... 298
Exhibition of advertisements on	A. 1890 s. 79	... 298
Erection during progress of buildings ...	A. 1890 s. 23	... 282
HOISTS		
Using improper or insufficient tackle ...	A. 1845 ss.153-154	150
HOLLAND		
Provisions relating to lands of the late Chas. Holland	A. 1896 s. 41	... 327
Provisions relating to lands of the late Edgar Swinton Holland	A. 1896 s. 42	... 329
HOLLAND ROAD		
Slipway to be made to shore from	A. 1896 s. 41 (4) ...	328
HORSES		
Power to license owners or drivers ..	O. 1852 art. 18 O. 1888 arts. 1 and 2	164 270 271
Provision for, crossing footways	A. 1890 s. 15	... 279
HOUSES		
Back yards of, to be paved	A. 1890 s. 27	... 283
Buildings improperly used as	A. 1890 s. 25	... 282
Certificate of compliance with bye-laws, &c	A. 1890 s. 20	... 281
Construction for prevention of fire, Towns Improvement Clauses Act, 1847, applied...	O. 1852 art. 17	... 163
Definition of	A. 1845 s. 327	... 155
Disinfection of	A. 1890 s. 59	... 292

	ACT.	PAGE.

Houses—*Continued*.
   Drainage and water supply before occupation ... A. 1890 s. 20 ... 281
   Duty to disinfect before ceasing to occupy ... A. 1890 s. 60 ... 293
   Electric Conductors, &c., may be attached to ... A. 1899 s. 38 ... 393
   Entering for disinfecting .. ... A. 1890 s. 68 ... 295
   Height of rooms ... A. 1890 s. 19 ... 281
   Inspection of building in progress ... A. 1890 s. 21 ... 281
   Notification of infectious disease to owner or intended occupier... A. 1890 s. 60 ... 293
   Numbering... A. 1890 s. 16 ... 280
   Obliterating or removing numbers ... A. 1890 s. 16 ... 280
   Occupied by labouring class, purchase restricted ...
      C.A. 1892 s. 2 ... 301
      A. 1896 s. 10 ... 320
      E.L.O. 1897 art. 7 ... 338
      A. 1899 s. 12 ... 385
   Overcrowded ... A. 1867 s. 39 ... 225
   Owners compounding for water... A. 1867 s. 18 ... 219
   Owners to obtain water supply ... A. 1867 s. 16 ... 219
   Owner to pay water rate for houses let less than quarterly ... A. 1890 s. 72 ... 296
   Precautions during construction and repair, Towns Improvement Clauses Act, 1847, applied ... O. 1852 art. 17 ... 163
   Purchase of, for streets ... A. 1864 s. 34 ... 207
   Purchase of portions of, only ... A. 1896 s. 7 ... 319
   Removal of projecting ... A. 1864 s. 33 ... 207
   Temporary shelter during disinfection of ... A. 1890 s. 66 ... 295
   Unoccupied not rateable ... A. 1845 s. 294 ... 154

HUMAN REMAINS
   Contents of notice of removal of... A. 1899 s. 51 (2) ... 401
   Council may remove ... A. 1899 s. 51 (6) ... 401
   Executor, &c., of deceased person may remove ... A. 1899 s. 51 (3) ... 401
   Expenses of removal and re-interment ... A. 1899 s. 51 (5) ... 401
   Notice of removal of, to be published ... A. 1899 s. 51 (2) ... 401
   Removal of, in Congregational Churchyard in Rake Lane ... A. 1899 s. 51 ... 400
   Removal of, under supervision of Medical Officer of Health ... A. 1899 s. 51 (8) ... 401

IMPROVEMENTS
   Application of Towns Improvement Clauses Act, 1847 ... O. 1852 art. 17 ... 163
   May be executed at expense of owners... A. 1858 s. 80 ... 185

	ACT.	PAGE.
INCLOSURE ACTS		
Awards under	—	{ 22 { 61
Text of Liscard Inclosure Act, 1809	—	13
,, Wallasey ,, 1814 ...	—	48
INFECTIOUS DISEASE		
Definition of	A. 1890 s. 3	... 277
Detention in hospital of infected person without lodging	A. 1890 s. 65	... 294
Sanitary precautions against	A. 1890 ss. 56 to 69	{ 291 { 295
INSPECTION		
Expense of pulling down buildings for ...	A. 1890 s. 22	... 281
Of buildings	A. 1890 s. 21	... 281
Of bye-laws, not permitting	A. 1858 s. 57	... 180
Of dairies, farmhouses, &c.	A. 1890 s. 57	.. 292
Of drains or sewers ...	A. 1890 s. 21	... 281
Of tramways by Board of Trade ...	{ A. 1899 ss. 18 and 23 (2) }	389
Of rails of tramway ...	A. 1899 s. 23	... 389
Of unsound food	A. 1890 s. 67	... 295
INVESTMENTS		
Power to invest	{ A. 1867 s. 34 { A. 1899 s. 63	} 223 { 406

Returns to Local Government Board of	{ O. 1881 art. 2;
	  O. 1883 art. 8;
	  O. 1892 art. 2;
	  A. 1896 s. 34;
	  O. 1897 art. 9
		} 259
		266
		303
		326
		372

JUSTICES		
Bye-laws examined by	{ A. 1858 s. 54; { A. 1867 s. 29	} 180 } 222
Detention in hospital of infected persons directed by	A. 1890 s. 65	... 294
Determination of objections by, private street works	A. 1890 ss.42&46(3)	{ 287 { 289
Dismissal or suspension of constables by	A. 1845 s. 256	... 154
Errors in deposited plans corrected by ..	{ A. 1896 s. 6 { A. 1899 s. 6	} 319 } 382
Establishment of testing stations directed by	E.L.O. 1897 art. 32	... 355
Inspection of buildings improperly used for habitation authorised by ...	A. 1890 s. 25	... 282
Inspection of farmhouses, dairies, &c. authorised by	A. 1890 s. 57	... 292
Not disqualified by contract or liability to rates	{ A. 1858 s. 83; { A 1867 s. 40	} 186 } 225

INDEX. XXVII.

	ACT.	PAGE.
Justices—*Continued.*		
Of Wirral to have jurisdiction over river offences	A. 1890 s. 76	... 297
Order to test gas by	A. 1858 s. 25	... 172
Removal and burial of infected body ordered by	A. 1890 s. 63	... 294
Security for gas and water determined by	A. 1867 s. 12	... 218
LABOURING CLASS		
Definition of	C.A. 1892 s. 2 ;	301
	A. 1896 s. 10 (2)	320
	E.L.O. 1897 art. 7	338
	A. 1899 s. 12 (3)	385
Purchase of houses occupied by, restricted	C.A. 1892 s. 2 ;	301
	A. 1896 s. 10 :	320
	E.L.O. 1897 art. 7	338
	A. 1899 s. 12	385
LAND		
Abutting on Foreshore protected	A. 1890 s. 12	... 279
Acquisition of, for electric lighting	O. 1892 art. 1 ;	303
	E.L.O. 1897 art. 7	338
„ for gasworks	A. 1867 s. 9 ;	217
	O. (No. 1) 1877, art. 5 ;	250
	O. 1892 art. 1	303
„ for refuse destructor	O. 1892 art. 1	... 303
Adjoining streets to be fenced	A. 1845 s. 118 ;	150
	A. 1890 s. 24	282
Certain lands may be sold, &c.	A. 1845 s. 84 ;	147
	A. 1858 s. 68 ;	184
	A. 1864 s. 20 ;	203
	O. (No. 1) 1877, art. 1	248
	A. 1896 s. 12	320
	A. 1899 s. 13	386
Compulsory purchase of part only	A. 1896 s. 7	319
	A. 1899 s. 8	383
Correction of erroneous description of, in plans	A. 1896 s. 6	319
	A. 1899 s. 6	382
Covered with sandhills, control of	A. 1845 s. 85	... 147
Definition of	A. 1845 s. 327	... 155
Enclosed lands, definition of	A. 1896 s. 3	... 319
Extinction of rights over "open lands"	A. 1896 s. 21 (6)	... 323
Laying out of "open lands"	A. 1896 s. 21	... 322
Of Dock Board protected	A. 1858 s. 10 ;	170
	A. 1890 s. 89	299
„ late Charles Holland, provisions relating to	A. 1896 s. 41	... 327
„ late P. M. Vaughan, provisions relating to	A. 1896 s. 13	... 331

	ACT.	PAGE.

Land—*Continued*.

"Open lands," definition... A. 1896 s. 3 ... 318

Period for compulsory purchase...
- A. 1858 s. 8; — 170
- A. 1864 s. 13; — 201
- A. 1896 s. 8; — 320
- A. 1899 s. 7 — 383

Power to grant easements affecting...
- A. 1896 s. 11 — 320
- A. 1899 s. 10 — 385

,, take ...
- A. 1864 s. 6; — 199
- A. 1896 s. 5 — 319
- A. 1899 s. 5 — 382

Proceeds of sale of surplus lands ...
- A. 1896 s. 35 — 327
- A. 1899 ss. 14 & 62 — 386
- — 406

Protection of owners of, in Seabank Road A. 1899 s. 17 ... 388

,, Wirral Railway Co., as owners of ... A. 1899 s. 49 ... 397

Purchase of additional ...
- A. 1896 s. 9 — 320
- A. 1899 s. 11 — 385

,, ,, for streets ... A. 1864 s. 34 .. 207

Security of district fund and rate for purchase, &c.... A. 1896 s. 23 ... 323

LANDING STAGE

Admiralty approval to construction, alteration, or extension ... A. 1864 s. 8 ... 200

Anchoring and Mooring near ...
- A. 1867 s. 28 — 222
- A. 1872 s. 14 — 239

Exemptions from Pier rates or duties ... A. 1864 s. 10 ... 200

Floating stage at Seacombe authorised.. A. 1872 s. 7 ... 237

Land acquired for, may be sold, &c., ... O. (No. 1) 1877 art. 1 — 248

Lease of Foreshore for ... A. 1864 s. 43 and schedule — 208 / 209

Lights to be exhibited on ... A. 1864 s. 9 ... 200

Period for completing at New Brighton A. 1864 s. 14 ... 201

Power to construct at New Brighton ... A. 1864 s. 7 ... 199

LANDS CLAUSES ACTS

Application of ...
- A. 1858 s. 5 — 169
- A. 1864 s 3 — 199
- A. 1867 s. 3 — 216
- A. 1872 s. 3 — 236
- A. 1896 s. 2 — 318
- A. 1899 s. 2 — 382

Enforced for approaches to Seacombe Ferry ... O. 1876 ... 244

Section 92 of Lands Clauses Act not to apply in certain cases ...
- A. 1896 s. 7 — 319
- A. 1899 s. 8 (ss. 2) — 384

LAUNDRY

List of customers to be supplied A. 1890 s. 58 ... 292

INDEX. XXIX.

	ACT.	PAGE.
LAVATORIES		
Provisions for public	A. 1890 s. 31	... 284
LEASOWES EMBANKMENT		
Protection of Commissioners of	{ A. 1845 s. 85 ;	} 147
	A. 1890 s. 11	279
LICENCES		
Of bathing machine proprietor, conditions	A. 1890 s. 9	... 278
,, drivers and conductors	{ O. 1852 art. 17 ;	} 163
	O. 1888 arts. 1 & 2	270
		271
,, hackney carriage	{ O. 1852 art. 17 ;	} 163
	O. 1888 arts. 1 & 2	270
		271
,, owners or drivers of mules ...	O. 1852 art. 18	... 164
,, porters ...	{ A. 1845 ss. 236,	} 152
	237, 240	
,, slaughter houses, period of ..	A. 1890 s. 77	... 297
Revocation of Wallasey Electric Lighting	E.L.O. 1897 art. 72	.. 365
LIGHTING		
Included in private street works	A. 1890 s. 40	... 286
Promenade	{ A. 1896 s. 18	} 321
	A. 1899 s. 56	402
Rate, how to be made and recovered ...	A. 1858 s. 33	... 174
Rate may be levied on separate districts.	A. 1858 s. 31	... 173
Rate, power to levy ..	A. 1858 s. 29	... 173
Streets	A. 1858 s. 17	... 171
Wallasey lighting account created	A. 1858 s. 29	... 173
LIGHTS		
Commissioners of Northern, exempted from pier rates	A. 1864 s. 10	... 200
Exhibition of, on piers or landing stage. .	A 1864 s. 9	... 200
LISCARD		
Act for inclosing waste lands in township, 1809, text of ..	—	13
Award of Commissioners under Inclosure Act of 1809 ...	—	22
Boundaries of township, award ...	—	22
LISCARD BATTERY		
Protection of rights of War department respecting	A. 1896 s. 16	... 333
LISCARD VALE		
Access to promenade and shore from	A. 1896 s. 11 (7)	... 328
Provisions relating to ...	A. 1896 s. 41	... 327

xxx. INDEX.

	ACT.	PAGE.
LOANS		
Application of	A. 1858 ss. 63 to 67	182, 183
	A. 1861 s. 3;	189
	A. 1864 s. 21;	203
	A. 1867 s. 37;	224
	A. 1872 s. 17;	239
	A. 1896 s. 36;	327
	O. 1897 art. 7;	372
	A. 1899 s. 62	406
Local Loans Act, 1875, applied to	O. 1892 art. 2 (2)	304
	A. 1896 s. 24;	323
	O. 1897 art. 2;	370
	A. 1899 s. 62	406
Protection of lender from inquiry	A. 1896 s. 37;	327
	A. 1899 s. 62	406
Repayment of	A. 1864 s. 27;	205
	A. 1867 s. 33;	223
	O. 1877 (No. 1.) art. 4;	249
	O. 1883 arts. 2 & 4 to 8;	264, 266
	O. 1892 art. 2;	303
	O. 1895 art. 1;	311
	A. 1896 ss. 27 to 29	324
	O. 1897 arts. 3 to 6	370, 372
	A. 1899 s. 61	405
Subject to trusts	A. 1896 s. 31;	325
	A. 1899 s. 62	406
LOCAL GOVERNMENT BOARD		
Approval to additional loans, promenade.	A. 1896 s. 23 (2)	323
Costs of local inquiries by	O. 1892 art. 2 (10)	306
	A. 1896 s. 38 (2);	327
	O. 1897 art. 10;	373
	A. 1899 s. 62	406
Direction as to repayments and sinking fund by	O. 1881 art. 2;	259
	O. 1883 art. 8;	266
	O. 1892 art. 2;	303
	A. 1896 s. 34;	326
	A. 1899 s. 62	406
Inquiries by inspectors of	A. 1896 s. 38;	327
	A. 1899 s. 62	406
Returns to, respecting repayment of loans and sinking fund	O. 1881 art. 2;	259
	O. 1883 art. 8;	266
	O. 1892 art. 2;	303
	A. 1896 s. 34;	326
	O. 1897 art. 9;	372
	A. 1899 s. 62	406

INDEX. XXXI.

	ACT.	PAGE.
LOCAL LOANS ACT, 1875		
Available for raising money	O. 1892 art. 2 (s.s. 2);	304
	A. 1896 s. 24;	323
	O. 1897 art. 2;	370
	A. 1899 s. 62	406
S. 15 not to apply to sinking fund under	A. 1896 s. 29 (6);	325
	A. 1899 s. 62	406
LODGINGS		
Persons letting, rateable as occupiers	A. 1845 s. 300	155
Persons infected without, may be detained in hospital	A. 1890 s. 65	294
MAGAZINE LANE		
Slipways to be made to shore from	A. 1896 s. 41 (4)	328
MAINS		
Altering position of	A. 1896 s. 17;	321
	A. 1899 s. 56	402
Distributing Mains for electric lighting	E.L.O. 1897 art. 17; and schedule 2	338 / 366
Laying electric lines near	E.L.O. 1897 art. 14	346
Requisition to lay distributing	E.L.O. 1897 art. 19	349
Sale of to outside authorities	A. 1890 s. 73 (3)	296
Testing of distributing mains	E.L.O. 1897 art. 30	354
MANORS		
Protection of manorial rights	A. 1814 s. 35	60
MARKETS		
Markets and Fairs Clauses Act, 1847, incorporated	O. 1852 art. 17	163
Power to provide	A. 1845 s. 198	151
MARKS		
Forging stamps or, of urban authority	A. 1890 s. 71	296
MARL		
Allotments for Marl	A. 1814 s. 17; Awards	54 / 22 / 61
,, ,, may be sold, &c.	A. 1845 s. 84;	147
	A. 1858 s. 68;	184
	A. 1864 s. 20	203
MECHANICAL POWER		
Board of Trade may make regulations for use of	A. 1899 s. 37 (2)	392
Electrical, for tramways	A. 1899 ss. 37-41	392 / 396
May be used for tramways	A. 1899 s. 37	392
Penalty for improper use of	A. 1899 s. 37 ss. 3 & 4	392
Works, subject to sec. 30 of Tramways Act, 1870	A. 1899 s. 41	396

	ACT.	PAGE.
MEDICAL OFFICER OF HEALTH		
Attributing infectious disease to milk	A. 1890 s. 56	... 291
Certificate of, as to cleansing and disinfecting	A. 1890 s. 59	... 292
Certificate of, as to retention of infected body	A. 1890 s. 61	... 293
Certificate of, as to removal of body from hospital for burial	A. 1890 s. 62	... 293
Certificate of, as to detention in hospital of infected person without lodging	A. 1890 s. 65	... 294
Inspection of dairies, farmhouses, by	A. 1890 s. 57	... 292
Removal of human remains under supervision of	A. 1899 s. 51 (8)	... 401
MEMBERS		
Of urban authority, qualification, note to	O. 1852 arts. 2 to 5	161
Protection of officers and	E.L.O. 1897 art. 68	... 365
MERSEY CONSERVANCY COMMISSIONERS		
Protection of	A. 1890 s. 90;	299
	A. 1896 s. 45;	333
	A. 1899 s. 57	403
MERSEY DOCKS AND HARBOUR BOARD		
Agreement as to river wall	A. 1872 sched.	... 241
Confirmation of agreement as to river wall	A. 1872 s. 13	... 239
Contribution to cost and maintenance of river wall	A. 1872 sched.	... 241
Liability to rates	A. 1858 s. 35	... 174
Marginal sewer of	A. 1867 s. 8	... 217
Protection of Estate, and rights of	A. 1858 s. 10;	170
	A. 1890 s. 89	299
Streets and roads of, protected from tramways	A. 1867 s. 6	... 216
To secure communication between Seacombe and Birkenhead	A. 1867 s. 7	.. 216
METER		
Consumption of gas by	A. 1858 s. 18	... 171
Regulations as to, in Electric Lighting Order	E.L.O. 1897 arts. 40 to 50	356, 358
Removal of, from unoccupied premises	A. 1858 s. 20	... 171
Tampering with	A. 1858 s. 19	... 171
Testing power by	A. 1858 s. 24	... 172
MILK		
Purveyors to furnish list of customers	A. 1890 s. 56	... 291
Supplying milk from prohibited dairies, &c.	A. 1890 s. 57	... 292

	ACT.	PAGE.
MILK SHOPS		
Inspection of	A. 1890 s. 57	292
Occupier of, or milk store, to furnish list of customers	A. 1890 s. 56	291
Supplying milk from, prohibited in certain cases	A. 1890 s. 57	292
MOORING		
Byelaws regulating, of vessels	A. 1867 s. 28;	222
	A. 1872 s. 14	239
MORTGAGES		
Application of moneys borrowed	A. 1858 ss. 63 to 67	182, 183
	A. 1861 s. 3;	189
	A. 1864 s. 21;	203
	A. 1867 s. 37;	224
	A. 1872 s. 17;	239
	A. 1896 s. 36;	327
	O. 1897 art. 7;	372
	A. 1899 s. 62	406
Charge on General District Fund and Rate	A. 1867 s. 36;	224
	A. 1890 s. 52;	290
	A. 1896 s. 23;	323
	A. 1899 s. 60	405
Issue and payment of Coupons for interest on	A. 1867 ss. 34 & 35	223
Local Loans Act, 1875, to apply	O. 1892 art. 2;	303
	A. 1896 s. 24;	323
	O. 1897 art. 2;	370
	A. 1899 s. 62	406
Mortgagees may appoint Receivers	A. 1896 s. 32;	326
	O. 1897 art. 8;	372
	A. 1899 s. 62	406
Power to Borrow: *Ferries*:	A. 1858 s. 60;	181
	A. 1861 s. 3;	189
	A. 1864 s. 21;	203
	A. 1872 s. 17;	239
	O. 1877 (No. 1.) art. 3;	249
	O. 1881 art. 1;	258
	O. 1883 art. 2;	264
	O. 1895 art. 1;	311
	O. 1897 art. 1	369
,, *Gas*:	A. 1858 s. 60;	181
	A. 1861 s. 3;	189
	A. 1867 s. 30;	222
	O. 1877 (No. 1.) art. 2;	249
	O. 1883 art. 1;	264
	O. 1892 art. 2;	303
	O. 1896 art. 1;	314
	O. 1898 art. 1	375

XXXIV.   INDEX.

		ACT.	PAGE.
Mortgages—*Continued.*			
Power to Borrow: Private Street Works		A. 1890 s. 52	290
		A. 1896 ss. 23 & 33	323
,, Purchase of land, promenade			326
		A. 1899 s. 60	405
,, Water		A. 1858 s. 60;	181
		A. 1861 s. 3;	189
		O. 1863;	194
		A. 1864 s. 28;	206
		O. 1870 art. 6;	232
		A. 1872 s. 17;	239
		O. 1894 art. 1	308
Priority of...		A. 1858 s. 62;	182
		A. 1861 s. 5;	190
		A. 1864 s. 23;	204
		A. 1867 s. 31;	222
		A. 1872 s. 19;	240
		O. 1883 art. 9;	267
		A. 1896 s. 30	325
Protection of lender from inquiry		A. 1896 s. 37;	327
		A. 1899 s. 62	406
Public Health Act to apply to		A. 1858 s. 61;	182
		A. 1861 s 4;	190
		A. 1864 s. 22;	204
		A. 1867 s. 32;	223
		A. 1872 s. 18;	240
		O. 1877 (No. 1.) art. 4;	249
		O. 1881 art. 1;	258
		O. 1883 arts. 1&2;	264
		O. 1892 art. 2;	303
		A. 1896 s. 26;	324
		O. 1897 art. 2;	370
		A. 1899 s. 62	406
Repayment of		A. 1864 s. 27;	205
		A. 1867 s. 33;	223
		O. 1877 (No. 1.) art. 4;	249
		O. 1883 arts. 2, & 4 to 8	264, 266
		O. 1892 art. 2;	303
		O. 1895 art. 1;	311
		A. 1896 ss. 27 to 29	324
		O. 1897 arts. 3 to 6	370, 372
		A. 1899 ss. 61, 62	405, 406
Returns as to repayments and sinking fund		O. 1881 art. 2;	259
		O. 1883 art. 8;	266
		O. 1892 art. 2;	303
		A. 1896 s. 34;	326
		O. 1897 art. 9	372
Subject to Trusts...		A. 1896 s. 31;	325
		A. 1899 s. 62	406
Surrender of		A. 1864 s. 26;	205
		A. 1867 s. 33	223

INDEX. XXXV.

	ACT.	PAGE.
MORTUARIES		
Removal of body of infected person to ...	A. 1890 ss. 62 & 63	293, 294
MULES		
Power to license owners or drivers of ...	O. 1852 art. 18	... 164
MUSICIANS		
In street, to depart when desired	A. 1845 s. 188	... 151
NAVY		
Service exempted from pier rates or duties	A. 1864 s. 10	... 200
NEW BRIGHTON FERRY		
Exemptions from pier rates or duties, at	A. 1864 s. 10	... 200
Lease of foreshore for pier	A. 1864 s. 43 and sched.	208, 209
Period to complete pier or stage	A. 1864 s. 14	... 201
Power to construct pier or landing stage	A. 1864 s. 7	.. 199
Power to lease or purchase	A. 1858 s. 36	... 174
NEW BRIGHTON PIER COMPANY		
Protection of ...	A. 1899 s. 59	... 404
NOTICES		
Authentication of ...	A. 1858 s. 82 / A. 1890 s. 84 / A. 1899 s. 67	186, 298, 408
Contents of, to treat	A. 1899 s. 8	... 333
Of removal of human remains ...	A. 1899 s. 51 (2)	... 401
Publication of notice or resolution	A. 1890 sched. II	300
Service of ...	A. 1890 s. 84; A. 1899 s. 67	298, 408
To be given to Postmaster General on laying electric wire ...	A. 1899 s. 40 (2)	... 394
Under Electric Lighting Order ...	E.L.O. 1897 arts. 54 & 55	360
NUISANCES		
Abatement of, s. 104 Towns Improvement Clauses Act, 1847, applied ...	O. 1852 art. 17	... 163
Committed in executing Provisional Order	E.L.O. 1897 art. 70	... 365
Council not to permit, on lands purchased	A. 1896 s. 9	... 320
Embanking offensive matter ...	A. 1864 s. 35	... 208
Entering premises for removal of	A. 1890 s. 68	... 295
Examination of drains, &c.	A. 1890 s. 36	... 286
Houses without water ...	A. 1867 s. 16	... 219
In streets, Town Police Clauses Act, 1847, incorporated ...	O. 1852 art. 17	... 163
On boats, suppression of ...	A. 1858 s. 51	179
Overcrowded houses	A. 1867 s. 39	... 225

INDEX.

	ACT.	PAGE.
Nuisances—*Continued.*		
Prevention of, s. 104, Towns Improvement Clauses Act, 1847, applied ...	O. 1852 art. 17	... 163
Prosecutions for	A. 1864 s. 40	... 208
Slaughter-houses prejudicial to health ...	A. 1890 s. 77	... 297
NUMBERING		
Houses, ...	A. 1890 s. 16	... 280
Obliterating or removing numbers ...	A. 1890 s. 16	... 280
NURSES		
For attendance upon infected persons ...	A. 1890 s. 66	... 295
OBJECTIONS		
Costs of, to private street works...	A. 1890 s. 42 (3)	.. 288
,, to notice to treat...	A. 1899 s. 8 (1)	... 383
Determination of, private street works...	A 1890 ss. 42 and 46 (3)	287 289
Final apportionment; to, private street...	A. 1890 s. 46 (2)	... 289
Frontagers to footways, by	A. 1896 s. 21 (2)	... 322
Private street works, to ...	A. 1890 s. 41	... 287
To sell parts only of certain lands, &c. ...	A. 1899 s. 8 (1)	... 383
OBSTRUCTION		
Of drains or sewers, penalty	A. 1890 s. 33	... 285
Removal of, in streets, Town Police Clauses Act, 1847, applied	O. 1852 art. 17	... 163
Removal of, in streets, Towns Improvement Clauses Act, 1847, applied ...	O. 1852 art. 17	... 163
OCCUPIER		
Cleaning of courts, and passages by ...	A. 1890 s. 28	... 284
Connecting drains at expense of... ...	A. 1864 s. 31; A. 1890 s. 35;	206 285
Correction in plans of misdescription of	A. 1896 s. 6; A. 1899 s. 6	319 382
Duty of, to disinfect house	A. 1890 s. 60	... 293
Failing to notify disease	A. 1890 s. 60	... 293
Fencing vacant or waste lands by ...	A. 1890 s. 24	.. 282
For less than a quarter may deduct water-rate from rent	A. 1890 s. 72	... 296
Of dairy or milkshop to furnish list of customers	A. 1890 s. 56	... 291
,, projecting building, compensation on removal to	A. 1864 s. 33	... 207
,, uncertified new house, penalty ...	A. 1890 s. 20	... 281
Repair of vaults, cellars, &c., by	A. 1890 s. 26	... 283

INDEX. XXXVII.

	ACT.	PAGE.
OFFICERS		
Protection of members and, from liability	E.L.O. 1897 art. 68; A. 1899 s. 70	365 408
OMNIBUSES		
Definition of	A. 1845 s. 327, note; O. 1888 arts. 1 and 3	156 270 271
Regulation of drivers and conductors	O. 1888 arts. 1 to 3	270-271
Town Police Clauses Act, 1847, applied	O. 1888 art. 1	270
OPEN LANDS		
Definition of	A. 1896 s. 3	319
Laying out, on Promenade as pleasure grounds	A. 1896 s. 21	322
Rights of way over, extinction of	A. 1896 s. 21 (6)	323
ORDER		
Appeal from	A. 1890 s. 81	298
Service of	A. 1890 s. 84	298
OWNER		
Agreement with, to bind successors	A. 1890 s. 32	285
Allowing occupation of uncertified houses, penalty	A. 1890 s. 20	281
Compounding for water rents	A. 1867 s. 18	219
Connecting drains at expense of	A. 1864 s. 31 A. 1890 s. 35	206 285
Correction in plans of misdescription of	A. 1896 s. 6	319
Definition of	A. 1845 s. 327	155
Displaying wares on unfenced land	A. 1890 s. 6	278
Fencing vacant land by	A. 1845 s. 118 A. 1890 s. 24	150 282
May borrow for private street expenses	A. 1890 s. 51	290
Notice before covering foundation or drain by	A. 1890 s. 21	281
Notice of commencing building by	A. 1890 s. 21	281
Notification of infectious disease to	A. 1890 s. 60	293
Objecting to final apportionment of expenses	A. 1890 s. 46	289
Objecting to private street works	A. 1890 s. 41	287
Of land abutting on Foreshore protected	A. 1890 s. 12	279
Of projecting buildings, compensation to	A. 1864 s. 33	207
Repair of vaults, cellars, &c., by	A. 1864 s. 30 A. 1890 s. 26	206 283
Required to pave back yards	A. 1890 s. 27	283
„ sell part only of land, &c.	A. 1896 s. 7 A. 1899 s. 8	319 383

	ACT.	PAGE.
Owner—*Continued*.		
Water rate of houses let—for less than quarter, payable by	A. 1890 s. 72	... 296
,, supply to be obtained by	A. 1867 s. 16	... 219
PARKS & PLEASURE GROUNDS		
Admission of societies and institutions to	A. 1890 s. 78	... 298
May be closed to public on special occasions	A. 1890 s. 78	... 298
"Open lands" at promenade may be used as	A. 1896 s. 21 (5)...	323
Provision of "ornamental enclosure" on promenade	A. 1896 s. 43(11)...	333
Public Health Act applied to enclosure on promenade	A. 1896 s. 21 (5) ...	323
PASSAGES		
Cleaning of	A. 1890 s. 28	... 284
Dedication of	A. 1864 s. 29	... 206
Purchase of land or houses for	A. 1864 s. 34	... 207
To be flagged, sewered, &c.	A. 1864 s. 29	206
PASSENGERS		
Bye-laws regulating embarkation and discharge of	A. 1858 s. 51 A. 1899 s. 42	179 396
Detaining	A. 1858 s. 49	... 178
Evading or refusing to pay ferry tolls	A. 1858 s. 46; A. 1867 ss. 26&27 A. 1872 s. 15; A. 1890 s. 74	178 221 239 297
Ferry steamers plying during fog	A. 1890 s. 75	... 297
Ferry tolls for	A. 1858 s. 39; A. 1867 s. 20; and sched. c.	176 220 226
Luggage of, on tramways	A. 1899 s. 30	... 391
Nuisances committed by	A. 1858 s. 51	... 179
Rates for, on tramways	A. 1899 s. 29	... 391
Refusing to produce contract or season tickets	A. 1890 s. 74	... 297
Using abusive language to	A. 1858 s. 49	... 178
PATENTS		
Power to acquire, for tramways...	A. 1899 s. 47	... 397
PAVING		
Definition of paving, metalling and flagging	A. 1890 s. 39	... 286
Included in private street works	A. 1890 s. 40	... 286
Of courts and passages	A. 1864 s. 29	... 206

INDEX. XXXIX

	ACT.	PAGE.
PENALTIES		
Application and recovery of	A. 1845 s. 246 (Note);	153
	A. 1858 ss. 84 & 85	186
	A. 1864 s. 39;	208
	A. 1867 s. 43;	225
	A. 1872 s. 5;	236
	O. 1888 art. 3;	271
	A. 1890 s. 83	298
	A. 1899 s. 69	408
Bathing machine owners infringing license	A. 1890 s. 9	... 278
Bye-laws, not permitting inspection of...	A. 1858 s. 57	... 180
Bye-laws enforcing of	A. 1845 s. 246 (Note);	153
	O. 1852 (sched.);	164
	O. 1888 art. 3 (2)	271
	A. 1890 s. 85;	299
	A. 1899 s. 42 (2)	397
Carrying infected body in public conveyance ...	A. 1890 s. 64	... 294
Constructing or continuing cesspool	A. 1890 s. 30	284
Dairy-keepers, &c., refusing list of customers ...	A. 1890 s. 56	... 291
Definition of Daily Penalty	A. 1890 s. 3	... 277
Driving across footways ...	A. 1890 s. 15	... 279
Enforcing agreement with owners	A. 1890 s. 32	... 285
Failing to make returns of repayments and sinking fund	O. 1881 art. 2;	259
	O. 1883 art. 8;	266
	O. 1892 art. 2;	303
	A. 1896 s. 34;	326
	O. 1897 art. 9;	372
	A. 1899 s. 62	406
Failing to notify infectious disease	A. 1890 s. 60	... 293
Ferry bye-law, breach of...	A. 1858 s. 53	.. 179
Forging stamps or marks of urban authority	A. 1890 s. 71	... 296
Gas, for defective power of	A. 1858 s. 25	... 172
Gas, for preventing testing of	A. 1858 s. 25	... 172
Improper use of buildings for habitation..	A. 1890 ss. 20 and 25	281 282
,, ,, mechanical power	A. 1899 s. 37	... 392
Neglecting to disinfect public conveyance	A. 1890 s. 64	... 294
,, ,, maintain rails and roads for tramways ...	A. 1899 s. 23	... 389
Obliterating or removing street names or numbers ...	A. 1890 s. 16	280
Obstructing disinfection of premises	A. 1890 s. 59	... 292
Obstructing drains or sewers ...	A. 1890 s. 33	... 285
Obstructing removal and burial of infected body ...	A. 1890 s. 63	... 294

	ACT.	PAGE.
Penalties—*Continued.*		
Occupying dwelling houses not certified	A. 1890 s. 20	... 281
Offences relating to street, buildings, sewers and sanitary provisions ...	A. 1890 s. 82	... 298
On local authority not cumulative ...	A. 1867 s. 44	... 225
Refusing names of customers of laundries	A. 1890 s. 58	... 292
Removal from hospital of infected body except for burial	A. 1890 s. 62	... 293
Retaining body on death from infectious disease	A. 1890 s. 61	... 293
Supplying milk from prohibited dairies, &c.	A. 1890 s. 57	.. 292
Throwing materials into street	A. 1845 s. 155	... 151
Toll collectors, offences by	A. 1858 s. 49	.. 178
Under Electric Lighting Order, 1897	{ E.L.O. arts. 10 to 14 ; 16, 23, 51, 60 and 61 }	{ 340-346 347,352 358,363 }
Under Electric Lighting Order, 1897, application and recovery of... ...	E.L.O. art. 66	... 365
Water, improper use of	A. 1858 s. 16	... 171
PERIOD		
For compulsory purchase of land ...	A. 1899 s. 7	... 383
,, completion of tramways ...	,, s. 28	... 391
,, ,, ,, street works ...	,, s. 52	... 401
,, objections to sale of portion of land, &c.	,, s. 8	... 383
PIER		
Admiralty to approve construction, alteration, or extension	A. 1864 s. 8	... 200
At Seacombe authorised	A. 1872 s. 7	... 237
Exemption from pier-rates or duties ...	A. 1864 s. 10	... 200
Extension at Egremont	A. 1872 s. 7	... 237
Land acquired for, may be sold, &c. ...	{ O. 1877 (No. 1), art. 1 }	248
Lease of foreshore for ...	{ A. 1864 s. 43, and sched. }	{ 208 209 }
Lights to be exhibited on...	A. 1864 s. 9	... 200
Mooring and anchoring at or near ...	{ A. 1867 s. 28 ; A. 1872 s. 14 }	{ 222 239 }
Period for completing	A. 1864 s. 14	... 201
Power to construct at New Brighton ...	A. 1864 s. 7	... 199
PIPES		
Altering position of	{ A. 1896 s. 17 A. 1899 s. 56 }	{ 321 402 }
Approval of	A. 1858 s. 12	... 170
Laying in adjacent districts ...	A. 1890 s. 73 (2)	... 296
,, electric lines near	E.L.O. 1897 art. 14	.. 346

INDEX. XLI.

	ACT.	PAGE.
Pipes—*Continued.*		
Person erecting or repairing, to notify urban authority	A. 1890 s. 70	... 295
Removal of, from unoccupied houses	A. 1858 s. 20	... 171
Sale of, to outside authorities	A. 1890 s. 73 (3)	... 296
Service, provision of	A. 1858 s. 20	... 171

PLANS

Alteration of plan of footways to promenade	A. 1896 s. 21 (3)	... 323
Correction of errors in deposited	{ A. 1896 s. 6 A. 1899 s. 6	} 319 382
Deposit of, void after certain intervals	A. 1890 s. 13	... 279
Deposit of plan of footways on "open lands"	A. 1896 s. 21 (2)	... 322
Deviation from	A. 1896 s. 14	... 321
Objections by frontagers to	A. 1896 s. 21 (2)	... 322
Of certain electrical works to be approved by Postmaster General or Board of Trade	E.L.O. 1897 art. 10	... 340
Of proposed Tramways to be laid before the Board of Trade	A. 1899 s. 20	... 389
Private street works of	{ A. 1890 s. 40 and sched 1.	} 286 300

POSTMASTER-GENERAL

Appeal to Board of Trade from, as to electric work in streets	E.L.O. 1897 art. 10 (c)	340
Approval by Board of Trade of electric work in streets	E.L.O. 1897 art. 10	... 340
Compensation to	A. 1899 s. 10	... 394
Compensation to, on failure to comply with requirements	E.L.O. 1897 art. 10 (f)	340
Notice to be given to, in certain cases	A. 1899 s. 40 (2)	... 394
Injuriously affecting telegraphic line of	{ E.L.O. 1897 art. 10 (f) A. 1899 s. 40	340 394
Protection of rights of	{ E.L.O. 1897 art. 69 A. 1899 s. 40	365 394

POLICE

Justices may dismiss or suspend constables	A. 1845 s. 256	... 154
Power to employ	A. 1867 s. 41	... 225
Power to make rules and orders for	A. 1845 s. 257	... 154
Town Police Clauses Act, 1847, applied	O. 1852 art. 17	... 163

POULTON-CUM-SEACOMBE

Allotment of commons and waste lands: Award	—	61
Inclosure of commons and waste lands	A. 1814	48

Poolton-cum-Seacombe—*Continued.*

	ACT.	PAGE.
Highways, roads, and footways set out: Award	—	61
Roads on Poolton Common: Award	—	61

PORTERS

Acting without license	A. 1845 s. 237	152
Licensing of errand, message and luggage	A. 1845 s. 236	152
Licenses may be suspended or revoked	A. 1845 s. 240	152
Power to make bye-laws regulating	A. 1845 s. 245	153
Recovery of fares by	A. 1845 s. 243	153
Return of overcharge by	A. 1845 s. 242	153

POST OFFICE

Service exempted from pier rates or duties	A. 1864 s. 10	200

PRIVATE IMPROVEMENT EXPENSES

Flagging or paving yards	A. 1890 s. 27	283
Recovery of	A. 1858 s. 80; A. 1890 s. 27	185 / 283
Works may be executed and declared to be	A 1858 s. 80	185

PRIVATE STREET WORKS

Adoption of streets after completion of	A. 1890 ss. 53 & 54	290 / 291
Amendment of specifications, &c.	,, s. 45	289
Borrowing powers for	,, s. 52	290
Contribution to expenses	,, s. 49	290
Costs of objections to	,, s. 42 (3)	288
Determination of objections	,, ss. 42 & 46(3)	287 / 289
Enumeration of	,, s. 40	286
Estimate of expenses	,, ss. 40 & 43(2)	286 / 288
Expenses and charge on premises	,, s. 47	289
Expenses, how apportioned	,, s. 44	288
Final apportionment and recovery of expenses	,, s. 46	289
Incumbent, minister, &c., exempted	,, s. 50	290
Limited owners may borrow for	,, s. 51	290
Objections to	,, s. 41	287
Objections to final apportionment	,, s. 46 (2)	289 / 300
Particulars to be stated in estimates	,, sched. 1	300
,, ,, plans	,, ,,	300
,, provisional apportionment	,, ,,	300
,, specifications	,, ,,	300

	ACT.	PAGE.
Private Street Works—*Continued.*		
Provisional apportionment	A. 1890 s. 40	... 286
Provisions relating to, text of	,, ss. 38 to 55	286-291
Publication of resolution approving ...	,, s. 40 (3) sched. 2	287 300
Recovery of expenses summarily or by action	,, s. 48	... 290
Register of charges	,, s. 47 (2)	... 290
Remedies under Conveyancing Act, for	,, s. 47	... 289
Resolution approving	,, s. 40	... 286
Separate account of expenses ...	,, s. 55	... 291
Specifications and plans of	,, s. 40	... 286

PROMENADE

	ACT.	PAGE.
A public highway... ...	A. 1896 s. 18 A. 1899 s. 56	321 402
Access for frontagers, to ..	A. 1896 s. 21 ; ss. 41 to 44	322 327-333
Band stand on	A. 1896 s. 20 A. 1899 s. 56	322 402
Bye-laws for preservation of order on ...	A. 1890 s. 79 ; A. 1896 s. 19 A. 1899 s. 56	298 321 402
Footways to	A. 1896 s. 21	322
Lands of C. & E. S. Holland, provisions relating to	A. 1896 ss. 41 and 42	327-329
,, P. M. Vaughan	A. 1896 s. 43	... 331
,, J. E. Rayner	A. 1899 s. 58	... 403
Lighting and maintenance of	A. 1896 s. 18	... 321
Ornamental enclosures on ...	A. 1896 s. 21 (5) s. 43 (11)	323 333
Period of completion of	A. 1896 s. 15 A. 1899 s. 56	321 402
Power to construct ...	A. 1896 s. 13 A. 1899 s. 55	321 402
,, deviate in construction ...	A. 1896 s. 14 A. 1899 s. 56	321 402
,, execute subsidiary works ...	A. 1896 s. 16 A. 1899 s. 56	321 402
Protection of New Brighton Pier Company	A. 1899 s. 59	... 404
Public Health Act to apply to bye-laws for	A. 1896 s. 19 (2)	... 322
,, s. 234 not to apply to	A. 1896 s. 25	... 324
Regulation of traffic on	A. 1896 s. 19	... 321
Shelters may be provided on ...	A. 1896 s. 20 A. 1899 s. 56	322 402

		ACT.	PAGE.
PUBLICATION			
Of byelaws		A. 1858 s. 57;	180
		A. 1867 s. 29;	222
		A. 1890 s. 85	299
Of notice or resolution		A. 1890 sched. II.	300
PUBLIC HEALTH ACTS			
		A. 1845 s. 246 (note);	153
Applied to byelaws		O. 1888 art. 3 (s.s. 2);	271
		A. 1890 s. 85;	299
		A. 1896 s. 19 (2);	321
		A. 1899 s. 65	408
Applied to the district		O. 1852 art. 1;	160
		O. 1877 (No. 2)	247
		A. 1858 s. 61;	182
		A. 1861 s. 4;	190
		A. 1864 s. 22;	204
		A. 1867 s. 32;	223
		A. 1872 s. 18;	240
Applied to mortgages		O. 1877 (No. 1) art. 4	249
		O. 1881 art. 1;	258
		O. 1883 arts. 1 & 2;	264
		A. 1896 s. 26;	324
		A. 1899 s. 62	406
Applied to pleasure grounds, promenade		A. 1896 s. 21 (5) ...	323
		A. 1858 s. 84;	186
		A. 1864 s. 39;	208
Recovery of penalties under		A. 1867 s. 43;	225
		A. 1872 s. 5;	236
		O. 1888 art. 3	271
Section 234 of Public Health Act, 1875, not to apply to borrowing powers for promenade		A. 1896 s. 25;	324
		A. 1899 s. 62	406
Wallasey Improvement Act, 1845, incorporated with		O. 1852 art. 11 ...	162
PUBLIC HOUSES			
Sunday closing		A. 1845 s. 156 ...	151
Urinals to be provided at...		A. 1864 s. 32 ...	207
PUBLIC OFFICES			
Power to provide ...		A. 1845 s. 88 ...	149
Rules for use of ...		A. 1845 s. 88 ...	149
PUBLIC PLACE			
Foreshore, a		A. 1890 s. 6 ...	278
Unfenced ground, a		A. 1890 s. 6 ...	278

INDEX. XLV.

	ACT.	PAGE.
PURCHASE		
Additional lands, of	A. 1896 s. 9 ; A. 1899 s. 11	320 385
Compulsory, limited	A. 1858 s. 8 A. 1864 s. 13 A. 1896 s. 8	170 201 320
Compulsory, of part of land, &c., only...	A. 1896 s. 7; A. 1899 s. 8	319 383
Ferries	A. 1858 ss. 36 & 38 A. 1861 ss. 6 & 7	174 175 191
Foreshore ...	A. 1872 sched.	241
Land for electric lighting	E.L.O. 1897, art. 7	338
Land for gasworks	A. 1867 s. 9 O. (No. 1) 1877 art. 5 O. 1892 art. 1	217 250 303
Land for street, &c.	A. 1864 s. 34	207
Steamboats	A. 1845 s. 86 A. 1858 s. 36 A. 1864 s. 17	148 174 202
QUALIFICATION		
Of members of urban authority ...	O. 1852 art. 1, and note to arts. 2 to 5	161
,, electors...	A. 1845 (note to repealed s. 15) O. 1852 note to arts. 2 to 5	146 161
QUARRY		
Allotments for stone, Inclosure Act of 1814, awards ...	A. 1814 s. 17	51 61
Allotments for stone may be sold, &c. ...	A. 1845 s. 84; A. 1858 s. 68; A. 1864 s. 20	147 181 203
QUARTER SESSIONS		
Appeal to ...	A. 1890 s. 81	298
Bye-laws to be allowed by	A. 1858 s. 54; A. 1867 s. 29	180 222
RAILS		
Distance required between, and footpaths	A. 1899 s. 25	390
For tramways to be approved by Board of Trade ...	A. 1899 s. 22	389
May consist of single or double lines	A. 1899 s. 25	390
To be level with surface of road...	A. 1899 s. 19	389

	ACT.	PAGE.
RAILWAYS		
Power to break up railways on highway for electrical supply ...	E.L.O. 1897 art. 8	... 339
Protection of, under Electric Lighting Order ...	E.L.O. 1897 art. 15	... 347
Restrictions on breaking up	{ E.L.O. 1897 arts. 11 and 12 }	341 342
RATES		
Assessments may be in one rate book ...	A. 1864 s. 41	... 208
Compositions for and recovery of water and lighting rates ...	A. 1858 s. 34	... 174
Compounding for water ...	A. 1867 s. 18	.. 219
District rate security for land purchase, &c.	A. 1896 s. 23	... 323
Estimates for general district	A. 1867 s. 36	... 224
Exemptions from rates or duties at landing stage...	A. 1864 s. 10	... 200
Ferry, may be altered	A. 1864 s. 16	... 202
For use of ferries or landing stages ...	{ A. 1858 s. 39; A. 1864 s. 16; A. 1867 s. 20 and sched. C. }	176 202 220 226
For use of Tramways ...	{ A. 1899 ss. 29 to 35 and sched. II. }	391 409
Liability of Mersey Docks and Harbour Board to ...	A. 1858 s. 35	... 174
Lighting rate ...	„ s. 29	... 173
Lighting and water works, how to be made and recovered...	„ s. 33	... 174
Lighting and water works, may be levied on separate districts...	„ s. 31	... 173
Owner liable for water, for houses let under a quarter ...	A. 1890 s. 72	... 296
Power to contract for ferry ...	A. 1864 s. 16	... 202
Priority in bankruptcy ...	{ A. 1867 s. 38 (note); A. 1872 s. 21 }	224 240
Revision of, for tramways ...	A. 1899 s. 35	... 406
Security for gas and water	A. 1867 s. 11	... 218
Wallasey water-works rate	A. 1858 s. 27	... 173
Water, payable quarterly ...	A. 1867 s. 17	... 219
RAYNER		
Protection of J. E. Rayner	A. 1899 s. 58	... 403
RECEIVER		
Appointment by mortgagees ...	{ A. 1896 s. 32; A. 1899 s. 62 }	326 406
Appointment to recover private street expenses ...	A. 1890 s. 47	... 289

INDEX.

	ACT.	PAGE.
REFUSE DESTRUCTOR		
Appropriation of site for ...	O. 1892 art. 1 (s.s.3)	303
RELIEVING OFFICER		
Duty to bury infected body	A. 1890 s. 63	... 294
RENEWAL FUND		
Creation of Depreciation and ...	A. 1872 s. 22;	241
	O. 1883 art. 3	265
RENTS		
Mortgage of water ...	O. 1863;	194
	A. 1864 s. 28	206
Power to compound for water	A. 1867 s. 18	... 219
Priority in bankruptcy ...	A. 1867 s. 38 (note);	224
	A. 1872 s. 21 (note)	241
Security for water...	A. 1867 ss. 11 & 12	218
Water, domestic supply	A. 1858 s. 11;	170
	A. 1864 s. 18	202
Water for additional baths, &c. ...	A. 1858 s. 14	... 170
Water for other than domestic purposes	A. 1858 s. 15	... 170
Water payable quarterly ...	A. 1867 s. 17	... 219
REPEAL		
Of Byelaws ...	A. 1858 s. 52;	179
	A. 1864 s. 37;	208
	A. 1867 s. 29;	222
	A. 1890 s. 85	299
RESERVE FUND		
Creation of, under...	A. 1899 s. 63	... 406
RESERVOIR		
Application of funds to purposes of ...	A. 1864 s. 21	205
Construction of	A. 1864 s. 7	... 199
Period to complete ...	A. 1864 s. 14	... 201
RIVER OFFENCES		
Jurisdiction of Wirral Justices over	A. 1890 s. 76	... 297
RIVER WALL		
At Seacombe Ferry, authorised	A. 1872 s. 7	... 237
Cost, maintenance and repair of (agreement with Dock Board)	A. 1872 (sched.)	... 241
Power to construct, to New Brighton ...	A. 1896 s. 13;	... 321
	A. 1899 s. 55	... 402
,, ,, Seacombe	A. 1899 s. 55	... 402

	ACT.	PAGE.
ROADS		
Commissioner empowered to set out and make, &c.	A. 1814 s. 15	... 53
Maintenance and repair of private or occupation roads, award	—	22 / 61
Over commons and waste lands, set out, award	—	22 / 61
Over "Wallasey Pasture," award	—	22 / 61
Public, over commons to be not less than 30 feet wide	A. 1809 s. 26	... 20
Public and private, in Liscard set out, award	—	22 / 61
ROCK POINT ESTATE		
Provisions protecting the...	A. 1896 s. 44	... 333
SALARIES		
May be charged to particular accounts...	A. 1864 s. 42	.. 208
SALE		
Certain lands of	A. 1845 s. 84; A. 1858 s. 68; A. 1864 s. 20; O. 1877 (No. 1) art. 1 A. 1896 s. 12; A. 1899 s. 13	147 184 203 248 320 386
Of mains and pipes to outside authorities	A. 1890 s. 73 (3)...	296
Proceeds of, surplus lands	A. 1896 s. 35; A. 1899 s. 14	... 327 ... 386
SANDHILLS		
Certain sandhills to remain open as protection against sea	A. 1814 s. 23	... 56
Common rights of, to cease	A. 1814 s. 29	... 58
Placed under control of local authorities	A. 1845 s. 85	... 147
SEACOMBE		
Roads on Seacombe Common—Award	—	22 / 61
Communication with Birkenhead	A. 1867 s. 7	... 216
Power to construct embankment to	A. 1899 s. 55	... 402
SEACOMBE FERRY		
Cost, maintenance, and repair of River Wall authorised	A. 1872 sched.	... 241
Embankment or River Wall authorised	A. 1872 s. 7	... 237
Lands Clauses Act applied	O. 1876	... 244
Pier and floating landing-stage authorised	A. 1872 s. 7	... 237
Power to lease or purchase	A. 1845 s. 86	... 148
Purchase of reversion	A. 1861 s. 6	... 191
Steamers plying during fog	A. 1890 s. 75	... 297

SEA WALL

	ACT.	PAGE.
Embankment or River Wall at Seacombe	A. 1872 s. 7;	... 237
	A. 1899 s. 55	... 402
Maintenance and repair of (agreement with Dock Board)	A. 1872 sched.	... 241

SEWERS

Altering position of	A. 1896 s. 17;	... 321
	A. 1899 s. 56	... 402
Connection of drains with	A. 1864 s. 31;	206
	A. 1890 s. 35	285
,, with marginal sewer of Dock Board	A. 1867 s. 8	... 217
Courts and passages to be sewered	A. 1864 s. 29	... 206
Inclusion in private street works	A. 1890 s. 40	286
Inspection of sewer or drain	A. 1890 s. 21	... 281
Notice of covering up	A. 1890 s. 21	... 281
Obstruction of	A. 1890 s. 33	... 285
Precautions during construction and repair, Towns Improvement Clauses Act, 1847, applied	O. 1852 art. 17	... 163
Turning steam, &c., into...	A. 1890 s. 34	... 285

SHELTERS

For families during disinfection of dwellings	A. 1890 s. 66	... 295
Provision of, on promenade	A. 1896 s. 20;	322
	,, s. 41 (10);	329
	,, s. 42 (8);	330
	,, s. 43 (9);	332
	A. 1899 s. 56	402

SHOPS

Conversion into dwelling-houses	A. 1890 s. 25 (s.s.2)	283
Lock-up shops not to be used for habitation	A. 1890 s. 25	... 282

SINKING FUND

	A. 1858 s. 61;	182
	A. 1861 s. 4;	190
	A. 1864 s. 22;	204
	A. 1867 s. 32;	223
	A. 1872 s. 18;	240
Public Health Act and other provisions as to, applied	O. 1877 (No. 1) arts. 2 to 4	249
	O. 1881 art. 1	258
	O. 1883 arts. 4	265
	to 8;	266
	O. 1892 art. 2;	303
	A. 1896 s. 29;	324
	O. 1897 art. 2;	370
	A. 1899 s. 62	406

	ACT.	PAGE.
Sinking Fund—*Continued.*		
Returns to Local Government Board	O. 1881 art. 2 ;	259
	O. 1883 art. 8 ;	266
	O. 1892 art. 2 ;	303
	A. 1896 s. 34 ;	326
	O. 1897 art. 9 ;	372
	A. 1899 s. 62	406
Under Promenade Act of 1896, s. 15 of	A. 1896 s. 29 (6 ;)	325
Local Loans Act, 1875, not to apply	A. 1899 s. 62	406

SLAUGHTER HOUSES

Markets and Fairs Clauses Act, 1847, applied	O. 1852 art. 17	... 163
Not exempted from general Acts	A. 1890 s. 69	... 295
Period of licenses for	,, s. 77	... 297
Prejudicial to health to be discontinued..	,, s. 77	... 297

SMOKE

Prevention of, Towns Improvement Clauses Act, 1847, applied	O. 1852 art. 17	... 163

SPECIFICATIONS

Amendment of, private street works	A. 1890 s. 45	... 289
Particulars in, of private street works ...	A. 1890 sched. I	... 300
Private street works, of ...	A. 1890 s. 40	... 286

STAMPS

Forging stamps of Urban authority	A. 1890 s. 71	... 296

STEAM

Turning, into drains	A. 1890 s. 34	... 285

STEAMBOATS

Plying during fog ...	A. 1890 s. 75	... 297
Power to lease or purchase	A. 1845 s. 86 ;	148
	A. 1858 s. 36	174
Power to provide, &c.	A. 1845 s. 87 ;	149
	A. 1858 s. 37 ;	175
	A. 1864 s. 17	202
Power to hire and charter	A. 1858 s. 37	... 175
Power to sell or let	A. 1864 s. 17	... 202
Wirral Justices jurisdiction over	A. 1890 s. 76	... 297

STREET

Definition of	A. 1845 s. 327	155
	A. 1890 s. 38	286
Deposit of plan of, void after certain interval	A. 1890 s. 13	... 279
Fencing of vacant land adjoining	A. 1845 s. 118	150
	A. 1890 s. 24	282
Foreshore a	A. 1890 s. 6	... 278

INDEX. LI.

	ACT.	PAGE.
Street—*Continued*.		
Laying of distributing mains in...	E.L.O. 1897 art. 17	348
Musicians to depart when desired	A. 1845 s. 188	151
Naming or altering name of	1890 s. 16	280
,, and improving line of, Towns Improvement Clauses Act, 1847, app.	O. 1852 art. 17	163
Obliterating or removing name or numbers	A. 1890 s. 16	280
Obstructions and nuisances in, Town Police Clauses Act, 1847, app.	O. 1852 art. 17	163
Obstructions, removal of in, Towns Improvement Clauses Act, 1847, app.	O. 1852 art. 17	163
Power to break up, adjacent to district	A. 1890 s. 73	296
,, ,, for electric purposes	E.L.O. 1897, art. 8	339
,, construct street boxes	E.L.O. 1897, art. 9	339
,, light	A. 1858 s. 17	171
,, vary position or direction of new	A. 1890 s. 14	279
Precautions during construction, &c., Towns Improvement Clauses Act, 1847, app.	O. 1852, art. 17	163
PRIVATE STREET WORKS:		
Adoption of streets	A. 1890 ss. 53 & 54	290, 291
Amendment of Specifications, &c.	A. 1890 s. 45	289
Borrowing powers for	A. 1890 s. 52	290
Contribution to expenses	A. 1890 s. 49	290
Costs of objections to	A. 1890 s. 42 (3)	288
Determination of objections	A. 1890 ss. 42 & 46 (3)	287-289
Enumeration of	A. 1890 s. 40	286
Estimate of expenses	A. 1890 ss. 40 and 43 (2)	286, 288
Expenses a charge on premises	A. 1890 s. 47	289
Expenses, how apportioned	A. 1890 s. 44	288
Final apportionment and recovery of expenses	A. 1890 s. 46	289
Incumbent, minister, &c., exempted	A. 1890 s. 50	290
Limited owners may borrow for expenses	A. 1890 s. 51	290
Objections to	A. 1890 s. 41	287
Objections to final apportionment	A. 1890 s. 46 (2)	289
Particulars to be stated in estimates	A. 1890 sched. 1.	300
,, ,, plans	,, ,,	300
,, ,, provisional apportionment	,, ,,	300
,, ,, specifications	,,	300

	ACT.	PAGE.
Street—*Continued*.		
Private Street Works—*Continued*.		
Provisional apportionment	A. 1890 s. 40	... 286
Provisions relating to ...	A. 1890 ss. 38 to 55	286-291
Publication of Resolution approving	A. 1890 s. 40 (3) and sched. II.	287 300
Recovery of expenses summarily or by action	A. 1890 s. 48	. 290
Register of charges	A. 1890 s. 47 (2)...	290
Remedies under conveyancing Act for	A. 1890 s. 47	... 289
Resolution approving ...	A. 1890 s. 40	... 286
Separate accounts of expenses	A. 1890 s. 55	... 291
Specification and plans of	A. 1890 s. 40	... 286
Repair of vaults, cellars, &c, under	A. 1864 s. 30 A. 1890 s. 26	206 283
Restrictions on breaking up	E.L.O. 1897 arts. 10 to 12	340-342
Straightening line of	A. 1864 ss. 33 & 34	207
Throwing materials into, penalty ...	A. 1845 s. 155	... 151
Tramways may be laid in	A. 1867 s. 6; A. 1899 s. 26	216 390
Purchase of land for... ...	A. 1864 s. 34	... 207
STREET WORKS :		
Authorized	A. 1899 s. 50	... 398
Removal of human remains during	A. 1899 s. 51	.. 400
Period for completion of	A. 1899 s. 52	401
Power to make	A. 1899 s. 50	... 398
Power to deviate	A. 1899 s. 53	... 401
Power to make subsidiary works ...	A. 1899 s. 54	... 402
Provisions relating to, text of	A. 1899 ss. 50-54	398 402
SUMMARY JURISDICTION		
Court of, may order testing stations ...	E.L.O. 1897 art. 32	... 355
Detention in hospital of infected person, directed by	A. 1890 s. 65	... 294
Determination of objections by, private street works	A. 1890 ss. 42 and 46 (3)	287 289
Establishment of testing stations, directed by	E.L.O. 1897 art. 32	... 355
SUMMONS		
Authentication of	A. 1858 s. 82	186
SUPERANNUATION		
Power to grant ...	A. 1864 s. 38	... 208

INDEX.

	ACT.	PAGE.
SURVEYOR		
Inspection of buildings by	A. 1890 s. 21	281
Power of, inspecting	A. 1890 s. 22	281
TELEGRAPH ACT, 1878		
Certain sections to apply to tramways	A. 1899 s. 40	394
TENANTS		
For less than a quarter may deduct water rate from rent	A. 1890 s. 72	296
Purchase of houses tenanted by labouring class restricted	C.A. 1892 s. 2; A. 1896 s. 10	301 320
TIDAL WATER		
Abandoned works affecting, may be removed	A. 1864 s. 12	201
TOLLS		
Alteration of	A. 1864 s. 16; A. 1867 s. 23	202 220
Collector of, liable for wrong detention of goods	A. 1858 s. 50	179
Contracts for ferry	A. 1864 s. 16	202
Disputes as to amount and weights	A. 1858 ss. 43 & 44	177
Ferry	A. 1858 s. 39; A. 1864 s. 16; A. 1867 ss. 19 & 20 and sched. C.	176 202 220 226
List of, to be printed and exhibited	A. 1858 s. 48	178
Offences by collectors of	A. 1858 s. 49	178
Passengers evading or refusing	A. 1858 s. 46; A. 1867 ss. 26 & 27; A. 1872 s. 15	178 221 239
Passengers refusing to produce tickets	A. 1890 s. 74	297
Piers or landing stages, for use of	A. 1864 s. 16	202
Recovery of	A. 1858 s. 42; A. 1867 s. 23;	177 220
Specified, not to be exceeded	A. 1858 s. 41; A. 1867 s. 22	176 220
Tramway	A. 1899 s. 43 and sched. II	397 409
Time and place for payment of	A. 1858 s. 42; A. 1867 s. 25	177 221
To be charged equally	A. 1858 s. 40; A. 1867 s. 21	177 220
TOWNS IMPROVEMENT CLAUSES ACT, 1847		
Sections incorporated with Local Act	O. 1852 art. 17	163
TOWNS POLICE CLAUSES ACT, 1847		
Sections incorporated with Local Act	O. 1852 art. 17; O. 1888 art. 1	163 270

TRAMWAYS

	ACT.	PAGE.
Additional Crossings, power to make	A. 1899 s. 24	390
Alteration of	A. 1899 ss. 25 & 38	390 / 393
Authorised	A. 1899 s. 16	386
Application of road materials excavated	A. 1899 s. 27	390
Application of revenue of	A. 1899 s. 63	406
Bye-laws as to	A. 1867 s. 28 / A. 1899 ss. 36 & 42	222 / 392 / 396
Council not bound to carry animals and goods upon	A. 1899 s. 32	391
Deficiency of Revenue of	A. 1899 s. 63 (2)	406
Definition of	A. 1899 s. 8	382
Electrical power for	A. 1899 ss. 37 to 41	392 / 396
Existing, not to be interfered with until required	A. 1899 s. 45	397
Gauge of	A. 1899 s. 21 (1)	389
Lands of owners in Seabank Road, provisions as to	A. 1899 s. 17	388
Lands of Wirral Railway Co.	A. 1899 s. 49	397
Motive power for	A. 1899 s. 37	392
Opening of, for public traffic	A. 1899 s. 18	389
Period for completion of	A. 1899 s. 28	391
Plans of mode of construction for, Board of Trade	A. 1899 s. 20	389
Power to acquire patents for	A. 1899 s. 47	397
,, work	A. 1899 s. 43	397
,, lay	A. 1867 s. 6 ; / A. 1899 s. 16	216 / 386
,, break up tramways for electrical supply	E.L.O. 1897 art. 8	339
Rails of	A. 1899 ss. 22 & 25	389 / 390
Railway carriages or trucks not to be used on	A. 1899 s. 21 (2)	389
Rates for passengers	A. 1899 ss. 29 & 33 to 35	391
,, ,, luggage	A. 1899 ss. 30 to 33	391
,, goods	A. 1899 s. 31 to 33 and sched. II	391 / 409
Restrictions on breaking up	E.L.O. 1897 arts. 11, 12	341 / 342
To be kept level with surface of road	A. 1899 s. 19	389
Temporary, may be made where necessary	A. 1899 s. 26	390
Waiting-rooms, &c., may be provided	A. 1899 s. 16	386

INDEX.   LV.

	ACT.	PAGE.
Tramways—*continued*.		
Width of engines and carriages used on..	A. 1899 s. 21 (1)	389
Works and conveniences therewith may be provided	A. 1899 s. 16	386
TRAMWAYS ACT, 1870		
Application of ss. 3 and 19 and parts II and III of	A. 1899 s. 2	382
Application of s. 26 of	A. 1899 s. 20	389
Mechanical power works to be subject to s. 30 of	A. 1899 s. 41	396
Penalties for non-observance of s. 28 of..	A. 1899 s. 23	389
Regulations authorized by, to be made by Council alone	A. 1899 s. 44	397
Secs. 30 and 34 of, not to apply in certain cases	A. 1899 ss. 21 (1) and 40 (1)	389 394
Secs. 8, 10 to 17, 37 to 48, and sched. of, to be repealed when tramways purchased	A. 1899 s. 46	397
URINALS		
Provisions for public	A. 1890 s. 31	284
Provision of, by Innkeepers	A. 1864 s. 32	207
VAUGHAN		
Provisions relating to lands of Philip Michael Vaughan	A. 1896 s. 43	331
VAULTS		
Repair of	A. 1861 s. 30; A. 1890 s. 26	206 283
VEHICLES		
Provision for, crossing footways	A. 1890 s. 15	279
VESSELS		
Anchoring and mooring of	A. 1867 s. 28; A. 1872 s. 14	222 239
VYNER		
Rights of R. C. De Grey Vyner in land and foreshore protected	A. 1890 s. 88	299
WAGES		
May be charged to particular accounts...	A. 1861 s. 42	208
WALLASEY DISTRICT		
Constituted for purposes of Public Health Act	O. 1852 art. 1	160
Extension of	O. 1877 (No. 2)	250
Sea and river boundary defined	A. 1890 s. 5	277
WALLASEY FERRIES ACCOUNT		
Application of	A. 1858 s. 67	183
Creation of..	A. 1858 s. 39	176
Deficiency in, provided for	A. 1867 s. 36	224

	ACT.	PAGE.
Wallasey Ferries Account—*Continued.*		
Mortgage of	A. 1858 s. 60;	181
	A. 1861 s. 3;	189
	A. 1864 s. 21;	203
	A. 1872 s. 17;	239
	O. 1877 (No. 1) art. 3;	249
	O. 1881 art. 1;	258
	O. 1883 art. 2;	264
	O. 1895 art. 1;	311
	O. 1897 art. 1	369

WALLASEY FREE GRAMMAR SCHOOL

Allotments to Master or Trustee, and Commissioner's Award	—	61

WALLASEY IMPROVEMENT ACTS

Text of Act of 1845	—	... 146
,, ,, 1858	—	... 165
,, ,, 1861	—	... 187
,, ,, 1864	—	... 196
,, ,, 1867	—	... 212
,, ,, 1872	—	... 233

WALLASEY INCLOSURE ACT

Text of Act of 1814	—	46

WALLASEY LIGHTING ACCOUNT

Application of	A. 1858 s. 66	.. 183
,, ,, gas rents to	A. 1858 s. 30	173
	A. 1867 s. 10	218
Creation of..	A. 1858 s. 29	... 173
Deficiency provided for	A. 1867 s. 36	... 224
Mortgage of	A. 1858 s. 60;	181
	A. 1861 s. 3;	189
	A. 1867 s. 30;	222
	O. 1877 (No. 1) art. 2;	249
	O. 1883 art. 1;	264
	O. 1892 art. 2;	303
	O. 1896 art. 1;	314
	O. 1898 art. 1	376

WALLASEY LOCAL BOARD

Boundary of jurisdiction...	O. 1852 art. 1;	160
	O. 1877 (No. 2) art. 3;	252
	A. 1890 s. 5	277
Constitution of	O. 1852 art. 2	... 161
First election	C.A. 1853 s. 3	... 158
Made a "Body Corporate"	A. 1861 s. 8	... 191
Property of Commissioner transferred to	O. 1852 art. 12	... 162

INDEX. LVII.

| | ACT. | PAGE. |

Wallasey Local Board—*Continued.*

Qualification of members	O. 1852 art. 4	161
Qualification of electors	O. 1852, note to arts. 2 to 5;	161
	A. 1864 s. 36 (note);	208
	O. 1870 art. 5	232
Superseded by Urban District Council	O. 1852, note to arts. 2 to 5;	161
	A. 1896, preamble (note)	317
To exercise powers of the Improvement Commissioners	O. 1852 art. 9	162

WALLASEY LOCAL BOARD ACT, 1890

Text of	—	272

WALLASEY TRAMWAYS AND IMPROVEMENTS ACT, 1899

Text of	—	377

WALLASEY PASTURE

Allotment of, Commissioner's Award	—	61
Highways and roads over—Award	—	61

WALLASEY URBAN DISTRICT COUNCIL

Creation of	O. 1852 note to arts. 2 to 5;	161
	A. 1896 preamble (Note)	317

WALLASEY URBAN DISTRICT COUNCIL (PROMENADE ACT) 1896

Text of	—	317

WALLASEY WATERWORKS ACCOUNT

Application of	A. 1858 s. 65	182
Creation of	A. 1858 ss. 27 & 28	173
Deficiency in, provision for	A. 1867 s. 36	224

WAR DEPARTMENT

Protection of Rights of	A. 1896 s. 46	333

WARES

Displaying, on unfenced land	A. 1890 s. 6	278

WAREHOUSES

Power to provide	A. 1867 s. 24	221

	ACT.	PAGE.
WASH-HOUSES		
Persons washing clothes to furnish list of owners	A 1890 s. 58	292
Powers of Towns Improvement Clauses Act, 1847, incorporated	O. 1852 art. 17	163
WASTE LANDS		
Allotment and division of commons, &c., in Liscard, award	—	22 / 61
Allotment and division of commons, &c., in Wallasey and Poolton-cum-Seacombe, award	—	22 / 61
Contents of, Wallasey and Poolton, award	—	22 / 61
Rights of common over, extinguished	A. 1809 s. 21 ; A. 1814 s. 29	19 / 58
WATER		
Additional baths and water closets, rates for	A. 1858 s. 14	170
Altering position of mains or pipes	A. 1896 s. 17 ; A. 1899 s. 56	321 / 402
Borrowing powers for	A. 1858 s. 60 / A. 1861 s. 3 / O. 1863 / A. 1864 s. 28 / O. 1870 art. 6 / A. 1872 s. 17 / O. 1894 art. 1	181 / 189 / 194 / 206 / 232 / 239 / 308
Breaking up streets adjacent to district to supply	A. 1890 s. 73 (2)	296
Bye-laws as to supply	A. 1867 s. 15	219
,, for testing and stamping fittings	A. 1890 s. 70	295
Cisterns, pipes, and cocks, approval of	A. 1858 s. 12	170
Compounding for rents	A. 1867 s. 18	219
Domestic purposes, for	A. 1858 s. 11	170
,, ,, terms for other than	A. 1858 s. 15	171
,, supply, rents for	A. 1858 s. 11 ; A. 1864 s. 18	170 / 202
,, ,, what it comprises	A. 1858 s. 13	170
Fittings, supply of	A. 1864 s. 19	203
Improper use of, penalty	A. 1858 s. 16	171
Laying electric lines near pipes	E.L.O. 1897 art. 14	346
Mortgages of rates and rents	O. 1863 ; A. 1864 s. 28	194 / 206
Owners to obtain supply	A. 1867 s. 16	219
Person erecting or repairing pipes to notify urban authority	A. 1890 s. 70	295

INDEX. LIX.

	ACT.	PAGE.

Water—*Continued.*

Rate for houses let under a quarter payable by owner	A. 1890 s. 72	... 296
Rents payable quarterly	A. 1867 s. 17	... 219
Sale of mains or pipes to outside authorities	A. 1890 s. 73 (3)	... 296
Security for rates and charges	A. 1867 ss. 11 & 12	218
Supply to houses before occupation ...	A. 1890 s. 20	... 281
,, outside authorities and others	A. 1890 s. 73	... 296
,, ,, ,, not to interfere with district supply	A. 1890 s. 73	... 296
Wells, power to sink ...	A. 1872 s. 16	... 239

WATERCLOSETS

Provision for public	A. 1890 s. 31	... 284
Water rates for additional	A. 1858 s. 14	... 170

WATERING PITS

Allotment of	{ Award —	} 22 / 61
When dried up may be sold, &c.	{ A. 1845 s. 84 ; A. 1858 s. 68 ; A. 1864 s. 20 ;	} 147 / 184 / 203

WATERWORKS

Application of loans on	A. 1858 s. 63	... 182
,, ,, Waterworks Clauses Acts	{ A. 1858 s. 5 ; A. 1864 s. 3 ; A. 1872 s. 3 ; A. 1890 s. 73 ;	} 169 / 199 / 236 / 296
Depreciation and renewal fund ...	{ A. 1872 s. 22 ; O. 1883 art. 3	} 241 / 265
Mortgage of	{ A. 1858 s. 60 ; A. 1861 s. 3 ; A. 1864 s. 28 ; A. 1872 s. 17	} 181 / 189 / 206 / 239
Period for completion of ...	A. 1858 s. 9	... 170
Power to construct	A. 1858 s. 7	... 169
Rate, power to lay	A. 1858 s. 27	... 173
Reservoir, application of moneys to	A. 1864 s. 24	... 205
,, power to make	A. 1864 s. 7	... 199
Wells, power to sink	A. 1872 s. 16	... 239

WAYS

Purchase of land for ways or passages ...	A. 1864 s. 34	... 207

	ACT.	PAGE.
WEIGHTS AND MEASURES		
Disputes as to ferry tolls and weights ...	A. 1858 s. 44	... 177
To be provided at ferries...	A. 1858 s. 45	... 178
Weighing goods and carts, Markets and Fairs' Clauses Act, 1847, app. ...	O. 1852 art. 17	... 163
WELLS		
Power to sink and maintain	A. 1872 s. 16	... 239
WIRRAL RAILWAY COMPANY		
Protection of rights of ...	A. 1899 s. 49	... 397
YARDS		
Back yards to be flagged or paved	A. 1890 s. 27	... 283

www.ingramcontent.com/pod-product-compliance
Lightning Source LLC
Chambersburg PA
CBHW051848300426
44117CB00006B/312